FRANK RAMSEY

CHERYL MISAK

FRANK RAMSEY

a sheer excess of powers

OXFORD
UNIVERSITY PRESS

OXFORD

UNIVERSITY PRESS

Great Clarendon Street, Oxford, OX2 6DP,
United Kingdom

Oxford University Press is a department of the University of Oxford.
It furthers the University's objective of excellence in research, scholarship,
and education by publishing worldwide. Oxford is a registered trade mark of
Oxford University Press in the UK and in certain other countries

© Cheryl Misak 2020

The moral rights of the author have been asserted

First published 2020
First published in paperback 2022
Impression: 1

Published in the United States of America by Oxford University Press
198 Madison Avenue, New York, NY 10016, United States of America

British Library Cataloguing in Publication Data
Data available

Library of Congress Control Number: 2019946130

ISBN 978-0-19-285675-3

Printed and bound in Great Britain by
Clays Ltd, Elcograf S.p.A.

Links to third party websites are provided by Oxford in good faith and
for information only. Oxford disclaims any responsibility for the materials
contained in any third party website referenced in this work.

CONTENTS

PART I. BOYHOOD

PART II. THE CAMBRIDGE MAN

CONTENTS

PART III. AN ASTONISHING HALF DECADE

TABLE OF GUEST BOXES

LIST OF ILLUSTRATIONS

LIST OF ABBREVIATIONS: ARCHIVAL SOURCES

ASP/FPR.1983.01	Frank Plumpton Ramsey Papers, Archives of Scientific Philosophy, University of Pittsburgh Library System
ASP/RC.1974.01	Rudolf Carnap Papers, Archives of Scientific Philosophy, University of Pittsburgh Library System
ASP/HR.1973.01	Hans Reichenbach Papers, Archives of Scientific Philosophy, University of Pittsburgh Library System
BL	British Library
BK	Kingsley Martin Collection, Sussex University
BR	Ludwig Wittgenstein Collection: Research Institute Brenner Archive, University of Innsbruck
BRA	Bertrand Russell Archive, McMaster University
BTTS	*Better than the Stars*, (Mellor, 1978)
CA	Cambridgeshire Archives
CUL	Cambridge University Archives
DA	Maurice Drury Archive, Mary Immaculate College, Limerick, Ireland
EC	Einstein Collection, Hebrew University
GCA	Girton College Archives, Cambridge
KH	Harrod and Keynes Notes and Memoranda, University of Tokyo Archives
KCA	King's College Archive, Cambridge
LRA	Lettice Ramsey Autobiography, courtesy of Stephen Burch
LWG	Ludwig Wittgenstein: Gesamtbriefwechsel / Complete Correspondence, Electronic Edition
MBP	Max Black Papers, Cornell University
MCA	Magdalene College Archives, Cambridge
OF	Ogden Fonds, McMaster University
TCL	Trinity College Library, Trinity College, Cambridge
TFL	Thomas Fisher Rare Book Library, University of Toronto

TFL MS/COLL/735	Laurie Kahn Ramsey Collection, Thomas Fisher Rare Book Library, University of Toronto
VCA	Vienna Circle Archives, Noord-Hollands Archief
WCA	Winchester College Archives

LIST OF ABBREVIATIONS: PUBLISHED WORKS OF FRANK RAMSEY AND LUDWIG WITTGENSTEIN

Details can be found in the Bibliography.

Ramsey

C	'Chance'
CN	Critical Notice of Wittgenstein, *Tractatus Logico-Philosophicus*
DP	'The Douglas Proposals'
DS	'On There Being No Discussable Subject'
EBFM	'The Foundations of Mathematics', *Encyclopedia Britannica*
EBM	'Mathematics: Mathematical Logic', *Encyclopedia Britannica*
EBR	'Russell, Bertrand Arthur William', *Encyclopedia Britannica*
FM	'The Foundations of Mathematics'
FP	'Facts and Propositions'
GC	'General Propositions and Causality'
K	'Knowledge'
KP	'Mr. Keynes on Probability'
ML	'Mathematical Logic'
NP	'The Nature of Propositions'
NPPM	*Notes on Philosophy, Probability and Mathematics*
NST	'Notes on Saving and Taxation'
OT	*On Truth*
P	'Philosophy'
RMM	Review of Ogden and Richards, *The Meaning of Meaning*
RT	Review of Keynes *A Treatise of Probability*
TH	'Theories'
TP	'Truth and Probability'
TT	'A Contribution to the Theory of Taxation'
U	'Universals'
UMA	'Universals and the "Method of Analysis"'

Wittgenstein

CV	*Culture and Value*
LAPR	*Lectures & Conversations on Aesthetics, Psychology, and Religious Belief*
LFM	*Lectures on the Foundations of Mathematics*
M	Letter to the Editor of *Mind*
MCI	'Arthur MacIver's Diary: Cambridge'
PG	*Philosophical Grammar*
PI	*Philosophical Investigations*
PPO	*Ludwig Wittgenstein: Public and Private Occasions*
PR	*Philosophical Remarks*
RPP	*Remarks on the Philosophy of Psychology, Volume I*
T	*Tractatus Logico-Philosophicus*
WCL	*Wittgenstein in Cambridge: Letters and Documents*
WPCR	*Wittgenstein's Philosophical Conversations with Rush Rhees*
Z	*Zettel*

TRUNCATED FAMILY TREE

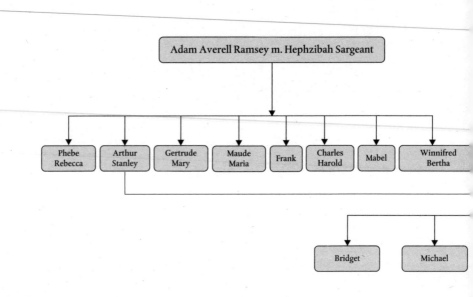

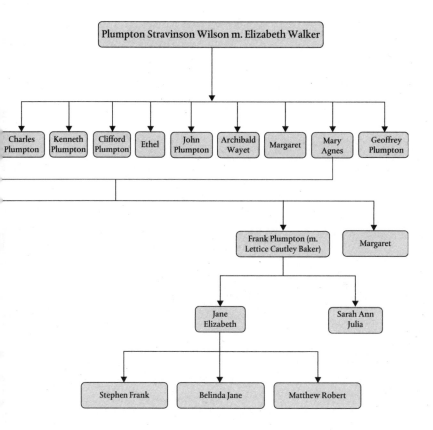

AUTHOR'S NOTE

I have endeavoured to trace copyright holders and obtain permission to quote from all material under copyright. (For permission to reproduce copyrighted images, see Illustration Sources) I gratefully acknowledge the following.

Stephen Burch granted me permission to quote the many passages from the private correspondence and diaries of Frank Ramsey and Lettice Ramsey. Permission to reproduce material from their collections, over which they hold copyright, has been granted by the Archives of Scientific Philosophy, University of Pittsburgh Library System; The Provost and Scholars of King's College, Cambridge; the Bertrand Russell Archive, McMaster University; the British Library Board; the Master and Fellows of Magdalene College, Cambridge; the Master and Fellows of Trinity College, Cambridge; the Noord-Hollands Archief; the Syndics of Cambridge University Library; the Thomas Fisher Rare Books Library, University of Toronto; and the Warden and Scholars of Winchester College.

ACKNOWLEDGEMENTS

In the attempt to make sense of the whole of Ramsey's work, I have had to call on considerable expertise. Various authorities on Ramsey contributed directly by writing guest boxes, in addition to providing feedback on my surrounding text: Simon Blackburn, Robin Boadway, Partha Dasgupta, Pedro Garcia Duarte, Juliet Floyd, Ronald Graham, Colin Howson, Mathieu Marion, Steven Methven, Michael Potter, Huw Price, Stathis Psillos, Ian Rumfitt, Markus Säbel, Nils-Eric Sahlin, Peter Sullivan, Robert Trueman, Timothy Williamson, and Richard Zach. I am grateful to them for their generosity and commitment to this project. Many other fine scholars commented on parts or all of early drafts: Anna Boncompagni, Gabriel Citron, John Davis, Dave Edmonds, Maria Carla Galavotti, Sue Howson, Michael Hallett, Joe Heath, Jim Klagge, Christoph Limbeck-Lilienau, Fraser MacBride, Kumar Murty, Allan Olley, Mary O'Sullivan, Josef Rothhaupt, Roger Sandilands, Margaret Schabas, Dirk Schlimm, David Stern, Tadeusz Szubka, and Roy Weintraub. This list no doubt omits many, such as those who made contributions when I presented material on Ramsey to departments and conferences. Of course, responsibility for mistakes resides entirely with me.

Some remarkable people were involved in more unusual ways. Amartya Sen convinced me to take on the project over lunch at Trinity College in 2015. Steven Methven, in addition to reading the manuscript twice, introduced me to Ramsey's grandson—Stephen Frank Burch. One of the pleasures in writing this biography was spending time with Stephen. He never knew his grandfather. But his grand-mother Lettice was a constant and loving presence in his life. Stephen trusted me with a large satchel of original material, despite the sensitivities and intrusions that inevitably arise when a stranger delves into the life of a family member. When it came to the decision to grant permission to quote, he was magnanimous. It was a pleasure also to meet Ramsey's nieces: one of them, Anne Paul Jones, granted me permission to reproduce the photo of the Ramsey family taken in 1919.

Partha Dasgupta, Ian Hacking, Hugh Mellor, Ian Rumfitt, and David Wiggins supported the book from beginning to end, and were excellent sources of advice. Laurie Kahn contributed her invaluable primary research, conducted in the early 1980s. Nils-Eric Sahlin organized a Ramsey workshop in Lund on the 87th

ACKNOWLEDGEMENTS

anniversary of Ramsey's death. Pedro Garcia Duarte organized two sessions on Ramsey at the History of Economics Society meetings. Brian McGuinness hosted me at his home in Siena to discuss Ramsey and Wittgenstein. Michael Nedo provided generous access to his extraordinary collection of Wittgenstein materials and a copy of a rarely seen four-page original manuscript in Ramsey's hand. The exceptional physicians David Naylor and Mark Tonelli figured out, as much as is possible, the cause of death, and Mark commented on the entire manuscript in draft. Roger Penrose provided insight into his father Lionel and Max Newman. Rainer Lackner of the Kirchler Hotel in Hinterux made our stay more informative and warned us to stay off the mountain when the weather locked in. Monika Gruber took me to Ramsey's flat and Gretl Wittgenstein's house in Vienna. Hermione Lee saved me from errors with respect to Virginia Woolf's *To the Lighthouse*. Ray Monk kindly answered queries about his biography of Wittgenstein, as did Henry Hemming about his biography of Geoffrey Pyke. Bernie Linsky sent me the complete set of the TLS *Wittgenstein in Red* letters.

This is the second happy opportunity I've had to work closely with archivists. Patricia McGuire and Peter Monteith at King's College, Cambridge provided endless support and information, and Patricia made excellent comments on sections of the manuscript. When I talked with them in the King's Archive Centre, I was standing precisely where Ramsey's old rooms had been. Jonathan Smith of the Wren Library at Trinity College, Cambridge pointed me to material not readily found, and cast his educated eye over parts of the manuscript. Suzanne Foster at Winchester was a wonderful guide, unstinting host, and careful reader. My old friend Jacky Cox, now Keeper of the University Archives at Cambridge, was a brilliant source of ideas as well as a reader of various sections of the manuscript. Lance Lugar in the Archives of Scientific Philosophy at the University of Pittsburgh went out of his way to find material in the Ramsey, Carnap, and Reichenbach collections, as well as to reproduce the letter from Ramsey to Wittgenstein. Catherine Sutherland and Matilda Watson in the Pepys Library at Magdalene College, Cambridge and Evan Fay Earle at Cornell University Archives also provided vital materials. Jennifer Toews and Mark Pellegrino at the University of Toronto Fisher Rare Books Library efficiently took in and archived the complex Laurie Kahn Ramsey Collection.

This book would not have been possible without vital institutional support, for which I am thankful. The chair of my department, Martin Pickavé, the Faculty of Arts and Science Dean's Office, and the Office of the Provost at the University of Toronto generously accommodated my many leaves. The book was started in 2014–15, when I was a very happy Visiting Fellow Commoner at Trinity College, Cambridge, the college of Russell, Moore, Wittgenstein, and the undergraduate Ramsey. In 2016–17,

xxii

a Humboldt Research Prize enabled me to spend 12 months in Stefan Gosepath's research group at the Free University in Berlin. During that year, in which I wrote a first draft, the librarians at the Wissenshaftskolleg zu Berlin fetched over 300 items for me, as the spouse of a fellow. In 2017–18, the Guggenheim Foundation supported the project with a Fellowship and the Oxford Centre for Life Writing hosted me as a Visiting Scholar. The Social Sciences and Humanities Research Council of Canada provided material support for travel and for my two superb primary graduate student research assistants. Soroush Marouzi came on board for the final two years and provided crucial help, especially with the probability and economics sections and the endnotes, and in the Cambridge archives. He also put countless hours into ensuring that the paperback edition was free of typos and the like. Griffin Klemick was with the book the whole way, providing terrific editorial support, saving me from countless mistakes, and taking on the yeoman task of compiling the index.

Oxford University Press's Peter Momtchiloff has always been a wonderfully supportive editor, and the perfect person with whom to discuss ideas over lunch or tea. This time round, he went many extra miles to ensure this biography looks and reads as best it can. That included an extraordinary line-edit of the entire manuscript and constant counsel. I am also indebted to Tom McKibbin for imaginatively and patiently locating photos and permissions; to Martin Noble for excellent copy editing; and to Kate Shepherd and Kate Roche for spirited work on the publicity.

This project required considerable archival work in the UK, and some dear friends and family made me feel at home in their homes: Hazel Mills and Andrew Freeman in Cambridge; Lois McNay and Murray Hunt in Oxford; and in London, Louise and Lewis Spitz, Richard Spitz and Jo Feary, Jonathan Lewis, and Jenna Darler. And without Hazel's superb historian's judgment, measured out in sprints in Cambridge and in a sustained way as she pored over a draft of the manuscript over a glorious two weeks in Umbria, this biography would be much poorer.

Finally, my thanks go to David Dyzenhaus. Both he, and our children Alex and Sophie, put up with Ramsey as a constant presence in our lives for five years. Then, on a long journey to New Zealand, David read the penultimate draft, corrected countless infelicities, and persuaded me it was good enough to let go. This book is dedicated to him.

PREFACE TO THE PAPERBACK

Since *Frank Ramsey: A Sheer Excess of Powers* was published in March 2020, many people have taken the time to alert me to typos and mistakes. In addition, over two dozen thoughtful reviews and blog posts have discussed the book. I thank this true community of inquirers for their interest and generosity. I'm especially grateful to those who pointed out flaws or suggested further lines of inquiry. Chris Collins dropped a bombshell revelation about Richard Braithwaite. Simon Blackburn encouraged me to talk about Newman's Problem. Vince Crawford prompted a tweak about what I say about von Neuman and Morgenstern and Tim Hazledine did the same for Joan Robinson. Paolo Mancosu corrected mistakes in my history of mathematics and in my recounting of Ramsey's visits to Wittgenstein and caused me to include Ramsey Cardinals and the Paris and Harrington Theorem. Graham Foster and Trish Greenhalgh provided further superb medical advice about the cause of Ramsey's death. Galen Strawson gave me insight into Margaret Paul and helped with the *Afterword* to this paperback edition. That *Afterword* discusses the revelations of Chris Collins, who had a special perspective, as he was Margaret Paul's research assistant while she was writing her own book about her brother.

The revisions to the text do not change the original pagination.

PREFACE

Beginning at the End

Any biography of Frank Ramsey must start with, and be haunted by, his death. He was one of the most powerful and influential thinkers Cambridge ever produced. Yet he died just shy of his twenty-seventh birthday, in January 1930. In November 1929, the young don at King's College, Cambridge was ill with jaundice. His family and friends weren't alarmed, as the ailment was not uncommon. A few weeks into his illness his wife Lettice herself came down with flu and Frank was moved across town to his father's house, his old family home. Lettice had their two little girls to look after, and needed a break. His brother Michael came home for Christmas, and on New Year's Day, wrote in his diary:

> Then to Frank. He was in bed with jaundice, poor fellow, and he looked very weak. We talked about the usual sort of topics and argued less than usual. He thought that a lot of unhappiness in the world was caused by 'unsatisfied lust'. I expounded to him the desire 'to contemplate a oneness' and he was tolerant, though he didn't understand. 'Have you had any more success at this trick?' he asked!

Michael, 'Mick' to the family, was at this time a vicar's assistant in Liverpool. He would go on to be Archbishop of Canterbury. Frank used to call him 'my little brother the curate'. Michael was very much given to the contemplation of 'oneness', and not at all given to regretting lust unsatisfied. Frank was a resolute atheist, immersed in bohemian culture and interested in Freud. He thought it both frustrating and comic that his brother, to whom he was so close, was devoting his life to a God that didn't exist. They often argued about it, mostly in a good-humoured way.

On 3 January, Michael noted that Frank 'still looks ill'. Frank wrote to Lettice from his new sick-room, both concerned about her and sounding the first note of alarm about his condition. He asked if she would consult someone in her physician-populated family and ask what he knew about jaundice. Lettice contacted her uncle Bobby, a senior surgeon at Guy's Hospital in London. Bobby was taken aback by Frank's condition and things then moved quickly. Frank was moved by ambulance to Guy's, where he was admitted to the Lazarus Ward for exploratory surgery. Two dear friends, Frances Marshall (later Partridge) and Ludwig Wittgenstein, joined Lettice at his bedside during these grim days. There was to be no miraculous resurrection from Lazarus Ward. Frank died in the early hours of Sunday, 19 January, leaving behind his family and a devastated set of friends and colleagues.

Also left bereft were great swaths of scholarship. If we include his undergraduate days, Frank Ramsey was an academic for ten years. In that short span, he made indelible marks on as many as seven disciplines, depending how you count: philosophy, economics, pure mathematics, mathematical logic, the foundations of mathematics, probability theory, and decision theory. The Austrian economist Joseph Schumpeter described him as being like a young thoroughbred, frolicking with ideas and champing at the bit to work out solutions to problems:

> Certainly, that young man was a true product of Cambridge at its best—nobody can have any doubt about it who ever met him, which the present writer did but once. In discussion he impressed one curiously like an overgrown two-year-old who misbehaves on the race-course from sheer excess of powers.

John Maynard Keynes struck a similar note in his obituary, describing a boyish enthusiasm and a lack of constraint in Ramsey's thinking, laughter, and relationships:

> His bulky Johnsonian frame, his spontaneous gurgling laugh, the simplicity of his feelings and reactions, half-alarming sometimes and occasionally almost cruel in their directness and literalness, his honesty of mind and heart, his modesty, and the amazing, easy efficiency of the intellectual machine which ground away behind his wide temples and broad, smiling face . . .

My subtitle and aim derives from these observations of Schumpeter and Keynes. I aim to articulate the quality of mind and heart possessed by this extraordinary young man possessed of a sheer excess of powers.

The Mind

As Schumpeter said, Ramsey was very much a product of Cambridge. It was a particularly luminous period for that university. During the three decades of Ramsey's life, Cambridge was home, off and on, to the philosophers Bertrand Russell, G.E. Moore, and Ludwig Wittgenstein; the economists J.M. Keynes, Arthur Pigou, and Piero Sraffa; and the mathematicians G.H. Hardy and J.E. Littlewood. Ramsey came into substantial contact with them all.

But although Ramsey was very much a product of his time and place, he was one of those rare minds whose ideas seem to bound over the thinking of his contemporaries, launching the discussion into a future that only he could glimpse. He has attracted an almost mythical status in all the disciplines he touched. One must keep in mind what early death can do to a reputation. It can amplify promise and project greatness, which, had death not intervened, might have been compromised by later disappointment. But even when we account for that, Ramsey's genius is clear.

He is perhaps most widely known for his trailblazing work on choice under conditions of uncertainty. His paper 'Truth and Probability' solved the problem of how to measure degrees of belief, and then provided a logic of partial belief and a model of subjective expected utility. These results underpin contemporary economics and Bayesian statistics, as well as much of psychology, artificial intelligence, and other social and physical sciences. 'Truth and Probability' was not published in Ramsey's lifetime, as he was in the middle of expanding on it, by writing a book with the same title, when he died.

In economics proper, Ramsey published two papers in Keynes's *Economic Journal*, one on optimum taxation and one on optimal savings. Each has become a classic, and each has launched a branch of economics and a sizeable handful of Nobel prize-winning ideas. He identified very modern problems and solutions to them, setting agendas that are still being pursued a century later. His workhorse model (now modified and known as the Ramsey–Cass–Koopmans model) is still a feature of most graduate course textbooks and his name in economics also lives on in Ramsey Pricing, Ramsey's Problem, the Keynes–Ramsey Rule, and more.

In philosophy, he made advances in logic, foundations of mathematics, philosophy of science, truth theory, philosophy of language, and decision theory. Donald Davidson, a leading philosopher of the twentieth century, in 1999 coined the term 'the Ramsey Effect': the phenomenon of finding out that your exciting and apparently original philosophical discovery has been already presented, and presented more elegantly, by Frank Ramsey. In addition to this wonderful catch-all label, philosophy, like economics, has named specific innovations and approaches after Ramsey: Ramsey Sentences, the Ramsey Test for Conditionals, Ramsification, Ramseyan Humility, and more.

In pure mathematics, we have a fruitful branch of combinatorics and graph theory. His discovery here was quite literally an aside. He had been working on the *Entscheidungsproblem* that the German mathematician David Hilbert had set in 1928. It asked whether there was a way of deciding whether or not any particular sentence in a formal system is valid or true. Ramsey solved a special case of the problem, pushed its general expression to the limit, and saw that limit clearly.

Shortly after his death, there would be great excitement when Kurt Gödel, and then Alan Turing, showed the limit to be hard and fast, and the problem to be unsolvable. But a theorem that Ramsey had proven along the way in his contribution, an important mathematical truth now called Ramsey's Theorem, showed that in apparently disordered systems, there must be some order. The branch of mathematics that studies the conditions under which order must occur is now called Ramsey Theory.

He also played a major role in the history of thought. Even as an undergraduate, Ramsey held his own in the impressive environs of Cambridge. He shook Keynes's confidence in his newly published probability theory; wrote a damning report on C.H. Douglas's Social Credit proposals; and perhaps most strikingly, had an immense influence on Wittgenstein. In 1921, at the age of eighteen, Ramsey was asked to translate Wittgenstein's early and difficult work, *Tractatus Logico-Philosophicus*. In 1922, he wrote a Critical Notice of it which still stands as one of the most important commentaries. Indeed, we will see that Ramsey's persistent objections to the theory of meaning and truth set out in the *Tractatus* were largely responsible for Wittgenstein's turn away from the *Tractatus* and towards what we think of as the later Wittgenstein. This was one of the most important shifts in the history of philosophy. Wittgenstein was himself largely responsible for the way philosophy unfolded in Cambridge and beyond. Ramsey's book, had it been completed, it might have reset the course of a major branch of philosophy.

Much of Ramsey's work had a delayed effect. That was partly caused by its prescient nature. The rest of the world had to catch up with him, especially on technical matters. We still struggle to work out some moves and proofs Ramsey declared obvious. The delayed effect was also caused by the fact that much of his work was unfinished, his ideas left in drafts or notes, alive with thought, but destined to stay in their raw state. His friend and colleague Richard Braithwaite published some of these drafts and notes in his 1931 selection of Ramsey's work, *The Foundations of Mathematics and Other Logical Essays*. Braithwaite tidied up some of the manuscripts and provided titles, in ways that subtly changed their meaning. He declined to publish any of the book manuscript, only coming to appreciate its significance much later. That manuscript and various other notes were published only in the 1990s. That is, only recently has the full and accurate picture of Ramsey's thought been available. One of the aims of this book is to bring to light the importance of the relatively unknown work, as well as the famous papers.

It will become clear that one of the ways in which Ramsey was so special—and radical—was that he saw it as a mark of a good theory that it be 'realistic', or able to make a difference in practice. His general approach was to move away from high metaphysics, mystical solutions to our deepest problems, unanswerable questions, and indefinable concepts, and move towards human problems that are in principle solvable in down-to-earth ways. As Steven Methven has put it, Ramsey dispensed with myth and metaphor, and instead placed human beings—'finite, fallible and yet extraordinarily functional'—at the heart of his theories. During Ramsey's time, Bertrand Russell, Wittgenstein, and the Vienna Circle were all engaged in a quest for certainty and logical purity. They conceived of truth in terms of our propositions getting right a reality wholly independent of us. Ramsey would retain a place for this kind of absolute truth for a very small class of propositions. But for the vast bulk of our beliefs, he stood in opposition to his contemporaries. He was engaged in a quest for beliefs that would work best for human beings.

The Heart

The first American Nobel Laureate in Economics, Paul Samuelson, rightly said that 'Frank Ramsey was a genius by all tests for genius.' But Ramsey was the antithesis of the kind of figure with which this label is often associated. He was not an enigmatic, cult-encouraging eccentric. He was that rarity among so-called geniuses—genial, open, and modest. He was, as his brother put it, 'very accessible to his fellow human beings'. 'Never a showman', said Ivor (I.A.) Richards, one of the founders of the new Cambridge school of literary criticism. Frances Marshall never heard anyone say a word against him—she didn't think it would be possible. Richards summed him up thus: 'Frank was never less than serious about anything and never solemn about anything either.' But the best one-liner is his brother Michael's: despite his being so clever and accomplished, Frank had 'a total lack of uppishness'. Wittgenstein told a story that also perfectly captures Ramsey's character. When Wittgenstein was a schoolteacher in a small village in Austria, Ramsey came to visit. In one of the classrooms there was a physiological diagram on the wall designed to show that certain 'bad habits' could give one an enlarged heart. Ramsey opined that a pupil's ambition should be to have as big a heart as possible.

Ramsey's own heart was outsized, as were his laugh and physique. His head, said Braithwaite in an obituary, was pentagonal and his smile gentle; his 'enormous physical size' was perfectly in proportion to 'the range of his intellect and his devastating laugh'. Moore, in his copy of that obituary, underlined 'devastating'. Patrick Wilkinson, who would be a colleague of Ramsey's at King's College, said that 'He shook with laughter'. So distinctive was his laugh that when his sister Bridget's son was a student in Ramsey's old undergraduate college, one of the college servants heard the laugh (without seeing the owner) and, in a state of astonishment, announced that it sounded just like Frank Ramsey had risen from the dead.

Ramsey thus comes across not only as one of the most impressive minds in the history of philosophy, mathematics, and economics, but also as one of the most attractive personalities. Even if we take into account the tendency to romanticize the traits of someone who died so young, there is overwhelming evidence of a simple, honest, hearty, and generous character. But there are flaws too, and I will not step around them. Indeed, Ramsey's naturalness and appetite for life, while usually being a strength of his character, was sometimes a weakness. It made him naïve and wretched in his romantic life, until he found his footing. While that is far from unusual in a young man, we will see that it was such a problem for Ramsey that it could spill into a bitter fault-finding with himself and his friends.

It might be thought that if Ramsey somehow managed all of his astonishing intellectual advances in a mere decade, he could not have had much room left for living, and that any biography must be mostly about his work. But that is not true. He lived an interesting life in interesting times. He started his Cambridge under-graduate degree in October 1920, not long after the First World War, with the surviving youth of Britain still struggling with the loss and with their re-entry into a peacetime world. He was part of the flow of a certain sort of English person who went to Vienna to be psychoanalysed, and was 'cured' by one of Freud's students. He was a vital member of the Apostles, the secret and elite Cambridge discussion society, during one of its most compelling periods, and part of the Bloomsbury set of writers and artists, with their open attitudes towards sex, their love of friendship, and their witty, gossipy, shocking conversation.

Indeed, Ramsey seemed not to know anyone who was boring or dull. Many of his friends went on to important lives. Lionel Penrose became the founder of modern British genetics. Kingsley Martin became the editor of *The New Statesman*. Max Newman went on to become a leading Second World War code-breaker and a computer pioneer. This biography will shed light on the lives of these, and many more, major figures in British modern intellectual history, as we see them intersect with Ramsey's life. We will also get an indication of how this remarkable group, in the hothouse that was 1920s Cambridge, played a key role in shaping the subsequent trajectory of philosophy, economics, and mathematics. By gaining a better under-standing of this history, we might improve our understanding of the intellectual disciplines in which we engage and thus improve our understanding of ourselves.

It may appear to the more austere academic that Ramsey's personal experience is irrelevant to what is really important about him—the intellectual advances. It might even be thought a violation to dredge up intimate facts about, for instance, his emotional life and his sexual relationships. But these sentiments are, I think, misguided. For one thing, it will become clear that Ramsey and his wife were uninhibited about such matters. Indeed, Lettice Ramsey deposited a copy of almost all the sensitive material in the King's College Archive Centre. This means that it has been widely available and that many of the intimate details are already in print. Ramsey's sister, Margaret Paul, reproduces some of the most painful letters and diary entries in her memoir of her brother. Henry Hemming, in his biography of Geoffrey Pyke, describes an early embarrassment in Ramsey's sex life. John Forrester and Laura Cameron have written and quoted much about Ramsey's psychoanalysis and the personal problems that caused him to seek treatment. But these matters have not always been placed in their full context—for instance, in the frame of reference of the free attitudes of Bloomsbury and the fashion for Freud. So one reason for including the intimacies of Ramsey's life in this biography is to rectify misleading impressions.

Another reason for including matters of the heart as well as the mind is that Ramsey's ideas become more distinctly focused when we see how they are aligned with his personality. His instincts, in all parts of his life, were straightforward and directed to the facts. We might go so far as to say that differences in the personalities between Ramsey and one of his most important interlocutors, Wittgenstein, manifest themselves as differences in their philosophy. Fichte famously said:

> What sort of philosophy one chooses depends . . . on what sort of man one is; for a philosophical system is not a dead piece of furniture that we can reject or accept as we wish; it is rather a thing animated by the soul of the person who holds it.

I will suggest that this is especially true of Ramsey and Wittgenstein.

Finally, those who are interested in people, as well as ideas, will want to see how Ramsey's apparent effortless superiority was set against a background in which he struggled with the full range of human emotion and anxiety. He was held in high esteem from the time he was a child and was moved ahead of his age group in school, with the consequence that he was always at least three years younger than the rest of his cohort. He would suffer for that. Though he may have appeared on the surface as a dispassionate logical brain, Frank Ramsey was as emotionally vulnerable as the next person. He was sharply aware of that fragility, and it interested him both personally and intellectually. In addition to being a superbly gifted technical thinker, he explored topics in psychology, ethics, politics, and the meaning of life. I will venture that Ramsey's poignant remarks on the timeless problem of what it is to be human are as fruitful to us today as is his work on more specialized topics.

The Challenges

One can understand why a full intellectual biography of Ramsey has been so long in coming. Many of the topics and problems he pursued seem impenetrable to all but a small number of specialists, and their range is staggering. Anyone who would try to fully understand Ramsey must be comfortable both in the minute crannies of technical scholarship and on the grand peaks of abstract thought. The task is daunting.

What we have to date is a wonderful BBC radio programme on Ramsey, a sister's substantive memoir, an electronically available trade biography, and biographical chapters in fine commentaries on Ramsey's work.* But no comprehensive biography has been undertaken. Because we have been waiting nigh on a century for it, I have tried to do what might be impossible. I have tried to satisfy all the parties interested in Ramsey for one reason or another—for his advances in decision theory, probability theory, and mathematics; his work on the deepest questions in philosophy, such as the nature of truth and meaning; his ground-breaking advances in economics; his relationship to Wittgenstein; his foray into psychoanalysis, and on and on. The result is an introduction to his work, as well as an account of his life.

My own expertise is in philosophy, and there is a plausible case to be made that this discipline provides the best basis from which to try to tackle the whole of Ramsey's thought, although a philosophically minded economist would also be suited to the task. Nonetheless, I will not attempt ham-fisted explanations of work that goes beyond my ken. I have asked some of the best people in, for instance, Ramsey Theory in combinatorial mathematics, optimal taxation theory, and optimal savings theory, to write short guest boxes. Indeed, even where something of interest to the specialist is within my range, I have asked guests to explain the brilliance of Ramsey's view, or show where sparks from his mind have alighted. My text is designed for a certain kind of general reader, whereas the material in the guest boxes is for those who know, or want to know, more. Those boxes will be invaluable for some, and unintelligible to others. They can be skipped without rendering unclear the line of thought in the main text.

Another challenge is that Ramsey's work comes into focus only when we see it as responsive to his contemporaries and to the moral, political, and economic affairs of

---

* See Hugh Mellor's *Better than the Stars* (BTTS) and 'Cambridge Philosophers I: F.P. Ramsey' (1995); Margaret Paul's *Frank Ramsey: A Sister's Memoir* (2012); Karl Sabbagh's *Shooting Star: The Brief and Brilliant Life of Frank Ramsey* (2013); Nils-Eric Sahlin's *The Philosophy of F.P. Ramsey* (1990a); Pedro Garcia Duarte's 'Frank P. Ramsey: A Cambridge Economist' (2009a); and Gabriele Taylor's 'Frank Ramsey: A Biographical Sketch' (2006).

his time. A fair bit of background of the likes of Russell, Moore, Wittgenstein, Keynes, Pigou is necessary. Separate and weighty books would be required to get each of these thinkers right. I have had to severely telescope their positions.

To make matters even more difficult, Ramsey often produced highly compressed arguments and proofs, expecting us to be able to fill in the gaps and keep up with his pace. He often made an important point by employing a witty remark, and generally did not belabour explanations. As Moore put it shortly after Ramsey's death:

> [he] had . . . an exceptional power of drawing conclusions from a complicated set of facts . . . But sometimes I feel that he fails to explain things as clearly as he could have done, simply because he does not see that any explanation is needed.

Twenty years later, Ramsey's friend, the economist and statistician Roy Harrod, captured his cerebral manner perfectly:

> The intellectual process is at white heat; but the style is delightfully cool, like that of some old naturalist taking one for a ramble in the country and making desultory observations.

Ramsey's early death also hinders our ability to provide the explanations that Moore and others have found missing. He might have done so, had he had more time. Moreover, we tend to interpret an individual's youthful thought through the lens of their mature or adult thought, and we cannot do that here. Ramsey had very little adulthood for us to go on.

The modern cast of Ramsey's ideas introduces a further challenge. It makes the danger of engaging in Whig history omnipresent. There is a temptation to read his work by viewing it from the perspective of contemporary theories, thinking that Ramsey leads inexorably to this particular present. Even contemporaries of Ramsey, who were interviewed in the early 1980s, had their recollections burdened with all sorts of more recent events and theories. I will place Ramsey in the context in which he found himself, in an attempt to avoid such distortions.

But I will also need to cautiously employ contemporary standpoints. Ramsey's thought is almost always described as being ahead of his time. So I will need to take a look back from where we are now and see what his contribution were, both to the way the history of ideas unfolded and to freestanding ideas. The first endeavour is made a little easier by the fact that Ramsey's questions and ways of answering them left a traceable mark in Cambridge. For many years after his death, when Wittgenstein and Moore held their philosophical discussions, they would pepper their remarks with 'Would Ramsey say this?' or 'Would Ramsey think that?' Moore would still be writing in his notebooks what Ramsey would say about various matters as late as 1953. Richard Braithwaite based much of his own work on Ramsey's, and Wittgenstein's turn away from his early position was largely caused by Ramsey. His influence, that is, continued to shape discussions long after his death. I will give indications of Ramsey's enduring effects by tracing connections of thought back to him when those lines are there to be seen. When there is a break in the lineage—when Ramsey's ideas reappear decades later without an obvious path back to him—I will offer explanations of that.

A related danger would be to succumb to the temptation of taking Ramsey to be a kind of god. It seems that intellectuals, like other breeds of humans, need heroes—those super-talented rarities around whom stories can be built. Such narratives no doubt simplify complex histories and vest too much credit in formational figures. Correctives can and should be administered, bringing to the fore those who have been relegated to the shadowy background. I have done some of that here, bringing to light some little-known figures, such as the Polish probability theorist Janina Hosiasson. But at the same time, we do require coherent accounts of how we arrived at where we are. We require maps of a discipline if we are to make sense of it, and those maps will point to iconic features in the landscape. A wilderness trail could be signposted every five feet, but it is a better trail if the directions are spaced out at important junctions. Ramsey merits prominent signposts in our histories of philosophy, economics, and mathematics.

One challenge seems trivial in comparison, but nonetheless proved difficult for me: I wasn't sure what to call him. I have decided to use 'Frank' when I discuss his life and 'Ramsey' when I discuss his work. There aren't too many photographs of him, as the most important album (from 1928 to 1929, when Lettice was starting to take a lot of photos) has gone missing. But in the surviving pictures, an unaffected character shines through. Referring to that kind of person by his surname seems stilted, especially when discussing his boyhood. But it would be equally odd to use 'Frank' when talking about his work, especially when his surname graces so many important theories and innovations.

Another small decision I have had to take is how to cope with the extended cast of characters, who, once introduced, often reappear on the scene. Rather than risk annoying the reader by fastidiously saying who is who at every reappearance, I will allow the index of names to carry the weight. The pages where the person is properly introduced (not necessarily the first mention) are in bold.

Finally, one cannot describe a life, nor a life's work, without bringing to it one's own interpretation, and describing its shape or arc. Otherwise we just have a tedious transcription of what was said, recalled, or written. I've endeavoured to seek out and enlist all the available sources, and to be as fair-handed as possible, so that my reading of Ramsey is as true as it can be. But the facts, both with respect to the life and the work, are partly lost to the past, and even those that are accessible require interpretation. At times, my own reading has had to be especially present. For instance, there is no discussing Wittgenstein's ideas without taking a stand on scholarly disputes.[†] Moreover, I came to be interested in Ramsey because he put forward the kind of philosophical pragmatism I had already thought right. In presenting him as a pragmatist of this particular variety, I have marshalled the texts, so as to prevent the impression that I am imposing an unwarranted interpretation on him.

For those who like a strong narrative, an overarching story tying everything together, that pragmatism happens to provide one. Ramsey rejected metaphysical and mystical answers to our most profound questions, preferring to offer solutions close to the human ground. In life too, he was a kind of pragmatist, always trying to work things out in the best and most optimistic way possible, for himself, for his friends, and for his relations with others. There are of course exceptions to this tendency, both in his thought and life, and I will not try to squeeze everything about Ramsey into this mould.

Note on Primary Sources

One might think that, given the brevity of Ramsey's life, there could not be much documentary evidence about it. That would be a mistake. Ramsey's father wrote not one, but two, accounts of his son's life—one in an autobiography at the end of his own life and another in a scrapbook, full of letters and school reports, put together shortly after Frank's death. In 2013, a fine memoir by Frank's younger sister, Margaret Paul, was published after her death. There is also a wealth of material from some of the most celebrated diarists and letter-writers of the period. A.C. (Arthur) Benson, Master of Magdalene College, essayist, poet, and nephew of Henry Sidgwick, whose diaries clock in at over four million words in 180 volumes, offers us insights into the young Frank and his family. Frances Marshall, who was the fourth in the ménage at the core of the Bloomsbury group (the Lytton Strachey–Dora Carrington–Ralph Partridge relationship) does the same for the adult Frank. There are illuminating materials in archives, such as those at Winchester College; Trinity College, Cambridge; the Ramsey, Keynes, Braithwaite, Partridge, and Sprott papers at King's College, Cambridge; the Ramsey–Schlick correspondence at the Vienna

---

[†] My reading of Wittgenstein and of his relationship to Ramsey differs, for instance, from the 'resolute reading' of Wittgenstein, pioneered by Cora Diamond (1995, 2011). See my *Cambridge Pragmatism: From Peirce and James to Ramsey and Wittgenstein* (Misak 2016).

Circle Archives in Amsterdam; the Ramsey, Carnap, and Reichenbach collections at the University of Pittsburgh Archives of Scientific Philosophy; and the Russell and Ogden papers at McMaster University. Hugh Mellor's 1978 radio portrait includes short interviews with people who knew Ramsey, and Ramsey's grandson, Stephen Burch, possesses private material not available elsewhere. Ramsey's diaries and letters were not occasions for creativity and were not meant for posterity. But they manifest the sometimes painful truth and honesty of his feeling, and allow us to see not just a remarkable mind, but also the whole person.

Finally, in what can only be described as an academic's fairy-tale, I discovered a priceless, and pretty much unknown, goldmine. I was already well into this biography when I came across a 1982 letter from one Laura Leavitt Kahn in the Max Newman papers at St John's College, Cambridge. She had written to Newman to say that she was an Oxford doctoral student, whose thesis was to be a biography of Ramsey. She wondered if he had any recollections he might share with her. She had a motor car, and would like to come to interview him. To make a long story short, I tracked down that student, Laurie Kahn, now an award-winning documentary filmmaker in Boston. The biography had never been written. But Laurie had done a tremendous amount of high-quality investigating and interviewing. Her materials had been lent out and it was an open question as to whether they still existed. Happily, they had been preserved, and now reside in the Thomas Fisher Rare Books Library at the University of Toronto, gifted by Laurie, with relevant copyrights.

Laurie said to one of her interviewees that she'd come to her project at the last moment possible, fifty-two years after Ramsey's death, when those who had known him were at least in their late seventies. I began my research well after that crucial period, after everyone who had known Ramsey was gone. Laurie interviewed Ramsey's widow, his siblings, his childhood and undergraduate friends, his students and colleagues, Wittgenstein's nephew, and more. By opening a window into the past for me, she made possible what had seemed impossible: access to direct questions and candid answers about Ramsey from those who were in a first-hand position to know. I am grateful to Laurie for her diligence and interviewing skills in 1982 and for her kindness in 2016.

In addition to all this, there is a significant quantity of hardly excavated intellectual work by Ramsey himself. Most of the important material has now been published—a set of papers in 1931 by Richard Braithwaite, reprinted and added to by Hugh Mellor in 1978 and 1990; the unfinished book manuscript in 1991, edited by Nicholas Rescher and Ulrich Majer; notes on philosophy, probability, and mathematics by Maria Carla Galavotti also in 1991; a note on the weight of evidence in 1990 by Nils-Eric Sahlin; and one on economics by Pedro Garcia Duarte in 2009. But many of the original manuscripts, with Ramsey's cross-outs and pencil edits, remain a treasure trove for anyone with a love for intellectual detective work. Most of them are housed at the University of Pittsburgh's Archives of Scientific Philosophy, which purchased the Ramsey papers in 1982. That collection consists of seven large boxes, each holding as many as thirty-eight folders, and are available digitally. A few of Ramsey's original papers are in the Cambridge University Archives, and some are in private hands. For instance, Lettice gave the Wittgenstein scholar Michael Nedo a short and undated manuscript on Wittgenstein's *Tractatus*. Very few people have laid eyes on that. Some of the original material is nowhere to be found, such as the important paper 'Theories'.

Some personal material has also been lost or destroyed. The most relevant of Lettice Ramsey's photo albums has disappeared. Laurie Kahn's inventory of it makes one feel very bad about that: there were pictures of Frank with Lettice and Frances Marshall frolicking on river banks; Frank horsing around and relaxing with his little girls; Frank visiting Keynes at his country house; Frank exercising on the beach, playing tennis, enjoying picnics with his friends, unclad with Lettice, and walking with Elizabeth Denby, the other great love of his life. Denby's own letters to Frank were burned, on her instructions, after her death.

While no doubt less than ideal for the scholar, I have kept the text uncluttered by consigning the citations of both primary and secondary sources to the back of the book. Anyone who wants to track down the original material, or investigate my warrant for a particular claim, can do so. My policy with respect to citation of the primary material is complicated, for what I hope are understandable reasons.

Sometimes an item is only accessible in photocopy or digital form, in more than one location. For instance, Ramsey's grandson holds the originals (as well as the copyright) of all the letters and diaries, but Lettice Ramsey gave not-quite complete and not quite identical copies to both King's College and to Laurie Kahn. My choice of source in these instances will inevitably be irritating to some, but not to others, the irritation likely being dependent on one's continent of residence.

Scholars in a number of fields have been to the various archives and have used material from them (often without securing permission). Sometimes a published version of a letter, diary note, or manuscript is inaccurate, or partial, or fails to register an important strikeout or hesitation on the author's part. In those cases, I cite the more accurate or more revealing source in the archive, rather than the published one. Where the published transcription is perfect, or where there is an utterly trivial error in it (such as a missing full stop) I cite the published version, silently correcting the text. I mark what is illegible by [ ]. If a letter is translated from, say, the original German to English, I give the name of the translator in the endnote, if it's not obvious from my text. Page numbers to Ramsey's collected papers are those of the 1990 Mellor collection, not the 1931 Braithwaite volume.

PART I

BOYHOOD

1

THE RAMSEYS

A Cambridge Family

Frank Plumpton Ramsey was born on 22 February 1903, in the family house on Chesterton Road, in the heart of Cambridge. He was the eldest child of Agnes and Arthur Ramsey. Arthur was a mathematics Fellow and President (vice-Master) at Magdalene College, Cambridge—a good textbook writer, but no great mathematical mind. Agnes, Oxford-educated, at a time when it was rare for a girl to be sent to university, was a social reformer. Arthur and Agnes expected success from their children, and they got it. Michael was born the year after Frank. He became Archbishop of Canterbury, the head of the Church of England. Then came Bridget, who would be a physician, and then Margaret, an Oxford economics don.

The family was part of what Noel Annan, Provost of King's College, Cambridge during the 1950s, called the English intellectual aristocracy. In the early 1900s, its Cambridge branch was composed of a complex web of people and families. Frank's nursery school teacher, Miss Sharpley, had been the governess of Frances Darwin, granddaughter of Charles Darwin. Agnes's political work brought her into the orbit of John Maynard Keynes's mother. The Keynes and the Darwin families were bound together by marriage. Edward Bevan, who would become Ludwig Wittgenstein's doctor and friend, had been a neighbour of the Ramseys, wrestling on the drawing room carpet with Frank and Michael when they were all youngsters. Charles (C.K.) Ogden, the influential editor and inventor of Basic English, was a family friend.

With such a background of cultural privilege, Frank's ascent to the heights of the English intellectual world might at first glance appear frictionless, and indeed, the bald facts support that view. He won a scholarship to Winchester, a top academic public (fee-paying) school, and then studied mathematics at Trinity College, Cambridge. Keynes, who had identified him as a major talent early on, snapped him up and made him a Fellow of King's College, Cambridge when he was only twenty-one. Apart from boarding school, holidays, and a half-year in Vienna, Frank spent his entire life in the warm embrace of Cambridge, in arguably the most glorious decades of the university's 800-year history.

But while it might have been an ascent up a ladder that had been placed there for him, no one could have expected Frank to climb so fast and high. As Keynes put it, 'One almost has to believe that Ramsey in his nursery near Magdalene was unconsciously absorbing from 1903 to 1914 everything which anyone may have been saying or writing in Trinity.' Moreover, the ascent wasn't without its hesitancies. We will see that there were personal struggles that might have tumbled him from those rungs.

Frank was of a very particular class and status, in that fine-grained English way. It was not upper class, but a confident, professional, upper middle class. He had the certainty of the vicarage, and the tools of an excellent education, in his baggage. We will see that some of the prejudices of that class were in there as well. But his socialist and egalitarian principles, his 'caring for the underdog', would make those biases inert in his actions. Since one of his philosophical triumphs would be to show how we judge what someone believes by their behaviour, we should do the same with him.

Vicars and Preachers

Both Frank's parents were the children and grandchildren of clergymen. On Arthur's side they were evangelical, low church, populist Congregationalists. Arthur's father, Adam Averell Ramsey, was a minister in Yorkshire, where Arthur spent his childhood until the family moved to build a new congregation in Hackney, London. Agnes was from a more traditional family, though just as devout. She grew up in villages in Norfolk, where her father, Plumpton Stravinson Wilson, was an Anglican vicar.

Not only did churchmen permeate Frank's lineage, religion also permeated his immediate family. They were regulars at the non-conformist Emmanuel Congregational Chapel in Cambridge, where Arthur was a deacon from 1914 until his old age. Arthur led daily prayers after the family's breakfast and Agnes sent Frank prayer and hymn books when he was away at boarding schools. Michael would make his life in the church. The one he chose, much to his mother's pleasure and his father's initial displeasure, was the Anglican Church of England. The young Frank, as you would expect, was a believer.

He rebelled, however, quite early on. Arthur gives the following account of Frank's state of faith at the age of thirteen:

> In the summer of 1916 we spent a few weeks at Old Hunstanton, our only family holiday together between 1914 and 1919. While there Frank talked to me about religious difficulties. He was thinking out things for himself. I think it was in the following term that he decided, much to his Housemaster's surprise, who thought him too young, that he wished to be confirmed.... [T]hat he should wish to take such a step after a good deal of thought about it was a great joy to us both.

He was at Winchester at a time when almost all the boys were confirmed in the Church of England.

But in June 1920, his final year at Winchester, Frank would write to his mentor back in Cambridge, C.K. Ogden, with a different story about his religious state of mind during his confirmation:

> Dear Mr. Ogden,
>
> I thank you very much for your letter, which I would have answered before, if I had had the opportunity. Mother and Bridget were here from Saturday till Tuesday and since then I have been writing a very bad essay for Mr. Williams which is sometime overdue.
>
> I think this might interest you about Williams. When I was confirmed 3½ years ago, I rather doubted if I believed all the things I was supposed to and consulted Williams about it as he was preparing me. So I went and told him I didn't believe in the resurrection of the body; he didn't seem to mind and explained to me that what I understood by 'the body' was really called 'the flesh' and that the body only means the personality, so that everyone believed in the resurrection of the body, but of course no one in the resurrection of the flesh, which was an absurd doctrine. I then showed him that in the baptismal vow which I renewed in confirmation it said not resurrection of the body, but actually resurrection of the flesh, which he had just told me was an absurd doctrine. I thought he would be rather at a loss but he didn't seem to mind a bit, but defended the resurrection of the flesh quite happily.... As far as I can see he is prepared to say he believes in anything if he thinks it will pay; he isn't a bit clerical and it looks as if he took orders as a step to a headmastership.

At the age of thirteen, Frank was already an atheist. He made his views known to his masters in an essay on whether the state should support sectarian education. His conclusion was that they must not do so:

> sectarian education is not education.... True education is broad and tolerant; it should make us feel the littleness of man, of our nation and of our creed. Moreover there is everything to gain from Christian and Parsee children learning ethics or comparative religion together... There is no harm in Bible reading; it is the best book anyone could read; what is objectionable, is the belief that the Bible or any other book represents final truth. People talk of education in the principles of the Christian religion; that is not really education, any more than education in the principles of Marx is education.

Frank's atheism was an unwanted first for both sides of the family, made even less welcome because his two younger sisters followed him. Michael, who was always close to Frank, was terribly unsettled when, on a family seaside holiday, he first heard from Frank that he had lost his faith. They had arguments about it all of Frank's life. Michael was always clear, however, that although Frank was certainly sorry that Michael had joined the clergy, it was never an issue that threatened their relationship. On his deathbed, Frank was still trying to persuade Michael that religion was irrational.

Frank was so known for his atheism that, after his death, when one of his friends embraced religion and got himself baptized, a close friend of both said 'B. could never have done that if Frank had been alive.'

Hearties vs Spartans

Frank's mother was from a family of hearties—vigorous, lively, and loud. Agnes was a Wilson, the second-youngest of nine, born in 1875. Her mother Elizabeth ('Meme') was the daughter of a successful merchant in North Lynn, Norfolk. Agnes's father, the Reverend Plumpton Stravinson Wilson, was head boy and cricket captain at Uppingham School in Rutland, then marched on to Exeter College, Oxford, where he lost his right hand in a gun accident. The name 'Plumpton' is a nod to the Wilson family's descent from the de Plomptons, knights who held considerable land after the 1066 Conquest. There's a village called 'Plompton' in Yorkshire named after the family—Sir Edward Plompton swapped the 'u' for the 'o' in the 1500s. There's at least one Plumpton in every generation of the Wilson family, although by Agnes's day it was relegated to middle-name status. Five of her six brothers had it bestowed on them. It's not clear why just one—Archie—escaped.

The Wilsons valued education for their sons and, unusually for the time, their daughters as well. Meme taught them gently till they were six, then the Reverend took over in what one of the boys—Charlie—called an 'exceedingly rigorous' way. But none of the brood seemed to mind, and they all reaped the benefits. The boys won scholarships to public schools and went on to become doctors, schoolmasters, vicars, and an organist of Ely Cathedral. One sister, Ethel, became a schoolteacher, as did Agnes, and another, an art-schooled painter.

The Wilsons were large, both physically and in personality. They managed to be 'ebullient members of the upper middle class', despite subsisting on a vicar's salary and his after-hours tutoring. Perhaps they were aided by money on Meme's side. Frank's sister Margaret described the Wilson clan as a friendly, amusing, noisy, and cheerful bunch, 'over-confident in their opinions'. They were a constant presence in the lives of Frank and his siblings. Meme was a wonderful grandmother, loved by the Ramsey children. The Reverend was terrifying, not least because of the hook that served as his prosthetic hand. When he was a young adult, Frank would complain about how loud and obnoxious his Wilson relations were, and how they simply shouted their opinions at each other. But as a child, he enjoyed going on vacation with the extended family. They were jolly affairs, with outside games and singing round the piano. Once, in Perranporth in North Cornwall, Frank read *War and Peace* to the cousins in the evenings. The clan also convened at uncle Kenny's house in Fettes in Edinburgh, where everyone would get angry at each other over bridge games. Arthur did not like being beaten at cards, or at billiards, on these family jamborees.

Frank's eldest Wilson uncle, Charlie, played a significant role in his life, as he was Frank's headmaster at his first boarding school. Charlie had taken his degree at Trinity College, Cambridge, where he represented the university in cricket and rugby. He was one of a very few Englishmen to earn international caps in both rugby and football. But in the Wilson family, that hardly distinguished him. Another of the boys, Geoffrey, was such a good footballer that the *Daily Mail* called him 'England's darling'. Every one of the Wilsons seemed to get a Blue (a place on their Oxford or Cambridge sports team). There is a photo of a holiday in which a pack of the boys of that generation stride through the surf. They are strong, athletic, and handsome. A couple of them look just like Frank.

Charlie became co-headmaster of Sandroyd, a highly regarded and well-equipped preparatory school. It had an indoor heated swimming pool and a nine-hole golf course. Charlie was an outspoken conservative who believed in the Empire. The Oxford archaeologist Christopher Hawkes, an ex-Sandroydian, remembered him as 'the great Victorian, athletically and scholastically towering'. Parents, he said, 'adored this kind of thing' and 'simply fell for him'. Charlie was 'genial and powerful and stumpy, occasionally wrathful but an extraordinary teacher'. He chose his Sandroyd boys on physical as well as intellectual merit. In his day, the school was in the Oxshott woods in Surrey. One had to come up from Cobham Station in horse-drawn buggies or else walk through the woods. Charlie would run a genetics test on prospective mothers. As he walked them back to the train station, he would bring out his pocket-watch at the half-way mark and said 'Oh, Mrs. So-and-so, we've missed the time—we shall have to run.' If the mother, in her corset and long skirt, said she simply couldn't, the boy was out. If she sprinted though the woods, Charlie would return to the school and say 'We'll have that boy.'

Charlie's account of the family—the 'Wilson Family Record'—is mostly an adventure tale stuffed with roaming, shooting, fishing, and general mischief. The only unwelcome break was said to be the Sunday regime, with its relentless talk of hell-fire and eternal punishment. Charlie's construction of the Family Record was of course the image he wanted to present, but all those sporting blues give it the air of truth. The girls are far in the background of this record, except when one marries 'an amusing pal' who engages with Charlie and the boys 'in quest of sport'. Agnes's marriage goes unmentioned. Arthur was not a sporting bonhomme.

The politics of the Wilsons as adults were all over the map. Agnes and Ethel were left of centre. Charlie and Kenny were the opposite, each holding a full deck of unpleasant views about class and race, against which their sisters would rail. Charlie thought that 'socialists and liberals' were 'miserable worms', whereas Agnes would remain a socialist and liberal (though hardly miserable) all her life. The following story of Charlie's illustrates the familial tensions:

The Matabele chiefs were on view in London. They were much admired by certain foolish ladies and one of them, reputedly rich, actually married Lobengula, a huge handsome savage.... I remarked that I would sooner see a sister of mine dead than so married. This caused an outbreak from Ethel and Agnes, who had rather advanced views. They argued that God had created coloured men as well as white. I proved right this time, as after a week of this unnatural union, Lobengula being in his opinion scantily supplied with cash by his wife, seized her hand and bit her thumb off! The union was promptly annulled. I had my triumph and made the most of it.

Lobengula was the Matabeleland ruler who eventually gave Cecil Rhodes permission to dig for gold on his lands. Charlie had met Rhodes while trying for a scholarship at Exeter, his father's old college in Oxford. The examination didn't go well and he reported that 'Cecil Rhodes, then an undergraduate, dug me out of the Clarendon Hotel and got me rooms at Oriel College.' They remained friendly—so much so that after Rhodes finished his degree he offered to take Charlie to South Africa with him, an offer Charlie declined.

Frank's father came from a very different sort of family, the kind that did not become mates with the likes of Cecil Rhodes. It was Spartan, strict, and austere. His mother, Hephzibah Sargeant, was from a class not dissimilar to that of the Wilsons, her father being a wealthy London coal merchant with a wharf on the Thames. But her marriage to the evangelical preacher Adam Averell Ramsey took her down in the world. He was first a minister in Hackney, on the outskirts of London, then in the smoky mill and mining town of Dewsbury, Yorkshire.

In old age Arthur and his sister Phebe would write in their own family records that their childhoods were full of nursery games and a father's affection. But they seem to have been looking back through rose-tinted glasses. In Margaret's description, the family was 'low-spirited', dour, straight-laced, and pious. The children had a strong 'sense of sin' and a 'formidable father' in Adam Averell. They also had a strong sense of the class difference between their parents. And Arthur's father, in Margaret's view, regarded all the women in the family as his slaves. All but one was a spinster, and they all suffered from a streak of hypochondria. One of them was told of a weak heart and stayed in bed for twenty years till the diagnosis was reversed, whereupon she got up and continued with life. After his wife died, Adam Averell's unmarried daughters stayed on to look after him. Lucy, who will reappear in these pages, begged her father for funds to take piano lessons and then taught piano in a boarding school, which she called a 'dog kennel', a different girl coming every half hour. Eventually she returned to fulfil her duty to her father.

The finances of the family were precarious, as were the children's lives and educations. Two of the three boys died in adolescence. One of them had been called Frank and would be the namesake of the first-born child of Arthur and Agnes. The education of the girls was not considered important, or at least it was not where money would be spent when in short supply. The two youngest nonetheless persevered and made schoolteachers of themselves, almost the only genteel route for the daughters of the hard-up middle-classes who were obliged to earn a living.

Agnes Ramsey

It is no surprise that Agnes, being a Wilson, was a powerhouse. After her excellent home-schooling, she got a place to read history at St Hugh's, Oxford, where she made an impression and a success of herself. Her sporting Blue was in hockey. She had met the mathematician and author Charles Dodgson (better known as Lewis Carroll) when her father did a stint at a vicarage in Oxford. When a little girl, she used to go boating with Dodgson, and when a St Hugh's undergraduate, she attended his logic lectures and went on further excursions with him. One of those trips, to the theatre in London, was taken with a fellow St Hugh's student, whose mother received a letter from Dodgson beforehand. Despite her being seventeen and Dodgson sixty-three, he wrote: 'I venture to ask if I may regard myself as on "kissing" terms with her, as I am with many a girlfriend a great deal older than she is ... Of course, I shall, unless I hear to the contrary, continue to shake hands only.' We don't know if he was on such terms with Agnes. He did give her a copy of *Alice's Adventures in Wonderland*, fondly inscribed. Much later, her young son Frank would be frightened of the picture of Alice with her arm out of the window and her leg out of the chimney. So Agnes cut out all the illustrations, destroying the book's monetary value, but making for a great family story.

After Oxford, Agnes taught at East Putney High School, in London, for a couple of years. She was known for an absent-mindedness that would have her covered head-to-toe in chalk. After two years, Agnes became 'fed up' with being a school-mistress and gave it up, going up to Fettes school to keep house for her brother Kenny. As Frank's sister Margaret said, the move is something of a mystery. Kenny was one of the Tory brothers she had always fought against, and housekeeping was not her strong suit. Nonetheless, it was momentous, for it would be at Fettes that she met Arthur. Perhaps to escape the housekeeping for her brother, perhaps because she felt it true love, Agnes married Arthur in 1902 and moved to Cambridge.

Only then did she find her stride, via her left-leaning political inclinations. She was a founder of the Cambridge branch of the Federation of University Women. She agitated for progressive causes. She put pressure on candidates for parliament to support the vote for women; gave talks in and beyond Cambridge on the topic; organized fund-raising stalls in the market; and was on the organizing committee of the Cambridge Association for Women's Suffrage. That was the non-violent group, unlike the suffragettes. She quickly became part of the nucleus of liberal Cambridge, along with Mrs Sidgwick, Mrs Keynes, Lady Darwin, and their progressive husbands. Agnes herself was always on the more radical part of the spectrum, more Labour than Liberal. She had suffragist friends come to stay and Labour Party gatherings in the garden. Graham Wallas, the social psychologist, educationalist, and major figure in the Fabian Society and the London School of Economics, was one of these visitors, as was Hugh Dalton, Labour Party economist and eventual Chancellor of the Exchequer. These leading figures in British left-wing politics had a warm respect for Agnes. Decades after her death, Dalton remembered Agnes and Clara Rackham as the women who made the Labour Party in Cambridge great.

Hardly a day passed without a committee meeting or three. Agnes was a school governor and a frequent letter-writer to the newspapers, advocating a women's right to birth control, the freeing of Irish political prisoners, and countless other progressive causes. She was elected to the Cambridge Board of Guardians and was involved in the Cambridge Workhouse on Mill Road. There was no state social safety net in those days, so Agnes went round on her bicycle putting milk on the doorsteps of the poor. She was instrumental in starting a children's home, connected with the workhouse, to save as many children as she could from being put to work. With her own offspring in tow, she would go to the grim workhouse on Christmas day to serve plum pudding. When she was speaking on political causes in the market square, you could hear her at Senate House, which, even at its nearest point, is a considerable shout away. Merely speaking in the square, never mind shouting, was a brave thing to do. Agnes's friend Leah Manning spoke of an occasion when she and Maurice Dobb, then an undergraduate, were addressing a crowd there:

> A score of undergraduates got between the shafts and ran us round and round the square. I couldn't keep my balance, and since I soon began, indelicately, to show my underwear, Maurice pushed me down on to a chair and clung desperately to it himself, while the men continued their frolic with cries of 'good old Ginger' and 'good old Bertie'.

Dobb, of whom we will hear more later, was called 'Band-Box Bertie' by his fellow students, his genteel familial roots buried under his sympathies for communism. The intelligence services had their eye on him, and he would later befriend and come under suspicion together with the Cambridge spies for Russia, Kim Philby and Guy Burgess.

Agnes's children were all devoted to her, and were perfectly happy being brought up to think that the Tories were 'the stupid party'. Michael found his mother flawless: radiant, friendly, outgoing, understanding, with a powerful sense of humour. He could always enjoy this unalloyed view of his mother, as he never rebelled against her. Agnes held on to her Christian beliefs and mores, and Michael's devotion to the Church of England meant that he never strayed from those principles. Frank also adored his mother, but when as a young man he felt the sharp end of Agnes's moral sensibility, he would rue her inflexibility. Publicly, she was involved in family planning and promoting contraception, which was thought not respectable at the time. But when it came to personal sexual morality, Agnes was not quite so fiercely progressive. Her daughter Bridget later said that it was a surprise to her that her mother would even know what family planning was, given that she would never discuss such intimate matters with her children. She told Bridget when she started studying at Cambridge that if she let a man kiss her, she must marry him. Bridget assumed that this was because a kiss could cause a pregnancy.

While many of their neighbours and other acquaintances had the view that Agnes was an effusive and charming woman, others saw her as formidable and over-bearing. She was tall and confident in her views, with no time or interest in being stylish or in mending her stockings. Her morals were uncompromising. During the war, she gave a talk to the British Women's Temperance Society on how spending anything that went beyond the truly essential was an evil. We should take pride, she said, in being shabby, and children should also feel the effects of wartime frugality— for instance, in their Christmas stockings.

Arthur Ramsey

The young Arthur Ramsey enjoyed football and cricket, although the pitches, organization, and equipment at his schools were nowhere near the standards of the Wilsons. That was the least of the hardships. Most critical was the fact that the mathematically talented and hard-working boy had to make his own way educationally. Arthur's mediocre schools hardly ever sent their pupils to universities. He recalled: 'If I succeeded in solving examples, well and good; but if I failed there was nobody available with the time and ability to show me how to do them.'

Nonetheless, the school encouraged him to apply for scholarships to Oxford and Cambridge. He tried, and tried again, until he succeeded in getting a scholarship to Magdalene College, Cambridge. He was of the first generation of Ramseys to attend university.

Magdalene back then was a small, poor college, with a dearth of good students. Its formal teaching didn't amount to much. During Arthur's undergraduate days, from 1886 to 1889, the mathematics students had just over two hours of lectures a week and were advised to hire private tutors out of their own pocket. Arthur did that, worked hard, and went to church twice a day. He ended up coming fifth in the final examinations, and after graduation, was encouraged to apply to teach at a good public school—but not in England, where his non-conformism would be an obstacle, if not an outright bar. So he applied to Fettes in Scotland and landed a position there in 1890. One of his colleagues was Kenny Wilson, one of the right-wing members of the high-spirited Wilson family.

If Agnes was a Wilson through and through, Arthur too was a chip off his family's block. He was a stiff man with a bald head and a big moustache, thin and wiry—as physically unlike the Wilsons as possible. He was pinched emotionally too, again, unlike the Wilsons. He would eventually become a fellow of Magdalene and Arthur Benson, the Master of the college, would say that when roused to anger—an all-too-frequent occurrence—Arthur Ramsey 'was all eye and moustache'. Arthur's father's severe, puritanical streak had also lodged itself in him. None of his fellow Magdalene Fellows, apart from Benson, called him by his first name: he was A.S.R. (Arthur Stanley Ramsey) to them. His obituary in the Magdalene College Record noted: 'He did not give intimacy easily—"I do not think", he once said, "that I have ever addressed anyone other than a relation by his Christian name."'

The story of how Arthur ended up a don at Magdalene is ironic, given that his wife would be a suffragist. In 1896, while he was a schoolteacher at Fettes, his old mathematics supervisor at Magdalene died. The possibility of filling the vacancy took up residence in Arthur's mind, despite a discouraging reply to an initial query. He soon had his chance to make an impression, during an especially low note in Cambridge University's sorry history around the admission of women.

Women had been successfully sitting the Cambridge exams since 1870, but they were not officially members of the University, and were not granted degrees. Rather, the women's colleges—Girton and Newnham—would award each student a certificate saying that she had done all the work, passed the exams, and would have obtained a certain class of degree. A proposal was made in 1897 to grant to women membership in the University and degrees. The women had their supporters, some powerful. Henry Sidgwick, the eminent utilitarian philosopher at Trinity, was on their side—he had co-founded Newnham in 1871. The women's colleges thought they might win the vote. After all, they had successfully established themselves and grown in size, demonstrating that their students could meet the University's standards. Indeed, a larger proportion of the women were now sitting the difficult final cumulative exam than their male counterparts, many of the latter content with the less ambitious, 'Ordinary' degree. Arguments raged pro and con in the national press.

Cambridge University was (and still is) governed by ancient rules. Any graduate (who had waited the requisite year and taken his automatic MA) was eligible to vote on this proposal. The ugly side of this radically democratic system was on full display, as old boys were called from near and far to come and vote down the proposal. Arthur was approached by a Fellow of Magdalene and offered a room in College if he would travel from Edinburgh, no minor journey in those days. On the account he gave when he was in his eighties, he initially demurred, after which another Fellow urged him to make the trip because the College was considering him for the vacant Fellowship. Here is Arthur's description of the day, a day which the anti-woman forces won:

> After lunching in the Combination Room we went round to the Senate House to vote. The streets were crowded with people especially near the Senate House and there was no lack of flags and such inscriptions as 'Get thee to Girton, Beatrice' hanging across Trinity Street, and a dummy figure of a woman in bloomers mounted on a real bicycle hung high above the ground..... The voting showed a huge majority against the proposal in the largest poll ever taken in the Senate House. A large body of undergraduates at once rushed round to Newnham College, I suppose to make a hostile demonstration, but the authorities had wisely shut the College gates. One man climbed a drainpipe and got in at an open window, to find himself in a room with about half-a-dozen young ladies who stared at him so scornfully that he could think of nothing better to do than climb out of the window and go back down the drainpipe, and the demonstration petered out.... The women's Colleges bore their rebuff with fortitude and dignity, and no further steps were taken in their interests until after the first world war.

Arthur neglects to tell us how he voted. That alone should raise suspicion. His daughter Margaret asserted that he voted against the women. Magdalene would be the last all-male college in the whole of Oxford or Cambridge to admit women (in 1988), and he was there to do its bidding. Arthur had his meeting with the Master and in due course was offered the job. In 1897, at the age of thirty, he left Fettes and returned to his old college and to Cambridge, where he was to spend the rest of his long life.

On occasion, he would return to Fettes to see Kenny Wilson and his other old colleagues. On one of those visits, he met Agnes Wilson, eight years his junior. He was so taken with her that he extended his stay and proposed marriage after a week. She asked him to return for an answer in a couple of months when her family would be visiting. The prospect of running her own house in Cambridge, rather than her brother's house in Scotland, was attractive, and so was the political and intellectual milieu. She was an intelligent woman with modest means, and staying at Fettes offered limited prospects. She decided on Arthur and Cambridge.

They married, and moved into a spacious house in central Cambridge, at 71 Chesterton Road, next to the river Cam.* When the Ramsey children were young, they were able to cross over the bridge and play on the common, Jesus Green. The issue of how the family was going to worship must have been talked about, for Arthur and Agnes were each committed to opposite sides of the conformist/non-conformist divide. The deliberations were resolved by a compromise. They all attended the Congregational church, very regularly, always in the same pew. But Agnes's Anglican father christened all the children and Agnes made her communion on holy days at Anglican churches. They prayed and read the Bible as a family every morning.

They also found work-arounds for their political differences. Arthur would always resent Agnes's suffragist garden parties, but never prohibited them. He would not be converted to the Labour Party, but he would often attend suffragist meetings, sometimes even publicly sitting on the stage with Agnes. They had an intriguing marriage. One of Frank's Winchester friends recalled that Agnes was the dominating party. But Arthur had his own bad-tempered ways of keeping the household under his control.

Arthur was never to be more than a journeyman mathematician. He was considered a boring teacher, his lectures 'read at a fast dictation speed'. His style is summed up nicely in his obituary in the Magdalene College Record:

> Let it be conceded that his relations with undergraduates were marked by a certain rigidity; but this, although it kept intimacy at bay, did not impair the great personal respect in which we held him. His standards were high, his rule austere; and the College prospered under his rod.

He became famous for adapting his lecture course notes in various branches of applied mathematics into clear, well-organized, and highly successful textbooks.

---

* The house currently has a blue plaque stating that it is the birthplace of Michael Ramsey, with no mention of Frank. There is also no plaque on Frank's Mortimer Road house, in which he lived as an adult.

He was also a pillar of college administration—steward and bursar, before a twenty-two-year run as President, or vice-Master, from 1915 until his death at the age of eighty-eight in 1954. When he arrived at Magdalene, the college was in dreadful shape. The quality of its students, fellows, and finances was at a low ebb. Although its inferior standards had enabled Arthur himself to get in, he made it his mission to raise that bar, and when Arthur Benson was made Master in 1915, the two spent the next decade turning the place around. Arthur Ramsey's obituary in *The Times* is titled 'Mr. A.S. Ramsey: Resurgence of Magdalene College Cambridge'. He also did more than his share for the University, including being chair of the Faculty of Mathematics, where he reigned in a competent but conventional way, always set against new notions and notations.

In writing the record of his life, Arthur described his career at Magdalene as productive, happy, and easy. But we get a different picture from Benson's diaries, which have Arthur conducting rude, self-righteous, and brainless arguments with his colleagues, and frequently losing his temper in meetings: 'R is very unconciliatory & scornful & his temper is bad—it's a pity, but he's a forcible man by virtue of those very qualities.' Benson himself got 'a look of hatred' all too frequently from Arthur. On one occasion, Benson complained to his diary:

> A beastly letter from Ramsey, saying that we were disgracing ourselves by selling drink to cadets and & advertising our wines. . . . This is very bad of Ramsey. Why not enquire first before he makes a row? It isn't for us to settle about total abstinence for cadets—& it comes from a man who wrecked his own health by indulgence in tobacco.

Two days later, Benson was still railing about Arthur, who wouldn't let the matter drop: 'The truth is that R believes himself to be a radical, & is really a Pharisaical bully & tyrant.' Eventually Benson had to reprimand Arthur for the 'violence' and unreasonableness of his campaign. Arthur's non-conformist conscience was hardening into an abhorrence of personal self-indulgence, and this became a running theme in Benson's diary. An undergraduate who was found too doctrinaire sparks the following remark from Benson: 'But of course he was Ramsey's pupil!' Benson thought 'The Ramseys of this world' are all about 'contemptuous virtue and complacent commonsense'.

But there was another side to Arthur's character. Benson thought that despite his 'violent Puritan mind, intensely self-righteous & self-sufficient & full of contempt & censoriousness', 'this disease is of his <u>reason</u> only; we unite as friends in the <u>lower</u> regions of the heart'. Benson had a soft spot for him. On the very day he was offered the Mastership of the College, he informally offered Arthur the Presidency, ensuring that he would work side by side with his frosty, narrow-minded, suspicious, and self-absorbed colleague for the next decade. Benson was so fond of him that he sent for Arthur as he lay dying. The fact that Benson, from one of Cambridge's most eccentric, radical, and accomplished families, was the colleague to whom Arthur was closest, is telling about Arthur's dual and duelling traits. Benson's diary makes the dual sides clear:

> He might, I think, be very hard if pushed almost cruel. But there's beauty about him within and without, which wins me. He is very ambitious, very nervous, wants to be someone, desires success. But with that he unites real affection and tenderness.
>
> Ramsey came out *at his best* like the sun from the clouds.... That is like R. to snap and growl till the last minute, & then walk out in a leonine sort of way and give one his paw.

Benson's diagnosis of Arthur was that he was so uncomfortable in his own skin and with his own education that he needed to look down on those who mastered the social and intellectual world. On a Thursday in the spring of 1924, Benson and Arthur took a walk before dinner. Frank had just finished his undergraduate degree and Arthur had just had the news of Frank's election to an Allen Fellowship, which would help him write a thesis:

> He talked about Frank and his own intellectually starved youth—a big family all at the local school—his lack of reading. R has been converted to a belief in culture by his clever family.

Arthur's struggles with his character may have been the product of his strange upbringing. He was completely out of place in any kind of social gathering. Benson never tired of reflecting on how Arthur could not cope in company:

> He exercised his usual dulling influence on the party: because he never follows anything up, or wishes to learn what anyone thinks about anything. If one questions him, he answers with pleasure; if one doesn't he simply sits; I never saw anyone less civilised or social.
>
> He has to be attended to like a child, or he sighs and says nothing.
>
> He has to be spoonfed all the time with such questions, & they are few, as he can understand. Ramsey is to parody Wordsworth 'Contented if he might despise the things which others understand'.
>
> Ramsey came to Hall. It is astonishing how his presence seems to flatten things out. He is narrow-minded & self-absorbed; & all his real goodness doesn't make him in the least sympathetic. He has no use for friendship – he's an individualist; & he prefers being what he calls sincere to feeling that other people are comfortable.

That last sentence should be kept in mind when we get to Frank's relationship with Wittgenstein. While he had his endearing side, Wittgenstein too was notorious for being sincere at the expense of the comfort of others. It may be that Frank's long experience of dealing successfully with his father helped him to manage Wittgenstein, when others could not or gave up.

While Arthur's character flaws might be understandable, that didn't make them easier to take. At dinner at home, he would be silent and sulky, or rage at the children and his wife. Agnes sometimes left the table in tears. When it got too much, Michael would leap up in the middle of a meal and run around the garden in an agitated state. Frank had a different strategy. Margaret says that 'He was an expert in slipping out of a room if the conversation bored or displeased him.' One assumes that Michael did not bolt from tables when he was Archbishop of Canterbury, but Frank employed his own particular escape mechanism all his life.

Arthur dined in College two or three nights a week, as was expected of a fellow. This was some relief to his family, if not to his colleagues at Magdalene. Agnes could have the luxury of making scrambled eggs instead of a big meal. When he was home in the evenings, Arthur would retire to his study to write his textbooks, ignoring his children, who followed him there, where the only fire burned. Like Benson, they could see that although he didn't show it much, their father was fond of them. Of all the children, it was Frank who was most aware of this side of their father, and who made the greatest effort. As Margaret put it, Frank was very nice to their 'very difficult, withdrawn, irascible' father. Arthur was a compulsive worker and his only interest was gardening and going for walks in the afternoon. Frank often accompanied him on those walks and both father and son seemed to enjoy them.

Family Values

'Thrift' was a family watchword. The Cambridge stipends might have been suitable for bachelors living in college, but not for men with dependants. Arthur experienced life as strenuous, taking a large number of private pupils and more than his share of examining and administrative work. He fretted about finances. Agnes was economical with the household budget, and the children followed suit. They all watched their small change.

Frank was born in 1903, shortly after Agnes and Arthur were married. Michael followed in 1904; Bridget, in 1907. Margaret was a late addition, coming fourteen years after Frank's birth. As was typical for their class and time, they had help—a nanny, cook, and housekeeper, all from the same family. Once the fees from private pupils expanded, along with the number of offspring, Arthur purchased a plot of land from Magdalene, just round Castle Hill. There he built a larger house which they called Howfield. It had three storeys, a big hall, three large rooms on the ground floor, and extensive servants' quarters with a separate staircase. When the Great War came in 1914, family finances became tighter, as private income from students evaporated as they left for the front. The Ramseys made ends meet by taking in and tutoring young Southeast Asian and Belgian lodgers who were studying for the Cambridge entrance exams. At times the house resembled a hotel.

Frank and Michael got on well with the lodgers, who they would ask for 'piggyback trots' round the gardens. A Prince of Siam once gave them a large toy ocean liner. Arthur got permission for his children to sail it in the Emmanuel College pond. When it sank, Frank sent Bridget behind a bush to strip to her bloomers so she could dive in and retrieve the prized vessel. Arthur had to write to Emmanuel and apologize.

Howfield felt old-fashioned, even though it was brand new. It was a tasteless house with heavy furniture—comfortable but unexciting. The dining room was decorated with drab sepia prints and the table centrepiece was a bowl of light bulbs. Margaret said that the house was decorated on the principle that one should be able to throw a cup of coffee over anything without it showing. The children, however, were oblivious to fashion, and found the house excellent for hide and seek because of the two staircases. The garden was even better. It had forty apple and other fruit trees, which Arthur took special care over, and a vegetable garden. Best of all for Frank, it had a lawn tennis court. Richard Braithwaite remembered that in those days it was thought not quite proper to give tennis lessons to boys, as it was a girl's game. Frank nonetheless got proficient at it with his siblings and the neighbour children. He and Michael also played an endless game of their own making, hitting a tennis ball against the wall above the veranda.

To outsiders, the inhabitants of Howfield appeared as strange as the décor. One of Wittgenstein's nephews, Thomas (Tommy) Stonborough, would be a frequent guest at Sunday lunches when Frank was a young don and Tommy an undergraduate. He called it 'old Professor Ramsey's home', The Ramseys were always kind and friendly towards him, but Tommy thought them odd and incomprehensible, especially Arthur and Michael. He found Agnes not so much odd as 'big and mighty', with a quiet and contained exterior. The food was always the same, leg of lamb, and Arthur's carving of it was a formal and ponderous operation. To Tommy, the Ramseys seemed 'from another planet', and in a way, they were. Tommy was part of one of Europe's most wealthy families, and was used to different standards of living, customs, and humour. The Ramseys talked about mathematics, politics, and other intellectual topics, whereas at the Stonborough/Wittgenstein Sunday lunches, the conversation was about music, art, and other forms of high culture.

But one did not have to be from a different world to find the Ramseys strange. After going to a Howfield Sunday lunch, Benson gave this glimpse into the household:

> Curious how the amenities are neglected. The drive is like a sea beach, the shrubs sprawl, dead leaves pile up, flowers struggle. The house is bare & unbeautiful. It was something of an ordeal. R. genial but a little frozen, Mrs. R. very voluble and emphatic, Frank solid and <u>very</u> clever, Michael a distressing object—so sharp-faced, dull-eyed, spotted—Bridget charming and long-legged & Margery (6) really pretty...I talked feverishly. They gave me an excellent lunch—fish, duck, marmalade pudding, cheese straws, and much whisky. But the silent circle was alarming & I grew nervous in the drawing-room after. But they welcomed me warmly and I'm glad I went.

Michael said, in his old age, when he heard this description, that it was unkind, but not unfair.

One thing that put Arthur in a good mood was the precociousness of Frank and Michael. One of the family stories has the three-year-old Frank 'much excited' about the General Election in January 1906. Banners of the Liberal Campbell-Bannerman and the Conservative Balfour were hanging from ceiling to floor in the Ramsey home, and as the results came in, Frank was allowed to move figures up the rungs of a ladder. Another story has Frank unwittingly summarizing the Oedipus Complex. Michael, still in the nursery, clung to his mummy and announced that when he was grown up, he was going to marry her. Frank replied 'How can you be so silly, Michael? Don't you know that you can't marry your mother till she's a widow?' Arthur told another story that showed Agnes's influence on Frank's politics when he was still in short trousers:

> Quite early Frank began to share his mother's keen interest in politics and one day came to her saying 'I'm afraid that after all Michael is a conservative'. You see, I asked him, 'Michael are you a liberal or a conservative?' And he said 'What does that mean?' And I said 'Do you want to make things better by changing them or do you want to keep things as they are?' And he said – 'I want to keep things'. So he must be a conservative.

Michael soon came to share his brother's interest in politics and lined up his toy soldiers not in actual war, but as a House of Commons war, 'and made them harangue one another'. They were unusual little boys, headed for unusual careers. They would both be on their mother's liberal-left side of the political spectrum, with a keen sense of justice and injustice. Michael's legacy, when he died in 1988 at the age of eighty-three, was that of one of the most liberal Archbishops of Canterbury.

Frank and Michael shared other characteristics. As adults, both were amusingly absent-minded gentle and genial giants, with a love for exercise and sport, despite being rather uncoordinated. They had guffawing laughs, subtle senses of humour, and soft voices and accents. Their handwriting was atrocious. Michael, especially, was plagued with a general clumsiness with his hands and he lived long enough to have the terminology of disability used to describe it. In Frank's case, his school reports bemoaned his penmanship from early on. While at Winchester, he was told to give up on cursive and stick to printing. His handwriting never grew up, as a Winchester school friend put it.

Agnes was said hardly to be able to boil an egg, but with help from the servants, she would host groups of Magdalene undergraduates twice during the week for lunch, and for tea on Sundays. Those Sunday open houses would often draw thirty students, who stayed on until Arthur reared up at 6:00 to say that it was time to go to Chapel. Kingsley Martin, Magdalene undergraduate and friend of Frank's, published a piece in *The Granta* about a Howfield tea, saying 'It was the usual don's dreary Sunday afternoon tea', with 'everyone trying to look as if they were enjoying themselves'. Agnes was understandably offended.

Arthur and Agnes were strivers and had clear ideas about appropriate behaviour and aspirations for their children. They worried over the education not just of the boys, but the girls as well. While his siblings kept up their end in terms of education and also behaviour, Frank would pull hard against his parents with respect to the latter.

The First Born

Frank did not come easily into the world. He was two weeks early, and there was anxiety over whether he would survive the birth. He was jaundiced and not easy to feed. As he grew, his parents continued to fret about his health. His personality, too, was delicate. Arthur recalled that he was 'a rather timid child', the sight of a headless lead soldier causing him to shrink to the other end of the nursery and turn pale with agitation.

But, even accounting for the distortion of parental pride, it was clear that their first born was highly intelligent. Arthur recalled:

> He learned to read almost as soon as he could talk. He learnt his letters from a bag of alphabet biscuits into which he could dive, extract one and hold it up to be named, chortling when one came up which he had had before.

It was soon 'tiresome' to take him out, as he insisted on identifying letters of the alphabet on billboards from his pram. But he was a normal little boy in other respects, growing rapidly and interested in trains and (intact) figurines of people and animals.

He was sent to Miss Sharpley's school when he was five years old—a modern-thinking school, largely for the children of academics. There were a dozen pupils at different stages in one room, with Miss Sharpley allowing them to read at their own pace and teaching them French verbs. Frank stayed at this cosy school till he was eight. Miss Sharpley noted that his exercise books were untidy, but she thought him a charming and wonderful pupil, soaking up novels and encyclopedias. He also made a good beginning at Latin and mastered recurring decimals. Agnes began to teach him the piano, although he had little aptitude.

In October 1911, at the age of eight, Frank started a two-year stretch at King's College Choir School. While a few of his contemporaries later described it neutrally as 'orthodox' or 'traditional', most of them remembered 'the tyrannies of the Jelf regime'. Jelf was the new headmaster, a strict disciplinarian with little sympathy for small boys, and with a determination to rid the school of all frivolity and joy. But all seem to remember getting a solid education, mostly delivered by Cambridge undergraduates. The Latin and Greek were excellent. The maths master, Reinhart, a German who was an undergraduate at Trinity, taught by hitting the students over the knuckles when they made a mistake. But he was a good mathematician and helped Frank advance. He was also the owner of an Indian motorcycle that could go 60 mph on the track and was rigged up so that he could drive it when sitting in the sidecar. The boys were suitably impressed.

Frank was a reserved, dishevelled little boy, shoelaces undone and hair askew. One of his classmates could tell even then that 'attention to sartorial matters had no place in his life'. What he had a 'tremendous zest' for, said his father, was cricket, football, schoolwork, and 'everything new'. His classmates recalled that his skill on the sports fields did not match his enthusiasm. But they saw that 'intellectually he outshone us all'. Frank did well in every subject, with special strengths in Latin and mathematics. He would ask to be excused from church so he could do trigonometry. None of his classmates was at all surprised when he became a renowned mathematician. He had it written all over him at the age of eight.

Then, as with so many English families of a certain class and financial means, the decision about boarding school was made. They chose Sandroyd, where Uncle Charlie Wilson was Headmaster. Frank was offered reduced fees, and although his parents were loath to see him go, they figured that Uncle Charlie and Aunt Lily would make this a soft landing for a first boarding school. In most ways, it was. Frank enjoyed the camaraderie of sport and the open-air life. He wrote home about goals scored, fouls committed, and chances missed. He caddied for golf and asked for a set of clubs for Christmas. The outdoor swimming pool was a special pleasure. He also loved the Boy Scouts, then a new organization, adopted by Sandroyd straightaway. Charlie's aim to recruit talented athletes to the school meant that Frank was in high-end company, and his success on the Sandroyd fields, pitches, and pool indicates some raw talent, if not the fluid athletic ability so characteristic of the Wilsons.

There were the usual public school privations of the time, such as cold baths, winter and summer. Frank got chilblains on his hands, a painful condition of the skin caused by cold. Fruit sent from home would often be nicked, which made him cross. But he wasn't anywhere near as miserable as Michael was when he arrived at Sandroyd a couple of years later. One letter home is so extreme, you don't know whether to laugh or cry:

Tuesday Evening just after tea

My dear mother,

I never were more utterly miserable. I have just had Greek before tea; It is horrid. we did translation, Xenophon, I do not know a word of it I do not think Greek alone makes me miserable, I am always miserable.

I cannot bear it any longer, I am crying now.

I cannot stand it any longer, if someone does not come to me I will give up and be miserable for ever and perhaps go home of my own accord, write or wire to Uncle C. and say you are coming at once pleas darling, and come on Saturday or I will give up altogether and always wretched.

Do not tell any about me nor anyone except father and possibly Frank, write at once if you are going to.

I am too miserable for words.

I beleive that you will take pity and come at once,

Your loving son

Michael

I am crying like anythinke

Come at once

never mind anything else

I am utterly miserable

Agnes rushed to the school. Michael said that his Uncle Charlie's response was to tell him that if he wrote another letter like that he'd beat him so hard he'd have no skin on his bottom.

This was no empty threat. Corporal punishment was delivered at Sandroyd by both the headmaster and the head boy. Frank detested the violence. The head boy, he wrote home, 'whips lots of people' and even worse was when the boys would have to decide themselves on the punishment. In Frank's first year, the class had to vote on how many strokes a boy was to get for a minor infraction, with the average to be meted out. Frank and another boy voted o, but the others didn't concur and the boy had two strokes with a hard cricket stump. Frank thought that terribly unfair. But as far as Charlie would have been concerned, this was all light stuff—nothing like what happened to him at Uppingham, where the small boys would endure 'roasting over the big fire in the hall on Saturday nights', so that for weeks Charlie 'could only sit askew, as my tail-end was lamentably short of skin'.

Frank kept quiet about whatever homesickness he may have experienced. He was especially young, having been sent away to school early because of his intellectual precociousness. The fact that he was a large boy may have obscured his youth to his classmates. He stayed, without major incident, at Sandroyd from 1913 to 1915. He sent letters regularly both to his parents and brother, sometimes even to little Bridget, writing of home matters and wishing success for his mother's suffrage meetings. On the whole, his letters bore out his parent's hope that their child was happy. He told them, in response to their questioning: 'I don't know if this is what you call sociable, but I'm kind of friends with lots of boys.' Those classmates remembered him decades later as being the top student, taking 'quite a prominent part of all other activities', and being 'very well liked and greatly admired'—a gentle, kind boy with an outsized head, a grin stretching between his big ears, and eyes blinking whenever he had to take off his glasses.

He raced ahead with the academic work, especially mathematics. One holiday, 'just for the fun of it', Arthur set Frank an advanced exam in mechanics. He scored a 70 per cent (a high grade even for those old enough to take the exam), often correctly guessing the kinds of solutions to problems he had never before encountered. It seemed time to move their young son ahead in the public school world. As Arthur recounted:

> It was decided that he should try for a scholarship at Winchester in the summer of 1915 – he was 12¼ at the time of the examination and staying in lodgings at Winchester made it rather a strain for him & he slept very badly while it lasted and consequently did not do himself justice on the harder mathematical paper though he was easily top in Classics. He made a good impression by his personality also. I met the outside examiner in Classics...some weeks later and he asked me if that round faced smiling boy who had done so well at Winchester was my son. He said that after reading his

papers he was rather expecting to find the writer to be a wizened little specimen of humanity all brains and no body, and when he came in smiling for his viva voce he was a joy to behold; and when he put him on to translate, he very honestly said 'Please I have done this piece before' and then acquitted himself well on a piece that was really unseen. The news of his great success came to us by wire on the Saturday after the examination. It was more than we dared to hope for & we felt overwhelmed by it. The news came to Frank as he was returning from a Second XI cricket match in which his side had won & they said that he seemed to think far more about the result of the match than the examination.

Their boy had placed first in the scholarship exam for one of the most rigorous schools in the land. Arthur Benson scribbled in his diary:

Little Frank Ramsey to lunch—just got in first at Winchester—a sensible & pleasant [boy]. He ate and drank little. Then fled.

Frank's history master wrote to Arthur, rather floridly:

It is delightful to find a head so full of brains and a heart so full of the milk of human kindness in one human unit.

The Sandroydian relayed the news about Frank's scholarship. It was the first time the school had produced the top scholar at Winchester. The article reported that Frank is 'leaving us all too early, as he is only 12½'. But the prediction was that he would 'hold his own easily at Winchester, as he is strong both in physique and common-sense'—not only 'brilliant', but 'strenuous in all games'. Uncle Charlie was pleased, as one classmate recalled:

I remember Frank Ramsey standing up and reeling off, by heart, a long piece of Latin verse—Wilson pretending to be gruff, but unmistakeably delighted. It must have been his scholarship year summer, so he'd have been 13. Tall long-legged, neck hunched and thrust forward from his shoulders: big smiling mouth, big ears, eyes blinking through his specs.

On the last night of term, when everyone was in their dressing gowns, those who were leaving the school were summoned to Charlie Wilson's room, where he gave an avuncular talk on the facts of life. Most of them were already adolescents, and they all were all moving on to single sex schools. Charlie warned, in a roundabout way, that they might be approached by older boys, especially if they were pretty. Frank needn't have worried about that—he wasn't very pretty. But his age and lack of guile would make going to the big boys' school a challenge in other ways.

Frank was to have joined a scout camp in the school grounds for the first week of that summer's holidays, but it was cancelled, due to the war. Casualty lists appeared with the names of old Sandroyd boys, and some of the masters left for the front. The boys felt they should knit for the soldiers, and Frank discovered he was hopeless at it. The war overshadowed everything, as it would for the rest of Frank's schooldays.

WINCHESTER NEARLY UNMADE HIM

Sweating, Chaffing, Ragging

A rthur and Agnes would have known that there was no soft landing to be had at Winchester College. Savage discipline and bullying were the norm in the traditional public schools. They could have chosen to send him to a new reformed school, but they went with Winchester, as it was generally thought to be the top academically. It wasn't particularly close either—well the other side of London and a journey of a good few hours by train.

Frank entered Winchester in the autumn of 1915, a year after the start of the Great War. Leah Manning, one of Agnes's friends and fellow Labourites, remembered the shattered hope that it would be a short war:

> 'Over by Christmas; over by Christmas' they kept chanting. But it seemed as if it would never be over. The battles became bloodier, the blunders more egregious, munitions shorter. Trench warfare, gas warfare; men coming off the trains coughing up their hearts—and those terrifying lists of names.

When Frank arrived at Winchester, the younger masters had already gone off to fight. The headmaster, Monty Rendall, had a difficult time keeping up a teaching staff. He started his annual report that year as follows:

> The Great War, whose issue now hangs in the balance, has profoundly influenced every aspect of our School life: not only have our thoughts and emotions been dominated by its influence, so that we seemed to live half in England and half across the seas, but every instrument and every department of School life has been coloured and affected by it: nothing has remained as it was. . . . No one who has not lived in Winchester can picture the military scene presented by the city and neighbourhood. Day and night we have lived in the presence of military sights and sounds: College Street, as well as High Street, has been crowded with men in khaki and military carriages of all sorts.

Frank's two homes, Winchester and Cambridge, were transformed into army camps and hospital sites. The Winchester school sanatorium was sometimes filled with wounded soldiers. An open-air military hospital had been set up in the cloisters of Trinity College, Cambridge, eventually moving to the King's and Clare playing fields, where it grew to 1600 beds. Winchester was full of students, and short on masters. Cambridge was almost emptied of both. The Officers' Training Corps, a section of the British Army Reserves, was compulsory for Winchester students during and after the war. But perhaps even more pertinent for the pupils, a country at war made Winchester, already an austere school, still more so.

The students—the Wykehamists—were called 'men'. Even Frank, the youngest boy in the school, was supposed to think of himself as grown up. While at some other public schools, boarders had their own rooms, at Winchester 12–14 boys of different ages were mixed together in a large chamber. Some of Frank's roommates would have been seventeen years old, a different kind of creature from the twelve-year-old Frank. The seventy scholarship boys lived in a damp and cold fourteenth-century building. The chambers were unheated— central heating was installed only in 1987, after the students built a snowman inside one of the chambers and it stayed intact for the duration of the term. Freezing morning baths, quickly in-and-out, were not optional. The commoners, or the pupils who paid full fees, lived in more modern houses outside of the main College.

But while cold in temperature, Winchester was an intellectual hothouse. This enclosed world was highly competitive, with many of the students battling to come out on top. Despite the staffing difficulites, they had good teachers, often real scholars, who took their work seriously. Some were extroverts and eccentrics who stirred things up and made things interesting for the boys. There were extracurricular entertainments to enrich the formal learning. Musicians came to perform, as did speakers, on topics ranging from the Treasury to fishing. The early promise of the boys was usually met. Frank's classmates included a disproportionate number of future eminent academics, distinguished diplomats, and successful businessmen.

The first term was partly taken up by learning the 'notions', an extensive language and set of customs, much of it traceable to medieval Winchester. The notions set out what was always to be said or done, or what was never to be said or done—or, at least, not until one reached the appropriate year for doing it. Some of the customs were standard fare for English public schools and no bother at all—the scholarship boys, for instance, wore gowns all day, except for games. Some rubbed against Frank's feeling for justice. He wrote home that it was 'infra dig'—beneath one's dignity—for a scholar to walk about with a commoner: 'I don't care at all. I walked about with Brown a lot.' Some were simply irritating, such as knowing which old boys were currently Oxford or Cambridge Blues, and for what sports they received their Blue.

The seniors, or prefects, conducted two examinations on the notions in the first fortnight of the first term. The practice had been officially banned, due to past excess, including brutal beatings upon failure. But it was not so easily dislodged. One of Frank's contemporaries expressed the received view:

> Senior boys regarded Notions as a heritage, and in their minds it was part of their duty to the place to pass that heritage on intact. There was nothing irksome in this. On the contrary, many of the Notions held great interest for boys of scholarly mind.

Frank did not share the received view. He wrote home to say that 'notions are frightfully queer'. His scholarly mind found them of no interest whatsoever. Frank's 'Pater', the student responsible for teaching his 'Son' the notions, and responsible for his misdeeds and failures during that first fortnight, had known him from Sandroyd. His recollection of Winchester was that the students 'were very much servants, if not the slaves, of tradition, and all these things were taken very seriously'. But not Frank. His answers, when examined, were flippant, and his Pater was concerned that he himself would be 'punished in the traditional manner'. Luckily for both of them, Frank was already taken to be 'mildly eccentric', and both were spared.

In perfect step with his previous schools, the pupils and masters thought Frank brilliant, modest, and honest. As one classmate put it, he was an 'exceptionally civilized and courteous man, especially courteous to his juniors, usually smiling and with beaming eyes and constantly engaged in argument of the friendliest kind'. His Housemaster's notebook registers him thus:

> math vy gd; otherwise a 'clever well-rounder'; likes games tho' short-sighted & bad. conscientious. father radical etc.

The reference to Arthur's radicalness was likely about his non-conformist religious affiliation.

But despite Frank's genial character, he became reserved at Winchester. He didn't take part in the rough and tumble of schoolboy life. One friend said that 'Ramsey was an adult at the age of twelve'. Some described him, in tension with the 'beaming' remarks, as a bit remote and self-contained. Whether it was a protective strategy developed to cope with his new school, or something more bred in the bone, Frank would in some ways always remain self-contained, not particularly concerned about being part of a conversation or not.

When Frank arrived at Winchester, his parents worried that their boy wouldn't cope with the harsh conditions. The winter of 1915–16 was wet and stormy, and Frank thought it 'absolutely beastly' that he wasn't allowed to change his boots and socks more often. All day his feet were cold and sodden. The war had a deleterious effect on the food, which at Winchester was at the best of times awful. Its quality had been known to give rise to correspondence in *The Times*. Breakfast, Frank thought, was an especially 'mucky meal'. The evening provisions were not only mucky, but meagre as well—bread and butter, and even that was rationed. Meat appeared just once a week. Once they were given boiled rhubarb leaves as a vegetable, only to discover the next day that they could have died from eating them. The biscuits were full of weevils, and one boy thought the soup they had on meatless days 'was made of juicy old toothbrushes as it was always full of bristles'. The boys who couldn't buy food from the school shop were always hungry. One of Frank's contemporaries said that after five years of disgraceful quality and quantity of food at Winchester, he remained hungry all his life. A brief spell in the infirmary during his first term was heaven for Frank. He was finally comfortable, fed well, and able to have a warm bath. 'I am having a ripping time', he reported.

After Frank's death, Arthur would write of this period:

> For some time he had been growing very fast & we had some anxiety about his health. He suffered a good deal from headaches and it was discovered by accident that his eyesight was very defective and that he was hardly able to use one of his eyes at all.... He suffered from indigestion & school food was not always the proper diet for him. When voluntary rationing was introduced in order to reduce the public consumption of food on account of the wartime shortage, the school authorities very unwisely cut down the boys' food—bread, meat etc, 'for the sake of example'.

If the physical life was harsh, the social life was even harsher. Students occasionally had to be taken out of the school because they were treated so badly in their chambers. Frank was the most junior 'man' in what could be a barbarous place. His size and abilities made him seem older than he was, sometimes to his detriment. For instance, while he found the mathematical work so easy that he called it 'potty', his Classics master, Mr Bather, spent the first couple of months thinking Frank not much good at all. Arthur travelled down to the College in February to talk to Bather and reported the following conversation:

> 'I hope you are satisfied with his work.' 'Well, there's not much form about it.' 'How much form do you expect from a boy of twelve?' 'Good gracious, is he only twelve? I thought he was fifteen.'

Frank wrote home after Arthur's intervention:

> Bather seems much nicer to me since Father spoke to him. Actually when I made a bad mistake instead of calling me very idle and cursing me he just said 'O, Ramsey, Ramsey'!

While the masters were eventually cognizant and understanding of Frank's youth, that wasn't the case with many of his fellow classmates.

The hierarchy at Winchester was a complex thing, as it was at all English public schools. As one of Frank's friends put it, the prefects or older members of each chamber, 'ran the school, and the masters simply taught'. The pupils were often of a higher social class than the masters, and would have had a kind of superiority. Hence the sharing of authority between teachers and older students—an uncomfortable compromise between social class and institutional role. But where the hierarchy most manifested itself was amongst the boys.

Each junior was the personal servant of an older student, and had to 'fag' or 'sweat' for him. That meant cleaning the buttons and boots of his Officers' Training Corps uniforms as well as his muddy cricket boots so they gleamed white again, along with as countless other tasks. The juniors had to make the prefects' tea, or afternoon meal, and wash up after; tend to the needs of any chamber-mate who was in the sick-house; shake the prefects awake in the morning; and fetch and carry when ordered. When a prefect wanted something done, he would melodiously shout 'Jun–ior!' and all twenty of the juniors would run, the last to arrive being charged with the task. All this was much more humane than what the previous generation had to cope with. No longer were the new junior boys given 'tin gloves'—forced to grasp a burning piece of wood, which scalded and then calloused their hands, under the rationale that it made them much better at washing up in hot water. But it was still pretty unpleasant, especially for sensitive boys like Frank.

The prefects regularly administered beatings and spankings to their 'inferiors'. The former were official punishments, sanctioned by a housemaster and administered by a prefect, of up to twelve strokes on the shoulders with an ash branch. Disobedience or a bad half-term report could warrant one of these beatings. The spankings were harder, unofficial punishments, a half dozen strokes on the backside with a cricket bat, the offender's head being lodged under the conduits to hold him still. The neglect of minor fagging duties was deserving of a spanking. The severest 'bottoming' was administered by the Headmaster for serious offences such as stealing. Frank was beaten at least once, for an offence that wasn't worth describing to his parents. But it was not just the assaults on his own person that bothered him. It was the whole culture of violence that he couldn't stand. He thought that Sylvester Gates, the Senior Prefect, was 'the nastiest man in College'—a fellow student called him 'a picturesque villain'. Frank eventually thought that Gates improved. But he would hate brutality, of any kind, for the rest of his life.

To make matters worse for him, a point of contention arose in which a bit of parental interference turned out to have unwanted consequences. Agnes did not buy into the myth that privations made men out of boys, and she acted on her principles. The primary issue was the length of the day, which officially started at 6:45 in the morning and went straight through to 8:45 in the evening. Lessons began at 7 am, and late risers did without their cup of tea and two weevily biscuits. But the junior boys had a much more arduous time of it than the official story let on. As one of the youngest, it was Frank's duty to get up at the first sound of the bell at 6 am and 'call' or wake up the dormitory. And by a gratuitious convention, the juniors were not allowed to wash up the prefect's 4:00 tea in their own chamber. A senior would sweat or require a junior from another chamber to do it, and then that junior would have to go off and wash up wherever he was beckoned. In the winter evenings, they had to procure hot water for the washing up basin, and light the fire. When his mother came to visit, Frank wasn't let off these chores. The whole arrangement did not please Agnes, although she must have known that such things happen in English public schools.

In the first term, Frank complained to his mother that he was so tired, he could hardly move. Arthur wrote to the Headmaster 'in strong terms', and Agnes went to the school to make the case to the Second Master for a revision of bedtime practices. Arthur reported the following response from the Headmaster:

> his reply was to the effect that he was newly in charge of College & it was too early to expect him to alter customs which had been in force for hundreds of years. The result of our protest however was that the Headmaster made a rule that small boys were to go to bed earlier—though nothing was done to make it easier for them to go to sleep.

As one might expect, the parental interventions did Frank no favours. He was at first elated, writing to his parents with glee about the extra '1½ hours more in bed' and relaying that Patrick Duff, a friend from both Miss Sharpley's School and King's College Choir School, 'sends you his heartiest congratulations'. Duff would go on to be Regius Professor of Civil Law at Cambridge. Seventy years later, the event stuck in his mind, and those of his fellow Wykehamists. They thought Frank's mother 'a fierce lady' and noted that Frank 'got the blame' from those who did not agree with the new bedtime regime. One recollected that once when Frank was washing up the prefects' tea, 'his mother—not an oil painting—went in there and helped with the washing up'. That had never happened within living memory, and was not looked upon kindly. At least she didn't make an issue about the fact that juniors could only use the indoor toilets for urinating—other business to be conducted at the outdoor toilets some distance from the main buildings. Frank's gut did not fare well under this regime, but his parents seem not to have brought up that embarrassing matter with the headmaster.

An unfortunate side effect of the new bedtime was that the sweating in the evening was even more rushed. Frank wrote: 'The worst of this new regulation is that we have 20 mins for supper, fires, getting water and undressing. Still, it is good to get to bed.' He also expressed surprise at the concern about his health, especially when it came from the headmaster:

> Yesterday the H.M. stopped and gave me a long harangue on overworking, talked about ruining my health for life etc (apparently I yawned up to books which made him think I was tired) !!!!!!??!?!?

Frank had learned enough of the Winchester notions to use them: 'I yawned up to books' means 'I yawned in class.' He reassured his parents about the amount of sleep he was getting and seemed to think that *they* were now the concern: 'However if you're very keen I might get to bed a bit quicker.' His letters home started to say that 'fagging is not so bad now but it is a nuisance':

> To-day all the fagging I have done is calling and making tea and I shall have to do my evening duties. Fires have begun which is an awful nuisance because I have to light one in the evening.

Sometimes Duff helped him: 'Even though he annoys people he is very good natured and if I oversleep does my fagging or if my fire won't burn helps me with it and he would do that for anyone.'

His parents remained anxious, with Arthur recalling that 'After spending a Sunday with him in his second term, I felt that Agnes and I ought to go and see him frequently, but it was very difficult to do as we had pupils resident here almost continuously.' But Frank was already a 'butt', an object of teasing, and he didn't want to make it worse with frequent parental visits. When his parents came, he was reluctant to take them to see his chambers and the other boys.

His parents weren't the only cause of his social troubles. As the aristocratic Gilbert Simon (later Viscount Simon, head of P&O steamships) recalled, Frank was an unusual boy, and unusual boys tend to get picked on. He was also three years younger than most of the others in his form (or class) and at that stage of life, as another of his classmates said, 'even a year or two mattered very seriously'. Another recounted that boys tend to go by exteriors and that Frank had an unusual exterior:

> Physically he was unlike any other boy we'd ever seen, with his long legs, and his rather stiff-legged stride, like it might be a crane or a heron…then on the top there was this beaming, blinking, broad visage that we had never seen on any other boy.

Another said that 'he strongly resembled a monkey or an ape, but he was quite nice & kind'. Another noted that Frank made no secret of the fact that he intended to eat as much butter as he possibly could, and was laughed at for that—'I think everybody treated it as a joke although I do not think that Frank did.' Some of his classmates called him 'Frink', and although nicknames were thick on the ground, this one has a bit of a sneer to it. His tormentors gave themselves the luxury in their old age of thinking that Frank was impervious to what they considered 'good natured chaffing'.

But as one classmate, Igor Vinogradoff, said, Frank took life seriously and did not like being made fun of. He had a hard time telling whether the other boys were 'ragging' or teasing him, and that made him insecure about himself. It didn't help that he was soaring above the others academically in a highly competitive environment. The other boys couldn't understand the mathematics he was doing, but they understood well enough that Frank was gaining extra respect from the masters. He was recognized to be a 'real egghead'—a 'phenomenon'. Another classmate said 'like many persons of genius he was, I think, regarded as an oddity, and though not exactly disliked, I doubt if he had many close friends'.

Some respond to being bullied by putting up a defensive shell that makes them seem (and sometimes become) impervious, if emotionally stunted. Frank tried that coping mechanism, but succeeded only to a very limited extent. Some respond to being bullied by tormenting others when they get the chance. Frank reacted in the opposite way. He was kind to those he might have belittled, and he developed a lifelong dislike of bullies.

As the first year drew to a close, his masters expressed the hope that their prodigy would return from the long holiday renewed. One of them reported to his parents:

> Conduct excellent in every way. He has plenty of character. I hope he will have a good rest.

Image 1 Frank, crop from Winchester College photo, 1916.

Digging In and Getting On

Frank did have plenty of character, and he drew on it by digging in and making the best of his time at Winchester. As at Sandroyd, he found new sporting enthusiasms almost by the week. At one point, he exclaimed in a letter home 'Fives is the best game in the world.' The court of Winchester Fives, one of many ancient handball and racquet games, was a thrill, with its 'hazard' or buttress jutting out on one side wall and causing the ball to change direction. Soon the best game was squash, until the moment it became golf. He played for the Second team at cricket, where he was described as 'a solid bat and good all-rounder'. He was a keen football player—the arduous Winchester variant, a cross between rugby and ordinary English football (or soccer). It was and still is the most important game in the College. Frank made the College Fifteen, so was a strong player. He performed perfectly well, not

34

attracting any of the abuse hurled by the captain in his notebooks, and scoring a decent number of goals. The captain, in his annual summing up of the players, described Frank as no more and no less than a decent player: 'Not a very strong front-row up but occasionally quite useful in the loose as he kicks the ball very fairly when he gets the chance'.

He also became an enthusiastic debater, on both serious topics, such as 'That the late press agitation on aliens is to be regretted', and lighter ones, such as 'A man is too old at 40.' He participated, in a half-hearted way, in the fancy-dress days in which some of the Winchester men dressed up as women, others as archbishops or sheiks. Winchester was a male place, and there were no mixed parties or dances. The only woman one regularly saw ran the College sick-house.

Frank made some good friends, not always from his year, as the boys coming up behind him were more his own age. One was Anthony ('Puffin') Asquith. He was the son of Rt. Hon. H.H. Asquith, the Liberal Prime Minister who had led the country into war. Gilbert Simon, who felt, like Frank, a loner, also became a friend. They shared a hatred of the Officers' Training Corps and the war. But his closest friend was Eric Siepmann, a volatile, charming boy from an Anglo-German family. Although he didn't feel German in the slightest, he was nonetheless met with the unpleasant gaze of suspicion. Siepmann was Asquith's best friend, and spent many of his holidays at the family's grand houses. Asquith would become a famous film director and Siepmann a less famous playwright and journalist, married to the novelist Mary Wesley.

In 1917, the youngest Ramsey child was born, and upon hearing that her name was to be Margaret, Frank cheekily wrote home to propose alternatives—Cordelia or Elaine, he thought, would be much better. He wanted to see her 'so badly', but had to make do with sending books as a christening present, as well as one for his mother. He asserted that he could afford them by eating less at the school shop. The age difference between Frank and his newest sibling was considerable, and he would always feel paternal towards her.

There was the usual Ramsey accounting of pocket money, heightened by the fact that Arthur had lost most of his extra tutoring fees, with the undergraduates off to war. Benson made a gift of £100 to Arthur to tide him over. It would amount to more than £7000 today. Frank worked during his vacations. In the summer of 1917, he picked fruit on a farm near Histon, a few miles outside of Cambridge. He earned what was for him a lot, and spent it buying books—mostly editions of English classics.

He was also working hard, perhaps too hard, trying to come first in his subjects and starting on a staggering course of extracurricular reading. The headmaster counselled moderation:

The great thing is to prevent him from doing too much. This I regard as very important. He is doing excellent work.

He was doing very well in everything, except penmanship. Although, as the terms rolled by, Frank would find himself not enjoying (and not coming first in) Divinity and Classics. Two things that were at the top of Winchester's list of priorities. He was much more interested in learning German during his holidays, in order to read books on philosophy and the foundations of mathematics in the original.

In mathematics, he was streets ahead of anybody else. He found both the level of difficulty and the method of problem-setting at Winchester frustratingly easy. In 1918, with much to-and-fro between Frank's father and the school, he was allowed to taper off Classics in favour of accelerated mathematics and extended essay writing on politics and economics. He found the advanced mathematics easy going too. One of the mathematics masters commented that, although his work was first-rate, 'He should however take more pains to explain himself; his answers are sometimes too condensed.' This plea would be echoed by many in the coming decades, for Frank Ramsey never grew out of his penchant for condensed proofs, the missing steps obvious to him, and only a very few select others.

When he was no longer a junior boy with significant sweating duties, either the chaffing abated a bit or Frank found ways of ignoring it. But neither that, nor all of his breezy academic success, dampened his parents' concern. At the beginning of 1918, Arthur and Agnes made a proposal to the headmaster: Frank's standing at school was not in question, and it would do his work no harm and his health good, if he stayed home for the Lent Term. He was given extraordinary leave to spend the spring in Cambridge.

The sick leave was not spent bed-ridden. Frank attended his father's university lectures on Dynamics three times a week. The wartime shortage of labour made it easy for him to find gainful employment as an errand boy for the bookstore Galloway & Porter (shuttered only in 2010) and as garden boy at Girton College. The Girton College Garden Committee minutes in February 1918, approved Frank's first college job:

A suggestion for engaging a reformatory boy to work in the garden was approved. The Garden Steward reported that she has asked Frank Ramsey to work in the garden in his spare time—approved.

Winchester certainly felt like a reformatory to the Ramsey boy, although that couldn't have been the suggestion of the Girton Garden Committee.

Image 2 Frank, happy at home, with his parents and sisters, *c.* 1919.

Image 3 Winchester College House, Frank in glasses, with chin up, near top row, 1919.

Fancy Dress Leaving Sport, Cloister Time 1919.

standing, l. to r.: Hornby, Gates, Radice, Ramsey, Birk-
beck, Mallett, Gibson, Boileau, Brown, Thring, Chitty.
seated, middle row: Forbes, Barker, Shirley, Watt, Sand-
ars, Overton, Vinogradoff, Duff, Foot: on ground, Campbell,
Constable, Bates, Monypenny

Image 4 Frank half-heartedly in fancy dress, 1919.

A Lifeline: C.K. Ogden

Some relief from the trials of school was provided by a family friend in his late-
twenties, who took Frank under his wing. Charles Kay Ogden was an energetic and
well-known character around Cambridge. He has now largely dropped off the radar,
despite having been extremely accomplished and interesting. He is sometimes
mistakenly referred to as having been a Fellow of Magdalene and, indeed, he often
put 'Magdalene College' after his name. The affiliation, however, was rather loose.
He had been an undergraduate at Magdalene, but in 1912 interrupted his degree mid-
course to take up an offer to edit a new periodical, *The Cambridge Magazine*. Only in
1928 would he be a kind of fellow of the college, and then only for one year on a
Charles Kingsley Bye Fellowship, designed to give young men a temporary stepping
stone. Agnes had been especially fond of him when he was a radical Magdalene
undergraduate, and they stayed friendly.

The Cambridge Magazine had been a parochial penny weekly reporting on events in academic Cambridge. Ogden turned it into a nationally respected paper governed by a strong principle of free speech, its fame reaching a peak during the Great War. Ogden was twenty-six years old when the hostilities broke out, but was given a medical exemption. He spent his war years soliciting progressive articles for the *Magazine* on women's rights, the Guild or Syndicalist brand of socialism, and the new discipline of psychology. This was in keeping with his own work and interests. In 1915, for instance, he co-authored *Militarism versus Feminism*, which argued that the military state oppressed women, and, in 1917 he wrote *Fecundity versus Civilization*, which argued in favour of birth control.

The Cambridge Magazine took a pacifist and anti-conscription line. Its 'Notes from the Foreign Press', including the German press, provided a rare bit of transparency about what the rest of the world was thinking. The readership shot up to 20,000 and Ogden had trouble obtaining the paper on which to print. He acquired war-emptied shops, started up second-hand bookshops in them (one called The Cambridge Magazine Shop, another called The Other Shop), and pulped the less valuable books so that his magazine could go to press. The foreign press survey became so important that in 1920 the *Manchester Guardian* took it over.

Pacifism was a tremendously unpopular stance. Before the war started, no one had wanted it. Arthur, for one, had helped to draw up a Cambridge neutrality manifesto, which, after the assassination of the Archduke in Sarajevo, urged the government not to be 'egged' into war. But once England was in, allegiance to the war effort was expected, indeed, it was a test of whether one was a patriot or a traitor. The ferocity of feeling is illustrated by Bertrand Russell's case. He was dismissed from Trinity College in 1916 for his anti-war stance, prosecuted twice for agitating against the war, and served a jail sentence of six months.

Ogden was also the founder and mainstay of the Cambridge Heretics Society. As befitted its name, it was notorious. He and some other undergraduates brought it into being in 1909 and Ogden nurtured it until he moved to London in 1925. It opposed the war, as well as school and college compulsory chapel (at Winchester it was twice a day). He was also the founder and promoter of the proposed world language of Basic English, which he wrote about tirelessly, sometimes in *The Cambridge Magazine* under the feminine pseudonym Adelyne More—'add a line more'. In 1922, he would start the excellent and expansive *International Library of Psychology, Philosophy and Scientific Method*, which published best-selling popular books by top psychologists, philosophers, and scientists, as well as more specialized academic monographs. A small sample of Ogden's authors during the 1920s gives an indication of the quality of the series: Moore, Jung, Adler, Vaihinger, Piaget, Malinowski.

Ogden was a secretive eccentric. He never went to bed till daylight. Even his sport was indoors—the young philosopher Max Black called him 'a king ping pong player'. He always wore one of forty pairs of high-heeled suede shoes with square toes. Keynes, who couldn't understand where he got his money, as no one seemed to go into his bookshops, used to joke that he must have smuggled heroin in the heels of those shoes. A rumour was put about that Ogden's expensive wardrobe was the gift of an American millionaire as a reward for philosophical instruction. But as Fredric Warburg, who ran Kegan Paul, Trench, and Trubner, the publisher of the *International Library*, put it, 'Ogden was not merely eccentric, he was hard-working, learned, witty, and highly mysterious.... His activity was immense.' He received a small royalty on each thing he published, and once the *International Library* was up and running, that amount was substantial. Warburg described him thus:

> The high-domed forehead, the deep-set serious eyes behind their spectacles, the thin mouth, the prominent chin, gave him a slightly vinegary look, and he could be sharp and tetchy when annoyed, which was not unusual...

Dora Black, the women's rights campaigner, experimental educator of children, and eventual wife of Bertrand Russell, drew a similar portrait:

> C.K., as his friends called him, was a small man with a round head thinly covered with fair hair, the forehead of an intellectual, gold-rimmed glasses over grey eyes, a round pink face with the complexion of a baby. There was something gnomish about him; I used to say that he was either a changeling, or had been born just like that, neither a baby nor a mature man. His chuckle was gnome-like too. He disliked fresh air and healthy pursuits... He would live in a stuffy room and then acquire a thing called an ozone machine, the artificial substitute being immensely preferable, as he would tell us, to the real article.

Ogden provided Frank an intellectual lifeline during the last years of his Winchester exile. During school holidays, Frank visited Ogden in Top Hole—his attic rooms in Petty Cury. It's now a bland shopping mall, but in Ogden's time Petty Cury was the site of Cambridge's most lively cafés and pubs. Top Hole itself was overflowing with Ogden's collections of clocks, masks, and books piled in high, precisely balanced stacks.

Frank's diary gives a good flavour of the relationship. On 5 April in the spring vacation of 1920, he 'Went to tea with Mr. C.K. Ogden', then on 12 April: 'Went to talk to Ogden he came to lunch.' Frank borrowed some books from him. Then on 14 April:

> Went to see Ogden at 9 p.m. Mr. Richards and Dr. Shearer a biologist...there. Talked (I mostly listened) of Driesch, Bergson, the reality of universals, german bookselling...Japanese and Chinese art and Russia. Left about 11:30.

On that evening, Ogden told Frank to read 'some stiff German book', and the next day: 'Ogden sent list of books in Univ Lib both English and German'. On 16 April, Frank got from the University Library Brentano's *The Origins of our Knowledge of Right and Wrong* in English, as well as the stiff German book—Mach's *The Analysis of Sensations*. These were two leading German philosophers of the previous generation (Mach died in 1916, Brentano in 1917). On the 25th, Frank saw Ogden and Richards at a Heretics meeting. On the 27th, he returned to Winchester. That's quite an extra-curricular education. This schoolboy, during his vacations, was reading difficult philosophy and physics, some of it in the original German. He was in the orbit of impressive Cambridge academics, attending meetings of the Heretics (on which there will be more later) with dons and undergraduates. All this was under the tutelage of Ogden.

The 'Mr. Richards' was I.A. Richards, at the time a young English don with a cross-appointment in Moral Sciences. He too was an old family friend from his Magdalene undergraduate days. A fine mountain climber, he often took his students along after teaching them how to traverse round a pillar in Trinity's Nevile's Court. His reminiscences of Frank, from those Winchester school holidays, have become lore. One story is about Frank's precocity in mathematics:

> I well remember the strange large-boned boy, with a head like the young Beethoven coming into Top Hole and Ogden producing C. I. Lewis's *A Survey of Symbolic Logic*. It contained in an Appendix a collection of problems in logic supposedly *not* solvable by extant logical procedure. Ogden asked young Ramsey what he made of them. Frank glanced through the first of them and said, 'I don't see that there is a problem. It tells you, as it goes on, all you need to know.' And then, one after another, he gave us the answers amidst bursts of laughter at our astonishment.

The story is not quite right, given that there is no appendix to the logic book he mentions, but it fits with what his students would later say about Frank's ability to solve difficult problems off the top of his head.

Richards also started a legend which had Ogden teaching Frank German, from scratch, by giving him Mach and a German dictionary. Richards said that Frank returned in just over a week with a list of philosophical mistakes made by Mach. But Frank did not get his German up to speed in such an amazing way. He had won the German Prize in his final year at Winchester. And Frank's diary shows that, while Ogden did indeed suggest during that Easter vacation of 1920 that he read Mach's

The Analysis of Sensations in German, it took him a month. He finished it when he was back at Winchester, on 18 May, having read much else in between, including some of his father's mathematics textbooks. It was still an impressive feat, but the story has spun out of control—for instance, when the economist Paul Samuelson repeated it, he substituted Kant's *Critique of Pure Reason*.

One thing beyond dispute is that Ogden's influence on Frank was critical. Frank's grey mood at Winchester was given some sparkle by Ogden sending him letters, books, and issues of *The Cambridge Magazine*. Frank's replies to those letters are chatty and confiding. The two corresponded about the value of metaphysics, causation, Ogden's theory of signs (of which the young Ramsey was sceptical and would remain so), the nature of probability, and on and on. Frank told Ogden about the debates with his classmates and vented to him about his divinity classes. In one letter, he remarked that he was reading something that mentioned Russell's *Principles of Mathematics*, the first he'd heard of it. Russell and his view of mathematics would come to shape Ramsey's future.

Bolshie

At the beginning of his Winchester years, Frank had had a schoolboy's enthusiasm for the war. But his attitude quickly matured. The casualty lists occupied the whole of the back pages of *The Times*. On Sundays, the Headmaster read out the names of Winchester men who had died. Some had left the school only six months before. On occasion, a current student's own father, brother, or cousin appeared on the lists. The masters were often on the verge of breaking down, and this affected the boys almost as much as the news being delivered. They had visitors from the front, as masters and old boys would come to College while on leave. Most had been in the trenches. They didn't want to talk about it, but one could get a glimpse of what they had gone through. The visitors would sometimes read in the papers that the village they'd been in a few days before had been captured. The influenza epidemic, or Spanish flu, was an added blow towards the end of the war. In Britain it affected a quarter of the population and killed something like 230,000. Frank's Aunt Lily exhausted herself caring for the ill Sandroyd boys and she too soon was stricken, and died. She had been largely responsible for the humane atmosphere of the school. Charlie was devastated.

Ogden played an important role in making the horrors of the war widely known in England. In 1917, *The Cambridge Magazine* published four of Siegfried Sassoon's anti-war poems from the front. 'Dreamers' spoke of the young soldier in the foul rat-infested trenches, whose small dreams of going to the picture show and to work at the office will not come to pass. The bitter 'Base Details' mocked the greedy, fat, bald majors who carelessly sent the young soldiers to their deaths. Frank joined Ogden in his pacifism.

That included a hatred of the Officers' Training Corps, in which Frank was required to participate. On 14 November 1918, just after Armistice Day, he started an over-excited letter home by making his feelings about the Corps clear:

> I hope soon to be able to chuck the corps. The only thing that prevents me is that under present conditions it gets one off 6 months military service. If I was certain conscription would be abolished I should resign.

He then gave a long account of how Winchester celebrated. 'At 11 a.m. Mr. Robinson told the news to the people waiting about in Flint Court...and we pretty nearly went mad cheering and rushing about.' Then they all 'rushed uptown and found everyone and everything covered with flags'. The Winchester students procured flags and toy trumpets. They met 'a great amalgamated military band marching down the high street' and raced around town, listening to speeches from the Mayor and singing 'God Save the King' and 'La Marseillaise'. Letting the boys loose in town was clearly an aberration, even if warranted by the occasion. The headmaster put up a notice 'asking people not to go uptown again in the afternoon I think very few did'. They had a service of thanksgiving, with the special treat of a cake with their tea:

> then we had a strange thing, organized cheering for the allies etc led by the H.M. It was quite successful. I happened, quite by accident, to be next [to] Evans-Pritchard the Bolshevik; he never opened his mouth to sing 'God Save the King' though he consented to stand up—all the time a lot of commoner prefects behind were kicking and hitting him and afterwards they rolled him in the mud etc. It seems most disgraceful bullying but he is very brave.

This was either Edward Evans-Pritchard, who would go on to a distinguished career in anthropology, or his brother Thomas (we don't know which).

One would think that at the war's end, the pacifists might be forgotten and forgiven. But on Armistice Day, one of Ogden's bookshops, located directly across from King's College, was sacked by an angry mob. Works by the Bloomsbury painters Vanessa Bell, Duncan Grant, and Roger Fry were tossed into the street, along with Ogden's two grand pianos. Ogden loved a good fight or 'rumpus'. But this went too far. From that day on, he started to move his work and lodgings to London.

Frank's strong feelings also did not die with the end of the war. In March 1920, he told his diary that he 'answered back' while on parade and 'raised considerable hump, especially off Vino'—he publicly challenged the Major and made the both him and the conservative Vinogradoff angry. In a letter to his father in June of that year, Frank said of his Officers' Training Corps obligations: 'I haven't much fear of being made to go to camp. I can always just get into the London train at the end of the term and Major Robertson can't prevent me by force.' Camp was in principle voluntary, but there was great pressure to attend, for if half the students declined, 'the corps suffers heavy financial and reputational loss, which I should gloat over'. On 4 July, he stated in his diary: 'Am not going to camp.' His position was infectious. The next day he wrote: 'Theory that the absence of people going to camp (voluntarily) is due to propaganda by Gates and myself. Feel rather flattered.' Some students went to the masters to complain about his influence. The incident was remembered into the 1980s, and remembered as highly unusual. Frank's independence of mind and heart was becoming well-established. As Tom Stonborough was to put it: Frank wasn't the typical 'public school product', he was an exception to it.

He had also become a socialist, and like Evans-Pritchard, was labelled a 'Bolshie'. These were fraught political and economic times, dominated by high anxiety about the recent Russian revolution, as well as increased Republican violence in Ireland. As the war ended, Britain started a gradual economic decline from its position of the world's chief producer of goods such as iron and steel. Imports came more easily from overseas, and when the goods and the grain containers arrived, dire consequences for the working class accompanied them. Labour troubles had been brewing before the war, with The Great Unrest—a wave of strikes by miners, transport workers, and dockers. The Labour Party had been born in 1900, amongst other socialist parties and factions. The war had provided a temporary economic boost, owing to the need to produce goods for the conflict. When that came to an end, industrial action started up again, and was brutally put down by the police. The police themselves went out on strikes during 1918–19. A revolutionary socialism now seemed a real possibility. The Stalin we know had not yet appeared on the scene, and one could still believe that Lenin would lead the world to a better future. To those who cared about equality, socialism was a beacon of light for the future.

Frank certainly thought so. He exchanged letters with the Glasgow Communist Party, which were sent to a general Winchester College address to keep him out of trouble. As one of his classmates put it, 'they all got to Frank without difficulty'. During a railway strike, a party of boys went to help keep the trains running, while Frank stood at the gate shouting 'blacklegs!' (The shout today would be 'scab!') One classmate recalled that Frank didn't parade or impose these views on others, and that his views were prompted not by emotion, but by reason. A sensible society, thinking the matter through carefully, would subscribe to socialism.

Frank did put his arguments forward in a number of Winchester college debates, the most divisive occurring three months after Armistice Day, in February 1919. The motion was 'That a whole-hearted policy of armed intervention in Russia ought to be adopted.' Frank and Evans-Pritchard lined up against Igor Vinogradoff and Richard Pares.* Although Frank had written home in advance of the debate 'I feel fairly confident of my ability to squash Pares, as I have often done in conversation', it got pretty rough. Vinogradoff argued that Russia had been of real service to the allies and suffered enormous casualties, and that the Bolshevik leaders, 'who were mostly Jews, had introduced a reign of terror and were ruining Russia'. The student editors of *The Wykehamist* thought 'This was a really interesting speech, and was a most formidable indictment of Bolshevism', before reporting, not kindly, that Ramsey

> was evidently an ardent Bolshevik. He drew a most delightful picture of the Bolsheviks as well-meaning statesmen, cruelly maligned by capitalist civilization. He described their difficulties and explained away all their misdeeds. He upheld them as true democrats, whose only wish was the welfare of the masses.

Frank and Evans-Pritchard were shouted down and defeated in the voting 34 to 18. In the following week's debate, the matter was not forgotten. When Frank got up to speak, the audience shouted 'Bolshie, sit down!' Later that month, there was another debate, with an old boy, Mr Ensor, 'the famous editor of the New Statesman', offering a defence of socialism. *The Wykehamist* reported that 'really eloquent' speeches were made against the motion, and that 'F.P. Ramsey made a short speech in favour of Guild Socialism, in spite of many interruptions and accusations of Bolshevism'. Guild socialism was a short-lived movement arguing for guild congresses (democratically elected by workers in their factories), which would form a representative body alongside Parliament.

Frank was immersed in political theory and in politics itself. In March, he made another short speech in favour of Guild Socialism. In November, he asserted in a debate that the government had only been successful in dealing with a miners' strike because they chose the time for it, and that further strikes were imminent. Another November debate had him arguing 'Our proper policy as capitalists was not to make a frontal attack on Trade Unions.' Here we see the seeds of his later position:

---

* 'Vino' had come second to Frank's first in the 1915 admissions to Winchester. He came from a highly educated Russian family—his father was the Oxford historian Paul Vinogradoff. He would marry Julian Morrell, daughter of Lady Ottoline Morrell, and as a young adult would become part of a fast set, along with two other of Frank's classmates—Sylvester Gates and Richard Pares (the future Oxford historian and lover of Evelyn Waugh). Vinogradoff, Gates, and Pares would not intersect much with Frank after leaving Winchester.

a reformed capitalism, in favour of private ownership, but one that made not the rich, but the poor, richer. Even as a schoolboy, Frank was not the sort of thinker to fall head over heels for any one theory. He rejected solutions to the world's problems that were 'fantastic dreaming', insisting that 'the world we live in is a real world and slow to change, and we must find some more reasonable prospect for the future'. In his view, that was education:

> The sovereign remedy for most of the world's evils is education. When the world is educated democracy will be inevitable; labour struggles will cease with fuller knowledge; and democracies are not inclined to aggressive war.

While that may still be idealistic, it is hardly a standard socialist line.

Frank's politics spilled into his academic and life interests. He started to express an intention to leave mathematics for what he saw as the real-world discipline of economics. His mathematic masters at Winchester and his father expressed their disapproval. The headmaster was more relaxed, writing that in addition to Ramsey's 'brilliant performance', modesty, and simplicity, 'It is pleasant also to reflect that he has an eager intellectual outlook & really cares about social questions.' Perhaps his mother was more supportive of his proposed change of plan, for Frank learned Labour Party politics at her knee—Arthur said that 'he inherited and imbibed from Agnes an inclination to take the side of the weak & to support the claims of the wage earner and was always on the side of liberty'.

Michael was taking a similar stance in his own public school debates, at Repton. When his Uncle Charlie got wind of his nephews' political inclinations, he disowned them, fuming to Agnes: 'When the bloody communists get into power, you will teach Frank and Michael to dance on my grave!' Frank had been going back to Sandroyd regularly for their old boy dinners, but Charlie's rage put an end to that. In his last letter from Winchester, Frank wrote to his parents:

> I'm not going to Sandroyd as it is too late, nor do I want to, after Uncle Charlie disowning me as a nephew it seems unnecessary.

Charlie would no doubt turn in his grave if he knew that the only reason anyone still reads his history of the Wilson family is to find out about those two left-wing nephews.

Finding His Way Home

In January 1920, Frank started a journal. It provides a good snapshot of his last months at Winchester. He recorded matters such as his income (largely from his relatives and from bets with other boys) and his expenditures; the time at which he fell asleep; the books he read; and his daily measures of work and exercise. There is also an accounting regarding 'food': whether it was about the quantity, the quality, or the amount he spent in the school shop, is unclear. He recorded his visits with his paternal grandparents and aunts in Enfield, in North London; his teas with various relations and family friends; the letters he wrote and received from home; and his frequent walks with classmates.

In some ways, Frank was now a typical English schoolboy. He had got over his aversion to Winchester slang, and peppered his diary with it. He was engaged with his chamber-mates and others at the school. He loved football ('Played in Senior House. Scored goals'); went out on his own to kick a ball in the net ('Shot at goal a bit'); and signed up for almost everything, including races ('Ran in Senior Steeple-chase... came in 34th') and cricket ('made 19, took 5 wkts'). He also remained keen on racquet sports. It was a dull, mild winter, and Frank played tennis almost daily. When the ground was frozen or wet, he played ping-pong in the evenings and took part in informal doubles Fives competitions.

The first entry in the diary is New Year's Day, 1920, while he was on Christmas vacation in Cambridge:

7. 15 Service at Emmanuel.
Tennis in Morning. Did no optics.
Read Industry and Trade (Marshall).
Invitation from Miss Huskisson.
Lost a bet about Monty's letter.

'Miss Huskisson' was a friend of his mother from her school-teaching days, who taught near Winchester and took Frank to tea during term-time. 'Marshall' is Alfred Marshall who, in 1903, took the lead in establishing economics as an undergraduate degree course in Cambridge. In his last months at Winchester, Frank read the marginal utility theory of the Cambridge school of economics—Marshall's three volume *Industry and Trade*, as well as material on what he called Keynes's 'pro-German' work on war reparations, *The Economic Consequences of the Peace*. He devoured much non-Cambridge economic material as well, including Marx and Lenin.

Frank was fully engaged in family life during the holiday. Bridget had contracted diphtheria and spent a spell in quarantine at the Infectious Diseases Hospital, which caused considerable worry. Frank tried to teach her maths. He nonetheless found time to read a staggering number of books, often one a day, during these holidays and continuing into the term. Some of them were Ogden's suggestions and were procured for him from the Cambridge University Library. Those were largely books in logic, science, the foundations of mathematics, and the analytic philosophy of Bertrand Russell. The ideas emanating from Germany—from Einstein's relativity to the mathematics of Hermann Weyl—were of special interest, and Frank read many of them in the original. When he returned to Winchester after the holidays, he wrote to his mother to say that if it wasn't for the aftermath of the war, 'I should clamber to get to Germany'.

Other books were borrowed from his masters, the young historian Williams, who was straight out of Oxford, and the Reverend Stewart McDowell. The boys called McDowell 'Guts'—derived from a kind of rhyming slang for the unpopular biology master who taught them dissection ('slack bowels McDowell'). McDowell's books were mostly science, economics, politics, history, and literature. His mathematics master L.M. Milne-Thomson, a bad teacher and 'bad explainer' in Frank's view, made up for it by lending him books such as Couturat's *Die Philosophischen Prinzipien der Mathematik*.

On the last page of his diary, Frank recorded the near fifty 'Books Read' in the three months from January till the end of March. The list is not even complete—he recorded, day by day, more books read than he summarized in the list. The day after he read Marshall's *Industry and Trade*, he read Lenin's *The State and Revolution*, some Kant, and a number of other things. On 3 January, we find Bruce Glasier's *The Meaning of Socialism* (Glasier was a friend of Agnes's) and Lord Acton's Lectures on the French Revolution. Skipping over a few days and a few books, we see him reading, on January 12, Drake: *Women in the Engineering Trades*, Shaw: *Androcles and the Lion*, Lecky: *History of the Rise and Influence of the Spirit of Rationalism in Europe*, and starting a book on trade unionism and the railways. He read some law as well, including Dicey's *Law of the Constitution*. Only on occasion did he register a comment on what he was reading. But he did write that Thomas Hardy's *Jude the Obscure*, a desperate tale of a scholarly working-class man, was 'the most depressing and powerful' book he'd ever read. Whatever his trials at Winchester, they were minute in comparison to those of the working-class Jude who had an impossible dream of being a scholar, and whose life spiralled into tragedy.

Politics and economics continued to be a staple in his diet for the remaining Winchester months, and alongside his reading lists, he noted important political events, such as the surrender of the White Russian Alexander Kolchak on 13 January 1920. When he won the Richardson Prize in mathematics, which was given in books, he asked for Trotsky, Marx, and Adam Smith. Trotsky was 'so exciting' for Frank at this point. In a long letter home that took him two hours to write, he expressed that excitement and delivered an enthusiastic analysis of the Bolshevik revolution, land nationalization, and pricing and taxation policies, ending with the proclamation: 'History is working for us.' 'A proletarian revolution in Europe and America will break out sooner or later' for 'the whole of suffering humanity'. But he tempered the socialism with some market ideas, arguing that 'we ought to help them do it better, not fight them'. Some of his masters started to assume that he would become an economist.

But his reading in philosophy and logic was just as heavy as that in politics and economics. In addition to Mach, Brentano, and Kant, which he read in the winter, early June found him reading W.E. Johnson's *Logic*, Hume's *Treatise on Human Nature* (in German, for some reason), Russell's *Problems of Philosophy*, Moore's *Ethics*, Weyl's *Raum, Zeit, Materie*, and much else. As he wrote to his mother: 'the number of things I want to read is legion'. At one point, he made a list for her of books he had read, well over thirty, 'a good deal for 5 weeks'. He kept up this pace till the day before his exams at the end of July, and only slowed down a little during the exams themselves. He badly wanted to 'get on'—to race ahead with work that went beyond the Winchester curriculum and to discover new things.

Frank's reading during this last year at school was a roadmap of how his mind would develop. He was instinctively landing on some defining features of his future thought. In addition to the melding of socialism and capitalism, he saw that philosophical questions are fundamental and unavoidable. He wrote home:

> I'm starting an Introduction to Logic by Joseph of New College, an immense book (a defense of trad. Logic against Jowett). It...ought to set me up with a sufficient knowledge of logic; but it seems that you get up against metaphysical questions nearly all the time in logic; already I have in the abstract and concrete questions.

He would always feel the deepest questions pressing in on logic, as well as on economics. 'The fundamentals', he would say 'are so philosophical.'

His last Winchester year also was a roadmap as to how his character would develop. This diary note, from 11 January, is especially telling: 'Decided to give up sweating juniors.' He made a bargain with the younger boy assigned to him that he would not be required to do any chores at all for Frank. In return, the boy was to pass on the favour to his own junior when he was a prefect. Frank cleaned his own muddy boots and did his own washing up. One's guess is that the chain of passing on the favour was broken pretty quickly. Defiance of this established custom did Frank no favours in the popularity contest. But he knew that would happen, in any event, he had already refused to enter that competition.

It is also clear from Frank's diary that the hurly-burly of activity could not completely erase the unhappiness of his Winchester life. The 16 February entry reads: 'Feel lonely'. His friend Eric Siepmann had been involved in a ruckus. One boy had written a stanza of 'Swinburnian English verse', presumably erotic, in a book that Siepmann had lent him. They all, including Frank, 'started composing similar things' and 'a rumour circulated that Gates, Siep, and Higginson were composing these poems to each other'. 'Gates demanded an apology, which never came'. Siepmann was 'rather in a stew' and thinking of telling one of the masters about the matter. This mini-scandal seems to have sparked desolation in Frank. The next day he recorded: 'Feeling appallingly lonely and unhappy'. The following day, a stab of religious feeling entered the picture, but did not help, and quickly dissipated. He made a list of resolutions—minor self-improvements to not bite his nails, get to sleep at a reasonable hour, and do more work. He then crossed them out.

What he really wanted was to get out of Winchester and back to Cambridge. Winchester tended to send its best scholars to New College, Oxford, also founded (in 1379) by William of Wykeham, bishop of Winchester. The year before he was due to finish at Winchester, at the age of sixteen, Frank, on his father's urging, had taken the New College entrance exams, and a few others, to see how well he could do. He came second in the New College General Paper and, Arthur reported, 'easily top, a long way head of the other candidates' in the mathematical scholarship paper for the Cambridge colleges Peterhouse, Queens', and Magdalene.

In December 1919, with this preparation under his belt, he took a run at a scholarship at Trinity, the largest, richest, and most eminent college in Cambridge. His thinking was that if he didn't get it, his age was such that he could apply the following year. As always, we have boastful reports from Arthur about the gap between Frank and the next best candidates. The mathematician Samuel Pollard, one of the two Trinity scholarship examiners, relayed to Arthur that Frank surprised the examiners in two ways. The candidates were asked to attempt twelve out of sixteen questions, and Frank 'answered the whole lot'. And for the mathematical essay, Frank went far beyond the brief of the question, making the examiners 'feel small'.

He came first, and when Trinity telephoned the news to the Ramseys, they were told that he was top not just in mathematics but in English and the General Paper. That is confirmed by the letters of congratulation to Arthur from the headmaster at Winchester. Thus it was that in March 1920 Frank was elected to a Senior Scholarship at Trinity, to begin the following Michaelmas (autumn) term.

Frank's Winchester journal stops on 11 August, just prior to his return to Cambridge. In July he had expressed to his mother the old canard that he was beginning to feel rather sad about leaving Winchester. But he immediately took it back:

> The reason people say this is the happiest time of one's life is simply that it is true for most people for e.g. Foot will never again possess despotic power as he does now.

He can be witness judge and executioner all in one; he can abuse juniors as he will never-again be able to abuse people . . . He can go about imagining he is upholding the foundations of College and talk rot about prefectorial dignity and people being above themselves and can beat people as he did Asquith for being 'solitary'.

He went on to say that he didn't like being at school at all and didn't like his schoolfellows very much, except for Siepmann and a few others, but he liked 'the place'. That vague positive note was also eventually overridden. At the end of his time at Winchester, he wrote home: 'There seems little to say except what I read.' Winchester nearly unmade him by undermining his easy-going nature. Even his relationship with Siepmann was fraying. This, from a diary entry in late June 1920:

Last night Siepmann made me really angry at his stupidity. He proposed to judge the theory of evolution not on the evidence but by his personal instinctive ideas on the subject. And held that his instinctive ideas were not to be shattered by arguing, even though he admitted he could be proved wrong.

Image 5 College prefects, 1920. Frank top row, third from right. Igor Vinogradoff next to him on the left; Richard Pares on the ground, right; Sylvester Gates, 'the nastiest man in College' seated third from left. Foot, seated, second from right.

Frank was ready to leave. In a parting letter, one of his masters, who could not know how things would tragically fail to bear out his last sentence, wrote to Arthur:

> Your boy is progressing in many ways and shows character as well as capacity. His grasp of social problems is remarkable—I feel sure that he would do well to combine math and economics. My only complaint is that he is too anxious to be on with the next thing, when all life lies before him.

'WE REALLY LIVE IN A GREAT TIME FOR THINKING'

The Greats I: Keynes

Cambridge University was a powerhouse when Frank arrived. As he would say at the end of his degree: 'We really live in a great time for thinking'. Perhaps unsurprisingly, the atmosphere was rather combative:

> [V]ictory was with those who could speak with the greatest appearance of clear, undoubting conviction and could best use the accents of infallibility. Moore ... was a master of this method—greeting one's remarks with a gasp of incredulity—*Do you really* think *that*, an expression of face as if to hear such a thing said reduced him to a state of wonder verging on imbecility, with his mouth wide open and wagging his head in the negative so violently that his hair shook. *Oh!* He would say, goggling at you as if either you or he must be mad; and no reply was possible. Strachey's methods were different: grim silence as if such a dreadful observation was beyond comment and the less said about it the better, but almost as effective for disposing of what he called death-packets. Woolf was fairly good at indicating a negative, but he was better at producing the effect that was useless to argue with *him* than at crushing *you*.

We have already encountered, in the *Preface*, the philosopher G.E. Moore and the writer Lytton Strachey. 'Woolf' is Leonard Woolf, writer, civil servant, and husband of Virginia. The author of the vignette is John Maynard Keynes, who would become the founder of macroeconomics and one of the most influential economists ever to have lived. Frank would become closely connected to these and other Cambridge luminaries. In order to understand his own development, we must understand the ideas of four figures especially important to him: Keynes, Russell, Moore, and Wittgenstein.

It might seem strange that this set of great minds into whose orbit the undergraduate Ramsey would enter consisted of an economist and three philosophers, for he would be a mathematics student and a mathematics don. His choice of mentors is less surprising when we remember that in his final year at Winchester, his interests were already shifting towards philosophy, the philosophical foundations of mathematics, and economics. He would become the singular mind who could engage each of those great thinkers—Keynes, Russell, Moore, Wittgenstein—on their own terms. There would be simply no one else who could do that, including these four themselves. At the least, Keynes and Moore weren't up to Russell's logical skills and Wittgenstein, Russell, and Moore weren't up to Keynes's skill in economics.

After a brief career as a civil servant, Keynes in 1909 became a Fellow of King's College, Cambridge. He was anti-conscription but had nonetheless played a significant part in the war, working for the Treasury and emerging a man of tremendous political influence and humane spirit. He had participated in the Paris peace talks, arguing against making Germany pay heavy reparations—against 'crushing' it. He was in favour of refinancing the international debt between the allies so that funds were available for German reconstruction and development. He only partially won—the debt was lowered, but not nearly by as much as he thought necessary. He was thus a forerunner of a united Europe and a foreteller of the ruin that was awaiting the world, as Germany heaved under the harsh and punitive reparation payments of the Versailles peace treaty. In 1919 he made his case famous in the hard-hitting and internationally bestselling *The Economic Consequences of the Peace*.

When Ramsey arrived in Cambridge, Keynes had recently returned. As Virginia Woolf put it: 'Maynard in disgust at the peace terms has resigned, kicked the dust of office off him, & is now an academic figure at Cambridge.' He was nonetheless frequently travelling down to London to advise the government, business leaders, the Bank of England, and the League of Nations, as well as lunch with Winston Churchill. He was a vociferous advocate of free trade, and he had a public opinion on most important matters of the day. Keynes's friend, Clive Bell, described him as being 'cocksure', laying down the law with authority on all subjects, and having a 'masterful' manner and 'a disregard for other people's opinions'. We will see, however, that Keynes was perfectly happy to have his authority challenged by a very young Ramsey.

The post-war economic situation was unstable. After financing the military effort, England was caught in a disastrous cycle of inflation, deflation, and unemployment. Over the subsequent few years, the prices of many goods doubled. There was labour unrest, and a depression from 1920 to 1922. When prices calmed down in 1923, the country was in a state of raging unemployment. No longer could it be taken for granted that the economy was self-stabilizing—that the existence of unemployment would naturally cause wages and prices to fall, in turn causing interest rates to fall, in turn stimulating investment and demand, in turn raising employment. Keynes devoted much of his energy in the early 1920s to these economic issues, developing ideas later expressed in *A Tract on Monetary Reform* (1923) and *A Treatise on Money*

(1930). His line was that government must intervene, reducing interest rates by issuing bonds and employing people directly in infrastructure projects, such as road-building. An international, managed currency was required to keep the world's economies steady and avoid the ruinous cycles of boom and bust. Keynes made these arguments not just in academic journals, but in the newspapers and in the rooms in which policy was made. We will see that he enlisted Ramsey's help, almost from the beginning.

The Greats II: Moore

George Edward Moore, called 'Moore' by his friends and 'Bill' by his wife, was in his early forties when war broke out. He held the philosophical fort in Cambridge while others were either fighting (Wittgenstein, for the other side), seconded to ministries (Keynes), or engaged in contentious conscientious objection (Russell). He was held in the highest regard by academic Cambridge and artistic Bloomsbury. The American philosopher Brand Blanshard chalked up the attractiveness of Moore to a set of related traits. First, he was strenuous—his philosophical discussions were never casual, but always 'full dress', with his whole mind given to them. The effort he put into his lecture courses meant that he never covered much ground, but rather broke down sub-problems into sub-problems of their own. He would be struggling with the problem at the end of the course much the same as he had struggled with it at the beginning. Second, he was honest, never pretending that he had solved a problem or drilled down to its bottom. Third, his passion for getting things right resulted in an intensity that was often withering for what he called the 'stupe' who was under scrutiny, and he did not exclude himself from being the stupe. Finally, he had a quest for clarity, always wanting to know what he, or anyone else, *meant* by this or that term. The result of all this was that his verbal style was weighty, his prose was 'needlessly wordy', and that he was happy, Blanshard said, 'when he was convinced that another, Wittgenstein or Frank Ramsey for example, was abler than he was'.

Countless anecdotes about Moore bear out this characterization. Keynes called him a 'puritan and a precisian'. Leonard Woolf, who thought Moore the only great man he had 'ever met or known', noted the 'streak of the "silly"' in Moore—the 'single-minded simplicity that permeated his life, and the absurdity which it often produced in everyday life'. A story from Margaret Gardiner is illustrative:

> Lionel [Penrose] told me that Moore was unable to pursue his thought when lecturing unless he had a piece of chalk in his hand and was making marks on the blackboard. So, in Lionel's day, one of the students hid the chalks to see what would

happen. But Moore was only briefly put out; then, undeterred, he wrote invisibly on the blackboard with his finger.

Moore was famous for exploding at mistakes—his own or another's. He would climb up the back of the sofa on which he had been seated to ask the speaker what he meant by what he had said, suggesting that the poor speaker was frightfully vague, and very muddled indeed. Kingsley Martin described one occasion:

> Once, when C.E. Joad...had read a paper, I watched its extraordinary effect on Moore, who, tearing his hair, demanded in astonished terms 'just what Joad could possibly mean' and demonstrated by a few Socratic questions that the luckless Joad had used a word in three contradictory senses in a single page.

But of course, there was much more to Moore than his manner. He was one of the founders of modern analytic philosophy, which arose in Germany and Austria (with Frege, and then the Vienna Circle) and in Cambridge (with Moore and Russell, and then Wittgenstein, and then Ramsey).

One of Moore's main philosophical occupations was an attempt to answer the ever-looming question of scepticism, or whether we can know anything of the external world. In the late 1800s, he argued against the idealism of his teacher J.M.E. McTaggart, and for a kind of direct realism. Consciousness, far from spinning in the void of the mental, has direct access to its object. We don't need to drive ourselves into philosophical despair with the old British empiricist question of how we could possibly achieve awareness of something outside of mental impressions. For to have a sensation *just is* to make contact with an external reality.

Moore also argued that propositions actually exist independently of any human cognition. They aren't mental entities, but are facts. Moore realized that this sounded strange: 'I am fully aware how paradoxical this theory must appear, and even how contemptible.' The question arises immediately: what makes a proposition true and what makes it false? Moore thought that we can't say, but we can know it when we see it: 'What kind of relation makes a proposition true, what false, cannot be further defined, but must be immediately recognised.'

In 1903, Moore had published *Principia Ethica* to great acclaim. In it, he described how to analyse a concept. First, you break it down into its simple terms—terms that correspond with the most basic items in the world:

> [T]hen you can no longer define those terms. They are simply something which you think of or perceive, and to any one who cannot think of or perceive them, you can never, by any definition, make their nature known.

The concept of the good, Moore argued, was an example of a simple, indefinable, objective concept. If you try to define it in terms of some other property, it can always be intelligibly further asked: But is that property itself good? The utilitarian attempt to translate ethical terms like 'good' and 'bad' into non-ethical ones like 'pleasing' and 'displeasing' commits what Moore called the 'Naturalistic Fallacy'. We value different kinds of things, not just one thing.

Moore's theory pleased the Bloomsbury set, who were happy to begin with their own perceptions or intuitions about what is good, rather than the morality of their parents. Moore was the only philosopher Virginia Woolf read closely (her first novel, *The Voyage Out*, has one of the characters reading *Principia Ethica*). Lytton Strachey wrote to Moore right after he read *Principia*:

> I think your book has not only wrecked and shattered all writers on Ethics from Aristotle and Christ to Herbert Spencer and Mr. Bradley, it has not only laid the true foundations of Ethics, it has not only left all modern philosophy bafouée [violated]— these seem to me small achievements compared to the establishment of that Method which shines like a sword between the lines.

That method was supposed to be the scientific method. Strachey was exaggerating terribly when he claimed that Moore was the first to apply it to philosophical reasoning. But to his group, it was Moore who, as Keynes put it, 'was exciting, exhilarating' and brought the 'beginning of a renaissance, the opening of a new heaven on a new earth'. If you wanted to take every ethical case on its own merits and not have it tried by some tribunal of utility or religion, then Moore was your philosopher. The Bloomsbury set was bucking trends, and as Leonard Woolf said, they used Moore's theory—the 'divine voice of plain common-sense'—as a guide and justification for the way they conducted their lives.

When one reads *Principia Ethica*, one is hard pressed to find any semblance of the Bloomsbury interpretation. Keynes later saw that clearly:

> Now what we got from Moore was by no means entirely what he offered us....There was one chapter in the *Principia* of which we took not the slightest notice. We accepted Moore's religion, so to speak, and discarded his morals....Nothing mattered except states of mind, our own and other people's of course, but chiefly our own. These states of mind....consisted in timeless, passionate states of contemplation and communion....The appropriate subjects of passionate contemplation and communion were a beloved person, beauty and truth, and one's prime objects in life were love, the creation and enjoyment of aesthetic experience and the pursuit of knowledge....How did we know what states of mind were good? This was a matter of direct inspection, of direct unanalysable intuition about which it was useless and impossible to argue.

Ramsey would throw a bucket of cold water onto Moore's indefinables.

The Greats III: Russell

Moore's co-founder of the British stream of analytic philosophy was Bertrand Russell: 'Bertie' to his friend Keynes, but 'Russell' to Moore, with whom he had chillier personal relations. He was less lovable than Moore. But in Ramsey's eyes, he was the better philosopher.

Russell came from one of Britain's most illustrious political and aristocratic families, and had entered Trinity as a mathematics student in 1890, joining Moore as a don there in 1910. By no means did Russell and Moore agree on everything. But they were in step on the philosophical problems of truth and knowledge. Both were devoted to trying to slay the dragons of scepticism and idealism, and to promoting the method of analysis.

Russell's pacifist activities had lost him his Trinity job during the war. Nonetheless, for the undergraduates in Ramsey's day, he was at least as, if not more, important than Moore. Braithwaite put it thus:

> In 1919 and for the next few years philosophic thought in Cambridge was dominated by the work of Bertrand Russell.... [T]he books and articles in which he developed his ever-changing philosophy were eagerly devoured and formed the subject of detailed commentary and criticism in the lectures of G. E. Moore and W. E. Johnson. Russell's statements on the various topics of philosophy were...the orthodoxy...

Johnson was the elderly and eminent professor of logic, with a side interest in economics. The young Ramsey would read all his work as well.

Russell's views, expressed in prolific writings, were forever evolving and changing. But we can capture the basic state of play when Ramsey started his undergraduate degree. Russell shared Moore's conception of the proposition as an objective entity, as well as his method of analysis. He argued that if we focus on a logically perfect, scientific, and transparent language, and show how the objects of all meaningful thought and language can be constructed out of experience, we can solve the problem of truth and knowledge. This was Russell's 'analytic realism' or 'logical atomism'. Philosophy must proceed by an analysis that bottoms out in simple, metaphysically fundamental, existents in the world: 'you can get down in theory, if not in practice, to ultimate simples, out of which the world is built, and...those simples have a kind of reality not belonging to anything else'. A proposition is true if it stands in the 'corresponding relation' with the objects it picks out. If we can attain knowledge about these atomic facts, then we can build up all the truths about more complex facts. At least in its strongest articulation, and at least in principle, the project aimed to provide certainty of all truths that could be built up from atomic ones.

The method of analysis could be employed not only to give us the above theory of meaning, truth, and knowledge, but also to solve local philosophical problems. We can reduce a complex statement to its real meaning by breaking it down and defining it in simple terms. One of the most brilliant pieces of philosophical analysis is Russell's Theory of Descriptions. A definite description picks out a unique individual, for example, 'the woman with the most open era Wimbledon titles'. But some definite descriptions, such as 'the present King of France', do not pick out anything that exists, and it is thus unclear what to think about the assertion 'The present King of France is bald.' Russell, in his 1905 paper 'On Denoting,' analysed the sentence and resolved the worry. 'The present King of France is bald' can be broken down into: 'There exists one and only one entity x such that x is a present King of France, and x is bald.' That statement is false because the first part is false: no King of France currently exists. As Ramsey would put it in his *Encyclopedia Britannica* article on Russell in 1929, Russell applied this method not only to non-existent entities such as the present King of France, but also to classes and numbers, arguing that if they are legitimate, they are 'logical constructions' of genuine entities. Ramsey himself, as an undergraduate, would briefly explore the idea that truth might be analysed as one of those incomplete symbols or expressions.

The Greats IV: Wittgenstein

Ludwig Wittgenstein, from one of Austria's wealthiest families, had been studying engineering at Manchester in 1908. A reading of Russell's *The Principles of Mathematics* and Gottlob Frege's *Grundgesetze der Arithmetik* (*The Basic Laws of Arithmetic*) had thrown him into what his sister Hermine called a 'constant, indescribable, almost pathological state of agitation'. Gripped by the hard problems of the foundations of mathematics, he went to see the elderly and ill Frege in Jena for advice about his future. Frege suggested that Wittgenstein abandon engineering to study with Russell. Wittgenstein arrived, unannounced, at Russell's rooms in Trinity in October 1911, while Russell was having tea with Ogden. Russell was in the early days of his logical atomist programme. Ramsey was an eight-year-old boy at King's College Choir School.

Wittgenstein was admitted to Trinity as an undergraduate in the Moral Sciences (philosophy) Tripos. He would sometimes call on Russell mid-afternoon and stay until dinner, talking philosophy even while Russell dressed, and returning after Russell's dinner in Hall. Russell called him 'his German', and at first thought him tiresome and argumentative. But he soon came to feel Wittgenstein fresh and bracing. So did Keynes and Moore, the latter not at all put off by Wittgenstein telling him that his lectures were bad. In fact, pretty much all of Cambridge was in awe. They thought him a true genius, a mind like no other.

Wittgenstein's pre-war intellectual problems—the foundation of mathematics, the nature of propositions, and the relationship between language and the world— were shaped by Russell. And like Russell, Wittgenstein wanted to solve them by developing a logical language so that confusions in philosophy could be made transparent and resolved. A gulf would eventually open up between Russell and Wittgenstein. But before the war, both were very much on the same page, influencing each other and arguing for a conception of truth that had an elementary proposition picturing the world.

Wittgenstein was a troubled man. Despair was either upon him or hovering nearby. After the war, he would give his immense fortune to his family, refusing to keep anything for his own upkeep or ever ask them for financial help. His siblings didn't need the money and tried their best to change his mind. One of his sisters described Wittgenstein's reaction to their incomprehension:

> Thereupon Ludwig answered with a comparison which silenced me for he said, 'You remind me of someone who is looking through a closed window and cannot explain to himself the strange movements of a passer-by. He doesn't know what kind of a storm is raging outside and that this person is perhaps only with great effort keeping himself on his feet'. It was then that I understood his state of mind.

Such states of mind were no doubt partially responsible for the strain Wittgenstein put on his relationships with Russell and others, as well as for the overpowering intensity that was to appear so attractive to many.

Wittgenstein fell into a serious depression a year after he arrived in Cambridge. Russell reported that 'Wittgenstein came to feel even more strongly that "nothing is tolerable except producing great works or enjoying those of others, that he has accomplished nothing and never will".' He decided to exile himself in order to produce that great work. He left Cambridge in the autumn of 1913 for a remote part of Norway and started what for him was a painful labour on logic. Moore visited him there for a fortnight over Easter 1914 and Wittgenstein dictated notes to him, which Moore made available to Russell and Keynes.

When the First World War erupted, Wittgenstein joined the Austrian army, despite having a medical exemption due to a double hernia. Most of his war was spent either on the front itself or operating a searchlight on a captured ship, in perilously dangerous conditions. He was commended twice for bravery in the face of heavy fire. He wrote what letters he could to his Cambridge friends, and he somehow managed to do a lot of philosophy. In October 1915, giving his address as an artillery field post, he wrote to Russell:

> Dear Russell,
>
> I have recently done a great deal of work and, I think, quite successfully. I'm now in the process of summarizing it all and writing it down in the form of a treatise. Now: whatever happens I won't publish anything until you have seen it. But, of course, that can't happen until after the war. But who knows whether I shall survive until then? If I don't survive, get my people to send you all my manuscripts: among them you'll find the final summary written in pencil on loose sheets of paper. It will perhaps cost you some trouble to understand it all, but don't let yourself be put off by that.

The fact that Wittgenstein was writing a treatise caused Russell great excitement, dampened only by fears for his safety. He was also concerned about the security of the manuscript—those loose sheets, written in pencil. Russell wrote back:

> Dear Wittgenstein,
>
> It was a very great pleasure for me to receive your kind letter—it arrived only a few days ago. I am absolutely delighted that you are writing a treatise and want it published. I hardly think that it is necessary to wait until the end of the war. Could you not have a copy of the manuscript made and send it to America? Professor Ralph Barton Perry, Harvard University...knows of your previous logical theories from me. He would send me the manuscript and I would publish it....How splendid it will be when we finally meet again. I constantly think of you and want to have news of you. Be happy, and may Fate spare you!

It is no surprise that Wittgenstein was unable to make a copy of his manuscript at the artillery field post. It is also no surprise that he was not 'happy' there. But Fate did spare him, and his manuscript.

At the war's end, Wittgenstein's Cambridge friends had no idea what had become of him. Russell had prefaced his 1918 book, *The Philosophy of Logical Atomism*, with this generous and emotional paragraph:

> The following articles...are very largely concerned with explaining certain ideas which I learnt from my friend and former pupil Ludwig Wittgenstein. I have had no opportunity of knowing his views since August, 1914, and I do not even know whether he is alive or dead. He has therefore no responsibility for what is said in these lectures beyond that of having originally supplied many of the theories contained in them.

Three months later, in February 1919, Wittgenstein was finally able to reply to Russell's letters, from a prisoner of war camp in Italy. He told Russell:

You can't imagine how glad I was to get your cards! I'm afraid though there is no hope that we may meet before long. Unless you came to see me here, but this would be too much joy for me. I can't write on Logic as I'm not allowed to write more than 2 cards (15 lines each) a week. I've written a book which will be published as soon as I get home. I think I have solved our problems finally. Write to me often. It will shorten my prison. God bless you.

In the next letter, Wittgenstein repeated his belief that he had solved all the problems they had been working on before the war, adding:

I've got the manuscript here with me. I wish I could copy it out for you: but it's pretty long and I would have no safe way of sending it to you. In fact you would not understand it without a previous explanation as it is written in quite short remarks. (This of course means that nobody will understand it; although I believe, it's all as clear as crystal...)...I suppose it would be impossible for you to come and see me here? or perhaps you think it's colossal cheek of me even to think of such a thing. But if you were on the other end of the world and I *could* come to you I would do it.

Russell, in his reply, started the discussion of how to get Wittgenstein's treatise out of a shattered Europe. He immediately wrote to various people. Russell himself, as he put it, had 'fallen out with the Government' and so was not much use. Keynes, on the other hand, had not blotted his copybook and could be deployed. Keynes wrote to Wittgenstein saying that he had 'begged the Italian authorities' to provide 'an absolutely safe way of conveying the MS. ... to Russell through me'. He was at that moment in Paris for the Peace Conference, and he wrote on the Italian delegation's letterhead. Keynes's influence and connections did the trick. Wittgenstein would be able to receive books and other privileges, and the manuscript would be sent to England.

Wittgenstein was not confident that the *content* of his manuscript would be successfully transmitted, even if the physical document arrived safely. He expressed to Keynes what he had written to Russell—that Russell wouldn't understand it without 'a very thorough explanation'. In June Wittgenstein wrote to Russell again, after receiving his book, *Introduction to Mathematical Philosophy*. The endearments were gone:

Some days ago I sent you my manuscript through Keynes's intermediary. At that time I enclosed only a couple of lines to you. Since then your book has reached me...I should never had believed that the stuff I dictated to Moore in Norway six years ago would have passed over you so completely without trace. In short, I'm now afraid that it might be very difficult for me to reach any understanding with you. And the small remaining hope that my manuscript might mean something to you has completely vanished. As you can imagine, I'm in no position to write a commentary on my book. I could only give you one orally. If you attach any importance whatsoever to understanding the thing and if you can manage to arrange a meeting with me, then please do so. If that isn't possible, then be so good to send the manuscript back to Vienna by a safe route as soon as you've read it. It is the only corrected copy I possess and is my life's work! *Now* more than ever I'm burning to see it in print. It's galling to have to lug the completed work round in captivity and to see how nonsense has a clear field outside! And it's equally galling to think that no one will understand it even if it does get printed!

Wittgenstein seems not to have had the faintest idea how equally galling his letter might be to Russell, whose programme, far from being the 'nonsense' that Wittgenstein now proclaimed it to be, had provided the initial spark and fuel for Wittgenstein's treatise.

Wittgenstein had expressed this kind of arrogance before the war. Russell had made allowances then and was even more inclined to do so now, after the hell that Wittgenstein had just been through. In what has to be one of the most mature responses in the history of philosophy, he ignored the abuse and replied that, indeed, he would have to work hard if he was to understand Wittgenstein's manuscript. He said that he would read it carefully upon its arrival and then try to meet with Wittgenstein at Christmas to discuss it. Before long, their letters returned to expressions of mutual devotion and concern, their friendship back on its rickety rails.

Keynes received the manuscript a few days later and sent it immediately to Russell. It *was* difficult. After two careful readings, Russell thought it was very good. He wrote to Wittgenstein: 'I am sure you are right in thinking the book of first-class importance'. He included queries about the complex philosophical ideas, such as Wittgenstein's contention that 'The logical picture of the facts is the thought.' He also included points of agreement, for instance, about what he called Wittgenstein's 'main contention': that logical propositions are tautologies, not true in the way that 'substantial' propositions are true.

A major change, however, had taken place in Wittgenstein's thinking. Or perhaps it was just an amplification of something that was present, but undeveloped, in his pre-war work. When Wittgenstein left Cambridge in 1913, it quite reasonably seemed to Russell that he was brilliantly carrying out their joint project with logical precision. But that was now not so clear.

Wittgenstein's nephew Tom Stonborough reported that before the war, Ludwig was the 'sunniest' of the five brothers. They were an unsunny lot—three of those brothers would kill themselves. Indeed, Russell remembered Wittgenstein having suicidal thoughts before the war. Now he was even more absorbed with questions about the meaning and value of life. Tommy noticed a difference in his uncle Ludwig after the war. He became more severe and intense, and his religious sentiments deepened. His philosophy changed as well. Now he thought there was something mystical or profound that could not be expressed, but only gestured at.

Wittgenstein injected this idea into the austere logical atomism he shared with Russell. Perhaps Russell could have agreed with Wittgenstein when he said in his manuscript that even when all possible scientific questions have been answered, the problems of life remain untouched. For Russell himself worried about how it is possible to think about the problems of life once we accept the cold facts of science. But Wittgenstein went further. He asserted that once we answer the questions of science and logic, there are no questions left, and that this itself is somehow the answer to questions about life. We cannot speak of the most important things, hence we must be silent about them. Russell took this to be an expression of mysticism or the idea that we cannot have knowledge of the Absolute, but only feel it. Russell would never be happy with that. Neither would Ramsey. Both were atheists. But while Russell kept his focus on the non-mystical part of the text—the account of how the primary language about atomic facts worked, Ramsey would eventually mount arguments against Wittgenstein's proclamations that we must be silent about the meaning of life, and that the human soul or subject lies outside of the primary world.

Wittgenstein wrote back to say that he couldn't provide answers at the present time—Russell should know how difficult it was for him to write about logic. That is why the manuscript was 'so short, and consequently so obscure'. But he was eager to correct Russell about its 'main contention'. Wittgenstein took his main point to be the distinction between what can be expressed and what cannot be expressed. That, Wittgenstein contended, 'is the cardinal problem of philosophy'. He also noted that he sent the manuscript to Frege, who 'doesn't understand a word of it at all', and that 'It is VERY hard not to be understood by a single soul!'

Wittgenstein was released from the POW camp in August 1919. After much difficulty, Russell got a visa, and the two met in The Hague so that Wittgenstein could explain his manuscript. Russell wrote the following to his lover Ottoline Morrell:

> I leave here today, after a fortnight's stay, during a week of which Wittgenstein was here, and we discussed his book every day. I came to think even better of it than I had

done; I feel sure it is a really great book, though I do not feel sure it is right. . . . I had felt in his book a flavour of mysticism, but was astonished when I found that he has become a complete mystic.

After his release, Wittgenstein stayed in Austria, teaching schoolchildren in a small village south of Vienna. During his undergraduate years, Ramsey would know Wittgenstein by reputation only.

The Shaky Foundations of Mathematics

Frank's burst of reading in his last year at Winchester had included a good deal of the foundations of mathematics and physics: Couturat's *Die Philosophischen Prinzipien der Mathematik*, Eddington's *Time, Space and Gravitation*, Helmholtz's *Origin and Significance of Geometrical Axioms*, Mach's *Analyse der Empfindungen*, Poincaré's *Science et Hypothese*, Russell's *Principles of Mathematics*, and Weyl's *Raum, Zeit, Materie*. The discipline was in a highly expectant and turbulent state. There was a kind of confidence in the air that the big problems were on the way to being solved. A leap had been made in the 1870s, with Frege in Germany developing a formal logic for propositions. Russell and other mathematically minded philosophers were swept up by the power of Frege's analysis of propositions in terms of unsaturated functions that can take various objects, his account of quantification, and his proof system.

But there was also a sense that mathematics was in crisis. It had been supposed to be the domain of almighty certainty. But in geometry, where Euclidian axioms had long seemed to have provided the fundamental moorings, alternative axioms had been discovered during the 1800s, giving rise to non-Euclidian geometries. Pressing questions arose: What is the essential nature of mathematics? Is it a discipline that deals with necessarily true propositions? Or is it a product of the human mind, only as good as we can deliver? The Germans had a word for the debate: *Grundlagenstreit*, or the dispute about foundations.

One approach was that of the logicist school. It came into being with Frege and was bolstered by Russell and his former teacher Alfred North Whitehead at the beginning of the new century. They rejected the idea at the heart of geometry—that the aim of mathematics is to discover what follows from a particular set of postulates. For the postulates themselves remain unproven. The logicists thought that we must start by defining the entities, or the mathematical objects, that the postulates are about. Frege and Russell's proposed definition was that a number is a class. Mathematics is based on an ontology of sets, so that the number 2 is not an elusive thing, but rather, the set of couples. They conceived of sets or classes as logical objects, and held that all mathematical truths can be defined as logical truths and all mathematical proofs can be recast as logical proofs.

But in the spring of 1901, when writing his *Principles of Mathematics*, Russell discovered a biting paradox in set theory, one that threatened the whole project, and one that both he and Ramsey would labour to solve. Russell and Frege held that every property defines a set. So *a set that does not contain itself* is a property that defines a set (the property of being the set of sets that don't contain themselves). But the existence of that set is contradictory. Russell employed an engaging informal example to convey the essence of the problem:

> You can define the barber as 'one who shaves all those, and those only, who do not shave themselves'. The question is, does the barber shave himself?

If we try to answer this question, we land in a contradiction. On the one hand, it seems the barber cannot shave himself, as he only shaves those who do not shave themselves. But, on the other hand, if the barber does not shave himself, then he is in that set of people who would be shaved by the barber. Thus, if he shaves himself, then he does not; and if he does not shave himself, then he does. Similar paradoxes had been discovered, but it was Russell's version that struck at the very concept of a class, a concept so necessary for the logicist.

Russell wrote to Frege, setting out the paradox. Frege's second volume of *Grundgesetze der Arithmetik* was in press, and he had to quickly add a postscript trying to deal with the disaster. In it, he said:

> Hardly anything more unwelcome can befall a scientific writer than to have one of the foundations of his edifice shaken after the work is finished.
> This was the position into which I was put by a letter from Mr Bertrand Russell as the printing of this volume was nearing completion.

Russell's first attempt at resolving the paradox was in an appendix to his 1903 *Principles of Mathematics*. His solution drew on what he called the Theory of Types. His strategy was to steer clear of the idea of self-membership or self-application that lies at the heart of the paradoxes. He arranged sets into a hierarchy of types. At the bottom were individual objects (Type 0); next were sets of objects (Type 1); above them were sets of sets of Type 1 (Type 2). Russell stipulated that a given set contains only entities of a single type: it may contain entities of Type 1 or Type 2, but it cannot contain both. He argued that this enables us to escape the paradoxes, for they arise only if it is a meaningful question whether a set is a member of itself, and this is

FREGE'S AND RUSSELL'S CRISIS

Richard Zach, Professor of Philosophy, University of Calgary

The aim of Frege's project was the reduction of the theory of natural numbers (0, 1, 2, . . .) to the laws of logic. This involved two crucial parts: the first was the formulation of the laws of logic on which this reduction rests. The second was the actual reduction, i.e., to define 'natural number' in purely logical terms and to prove that the basic principles of number theory (such as every number other than 0 is the successor of some number) follow from the laws of logic provided in the first part and the definitions. In the second part, Frege was successful: he found a way to define the natural numbers logically and was able to derive the axioms of number theory that Dedekind had given from his logical system. Frege's definition of numbers constitutes a fundamental insight: numbers are properties of concepts, namely of all those concepts that have exactly that many things falling under them. For instance, 'eight' is a property of the concept 'planet', and of the concept 'leg of a spider'. But numbers are also things, and Frege did not count properties and concepts as things. So he needed his logic to provide objects that could go proxy for these properties of concepts. This he did using *extensions*: in Frege's logic, every concept or property has an extension: the class of all things that falls under the concept in question. And extensions are objects. So to solve his problem, Frege stipulated that a number—the extension of a number concept, e.g., the number 8—is the class that consists of all concepts that have, e.g., eight things falling under them.

In order to guarantee that every property (such as 'eight') has an extension (such as 8), Frege's logic assumed as a basic logical law that every concept has an extension, i.e., for every property there is a class consisting of exactly the things that have the property. This principle, together with the rest of Frege's system, was strong enough to allow Frege to carry through his reduction. Unfortunately, as Russell realized, it was too strong: it made Frege's system inconsistent. Consider the property 'is a class that does not contain itself as an element'. Let's say a class with this property is 'normal'. The class of natural numbers is normal, since it is not itself a natural number. The class consisting of all classes does contain itself, so it is not normal. Frege's Basic Law V requires that the property 'normal class' has an extension, viz., the class of all those classes that do not contain themselves as elements. Suppose it does; let's call the extension R. If R is normal, then it has the property that defines R (normality), so R is an element of the extension of 'normal'. But that extension is R, so R is an element of itself, and thus not normal. On the other hand, if R is not normal, then (like the class of all classes) it does contain itself as element. But the elements of R are all and only the normal classes, since R is the extension of 'normal class'. So, R must be normal after all. This is now known as Russell's Paradox.

Russell set himself the task of fixing Frege's system, i.e., of producing a system of logic that avoids Russell's Paradox and yet suffices to derive the laws of number theory using (something close to) Frege's definition of number. To avoid the contradiction, Russell did away with extensions. Everything was done with objects and concepts—which Russell called 'propositional functions'—but the problematic talk of classes was avoided by, e.g., paraphrasing '3 is an element of the class of prime numbers' as '3 is prime' (so 'element of' and 'class of' is replaced with 'falls under'). This is Russell's so-called no-class theory. In Russell's system, numbers are not objects but propositional functions, carrying on Frege's idea that numbers are concepts of concepts. To avoid the contradiction that scuttled Frege's logic, Russell had to require that no propositional function can meaningfully be attributed of itself. This is the *theory of types*: there are objects, propositional functions (of level 1) which apply to objects, propositional functions (of level 2) which apply only to propositional functions of level 1, and so on. In particular, the theory of types prohibits propositional functions analogous to the contradictory class of normal classes R.

precluded by the stipulation that a set must only contain entities of its assigned type. As Ramsey would put it, Russell requires us to maintain that 'a sentence which is perfectly grammatical English'—namely, 'The set of all sets that are not members of themselves is a member of itself'—'may yet be literally nonsense'.

Russell and Whitehead's three-volume *Principia Mathematica* was published between 1910 and 1913. In it, they argued the paradoxes could be avoided only by adding to the hierarchy of types a hierarchy of orders within a type. But there was a problem with this 'ramified' Theory of Types—it precluded some important mathematical definitions and proofs. To avoid this further problem, Russell introduced something called the axiom of reducibility. Ramsey, in his undergraduate thesis, would explode this escape route and suggest a revision in the theory of types. (One result is that the simpler, revised, theory of types is now, rather confusingly, called a 'ramseyfied', as opposed to a 'ramified' theory.)

The German mathematician David Hilbert had a competitor programme to logicism. His formalism had it that pure mathematics requires no commitment to the existence of mathematical entities, such as sets. Rather, numbers are realized by quasi-concrete objects, and the arithmetical relations between them are grounded in human intuition of those objects. The problem for Hilbert was that some higher mathematics cannot be explained this way. Set theory, for instance, tells us that the set of numbers is an actual infinite set, but infinity goes beyond the actual, concrete number of objects. Hilbert's solution was to treat the truths of higher-order mathematics as strings of symbols. Mathematical proofs manipulate these symbols according to agreed-upon formal rules. The most that can be done to show they are in good order is to show that the formal systems they deploy are consistent, or characterized by a kind of internal necessity, and are good instruments for our purposes. In Cambridge, formalism was derided as taking higher mathematics to be like a game, with no subject matter beyond its own symbols.

The third idea in the dispute about the foundations of mathematics was that of L.E.J. Brouwer and Hermann Weyl. They advocated intuitionism about mathematics, which is unrelated to intutionism in ethics. Moore's ethical intuitionism had our intuitions discovering objective facts, whereas Brouwer and Weyl held that mathematics is *not* the discovery of objective or independently existing entities and facts. Numbers and other mathematical entities are human constructions: a putative mathematical object or fact does not exist unless we can see our way to a procedure for constructing it. A mathematical proposition is true if we could prove it, false if we could disprove it, and neither true nor false if it could not be proved or disproved. Intuitionists thus reject the principle of excluded middle—that every declarative proposition is either true or false. Ramsey would start out disparaging intuitionism, but would eventually be drawn to it.

PART II

THE CAMBRIDGE MAN

4

UNDERGRADUATE LIFE

Post-War Wreckage and Jubilation

In the autumn of 1920, a year after the war's end, the seventeen-year-old Frank Ramsey began his undergraduate mathematics degree—the three-year Mathematical Tripos. He may have been too young for the Front, but the war nonetheless had a dramatic effect on his life. His politics were shaped by it. So were his social circumstances. A million British men had been killed in action. Many of those who survived and were in a position to attend university had shrapnel in their bodies, medals in their dresser drawers, and memories of corpses rotting in the mud. The minute book of a Trinity undergraduate debating society, the Wranglers, lists the military rank of members who had been to war; how many times they had been wounded; and whether they had been taken prisoner. Almost all of them were marked in some way. The future Prime Minister, Harold Macmillan, made clear the traumas for returning students:

> I did not go back to Oxford after the war. It was not just that I was still a cripple. There were plenty of cripples. But I could not face it. To me, it was a city of ghosts. Of the eight scholars and exhibitioners who came up in 1912 Humphrey Sumner and I alone were alive. It was too much.

Cambridge, too, was a city of ghosts. Especially missed by the gang of friends Frank would join were two prominent young King's College men—the poets Rupert Brooke and Ferenc Békássy.*

Frank would be spun into the orbit of the returning veterans. Now, instead of being three years younger than his classmates, the gap widened even further. When his fellow mathematics student Max Newman first met him, he thought Frank quiet and not inclined to join easily in conversation because 'he was much younger than anybody else there'. Newman, a pacifist, had spent the war in the pay corps and was

---

* Békássy, a Hungarian History undergraduate at King's, had died fighting for the other side. Keynes had helped him return to the continent so he could fight the Russians.

six years Frank's senior. Most of Frank's new friends were pacifists, but nonetheless brutalized by the war. They allowed themselves to enter the fray, avoiding jail, on the condition they were given a job that did not involve killing. Many served in the Friends' Ambulance Unit. Four of these ambulance men would become especially close to Frank: Richard Braithwaite, Joseph Fryer, Kingsley Martin, and Lionel Penrose. Kingsley had been a medical orderly for soldiers shot in the spine. His war had not been easy:

> In my ward, there were twenty-five men who were literally half dead. They were very much alive in their top halves, but dead below the waist. The connection between their brain and their natural functions were broken. They could feel nothing in their hips or legs, and in spite of being constantly rubbed with methylated spirit, they had bedsores you could put your hands in.

Lionel's brother Alec was invalided out of the Ambulance Unit after a harrowing time in Flanders, with a shell shock that became lasting depression and breakdown. Frank's friends had experienced too much and Frank himself had experienced too little.

Some of the ex-servicemen behaved appallingly, talking and shouting in lectures. Margaret Leathes (who would later marry two of Frank's friends, first Lionel Penrose and then Max Newman) remembered one lecturer who couldn't make himself heard jumping over the table in front of him and shaking a misbehaving student. The ex-servicemen were also intolerant of those who they saw as having shirked their duty during the war. Braithwaite recalled that the conscientious objectors huddled together for self-protection.

That community of pacifists and socialists was the one Frank joined, by natural inclination. They were no longer a tiny minority. Disillusionment with the war-makers had solidified and the old Liberal order was losing some ground to the Labour movement. The political divisions between those on the left and those on the right were only deepening, the positions taken on the Russia question forming the canyon. Not much was then known about the Soviet Union, as it was just coming into existence in 1922. In the elite world of Cambridge University in the early 1920s, being vaguely pro-Bolshevik was not a particularly radical stance. That's not to say there wasn't a radical wing of socialism in Cambridge. The infamous Cambridge spies of the 1930s would be drawn from the circle of Frank's friends.

Cambridge was undergoing massive change in other ways as well. The war had interrupted the system in which students paid individually for their teaching. State support for universities was introduced in 1919, with the proviso that the results of a 1920 Royal Commission on the role of universities in modern Britain be heeded. In response to that Commission, Cambridge University entered a period of self-scrutiny. Its formal institutions began moving in democratic directions. No longer would Cambridge be largely a finishing school for the rich, who would often not take the difficult Tripos degree, but instead would take the Ordinary degree with its less taxing exams. The University would train a broader swath of people, and train many of them in engineering and other sciences. Faculties were created, the PhD was introduced, and the growing number of graduate students now had a formal place in the University. There was renewed pressure to reform the status of women. Oxford in 1920 had formally admitted them. Cambridge, in 1921, after another passionate campaign, would not follow. Presumably Arthur, under the influence of Agnes, voted the right way this time.

Cambridge's less formal cultural institutions were also undergoing a transformation. There was a revolution pounding at the doors of conventional morality. Amidst the horror of the lives lost and the traumas suffered, the mood remained celebratory. Cambridge undergraduates had raced around even more freely than Frank and his fellow public school juniors on Armistice Day, drinking and ringing bells on tops of buses. The jubilant atmosphere continued, as the League of Nations offered the possibility that peace would be permanent. As Roland Penrose, another brother of Lionel, put it, 'there was a ridiculous sense of hope. We had had the war to end all wars.' Frank's future wife would say:

Everyone was dancing mad after the First World War. They thought here is peace, everything is going to be wonderful. My time at Newnham was spent dancing.

Frances Marshall, who started her studies at Newnham in 1918 and would become a central member of the Bloomsbury circle and a great friend of Frank's, said the same thing: 'all England had gone dancing mad and so had Cambridge'; 'all we cared about in our partners was their technical ability'. One imagines that the clumsy and intellectual Frank Ramsey, not as old or as sophisticated as the other men by a good measure, may not have been the most sought-after partner. Nonetheless, he was anxious to join the post-war freedoms.

Those freedoms, in the decade that would become known as the roaring and golden twenties, included sexual liberties. Women had been employed in various ways during the war, including in manual labour, and were not keen on giving up their independence. There was much enthusiasm for breaking down barriers. Some of the dons sympathized and helped the students skirt round the rules. Dorothy Pilley Richards, prominent mountaineer and wife of I.A. Richards, recalled that the undergraduate men used to come to her and Ivor for advice, sometimes in the middle of the night, about their agonized love affairs. This was a new fast crowd, set against outmoded prescriptions of right and wrong.

The war and the death of the old world order can't be given all the credit for the new, self-described modernist way of living, writing, and painting. A paper Virginia Woolf would read to the Cambridge Heretics Society in 1924, located the change earlier than that:

> in or about December, 1910, human character changed.... All human relations have shifted—those between masters and servants, husbands and wives, parents and children. And when human relations change there is at the same time a change in religion, conduct, politics, and literature.

British novelists, she thought, need no longer set out to entertain, or to 'preach doctrines', or to 'celebrate the glories of the British Empire'. They could express individual personalities, using them as a vantage point on life itself. This was a theme amongst the Bloomsbury set of writers and artists, to which Woolf belonged. In his *Eminent Victorians*, another core member of that set, Lytton Strachey, put the change at around the same time. In 1912, he wrote to Virginia Woolf that their Victorian predecessors 'seem to me a set of mouth bungled hypocrites'. Strachey, with his tall, bendy frame and high-pitched voice, incongruous with his sharp intelligence, had lived an openly homosexual life before the war, as had Keynes. Not for them the staid regime of monogamous marriage and breeding. Keynes would make an about-face, marrying in 1925. But he would not change his mind about the principle that the hidebound sexual mores of society ought to be overturned. Woolf's great niece, Virginia Nicholson, said that her great-aunt's generation was conducting 'experiments in living' of the sort John Stuart Mill had discussed, trying out radical versions of equality, sexual freedom, and friendship, and talking about such matters in explicit terms that would have made their parents faint. This was the Cambridge Frank returned to, a Cambridge in which radical forms of living and loving were the norm amongst those who would become his friends.

Those who made use of their new freedoms, however, walked on a tightrope between the old and the new, always ready to fall off and lose all. Homosexuality was illegal. Extra-marital heterosexual relationships were still the subject of moralizing, well after the war. A don could lose his job for engaging in either. Margaret Gardiner, the artist and eventual lover of the eminent crystallographer Desmond Bernal, remembered that a house in Little St Mary's Lane was deemed out of bounds because a decade ago it had been the location of a seduction of a Newnham girl. She also recalled that Russell was thought to be so immoral that when he came to give some lectures at Girton it was 'nearly cancelled on the day', and when it went ahead 'the wretched man was not to be given tea' and 'no student might be allowed to accompany him from lecture room to door'. Nonetheless, Gardiner and many of the other female students in Frank's day scoffed at these restrictions and felt 'free and authentic'.

Friendship

When Frank started his degree, he kept in close contact with his family, going to Howfield for Sunday lunches and tennis games, and inviting his siblings to tea in his rooms at college. But, like most new undergraduates, he was eager to start living more independently, and did so. He moved into rooms on the second floor of Trinity's Whewell's Court, overlooking All Saint's Passage and the gates of St John's College. This gorgeous stretch of Cambridge, from the Flemish diagonal bond brickwork of St John's to the late Gothic magnificence of King's, would be the backdrop for the rest of his life. He may well have simply taken all that beauty for granted, having spent most of his years with it. What did amaze him was just how quickly his life turned around, and became the life of an adult. He attended College chapel on the first Sunday morning of term, under the impression that all students would be required to do so, as they were at Magdalene. But he soon learned that there was no such obligation at Trinity. Thereafter, he abandoned all vestiges of religion. His parents accepted his decision, despite the fact that Arthur was one of those who kept Magdalene's outdated requirement in place. They, or at least Agnes, had encouraged their boy to think freely, and he thought his way straight out of their ecclesiastical world.

Word quickly got around that, as Richard Braithwaite put it, 'a remarkable young man has just come up', and it was thus that Frank immediately made a pack of friends. He met Braithwaite, a philosophically minded mathematics undergraduate at King's, right away. He had been one of those Quaker Ambulance men who had started his degree right after the war, that is, a year before Frank. Genial, with a barking voice and an open door, he was already a member of the societies to which Frank would gravitate. Braithwaite went on to be Knightbridge Professor of Philosophy at Cambridge, bringing philosophy of science and game theory to ethics, and collected and edited a selection of Frank's papers for publication after his death. He was a steady presence for the rest of Frank's life, and one of Frank's few actively Christian friends.

Soon Braithwaite came to Frank's rooms to inform him that Lionel Penrose wanted to meet him. Penrose, too, was a Quaker and older than Frank (three years in Braithwaite's case, five in Penrose's). Lionel had come up to St John's the year before Frank to read for the Moral Sciences Tripos, with a special interest in psychology. He is described during this period as impish and inventive, full of 'bubble and fizz'—a 'queer prickly hobgoblin of a chap, with a terrific hearty laugh and a total disregard of the conventions'. He was a great chess problemist, and was always inventing things, abstract and concrete, such as the Penrose endless stair, which M.C. Escher would make famous. Lionel would go on to be a renowned medical geneticist.

The Bloomsbury writer David Garnett asserted that 'At Cambridge [Penrose] discovered that Frank Ramsey, then a fellow undergraduate, had the most remarkable mind in the university and he was profoundly influenced by him.' Lionel influenced Frank as well. He and two of his brothers, Roland and Bernard (called by his childhood nickname Beakus), were already starting to become enmeshed in the Bloomsbury circle. Beakus would become the lover of the Bloomsbury painter Dora Carrington; Roland a surrealist artist and co-founder of London's Institute of Contemporary Arts. Beakus and Frank were the same age, but when they first met, Beakus felt that Frank, with his talent and confidence, must be older. He described Frank as an intellectual, but a friendly one. This coheres with Frank's brother Michael's account—that Frank was never in the habit of revealing his intellectual status or lording it over anyone.

Sebastian Sprott also became an immediate and great friend. He was a hugely popular psychology student at Clare College—elegant, flamboyant, homosexual, sporting a cameo ring and a flowing cape. He too was a part of the Bloomsbury set. Frances Marshall thought him an 'original'—a charming, amusing, affectionate person, and 'rather fantastic'. His conversation, as unlike Frank's as possible, was highly stylized. When Frank came up to Cambridge, Sebastian was already Keynes's lover. The Bloomsbury set took them to be 'married' from 1920 till Keynes abruptly re-oriented his sexuality and his life in 1925, marrying the Russian dancer Lydia Lopokova. Frank took immediately to Sebastian, despite himself being inelegant and heterosexual. They did share some things, including fine intellects. Frances Marshall characterized Sprott by his

> extraordinary charm, his gaiety, the ruthlessness of his logic, . . . the eccentricities of his life. No man ever saw more quickly than he did through cant and flapdoodle.

Frank, too, had a devastating nose for weak and sanctimonious thinking. And like Sprott, he managed to avoid being aggressive or nasty while pointing it out.

Others were also fixtures from the beginning. Indeed, Kingsley Martin, because he was a history student at Magdalene, met Frank before he started his undergraduate degree:

> Frank came round to see me in my rooms when he was seventeen, a senior maths scholar of Trinity, straight from Winchester...he had read widely; he had digested the economists from Marx to Marshall. I suppose he had a mind such as any generation is lucky to produce. He argued with Moore on equal terms when he was still in his teens...

They remained friends. Kingsley was more Frank's sartorial style. He was thought to have only one set of shabby clothing, and being a passionate member of the Fabian Society, he didn't care a whit. He would go on to an illustrious career in publishing.

Joseph Bentwich was a philosophy undergraduate—he and Frank attended Moore's lectures together and went out for meals and walks. His father was an important figure in the founding of Israel, and Joseph would follow in his footsteps, playing a key role in setting up Israel's educational institutions. During Frank's time as an undergraduate, Joseph's sister Naomi was a philosopher as well, and had assisted W.E. Johnson in the completion of his *Logic* (and indeed, been engaged to him). She was now in the midst of an unfortunate romantic obsession for Keynes. Frank was in a new world of complexity, an adult world of great interest to him.

Some of Frank's new friends were radical socialists—Marxists and Communists—identities not easy to carry after the war. Maurice Dobb, an economics undergraduate student who started his degree at the same time as Frank, was another immediate companion. Dobb was subjected to an unpleasant pastime of the student 'hearties'—being dumped fully clothed in the river Cam for his Marxist convictions. While Frank wasn't as far along the socialist spectrum as Dobb, who joined the British Communist Party in 1920, he was most definitely in the Cambridge left-wing set who met to discuss politics. Their debates contributed to the formation of the Cambridge University Labour Club in 1920. In 1923 Braithwaite would be its treasurer, with Frank and Kingsley Martin active members.

Frank also became very friendly with Tsemou Hsu (or Xu Zhimo), an important modernist Chinese poet, and a bridge between English and Chinese culture. He had been educated at Clark and Columbia Universities in the US and was a research scholar at King's in 1921 and 1922. In his brief time in Cambridge, he was embraced by Bloomsbury and by Frank and his friends. He taught the more mathematically inclined how to play the ancient and highly complex strategic board game wei-chi, or Go. Frank, Newman, and Penrose became experts. After Frank died, Richard Braithwaite inherited his wei-chi board.[†]

Unlike many undergraduates, Frank did not confine himself to his college—most of the Trinity students who coincided with him recollected no personal contact. In an about-face from his Winchester days, he gravitated towards fun-loving, outgoing friends, at whatever college they happened to attend. They also were, almost to a man, kind, generous, smart, and left of centre. And they were all men. He would later have good relationships with the Girton philosophers Dorothy Wrinch and Susan Stebbing, with Ivor Richards' wife Dorothy, with Richard Braithwaite's wife Dorothy, and other women in his set. He would form lasting and deep romantic relationships with two highly intelligent women. But at this point, his best friends were always men, both heterosexual and homosexual. Frank would often bring them to Howfield for Sunday lunch. Michael recalled them as an awfully nice circle, and all happily integrated with the rest of the family. Frank's life was coming together. He finally had a community which valued him as a person and treated him well. The misery he had felt at Winchester was put aside (at least temporarily).

Cambridge lectures in those days were in the morning. Then someone might have a little lunch party, the College kitchen sending food up to the student's rooms. They would talk all afternoon. Many of Frank's friends were financially stretched and, while College meals were inexpensive, alcohol was not easily affordable. The liquid was mostly tea and, if the conversation went late, cocoa. Only on occasion would someone produce a bottle of port. They played chess, bridge, and wei-chi; went to opera and concerts; had parties in the evening; and took long walks during the day. Often those walks were to Grantchester, a village made famous by the poet Rupert Brooke's *The Old Vicarage, Grantchester*. Its Old Orchard Tea Room was frequented by Virginia Woolf, E.M. Forster, Lytton Strachey, Augustus John, Russell, Keynes, Wittgenstein, and students and academics to this day.

Frank was having a wonderful time. He found that even though he was buying lots of books, he could live comfortably on his £250 scholarship. He worked out what sport he could maintain. He found it difficult to get regular football games, not being prepared, as his father put it, to 'hold himself in readiness to play at short notice anytime'. But lawn tennis worked out nicely. He was good at it, steady—if not brilliant—and most of the people he played with found him hard to beat. He moved quite fast for a large man. Braithwaite was often on the other side of the net. They

---

[†] Hsu's life was cut short in an airplane accident in 1931. His poem 'Leaving Cambridge' is still a school staple in China, and King's College has a memorial stone and an annual Poetry and Arts Festival in his name and honour.

usually played doubles, and as they progressed through their undergraduate degree, they would go to the house of an older, married woman in their set, Margaret Pyke, for tennis parties. We will hear more of her later.

Frank also developed close relationships with two of the great figures of Cambridge—Moore and Keynes—and a good relationship with Russell, who was living in London, but sometimes travelling to Cambridge. He met Moore when he started to attend his lectures in his second term. The meeting with Keynes happened around the same time. On a Saturday in January 1921, Braithwaite invited Frank to lunch with Keynes. They then went on a walk. Frank was impressed:

> He is very pleasant…Talked of difficulty of writing, Philosophy (epistemology, Occam's Razor), History of Mathematics, Probability in Mathematics, Objective Interest, puzzles, games, History of Economics, Marshall, books to appear shortly, Keynes probability, Keynes said that probability was at present on the level of astrology.

That's a lot to talk about in a few hours. The conversation would continue for the next nine years.

Image 6 Richard Braithwaite.

Image 7 Lionel Penrose.

Image 8 Tsemou Hsu/Xu Zhimo.

Mathematics Takes a Back Seat to Socialism and Philosophy

Frank's interests continued to move away from mathematics and towards philosophy and economics. Upon arrival in Cambridge, he had been inclined to change his subject from mathematics to economics. His tutor—the Trinity don assigned to him to help him with general matters about his degree—was the classicist Ernest Harrison. He 'urged' him not to switch, saying, in Arthur's recollection, that 'he would exhaust such a subject as economics in a couple of years, whereas mathematics would always provide him with something to work at'. The mathematical Tripos, like Classics, had a much higher status than a new Cambridge subject like Economics. A 'Wrangler'—someone who got a first-class degree in the Mathematics Tripos—was respected, whatever else he might go on to do. With his college not keen on a change of degree course, he stuck with the Mathematical Tripos.

In the nineteenth century, those who aspired to be Wranglers had trained under hired coaches, preparing for the final marathon exams in which they solved problems against the timer and trotted out the formulae they had memorized. In 1909, G.H. Hardy had pushed reforms through the University Senate, trying both to humanize the Mathematical Tripos and to make the curriculum more sophisticated. He was determined to move the course away from applied, and towards pure, mathematics. He and his Trinity colleague J.E. Littlewood were presiding over a renaissance of pure mathematics in Cambridge, dominating the landscape with their number theory.

But the reforms only got so far. In 1920, the Mathematical Tripos was still a dreary business, still criticized as an archaic exercise in rote memorization, dull, arduous, and disconnected from the new abstract mathematics coming out of continental Europe. Frank felt it was just like maths at Winchester, always geared to examinations and scholarships. In his second year, he would be on the speaker's card of the Trinity Mathematical Society, engaged in a debate about whether applied mathematics 'should be instantly and radically revised'. He argued—alongside his supervisor Samuel Pollard (the Trinity don who had told Frank's father of his success in the entrance examination) and his fellow Trinity undergraduate Frederick Maunsell—that it would be better to do away with applied mathematics as a subject of study, as it 'is merely a collection of standardized puzzles'. Pollard gave the current textbooks a rough ride, some of them authored by Arthur Stanley Ramsey.

The final exams for Part II of the Tripos were taken in early June in the Examination School, at the end of the third year. One aim of the reforms had been to dampen the sporting excitement that used to attend this examination. Cambridge started naming its 'Senior Wrangler' in 1748 and the tradition had been to lay bets on who would score the top marks. Not only was the announcement of the victor a public event, but the Senior Wrangler was also celebrated with torchlit parades, and newsagents selling penny postcards with his picture. The unfortunate who scored the lowest pass mark was publicly awarded the 'Wooden Spoon'. All those who took not the Tripos, but the Ordinary Degree, or took the Tripos exams and failed, were branded 'poll men'.

Hardy's reforms had ensured that by Frank's time, the public reading of the order of merit from the balcony of Senate House had been abolished and the labels 'Senior Wrangler' and 'Wooden Spoon' were no longer in official use. The ranking was no longer published. But word of who was in effect the Senior Wrangler would often get out, by the examiner tipping his hat to the candidate who earned the top marks, when reading out that name off the alphabetical list. Frank had always come first in mathematics, and even though his interest in mathematics was flagging, he didn't lose his instinctive ambition to do better than everyone else. That ambition was made harder to realize by Frank's taking the Tripos to be a 'sideshow', as his brother put it. On the main stage were philosophy, economics, and politics.

Frank had met Hardy as a final year Winchester student, through his Cambridge connections. Had Hardy not decamped from Cambridge for Oxford in 1919, perhaps Frank would have been more engaged with his degree course. Hardy was shy, intense, cricket-mad, and politically and socially radical. Frank liked him. But there are signs that even Hardy being on site might not have mattered much to Frank. Hardy had been responsible for bringing the Indian mathematical prodigy Srinivasa Ramanujan to Trinity in 1914, through to 1919. Ramanujan had been an occasional guest at Howfield, and when Frank started his Cambridge degree, he overlapped with Ramanujan for six months before his return to India. But there is no mention of Ramanujan in Frank's letters or diaries, suggesting a real lack of interest in what was happening in mathematics at Trinity and Cambridge.

Having settled with the Mathematical Tripos, Frank selected the lectures he would attend. He had free rein, as Trinity was a wealthy college and could pay for whatever lecture courses he wanted. (In those days, there was a charge for each lecture course, and in the poorer colleges the burden fell on the student.) Arthur helped Frank choose Analytical Geometry as one of his first-term lecture courses, as Ramsey senior had been impressed by a Mr Welsh's lectures on the topic. Arthur later said that his advice was 'a mistake', for Welsh's method—walking up and down while ponderously dictating—was too slow for Frank. Arthur also sent Frank to G.P. Thomson at Corpus, who was starting a new course of lectures on Electricity, thinking that Frank might 'get from him the most modern presentation of the subject; but the course was not a success and he gave it up'. Other lecture courses were selected purely on the basis that in taking them, he could avoid his father's lectures.

Things went better when he followed his own nose. He attended the Trinity Analysis course, taught by Littlewood and Pollard, and thought well of it. Littlewood was Frank's supervisor for analysis. He had a magnetic and sometimes off-beat personality—at reading parties in the country he would terrify the company by standing on one leg on the edge of a sheer cliff. But not even Littlewood could turn Frank's attention back to mathematics. Frank was already on Russell's path of moving away from mathematics to the philosophical study of its foundations, and to philosophy more generally.

Like many off to a fresh start in a new place, Frank kept a diary. It began in the December vacation of 1920, right after his first term. The first page reads:

> Preliminary Remarks.
> This is meant to be a full diary. Last year I started a diary of bald facts, but it was very dull and in August I dropped it.
> I am now 17 and in my first year at Trinity.
> This vacation I am by way of working to make up for idleness last term.

His idleness is a thread woven throughout the diary. But what Frank mostly meant was not working hard enough on mathematics. He was reading politics, philosophy, and economics at a pace that would fell almost anyone. This included books and articles about current political affairs and trade unions, the foundations of mathematics, the theory of knowledge, and ethics. With respect to all these subjects, Frank immediately started to chart his own course. For instance, that term he argued with his brother, who seemed to Frank to be 'an Intuitionist proper', having adopted Moore's view of ethics. Right from the beginning, Frank thought the received ethical theory was wrong. He would keep moving in the opposite direction from Moore, arguing that the good is not something objective that we can have access to, but is based on human psychology and needs. He would, however, agree with Moore's value pluralism—that there are many kinds of things that matter, not just utility.

One day, early on in his diarizing, we find him doing some mathematics—specifically, rigid dynamics. But the dynamics merits a lone sentence, whereas roaming in the University Library for books on Guild Socialism gets an excited paragraph. He noted that Guild Socialism was going to be discussed at CUSS—the Cambridge University Socialist Society—next term, and recorded that he would like to be asked to read a paper there, but thought it unlikely to happen. Kingsley Martin later described his and Frank's Cambridge political scene thus:

> There were the communists, to whom Bernal was an early and distinguished convert. The youngest ever Fellow of the Royal Society, he forfeited much of his early promise

as one of the great scientists by his political involvement.... At the other end of the spectrum was the Labour Club, a large amorphous body which desired a Labour government but minded not at all about the niceties of dialectics. In between was the Socialist Society, of which I became chairman.... Its leading spirits dismissed Communism as immoral, and unnecessary in England; they were prepared to work with Communists if politically necessary, as long as Socialists did not lose their identity and faith. It saw that Communism, by confusing ends with means, would become a system of society which forgot that the object of social change was the happiness of the people, and not the form of Government.

Like Kingsley, Frank was a socialist. In his first year, he hardly ever missed a meeting of CUSS.

On New Year's Eve, 1920, Frank told his diary that he did a little mathematics, but again, his mind was elsewhere. He went to the Library and read a review of G.D.H. Cole's *Chaos and Order in Industry*, as well as material on the coal strike. Cole was a political theorist and a rising star in the socialist firmament. He was the intellectual leader of Guild Socialism, and on his way to becoming the first Chichele Professor of Social and Political Theory at Oxford. The Guild movement's gradual revolution was not to happen. As Kingsley Martin later put it, Black Friday—the crumbling of the alliance between miners and transport workers in 1921—dealt a blow to the movement, and the General Strike of 1926 killed it, as the government moved to 'smash the unions'.

Frank's diary, essays, and notes give us a sense of his developing independence of thought in his first year at Trinity, as well as his aversion to embracing theories as pre-bundled and dubiously consistent wholes. He says, a propos the review of Cole: 'Am sceptical about class war theory.' He was also, unlike most of his socialist friends, sceptical of Functionalism, the idea that a society is a complex and adaptive organism whose parts work together to promote stability and solidarity. Frank was a down-to-earth socialist, interested more in political reality, than theoretical Marxism, or Communism, or Functionalism. He doubted that any such theory was the science of society.

Cole's appearance in Cambridge was a highlight of Frank's first year. He thought it a 'great' speech and got to spend time with the speaker afterwards. But he wasn't shy of taking on Cole, in a paper titled 'Mr. Cole's Social Theory', read to CUSS at the end of his first year. The paper argued in favour of a democratic bureaucracy chosen by careful methods, with worker representation all the way up and down, from parliament to administrative boards. He summarized:

> The chief difference between Mr. Cole and me is this. Mr. Cole proposes that when two groups differ they should bargain, and for bargaining to be effective involves the strike or war of some sort in the background. I propose that they should settle the matter by

referring it to independent judges or experts. Mr. Cole's idea of a good law court is a
Sankey Commission without a chairman, a body which it is known beforehand how
everyone will vote and the only thing that matters is the proportions in which the
various parties are represented.

The Sankey Commission had been set up by Parliament in 1919 to address the future
of the coal industry, as well as working conditions, wages, hours, and disputes
within it. Frank suspected that Cole's social theory boiled down to rule by party
politics. It is clear from the above passage that he thought that union politics were
also partisan. He saw the rule of law as being the most important thing, and in this
he differed from most of his socialist friends.

Frank's practical commitment to some kind of socialism, however, was strong.
He spent a lot of time with Maurice Dobb, already a prominent Cambridge communist. Dobb would leave for London after his undergraduate degree to do a PhD,
quickly getting it under his belt and returning in 1925 to a Cambridge teaching
position and a leading role as a Marxist economist. While it's not clear how much
Frank had to do with Dobb after their undergraduate years, during that time they
were great friends. Frank's neglect of his mathematics often took the form of
engaging in on-the-ground political activities with Dobb.

One afternoon was spent at the 'Coop works'. The local Co-op or Cooperative
Society was enmeshed with the Labour Party and was occupied with important
post-war practical affairs: how best to accommodate workers who were disabled on
the job; how to end child labour in the fields now that there was a decent supply of
adult workers; and so on. Frank enjoyed the day:

> Most awfully interesting, entertained to tea by the general manager and the secretary.
> Good tea. Nice men. The secretary is going to let me into the quarterly meeting
> to-morrow evening.

Frank said that at that meeting, the secretary of the Co-op education committee
'read a marvellously ungrammatical report'. Dobb suggested that he join a socialist
research group and that appealed to him. Most likely as part of this research group,
he made a long and detailed report of the working conditions of various professions
in Cambridge, noting their union status and benefits, strike history, their members'
political affiliations, and whether and at what rate women were employed. He did a
fair bit of editorializing, finding some unions, such as the National Union of Asylum
Workers, strong and excellent, but the unions of Shop Assistants, Warehousemen,
and Clerks 'extremely weak...hopelessly disorganized...absolutely impotent'. He
noted that 'the organizer declared it was often easier to organize managers than

assistants', but Frank thought that was partly because the assistants 'fear the sack'. Frank wasn't a member of the working class, but he was committed to its cause in theory and in fine detail.

Frank's socialism has been largely forgotten (or was never known) by those who carry forward his work on decision-making under uncertainty. That work became interesting to economists who believe that the best economy is one generated by the decisions of individuals, with minimal government intrusion. It also became interesting to game theorists, who attempt to understand economic and political outcomes by studying mathematical models of conflict and cooperation between individual decision-makers. But Frank's politics were not such utilitarian, purportedly value-neutral frameworks. He saw that human beings would make flawed decisions and was in favour of government intervention to help the disadvantaged in society. One group of economists did seem to understand the socialist background of Frank's work in the two branches of economics he founded: optimal savings and optimal taxation. These economists tend to be left-leaning and suppose a more benevolent view of the role of government than is the norm in economics.[‡] I will be arguing that, while Frank Ramsey may have provided the theoretical basis for what might be called a kind of conservative economics, focused on the rational and self-interested person, that was not how he himself understood his findings.

As an undergraduate, his interest in economics was very clearly in lock step with his interest in socialism. In his first year at Cambridge, Frank was drawn not only to the economics of the socialist Cole, but also to the work of Major C.H. Douglas, who had just published a book that launched the Social Credit movement. His proposals were attracting a good deal of attention, including from the Labour party and the Guild Socialists. Frank was let down by Douglas: 'Wasted 7/6 on Douglas Credit Power and Democracy. Seems confused rubbish.' A few days later, he went to the University Library to read Douglas's *Economic Democracy*, in case it might shed light on *Credit Power and Democracy*: 'Douglas seems rot but I have still hope in finding therein a great idea.' While still an undergraduate, Frank was to have an opportunity to expose the rot in print.

During the weeks he was feasting on works in politics and economics, Frank was also reading vast quantities of philosophy. He borrowed books by Moore and he finished reading Russell's *Our Knowledge of the External World*. Braithwaite said that he and Frank were 'almost word perfect' on Russell. Russell wasn't

---

[‡] Some examples are Partha Dasgupta, James Mirrlees, Joseph Stiglitz, and Thomas Piketty.

around much. He had been dismissed from Trinity in 1916 for anti-conscription activities, and although the college was in the process of trying to reinstate him, he was busy in London, standing for Parliament and starting a family. Trinity was still reeling over the drama of his dismissal. The philosopher John McTaggart had been in favour of it, causing G.H. Hardy to refer to him in a letter to Russell as 'that ghastly shit McTaggart'. Hardy had been one of Russell's most tenacious supporters and he left Cambridge for Oxford partly because of disgust over his college.

While Russell's presence in Frank's life was intermittent, it was significant. Frank availed himself of every opportunity to hear Russell lecture and they made time for one-on-one conversations. His work was a leading cause of Frank's thinking that, after all, philosophy, rather than economics, might be his final destination. He decided to attend Moore's lectures, 'as Richards and Ogden will be there arguing'. He took notes in a clothbound book, the first page of which reads:

Lectures by Dr. G.E. Moore on Metaphysics.

I missed the first term.

[ ] indicates my insertion.

He had been 'unable to go' to the lectures in the autumn term. But something in his Tripos schedule must have changed. For the rest of his first year, he faithfully attended Moore's lectures, as well as the follow-up discussion classes.

Braithwaite said of Moore's classes during this period:

we hunted the correct analysis of propositions about the self on Monday, Wednesday, and Friday mornings and the correct analysis of propositions of the form 'This is a pencil' on Tuesday, Thursday, and Saturday mornings throughout the year....The lectures were quite inconclusive: Moore saw grave objections to any of the analyses he had discussed being the *correct* analysis, and the audience dispersed to sit their examinations, or to return to their homes across the Atlantic, without any idea as to which of the analyses had the best claim to correctness.

The subject matter of Moore's lectures that term was our knowledge of the external world. On the slate for discussion was Russell's position that we come to know sense-data by acquaintance and construct from them all the objects of which we have knowledge. Moore also spent considerable time working through Russell's Theory of Types—the idea that some terms are of different types and we cannot meaningfully mix them. Moore took that to entail that we can say 'This box is triangular', but we cannot meaningfully say 'Virtue is triangular'. That would be to mix types, or apply a predicate of an inapplicable type to a subject. After painstaking discussion, Moore concluded that he couldn't see why Russell thought that type-mixing sentences are meaningless, rather than simply false. Moore's style of doing philosophy comes out beautifully in Frank's notes:

> 'Virtue is not triangular'. Moore gives up; can't see why meaningless but prepared to believe it is. 'Round square' is a concept that applies to nothing.

The discussion classes turned to the views of Russell, Bradley, Kant, and Berkeley on space, time, objects, and events. They all got 'refuted' by Moore. There was also the topic of the nature of meaning and propositions. Frank reported Moore as saying:

> Meaning
> What do I mean? To answer it I must find out what is before my mind. I may be mistaken because I may not distinguish correctly the things before my mind.
> Judgment and Propositions
> Russell's view is muddled. a proposition would appear to be a new sort of logical construction.

What is the meaning of a proposition? Is it the experience of something, which I then try to capture in a sentence? Is a proposition a logical construction from sensations in front of me? Or is a proposition some kind of independently existing entity that stands in relations to other entities? These issues would occupy Frank over the next decade, and he would reject all these contenders for a theory of meaning in favour of his own, completely different, account.

Midway through the lectures, something changed in Frank's notes. During the first term of his attendance, he did not add many '[ ]'—those insertions of his own. But by the time the spring term came along, he was confidently challenging Moore, adding '[He spoke strangely as if these were the only alternatives]' or '[This is not quite right surely; we only need suppose particulars temporally infinitely divisible as they are spatially]'. Frank didn't confine his critical thoughts to his notebooks. Moore would recall:

> In the early twenties, F.P. Ramsey attended at least one course of my lectures. I had soon come to feel of him, as of Wittgenstein, that he was very much cleverer than I was, and consequently I felt distinctly nervous in lecturing before him: I was afraid that he would see some gross absurdity in things which I said, of which I was quite unconscious.

Frank also went to Keynes's lecture course on statistics and again took dense notes. One of his exercise books was dedicated to summaries of Keynes's *Theory of Probability* and to Russell's *Introduction to Mathematical Philosophy* and Whitehead's *Principles of Natural Knowledge*. He didn't get far with Whitehead, writing on two pages and then leaving the next ninety-eight pages blank.[§] But Keynes and Russell he wanted to get just right. Both probability theory and mathematical philosophy would be touchstones in his thought for the rest of his life.

While Frank's diversion into the work of Russell and Keynes was related to mathematics, it was not part of the syllabus. His neglect of his actual coursework caused him some anxiety. In January, after a day in the University Library reading about current economics, he wrote a diary entry expressing his uncertainty about what options to take:

> Did a little work.... Wonder what I shall do for Schedule B. Feel inclined to geometry but am such a bad visualiser. Depressed about myself. Seem to have no energy to learn ... any maths. Bad failure in the schol exams will I suppose stir me up.

In Frank's day, Part I of the Mathematical Tripos exams were taken at the end of the first or second year, depending on how advanced the student was. Frank took them at the end of his first year. Arthur reported that Russell figured in Frank's exam answers. 'In Part I of the Mathematical Tripos he quoted the principle of Mathematical Induction in the symbolism of *Principia Mathematica* and rather baffled the examiners for they had some difficulty in finding anyone who could say whether it was correct or not.' They must have found someone, for Frank obtained Honours. That entitled him to get the BA Hons by simply completing nine terms (three years) of residence. Ambitious students, though, would go on to Part II Maths, in which Schedule A consisted of six exams (each three hours' duration) on subjects all the students had to take, and Schedule B was an optional set of exams, for an additional 'mark of distinction'. Frank was ambitious and was most certainly going to take Part II Maths. Thus his anxiety about not doing well in the Part I exams. He needn't have worried. He came first in them, and was elected to a further Trinity scholarship after the end of his first year, in the spring of 1921.

[§] Alfred North Whitehead moved to Harvard and away from formal logic in 1924. He was not very much on Ramsey's radar.

Image 9 G.E. Moore.

Image 10 I.A. (Ivor) Richards.

Heretics and Apostles

Frank's friendships were often forged in the small societies that dotted Cambridge. He wasn't clubbable in the usual meaning of the word—he always would be uninterested in joining the elite London clubs. But as an undergraduate he was keen to join those societies in which he would find real and intelligent friendship. Like many first year undergraduates, he signed up for an excess, quickly winnowing down to those that most suited him.

He tried out the Cambridge Union—the debating society at which future politicians cut their teeth. These meetings made Kingsley Martin so nervous that he 'usually had to run to the lavatory instead of speaking'. Frank spoke off the cuff in the first debate of his first term. A few weeks later, he argued for prohibition. He was still under the influence of his parents' ideas about alcohol. (He would soon take a sharp turn away.) He spent a long time preparing a speech on state ownership for a debate the following term. At that event, Dobb gave what Frank thought the only good speech. After three hours 'of listening to by far the dullest debate' he had ever heard and trying vainly to get an opportunity to deliver his own remarks, he concluded that the Union was largely a waste of time. He dropped it.

He also joined the Decemviri Society, another debating club, this one with a lively social component. But that too didn't last long. Neither did the Trinity Magpie and Stump Debating Society. The minutes show Frank in November 1920 making 'a fluent speech' about the 'volcanic possibilities' of socialism, and the following May, 'a nice little speech' on the set topic 'That Democracy is the Rule of Force and Fraud'. But his attendance then fell off. That kind of oratory, he told his diary, was not one of his 'things'. His strengths, he was coming to see, resided in 'mathematics, philosophy, and political & economic theory'. He loathed his 'perverted ambition' to excel at debating merely for the 'recognition'. He found he had better debates in less formal settings. Kingsley, for instance, sometimes asked him to tea 'to argue with Dobb'. And he found societies that were precisely to his taste.

Ogden continued to help him find his way. He suggested that Frank get himself into the left-leaning, anti-Church, Heretics Society, of which he was president. Dora Black, future women's rights campaigner and wife of Bertrand Russell, then a student at Girton, called it 'specially naughty' that their meetings were on Sunday nights. Unusually for Cambridge societies in those days, it did not elect members, but was open to all Cambridge undergraduates and gave honorary memberships to those who didn't fit that criterion. Also, unusually, the Heretics welcomed women, and their presence moderated the public-schoolboy silliness that permeated many of the debating societies.

The Heretics attracted a sizable crowd. In 1913, roughly 200 undergraduates were members. The regulars were of high quality. There was a stellar set of older honorary members, such as Keynes, Hardy, Moore, and the historian G.M. Trevelyan. The economics undergraduate Joan Maurice, who, under her married name, Joan Robinson, would become a famous left-wing economist, was a frequent attendee. She was a heretic with respect to convention as well as belief—hailing from an eminent academic and military family, she cut her own vegetarian, chain-smoking, direct-speaking path.

They crammed into Ogden's 'fantastically cluttered' Top Hole, where the smell of the fishmongers below made for a heady mix with the views expressed. Dora Black described it:

> We were a trifle cramped for space at these meetings, for Ogden had a great many books which lay in piles, and there were besides piles and piles of papers and letters through which one waded or sat on. This was Ogden's method of filing, one which I am sure would commend itself to anyone who knows that, once a thing has got into a folder of a filing cabinet, it will never be found again.

Ogden presided with a generous spirit, boosting the self-confidence of the less well-known members. The women, especially, relished the defiance and liberation.

The Heretics' list of speakers in Frank's first year included Keynes, Moore, the Bloomsbury painter and art critic Roger Fry, the poet Walter de la Mare, the philosopher-logician Susan Stebbing, the birth-control advocate Marie Stopes, the novelist and former King's student E.M. Forster, and the physicists Ernest Rutherford and Arthur Eddington. Margaret Gardiner remembered Gertrude Stein coming to Cambridge to give a talk to the Heretics, 'looking and speaking like a disapproving governess, her hair severely scraped back to match her attitude to her audience'. Other speakers included Frank's undergraduate friends Dobb, Newman, and Penrose.

It was precisely to his taste. He wrote the following in his diary after Moore gave a talk in which we get insight into Moore's way of being as well as Frank's:

> Moore talked to Heretics on Ethics; good paper; discussion not very good at first but then I asked some questions and got illuminating answers but most people bored. the meeting was dissolved and Moore, Ogden, Richards, Sprott, Martin and I adjourned upstairs where there was a most interesting discussion, in which Moore showed to

great advantage. Sprott went soon. I talked a little. Moore seemed happy and wasn't overexcited. (It sounds as if he was a child I had care of.)
I think he's great.

The next day, Frank wrote a page about ethics and showed it to Ogden. Ogden and Richards were attending Moore's lectures and were working on a book together, published in 1923 as *The Meaning of Meaning*. In it, they argued, contra Moore, that 'good' is not objective and indefinable, but simply an 'emotional aura'. When we call something good, those sentences do not in fact express genuine propositions or refer to anything. They merely express emotional attitudes. Their emotivism would be later taken up by members of the Vienna Circle and beyond. But at the time *The Meaning of Meaning* was published, it was a strange, new view, opposed to the received view of Moore. Frank was attracted to Ogden and Richard's position, as he simply didn't buy Moore's. Braithwaite recalled that before Ramsey, Ogden, and Richards criticized Moore's *Principia Ethica*, everyone in Cambridge just accepted it. Braithwaite was pretty sure that he got his own criticisms of Moore from Ramsey.

Between 1921 and 1927 the Heretics Society ran an economics section, which met in the house of the economist Philip Sargant Florence, brother of Alix Strachey. Sargant Florence characterized the economics section as being 'heretical in criticizing theory based entirely on the assumption of a rational economic man'. It was the only economic forum Joan Maurice could attend, as Keynes did not invite women to his Political Economy Club. He said to Joan that he disliked 'Mrs. Hollond' very much and if he asked Joan, he would have to ask her as well. A rather feeble excuse, and rather hard on the American Marjorie Tappan-Hollond, who was the first woman appointed to a Lectureship in the Cambridge Faculty of Economics, and Joan's supervisor at Girton. In any event, the Heretics economics section suited Joan. She said neo-classical economics 'stuck in my gizzard as a student'. Frank too was a regular. In his second year, he read a revised version of 'Mr. Cole's Social Theory', in which he argued for Guild Socialism. Despite the tools he would later give the theorists of the 'rational economic man', he was not one of them as undergraduate (nor, I shall argue, later).

Kingsley Martin told the following story about Frank when he was secretary of the Heretics:

> It is Frank Ramsey who comes back most vividly to my mind when I speak of the Heretics. I am remembering an occasion when, as secretary of the society, he read from the minute book a very learned and complete summary of a philosophical lecture we had listened to the previous week. He passed the book for signature to Ogden, in the chair, who stared in astonishment at finding the pages completely blank.

Not the best secretarial practice, perhaps, but impressive in a different way.

One member of the Heretics would become especially important in Frank's life. The first mention of the society in his diary is as follows:

> Heretics committee consists of Ogden President Miss Baker Treasurer Sprott Secretary...Miss Baker very beautiful and rather nice Sprott very nice...Miss Baker and Sprott are Moral Scientists.

The very beautiful and rather nice Miss Baker was then completing her time as a student of Newnham. She seems not to have attended many of the Heretics meetings, but Frank would keep a mental note of Lettice Baker.

Baker and Sprott were regulars at the Moral Sciences Club—the serious philosophy colloquium series that had started in the 1870s and, unlike the Heretics Society, still thrives. It was at an apex in the 1920s when at various times, Russell, Moore, Wittgenstein, and Ramsey were holding court. Topics in Frank's time were not so different from topics today—whether truth and beauty are human inventions; whether materialism is incompatible with ethics; how physics constructs the world; the nature of experience, causation, and logic. This was hearty, substantial fare for the philosophers. The papers were meant to be short introductions to longer discussion periods, although more often than not, the papers couldn't be crammed into what was then a ten minute limit. Frances Marshall recalled the atmosphere being marvellous, enthralling, and frightening, with concentrated thinking being conducted in a cloud of tobacco smoke. The meetings were held in someone's college rooms and were open to women, who would in theory require permission from their colleges and be expected not to go alone to the men's rooms. Most of the participants sat crammed on the floor, Moore included, contorting himself with the effort of answering a question. Almost all of the philosophers attended, except C.D. (Charlie) Broad, who could not abide cigarettes and so often boycotted the Moral Sciences Club. As a result, he was taken to be a bit of a recluse, interacting mostly with his colleagues at Trinity.

Frank and Braithwaite also joined the eminent Cambridge Philosophical Society, where science, not philosophy, was discussed. Physics was abuzz with the new quantum mechanics which was often the topic. Perhaps it was here that Frank met Pat Blackett, one of Rutherford's star young physicists, or perhaps they met because Blackett was a Magdalene student who had been swept up by Kingsley Martin. In any event, they would be friends to the end. Blackett had been a schoolboy at the Royal Naval College, and he had had a hard war, joining the navy at the age of sixteen and coming under fire in the fatality-strewn Battle of Jutland. By 1922 he was a member of the Heretics and CUSS. He would go on to win the Nobel Prize for his work on cloud chambers and cosmic rays. In 1925 he had the odd distinction of having his visiting (and mentally unwell) American student Robert Oppenheimer try to poison him by leaving an apple, laced with laboratory chemicals, on his desk.

Frank was invited to join Keynes's Political Economy Club—the undergraduates called it Keynes's Club or the Monday Club, as it was held on Mondays at 8:30 pm in Keynes's rooms. A restricted number of the best (male) economics students were invited, with a waiting list constructed for those deemed also worthy. Fellows and research students could come along if they liked. If Keynes had a visitor from abroad, he would bring him. Keynes was the powerful editor of the *Economic Journal* at this time, and his club provided him not only an opportunity to get to know each generation of Cambridge economists, but a venue for talent-spotting for the *Journal*. Someone read a paper. The undergraduates drew numbers from a hat. If they drew a blank, they didn't have to speak. But if they drew a number they would stand on the hearthrug and put questions to the speaker. The dons spoke after the undergraduates. Then Keynes told everyone where they were right and wrong.

The talk at Keynes's Club was often of current economic affairs, the politics of Germany and Central Europe, and whatever else Keynes happened to be interested in. There was a kind of general agreement amongst the members that Keynes was right on foreign politics. Brian Reddaway, a childhood friend of Frank's, who would in time himself become the editor of the *Economic Journal*, remarked of these special, much-loved sessions, that Keynes 'could be rather devastating if people advanced silly views'. Austin Robinson, who would become Keynes's right-hand man on the *Journal*, described the club thus:

> To the undergraduate of the early twenties, I can say from experience, Keynes' club was fascinating but alarming. Fascinating because here one heard Keynes, a large part of the Faculty, and all the best of one's rivals discussing in realistic detail all the real and most urgent problems of the world. Alarming because if one read a paper one was likely to find one's undergraduate efforts (I speak from painful memory) being dissected by a visiting Mr. Hawtrey, destroyed by the full power of Frank Ramsey's dialectical analysis, and when one had maintained one's position to the best of one's ability for three hours, Keynes would sum up in friendly but utterly devastating fashion.

Despite Frank not being an economist, he quite clearly took an active part in the discussion. Robinson encountered Frank frequently at Keynes's Club, and was awed by his 'immense ability'. He said that Frank never dominated the discussion, never tried to refute someone for the sake of it. But when it was Frank's turn, or if he was asked his opinion on something, or if he simply had something to say, everyone looked forward to it. He shared with Keynes the distinction of uttering the final word in conversations.

But the most important of all the societies for Frank was the Cambridge Conversazione Society, better known as the Apostles or simply The Society. It too was a venerable institution, founded in 1820. But it was far from open to all (and not open to women until the 1970s). Every year, one or two of the cleverest undergraduates would be identified as 'embryos' or potential members. They were scouted by the 'angels'—Apostles who were no longer undergraduates. Once elected or 'born' into the Society, it was for life, with each new member adding his signature to the book of all those who had come before him.

On occasion, an old paper would be pulled from the Ark, a cedar chest that was the repository of papers. But the standard practice was for someone to read a short paper on a subject determined in advance. The paper would be read on the hearthrug of whatever room happened to be the venue of the meeting, and discussed. Then a question would be put to the vote, although that question was almost always droll and not obviously connected to the subject matter of the talk. The angels were no longer expected to give papers, nor participate regularly, although many remained active. There was an annual dinner held in London, in the private dining room at the Ivy restaurant in Covent Garden.

It was supposed to be a secret society, although as James Doggart, an Apostle also elected in the early 1920s, would say:

> Even the stricter Apostles conceded that it was permissible for wives of members to know of the Society's existence. Otherwise their attendance at the Saturday meetings of the Society, which seldom ended before one a.m., might give rise to domestic mystification or even discord.

Since undergraduates had to get permission to be out of college after midnight, college Tutors also knew about the Society, as did many of those who wondered where their friends disappeared on Saturday nights. Virginia Woolf, getting her information from the not-very-secretive painter Roger Fry, called it 'the society of equals enjoying each other's foibles'.

Henry Sidgwick said the Apostles were engaged in

> the pursuit of truth with absolute devotion and unreserve by a group of intimate friends, who were perfectly frank with each other, and yet indulged in any amount of humorous sarcasm and playful banter.... No part of my life at Cambridge was so real to me as the Saturday evenings on which the Apostolic debates were held; and the tie

of attachment to the Society is much the strongest corporate bond which I have known in my life.

While the pursuit of truth was highly valued by the Apostles, so were cleverness and provocation. In Russell's words, the group held to the principle that

there were to be no taboos, no limitations, nothing considered shocking, no barriers to absolute freedom of speculation. We discussed all manner of things, no doubt with a certain immaturity, but with a detachment and interest scarcely possible in later life.

The Society was also a place of open homoeroticism where being 'in love' with another man, whether a sexually oriented love or not, was not just commonplace, but in vogue. McTaggart, Keynes, Hardy, and both Strachey brothers held up 'higher sodomy' as the ideal way of life.

In February 1921, Sprott proposed Braithwaite for election. Lionel and Alec Penrose were already in. On 15 October of that year, Braithwaite gave notice that he was proposing Frank for membership. He was elected the following Saturday. Kingsley Martin was rather hurt at remaining on the outside looking in. In addition to the close friends already in The Society, Frank would make new strong connections there—for instance, with the future literary scholar, code breaker, and Fellow of King's, Peter (F.L.) Lucas.

Shortly before Frank joined, the Apostles had taken a hard look at themselves and asked whether they wanted to continue admitting members on the grounds that one of the group was sexually attracted to them, or, rather, on brains. The conclusion was to go with brains, not looks. Lytton Strachey wrote to his brother in November 1921, reporting that keeping up with Keynes's "social" (i.e. sexual) activities was exhausting him, and noting that the Apostles had taken an interesting turn:

The new additions to the Society, however, are by no means of the exhausting kind—except mentally. They are by name Braithwaite and Ramsey—both almost completely intellectual...the latter very young, very large—something like (to look at) an immense Franklin, and both very nice and liking the society.

In the same letter, he described Lionel Penrose as 'a complete flibbertigibbet, but attractive in a childish way, and somehow, in spite of absence of brain, quite suitable in the Society'. Strachey took Lionel to be one of the aesthetes, as opposed to one of the new intellectuals. Whether he was right or wrong about Lionel, he certainly was spot on in taking Frank to be one of the brains.

The 1920s were a singular time in the Apostles' history. The post-war angelic membership included Keynes, Russell, Moore, McTaggart, Hardy, Lytton Strachey and his brother James, Leonard Woolf, E.M. Forster, and Goldie Lowes Dickinson, the writer and architect of the League of Nations. The Society was a venue for pacifism, the rejection of old values, and the rise of free thinking about morals. Psychology, Freudian and experimental (such as the question of whether IQ tests were valuable or not), was of intense interest to the group. Freud's theories were thought to be one of the decisive scientific advances of the century. The Hogarth Press, run by Virginia and Leonard Woolf, was Freud's English publisher. James Strachey and his wife Alix would become Freud's translators, as well as psychoanalysts themselves, spending sustained periods in Vienna being analysed by Freud.

The generation just below theirs—Frank's—took up these topics with an enthusiasm that spilled out of the meeting rooms of the Apostles. Sprott tracked Freud down on holiday in Austria in 1922 and issued an invitation for him to come and speak in Cambridge, which was politely declined. Kingsley Martin recalled that his and Frank's undergraduate life revolved around staying up till the middle of the night, talking about God, Freud, and Marx. Believing in Freud was better than believing in God:

> The importance of Freud was that he engendered a new type of thinking. The discovery of the unconscious made Victorian thought seem childish. If people were driven by their unconscious it was foolish to blame them, and the world was much less easy to reform by reason than our fathers had imagined....On the other hand, you ought to be able to get rid of guilt...

One of Kingsley's 'illuminating' Freudian discussions was with the psychoanalyst John Rickman in the summer of 1922, in which Rickman described world politics in terms of buried traumas resurfacing in nervous conditions. France's exaggerated fear of Germany was partly due to the sexual inclination of the French for coitus interruptus; Russia had an oral fixation, and so on. It sounds pretty unpersuasive now, but in Cambridge in the early 1920s, this kind of talk was all the rage. Freud was both liberating and frightening: liberating because one could discuss sex in intellectual terms; frightening because, as Kingsley put it, the war had shown that 'our progress was leading to the destruction of civilization' and Freud seemed to say 'perhaps we were not really "directing ourselves" at all'. The very idea of intellectually conscious decision-making had been put in question by Freud's hidden springs of motivation.

Frank's first Apostles meeting, on 22 October 1921, was held in Keynes's room. Braithwaite read a paper addressing the question 'Is Russell's book deserving of our approbation?' The text under discussion was likely what Russell called his 'shilling shocker', the popular 1912 *The Problems of Philosophy*. The minutes record that Moore, Lionel Penrose, Desmond MacCarthy, H.O. Meredith, and James Doggart voted Yes, as did Braithwaite, with the qualification 'As philosophy, no: as a penny dreadful, yes'. Sprott, Keynes, and Ramsey voted No. Peter Lucas was undecided. From that point on, Frank was a regular every Saturday evening. Like Sidgwick before him, Frank loved everything about the Apostles, especially staying up till the wee hours talking about politics, and the late breakfasts on Sunday.

Frank read his first paper to the Apostles, on 3 December 1921. In it, he argued that mathematicians must not shirk their duty to engage the 'task of alleviating the suffering of humanity'. Along the way, he threw humorous barbs at G.H. Hardy, who apparently had argued, in an inaugural lecture, that the pure mathematician must leave that task to others. Perhaps Hardy was merely defending the pure mathematician from the charge that the discipline itself was useless, for he was no slouch politically. Whether fair or not to Hardy, Frank argued against the claim that a contemplative don's time, experiences, and achievements should outweigh that of the uneducated person: 'what I feel confident of is that, though they may be incapable of great good, all men can suffer, and that pain and misery are great evils'.

The minutes for this paper are, on the surface, baffling. The question voted on was: 'Can we stand the voice of God as a father-in-law?' Peter Lucas and Keynes voted Yes, 'provided its daughter is dutiful to me'. Gordon Luce voted Yes, 'If she will insist on raping me, and so long as she is not, to my knowledge, giving me siph.' Lionel Penrose voted No, 'unless she is a virgin'. Braithwaite voted No, 'not unless there is a handsome dowry to compensate for her barrenness'. Sprott voted No, 'It's impotent'. We have to worm our way into this self-consciously clever discussion, with its public-school-boy desire to shock and its reprobate language. When we do so, we get something like the following. The question was whether the most abstract kind of thought can drive, or is even compatible with, a life of concrete political action. A variety of answers were given. These included yes, if those actions are pure; yes, if those actions don't infect our fine minds; no, unless theory gets something out of the concrete actions; and no, as theory has no effect on action. Ramsey voted No, with the comment: 'Deteriora sequor'. The reference is to Ovid: 'I see the high way, but follow the low way.' Frank could make his way easily in on the path of abstract mathematical thought, but preferred concrete political action. That low path took him to socialism and economics, two things which were diverting his attention away from the Tripos.

Frank's next papers to the Apostles were difficult papers about truth as an incomplete symbol and inductive inference. He could tell his tone was a little too serious. (In a later paper to the Apostles, he would consider apologizing at the beginning for choosing a subject as 'dull' as 'Socialism and Equality of Income', in which he argued that a planned economy, with state ownership and control of industry would result in more employment and greater equality and fairness than a liberal, laissez-faire one.) In these early papers, he was not yet into the spirit of taking a flyer on a topic, scoring points on wit, and making insider references to previous discussions.

It was that lack of seriousness that Wittgenstein had hated about the Apostles. He had been elected to The Society shortly after his arrival in Cambridge in 1911. This was despite Russell's premonition that it would end in tears. But Wittgenstein was a sensation in Cambridge and the others overruled Russell's concerns. Russell, however, was right. He wrote to Keynes after Wittgenstein's first meeting, to say that Wittgenstein had declared the Society a complete waste of time. He thought the undergraduate members were untrained infants (they 'had not yet made their toilets'). As one of Wittgenstein's biographers, Brian McGuinness, put it: 'The brittle arguments of the Society, where the paradoxical or the scandalous would be defended for sheer love of argument seemed to him intolerable.' One Apostle

Image 11 Bertrand Russell and Dora Black.

(Saxon Sidney Turner) wrote to another (Lytton Strachey) on 5 December 1912, recounting the fateful meeting:

> Wittgenstein complained that there was nothing to discuss and that the proceedings were futile: reminded that he had said the same a week before he replied that he would not have if he could have then imagined this. We left together and I spent a few minutes in his rooms: he said he was thinking of resigning. I tried to be soothing. What will happen I don't know.

By the Society's rulebook, members would be 'cursed' if they resigned. The only resignation the Apostles knew of had been in 1855. Russell's suggestion to Keynes was taken up: they would confine Wittgenstein's resignation to practice only, retaining his name on the official roster.

Frank would explore Wittgenstein's assertion—that there was nothing to discuss—in his final paper for the Apostles. By that time, he had fallen into step with the tongue-in-cheek spirit of the Society, and real care will be required when it comes to interpreting this compelling paper.

Adventure and Misadventure

Frank settled comfortably into his new world of friendship. In the long vacation in 1921, he went on a hiking holiday with some of his mates. It was his first trip abroad. They were off first to the Austrian Alps and then to Germany. Frank was already impressed with the intellectual ideas coming out of this part of the world, and the trip would be the beginning of a lasting fondness for its physical and cultural landscapes. The vacation was organized by Kingsley Martin and his older sister Irene,** with Frank, Richard Braithwaite, and two other friends, Paul Redmayne and Joseph Fryer, completing the party. Frank was the youngster in the group by as many as nine years. Martin recalled:

> We went, full of excitement, young men with our exams behind us and in front a world of hopeful adventure. One of our ideas was to start a new weekly paper with Joseph's money—he had quite a lot of it—based on the idea of telling the unpopular truth...

Frank wrote to his parents en route, describing the trip from London by train and ship to Ostend, then through Germany. He was surprised and heartened by the fact that they were kindly treated by the Germans, so soon after the bitter and humiliating war.

** Irene Barclay would become Britain's first woman chartered surveyor and an advocate for improved housing conditions for the poor.

They arrived at their destination, Hintertux, on Monday, 4 July. The Tuxer is a picturesque line of small alpine villages on a beautiful valley floor. As the name suggests, Hintertux is at the end—the back of beyond. It is nestled at the bottom of a steep glacier and boasts the highest thermal springs in Europe. In 1921, all that was to be found there was Kirchler's Hotel, a simple wooden structure accessible by horse and cart over a recently built road.[tt]

Frank's holiday companions were able hill walkers. Kingsley Martin was nicknamed 'the goat' due to his 'uncommon agility on mountains'. He could put on gym shoes and run 'up and down a Lake District peak each day, just for the fun of the thing'. The same could not be said of Frank. While he loved walking, at this point in his life he had little experience with strenuous climbs. In his first letter from the hotel on Wednesday, 6 July, he told his parents that they had just returned from a walk to Lanersbach, a village a mile away, where they left their boots for nailing. Late on Thursday he wrote that they were wondering whether the boots had been returned. The plan was to walk up part of the glacier where proper treads would be essential. But the absence of boots hadn't stopped them from spending Thursday climbing some steep slopes. They ascended Frauenwand, four hours straight up from the hotel, with significant snow patches even in the summer. At the top, they were rewarded with a magnificent view over the Brenner, the range along the border between Austria and Italy. There was a hut just before the big ascent begun. Frank wrote home: 'We stopped at an inn at lunch time and I was dog tired and drank 2 glasses of red and 2 of white wine straight off much too fast which made me dizzy for a bit but not long.' (In his first letter from the hotel, he had reported: 'I am getting rather fond of alcoholic liquor.') It sounds like an accident waiting to happen. And happen it did—not to the green, eighteen-year-old Frank, but to one of his friends.

On Thursday evening, they had a jovial time arguing and dancing with the other guests at the hotel. Amongst them were an Austrian brother and sister and an English family named Bully—husband, wife, and daughter. Friday saw the weather turn wet and cloudy. In the morning, Frank, no doubt still tired from the big climb the day before, hunkered down in the inn and studied his notes of Johnson's *Logic*. Fryer and Irene Martin struck out on their own, taking a packed lunch. In the afternoon Frank went walking with Braithwaite, Kingsley Martin, Redmayne, and the two Austrians.

When Frank's party returned to the hotel at around 6:00, they were met with the news that Fryer had broken his leg. They were told there was nothing for them to

[tt] Almost a hundred years later, the inn, much expanded and upgraded, remains one of the main hotels in Hintertux and is still run by the Kirchler family.

do, as mountain rescue had gone out with a stretcher to bring him back. But after they had bathed and dressed, Mrs Bully urged them to go up the mountain and meet the stretcher-bearers. Fryer's friends raced up, with Frank quickly falling behind. He came upon a relay man waiting for the stretcher and stayed with him. They spotted the group up the mountain and saw Braithwaite walk away on his own. They wondered what could possibly be going on. Then Miss Bully came to tell them what had happened, and Frank and Miss Bully returned to the hotel. Frank wrote to his mother on Saturday morning:

> Dear Mother, Fryer yesterday afternoon slipped on wet grass, fell over a precipice and was killed. I have never known a quicker descent from heaven to hell than this.

He had already sent a telegram announcing that he was safe, as the incident would be reported in the English papers before the post arrived. In his next letter, he was a little more expansive:

> He and Irene were on the precipice and he slipped and she saw him fall and felt sure he was dead. When she got down she was overjoyed to find him sitting up. She by great luck was seen by Mr. and Miss Bully. Miss Bully ran home and got a doctor, stretcher, etc and Irene and Miss Bully stayed with Fryer. He lived about an hour not in any pain. He said over and over again 'I am a fool' and one or two other remarks.

Fryer's accident occurred above one of the several waterfalls cascading down from the glacier. Even on a good day the spray surrounding these falls makes the area treacherous. Their boots were still at the shoemaker.

The next days were 'misery', with Irene beside herself and the others in various states of emotional disturbance. Fryer was buried on the following Monday at Lanersbach. Frank, not unfairly, reported it 'a horrid graveyard full of beastly little metal images, and the church inside is full of hideous pictures'. The Martin siblings and Redmayne travelled to Innsbruck that day. Frank wrote home: 'Braithwaite and I follow them there on Friday when the last of the other English go. Braithwaite will probably go home and the rest of us into Germany.' Braithwaite was Fryer's second cousin, and went home to be with Fryer's mother.

Despite being disconsolate about Fryer, the remaining party did their best to pull themselves together. Martin described their mood. They

> went off walking in the ripening cornfields of Bavaria. In that wonderful summer of 1921, we larded the ground with our sweat, drank quarts of beer, slept under pine trees, but realized that a carefree youth was over. For a moment we had believed, or most of

us, that the world was at our feet, an oyster to be opened with the sharp sword of Cambridge intellectualism.

Perhaps the fact that they were able to continue on so happily suggests they were not terribly mature. But perhaps it is also partly explained by the recent war. A young man losing his life was not a rare occurrence. Everyone would have known a family who lost a son.

Martin wrote to Agnes on 19 July from Munich to reassure her that they were 'in spite of everything' enjoying Germany, 'although there can be no zest in this broken holiday'. He noted, in closing, 'I remember that Mr. Ramsey is always very pessimistic on the subject of holidays.' He later remembered Frank and the holiday in these terms:

> He was a wonderful human being, utterly simple, unselfseeking and candid. He was a large, bulky man, and the sort of person who always looks untidy whatever he wears. When we were walking in Germany, he wore a straw hat to keep the sun from his eyes. It disintegrated, and the German police took him for a lunatic because he had straw in his hair. His flannel trousers also disintegrated, and large chunks of pink Frank were always showing through.

In the cities, Frank roamed through bookshops, coming to the conclusion that the Germans were interested in three things: the peace treaty (and Keynes), Spengler, and sexual ethics and hygiene. The only thing that marred the rest of the trip was German officialdom, which required them to stand in queues when they arrived in a city to report to the police, and then do the same on departure.

The Easter vacation of 1922 found Frank again on a mountain holiday, this time with Kingsley Martin and Lionel Penrose in Italy. Although not as proficient as his German, his Italian was quite good. (He could read the mathematician Peano in the original.) Ivor Richards then took him climbing in North Wales in the Christmas vacation of 1922. He would remain a keen mountain walker for the rest of his life. But he had learned his lesson about the need for good boots and a head not muddled by mid-climb wine. And he would always be afraid of cliff faces and any kind of dangerous drop.

He would have more frights on mountains. On that winter trip to Wales, they climbed Glyder Fawr in soft, knee-deep snow, with ice pellets driving into their faces near the top. Frank wrote to his brother: 'I had to receive a lot of assistance from the rope . . . it started to hail furiously; I hadn't nearly got enough clothes on as so many of mine were wet and it was very cold and I got panic stricken like mother on a mountain.' Even the experienced Richards got them lost in the blinding snow, only finding some old tracks and returning from the mountain just before dark. Richards was made of tough material. Frank told Michael: 'Near the bottom Richards bathed

Image 12 Frank with Irene Martin and Kingsley Martin, on holiday in Bavaria, 1921.

in a lake and put on his clothes without drying and stayed in them all evening!' Once, in 1924, lost in the dark with his father and brother in the Dolomites, they had to navigate a 100 yard narrow ledge with a deadly drop. Arthur kept his cool and talked them through it. In the autumn of 1927, Frank and his wife Lettice went to the Pyrenees and got lost on the Spanish side of the mountains. They had to cross back into France, where they struck a snowstorm and were rescued and thawed out overnight by some locals, who guided them over the frontier the next day. Lettice had to hold his hand when they encountered a narrow path with a drop on one side. Frank's fear of heights, however well-founded, made his love of mountain walking a rather fraught pastime.

Smooth on the Surface, Roiling Underneath

Most of Frank's friends thought, as Frances Marshall put it, that he had a very simple character. But he was more psychologically complex than he let on. While Frank seemed to be sailing smoothly on the surface, there was turbulence below. Sometimes he was ebullient and confident; sometimes raw and despondent; at other times, flat. His friends found him easy to know, and thought his intellect superior, without being accompanied by a desire for getting ahead. They would have been surprised at how many of his emotions were hidden from them. Frank had during this year what can best be described as a breakdown.

He agonized over his academic ambition. Early in his undergraduate degree, he confessed to his diary a concern about his motives for doing well: 'Damn my ambition: it is so much the rotten kind—more desire to be recognized as able than to be able.' He was a little jealous of those who had 'the gift of the gab', although he suspected it led to vacuous thinking. He thought that he was as good as Dobb, and better than many others who spoke so well at the Union, but he couldn't imagine how he could ever be as 'swell' as they were.

But his main cause for fretting was his intimate relations with other people. He felt terribly behind with respect to sex. The day after his diary entry about his ambition, he wrote:

> Really angry with myself re sex. Woe unto them that desire things that give no satisfaction. Will be a Puritan. I do hope I'm not injuring my health but haven't the guts to talk to a doctor.

He was finding release in the manner usual to young men his age. But he was not happy about it, as self-service gave him the opposite of what he was looking for: 'It is much more impulse than desire.'

On 1 November 1922, Frank wrote a corrosive note to himself. First, he recalled a rare Winchester friendship and echoed his sense of apartness at school.

> I feel lonely; I would rather be a mental eunuch...I need some satisfactory human relation and I have none. I feel this more than ever before. Before I have felt keenly the unsatisfactoriness of some particular relation; but this is more; it is a general feeling of isolation. I am not more isolated than I was at school, but then I was troubled by my passion for Siepmann more than general loneliness; and my emotional nature was then much less developed, I was much less dependent on other people.
>
> For a satisfying relation I know not where to look; it could be either of two kinds, friendship or love. Love with a woman would be best as it would satisfy me sexually, if consummated, but I have found that in any case passion even without intercourse to some extent relieves the sexual impulse.

Frank's 'passion' for Eric Siepmann appears to have been platonic. A 'passion', for Frank, was what Richard Braithwaite called 'a click'—something like an authentic and honest connection. Indeed, Frank implies in this note that passions for men would not be sexually satisfying to him. He still valued and yearned for them.

The note also has Frank's unhappiness about sex spilling over to an unhappiness about his friends. He remarked that his loneliness was of his own making: it 'is largely due to my fickleness resulting from a steady rise in my standards certainly for other people and I think for myself'. Then, in a painful way, he enumerated the defects of most of his friends. Kingsley Martin had now finished his degree and was abroad in Princeton for the year, but Frank said that he had been put off him before he left. Martin's diary entry the day before his departure confirms that his relationship with Frank (and Richard Braithwaite) was drifting:

> I like seeing Richard often, and Frank is better than anyone I know; and yet their minds work so differently, really, that I doubt if I should find enough permanent satisfaction in them. I feel so very much older in many ways.

Frank went on to say that his oldest friend in Cambridge was Bentwich, whom he now positively disliked, as he was becoming so religious that he 'presides in the local synagogue'. His treatment of Braithwaite further illustrated his brutal and candid mood. It was amplified by the kind of envy a young, unsophisticated man can have for a slightly older, more socially adept, competitor:

> Then there is Richard Braithwaite whom I know best, inside out in fact. Too well. I used to be fond of him, but never got what he calls a 'click' and I call passion for him. Till I really knew him I admired his brains; but now he seems to me intolerably superficial. Partly this is jealousy; he has much more of a certain kind of ability than I have, and I envy it, or perhaps the worldly success it gets for him (not that this is great, but greater than mine). My liking for him really started to decline at the end of the last term; I wanted him not to get a first without admitting it to myself, now I can no longer conceal it. He is so self-satisfied with so little ground; good God so am I but not as bad as he. I am three years younger and have more knowledge of every kind than he has. But I think he still likes me and thinks it not unreciprocated, and in fact I shall probably keep this dislike of mine to myself.

Lionel Penrose was still in his good graces, but he was in Vienna and, in any event, made a bad discussion partner regarding philosophy: 'he is mulish about it'. Newman 'would be first rate, but he too is in Vienna, and too ugly to love'. He continued:

> Hsu is gone and anyhow he is a Chinese, though I miss him. But somehow East and West don't... Yes indeed I do. Then I come to Sebastian who is perfect. I should like nothing better than to go round the world with him; but I never feel I matter enough to him.... But now I am sleepy and sentimental. And must stop. I have enjoyed an hours

thinking on paper; shall I keep this or will it like similar things I have written be destroyed tomorrow?

With respect to the 'perfect' Sebastian, Frank didn't matter enough to him because Sebastian's homosexuality was at the centre of his life, and Frank felt his friendship could never compete with that. At least, that's what he felt during this particular bout of misery.

He did keep his caustic thoughts to himself, and his friendships remained intact. Frank and his father went on a walking holiday with Hsu in the Lake District the following year, proving Frank right in reconsidering the idea that there might be an East–West divide getting in the way of their bond.[‡‡] Frank reported to Braithwaite after the holiday that 'Dear Hsu said he couldn't quite bear the smell of Englishmen', delighting Frank because it proved these kinds of judgments were entirely subjective.

The acute need to shed his inhibitions about sex could not be as easily overcome as his worries about his friendships. Exercise, he found, was no substitute, although travel did some good. Frank's older friends, on matters of sex if not on matters of intellect, were effortlessly superior to him. Hence his assertion that he would rather be a mental eunuch than a physical one. When it came to the desires of the body, he was a floundering and vulnerable young man, desperate for experience in a world populated by the sophisticated and free-thinking. He had been chosen for the Apostles, and had the respect and friendship of both the undergraduates and the dons. But something was missing.

[‡‡] Frank was probably friendly with the Chinese philosopher Jin Yuelin as well. Jin was in London and Cambridge from 1922 to 1925, and later made it clear that he was deeply influenced by Ramsey during this time. He became one of China's most famous analytic philosophers, and another bridge between the thought of East and West. The logician Hao Wang was his student, before going to Harvard for his doctorate.

'TO MY GENERATION, HE WAS RATHER FRIGHTENING'

The Border Country

When it came to organizing his time, mathematics, philosophy, and economics might have competed for Ramsey's attention. But when he was thinking through specific issues, these activities were in perfect harmony. He was melding disciplines together in ways that would pay major dividends. According to Braithwaite:

> By his second year he was accepted as the arbiter of good reasoning on every abstract subject: for eight years, if an abstruse point arose in philosophy, psychology, logic, economics, the question was 'What does Frank Ramsey think of it?' At conferences of philosophers, at the High Table or at undergraduate parties, his opinion on the value or relevance of an argument carried a peculiar and decisive authority.

Austin Robinson put it thus, in some contradiction to those reports of Frank being sweet to people while pointing out their errors:

> To my generation, he was rather frightening. He'd got that extraordinary sharpness of mind that you knew that if you said anything silly, you would get punctured pretty quickly.... He didn't think about his effects on *you*, so much as the pursuit of truth.... If you'd said something silly, he would just point it out.

And here is Roy Harrod:

> His main interests were in the difficult and recondite reaches of logic, but he discussed philosophy in an extraordinarily easy style. Subtle thoughts were distilled into simple straightforward sentences. In an entirely effortless and almost gossipy way he set out the quintessentials of a problem.... He had a genial contempt for the doctrines that had plagued me so much at Oxford; but he always gave the warning that it was necessary to understand mathematical logic, and believed that, in order to do so, it was necessary to have advanced some way into mathematics.

The philosophers knew Ramsey was an exceptional philosopher—recall that Moore was nervous about lecturing when he was in the audience. The mathematicians knew, from his performance on exams, that he was an exceptional mathematician. The economists also quickly realized that Ramsey was special, and that he would bring his brilliance in mathematical logic to economics.

Keynes relied on him for mathematical help almost from the outset. One instance, which brings out the respect the eminent economist had for the undergraduate, occurred at the beginning of 1922. Keynes was trying to figure out whether C.D. Broad, in his review of *A Treatise on Probability*, was right that Keynes had made a mistake in a bit of mathematics. Keynes wrote to Broad, who was then a member of the Bristol philosophy department:

> I think your solution is very near right, but not quite. I have discussed the matter with a mathematical friend, F.P. Ramsey of Trinity (have you met him? – certainly far and away the most brilliant undergraduate who has appeared for many years in the border-county between Philosophy and Mathematics), and he has worked out the enclosed solution, which is identical to yours, except that, according to his account, you have omitted one item in the equation. Could you let me have his manuscript back when you have finished with it.

Broad expressed surprise at not having come across Ramsey, for he frequently visited Trinity. Keynes's next letter said it wasn't surprising, since Ramsey 'is still an infant, aged about 18, and cannot remember before the war'.

Ramsey was happy to help Keynes with the maths. It was no work at all. While Broad was right that Keynes had made a mistake, so had Broad: 'Here are the calculations of those numbers. Broad seems to have made the same mistake each time.' The border country was indeed Ramsey's territory. He roamed freely over philosophy, mathematics, logic, probability theory, and economics. Perhaps no one would ever again do so with such intelligence and skill.

Taking on the Greats: Keynes on Probability and Induction

By the time Ramsey started his degree in 1920, Keynes had made a considerable fortune on the stock market. In 1922, he resigned his Ordinary Fellowship and became its Bursar. He now could live precisely as he wanted. He split his time between Cambridge, Gordon Square in London, and a country house in Sussex near the Bells' and the Woolfs' summer houses, all nerve centres of the Bloomsbury set. In his personal life, he was in full revolt against the pinched and heterosexual mores of the time. In his intellectual life, he solved difficult problems with technical sophistication and a humanistic sensibility.

Keynes was still bursar of King's, making money for it as well as for himself. But that was on an unpaid basis, so he wasn't tied to rules and academic schedules. He was usually in Cambridge only during term-time, from Thursday evening till Tuesday afternoon. He no longer supervised undergraduates, but engaged with some of them at his Political Economy Club and invited them to lunches in his rooms. Nonetheless, he seemed omnipresent—Kingsley Martin opined that Cambridge should be renamed 'Keynesbridge'. He most certainly was a major presence in Ramsey's life.

Keynes's eminence did not stop the young Ramsey from challenging him. His *Treatise on Probability*, published in 1921, was lauded by those in the Cambridge tradition. Russell called it 'undoubtedly the most important work on probability that has appeared for a very long time', a book which 'it is impossible to praise too highly'. The philosopher C.D. Broad and the statistician Harold Jeffreys also praised it. Such a reception should be unsurprising, given that the *Treatise* was in step with Cambridge's dominant paradigm. In the preface, Keynes acknowledged his debt to Russell and Moore, as well as to their British empiricist predecessors, Locke, Berkeley, Hume, Mill, and Sidgwick. All were united, he said, in their preference for matters of fact over high metaphysics. He included the logician John Venn in that tradition, writing to him that his *Treatise* 'was the latest link in the very continuous chain... of Cambridge thought'.

One of the *Treatise's* questions was: how is knowledge of probabilistic truth possible, given that it seems not to be moored in direct acquaintance or indubitable perception? This was an old question in Cambridge and in British empiricism more broadly. How can we explain the truths of mathematics and logic, when they have no foundation in experience? Hume had invoked a too-convenient separation of matters of fact and relations of ideas, with statements concerning the latter, including mathematical and logical statements, simply being exempted from the observational criterion. Mill had made an unsuccessful attempt to treat mathematics as an observable science.

Keynes's solution was to argue that we can indeed find a foundation for probabilistic truth in direct perception. There is one true probability—an 'objective relation'—between any set of premises and a conclusion in virtue of which, if we know the first, we will be warranted in accepting the second with some particular degree of belief. A probability statement is about a degree of partial entailment, part of the formal machinery of drawing conclusions from premises. Keynes then argued that it is not something that can, or need be, further defined: 'We cannot analyse the probability-relation in terms of simpler ideas.' The probability-relation denotes a unique quality, just like Moore's 'good', which we can know by perception or direct acquaintance.

Keynes thought that probability theory must be able to tell us to what degree we ought to hold beliefs. In his system, not all probabilities are numerical, measureable, and comparable. But to get measurement off the ground where we can, he maintained that we need to assume the Principle of Indifference, which

> asserts that if there is no *known* reason for predicating of our subject one rather than another of several alternatives, then relatively to such knowledge the assertions of each of these alternatives have an *equal* probability.

Ramsey was less than impressed. Despite the fact that he was himself in the lineage of Keynes's continuous chain of Cambridge thought, he had no qualms about knocking down parts of it. Keynes's theory of probability was his first target.* His attack was mounted in a review of the book in the January 1922 issue of Ogden's *Cambridge Magazine* and in less formal settings. Braithwaite's reaction indicates just how effective it was. He recalled that he read Keynes's *Treatise* in the long vacation, immediately after it came out, and said that he swallowed it whole: 'Whereupon Ramsey produced some pretty serious criticisms of it and shook my beliefs about it.'

Ramsey peppered the *Treatise* with problems. He objected to the attempt to provide a logical foundation for the Principle of Indifference. He objected to the idea of an unmeasurable non-numerical probability and would later, in the 1926 'Truth and Probability', offer an account of how all probabilities are measurable. And he objected to the very idea of Keynes's objectively fixed probability relations— the idea that all statements stand in logical relations to each other. As Ramsey put it, there is no such probability as the probability that 'my carpet is blue' given that 'Napoleon was a great general'. In some notes that Ramsey wrote either in preparation for his review, or in summary of it, he set out his objections to these supposed probability relations in a snappy way:

> There are no such things as these relations.
>
> (a) Do we really perceive them? Least of all in the simplest cases when they should be clearest; can we really know them so little and yet be so certain of the laws which they satisfy? ... All other logical relations are easily describable ... all we have to judge is that

---

* Wittgenstein's theory of probability and account of induction was also in Ramsey's sights. On Wittgenstein's theory, induction has "no logical basis".

something is an instance of a rule. Here there are no rules: Keynes Princ of Indiff is not such (owing to irrelevance) even if it is sound, which it is not.

(b) They would have to be relations between propositions and there are no such things.

(c) They would stand in such strange correspondence with degrees of belief.

In his first point, Ramsey is raising the problem that Wittgenstein would make famous—what we now call the rule-following problem. Ramsey would address it by suggesting that reliable habits of mind underpin our rules. His last point was especially hard for Keynes to take. It was Ramsey's intention to give a better account of how probabilistic or partial belief could be rational.

Here we have the first articulation of a core feature of Ramsey's way of thinking— a suspicion of anything indefinable or unanalysable. In 'Truth and Probability', he would put his point about Keynes's probability relations even more disarmingly: 'I do not perceive them, and…I…suspect that others do not perceive them either because they are able to come to so very little agreement as to which of them relates any two given propositions.' If someone were to ask him what probability one proposition gave to another, he 'should not try to answer by contemplating the propositions and trying to discern a logical relation between them'; 'no one esti- mating a degree of probability simply contemplates the two propositions supposed to be related by it; he always considers *inter alia* his own actual or hypothetical degree of belief'.

After Ramsey's review appeared, he and Keynes were locked in a discussion of the matter. A month later, in February 1922, Ramsey wrote to Keynes to tell him that he *still* thought Keynes was wrong to hold that one statement can support another only if there is a logical relation between them that constitutes such support. In the autumn of 1923, Ramsey read a paper to the Apostles on inductive inference, in which he mounted another attack—this time on the allied account of induction Keynes had set out in the *Treatise*.

Inductive inference is the kind of reasoning which moves from the observed ('Every human I've ever encountered is mortal') to the unobserved ('Every human is mortal'). The problem of induction, whose classic description was given by Hume, is that such conclusions—such generalizations—seem not to be fully justified by their premises. One problem in this vicinity is that the inference can be upset by one instance, as was the inductive conclusion 'All swans are white', when black swans were discovered in Australia. But the problem of induction runs deeper, for we can ask why the observation that many swans are white ever lent support to the conclusion in the first place: what bearing has the whiteness of each swan I have observed on the colour of a swan I have never observed? Hume suggested that there can be no non-circular answer to this question. Keynes tried to offer a non-circular justification in the *Treatise*: inductive inference is grounded in the principle that there is a limited variety of properties in nature. A generalization will arise from a small number of properties, and there will be a definite probability relation connecting any two properties. The more (unpredicted) observations we make, the more credibility for the generalization. His position was not dissimilar to the hypothesis of the uniformity of nature, offered by Mill as a grounding of induction.

Again, Ramsey was unimpressed. Keynes attended the meeting of the Apostles in which his young challenger set out his doubts. One was about the hypothesis of the principle of limited variety. Ramsey stated that there is

> no logical reason for believing any such hypothesis; they are not the sort of things of which we could be supposed to have a priori knowledge, for they are complicated generalizations about the world which evidently may not be true.

Hume and Ramsey are right: Keynes's principle about limited variety is itself an inductive generalization, and hence his justification is circular. Ramsey also made the point in a brasher way:

> To say that those who use induction are reasonable because they know subconsciously some big fact about nature, necessarily very complicated, as is shown by the failure of attempts of formulate it, is hardly good enough.

Nonetheless, Ramsey said, we all regard induction as reasonable—if we didn't, there could be 'nothing to distinguish the wise man from the fool'. This is another idea that will appear frequently in his work. He kept at the centre of his various theories the idea that if something seems essential to human thought and flourishing, scepticism about it should not be our first instinct. We can make a good guess as to why the question put to the vote was 'Is the belief in Induction philosophically similar to the love of copulation?' Both are things we think we cannot do without. Ramsey and Sprott voted Yes. Keynes, Braithwaite, Lucas, and Rylands voted No.

In this Apostles paper, Ramsey again went after Keynes's conception of probability, on which his defence of induction relied. He noted that Keynes's 'pure objective theory' is 'blurred' by his admitting in a few passages that probability is relative to the principles of human reason:

> with the word human we pass from a purely logical notion to one which is in part, at least, psychological, and in consequence the theory becomes vague and muddled.

Ramsey concluded the paper by sketching his own solution. He said, in this informal brotherly setting, that it has just occurred to him and since he is tired, he can't 'see clearly whether it is sensible or absurd'. His solution, which he thought was 'more plausible psychologically', would in fact turn out to be an acute line of thought:

> Roughly it is that a type of inference is ~~reliable~~ reasonable or ~~unreliable~~ unreasonable according to the relative frequencies with which it leads to truth and falsehood. Induction is reasonable because it produces predictions which are generally verified, not because of any logical relation between its premise and conclusion. On this view we should establish by induction that induction was reasonable, and induction being reasonable this is a reasonable argument.

It is likely that this solution had just occurred to him because he had been reading, via Ogden, the work of the American pragmatist C.S. Peirce. Indeed, Ramsey's first sentence is straight out of Peirce. Hume, Peirce, and Ramsey see that a non-circular justification of induction is impossible, and argue that is it a mistake to seek such a grounding. A few years later, in 'Truth and Probability', presumably when he was less tired, Ramsey would carefully circumvent the circle by putting the idea of reasonableness in terms of praising or blaming *a habit*.

'Truth and Probability' would sketch Ramsey's alternative to Keynes's conception of probability and set the course for subjective probability theory and decision theory. But it is clear that his position was already gelling when he was an undergraduate. In the same month that Ramsey's 1922 review of the *Treatise* appeared, Keynes wrote to Broad:

> I find that Ramsey and the other young men at Cambridge are quite obdurate, and still believe that *either* Probability is a definitely measurable entity, probably connected with Frequency, *or* it is of merely psychological importance and is definitely non-logical. I recognize that they can raise some very damaging criticisms against me on these lines. But all the same I feel great confidence that they are wrong.

Braithwaite would have been one of the young men leaning towards the frequency theory. The frequentist says that probability is objective: it is the relative frequency with which, say, a coin would land heads, were it tossed a great number of times.

Ramsey, on the other hand, would criticize the frequency theory as a general account of probability, but preserve a role for it in physics and other sciences. He thought that probability is multi-dimensional: it is measurable *and* psychological, though not *merely* psychological, and at times we require a non-psychological frequency account of it. But for Ramsey, the main event was to emphasize the subjective aspect of probability. In 'Truth and Probability' he would show how to measure partial belief by using a subjective interpretation of probability, one of his major contributions to modern thought.

Keynes was shaken by Ramsey's criticism. Clive Bell, who wasn't a logician, but had lived in the same house as Keynes when he was finishing his book, said that 'Ramsey made a rent' in Keynes theory, 'which caused the stitches to run'. Roy Harrod, who did understand the arguments, said that while Keynes took a negative review of Joseph's to be irritating and off the mark, he thought that Ramsey's was neither:

> The only criticism which disturbed Keynes at this time came from another quarter. There was an undergraduate at Trinity, Cambridge, who had recently arrived from Winchester, the son, like Keynes of a Cambridge don. This was Frank Ramsey. Keynes quickly spotted him as a young man of outstanding genius. Although he was still an undergraduate when the *Treatise* appeared, his criticism carried more weight with Keynes than any other, and it is not clear that Keynes felt that he had a satisfactory answer to it.

The *Treatise on Probability* was an important book for Keynes. It shaped his later views of what we now call risk and uncertainty. It was also important to Ramsey, shaping, in a negative way, his own ideas about uncertainty and how to measure it. The debate in 1922 set the tone for the future relationship between these two distinguished probability theorists. Keynes had been hearing from almost everyone that the *Treatise* was a major achievement until it fell apart under the criticism of his favourite undergraduate. From then on, Keynes would rely on Ramsey's judgment, for instance, in working out mathematics that went beyond him and in vetting papers for his *The Economic Journal*.

Taking on the Greats: Moore and Russell

The waves of Cambridge analysis would gain force and roll, via Wittgenstein, from England to Vienna, to the 'Circle' that was gathering around Moritz Schlick. An idea was taking hold. All of science can be reduced to (or be constructed from) a language of observation and formal logic, and anything that doesn't fit into that language is meaningless, including a fair number of apparently well-formed sentences. From his first exposure to this idea, Ramsey had reservations.

On 18 November 1921, he read a confident paper to the Moral Sciences Club titled 'The Nature of Propositions'. The meeting was held in Joseph Bentwich's rooms, with Susan Stebbing in the chair. Russell and Moore's domination of the topic seemed secure. But this second year undergraduate made a bold, if unfailingly polite, challenge. Ramsey attacked Russell's early view of propositions, facts, and truth and he pointed toward a new way of thinking of these fundamental matters. There was a lot in the paper, and it certainly broke the ten-minute rule. The entry in the minutes concludes: 'Though somewhat abstruse the paper was not too technical for a valuable discussion.'

Ramsey argued that Russell had been wrong to think that a belief is a dual relation between something mental and an objectively existing proposition, and was still wrong, in his version of a multiple relation view. Ramsey claimed that there simply are no such 'mysterious entities' as propositions in Russell's sense, 'so unlike anything else in the world'. (Notice the similarity to his objection to Keynes's mysterious objective probability relations.) Russell's idea that propositions are objects introduces more problems than it solves. In his multiple relation analysis, even 'the simplest case is so complicated' and some cases, such as general propositions (for instance, 'All men are mortal'), are 'infinitely complex' because there is an infinite number of objects (an infinite number of human beings stretching back in time and forward to the future) to be related. Ramsey thought it 'self-evident' that 'no proposition entertainable by us can be infinitely complex'.

On his alternative picture, Ramsey distinguished 'two kinds of characters' of any mental state, such as 'a belief, a doubt, or an assumption', each of which is 'of great importance'. The first consists of a psychological factor, such as the 'the presence or absence of feelings', which Ramsey called the 'pistic' character. 'Pistic' comes from a Greek word, transliterated as *pistis*, associated with persuasion and faith. A mental state's pistic character pertains to the degree of commitment. It is this character that distinguishes a belief that it will rain tomorrow, from a doubt that it will do so, or from an assumption that it will (say, because we are in Scotland in April). The second character is a belief's 'referential characters or references'. When we assert of a belief that it is a belief that it will rain tomorrow, we assert that it has the character of referring to precipitation and our location.

Ramsey didn't spend much time in this early Moral Sciences paper on the pistic character of belief. But he wrote at length about its referential character and about the nature of truth. He dismissed Moore's idea that 'truth is indefinable' (another of those mysterious, objective, relations). But he nonetheless thought that 'true beliefs do have a certain relation to facts which false beliefs do not have'. And he argued that Russell's 'propositional view' is wrong—to have a reference is not to point to an objective proposition. For one thing, Ramsey noted, Russell's theory, far from making the relations of 'pointing toward' and 'pointing away from' transparent, 'only pretends to have analysed' them. For another thing, Russell's theory is committed to the existence of facts corresponding to each true sentence. Ramsey thought it would be much better to dispense with nebulous facts in favour of things we can understand: real objects, properties, and events in the world. Three years later, Ramsey was pleased to hear from Braithwaite that Susan Stebbing had hoped the paper would be published.

Ramsey started to dimly discern a positive proposal in this paper, which he would continue to develop the whole of his life. At the end of it, he dealt 'as briefly as possible' with the idea of truth. He noted that to say 'it is true that *p*' is equivalent to asserting *p* itself:

> The most certain thing about truth is that '*p* is true' and '*p*', if not identical, are equivalent. This enables us to rule out at once some theories of truth such as that 'to be true' means 'to work' or 'to cohere' since clearly '*p* works' and '*p* coheres' are not equivalent to '*p*'.

Such passages have led many philosophers to take Ramsey to be a founder of the redundancy theory of truth (or its cousin, the prosentential theory), in which the concept of truth is superfluous and can be eliminated. Ramsey also seems decidedly set against the coherence theory of truth (a true belief is one that coheres with the rest of our system of belief) and the pragmatist account of truth (a true belief is one that works). But Ramsey would later put a different spin on his idea. He would say that the question 'what is the nature of truth?' is in the first instance answered by the redundancy equivalence idea, but that idea points us to the concepts of belief and assertion, which do all the heavy lifting for the concept of truth. And in that heavy lifting, pragmatism does some work as well.

Ramsey wrote another paper on Russell, which he read to the Apostles on 29 April 1922. Here, he tried to fit complex properties and relations, as well as propositions asserting probabilities, into Russell's logical analyst framework—into the view that everything can be explained in terms of its simple constituents. He found that Russell's theory stumbled on mathematical propositions, general propositions ('All A's are B's'), and even our belief that the cat is on the hearthrug:

> How are we to analyse them so as to avoid all complex entities? It is very difficult to see.... to get a coherent account of belief in this way is awfully difficult...

Moreover, Russell's account will rest upon 'the assumption that there are one or many indefinable belief relations'.

With respect to Moore's indefinable concept—that of the good—Ramsey sent off his first volley in his 1923 Apostles paper on induction, in which he noted an analogy between the problem of induction and the question of objective goodness. In induction, we consider the justification of our inferences from the observed to the unobserved. Keynes employed mysterious probability relations to make those inferences objective. In ethics

> we consider the justification of our actions, and are at once presented with the simple solution that this lies in their tendency to promote intrinsic value, a mysterious entity not easy to identify.

Both Keynes and Moore offer us a snare and a delusion. The solution to both problems, Ramsey suggested, is not to be found in a mysterious entity, but in 'psychology'.

Ramsey's opposition to Russell's idea of propositions and Moore's idea of indefinables only deepened, and he would continue to work through these issues, and what he meant by 'psychology', until the end of his life. But in carving out his alternative position, he would find inspiration in something Russell had written in the 1921 *The Analysis of Mind*, which seemed to Ramsey (although not, in the end, to Russell) to provide the key to the right account of truth and its relation to reality. For in that book, Russell toyed with the idea that a belief is a disposition to behave. Ramsey was, and would remain, attracted to it.

The Douglas Social Credit Proposals

We have seen that Ramsey, as a first-year undergraduate, had been interested in, yet unimpressed by, the political and economic ideas floated by Major C.H. Douglas, the founder of the Social Credit movement. He had thought them a load of 'rot'.

Douglas was a Scottish engineer, who in 1910, at the age of thirty-one, had started (and eventually quit) a Cambridge degree. During the war, as a major in the Royal Flying Corps, he had been sent to the Royal Aircraft Factory in Farnborough to organize supplies. He observed that what it cost to purchase the goods produced each week exceeded the weekly sums paid to all individuals and companies for labour, salaries, dividends, raw materials, and so on. That observation seemed to him to refute current economic thinking, which had it that costs and purchasing power are aligned. After retirement, he was appalled by the post-war labour unrest and inhumane conditions amongst the poorer classes, and he decided to apply his engineering skills to arrive at a system that ensured economic security for all. He surveyed hundreds of British businesses and believed his wartime experience was confirmed.

In any production of goods, he argued, companies distribute two types of payments. Group A payments are those made to other organizations for things like raw materials and bank charges, and Group B payments are those made to individuals in the form of wages, salaries, and dividends. Since all payments flow into prices, the price of goods must be at least A + B. But since A + B will always be greater than B, consumers over any period of time will never have the income to buy all the goods produced. Douglas thought that technological advances were only going to widen the gap between what is produced and what can be purchased, and he concluded that the economic system was on the verge of breakdown.

The problem of wage slavery, against which the left was united, was, in his view, caused not by industrial capitalists, but by the way credit and finance were structured. His solution was not the usual socialist one of nationalization of industry and increased wages for the worker. It was rather to be found in how the cost of goods is financed. Lending should be taken out of the hands of the private sector and given to the government. Douglas advocated what he called a 'Compensated Price Mechanism' or national dividend (not to be confused with the national dividend of Marshall and Pigou, who were talking about the national income or the yearly amount of goods and services produced). Douglas's idea was that the government should subsidize price reductions for goods. Domestic coal, for instance, should be sold at less than cost (less than A + B), with the government reimbursing the colliery owners for the difference. Alternatively, the government could issue additional money to consumers, and this credit would provide them with sufficient purchasing power. A just price, he suggested, is a quarter of cost price.

Sitting behind this analysis was a claim that Jewish bankers were behind the world's problems. When Douglas's ideas were applied by the first ever Social Credit government in 1935 in Alberta, Canada, that party was anti-Semitic, conservative, populist, and evangelical, and today the Clifford Hugh Douglas Institute for the Study and Promotion of Social Credit has tethered itself to Christian theology. In 2006, the Princeton game theorist Harold Kuhn described Douglas thus:

> Who was this Major Douglas? Briefly, he was one of those crackpots who exist on the fringe of academic economics and whose theories promise a redistribution of wealth that appealed to a large part of the public (including, in Douglas's case, Ezra Pound and T.S. Eliot). Like many of those offering a panacea for the Great Depression, he was also an anti-Semite who invoked the theses expounded in the Protocols of the Elders of Zion in defense of his economic theories.

This crackpot was on the verge of enormous power in the early 1920s. Some of the big Labour Party thinkers, such as G.D.H. Cole, Hugh Dalton, R.H. Tawney, were suspicious. But Douglas's impact on the left was so strong that in December 1920, an Extraordinary Conference of the National Guilds League considered (and in the end rejected) a re-positioning of the movement along Douglas's lines. One member, the prominent socialist Samuel Hobson, said that 'this was the first time he had heard of an ethical proposition coming out of a mathematical formula, and he thought that Bertrand Russell should be told of it'.

Ogden and Keynes thought it would be good to have the Douglas proposals analysed, and in their view, Ramsey was the one to undertake the task. Ogden commissioned him to write an article for *The Cambridge Magazine*. Braithwaite's recollection was that Ramsey was paid £100, a huge amount at the time, especially for an undergraduate. In his paper, and in an earlier draft which was circulated to his friends, Ramsey upended the Douglas proposals. While he agreed with Douglas that 'capitalism is obnoxious', he thought that Douglas's attempt at making it less so was no good at all.

Ramsey's wry style and crisp confidence is already in evidence in this early paper, as is his wariness about buying whole theories off the shelf, even Guild Socialism. He argued that Douglas had developed 'an original analysis of the capitalist system', but Ramsey did not mean that in a good way. Douglas, he said,

> regards financial systems as responsible for parts of human nature; much as some Socialists imagine that capitalism makes men grasping, he imagines that the credit system makes men constitutional saboteurs: change the financial system and you change human nature. 'Economic democrats will always adopt improvements' says Major Douglas. 'Guildsmen will never be greedy' says Mr. Cole.... [Douglas] is emphatic that our present discontents are due not to the idle rich who eat without working, or to bad distribution, but to 'the most gigantic and organized sabotage on the part of the capitalistic system and of Labour itself'.

Douglas's proposals, says Ramsey, amount to:

> 'A ought to be able to equal A plus B', since all purchases (A plus B) are purchases of the product of some factory, and the public cannot buy more than A, for A is all the money it gets.... Moreover B cannot be a zero without a complete return to barbarism, for when a market gardener buys a spade, he is making a payment B... Hence.... Major Douglas... is saying 2 ought to equal 3. If he convinces the Almighty he may get his way.

Ramsey noted a slew of problems, in addition to the point that perhaps not even God could make 2 equal 3. For one thing, if the state poured money into the system to subsidize lower prices, then A would be diminished, for the only way to get that money into the system is by taxation, not by printing notes as Douglas suggested. For printing money is 'an unequal and hidden form of taxation since it dilutes all existing purchasing power and so diminishes A by precisely the amount it increases it'. Ramsey also argued, crediting the point to Mill, that 'the boom caused by an issue of currency notes or an expansion of credit is only due to the failure of people, particularly investors, to realize that if prices are rising, £105 next year may be worth no more than £100 if prices are stationary'. On Ramsey's view, commodities are more or less useful, and their usefulness, along with productivity, interest, and capital, can be expressed mathematically. When we take all of this, and the cost of loans, as an element in cost, we see that prices are indeed more or less in line with cost.

In the published version, Ramsey began by recommending the reader to turn not to Douglas, but rather to W. Allen Young's 1921 pamphlet *Dividends for All: Being An Explanation of the Douglas Scheme*, as Major Douglas, he held, 'is always obscure and often absurd'.

RAMSEY ON THE DOUGLAS PROPOSALS

Pedro Garcia Duarte, Professor of Economics, University of São Paulo and INSPER

Ramsey examined the argument of critics of Major Douglas presented by Young, that the existence of intermediary firms selling goods for producing final goods implies that there are wages and dividends unaccounted by Douglas's theorem. In a given period of time, this additional purchasing power might 'enable the surplus consumption goods to be bought'. Ramsey stated that this argument 'is very simple and seems to show a genuine flaw in the Douglas argument'.

Ramsey defined 'cost price' 'to include the maintenance of capital, but not the cost of increasing it', which he considered to be 'obviously the correct usage' and 'that of Douglas and his followers'. The veracity of Douglas's analysis turns on whether the ratio of selling (final) price to cost price is less than unity. For Ramsey, 'there is...a strong and simple argument for supposing that the ratio does not differ appreciably from unity': in a stationary state, when 'production goes on at an unchanging rate and prices, wages and the national wealth never alter', 'the rate of flow of the cost of consumable goods produced is $A + B$' and purchasing power is distributed at a rate B by the final producers and as they spend A with intermediary goods, this represents purchasing power distributed 'at some previous time by other factories producing intermediate products'. Thus, in such a stationary state, 'the total rate of distribution of purchasing power is $A + B$, which equals the rate of flow of cost prices of consumable goods' and the ratio is unity.

Ramsey's main contribution was to show that the ratio is also unity off a stationary state, under wider conditions of changing the quantity produced, changing wages, the productivity of labour and the national wealth. For this he argued that labour produces commodities which are expressible in terms of the 'unity of commodity'—with less useful goods having fewer units—and productivity of labour at given period being the number of such units that result from a unit of labour. Thus, at time T, the cost of producing one unit of commodity is wages paid over labour productivity. But units of commodities are added at T to goods available for consumption at $t > T$. Ramsey abstracted from fluctuations and assumed a constant interest rate to derive national wages and dividends and the rate of flow of cost prices. Finally, he showed that the only mathematical solution for the equality between the purchasing power distributed and the selling prices of the final goods is a ratio of unity.

In mathematical terms, he showed that, for the case of perpetual constant rate of interest, r, and taking into account that the dividends paid to the public are simply $r \cdot C(T)$, where $C(T)$ is the national capital at time T (in real terms), $x(T) = 1$ is the only solution to the equation below, i.e., the ratio is unitary:

$$\int_0^{t_0} B(T) \cdot f(t)dt + r \cdot C(T) = x(T) \int_0^{t_0} B(T-t) \cdot f(t) \cdot e^{rt}dt + dC(T)/dT$$

where $\int_0^{t_0} B(T-t) \cdot f(t) \cdot e^{rt}dt$ is the 'rate of flow of cost prices of goods which become available for consumption at time T,' and $\int_0^{t_0} B(T) \cdot f(t)dt$ is 'the rate at which wages are being paid at time T'.

However, the results were not yet entirely general. He then considered a variable interest rate ('by calculating the dividends at rate r on a *nominal capital*,' $Q(T)$) and dispensed of another assumption about new investments and national capital. He defined $L(T)$ as 'the rate (positive or negative) at which the public is investing money' (which does not necessarily equal investments, $dQ(T)/dT$), and obtained the modified equation:

$$\int_0^{t_0} B(T) \cdot f(t)dt + r \cdot Q(T) = x(T) \int_0^{t_0} B(T-t) \cdot f(t) \cdot e^{rt}dt + L(T)$$

which has a solution $x(T) = 1$ only when we substitute $C(T)$ for $Q(T)$ and $dQ(T)/dT$ for $L(T)$. Under more general conditions, we obtain two cases in which the ratio of selling to cost price is less than unity: 'when dividends are paid on less than the national capital' (supposing that $(LT) = dQ(T)/dT$, then $x(T) < 1$ if $d(Q(T) - C(T))/dT > r \cdot (Q(T) - C(T))$); and 'when the rate of interest on new investments is less than that at which interest is reckoned as an element in cost' (supposing that $Q(T) = C(T)$, then $x(T) \langle 1$ if $L(T) \rangle dC(T)/dT$). But they are 'obvious to common sense' and 'clearly irrelevant to Major Douglas' contention that "just price" is today a quarter of cost price'.

Young replied, on Social Credit Movement letterhead. He found objectionable both the backhanded compliment and the idea, which he attributed to Ramsey, that the consumer is charged for the cost of loans for the building of capital as if they were a debit against him. Ramsey wrote to the editor (Ogden) that he assumed that only the maintenance of capital, not the cost of increasing it, is built into consumer price. He thought Young so far off the mark that a formal reply would be of very little interest. Ogden declared the controversy closed.

Ramsey's paper appeared in the January 1922 issue of *The Cambridge Magazine*. It was a memorable volume. It also contained Ramsey's review of Keynes's *A Treatise on Probability*; a preview of *The Meaning of Meaning* by Ogden and Richards; 'The Remedy for Overpopulation' by Marie Stopes, the famous advocate of birth control; and an illustration by Augustus John. A month later, Ramsey's friend Dobb published his own trouncing of Douglas in the *New Statesman*. Douglas's social credit movement was intellectually forced from its home ground, and moved it to the colonies.

Braithwaite recalled that it was Ramsey's analysis of the Douglas scheme that made economists sit up and notice that he was exceptional. Kingsley Martin had a similar recollection of the discussions of 'Douglasism': 'The controversy was usually conducted on a lofty plane of abstraction...The climax of these discussions was, I believe, Frank Ramsey's complicated mathematical analysis.' The mathematics were in fact pretty rudimentary, nothing so fancy that Bertrand Russell should be told of it. Ramsey would later really show how abstract mathematics has real-world applicability to our ethical questions. He did that in the two further papers he would publish in economics, not in *The Cambridge Magazine*, but in the prestigious *Economic Journal*. After the Second World War, when Ramsey's ideas crossed the Atlantic, to be picked up like messages in a bottle by American economists, they would be the founding ideas of the sub-disciplines of optimal taxation and optimal saving.

In the commission on the Douglas proposals, the hand of Ogden was still guiding Ramsey's career. He also asked Ramsey to write a pamphlet on the causal factors affecting commodity exchanges, which were at that time fluctuating widely. The idea was 'to provide matter for discussion at a conference of Chambers of Commerce'. This was likely the first meeting of the International Chamber of Commerce held in London in June 1921. The members of the conference had no idea they were discussing the work of someone still in his teens. Ramsey had suggested that if certain things happened politically, the exchange would move in a certain direction. When, later in the summer, that actually happened, one member of the conference took the trouble to find out the identity of the author of the pamphlet, and offered him the sum of £30 if for three months he would read trade journals and give his opinion as to the likely trend of prices. Ramsey started to do this, but felt that he was able to render 'very little service in return for the money' and he soon told the man not to waste his pounds. One of Ramsey's fundamental character traits was honesty. It had been expressed as a schoolboy when he told his scholarship examiners that he had already seen the Latin passage that was to be translated, and here we see it expressed again, turning back a welcome and easy income because he, and he alone, thought he was not doing enough to merit payment.

There was one more commission from Ogden, of rather greater significance. At the end of a letter in which Ramsey expressed hesitancy about Ogden's encouragement to dig further into Douglas, he wrote:

> Can you send me a copy of Wittgenstein?? As soon as ~~possible~~ convenient? I don't mean when it is out, but a proof as soon as you have one not being used. I'm thinking of giving a week to those problems.

Ramsey was asking for the galley proofs of the *Tractatus*, which he had just translated for Ogden.

6

RAMSEY AND THE EARLY WITTGENSTEIN

An Undergraduate Translates the *Tractatus*

When Wittgenstein wrote to Russell from the prisoner of war camp, he said: 'I believe I've solved our problems finally. This may sound arrogant but I can't help believing it.' Russell didn't think Wittgenstein had solved all their problems with such finality, and didn't agree with some things in the book. But he did think that the manuscript was a work of genius. When it finally made it out of war-torn Europe to the safety of Cambridge, the urgent question was how to publish it. Moore, who had titled his own book *Principia Ethica* and sparked Russell and Whitehead to title theirs *Principia Mathematica*, suggested a similarly grand headline for Wittgenstein's masterwork: *Tractatus Logico-Philosophicus*. Moore later told Gilbert Ryle that this title had 'a Spinozistic ring' (referring to Spinoza's *Tractatus Theologico-Politicus*).

The manuscript turned out to be a hard sell with publishers. Wittgenstein was in Austria and would not visit England until 1925. He was in discussions with the German firm Reclam. As Wittgenstein put it, they required 'the judgment of some expert in order to be sure that the book is really worth printing'. He asked Russell: '*you* would perhaps be kind enough to write ... a brief assessment of the value of the work' and asked him to 'please write ... a few words—as much as your conscience will allow you to'. Russell wrote words full of high praise. Reclam then wanted Russell to write an introduction to the book. He was again happy to comply and began the task, which took him some months. He sent a draft to Wittgenstein, saying that if there was anything unsatisfactory in his remarks, he would try to remedy it. Wittgenstein replied:

> Thank you very much for your manuscript. There's so much of it that I'm not quite in agreement with—both where you're critical of me and also where you're simply trying to elucidate my point of view. But that doesn't matter. The future will pass judgment on us—or perhaps it won't, and if it is silent that will be a judgment too.

When Wittgenstein saw the German translation of Russell's introduction, he was less sanguine and wrote to Russell: 'I couldn't bring myself to let it be printed with my work.' He informed Reclam of his decision, and they abandoned the project. Russell, used to such rough treatment from Wittgenstein, responded magnanimously. He offered to try to get an English or American publisher interested. He was setting off for China, and left the matter with his research student Dorothy Wrinch, a mathematician-philosopher at Girton. She had participated in a weekly study group with Russell on his *Principia* in 1916, and was one of a handful of people who would be able to understand Wittgenstein's manuscript and its importance. That handful was getting smaller, as Wittgenstein had declared that not even Russell (nor Frege) understood him.

A number of publishers turned down the manuscript, including Cambridge University Press—a decision which must count as one of the worst mistakes in its history. Wrinch then got the chemist Wilhelm Ostwald to take it for his journal *Annalen der Naturphilosophie*. Wittgenstein put aside his objections to Russell's introduction, and his qualms about Ostwald, whom he thought an 'utter charlatan', and expressed his pleasure that the manuscript was going to be printed. It appeared in 1922 (with a 1921 date on the cover) in German and with Russell's introduction, under the title *Logisch-Philosophische Abhandlung*. Neither Russell nor Wittgenstein was given the opportunity to see the proofs, with the result that typesetting errors were missed.

Wittgenstein's friends were still eager for the book to be published in English. One way or another, Ogden became involved. Perhaps Wrinch approached Ogden— she knew him from the Heretics Society. Perhaps Russell contacted him when he returned from China. Or perhaps Ogden, who had great publishing instincts, came up with the idea himself. In any event, Ogden snapped up the *Tractatus* for his new *International Library of Psychology, Philosophy and Scientific Method*. It would become one of the most important books of the century. It, along with Moore's *Philosophical Studies*, was the first of Ogden's acquisitions for that illustrious series—both would roll off the press in 1922. Wittgenstein was pleased, as he too remained keen that his manuscript be published in English.

A problem, however, loomed. Who would manage the task of translation? A translator of a work of philosophy needs to know the argument inside and out, and Ogden was not a philosopher, never mind a logician. His degree was in English, and for all his abilities, Wittgenstein's work, with its symbolism and its arguments about the nature of logical form, was beyond him. Indeed, the *Tractatus* was so beyond Ogden that he thought he understood it perfectly. He wrote to Russell, shortly after he received the *Annalen* version:

Looking rapidly over the off print in the train last night, I was amazed that Nicod and Miss Wrinch had both seemed to make so very little of it. The main lines seem so reasonable and intelligible—apart from the Types puzzles. I know you are frightfully busy at present, but I should very much like to know why all this account of signs and symbols cannot best be understood in relation to a thoroughgoing causal theory. I mean the sort of thing in the enclosed . . .

Jean Nicod, the French logician, and Dorothy Wrinch both had trouble figuring out what Wittgenstein was saying, but, after a quick read on the train, Ogden's impression was that the *Tractatus* was clear, reasonable, and intelligible. That in itself is an indictment of his claim to understand it. Moreover, that quick read made Ogden think that the *Tractatus* was similar to a chapter of his and I.A. Richards's *The Meaning of Meaning*, which was then in press (that was 'the enclosed chapter'). Wittgenstein certainly did not think there was any resemblance between his work and that of Ogden. He wrote to Russell:

A short time ago I received "The Meaning of Meaning". Doubtless it has been sent to you too. Is it not a miserable book?! No, no, philosophy, after all, is not as easy as that! But it does show how easy it is to write a thick book.

Ramsey also had concerns about *The Meaning of Meaning*. Ogden and Richards had given him drafts for comment. Richards wrote to Ogden after the completion of one chapter: 'it will now stand Ramseying', and he quite expected 'Ramsey will say "all wrong" now leaving us all alone in our opinions'. When the book was published in 1923, Ramsey reviewed it. He found the distinction between emotive and factual uses of language interesting, as well as the appendix on C.S. Peirce. But Ogden and Richards 'do not see the existence of logical problems'; their theory of signs is 'valueless'; and some of their criticisms of philosophers 'suffer from insufficient understanding of the difficulties which their victims are trying to solve'.

Richards later admitted that they didn't understand Wittgenstein:

Neither he [Ogden] nor I could much esteem what—obscurely—came through its [the *Tractatus*'s] pontifical pronouncements. . . . [The] *Tractatus* was plainly a magnificent specimen of the unintelligible, certain to be the occasion of rich misunderstandings of the sort we were studying [in *The Meaning of Meaning*].

His recollection of the process by which a translator was found was as follows:

All sorts of people were called in . . . They couldn't make it make as good sense in English as, if it made any good sense in German, they thought it should. Moore had been insisting very much that it wasn't translatable—it would be much better left just as it was.... [It] got into a kind of discord; and then I don't know who suggested that Frank ought to have a try at it, and as soon as Frank and Wittgenstein got together over this it was clear that there was a possibility.

Richards got it slightly wrong—Ramsey would not have any engagement with Wittgenstein until after the decision had been made that he would translate the manuscript. Ogden wrote to Wittgenstein to say they had found a translator, and described Ramsey as 'the Trinity mathematical prodigy'.

We have seen that Ramsey had won the prize in German at Winchester and that by the end of his school days, he was reading widely in German. But more important than linguistic fluency was his fluency in logic and philosophy, above all, the new kind of logic and philosophy that Wittgenstein was putting forward. Ramsey was at the time one of a small handful with the skill and background required to get inside Wittgenstein's system. (The obvious others were Russell, Moore, and Frege, despite Wittgenstein's claim that none of them understood his work.) Even in the late 1920s, after philosophers had time to study the volume, the *Tractatus* scholar Max Black could say: 'the general notion was that the *Tractatus* was a book of tremendous mystery and only Wittgenstein himself could have known what he meant by it, but he'd forgotten'. The book was extraordinarily difficult. It seemed in the empiricist spirit of Russell's work, but its conceptions of 'logical form' and its attempt to set the necessary conditions of knowledge sounded more like Kant.

Ramsey was keen to take up Ogden's suggestion. He had read the manuscript and it interested him very much. Russell wrote to Wittgenstein: 'The translation is being done by two young men at Cambridge who know mathematical logic, and I am telling them all that you and I agreed on as regards translation of terms.' The best guess as to the identity of the second young mathematical logician would seem to be Braithwaite, but he later said that he had been in the dark about the translation. In any case, nothing more was heard of the second translator.

Ramsey went to Miss Pate's secretarial agency in the winter of 1921–22 and translated the manuscript. He read it off an *Annalen* offprint to a shorthand writer who then typed it up. Ogden was at his side. It is hard to adequately convey how astounding an accomplishment it was to more or less straight away translate this immensely difficult text from the German to English. Ramsey turned nineteen in the middle of the translation, in January 1922.

Wittgenstein was then sent the typescript. He went over it carefully (as he did the proofs when they were ready). In the end, Wittgenstein wrote to Ogden saying that he couldn't think of any more changes and asked Ogden to give his 'best thanks' to the 'translators', who had 'done their work excellently' despite having 'an awful job'.

He had never before said of anyone that they had understood the book and, as far as I know, he would never say it again. Wittgenstein declared that the translation had 'equal authority with the original', which was printed side by side with the translation.

In 1961, controversy broke out about whether Wittgenstein had indeed approved the translation. A new set of translators, Brian McGuinness and David Pears, as well as the philosophers Elizabeth Anscombe, Rush Rhees, P.F. Strawson, and G.H. von Wright, bemoaned the 'badness of the original translation'. They claimed that Ramsey had quickly 'mugged up German' in order to translate the manuscript and that Wittgenstein had told his friends later in life that he had not been at all involved in the process. A decade-long firestorm of correspondence appeared in letters pages of *The Times Literary Supplement*, under the title 'Wittgenstein in Red'. Red was the colour of the Pears/McGuinness cover, in contrast to the dark green of the Ramsey/Ogden cover. Ogden's executors, Russell and Dorothy Wrinch, defended the original translation against the accusations of the new Wittgensteinians. Russell confirmed that Wittgenstein had taken 'great pains' over the English version, and that on numerous occasions he had 'altered the translation and found out afterwards that the translation had been right as it was'. Russell also confirmed that Wittgenstein sanctioned the translation point by point and where it differed from the German, it did so by his wish: 'the translation as it stood expressed what he wished to say better than a more exact translation'. The penultimate typescript of Ramsey's translation bears this out. Wittgenstein made changes on almost every page, the bulk of them minor, but many showing that he was making sure the philosophy was just as he wanted. So does the correspondence between Ogden, Ramsey, Wittgenstein, and to a lesser extent Russell, showing much back-and-forth about translational matters. The contemporaneous evidence, when produced by Ogden's executors, was decisive. When the defenders of the new translation saw the substantial correspondence between Wittgenstein and those involved in the Ramsey-Ogden translation, they issued a *mea culpa* and retracted their claims. Von Wright edited and published the correspondence. Future printings of the Pears/McGuinness version were modified in light of what they learned from those letters.

In the preface to what is known as the 'Ogden Translation', Ogden wrote:

> The Editor further desires to express his indebtedness to Mr F. P. Ramsey, of Trinity College, Cambridge, for assistance both with the translation and in the preparation of the book for the press.

That Ramsey was not given credit for the translation, nor even listed as a co-translator, doesn't show Ogden in a good light. Nor does the fact that Ogden appears not to have paid him. It might have seemed at the time that various publishers were right in their assessment that this book was not going to make any money. But Ogden knew better, and the revenues ended up being considerable. Wittgenstein was left out of the royalties as well. When, in 1933, the book was reprinted, he wrote to the publishers arguing that, now that the book was selling, shouldn't some of the royalties come to him? They didn't answer.

Ramsey was unbothered by not earning money or public praise. What interested him were the logical and philosophical issues in Wittgenstein's thought. The translation was simply a step on the way to those demanding matters. While Ogden would never express any further interest in the substance of the *Tractatus*,

Image 13 Dorothy Wrinch.

Ramsey would remain engaged with it for the rest of his life. Wittgenstein was a significant and fruitful influence on his young translator, even if Ramsey would end up jettisoning most of the *Tractatus*, in advance of Wittgenstein jettisoning it himself.

Taking on the Greats: Wittgenstein on Saying and Showing

The *Tractatus* is one of the most important philosophical texts of the twentieth century. In 1924 Braithwaite told the Oxford philosopher H.H. Price that it was the most important book since Kant's *Critique of Pure Reason*. That same year, Keynes wrote to Wittgenstein:

> I still do not know what to say about your book, except that I feel certain that it is a work of extraordinary importance and ~~peculiar~~ genius. Right or wrong, it dominates all fundamental discussions at Cambridge since it was written.

The *Tractatus* is an attempt to specify the exact relationship between language and reality. The book is structured in an unusual way, as a set of seven numbered primary assertions, each followed by sub-numbered assertions. Put extremely briefly, the position is as follows. The world divides into facts, and most fundamentally into 'atomic facts' or existing states of affairs. These states of affairs consist of absolutely simple objects that are in a definite set of relations with each other. Language, like a picture, represents that objects are a certain way. It too divides into simple parts—elementary propositions assert the existence of particular states of affairs, and these propositions are true if the world is as they say it is. If a proposition is to assert a fact, there must be something identical or shared in the picture and the depicted, and what is shared is a logical form. Wittgenstein provided a number of metaphors for this idea of correspondence: a picture is 'linked with reality'; it 'reaches up to it'; 'the picture agrees with reality or not'. The conjunction of all true elementary propositions constitutes a complete picture of the world, with more complex propositions built up logically from simple ones. Moreover, each elementary proposition is true independently of each other, providing a total, locked-in picture of the world.

Wittgenstein wasn't clear in the *Tractatus* (perhaps because he wasn't clear in his own mind) whether simple objects were particular existing entities or whether they could be universals, such as the property of redness. But we do know which propositions he thought did *not* link to reality—the propositions of logic, mathematics, philosophy, ethics, and religion. He declared these to be without sense.

If genuine propositions refer to reality and if reality is accessed through immediate experience, then it seems that only present experience can be known. We can't get away from ourselves to anything outside. Wittgenstein embraced this solipsism and the tension that seemed to be embedded in his position: 'The limits of my language mean the limits of my world'; 'solipsism strictly carried out coincides with pure realism'. The twist is that, since this is a philosophical idea, 'what solipsism means, is quite correct, only . . . it cannot be said, but shows itself'. Ramsey would find this intolerable.

It might be thought that Wittgenstein had delivered a unified account of meaningful and meaningless propositions. But in fact, he gave a slightly different account for various kinds of senseless propositions. Logical truths do not represent contingent facts in the world. Wittgenstein made a lovely move here, and took a logical truth to lack sense in that it is a tautology—it is always true, whatever the state of the world is, and hence is entirely independent of what the world is like. He gave the informal example that he knows nothing about the weather when he knows the truth that it is raining or not raining. True propositions in logic, that is, are not true in the way that empirical propositions are true. They are not pictures of reality. They 'say nothing'. In this very particular way, they are senseless, as opposed to being nonsensical. But to say this is not to say that they are useless for our thinking. 'Logic is transcendental', as it is the 'scaffolding' on which elementary propositions must rely if they are to depict the world. Indeed, logic is required to build up complex propositions from simple ones.

On Wittgenstein's view, all necessity is logical necessity. A mathematical truth such as $2 + 2 = 4$ might sound as if it expresses a tautology or necessity, but it doesn't. 'The propositions of mathematics', he says 'are equations, and therefore pseudo-propositions.' In the initial draft of the manuscript, Wittgenstein had written that 'Russell, Whitehead and Frege have not understood the essential of mathematical method, that is, working with equations.' He dropped mention of his opponents in the English translation, but the differences in Wittgenstein's view of mathematics and that of the others would remain a sticking point.

Other kinds of nonsense propositions received different treatment. Philosophical, ethical, and religious propositions are nonsensical because, in uttering any of them, we make a misguided attempt to say what can only be shown. Even within this group, Wittgenstein makes a distinction. He notes that ethics and the meaning of life do not reside in the world—'If there is a value which is of value, it must lie outside all happening and being-so.' But these propositions are somehow 'higher' than what one can say in the elementary language, despite the fact that we cannot express them. Ethics, like logic, is 'transcendental'—'God does not reveal himself in the world.' But such matters are not transcendental in precisely the same way that logic is, for they aren't the scaffolding for our thoughts. Wittgenstein says of ethics, religion, and the meaning of life:

> We feel that even if all possible scientific questions be answered, the problems of life have still not been touched at all. Of course there is then no question left, and just this is the answer. The solution to the problem of life is seen in the vanishing of this problem.... There is indeed the inexpressible. This *shows* itself; it is the mystical.

Wittgenstein saw himself as making space for the ethical and religious spheres of experience. One can have impressions of the good, or the beautiful, or the value and significance of one's life, but those impressions are ineffable. We must say no more than we can—we must not pretend to know what we cannot know. All we can do is speak about the things in the world. Recognizing the limit of the thinkable or sayable evokes a sense of mystery and awe of what lies on the other side of it.

For Wittgenstein, what can be expressed in the primary language are the natural sciences. A problem then haunts the project (it would haunt the project of the Vienna Circle as well). Scientific theories, laws, and causal hypotheses such as *All humans are mortal* and *A deficit in vitamin C causes scurvy* talk about all instances—past, present, and future. They go beyond actual objects in the world, and so they too cannot be expressed in the elementary or primary language. Wittgenstein treated the general quantifier $\forall$ ('all') as depending '*palpably* on that of the elementary propositions'. A generalization is an infinite conjunction of its instances. To say that all humans are mortal is to say that Bertrand Russell is mortal, and G.E. Moore is mortal, and on and on. He argued that to take it to be anything more would be superstition. A scientific theory, moreover, with its causal hypotheses, is something like a mesh applied to a surface, giving it form. We can apply a variety of such 'networks' to describe the world.

While Wittgenstein made an attempt to show how the laws of science fit into his picture, he thought that philosophical propositions really have to be ditched:

> The right method of philosophy would be this. To say nothing except what can be said, i.e. the propositions of natural science, i.e. something that has nothing to do with philosophy: and then always, when someone else wished to say something metaphysical, to demonstrate to him that he had given no meaning to certain signs in his propositions. This method would be un-satisfying to the other—he would not have the feeling that we were teaching him philosophy—but it would be the only strictly correct method.

One might ask about all the philosophy that Wittgenstein himself has just articulated, in the sentences of the *Tractatus* itself.

His answer was that he intended his own propositions to put the reader in a position to see things aright, and once we see things aright, we must see that it is a mistake to engage further with philosophy. He ended the *Tractatus* as follows:

> My propositions are elucidatory in this way: he who understands me finally recognizes them as senseless, when he has climbed out through them, on them, over them. (He must so to speak throw away the ladder, after he has climbed up on it.)
>
> He must surmount these propositions; then he sees the world rightly.
>
> Whereof one cannot speak, thereof one must be silent.

Philosophy demarcates the distinction between what can be said, and what can only be shown—the limits of the 'thinkable'. With that accomplished, philosophy, Wittgenstein held, is 'not theory, but an activity' producing 'elucidations' that might clarify thoughts.

Shortly after the publication of the *Tractatus*, Ramsey wrote a Critical Notice of it, published in the October 1923 volume of *Mind*. It provided the reader with a useful summary of the complexities of Wittgenstein's picture theory of representation and logical form, and praised the book for its originality, extraordinary interest, and 'remarkable' treatment of the propositions of logic as tautologies. He also said that Wittgenstein had 'incidentally' solved the problem of truth, or made it 'evident that there is no such problem'. What it is for a proposition to be true is for its elements to be arranged just as the elements in the world are arranged. Ramsey put it thus: 'if a thought or proposition token "p" says p, then it is called true if p, and false if ¬p'.* Nonetheless, Ramsey thought that Wittgenstein's system was 'altogether unsound' and that the book did not, as its author claimed, finally solve all philosophical problems.

Ramsey remarked that Russell's introduction might not be 'an infallible guide to Mr. Wittgenstein's meaning', for Russell said that Wittgenstein was concerned with a logically perfect language. Russell certainly could be forgiven for this. But as Ramsey noted, Wittgenstein 'seems to maintain that his doctrines apply to ordinary languages in spite of appearances to the contrary'. Wittgenstein had asserted that 'All propositions of our colloquial language are actually, just as they are, logically completely in order.' Ramsey took this declaration seriously, but thought it in tension with Wittgenstein's idea that meaningful propositions are those which mirror the world:

---

* Moore's lecture notes, before and after Ramsey's death, make it clear that Ramsey's rejection of Wittgenstein's distinction between sign and symbol in favour of Peirce's distinction between type and token was thought to be one of Ramsey's most significant moves. See Methven (2015) for an excellent discussion of it.

This is obviously an important point, for this wider application greatly increases the interest and diminishes the plausibility of any thesis such as that which Mr. Russell declares to be perhaps the most fundamental in Mr. Wittgenstein's theory; that 'In order that a certain sentence should assert a certain fact there must ... be something in common between the structure of the sentence and the structure of the fact.'

Ramsey agreed with Wittgenstein that his theory *should* apply to ordinary language. This wider application increased the interest of the theory. But ordinary language is full of propositions that seem not to share the same logical form as a concatenation of objects. As Ramsey would later put it, Wittgenstein's claim that language is in perfect order 'is like saying it is impossible to break the rules of bridge because if you break them you are not playing bridge'.

The Critical Notice focused on two aspects of the *Tractatus*. One was 'the non-mystical deductions' that occupy most of the text—the arguing in detail for 'the necessity of something in common between the picture and the world'. The other was gesturing at all the things that are 'intrinsically impossible to discuss'. He saw difficulties arising for both. He threw spanners into the works of Wittgenstein's non-mystical elaborate machinery (the picture theory of meaning) and he doubted the main contention of the book, as Wittgenstein himself saw it (the distinction between saying and showing).

The issues Ramsey raised for the picture theory were themselves of two kinds. Some were particular problems that struck at the heart of Wittgenstein's account of how we represent the simple world of actual objects—in Ramsey's words, his 'account of the proposition as the expression of agreement and disagreement with truth-possibilities of independent elementary propositions so that the only necessity is that of tautology, the only impossibility that of contradiction'. One 'great difficulty' with this account is what is now known as the colour exclusion problem. Ramsey pointed out that it is not a tautology that red and blue cannot be in one place at the same time, although when I say that x is red all over, that necessarily excludes x's being blue all over. There is more to necessity than Wittgenstein's truth-functional tautologies. Wittgenstein worried a lot about this 'great difficulty'. Under pressure from it, he would modify the picture theory, for instance, by dropping the independence requirement. He would eventually find the problem, and others that Ramsey threw at him, unsurmountable and would abandon the *Tractatus* altogether.

Some concerns Ramsey had about the *Tractatus* were more general. Wittgenstein had said:

The object of philosophy is the logical clarification of thoughts. Philosophy is not a theory but an activity. A philosophical work consists essentially of elucidations. The result of philosophy is not a number of 'philosophical propositions', but to make propositions clear. Philosophy should make clear and delimit sharply the thoughts which otherwise are, as is were, opaque and blurred.

Ramsey was adamant that 'we cannot be satisfied with this account without some further explanation of "clarity"'.

He was also suspicious about the very idea of representation in the *Tractatus*—that a picture has the same structure, or the same logical form, as reality. At the time of writing the Critical Notice, Ramsey was not sure if Wittgenstein meant that there was one general logical form or many. But one thing he was sure of was the following:

> it is evident that, to say the least, this definition is very incomplete; it can be applied literally only in one case, that of the completely analysed elementary proposition.

Many vital propositions cannot be completely reduced to simple atoms that correspond to objects. For instance, what about those containing logical connectives, such as '¬' ('not'), 'v' ('or')? The connectives seem not to have objects to represent. Wittgenstein treated these as *operators* on propositions, used to construct complex propositions. Ramsey thought this subverted the isomorphic structure that Wittgenstein was supposed to be putting in place. The negation operator '¬' illustrates the problem perfectly. The *Tractatus* gives us an account of representation, understanding, and truth that is essentially positive. To understand a proposition is to see how things are *if it is true*. All elementary propositions depict positive facts, and the world is fully described by one unique set of such propositions. Ramsey noted that it would be 'absurd' to represent ¬(aRb) (it is not the case that a stands in relation R to b) as mirroring a negative fact, and was not mollified by Wittgenstein's rendering of '¬' as saying that there is no such combination between objects or things.

Unlike Russell and (later) the Vienna Circle, Ramsey didn't turn his back on what, for Wittgenstein, was the most important claim in the book. He said in his Critical Notice: 'We must now turn to one of the most interesting of Mr. Wittgenstein's theories, that there are certain things which cannot be said but only shown, and these constitute the Mystical.' Then he argued that Wittgenstein's form of representation itself was an 'elusive entity which is intrinsically impossible to discuss'. That is, Wittgenstein's own discussion of what representation is goes beyond elementary propositions. Wittgenstein of course saw this, saying that his philosophy had to be used like a ladder and then kicked away. Ramsey thought this an unacceptable move. He registered what would later become a more fully-formed unease about Wittgenstein's conception of philosophy as needing to be silent, once Wittgenstein himself had set the limits of thought: 'we cannot be satisfied with a theory that deals only with elementary propositions'.

Post-war Cambridge philosophers knew the work of Russell and Moore inside out. But their knowledge of Wittgenstein, given that he had been away since 1913, consisted of the notes Moore took in Norway, the *Tractatus*, Russell's Introduction to it, and Ramsey's Critical Notice. Wittgenstein had asserted that Russell and Moore didn't understand him at all. That was unfair to Russell. In any event, Russell was in London, and that left Ramsey standing as the only figure in Cambridge who comprehended Wittgenstein, and who could genuinely evaluate his work. Moore himself employed Ramsey's Critical Notice when he was lecturing on Wittgenstein, at least up until 1929. Ramsey would remain critical of elements in the *Tractatus* all his life. But he would spend the next three years building on other parts of it, and he would never lose sight of its importance.

1923 Visit to Puchberg

When he translated the *Tractatus* and wrote his Critical Notice, Frank had yet to meet Wittgenstein. That would finally happen in September 1923, a couple of months after he wrote his final, Part II, Mathematical Tripos examinations. Frank breezed through them, getting a 'distinction' or a first-class degree, despite paying them only a fraction of his attention. His father later learned from the examiners that they found him to be 'easily the best candidate'. Frank had considered sitting the Moral Sciences, or philosophy, exams as well. But they were held a few days after the Mathematics exams, and he thought he would feel rather silly, if after making such a bold move, he failed to get a first in either or both. But his mind was nonetheless focused on philosophy—especially on Wittgenstein.

After Wittgenstein had been released from the POW camp, and over the protestations of his family, he had returned his part of his inherited fortune to them. Wanting to pay his own way through life, he would remain immovable about not letting them aid him financially, even when he was penniless and they were desperate to help. In 1920, he obtained a schoolteacher's position in the mountain village of Trattenbach, and then moved to a school in Puchberg am Schneeberg, in the mountains close to Vienna.

In the spring of 1923 Ogden wrote to Wittgenstein, saying that Frank Ramsey would be coming to Vienna and would like to meet him. Wittgenstein wrote to Frank:

Dear Mr. Ramsey,

I've got a letter from Mr. Ogden the other day saying that you may possibly come to Vienna in one of these next months. Now as you have so excellently translated the *Tractatus* into English I've no doubt you will be able to translate this letter too and therefore I'm going to write the rest of this one in German.

Towards the end of his summer vacation, right after finishing his Critical Notice of the *Tractatus*, Frank went to Austria. His travelling companion was Dick Pyke, who was studying economics at King's, and of whom we will hear more. Once they parted, Frank made his way from Vienna to Puchberg, three hours by the slow, off-season trains. He found Wittgenstein living in Spartan circumstances:

> He is very poor, at least he lives very economically. He has one <u>tiny</u> room whitewashed, containing a bed, washstand, small table and one hard chair and that is all there is room for. His evening meal which I shared last night is rather unpleasant coarse bread butter and cocoa.... He looks younger than he can possibly be; but he says he has bad eyes and a cold. But his general appearance is athletic.

Frank walked in the mountains every morning while Wittgenstein taught his school-children. Then they talked philosophy from lunch to dinner. In the evenings, Frank would read Gibbon and go to bed early, falling fast to sleep. Ludwig introduced him to his friend the pianist Rudolf Koder. The two philosophers spent two weeks going through the *Tractatus* line by line, at the rate of a page an hour. As the discussion progressed, a number of corrections and marginalia were made in Frank's copy of the *Tractatus*, by both of them. At 4.461, for instance, Frank crossed out 'senseless' in the following sentence and replaced it with 'nonsensical': 'Tautology and contradiction are, however, not senseless; they are part of the symbolism.' It is clear they were trying to get straight on the kinds of non-sense Wittgenstein distinguished. Frank also made fifty-five pages of notes and reflections. Forty or so changes in the second printing (1933) of the *Tractatus* resulted from these prolonged discussions.

Frank was full of youthful enthusiasm. In the same letter home, he wrote:

> In explaining his philosophy he is excited and makes rigorous gestures but relieves the tension by a charming laugh. He has blue eyes. He is prepared to give 4 or 5 hrs a day to explain his book.... He has already answered my chief difficulty which I have puzzled over for a year and given up in despair myself and decided he had not seen.... He is great. I used to think Moore a great man but beside W!

As Wittgenstein's nephew Tommy put it, everyone felt the impact of the 'radiation' and the 'immense seriousness' of his uncle. One could rail against it (as had Tommy when he was young), but no one could deny it. Tommy said he 'bewitched' many people, including Frank. We will see however, that the spell was less strong as the years went by. For as Tommy also said, Frank 'had the guts' to stand up to his uncle.

The 'chief difficulty' that Frank was talking about was that propositions containing logical constants seem to be relative to the language in which they are expressed.

We will see that he did not, in the end, think that Wittgenstein solved it. Three years later, in 'Facts and Propositions' he would offer a competing—dispositional—account of logical constants.

In addition to the chief difficulty and the other concerns already discussed, Frank found parts of the *Tractatus* opaque even after their marathon sessions. He placed some of the failings on Wittgenstein's shoulders. In the same letter home, he wrote:

> It is terrible when he says 'Is that clear?' and I say 'no' and he says 'Damn its horrid to go through all that again'. Sometimes he says I can't see that now we must leave it. He often forgot the meaning of what he wrote within 5 mins, and then remembered it later. Some of his sentences are intentionally ambiguous having an ordinary meaning and a more difficult meaning which he also believes.

Frank was interested in extending some of Wittgenstein's ideas for his own work. He wrote that he wanted to 'pump him for ideas for further development which I shall attempt'. Wittgenstein, for his part, had asked Frank to pump Cambridge University on the matter of whether he might be able to get a BA on the basis of the *Tractatus*, and the six terms' work he had done with Russell before the war.

Wittgenstein gave a report of Frank's visit to his sister Hermine:

> For a few days, I too could hardly speak as I have had to talk the whole day. Mornings at school and in the afternoon with Ramsey from Cambridge, who has stayed here for nearly a fortnight. It was a pleasure for me too, but at the same time a huge effort. – Ramsey will send me a copy of the Tractatus, which then you can have.

On 15 October, back at Trinity, Frank wrote a chatty letter to Wittgenstein, remarking on his journey home, relaying bits of Cambridge news, and saying that he hadn't had a chance to talk to Keynes about the possibility of Wittgenstein taking a Cambridge degree. The letter closed with: 'I haven't yet found myself out in having forgotten anything you explained to me.' He also hadn't found reason to abandon his concerns. When Frank was in Puchberg, his Critical Notice was in press. It was published a few months later, and Frank remarked to his diary:

> Read my review of W written in August; jolly good seeing I hadn't talked to him then; decide certainly to send it to him.

On 11 November, Frank sent another amiable letter, in which he told Wittgenstein that money was available to pay his expenses, if he would come for a visit. He also gave an update on the status of Wittgenstein's request to take a Cambridge degree. The PhD, not available before the war, now seemed the route to take.

Keynes at this time was in a phase in which he studiously avoided corresponding with Wittgenstein, knowing how intense and demanding that might be. In December 1923, Frank again wrote to Wittgenstein, answering a query Wittgenstein had made about just who was proposing to pay his travel expenses:

> First, the £50 belong to Keynes. He asked me not to say so straight away because he was afraid you might be less likely to take it from him than from an unknown source. I can't understand why he hasn't written, nor can he explain, he says he must have some 'complex' about it. He speaks of you with warm affection and very much wants to see you again.

During his visit to Puchberg, Frank had discovered from Wittgenstein, much to his surprise, that 'Keynes has never written to W'. He still hadn't.

Frank also tried to make Wittgenstein feel less ill at ease about being so ill at ease:

> I quite understand your fear of not being fit for society, but you mustn't give it much weight. I could get lodgings in Cambridge and you need not see more of people than you like or feel able to. I can see that staying with people might be difficult as you would inevitably be with them such a lot, but if you lived by yourself you could come into society gradually.

Frank would eventually see that it was company his new friend craved, not solitude. Wittgenstein's nephew Tommy was now a Cambridge undergraduate, and Frank recruited him in the endeavour to get Wittgenstein to Cambridge, explaining it all to Tommy in a letter, and adding a postscript that shows how familiar they were by this time: 'I hope you weren't late enough on Monday evening to get into any trouble.'

Frank also told Wittgenstein that he hadn't made much headway on extending Wittgenstein's views, 'partly because I have been reading miscellaneous things, a little Relativity and a little Kant, and Frege'. He would soon get to work. One of the most important intellectual relationships in the history of philosophy was up and running.

A Bolt from Cambridge, Massachusetts

It is crystal clear that Wittgenstein was a major influence on Ramsey. But another philosopher made a similar impact on him at the very same time and from a very different direction. In 1923, Ramsey read the work of the American founder of pragmatism, C.S. Peirce.

Peirce's rocky personality and career had cast him into obscurity in his lifetime, and Ogden was one of a small number of people who knew and appreciated his work.[†] Peirce died in 1914, and only in 1923 was a volume of his papers published by the American firm Harcourt Brace. Ogden brought out a simultaneous edition in his *International Library of Psychology, Philosophy and Scientific Method*. Putting the volume in Ramsey's hands would be the final mark Ogden would make on his young friend.

We find Ramsey on 23 January 1924 writing in his diary: 'Read some Hobbes Logic, and Peirce, who is surprising good in parts.' Over the following week, he read the whole volume, taking extensive notes. He had just completed his undergraduate degree, thinking about what he would write for his Fellowship dissertation, which the most promising undergraduates would write after their exams were finished. Ramsey now thought that he might write his dissertation on probability 'partly because interested in it again by Peirce'. On 29 January, he wrote that he 'Finished Peirce', but on the 31st, he was still making notes on the book.

Ramsey's notes begin with a passage from Peirce: 'Let us not pretend to doubt in philosophy what we do not doubt in our hearts.' This is the central insight of pragmatism and, whether Ramsey had identified it as pragmatist or not, it had already been present in his vindication of induction as a method that we cannot help but use. The idea of starting with what we find reliable and do not doubt would continue to drive his philosophy. When Ramsey next wrote on probability, in the famous 1926 'Truth and Probability', Peirce's ideas would be of the utmost importance. And he would be attracted to Peirce's account of truth as the best system we could have—the system that would stand up to all the experience and argument we could put to it, were we to inquire as far as we fruitfully could.

Russell, Moore, and (the early) Wittgenstein were highly critical of the pragmatism that was articulated by the other founder of the tradition, William James. He was more subjective about truth, and not a logician like Peirce. They shared the insight that science, mathematics, logic, ethics, and aesthetics are all human inquiries, and that our philosophical accounts of truth and knowledge must start with that fact. As James was fond of putting it, the trail of the human serpent is over everything. But James sometimes put his idea more radically, and that's what the Cambridge philosophers reacted against. In his famous paper 'The Will to Believe', James suggested that truth is what works for me or for you. When the question of

[†] Ogden was introduced to Peirce's thought by the independent scholar Lady Victoria Welby. For the full story, see *Cambridge Pragmatism: From Peirce and James to Ramsey and Wittgenstein* (Misak 2016).

God's existence is pressing, and isn't determined by the evidence, you are justified in believing in God if that belief is good for your life. His more moderate expressions of pragmatism were overshadowed by these more extreme remarks. But even in its modest form, pragmatism was in sharp disagreement with both Wittgenstein's picture theory and Russell's logical atomism.

James had a disciple in Oxford, F.C.S. Schiller, who was even more of a maverick and provocateur. His 1901 spoof *Mind! A Unique Review of Ancient and Modern Philosophy. Edited by A. Troglodyte, with the Co-operation of the Absolute and Others* was a parody of the esteemed journal *Mind*'s devotion to what Schiller took to be the establishment position. Schiller brought his version of pragmatism—'Humanism'— not just to the concept of truth but also to the concept of reality. The 'metaphysic which is true for one man, because it seems to him to synthesize his experience, may be false for another, because his personality is different'. Schiller held that truth and reality are 'wholly plastic'.

All of this enraged Russell and Moore. While Russell had a lot of time for Peirce, he wrote something scathing about Jamesian pragmatism every year from 1908 to 1912. Moore chimed in with a few choice papers. They took pragmatism's 'cardinal' and 'genuinely new' point to be its theory of truth, and Russell and Moore thought that truth was far from being 'plastic'. It was as inflexible as could be. The following letter from James to Schiller exemplifies the state of play in 1909:

> I give Russell up! That a man of his years should be so childish as to ignore the existence of probable reasoning, and the frequent need and right to decide somehow, puts him out of the pale of serious discussion. Moreover he is rabid on the subject of the Will to Believe . . . and smells it where it doesn't exist . . . Good bye, Russell!

While Moore was intensely charming and lovable to his friends, to his philosophical enemies, he could be sneering. James hated his nit-picking:

> Poor childish Moore! . . . He is too weak & silly for any comment at all, so I wont waste a minute on him. . . . He crawls over the outside of my lecture like a myopic ant over a building, seeing only the spot he touches, tumbling into every microscopic crack, and not suspecting even that there is a centre or a whole at all. Bah!

Ramsey came on the scene after the death of James and Peirce. He too didn't think much of James's view of truth. But he thought that there was something important in the pragmatist commitment to taking the human perspective seriously and he thought there was a lot of good to be found in Peirce. He would buck the Cambridge trend and declare himself a pragmatist.

What Ramsey found most compelling in Peirce was his account of belief. Peirce argued that a belief is in part a habit which cashes out in behaviour. The way we evaluate a belief is to see whether it is a good habit—whether it works, in a robust sense of 'works'. A true belief is one that would be 'indefeasible', and Peirce insisted that part of being immune to defeat is that the method that put the belief in place was not 'extraneous to the facts'. If you see that your belief was put in place by a method that cared nothing for the facts, you must put that belief into doubt.

In the end, Ramsey did not choose to write on Peirce and probability in his undergraduate thesis. As he announced after his visit to Puchberg, his thesis would be an extension of some of Wittgenstein's ideas. But Ramsey would become something of a Peircean pragmatist, and he would press the pragmatist case to Wittgenstein.

VIENNA INTERLUDE

Bloomsbury

On his birthday in his first year at Cambridge, a friend of Frank's mother, Miss Huskisson (age unknown), had taken him to tea. His verdict: 'nice, but religious'. Frank was keen to leave his parents' stodgy morality behind. That very evening, Lytton Strachey, who was anything but nice and religious, gave a talk to the Heretics Society. The paper was 'Art and Indecency', setting up an almost absurd contrast with the prim Miss Huskisson. The paper, Kingsley Martin said,

> discussed the proper attitude to sex and had the great advantage from our point of view of breaking all conventions about the value of 'the bawdy'. His extraordinary voice, which rose to an unexpected squeak, his ungainly appearance, and the brilliance of the phraseology were not things you could ever forget. I remember now my envy when after the meeting a number of undergraduates, of whom I was not one, were invited to continue the argument in Maynard Keynes's rooms in King's.

Frank was one of those invited to Keynes's rooms, along with Sprott, Moore, and Braithwaite. His verdict on Strachey: 'expurgated but highly amusing'. Frank seemed to think Strachey should have been bawdier.

Frank threw his lot in with Bloomsbury, although he could never be called a real Bloomsburian. The snobbery and snarkiness of Bloomsbury did not appeal to him, and there is no way he could have kept up with the clever talk about art. He never picked up their exaggerated accent—Max Newman said that he was far too serious for that. He did not agree with them that Moore's *Principia Ethica* underpinned the new freedoms. But nonetheless, he liked Bloombury's attention to friendship and their candour about taboo topics such as sex and godlessness. And they liked him.

He met Virginia Woolf first in February 1923, at a dinner in Keynes's rooms in King's. Woolf described Frank, and misnamed him Ramsay, in her diary:*

---

* In 1927, Virginia Woolf's *To the Lighthouse* was published, with a family called Ramsay at its centre. While she later said she did not consciously model the Ramsays after anyone in particular, she was also clear that various real characters 'leaked in' to her fictional ones and she liked to mine

Ramsay, the unknown guest, was something like a Darwin, broad, thick, powerful, & a great mathematician, & clumsy to boot. Honest I should say, a true Apostle.

Frank would become a frequent visitor to Tilton, Keynes's Sussex cottage. For the fit, it was within walking distance, over the rolling South Downs, of Virginia and Leonard Woolf's Monk House, and just down the road from Vanessa (Virginia's sister) and Clive Bell's Charleston farmhouse. Virginia's nephew, Quentin Bell, says that in the early 1920s his aunt 'began to see' Frank and other 'young and brilliant people'. Frank was also invited for weekends at Lytton Strachey's country house, Ham Spray. He would become closer still to the younger Bloomsbury generation, especially Dadie Rylands, his colleague at King's, and David (Bunny) Garnett, who had a country house just outside Cambridge.

The Bloomsbury group were in the process of making 'Victorian' a term of abuse. In 1918, Strachey had published *Eminent Victorians*, arguing that those supposedly upstanding citizens were hypocrites and defenders of a morally bankrupt system. Braithwaite said that he and his fellow undergraduates all thought Strachey's book 'very amusing indeed'. As Kingsley Martin put it, 'Its satirical handling of the lives of people who it was conventional to revere exactly satisfied the mood of revolt which was the common bond of Cambridge intellectuals.'

However it may have seemed to the young, Victorian morality was not a block universe of repression. There had been plenty of anarchist, socialist, and moral breakaways amongst a certain upper-class bohemian set. In Frank's day, the intellectual elite was also participating in such lifestyles. Free love, as Desmond Bernal put it, was the new religion. Frank was a convert. But not yet a practising one, and that made him miserable. His sex life stood in sharp contrast to those of his new friends. Lytton Strachey was involved in the most famous ménage of Bloomsbury, along with Dora Carrington, Frances Marshall, and Ralph Partridge. Carrington, just

---

her Cambridge acquaintances for this use. There is speculation that Ramsays were modelled after her parents; there is also speculation that they are modelled after Frank and his wife Lettice. But the fit is poor. Woolf's Mrs. Ramsay is thoroughly invested in seeing everyone in her orbit conventionally married and in doing things right by current standards. Lettice was thoroughly rebellious and counter-cultural. Woolf's Mr. Ramsay's early academic promise comes to nothing, leaving him disappointed in his career. Frank's achievements were widely recognized throughout his life. It is more likely that, if there are some non-fictional Ramseys in the novel, they are Frank's parents. Arthur Tansley, a friend of both Frank and Virginia, provided the names of 'egregiously academic types' in *To the Lighthouse*. Tansley was at the heart of the Cambridge branch of psychoanalytic theory, and in 1925 founded a group in which those who had been analysed met to discuss topics in psychoanalysis. Frank was a member, and so Tansley had access to Frank's intimate thoughts about his family. It is not too much a stretch to suggest that he delivered up caricatures of Frank's parents to Virginia Woolf to use as she pleased. The fit between the Ramsays and Agnes and Arthur is near perfect.

before she met Frank in May 1923, invoked his name in an effort to make an old lover jealous:

> I can quite see if I met someone new—Mr Ramsey of Cambridge, perhaps, who they all say is a paragon of intellect and beauty—I should, if he fascinated me and begged me to write to him every week, write probably less to you.

A couple of weeks later, when Carrington met Frank in the flesh, she wrote to Lytton Strachey:

> Just as we were leaving Sebastian and Frank Ramsey came in. I was completely captivated by the Ramsey Island. Even Ralph was moved! He is so charming to look at and very friendly. All you said of him was true. We left fortunately before his devastating intellect began—as I suspect it did—to wreck the party. Sebastian was very sweet but looked such a reed in the water's edge by the side of the great ox Ramsey.

But not Dora Carrington, nor any other of that free-loving group was inclined to be anything but platonically friendly with the Ramsey Island. They thought him a little naïve, in Lytton's works, 'one of the few faultless people, with a heavenly simplicity and modesty'. A letter of thanks after a 1923 visit to Ham Spray gives us a nice picture of the polite and absent-minded undergraduate, writing to Lytton, who was then forty-three years old:

> Dear Lytton,
> I ought to have written to you before to thank you for having me for the weekend, especially as I enjoyed it extremely, but I have been very occupied 'scrambling' about the Welsh mountains. 'Scrambling' is what the climbers call it when they think it easy and don't need a rope; but I have to be given shoves up every now and then.
> I lost all the benefit of my early departure from Pangbourne, because I was so absorbed in the Times that I got into a down train and only noticed at Didcot!
> Thanking you and Mr. and Mrs. Partridge again.
> Yours fraternally,
> Frank Ramsey

The same held for the younger, just as unchaste, Bloomsburians. Frank's dear friend Sebastian was utterly homosexual, and so not a possibility for Frank. On one occasion, as he and Frank strolled through Oxford on a trip to visit Richard Braithwaite's family, Sebastian talked about what was currently going on in his life. In Frank's recounting, 'Seb' was in love with Stephen Morland, but Morland fell in love with Beatrix Tudor-Hart and didn't want to go to bed with Seb; Seb thought

Image 14 Dora Carrington, Steven Tomlin, Sebastian Sprott, and Lytton Strachey.

he and Stephen might as well have sex, as they both were having sex with many men, including relative strangers. Frank was impressed that Sebastian's mother knew 'about his homosexuality' and was 'very tolerant'. Frank, on the other hand had a 'conversation with Mother about copulation being wicked, as she thinks. Wish she were more sensible.'

Such were the times. There was a lot of sex being had, but sadly, it did not involve Frank. Perhaps it had something to do with that simplicity of character. Perhaps it had to do with his massive size. His friend Austin Robinson thought he was like a 'large sort of woolly bear, a lump of a man, extraordinarily different from the sharpness of his intellect'. In any event, the result was an 'unhappy passion'.

The Pykes

In his letter to Wittgenstein after their two weeks of talking philosophy together in Puchberg, Frank included a rather intimate paragraph. Perhaps no one had told him about Wittgenstein's censorious streak. Frank wrote that it wasn't only his reading material that was preventing him from 'reconstructing mathematics':

> I am awfully idle; and most of my energy has been absorbed since January by an unhappy passion for a married woman which produced such psychological

disorder that I nearly resorted to psychoanalysis, and should probably have gone at Christmas to live in Vienna for nine months and be analysed, had not I suddenly got better a fortnight ago, since when I have been happy and done a fair amount of work.

The object of his passion was Margaret Pyke. She was a decade older than Frank, but not much older than many of his undergraduate friends. An Oxford-educated member of the Heretics, she was highly intelligent, involved in family planning and other progressive movements, and had held a good civil service job during the war. She was also two years into a marriage with Geoffrey Pyke, one of Ogden's good friends, and *The Cambridge Magazine's* London advertising manager. The Pykes were a physically striking and sensational couple. They were well-known in Cambridge. Agnes, for instance, was engaged in the same kinds of good works as Margaret Pyke, and knew and admired her.

Geoff's story is intriguing, almost crazily so. His father, a Jewish lawyer in London, died when he was five. In a fit of grief, his mother sent her eldest, rather unreligious child, to Wellington, a public school for the sons of army officers. She required—and required the school to accommodate—his obedience to strict laws. No Orthodox Jewish boy had ever gone to Wellington before. Geoff had a very rough time, with great masses of awful boys chasing him down the corridors with shouts of 'Jew Hunt!' or 'Pyke Hunt!' He acquired an understandable hatred of public schools.

At the outbreak of the war, Geoff interrupted his second year of law studies at Cambridge and convinced the editor of London's *Daily Chronicle* to employ him as an undercover correspondent. He travelled to Berlin on a false passport at a time when even the British secret services were having trouble planting their agents in Germany. After a few chaotic days with his minimal linguistic skills, he was arrested, taken to a prison, and told that he would be shot. Instead, he was moved to Ruhleben, an overcrowded but relatively civilized internment camp in the woods outside Berlin for British 'enemy' civilians who happened to find themselves in Germany when the war broke out. He and a friend escaped, winding their way through the Netherlands back to England. The *Chronicle* made headline news of its correspondent's 'ESCAPE from RUHLEBEN, TRAMP BY NIGHT THROUGH THE ENEMY COUNTRY and SUFFERING IN A PRISON CELL'. Pyke published *To Ruhleben—and Back: A Great Adventure in Three Phases* in 1916. It was a best-seller, widely (and well) reviewed, and published also in America. Geoff Pyke was famous.

The British security services, however, found it all unbelievable and suspected that the escape had been aided by the Germans. Shortly after his return, Pyke was placed under surveillance and banned from travelling out of the country. As his apparently suspicious activities piled up, the authorities became more convinced that he was a German spy. Whatever the truth may have been, he certainly was an adventurer. He became a successful commodities speculator, and in 1924 founded the Malting House, an experimental school in Cambridge for children aged two to seven, run on Freudian lines: no rules, no curbing of desires, no censure, no punishment. His motivation was partly scientific—he was interested in educational theory—and partly personal. He didn't want to send his young son David into the private school system. Moore's boys were enrolled in the Malting House, as were Rutherford's grandson and Philip Sargant Florence's boy.

Geoff put ads in the *New Statesman*, *Nature*, and *The British Journal of Psychology*, advertising for a head of school for a high salary. Geoff was heavily into the new psychology. He had organized the developmental psychologist Jean Piaget's first trip to England and arranged for the eminent child psychologist Melanie Klein to analyse David at the age of three. He was very happy to be able to recruit Susan Isaacs, another distinguished psychologist, who used the data she collected at the Malting House to make her name in educational theory. The school's ideology had the children considered as 'plants', to be left in their natural state, and the teachers mere 'observers'. There were many bright pupils, but there was a disproportionate number of difficult, disruptive ones who did not fit into any other establishment. Unsurprisingly, the result resembled a state of nature. James Strachey, uncle of the Sargant Florence boy, was bewildered, despite his own commitment to Freud:

> I must say I can't make out the point of it. . . . all that appears to happen is that they're 'allowed to do whatever they like'. But as what they like doing is killing one another, Mrs. Isaacs is obliged from time to time to intervene in a sweetly reasonable voice: 'Timmy, please do not insert that stick in Stanley's eye'.

There was also rather a lot of spitting, including in Susan Isaacs' face, and experimentation with faeces and what non-Freudians might call private body parts. One story, perhaps hyperbolic, circulated widely: the school was so permissive that when one boy didn't feel like getting out of the taxi at the school gates, he was allowed to remain in the vehicle, driven round Cambridge all day with a whopping bill delivered to his parents. The freedom was often too much for everybody, except perhaps for Geoff. It was said that the children organized a deputation to ask the staff: 'How can *we* make *you* make *us* do what we don't want to do?'

It was Margaret Pyke for whom Frank had his unhappy passion. Braithwaite recalled that she was 'an extremely handsome and remarkable woman' and that he and Frank had a wonderful time at her tennis parties. Braithwaite said that he too was quite in love with her, and that Frank's being so much in love with her showed good taste. Margaret Pyke was 'exceedingly handsome', with 'a perfect classical profile'. Frank's approach to Margaret Pyke, however, was in rather poor taste. The shy boy who had fled A.C. Benson's gentle conversation and who, at Winchester, had been so out of place, was now an undergraduate still without a certain kind of social grace. He was easy with great men like Russell and Keynes, and with his undergraduate friends, almost all of whom were male. However, more so even than most inexperienced young men, he was nervous about women and sex. He found himself in lust with Margaret Pyke and the only way he knew how to deal with the situation was to be completely (one might say, absurdly) honest.

Frank knew the Pykes well—both Geoff and Margaret, and Geoff's younger brother Dick. By mid-way through his undergraduate degree, he was seeing a Pyke nearly every day. Geoff and Margaret had a small son, and Frank was his godfather—his sisters remembered him playing with David in the garden at How-field. He knew them so well that he went on holiday to Italy with the family in the Easter vacation of 1922. One afternoon on that holiday, Frank and Margaret went to Lake Orta. On their return, they retired to one of their hotel rooms, each lying on a separate bed, nothing much happening. Margaret read and Frank lusted. ('She was wearing her horn spectacles and looking superlatively beautiful in the Burne Jones style.') He eventually came straight out with his question. He reported the exchange in a long note to himself:

> 'Margaret, will you fuck with me?' She didn't hear and I had to repeat it, then she said 'What? Will I?', and I said something about expecting her to say no, and now I said it to relieve the conflict about saying it, and she said 'Do you want me to say yes or no?' and I said 'Yes, or I wouldn't ask you' and she said 'Do you think once would make any difference?'

As a seduction technique, this might sound gauche and outrageous, and since a copy of this note is easily accessible in the King's College Archive (Frank's widow deposited it there), it has with some frequency been portrayed as such.

But it is far less shocking when placed in context. For one thing, the word 'fuck' was not taboo among Frank's Apostles and Bloomsbury friends: they used the term in a straightforward, casual way, to describe their frequent and open sexual activities. Margaret and Geoff were part of that circle, radically open about matters of sex. Geoff was having an affair with Susan Isaacs, his head of school. Margaret, who ran the school's daily business, seemed not to mind at all. Margaret Gardiner told the following story about a friend's experience at a Pyke tea party:

> David—who would have been, I think, around three years old—wandered up to her and demanded, 'Want to see Dorothea's thighs'. Immediately the circumambient adults urged her earnestly, 'Don't be embarrassed. Go on, show him your thighs'. Morris was embarrassed, but she obligingly lifted her skirt and David made his inspection.

It's not surprising that Margaret was not offended by Frank's proposal at Lake Orta. After some discussion, and after asking for time to think about it, during which Frank went for a walk, her answer was negative. She said she didn't want to do it out of feeling sorry for Frank. But she also told Frank she was not sure that her negative answer was final, and indeed, there was some physical intimacy between them when they returned to Cambridge. Geoff was not bothered. He said he'd give his blessing to any relationship of Margaret's. As Frank put it: 'He felt he had no property rights in her.'

Frank, however, was very bothered. In an attempt to address his situation, which included terrible insomnia, he started to see the London psychologist Edward Glover, who founded what would later be called the Portman Clinic. Glover prescribed a 'sleeping draught'. He also suggested to Frank that he had an Oedipus fixation, drawing on the Freudian contention that every son wants to kill his father so that he can have sex with his mother. Glover told Frank to have a talk with Margaret, and that seems to have helped: 'I did and she was awfully nice.' But his three months or so with Glover were on the whole not working: 'It wasn't really improving my mind very much, so I decided to stop it and go back to sea.' Margaret too was being psychoanalysed, by Dr James Glover, the brother of Frank's therapist. James Glover was also psychoanalysing Dick and Geoff. Their analysts had no qualms about discussing a patient's analysis not only amongst themselves, but also with other patients.

A year after the Lake Orta incident, the situation was still unresolved, at least in Frank's mind. He was about to write his final Part II Tripos exams. He often fell asleep after 2 am and once after 5:30. His parents fretted that he might have a breakdown. Arthur said that Frank's anxiety wasn't about the upcoming exam, 'but deeper problems about the meaning of life and his relation to other people'. Frank reported that Margaret

> was awfully nice and used expressions of affection to which I gave exaggerated significance. But I felt happy and exalted, and kissed her for the first time. She was frightfully nice to me during my trip[os].

Perhaps Margaret Pyke's kind attitude towards him during this period helped. When all was said and done, he was on the alphabetical list of the twenty Wranglers, and was, in effect, Senior Wrangler. The ranking and the title had gone out of existence with the 1909 Tripos reforms, but there was still considerable interest in who earned the top marks in the Part II exams. Indeed, the Senior Wrangler was said to be revealed by the examiner tipping his hat to the winner when reading out that person's name. There is no extant evidence that the hat was tipped in Frank's (or anyone else's) direction in 1923. But we can nonetheless answer the question. Arthur had access to the marks book and reported that Frank came first in Schedule A 'with a good margin to spare', and just missed coming first in Schedule B. The regulations for the ranking are clear: the examiners 'will look at performance in Schedule A papers', and 'in cases of doubt' also those in Schedule B'. Frank would produce a nice piece of philosophy six years later, arguing that we can make sense of the truth of some counterfactual conditionals (were A to have been true, B would have been true). We can safely say that this is one such counterfactual: were there still to have been a Senior Wrangler, Frank would have been it.

After the exams were over, Frank went on holiday with Dick Pyke to Germany. This was the holiday after which he spent the fortnight with Wittgenstein. He had managed a great feat of compartmentalization. He had been in an emotional and sleepless crisis about Margaret, but nonetheless came first in the marathon Mathematical Tripos exams and wrote his critical notice of the *Tractatus*. Now he would do some heavy philosophical work with Wittgenstein and enjoy himself on holiday. Frank and Dick visited Salzburg and Munich, where Frank's love of theatre and opera were ignited. On three consecutive nights, they saw *The Taming of the Shrew*, *Die Walküre*, and *Don Giovanni*, with Dick tutoring Frank on the finer points and insistently paying for everything. Germany and Austria were crippled by hyperinflation and food shortages, Keynes's warning about war reparations having not been heeded, and if one came with English pounds, one could live like a king. As soon as they changed their money, Frank wrote that they moved 'from the nasty hotel we went to first to the swaggerest in the town'. He was alarmed by the political and economic situation he witnessed. He wrote to his father from Augsburg, a small city in Bavaria:

> One expects a thunderbolt all the time to bust things up; it can't last; it is like 1789 must have been except that it is not the aristocracy but the whole nation that is going to suffer. They all cling to foreign money as a standby and try to accumulate it.

On return, his relationship with Margaret continued in its tortured and 'disastrous' way. Dick proposed a policy of 'avoiding intimate conversation with her but seeing her at tennis etc.'. This just made Frank feel that 'she only cared for me as for other tennis partners' and as a last-minute fourth for bridge. Geoff finally put an end to the affair, such as it was, and to Frank's misery, by telling him that he, Geoff, probably only had two years to live. Frank decided that, in that light, Margaret's conflicted and mostly spurning attitude towards him was completely reasonable. He ceased his pestering, although he remained discombobulated and miserable. Geoff lived many more than two years.[†] But whatever his illness might or might not have been, Geoff put the idea to good use in getting Frank to readjust his hopes.

The semi-relationship between Frank and Margaret was not very secret. Some Fellows at King's knew about it, and one of them, Frank's friend Peter Lucas, told him that Keynes was worried that one particular don might hold it against Frank when it came to giving him some teaching. Frank's sister Bridget later said that their parents never knew, and that they would have been shocked. But Agnes, certainly, was not as unaware as Bridget thought. To Frank's horror, Geoff joked to Agnes about Frank's fondness for his wife. Frank was appalled by the breach in confidence, but since his mother knew at least part of the story, he talked to her about the strain of it all. He thought perhaps he should go to Vienna to be analysed. His mother 'seemed to think it might be a good idea'.

Frank's main confidant, however, was Sebastian Sprott, though there were constraints even within that friendship when it came to this painful matter. Frank wrote in his diary in January 1924: 'Very hard to tell S anything about myself except that I am unhappy and very ashamed of myself... And he is so open with me even about things of which I should be ashamed.' But Frank got over his hesitancy and got some good advice:

> S. says first stage in stopping to do or say dreadful things is the one I have reached—to be appalled at it afterwards; next is to be appalled at them while you are doing them; and last, not to do them.

He wanted to stop blurting things out, with little regard to how they might be received.

[†] Geoff Pyke's luck with the stock market deteriorated, and in 1927 the Malting House School was shuttered. During the Second World War, he had a fascinating career as an inventor of machines to transport soldiers in the snow, and of the material Pykrete (to rhyme with concrete), a mix of ice and sawdust designed to enable the construction of a floating aircraft carrier. He was again suspected of being a spy, this time for the Russians. He committed suicide in 1948, an act *Time* magazine reported as 'the only unoriginal thing he had ever done'.

His father Arthur looked back on the winter of 1923–24 as, for him, 'a very happy time, in which I saw Frank more regularly than at any other time since his boyhood at home'. But he admitted that his son 'was not very happy himself'. Frank was determined to do something about the state of his sexual anxiety, and a more serious course of psychoanalysis seemed the best bet. He reported to Sebastian that Lionel had been to Vienna and returned the previous summer 'bursting with information about psychoanalysis, which often seems to me hardly to correspond with the writings of Freud, which I have been reading'; 'I feel the world rather impossible until I can get analysed which alone may release me from this or some other more unsatisfactory attachment.'

Frank decided to follow in Lionel's footsteps. He would go to Vienna to be psychoanalysed. He wrote to Wittgenstein at the beginning of January 1924 (all the underlining seems to be Wittgenstein's):

> Thanks for your letter; except that I think you might enjoy it, I no longer want you to come here this summer, because I am coming to Vienna, for some and perhaps the whole of it! I can't say exactly when and for how long, but, very likely, next month, so I shall hope to see you quite soon now.

He set out 'various reasons' for his trip:

> I hope to settle permanently in Cambridge, but as I have always lived here, I want to go away for a time first, and have the chance now for six months. And if I live in Vienna I can learn German, and come and see you often, (unless you object) and discuss my work with you, which would be most helpful. Also I have been very depressed and done little work, and have symptoms so closely resembling some of those described by Freud, that I shall probably try to be psychoanalysed for which Vienna would be very convenient, and which would make me stay there the whole six months. But I'm afraid you won't agree with this.

For the next few months, Frank buckled down to work. Agnes prevailed on him to teach Bridget some mathematics, which he was happy to do, as Bridget seemed to be falling behind, over-interested in tennis and under-interested in schoolwork. He had more formal teaching at Girton College two afternoons a week, where he learned, at some expense to the women students, how to communicate basic mathematics. His father often accompanied him on walking the two miles to Girton, for the exercise and company, waiting for his son in the road until he was finished with his pupils. While Arthur fondly recalled 'his smiling face ... as he came in sight and recognized me', it was a far cry from the company Frank really wanted to keep. The Girton girls, however, just a shade younger than him, did not figure in his range of romantic possibilities. Frank was twenty years old. He had a brilliant reputation. But he was right now spinning his wheels, with no idea of how to develop a good and sexual relationship with a woman, nor of how to turn his brilliance into a good life.

He thought he would work on a dissertation that might get him a Fellowship in Cambridge, preferably at Trinity. The usual route was to wait a year or so after one's undergraduate degree, and then to submit a thesis or long paper. Keynes's *Treatise on Probability* had started off as a dissertation that won him his King's Fellowship. A newer route, introduced in 1919, was to do the PhD. Its value was still up for discussion in Cambridge college common rooms. Frank preferred not to do the PhD, for rather grandiose reasons:

> Anything I wrote now covering the field as a whole whether in outline or detail would not be the least good; one must have time for such great problems. Wittgenstein took seven years writing his book.

Frank put together an application for an Allen Scholarship, which would provide him funds while he wrote a dissertation that might get him the coveted college Fellowship. That amount would enable him to make do without teaching for a year, after which he was placing his hope in Keynes's plan to get him a one-year teaching post at King's. But King's had already turned down Max Newman for the temporary post, so such an appointment was far from certain. Keynes was doing what he could. He ran into Frank at a party at the economist Dennis Robertson's in February 1924: 'J.M.K. came in, explained to me I must appear at King's to be interested in teaching, not merely doing it to avoid starvation.'

Littlewood thought Frank had a good chance at the Allen Scholarship and said he would write a reference for him about his mathematical abilities. Frank wrote to Moore to ask him if he might do the same with respect to philosophy. He was so friendly with Moore by now that he felt free to express his hope that Moore wouldn't judge him by his 'intoxicated outpourings' after a Commemoration Dinner. His proposed course of research was the foundations of mathematics. Keynes would also write for him, but for a time Frank considered asking Russell instead.

He left for Vienna in the spring, once Lent Term and his exams were over, with the Allen still undecided. His parents gave him some funds to help pay for the psychoanalysis. He wrote to Sprott soon after arriving: 'I had a very affectionate parting from Margaret. She was more responsive than ever before.' The ending that Geoff had engineered seemed not to have fully succeeded. Frank really did need to get out of there.

Image 15 Margaret and Geoffrey Pyke.

A Full Viennese Calendar

Frank's guess that Wittgenstein would not approve of his being psychoanalysed was full of portent. A year later, they would have a disagreement of some consequence about Freud. Having been through mental anguish himself, Wittgenstein was tolerant of those friends and relations who were ill, and who benefited from Freud's help. But it may have seemed from Frank's breezy letter that he was not in such pain, and that he was simply indulging in what Ivor Richards's wife Dorothy called the 'fashion' to be psychoanalysed. She said that chasing the cure did not mean that one was seriously ill, but only a little 'unbalanced'. Only Frank's parents, the Pykes, and Sebastian had any idea of the distress that lay beneath Frank's cheeriness.

Perhaps 'fashion' isn't the right word, for there was also a desire in the Cambridge air to experience the newest scientific advance in psychology. A significant number

Image 16 Frank, *c.* 1924.

of Frank's friends were already in Vienna, many of them keeping Freud and his students busy. Like Germany, Austria was in a state of hyperinflation, and Freud was keen to have students who paid in stable currency. Foreigners made up to forty per cent of his patient load. One of his patients was the Cambridge ecologist Arthur Tansley, then in his fifties and the author of a well-known book on psychoanalysis. Lionel Penrose was again in Vienna, both being analysed and studying psychoanalysis, as was the aristocratic Roger Money-Kyrle. Roger had been a Trinity undergraduate just ahead of Frank, and he was combining his analysis with a doctorate, supervised by Schlick. Lionel's youngest brother Beakus was also in Vienna being analysed, and Braithwaite, Newman, Sprott, Margaret Gardiner, and Philip Hall[‡]

[‡] Philip Hall was only a year younger than Frank, but would later, as a mathematics student, attend Frank's 'Foundations of Mathematics' course and eventually become his colleague.

were there for other reasons. Vienna, despite the difficult post-war economic situation, was an exciting place artistically and politically. Others came to visit, once for a conference on psychoanalysis at Salzburg. Frank wrote home:

> This place is full of English psychoanalysts come on from the Salzburg conference. I saw Glover for a few minutes yesterday…James and Alix Strachey are here for a week, which is nice, as I like them.

It was the year in which the London Institute of Psychoanalysis was founded, and taking the cure in Vienna was a common thing for young Cambridge academics. In 1929, Frank's student, the extraordinary geometer Donald Coxeter, would be taken by his father to Vienna and left for two months 'in the useful hands of the great psychoanalyst Dr. Wilhelm Stekel'. Coxeter's trip was at the tail end of this flow across the channel. The accelerating winds that forecast the storm of the Second World War put an end to it.

Frank arrived on 16 March 1924. Richard Braithwaite and Lionel Penrose met him at the station, 'Richard bubbling over with glee' at the breaking news he had just been elected to a King's Fellowship in mathematics. To celebrate, he took his friends to the opera and poured them wine till 3 am.

Frank immediately got one thing out of the way. He wrote to Sprott:

> To my surprise the other day I went home with a whore, and enjoyed it. Though I shook all over with fear and she said I ought to go to a doctor. She was rather nice and after a little I lost my fear.

He would tell the woman who would become his wife that the professional was 'charming and good-natured', and that he had been to bed with her two or three times, all the time worrying that he would contract gonorrhoea.

Frank lived with Lionel in a large apartment, at Mahlerstrasse 7, a grand building a stone's throw from the Opera. Lionel's mother hailed from the wealthy Quaker Peckover banking family, and he could afford to live in a magnificent flat. Frank had no money, but the Austrian currency remained in free-fall and he could live grandly on very few pounds. Lionel remembered them having great fun, going to the opera almost every night. Max Newman was in Vienna not for psychoanalysis, but mathematical analysis. The three of them spent a lot of time together, Max and Lionel walking along the streets of Vienna playing chess in their heads, no board needed.

Soon Frank had his own good news—he was awarded the Allen Scholarship. Wittgenstein's sister Margaret Stonborough (known as Gretl to the family) took a box at the opera to mark the occasion. Gretl was the youngest of the Wittgenstein girls, and Ludwig was the youngest of the boys. One of Gustav Klimt's most famous portraits is of her. Frank had met and been kind to Gretl's son Tommy in 1923, when the boy arrived as a mathematics undergraduate at Trinity. The favour was now returned. Frank went to see her within days of his arrival in Vienna and they got on splendidly. He dined at what he called her 'baroque palace' every Wednesday, and attended music events and parties there, slightly out of place in his informal clothes, but no one minding. He was taken aback by Gretl's being 'colossally wealthy', as he now fully understood what Ludwig had given up. She was 'a little exhaustingly intense', but not as exhausting and intense as her brother. One sometimes hears a rumour that Frank had an affair with her, perhaps sparked by Brian McGuinness saying that while in Vienna, Frank 'seems to have fallen in love with Wittgenstein's powerful sister'. But McGuinness didn't mean to suggest they had anything like an affair.

Frank also spent time with Ludwig's other siblings, including Paul, the one-handed pianist for whom Prokofiev, Strauss, Britten, and Ravel created piano concertos. Everybody in the Wittgenstein family liked Frank, but Gretl was especially fond of him. She liked his boyishness and mothered him a bit. He had an intelligent, odd sense of humour that struck the family in just the right way, and they considered him a clever and good-natured friend of Ludwig's—as Tommy put it, 'an exception to those English types who had the feeling of superiority towards foreigners'.

But the real aim of his visit was not to socialize, even with Wittgenstein's extraordinary relations. It was to be cured. The doctor Frank wanted was Freud himself.[§] But that proved impossible, as did an arrangement with the next-best, Otto Rank. He ended up with Theodor Reik, an important enough figure in the psychoanalytic movement. Reik wrote the first PhD dissertation on psychoanalysis, and was one of Freud's earliest pupils, although Freud himself didn't like him much. Freud thought Reik 'in every way unsuitable for therapeutic work, where his irresponsibility towards his patients and unscrupulousness towards his colleagues have so often been demonstrated'. The bad impression seems to have been shared all round. Here is Alix Strachey to her husband James, describing Reik at the dinner at that Salzburg conference:

Reik, in a positive sweat of—of—what is it, eigentlich? He could hardly contain himself, his fat & his exhilaration. I can never make out whether it is pure joy in his breast or a pin in his bottom that makes him bound like a jelly & snort like a porpoise. He was enthusiastic about Frank Ramsey's beautiful character, & seemed to think, analytically, that all was for the best.

[§] Forrester and Cameron (2017: 399) assert that Frank had a brief meeting with Freud, but I can find no primary evidence of that.

When Frank said to Reik: 'you're the ugliest person I've ever seen', Reik replied 'Everyone has to say that before we can get started.'

Frank wrote to Sprott early on in his stay:

> Today I went to see Rank; he had never got Glover's letter, and could not possibly take me....I went on to Reik, Glover's 2nd suggestion, who will have me, starting tomorrow, and going away for part of the summer to the mountains taking me with him. Lionel says he is very learned and has written an amusing book on the history of religion: but neither he nor I like the look of him. It is mostly prejudice against foreigners I think.

A couple of weeks later, he wrote again to Sprott, the prejudice against foreigners made more explicit:

> So I went to Dr. Reik, an unpleasant looking Jew, with whom I have had a fortnight. It is surprisingly exhausting and distinctly unpleasant. For about two times I just said what came into my head, but then it appeared that I was avoiding talking about Margaret, so that was stopped and I was made to give an orderly account of my relations with her, which went on till this morning. I think its time he said something; perhaps he will to-morrow. I rather like him but he annoyed me by asking me to lend him Wittgenstein's book and saying, when he returned it, that it was an intelligent book but the author must have some compulsion neurosis!
> You must read Rank's Das Trauma der Geburt. It is superb.

In the next letter to his mother he said he liked Reik 'though he is a Jew (but all the good ones are)'.

The whiffs of anti-Semitism coming off Frank's pen are no less unpleasant for being common in his circles. His parents were of the view that, while one could admire and be friends with Jews, their religion counted as a point against them. After having Harold Laski, a family friend, to lunch, Frank's sister Margaret remembered that Arthur made a disagreeable joke about his nose. Newman had changed his name (from Neumann) by deed poll during the war in an effort to avoid the seemingly omnipresent, if often casual, anti-Semitism. Fredrick Warburg was subject to it at Winchester and Oxford, and his view was that the anti-Semitism of the British upper and middle classes 'was then substantial if superficial'. The letters of Keynes, Alix Strachey, and others who showed no overt animosity towards Jews are marred by anti-Semitic remarks. Even Virginia Woolf, who was married to a Jew, wrote in her diary about her sister in law: 'I do not like the Jewish voice; I do not like the Jewish laugh; otherwise I think...there is something to be said for Flora Woolf'.

Despite Tom Stonborough's perception to the contrary, and despite Frank's arguing at Winchester that 'True education is broad and tolerant; it should make us feel the littleness of man, of our nation and of our creed', he did seem to be prone to thinking that the English were the height of the species. (He also thought the Irish different, and not in a good way.) But his 'prejudice against foreigners' was mitigated by his being aware of it and it was far from that of, say, the Trinity economist Dennis Robertson, who was known for saying violently anti-Semitic things. Also, to use the old bromide, some of his closest friends were Jewish—Joseph Bentwich, Dick Pyke, and, eventually, the woman Richard Braithwaite would marry— Dorothea Morison. Wittgenstein, as well as many members of the Vienna Circle, had Jewish ancestry.

Most importantly, Frank recognized these sentiments for what they were—'a prejudice'. He deplored the tendency of Austrians to blame the Jews for everything—to say 'it's the Jews'. He had arrived in Red Vienna, where the post-war municipal government was experimenting with radical democratic reforms in housing, healthcare, education, childcare, and worker's rights. The rest of Austria was conservative, and already in 1924, the right was on the rise. Frank was distressed to see it. He was upset about the violence and moralism of the police; about religion playing 'such an enormous part in politics here'; and about the fact that university appointments were made on the basis of political and religious affiliation. It's pretty safe to say that, had he lived to see the Second World War, Frank would have been shoulder to shoulder with Keynes, Stebbing, and Braithwaite, who worked to get Jewish academics out of Vienna and support them upon arrival.

Frank spent six months working with his Jewish analyst Reik, and became impressed by him. At first, he was a bit suspicious of psychoanalysis. He wrote to Sprott: 'I live with Lionel, whose brains, if he ever had any, have been analysed away pretty completely, so that serious conversation is almost impossible.' He repeated those complaints in a letter home. Lionel

is impossible to talk to. Psychoanalysis has destroyed his brain altogether. He is so self-confident and obstinate and silly, though rather amusing. [He] won't ever do for an analyst as he has no critical capacity or commonsense!

Lionel Penrose in fact went on to become an eminent geneticist, developmental psychologist, and the founder of British genetics. But in the 1920s, he was indeed rather too enamoured of psychoanalytic explanations. He suggested that chess might be:

1. A homosexual activity
2. A sadistic activity
3. Masochistic activity, & castration complex
4. An Anal Erotic Activity

5. Another sexual satisfaction given by chess play
6. Chess as oral activity
7. A chess problem as a dream of family conflict

Lionel had it in mind to write a treatise on the psychology of mathematics and the laws of formal logic. In the end, he wrote just a paper, in which assertion and negation represented pleasure and pain, and inductive reasoning was where the erotic resided.

While Frank would on occasion toy with such ideas, he was on the whole sick of this kind of talk. It wasn't how he thought of the foundations of mathematics and induction. He started to hope that he might live instead with another recent Cambridge graduate who was in Vienna. That was Adrian Bishop, who had been an undergraduate at King's in Braithwaite's and Penrose's year, and who Frank had somehow not met there. He wrote to Sebastian:

> It seems to me monstrous that I didn't know him at Cambridge; he says he made efforts to meet me but was never allowed to; and I was given quite a wrong impression of him. Also it's monstrous that he wasn't elected to the Society. I've lived three months with him and Lionel and it's absurd to me that anyone knowing them should have elected Lionel to the Society and not Adrian. He has a so much better brain than Lionel in every way that I can think of except ingenuity, and is so wise about people, and oh! I like him awfully.

Bishop was an Irishman known for his infectious humour, literary puns, and louche lifestyle. He was from an aristocratic background, and was openly and promiscuously homosexual.** He and Sprott had indulged in the Berlin nightlife written about by Christopher Isherwood in *Goodbye to Berlin*. We may suppose that Bishop would have been participating in whatever homoerotic adventures Vienna had to offer. Maurice Bowra describes him as he was in 1921:

> He was tall and heavy and dark, with a slightly curly hair, a receding forehead, and noticeably bad teeth. He was used to dominating any group in which he mixed, and in this, as in other ways, he resembled Oscar Wilde, who came from the same layer of Dublin society. I relished his overpowering vitality, his gift for juggling with words, and his quick, satirical wit.

** He would go on to be a spy in the Middle East and either fell or was pushed to his death from one of Tehran's most expensive hotels.

Adrian sorted out some tennis for Frank and himself in Vienna, and Frank started to spend considerable time with him.

Frank tried his best to resist his mother's instructions to see old family friends and other worthies, such as the visiting 'Penrose parents'. Frank found them stuffy—their use of 'thee' for 'you' was just scratching the surface of their formality. He was glad to have managed to encounter them only once, for a few minutes. Margaret put her brother's avoidance of the Penroses down to an enduring 'dislike of meeting people with whom he might not want to make friends', and took this to be a flaw in his character. But this doesn't seem quite accurate. Frank was happy to meet endless numbers of people, without prior judgment about whether he would get on with them. But he was not happy to socialize with the tightly wound Penrose parents just because his own parents thought it suitable, and perhaps advantageous.

Much more to his liking were weekend visits he, Lionel, and Adrian made to A.S. Neill's experimental school on a mountaintop, and to Melk and Budapest. Frank was impressed with Neill:

> They are mostly children no other school would take, pathologically naughty or neurotic. He seems to me a remarkable man in the way he deals with them, rather based on psychoanalysis.... This [letter] is being interrupted by Bishop teaching the two biggest boys arm drill to the great amusement of everybody. He can imitate a sergeant major superbly.

Frank also enjoyed making connections with members of the Vienna Circle. Newman took him to see 'Professor Hahn', who arranged for him to use the University library and invited him to attend his seminar on Theory of Functions of a Complex Variable. Hans Hahn was a sophisticated mathematician and one of the founders of the Circle. He supervised Kurt Gödel's doctorate in 1928. Frank didn't attend Hahn's seminar, but he did rue that he wouldn't be in Vienna the following year, when Hahn was to give a seminar on *Principia Mathematica*. He saw quite a bit of Hahn during these months, both independently, and at the Stonboroughs'. He also met Schlick, at dinner at the Stonboroughs'. Frank's first impression of the urbane Schlick, Berlin-born and married to an American, remained steady throughout his life: 'he didn't seem to me much of a philosopher, but a very nice man'.

In addition to all this socializing, Frank was hard at work on the paper he would submit for fellowships, devoting three or four hours a day to it. He was hoping for a position in Cambridge and needed to produce evidence that he was deserving of one.

Psychoanalysis

The main item of business, however, was an hour a day with Reik at noon. Frank found the descent into the minute particulars of his psyche hard going. To his mother he wrote:

> being analysed is different from what I expected in being at any rate at first much more exhausting and unpleasant.
>
> I talk all the time and find it strangely difficult. After the first 2 times I felt a wreck but by yesterday not nearly so bad.

It soon got a little better:

> I have no opinion about my analyst except that he is probably intelligent. He says almost nothing, but makes me narrate; but I think this won't go on for more than a few more days. I dislike it and try to wander from the point but he pulls me back. It isn't as exhausting now as it was at first.
>
> It is very interesting, and confirms a lot of what they say; but I don't believe a lot of the things he says; we don't argue much but go on to something else.

He added in the margin of a letter home: 'I'm quite happy you needn't worry.' To Sprott he wrote:

> One has to make sacrifices for psycho-analysis. At the moment I'm 'resisting' so that I don't see any good in it, but sometimes I think it's important, and am buttressed up by Adrian also thinking it important . . . I feel rather trapped by psychoanalysis. I am lonely here and don't want to go on but can't stop . . .

He later told a friend that in psychoanalysis you spend so much time talking about yourself, you get bored with the subject.

The prescription of uncensored talk could not have been comfortable for Agnes and Arthur. As Arthur Tansley put it, that generation (and class) tended to think that Freud's theories were 'bizarre and grotesque to an extreme degree', and felt a sense of 'disgust and repugnance at them'. Sex and the body were regarded with some horror. When the Heretics started to talk about contraceptives and psychoanalysis, some of their non-undergraduate members resigned in protest. And these were the Heretics, by choice on the wild side. An extreme example of this moral sensibility was Lionel's mother. Happily married to James Penrose, she found herself pregnant. A cousin of Lionel's tells the tragic story:

With a great deal of help from God, she learnt to endure dear James's love-making, and pretty soon in their wedded life discovered, with *frissons* of horror, that she was pregnant. Now all the intellectual argument in the world, about how the human race survived, the necessity of Woman playing her divinely ordained part in this, and so on, was of no avail to reconcile Mrs Penrose to the dread fact that this terrible thing was happening to her own body. The best thing to do was forget it and behave as if nothing was happening. ... The moment came. With the first unmistakable gripes of labour she locked herself in the lavatory. She could not, would not, allow a man, a doctor, to see the most private part of her body ... a small, male, baby was born, dead. The verdict as to its death: under-nourishment.

Frank's parents were not as extreme. But they were on that side of the continuum, and their children, like that of the Penrose parents, were swinging to the opposite end, openly talking about 'fucking' and 'masturbation' and all the intimate things their parents repressed.

Such sentiments would have been amplified when Frank wrote home, relaying Reik's questions about his early bowel movements and enemas, the time-point at which he was weaned, and so on. His parents supplied answers, adding information that might be helpful about suppositories and circumcision. Frank reported back that 'Reik doesn't think the circumcision could have any permanent effect; I mean, any longer than a day or two.' Agnes and Arthur felt that if all Reik was doing was dredging up facts about Frank's childhood, they could do it better. Frank had to tell them: 'You could naturally supply information about my childhood more reliable than (though agreeing with) Reik's conjectures, but that isn't psychoanalysis.' All that is embarrassing enough. They must have been more upset at the possibility that Reik was uncovering submerged sexual desires or hatred for his parents or, worse, a combination of the two. When he returned to Cambridge, Frank would give a talk to the Apostles, saying the following about such submerged desires:

In my own case I think that my interest in philosophy and all kinds of criticism, which is much greater than my interest in constructive thought, is derived from a fairly well repressed infantile rivalry with my father and my wish to kill him. This means that I can never get any great satisfaction from philosophizing, never anything like the pleasure I should have got from killing my father, which my conscience or rather my love for him forbade me to do when I was small. This has incidentally another unfortunate consequence, namely that my philosophical criticisms should always be regarded with suspicion, as I am probably identifying the man I am criticizing with my father, generally in his hostile aspect, so that I am biased against the philosopher who in my unconscious mind represents my father. I am also liable to identify someone like Wittgenstein with my beloved father and attach a most exaggerated importance to his every word.

This is written in the Apostles' style to amuse and entertain. Thoughts of patricide (and Wittgensteincide), if they existed at all, remained tucked away.

The question of homosexuality surely would have been discussed during his analysis. Some of his best friendships at the time were with emotionally open, witty, homosexual men—Sprott and Bishop—and during his analysis, Frank wrote to Sprott, of Lionel: 'I am slightly attracted to him physically.' But it seems that any such physical attractions were indeed slight, whereas his heterosexual attractions were the opposite. Frank may have been hoping to get Sprott to think that he wasn't as boringly heterosexual as he in fact was.

Frank's parents were also unhappy with him about money. The Allen Scholarship was worth £250, and in those days a single person could live comfortably on that. But to Agnes and Arthur, their son was blowing away his scholarship funds on psychoanalysis and opera tickets. Frank too was worried about how he was going to manage financially, but he was unwilling to miss the chance to attend great opera and theatre at bargain prices. He wrote home:

> now I am more settled and industrious and shan't go so often. But if you feel incapable of working and haven't many people to talk to or any light literature in English you rather want an entertainment in the evening, and this is such an opportunity for hearing opera really well done which makes a lot of difference.

His letters to his parents and to Sprott, unsurprisingly, differ in tone and substance. To Sprott he wasn't going to the opera and theatre because he was at a loose end in a foreign country. He was a young man on a grand adventure in a city he loved.

Arthur tried a different tack, suggesting that Frank was going to be in trouble for wasting all this time on analysis, rather than on his career. On 24 September, in what seems to be his last letter home before he left Vienna, Frank wrote:

> I don't see how there can be any such inquisition into my conduct in Vienna as you ~~suppose~~ seem to want to guard against.... No one can suppose that you can't research for six months without having a paper ready by the end. If everyone wrote a paper every six months the amount of trivial literature would swell beyond all bounds. Given time I shall produce a good paper. But if I hurry it will be ill written and unintelligible and unconvincing.
>
> It seems to me perfectly proper to spend a scholarship being analysed, as it is likely to make me cleverer in the future, and discoveries of importance are made by remarkable people not by remarkable diligence. My analyst is jolly clever; some of the things he says aren't at all convincing but others are very smart and once he astounded me by inferring that something had happened to me (not important) and saying so before I told him about it, and I haven't the least idea how he did it.

While it may not be persuasive that psychoanalysis makes one cleverer, Frank was prescient that the numbers of journal articles would eventually swell and he was right that diligence isn't enough to produce discoveries of importance. He also made an interesting point about the need to examine one's motivations for adopting a particular theory or approach to a problem:

> Psycho-analysis is very important even I think to one's work. You see obscure unconscious things may decide your attitude about certain things, especially personal factors in a controversial subject. Lots of work on the Foundation of Mathematics is emotionally determined by such things as
>
> 1. love of mathematics and a desire to save it from those (villainous and silly) philosophers
> 2. whether your interest in mathematics is like that in a game, a science, or an art
> 3. General Bolshevism towards authority
> 4. The opposite, timidity
> 5. Laziness or the desire to get rid of difficulties by not mentioning them
>
> If you can see these in other people you must be careful and take stock of yourself.

At the end of his time in Vienna, Frank was taken aback by the results of his analysis—he hadn't thought 'people were as complicated as that'. Over time, the chains of causation posited by Freud became less believable to him. But if people were not complicated in quite the way that Freud thought, they were still mighty intricate, and talking about his own complications certainly helped Frank.

'He Is No Good for My Work'

Frank's reasons for going to Vienna included a desire to visit Wittgenstein. He contacted him the day he arrived, and went to Puchberg at least three times. But it turned out that once Frank started to see Wittgenstein, it became clear to him that he preferred the company of his more freewheeling friends. On one occasion, he stayed just a night. He was finding Ludwig trying, something that was completely absent during his 1923 visit to Puchberg, when he was younger and less sure of his own philosophical views. Frank thought it a healthy life, in addition to being pleasant and inexpensive.

Frank reported on these visits to his friends in Cambridge. Keynes wrote to his lover Lydia Lopokova:

> I have a letter from Frank Ramsey from Vienna about the mad philosopher genius Wittgenstein. It seems that *three* of his brothers have committed suicide: so perhaps it is better not to be so wise and to be unphilosophical.

Keynes had made Frank his emissary in the quest to persuade the mad philosopher genius to return to Cambridge. In the letter to Wittgenstein in which Frank announced his intention to be psychoanalysed in Vienna, he went on to explain why Keynes had refused to answer Wittgenstein's correspondence: 'Keynes still means to write to you; but it really is a disease—his procrastination; but he doesn't (unlike me) take such disabilities so seriously as to go to Freud!' Keynes's procrastination stemmed from the knowledge that once he made contact, he would be caught up in the difficulties that accompanied relationships with Wittgenstein. Braithwaite captured the sentiment at the time: knowing Wittgenstein was a full-time job, as he was the most selfish man he had ever met. Wittgenstein had already had fractures with Russell and Moore. He told his nephew Tommy that he broke with Russell because Russell was not a decent, moral man. Tommy said that this judgment was due to Russell's 'loose' ideas about marriage and relationships between men and women—ideas which would make his uncle 'blow up'. As Tommy put it, 'He was not tolerant.'

Frank was starting to understand the challenging nature of his friend, and the differences in their personalities. Wittgenstein was anything but loose about sexuality, whereas Frank wanted to not be so uptight about it. Wittgenstein held the ideas of guilt and sin at the heart of his life, whereas Frank was keen to shake off those chains. This difference in moral temperament would cause some strain between them. Almost as dangerous to their relationship was the fact that, as Tommy put it, Wittgenstein was attracted not to equals or superiors, but to softer types, whom he could dominate and who would imitate him. There were a few exceptions—for instance, the economist Piero Sraffa. But Frank's refusal, or inability, to bend to Wittgenstein's ideas would cause some tension.

During Frank's first sojourn to Puchberg, in 1923, it might have seemed to Wittgenstein that Frank would become a disciple. Like Moore on his visit to Norway in 1914, Frank spent that first encounter taking notes and trying to understand the difficult material produced by the master. But there were already indications, in the Critical Notice that was then in press, that Frank wasn't going to defer to Wittgenstein. Tommy put it thus. Frank 'would stand up to God himself' if he thought God got something wrong; 'he was capable of seeing clearly where other people made mistakes in thinking and when he saw that, he just mentioned it'. From the 1924 visits on, there would always be the friction of disagreement between them. For during this period, Frank came to a less awe-struck understanding of Wittgenstein. He wrote to Keynes lucidly, yet humanely, summing up how things stood with their friend:

> With regard to Wittgenstein I do not think it is any good at all trying to get him to live any pleasanter a life or stop the ridiculous waste of his energy and brain. I only see this clearly

now because I have got to know one of his sisters and met the rest of the family. They are very rich and extremely anxious to give him money or do anything for him in any way, and he rejects all their advances; even Christmas presents or invalid's food, when he is ill, he sends back. And this is not because they aren't on good terms but because he won't have money he hasn't earned except for some very special purpose like to come and see you again. I think he teaches to earn money and would only stop teaching if he had some other way of earning money which was preferable. And it would have to be really earning, he wouldn't accept any job which seemed in the least to be wangled for him.

In early March, Frank wrote to Keynes that Wittgenstein might come to Cambridge, but only if he could stay with Keynes. Frank could see how that would unfold, and his letter suggests he was beginning to find Wittgenstein personally trying:

I'm afraid I think you would find it difficult and exhausting. Though I like him very much I doubt if I could enjoy him for more than a day or two, unless I had my great interest in his work, which provides the mainstay of our conversation.

He wrote home a couple of weeks after the letter to Keynes, registering an indication that even their philosophical conversations were trying:

I stayed a night at Puchberg last weekend. Wittgenstein seemed to me tired, though not ill; but it isn't really any good talking to him about work, he won't listen. If you suggest a question, he won't listen to your answer but starts thinking of one himself. And it is such hard work for him like pushing something too heavy uphill.

He went again in May and wrote:

Wittgenstein seemed more cheerful...But he is no good for my work.

With each trip to Puchberg, Frank became less enamoured with Wittgenstein's way of doing philosophy.

It's important to remember that when Frank was making his visits to Puchberg in 1924, he was the sole contact between Wittgenstein and his Cambridge friends. Moore hadn't seen him since the war. Russell had met him in The Hague right after the war and talked about the *Tractatus,* but hadn't seen him since. Keynes wasn't even writing to him. Before he arrived, Frank had the feeling that he and Wittgenstein were the vanguard. The following is from a letter, in advance of his trip:

I went to see Russell a few weeks ago, and am reading the manuscript of the new stuff he is putting into the Principia. You are quite right that it is of no importance....I felt he was too old: he seemed to understand and say 'yes' to each separate thing, but it made no impression so that 3 minutes afterwards he talked on his old lines.

Russell and Frank had talked about identity in mathematics and the theory of types. Frank thought—although this was said only to his diary, not Wittgenstein—that while Russell was 'poor on types', he was 'rather good against W's identity'. The paper he would write while in Vienna argued against Russell's new theory of types—the theory that was designed to block the set-theoretic paradoxes threatening the project of logicism. Russell would be magnanimous when presented with the dissent. Wittgenstein would be less so when Frank disputed his theory of identity.

The *Tractatus*, Ramsey, and the Vienna Circle

When Ramsey was in Vienna, he played an important role in introducing the *Tractatus* to the Vienna Circle and to the kindred Berlin Circle. Rudolf Carnap, who would become one of the most influential members of the Vienna Circle, had been in New York in 1923. Some mathematicians told him about Russell's influence on the new 'mathematical philosophy'. Carnap wrote to Hans Reichenbach, around whom the Berlin Circle turned, about the people connected to this new philosophy. The list was long. It included Wittgenstein, Keynes, and Broad, but gave no particular importance to Wittgenstein. Reichenbach immediately forwarded Carnap's letter to Schlick, and asked Schlick to write to Russell (with no mention of Wittgenstein) to see if Russell might be interested in being involved in a journal they were planning. Schlick's reply to Carnap noted that one of those new mathematical philosophers was nearby: 'Wittgenstein, whose book is edited by Russell, lives here close to Vienna.' Schlick did not yet have a copy of that book. We know that his University Library had one copy of the (less than accurate) *Annalen* printing, but it isn't clear whether Schlick had looked at it at the time he was exchanging these letters in 1923.

The Circle's attitude to Wittgenstein changed dramatically in the summer of 1924, when Schlick met Ramsey. Schlick wrote to Reichenbach on 5 August, during Ramsey's stay in Vienna. Schlick had now read the *Annalen* version of the *Tractatus* and was fired up about Wittgenstein:

> Do you know the 'Tractatus-logico-philosophicus' from L. Wittgenstein, which appeared in the Annals of Natural Philosophy and which has been edited by Russell in a book version in German and English? The author lives close to Vienna, and is highly original, also as a human being; the more one studies his treatise, the more one is impressed by it. The English translator, a mathematician from Cambridge, whom I met in the summer, is also a very intelligent and sophisticated mind.

Schlick then wrote to Wittgenstein on Christmas Day, expressing his admiration of the *Tractatus* and his desire to meet its author. He told him that the mathematician and Circle member Kurt Reidemeister had recently given a talk at the University of Vienna about the *Tractatus*, and mentioned that 'last summer I had the pleasure to meet Mr. Ramsey, the translator of your work, during his last stay in Vienna'. Schlick asked Wittgenstein how he and Reidemeister might get their own copies of the Ramsey translation of the *Tractatus*. Wittgenstein wrote back, saying he himself didn't have spares, but Ramsey 'would certainly be kind enough to arrange for some copies'. Schlick replied that he might be able to purchase it in Vienna bookshops: 'The book sells quite well in England, as Mr. Ramsey tells me.' By early 1925, the Circle was in possession of the Ramsey translation, with the revised German and English text side by side.

The *Tractatus* was taken to be a kind of founding document of the Vienna Circle. Schlick told Einstein that it was the 'deepest' work of 'the new philosophy'. One can see why the Circle took the *Tractatus* to be so harmonious. The Circle aimed to stake out the boundary of meaningfulness: a meaningful sentence is one that is reducible, via truth-preserving logic, to an elementary language of simple, basic observation statements. While there were differences between various Circle members, it is fair to say that they put an empiricist spin on this idea—all knowledge is constructed from immediate experience. They consigned to the dustbin of meaninglessness all unverifiable, non-observable propositions. Metaphysics, ethics, religion, and aesthetics were all either to be revised so as to be stated in scientific language, or else to be abandoned as nonsense.

They were understandably interested in Wittgenstein's idea that in order to tell whether a picture is true or false, we have to 'compare it with reality', and this is the province of the natural sciences: 'The totality of true propositions is the total natural science.' Carnap thought that two insights of Wittgenstein's were especially important. First was the idea that metaphysical propositions are pseudo-propositions, devoid of content. The other was the idea that the truths of logic are tautologies—true, come what may—and hence are exempt from the empirical standard of meaningfulness.

That there was some tension between Wittgenstein and the Vienna Circle is also understandable. They shared a project—what Ramsey called in his Critical Notice the 'non-mystical deductions' in the *Tractatus* or 'new theories of propositions and their relations to facts'. That was a source of mutual attraction. But Wittgenstein thought that indicating or gesturing at all the things that are, as Ramsey put it, 'intrinsically impossible to discuss', was his most important contribution. The members of the Circle tended to sweep under the rug Wittgenstein's bookend remarks, in the preface and at the end of the *Tractatus*, about the importance of ineffable ethics and religion. Like Russell, they didn't know what to make of them. Wittgenstein was unimpressed with the Circle's disregard of what he took to be the main contention of his book. Nonetheless, Wittgenstein would meet with members of the Circle, on and off from 1927, until 1936, when Schlick, with whom he was especially friendly, was killed by a mentally unstable ex-student.

Cured!

In July Frank had gone, as planned, with his analyst Reik and some other patients to a lake resort—Wörthersee in Austria—and then to the Italian Alps in Dobbiaco. He wrote to Sprott from Wörthersee:

> I've come to this place with my analyst with the prospect of staying here 4-7 weeks; it is beastly hot and there is no one to talk to except another patient of Reik's who is infuriatingly stupid and repeats the same idiocies at one indefinitely.

He filled his time. He bought a tennis racquet to play on the clay courts, a change from the English grass; swam in the lake; and walked in the hills. He also got a lot of work done, including reading Kant (which is 'rather dull'). He wrote to his parents about politics, both of home and Europe. Respite from the boredom arrived when the historian Lewis Namier joined Reik's party of patients. Namier was much older than Frank and, while his reputation is for being abrasive, Frank found both his personality and mind first-rate. After listing his many accomplishments, he summed up to his parents: 'He is a very clever Jew, amusing and interesting.' They would remain friends and go on a walking holiday a few years later.

Dobbiaco is part of the Tyrol, as is Hintertux, where Frank had spent his first disastrous mountain holiday. He again had a 'rather bad experience' on the mountains, this one caused by not turning back before sunset. He reported the incident to his parents:

> Hill and I set out for a walk about 3pm; it was hot and I left my coat behind and went in a shirt only. We walked ½ hour to the foot of a mountain called Sambock and then thought we would start up it. We found a path, but as it seemed only to be going round but not up, we left it and scrambled up a steep place through a wood for about an hour. Then we got to a farmhouse and had some milk hot from the cow, and asked how far it was to the top of the mountain and the woman said ½ hour! We found a clearly marked path and went on. As we got up we got a lovely view out of our valley. In fact the mountain was 2394 metres (7800 ft) and we couldn't resist going on, and eventually, a little after 7 were on the final ridge; then I felt it was good enough and sat down to look at the sunset while Hill went on the 20 mins left to the top. But I had only a

shirt and had sweated a lot and it was evening at 7500 ft so I soon felt cold and started
at once to go down without waiting for Hill.

He went on to describe how he made his way, cold and hungry, and in the dark,
back to the farm, all the while panicked about how he and Hill were going to meet
up. The boy at the farm started him on a path and, after losing his way a few times, he
found Hill. Now both were properly frightened of slipping down that steep bit and of
getting chilled to the bone. When they were almost down the mountain, in the moonless
night, they still had no idea how to get to civilization. It started to pour with rain:

> All this time Hill was very slow as he was so hungry and he only had rubber shoes which
> was awkward in the dark when it was stony. We got out the other side of the wood and
> then I had a narrow escape. I was in front (he could follow because my white shirt
> showed, but I couldn't see him) and happened to pause and put my foot forward slowly
> (I suppose I unconsciously noticed something odd). There was no ground at all in front!

They made it back after midnight, lucky to have not been felled by hypothermia or
by stepping off a precipice.

Frank was keen to arrange for his parents and Michael to come for a side holiday. Reik
objected to the break in his analysis, and caused much uncertainty for the holiday by
leaving Frank up in the air as to how long he could absent himself. In the end, his family
stayed at Dobbiaco for a week and then went away with Frank for a week. Frank told
them how to get a visa, how to clear customs, precisely what trains to take, which hotels
to stay in, and what kind of wine to drink. His taste had already outstripped his parents':

> [I]f you like the kind of wine I do drink Meursault (white burgundy) 7 francs for ½
> bottle. But I don't think you would like it (its really worth the money). I expect you like
> it sweet like Graves.

When his family arrived, more walks were undertaken, and on one, Frank, Michael, and
Arthur found themselves on a frightening ledge, again with any misstep a fatal one.

Such near-misses couldn't put Frank out of his good frame of mind. He was
feeling better about his life. Indeed, he was declared cured. After he returned to
England in September, full of confidence about his mental state, Alix Strachey
reported on Reik's verdict:

> He said to me that he'd done all he could to Frank *in the short time* at his disposal—that
> the analysis had gone very well owing to Frank's crystal-clear mind & soul—was
> enthusiastic about him; & wound up by saying that there'd never been anything
> much wrong with him. All of which seems fairly reasonable.

James Strachey wrote to Alix:

> Glover said Ramsey (so the story went) is under the impression that he's completely analysed, & and that Reik said—'if you'd had unlimited time and money, we couldn't have gone deeper'.

One suspects that Frank's progress was made largely by his losing his sexual inhibitions with the help of that kind professional woman at the outset of his Vienna stay. But whatever the cause, he was indeed cured.

The rumour mill was now in full grind in Bloomsbury. In a letter to Alix, James reported some gossip he heard from Lytton:

> Ramsey (who, before he went to Vienna didn't know that he wanted to fuck Mrs. Pyke) discovered there that he did, but thought himself cured of such wishes. On returning and meeting her, however, he was more bowled over than ever; but asked her to go to bed with him—which she declined.

This is completely wrong, although that hasn't stopped some from repeating it. Frank certainly knew his desires for Mrs Pyke before he went to Vienna and had expressed those desires rather bluntly to her. Reik had forbidden Frank from writing to Margaret Pyke during his time in Vienna. By the end of his stay, his desires for Margaret abated and were replaced by more appropriate ones.

A couple of months after the misleading gossip was spread, Sprott set the record straight. After a weekend at Ham Spray, James Strachey wrote to Alix:

> I and Sebastian retired to the library, where he made me tell him snippy 'anecdotes' about psycho-analysis. Incidentally, he said that Ramsey *has* been cured. He's abandoned Mrs. P; has taken on a new lady with whom (though, before, the idea had filled him with repulsion) he proceeds to the furthest limits. Perhaps we'd better all go on to Reik.

Sprott was Frank's closest confidant and it is unsurprising that he had the story right. The 'new lady' was Lettice Baker, whom Frank had admired from afar since 1920. He finally found a passion, and consummation of it.

Kingsman!

Another important thing was resolved during Frank's time in Vienna. Braithwaite, who had been a year ahead of Frank in the mathematical Tripos, and three years ahead in age, had been elected to a Fellowship at King's that spring. The College was also interested in Frank. Keynes had made a quiet proposal in April, just after Braithwaite's appointment and soon after Frank's arrival in Vienna. Might Frank want to come to King's next year as a supervisor of undergraduates in mathematics, with the possibility of the post becoming permanent? Frank found this a difficult decision, as he took it to mean giving up on trying to secure a Trinity Fellowship, and that would be an exceedingly high price to pay if the King's position dried up after a year. He also didn't want to resign the Allen Fellowship for a temporary job at King's. To further complicate matters, new University statutes were being contemplated (and would be put in place in 1925), establishing faculties and departments—more or less the structure we know today. Frank was trying to get a job in a system that was in transition, in which the old rules and conventions might no longer apply.

He expressed his agitation and hesitation to Keynes. It had a dramatic effect. Keynes swung into action and was able to almost immediately write: 'The wind now blows favourably here from your point of view: I expect you will hear something definite within two or three weeks.' Not long after writing to Frank, Keynes was dining at Magdalene and told Arthur that King's had decided to offer Frank a Lectureship and a Fellowship, with the Lectureship to begin in October and the Fellowship to begin as soon as one fell vacant. Keynes authorized Arthur to inform his son. The day before Arthur's letter arrived in Vienna, one arrived from Arthur Berry, a King's mathematician with an economics bent, officially conveying the news.

Frank was thrilled. He wrote home: 'It is a most wonderful thing; it just bowled me over. Now I'm rich I go to the opera even more often.' His stipend would be £300 in the first instance, with a further £300 coming when he received the Fellowship. His financial worries were over. He was also pleased to not have to take the PhD route:

> I'm glad too not to have to write a thesis. I shall write out part or parts that might make an article or articles, but I haven't got to the stage of making a whole theory and it would be a bore stringing together patches to make them seem a connected thesis. I just haven't solved the main difficulties and don't seem likely to just yet.

Braithwaite was surprised when Keynes 'pounced' on Frank before Trinity could do it. He didn't realize that Keynes, or anyone in Cambridge, had the ability to snap someone up like that. Decades later, the economist and Kingsman Richard Kahn would say that when Keynes brought Ramsey from Trinity, he upset the natural order of things. Ramsey would have been offered a Fellowship at Trinity, had Keynes not pipped them to the post.

Braithwaite was right that the appointment was unusual. It appears to have been the result of sophisticated machinations by Keynes. The King's College Electors to Fellowships minutes book for Friday, 9 May is downright secretive:

A discussion took place of an election under Statute E.II.5.

Proposed by Mr. Berry—That on consideration of a resolution from the Council the Electors are prepared to make the election suggested under Statute E.II.5.

Carried Ayes 12. No 1

Statute E.II required Fellows to be King's graduates, unless the Governing Body decided to open the position to all, or decided to elect someone who didn't meet the criteria but was 'specially fit to be a Fellow of the College'. The College had only the year before advertised the first external Fellowship. Frank's friend Pat Blackett won that competition, with his other friend Kingsley Martin out of luck, and out of sorts, in second place.

This position was not going to be advertised—it would have to be filled under the 'specially fit' clause. We don't know who was the lone vote against Berry's proposal. The objector may well have simply had enough of Keynes' ruling the College by creative interpretation of its rules. At that point, King's didn't have Law students, partly because, as a history of King's College put it, 'Keynes was passionately opposed to having a Law don in the College, fearing pedantic interpretation of our statutes.' Frank had heard from one of the Fellows, his good friend Peter Lucas, that 'there had been some terribly anxious moments'. But Keynes was unflustered. Later that day, sitting in his garden, he wrote to Lydia: 'This afternoon we decided to elect Frank Ramsey to a fellowship, which satisfies me.' That letter is the only bit of written evidence that it was Ramsey who was the subject of the proposal involving Statute EII.5.

Three weeks later at College Council, Ramsey was officially appointed as a Lecturer for one year, no mention made of his filling a Fellowship when one became vacant. In September, though, Frank could write to Wittgenstein: 'I don't know if I knew when I last saw you or told you that I have been made a Fellow and Lecturer in mathematics at King's starting with this coming term.' And he wrote to his family: 'there is no vacant fellowship yet but will be in a few months'. As far as he was concerned, it was all sewn up. And it was. On 18 October, just after Frank's first term at King's had begun, his name finally appeared in the King's Electors book:

Agreed that the Fellowship now held by Mr. Baker be treated as vacant under Statute E iii.

The Electors severally made the declaration required by Statute E. III.7.

Proposed by Mr. Berry and seconded by the Vice Provost to elect Frank Plumpton Ramsey, B.A., Scholar of Trinity College, Mathematical Lecturer in the College, into the Fellowship now held by Mr. Baker.

Carried. Ayes 11, Noes 1.

Philip Baker was an international scholar, who in 1924 went to the University of London, thus vacating a place for Frank to fill. Trinity didn't even get a chance to make a bid. Braithwaite was delighted to have Frank join him, and the fact that the election came through in the same year as Braithwaite's pleased Frank, who didn't like to be behind his friend. His duties were set at ten hours a week teaching and lecturing, the latter ramping up slowly to ease him into the job. He was told he could keep the Allen Fellowship. Part of the reforms of Cambridge University was a newly established category of University Lectureships set to begin in 1926. Frank would get one in the first tranche, against the tendency for them to go to people already established in their field. He would be the youngest University Lecturer in the Faculty of Mathematics.

When Frank got the news of the King's position, he was almost half-way through his analysis. His parents nagged him to come home and prepare for his lectures. But Frank returned to Cambridge on October 4, just in time for term. He was breezy about cutting it so close, and determined to return not a minute sooner than he had to. His reply must have exasperated Arthur, who worked so hard at his own lecturing:

> I needn't bother about getting any new furniture till I have leisure, my books and pictures can be arranged in a day. I can prepare a few lectures pretty quickly. Its no good preparing a whole course till I have some experience of what its like lecturing, how fast I go etc.

His first night as a Fellow, he and his King's friends dined in Hall and played bridge afterwards. He was twenty-one years old, and part of what his analysis had done for him was allow him to loosen the strings that tied him to his parents' wishes and demands.

Trinity was famous for its philosophers. But at King's, Keynes was building an economics empire. Marshall had hived off economics from Moral Sciences in 1903 and established the Economics Tripos. King's was now its centre. Arthur Pigou, Marshall's successor in the Professorship of Political Economy, was a Fellow. Keynes's Apostles and Bloomsbury friend, the economist Gerald Shove, had been made an Assistant Lecturer in 1923 and took the bulk of the undergraduate economics supervisions. Keynes had reason to believe that in bringing Ramsey to King's, he would be laying another foundation stone on which that empire could grow. The young man had contributed to the debate about Douglas and economists were already relying on him for technical advice. Like so many of Keynes's bets, this was to prove a good one.

Image 17 Moritz Schlick.

Image 18 Hans Hahn.

8

'THE FUNDAMENTALS ARE SO PHILOSOPHICAL'

The Foundations of Mathematics and the Theory of Types

Despite his parents' anxiety about his work, and his own desire to not rush things, Ramsey got a lot done during his six months in Vienna. Near the end, on 22 July 1924, he had written to his mother from Wörthersee, in a state of optimism about his work:

> It seems to me likely now that say in a year or two I shall have solved all the main problems and then I shall write a book. At the moment I haven't got absolutely clear stuff for more than an article which I would rather save up for my book. Wittgenstein took 7 years over his book; so far I've only had one year.

He was aiming rather high, but not without some reason. It was a remarkable time for logic and philosophy—as Ramsey said, he lived in a great time for thinking, 'with Einstein, Freud and Wittgenstein all alive (and all in Germany or Austria, those foes of civilization!)'. Ramsey was set to join the trailblazing. With respect to philosophy and logic, he was Wittgenstein's main interlocutor. Russell too held him in high regard, enlisting Ramsey to help with his own work. He was starting to make his way through the problems of his heroes, trying to correct errors and offer a different approach. It was not hubris to think that he might be on his way to solving the main problems of philosophy.

Ramsey's catalogue of great thinkers extended to others in the foundations of logic and mathematics. In his December 1923 letter to Wittgenstein, he said that he thought that Frege was finally getting the attention he deserved. For one thing:

> two great mathematicians Hilbert and Weyl have been writing on the foundations of mathematics and pay compliments to Frege, appear in fact to have appreciated him to some extent. His unpopularity would naturally go as the generation he criticized dies.

Frege, Russell, Hilbert, Weyl, Wittgenstein. Ramsey's name eventually would be added to this illustrious list.

He had been thinking hard about the foundations of mathematics. On 17 January, in the winter before his Vienna interlude and in the middle of his crisis about Margaret Pyke, he wrote in his diary:

> Hit on Russell's articles on logical atomism which I had forgotten. Explained to Sebastian Witt's theory of generality and Russell's and my theories of types...thought about identity and infinity axiom till 1a.m. Rather excited but got nothing out. Slept 2-9 without breakfast; a very hard day's work.

At the beginning of February, he went to London for a weekend. Ogden said he would pay all his expenses, if Ramsey corrected part of a translation of Hans Vaihinger's *Die Philosophie des Als Ob* (*The Philosophy of As If*), which Ogden was publishing in his *International Library*. Ogden put him up in a good hotel and the two of them had a grand time dining out and going to the theatre. But the point of the excursion was to see Russell. Over two days, Ramsey and Russell talked about logical topics such as vagueness, identity, and propositional functions. Russell lent him a typescript by his friend, the American logician Henry Sheffer. That was Sheffer's short monograph "General Theory of Notational Relativity" in which Ramsey reported to Wittgenstein that Ogden 'talked his rot and Russell thought it silly', but of Russell he said: 'I liked him very much.'

One assumes that Ramsey looked over the translation of *Als Ob*, as promised. But another task was more interesting to him. He agreed to review and correct the page proofs of Russell's revisions for the second edition of *Principia Mathematica*. There was a flurry of friendly letters between them, in which Ramsey verified references for the new edition and corrected the mathematics. He told Russell 'It seems to me an awfully good theory.' But he asked: 'Why not put Wittgenstein into the bibliography?' In the introduction to the second edition, Russell and Whitehead asserted that they were 'under great obligations to Mr F.P. Ramsey...who has read the whole in MS. and contributed valuable criticisms and suggestions'.

But Ramsey had some doubts about the manuscript. He wrote to Wittgenstein that he had read 'the new stuff' Russell was 'putting into Principia'. He felt that Russell's changes were cosmetic and that he (Ramsey) had 'made out the proper solution rather in detail of some of the contradictions which made Russell's Theory of Types unnecessarily complicated, and made him put in the Axiom of Reducibility'. That was the work he did in Austria—he tried to show how Russell's *Principia* could be 'rendered free from the serious objections which have caused its rejection by the majority of German authorities, who have deserted altogether its line of approach'. Those authorities were Hilbert, Weyl, and Brouwer.

Ramsey's paper was titled 'The Foundations of Mathematics'. It was written as a submission for a Smith's Prize, for which the best-placed wranglers could compete by writing a dissertation in a higher branch of mathematics. Ramsey explained the project to Moore:

> I am working on the basis of Wittgenstein's work, which seems to me to show that Principia is wrong not merely in detail but fundamentally. I have got Russell's manuscript of the stuff he is inserting into the new edition, and it seems to take no account of Wittgenstein's work at all.

His intention was to explain 'such parts of Wittgenstein that I want to use for my own stuff'.

Ramsey found 'important defects' in *Principia*. Most important was the 'failure' of Russell's Theory of Types to overcome the difficulties generated by the paradoxes. Russell, recall, had discovered contradictions that threatened his (and Frege's) logicist project of deriving all of mathematics from the principles of logic. His evolving Theory of Types was designed to avoid these contradictions. Ramsey wasn't convinced by it, especially by the fact that Russell relied on the 'doubtful' axiom of reducibility. Ramsey's paper was thus partly in the spirit of Russell's *Principia*—he wanted to save it—and partly in the spirit of Wittgenstein's *Tractatus*—he wanted to use ideas in the *Tractatus* in order to save Russell. But, as was his wont, he struck out on his own.

Ramsey began 'The Foundations of Mathematics', by agreeing with the logicists that mathematics is a part of logic. Invoking the received Cambridge interpretations of logicism's opponents, he argued against both formalism and intuitionism. Against the formalist view of Hilbert, he said that mathematics does not consist of 'meaningless formulae to be manipulated according to certain arbitrary rules'. Whatever you think of formalism as an account of mathematical propositions, such as '2 + 2 = 4', it is 'hopeless' as a theory of mathematical concepts. The concept <2> occurs 'in everyday life', as in 'It is 2 miles to the station', and it has as much 'ordinary meaning' as any other concept. Against the intuitionists Brouwer and Weyl, he asserted that in restricting themselves to what can in principle be constructed by human mathematicians, they give up 'many of the most fruitful methods of modern analysis, for no reason, as it seems to me, except that the methods fail to conform to their private prejudices'.

Ramsey, being a logicist, needed to deal with the paradoxes. He thought the first part of Russell's Theory of Types was fine. It asserted that to apply a predicate to the wrong type of subject does not produce a falsehood—rather, it produces something that is literally nonsense. But Ramsey found a 'blemish' in the second part of the Theory of Types. It invalidated an important piece of accepted mathematics, and that 'catastrophe was only averted' by the introduction of the axiom of reducibility, which asserts that for any predicate of a higher order there is a predicate of a lower order which applies to the same set of subjects. But, as Ramsey noted (following something Wittgenstein said in the *Tractatus*), this is a genuine proposition, set out in words, 'whose truth or falsity is a matter of brute fact, not of logic'. This so-called axiom 'is certainly not self-evident, and there is no reason whatever to suppose it true'. Ramsey, that is, thought that Russell had thrown the baby out with the bathwater. Russell had introduced an axiom that was not a tautology, in order to save the theory from contradiction. But in doing so, he had abandoned the project of building a self-evidently true theory,

Ramsey began his own solution by distinguishing between classes of contradictions. He thought Russell had mashed them together in 'a rather sloppy way', by saying that they all were examples of a vicious-circle principle. Ramsey divided the paradoxes into those that involve logical or mathematical terms and those that are not purely logical. Paradoxes belonging to the second category 'contain some reference to thought, language, or symbolism', and hence are 'due not to faulty logic or mathematics, but to faulty ideas concerning thought and language'. Take, for instance, the Liar Paradox. Suppose I assert 'This sentence is false'. If it is false, then it is true, which makes the assertion false.

For contradictions of a purely mathematical nature, such as paradoxes that arise by considering classes that are members of themselves, Ramsey held that Russell's Theory of Types would suffice. But Russell's theory doesn't work for the second category of paradoxes, which involve 'meaning' or 'ambiguities of language'. Such paradoxes rely on the meanings of words, like 'true' and 'false', and it is here, to deal with these meaning-based paradoxes, that Russell brought in the axiom of reducibility. Ramsey argued that it is not required. All that is required is the simple extensional or truth-functional hierarchy of individuals, predicates, and classes.

THE THEORY OF TYPES

Michael Potter, Professor of Logic, Cambridge University

In *Principia* Whitehead and Russell tried to derive mathematics from a form of logic known as the 'ramified theory of types', which divides propositional functions into types in accordance with two principles of classification: first according to the types of their free variables; then according to the types of their bound variables. They found, however, that they needed an extra axiom (the axiom of reducibility) in order to fulfil their logicist ambition.

The *Tractatus* opposed the logicism of *Principia*, but did not propose a convincing alternative. (The only part of mathematics of which it offered any account was elementary arithmetic.) In 'The Foundations of Mathematics' Ramsey aimed to fill this gap by making use of the idea, originally traceable to Frege, that because the aim of logic is not that of grammar, the notion of content logicians use should be coarser-grained: it should ignore those features of the content of an expression that are irrelevant to inference. Frege called the part that remains the expression's 'sense', but left the precise characterization of this notion somewhat uncertain. It was left to Wittgenstein in the *Tractatus* to give a precise definition: two propositional signs have the same sense (express the same proposition) if they are true in the same circumstances.

What Ramsey did was to generalize this distinction between propositional sign and proposition to propositional function signs: two such signs express the same propositional function, he said, just in case they express the same proposition when their argument places are filled with the same names. His central idea was then that if logicians should ignore the difference between two propositional signs that express the same proposition, they should equally ignore the difference between two propositional function signs expressing the same propositional function. If we apply that idea to the theory of types, we discover that of Russell's two principles of classification, only the first (according to levels) remains; the second classification (according to orders) makes sense only at the level of propositional signs. It is, Ramsey noted, just like talking about the numerator of a fraction, which makes sense only at the level of signs. It follows that if we accept Wittgenstein's criterion of sense, we should adopt a simple rather than a ramified theory of types. This is of great significance for logicism, because in the simple theory Russell's problematic axiom of reducibility is no longer required.

What, though, of the paradoxes which compelled Russell to adopt the theory of types in the first place? Just as we may distinguish two principles of classification, so we may distinguish two sorts of paradox: the first class requires the simple theory of types; the second the ramified theory. Ramsey's simple theory avoids paradoxes of the second class not in the theory itself but indirectly by pushing them into the metalanguage: they all make use of some non-extensional notion such as meaning, which is not expressible in an extensional language such as that of the *Tractatus*.

Ramsey argued that mathematical truths, like logical truths, are tautologies in Wittgenstein's sense, even though Wittgenstein himself didn't accept it. Russell wanted to build up the whole edifice of mathematics from primitive principles, and Ramsey thought he should do it by taking primitive mathematical propositions to be tautologies, so that everything that he built up would be necessarily true.

There are plenty of problems with Ramsey's paper, and indeed, even while looking at the page proofs, he worried that part of it (we don't know which) 'may be wrong'. He told Wittgenstein: 'My article seems far away and rotten though I corrected the proofs 2 days ago.' In September 1926, Ramsey would write to

Keynes, thanking him for his kind words about the paper and saying that he had signed a contract with Ogden to publish a book about the topic. But he said he had become 'rather tired' of it, unable to get over 'some obstinate difficulties'. He would find those difficulties unsurmountable and would reject much in the paper, including logicism. So would subsequent mathematicians. Unlike the bulk of Ramsey's work, the arguments in 'The Foundations of Mathematics' do not really speak to us today. But at the time, the paper was a bit of a sensation.

The Reception of 'The Foundations of Mathematics'

Ramsey had written about whether his paper was mathematical enough for the examiners of the Smith's prize. He wrote home from Vienna that it 'won't seem at all mathematics as I shan't have got past the fundamentals which are so philosophical...So it won't perhaps do for the Smith's prize.' He was right—he didn't get the Smith's Prize. That caused some consternation amongst the philosophically inclined mathematicians in Cambridge. It 'leaked round' to Harold Jeffreys, a mathematics fellow at St John's College, that the committee had consulted someone who said that the paper wasn't very good. But Jeffreys and others knew that Russell himself had praised the paper. (Russell had told Ramsey that although he wasn't entirely convinced, that was only because Ramsey's moves were unfamiliar and he found it hard to look at the matter in a new way.) As Jeffreys put it, Russell said that it was first rate, 'which made various people wonder who the hell was the expert that they had consulted!'*

Ramsey had written to his mother that he didn't care much about the Smith's Prize. But he did care that the article be published in a good venue, and he feared that it was too long. The secretary of the science-focussed Cambridge Philosophical Society told him that they would love to publish it, but they were short of funds and couldn't often bring out a monograph. Ramsey was most keen to have the London Mathematical Society publish it, as he took their *Proceedings* to be easily the leading English journal of mathematics. Once he had finished the paper, back in Cambridge, he sent it to Russell, deferentially asking for advice about whether it was publishable:

> It doesn't seem at all a popular subject with the professors of mathematics here, as they turned it down without even an honourable mention when I sent it in for the Smith and Rayleigh prizes.... The German papers especially Mathematische Annalen, which Hilbert runs, often print long papers on mathematical logic mostly devoted to the controversy between Hilbert and Brouwer and Weyl. Both sides to this controversy

---

* The Smith's Prize winner was no pushover—it was Thomas Room, who went on to be an eminent geometer.

dismiss Principia Mathematica principally on the ground that it cannot get over the difficulties of the Axiom of Reducibility; so that if they were to read my dissertation it might have a wholesome effect.

I wonder whether if you think it might be a good scheme to send it to Mathematische Annalen, which does sometimes contain papers in English, you would be so kind as to send me a little note which I could send with it, saying either that it seems to you to solve the difficulties or at least that it deserves careful consideration. Because I think they would be more likely to bother about a thing you recommended than one coming from an unknown Englishman and repeatedly referring to Wittgenstein of whom they have never heard....

I am sorry to bother you about this but there is no one here who knows enough about it to give me useful advice.

Much to his credit, Russell was happy to write a recommendation that this paper, which was delivering blows to his own work, be published.

G.H. Hardy also stepped up. Ramsey reported: 'Hardy the great mathematician was dining here the other day and asked me to dinner on Wednesday, which pleases me because I shall probably be able to interest him in my work, and he might help to get it published.' Hardy followed up on the conversation: he thought 'the L.M.S. will publish my thing though he can't promise as it depends on the council. I am to send him it with Russell's letter.' Hardy arranged for Ramsey to present the paper first in Oxford on 10 August 1925, and then at the London Mathematical Society on 12 November 1925. It was indeed published in the Society's *Proceedings*.

Ramsey sent it to a number of people he thought might be interested, including Heinrich Behmann in Halle; Wilhelm Ackermann, who was then an assistant to David Hilbert at Göttingen; and the Polish logician Leon Chwistek. Despite Ramsey's worry that it was rotten, the paper received a lot of attention. C.D. Broad made fourteen pages of close notes on it. Russell accepted the suggestion that he should extend Wittgenstein's definition of logic as tautology to mathematics. The great Swiss mathematician and collaborator of Hilbert's, Paul Bernays, referred to the paper in a 1930 essay. Soon Ramsey was corresponding with the German mathematicians Henrich Scholz, as well as with Ackermann and Behmann. The latter two had been students of Hilbert, bearing out Ramsey's prediction to Russell that the Hilbert school would be interested in his paper. In January 1928 Ramsey reported, tongue slightly in cheek, that he was 'asked by a German professor to read the proofs and criticize a section of a new edition of his book, in which he has made great use of my important and highly interesting article in the London Math Soc'. Adolf Fraenkel is 'the German Professor'. He and Ramsey had been writing to each other, and the 3rd edition of Fraenkel's *Einleitung in die Megenlehre* (*Introduction to Set Theory*) appeared in 1928, quoting Ramsey. The preface, dated summer 1928, thanks Ramsey (along with Carnap, Bernays, Tarski, among others) for his kind help in making corrections.

The Vienna Circle also took notice. They were remarkably open to new ideas, from Cambridge especially. They had eagerly read Russell and Whitehead's *Principia* and Wittgenstein's *Tractatus*. Ramsey's 'The Foundations of Mathematics' provided the next discussion point between Cambridge and Vienna. Ramsey sent Schlick a copy, writing 'With the compliments of the author' on the first page. Carnap transcribed parts of it and Schlick scribbled comments on the whole of his copy. We can see from Carnap's *Tagebuch*, or private journal, that the Circle talked about the paper for two weeks in January 1927 and then intermittently right through to 1929. One of the first entries about Ramsey says: 'We talked about Wittgenstein and Ramsey. Very interesting.' Carnap read the paper to Olga Neurath, Otto Neurath's mathematician wife, who was blind.

What they found most interesting was Ramsey's extension of Wittgenstein's idea of tautology. Like all empiricists, the members of the Vienna Circle struggled to say why the statements of logic and mathematics are legitimate. They can't be verified by experience, and hence don't satisfy the Circle's observational criterion of meaningfulness. The Circle was happy to find their answer in two moves, the first Wittgenstein's, and the second Ramsey's. Wittgenstein characterized the propositions of logic as tautologies. Logic does not make any claims about the world, and for that reason, it is exempted from any verifiability criterion. But Wittgenstein held that mathematics consists of purely syntactic or formal equations, that is, he did not think that mathematics was tautologous. In his dissertation, Ramsey declared Wittgenstein's position 'obviously a ridiculously narrow view of mathematics', as it is confined to simple arithmetic. Mathematics, Ramsey asserted, 'consists entirely of tautologies in Wittgenstein's sense'. Wittgenstein himself staunchly resisted the suggestion.

PROPOSITIONAL FUNCTIONS IN EXTENSION

Rob Trueman, Lecturer in Philosophy, University of York

Ramsey's aim in 'The Foundations of Mathematics' was to reduce mathematics to logic. His strategy was broadly Principian: first reduce mathematics to type-theory, and then show that the type-theoretic reductions of mathematical truths are logical truths. However, Ramsey's conceptions of logic and of type-theory were quite different from Russell and Whitehead's. Ramsey took his conception of logic straight from the *Tractatus*: all logical truths are tautologies, and vice versa. But Ramsey's conception of type-theory was all his own.

For Ramsey, type-theory was the theory of propositional functions, and he spent much of FM developing an account of what he called *predicative* propositional functions. These functions were 'predicative' in the sense that they behaved in roughly the way that predicates are meant to behave: if $\varphi\hat{x}$ is a predicative function, then 'φa predicates the same thing of a as φb does of b'. (Importantly, this use of 'predicative' is utterly unrelated to its modern mathematical sense.)

Ramsey's definition of a predicative function ran along the same lines as the Tractarian definition of a proposition. He started with the definition of an *atomic function*, which is 'the result of replacing by variables any of the names of individuals in an atomic proposition expressed by using names alone'. So if 'fa' is an atomic proposition expressed using names alone, and 'a' is the name of an individual, then $f\hat{x}$ is an atomic function. A *predicative function* is then any truth-function of atomic functions and propositions. So if $f\hat{x}$ and $R\hat{x}\hat{y}$ are atomic functions, then all of the following are predicative functions:

$$F\hat{x}\vee R\hat{x}\hat{y}; \quad F\hat{x} \rightarrow \neg Rab; \quad \forall x Rx\hat{y}$$

The predicative functions are a well-behaved totality of propositional functions. Unfortunately, however, that totality was far too narrow for Ramsey's logicist project. This project could not be completed unless it were a tautology that some propositional function is true of exactly one individual. But it is not a tautology that some *predicative* function is true of exactly one individual. To see this, we need only note that it is not contradictory to suppose that every individual satisfies *every* atomic function. On this supposition, every predicative function would either be true of *every* individual, or be true of *no* individuals at all. So, assuming that there are at least two individuals, no predicative function would be true of exactly one individual.

Ramsey was thus forced to broaden his range of propositional functions. He proposed to do this 'as radically and drastically as possible; [by dropping] altogether the notion that φa says about a what φb says about b'. On this broader conception, a propositional function 'results from any one-many relation in extension between propositions and individuals'. Ramsey called this new broader range of functions the *propositional functions in extension* (PFEs), and illustrated what he has in mind with the following example:

Thus φ(Socrates) may be Queen Anne is dead,
φ(Plato) may be Einstein is a great man;
$\varphi\hat{x}$ being simply an arbitrary association of propositions φx to individuals x.

With the help of PFEs, it is easy to show that it is a tautology that some propositional function is true of exactly one individual: for each individual a, there is some PFE which maps a to a tautology and everything else to a contradiction.

According to Ramsey, his definition of the predicative functions was 'the most important definition in [his] theory'. Be that as it may, PFEs were surely his most radical idea. This might not be immediately obvious to a modern reader. Ramsey tells us that PFEs are just arbitrary mappings from individuals to propositions, and arbitrary mappings are the stock-in-trade of modern mathematics. However, it is important to remember that a propositional function is *not* a mathematical function in the modern sense. Mathematical functions are denoted by functional symbols, like 'the successor of *x*' and '*x* + *y*'. But Ramsey is clear that propositional functions are *themselves* symbols, not things that we denote with symbols. What is more, propositional functions are an altogether different kind of symbol. Functional symbols are *term-forming* operators: when we substitute the term '0' for the variable '*x*' in 'the successor of *x*', we get 'the successor of 0', a term which denotes the number 1. By contrast, propositional functions are *sentence-forming* operators: when Ramsey says that the propositional function *Fx̂* maps the individual *a* to a proposition, he means that '*Fa*' is a *sentence* which *expresses* that proposition.

So a PFE is meant to be a *symbol*, which combines with names to produce *sentences*. But the propositions you can express by combining a given PFE with different names need not bear any relation to each other. Returning to Ramsey's own example, *φx̂* is meant to be a symbol such that '*φ*(Socrates)' *says that* Queen Anne is dead, and '*φ*(Plato)' *says that* Einstein is a great man. PFEs are, then, very different from the kind of arbitrary functions that we find in modern mathematics. The remaining question is whether Ramsey was right to think that his PFEs form 'an intelligible notation'.

As far as the Circle was concerned, the two moves taken together—first logic, then mathematics being seen as tautologies—were a fundamental turning point in philosophy. Hans Hahn, the 'Professor Hahn' whom Ramsey saw while he was in Vienna, was especially clear that the tautological character of mathematics is absolutely essential: 'If this position can be made out . . . the existence of mathematics is then also compatible with the empiricist position'. They took Ramsey to be very much on their side, trying to make even better the view they thought they shared with Wittgenstein. Ramsey was listed in the Vienna Circle's 'manifesto' as one of those 'sympathetic' to their mission, and that is still a frequently expressed opinion. Ramsey certainly did share some things with them. The Circle was interested in logicism, and hence with Ramsey's attempt to save *Principia*. Their views were all shaped by Russell and Wittgenstein. They all employed logical techniques. We shall see that some of Ramsey's logical innovations would later be used as tools by the Circle. But while Ramsey, like the Circle, was interested in the relationship between propositions and reality, even as an undergraduate he was rejecting the primacy of the primary language and suggesting that we should not be obsessed by word–world relationships.

Ramsey's revision of the Theory of Types was discussed also in Cambridge. Moore, in his copy of Ramsey's posthumously-published papers, marked up 'The Foundations of Mathematics' heavily, and was still discussing it in his lectures years after Ramsey's death. Ramsey would, in 1929, decide that the project of logicism and its Theory of Types was at a dead end as a theory about the nature of mathematics. (Type Theory, however, would continue to be a fruitful field in itself and is now employed to get rid of bugs in programming languages). He would continue to engage Heinrich Behmann on the matter of how to solve the set-theoretic paradoxes for Russell right through 1928, with Ramsey remaining sceptical of Behmann's alternative proposal for solving the problem. Russell had tried to repair Frege's logicism, and Ramsey tried to repair Russell's. But Ramsey eventually saw there was no fix to be had and he would give up the project altogether.

THE NEW DON

A King's Life

Frank cleared his things from Trinity and moved them straight to rooms in the Wilkins Building in King's. Pigou had the rooms next door, and that proximity was to have significant consequences for the discipline of economics. Ramsey's rooms, in which he would both live and teach, were rather plain, but he was nonetheless excited about how he might furnish them. His good intentions came to nought. His rooms, like Howfield, had the minimum of decoration.

Politically, King's was a liberal, non-conformist place, tolerant of its in-house atheists. Talk amongst the Fellows was often about politics. Keynes, the most powerful man in college, and a significant participant in liberal politics and government, would frequently hold forth at high table about the current political situation, and he gave an annual speech at Congregation about the financial situation of the world. Berry was a great supporter of women's suffrage. Goldie Lowes Dickinson, a history Fellow and good friend of Frank's, was active in promoting the League of Nations and defending the idea of collective security. But it wasn't all serious, and the talk could just as easily move to gossip, especially about sex. The classicist John Sheppard, who would go on to become Provost of King's in 1933, was inspiring and comic. He was especially welcoming of undergraduates, who were well-integrated into college life, with less of a gap between them and the dons than found in most other colleges. Keynes brought interesting guests to dinner, which further enriched the conversation at high table. According to Richard Braithwaite, Frank loved dining in College and his 'joy of life' added to the pleasure of the company. He liked making jokes and mocking political affairs, but he quite literally went out of his way not to do it at the expense of others, tending to unobtrusively slip out of a room if the conversation displeased or bored him. For Braithwaite, this was one of Frank's most distinctive traits:

> He was the least malicious person I've known. I've never heard him make a malicious remark. But he avoided people he might have been malicious about.

Frank especially liked the College Feasts, at which great quantities of good food and alcohol were served. Braithwaite said he enlivened those feasts with his hearty laugh—'a very fine noise'. Frank would get good intellectual ideas when he was slightly drunk, roaring with laughter at them during the feast and waking up the next morning with the thoughts still percolating.

The misery that had propelled him into psychoanalysis was gone. His treatment, as well as simply some time away from home and school in which to grow up, had loosened the unease he had often felt in social situations, especially those involving women. With his new emotional balance, his new job, and his new salary, he settled into a good life. The guiding hand of Ogden moved to London almost simultaneously with Frank's appointment, but it was no longer needed. If anyone played something of that role in Frank's life now, it was Keynes.

Some things remained the same. Frank spent time at Howfield, although his tolerance for the loud and argumentative Wilson family visits was fraying. His brother Michael was now an undergraduate at Magdalene, and so the family was reunited, the boys having returned from their boarding school exiles. Frank invited Michael to lunch in his rooms, where he introduced him to his new colleagues one at a time—Keynes, Sheppard, Lowes Dickinson. Keynes's verdict on Michael: 'not so interesting as Frank'. Michael was active in the Union debating society and would eventually become its President. From that pulpit, he preached liberalism. In Frank's first year as a Kingsman, former Prime Minister Herbert Asquith publicly suggested that Michael Ramsey would be the next leader of the Liberal Party. Frank hoped he would take the political path, rather than the one he did. Michael would switch from Classics, to Law, and then to Theology, with the intention of preaching from a different sort of pulpit. He wanted to be ordained an Anglican priest. Frank regretted that decision, but his arguments with his brother about religion had no impact.

The mostly male socializing with his friends from his undergraduate days continued. There were a few departures. Most significantly, in March 1925, Sprott left for a job at the University of Nottingham, after a big farewell party. His friends were disappointed. They would miss the Sebastian-hosted breakfasts, his landlady serving a full English fry-up with eggs, sausages, porridge, and beer. They also thought he could do better than Nottingham. But Sprott did very well there, ending up an eminent psychologist and sociologist. He kept in touch with his old Cambridge friends, so much so that he became E.M. Forster's literary executor.

He and Frank arranged visits back and forth between Cambridge and Trimingham, on the Norfolk coast, where Sebastian had a place. When Frank visited, he brought his tennis racquet, even though his friend was a formidable player.

Frank widened his circle. Kingsley Martin became friendly with people at the London School of Economics, and included Frank in various social and political activities with them. Frank also started to make more connections in Oxford. The mathematician G.H. Hardy was there. They knew each other through the Apostles, but now they had an independent relationship around their work. By 1928, Hardy would report to Moore about one of his (Hardy's) more philosophical efforts: 'Ramsey passed it as substantially sensible'. Most important was Roy Harrod, a young left-leaning economics don at Oxford. He and Frank had known each other since 1922, when Harrod spent part of the year at King's. Frank had taken Harrod under his wing then, introducing him to Moore and others. The friendship was now renewed, and they travelled between Oxford and Cambridge for intellectually rich weekends.

The Moral Sciences Club still met often in Braithwaite's room, now in King's, not Trinity. Braithwaite seems to have paid more attention to decorating it, or at least inherited it from someone who did. A visiting graduate student from Oxford said of Braithwaite's King's lodging:

> The room is one that I could not live in, with painted panels from ceiling to floor— huge nudes—looking like decorations for a café by an imitator of Marie Laurencin.

Marie Laurencin was a French avant garde Cubist painter, known for extravagant design. It seems Braithwaite had the famous rooms over the Webb's gate, painted by Vanessa Bell and Duncan Grant and later occupied by Keynes.

Teacher

One thing different in Frank's new life was the mountainous amount of teaching that was now expected of him. Unlike his father, who wanted extra pupils and the revenue that came with them, and who loved College and Faculty administrative work, Frank found himself desperate to preserve more time for his own writing. His teaching duties quickly built up to a staggering sixteen hours of supervisions and lectures a week. Frank wrote a nervous letter to Keynes on 11 December 1925, asking if he might arrange to have fewer undergraduate supervisions:

> Dear Maynard,
>
> I hope you won't mind my writing to you about this, but I am worried and want your advice.
>
> It now seems to me clear that if I go on doing as much lecturing and teaching as at present, I shall never do any important original work, which I think I might do otherwise.... In John's for instance, they do 9 hours a week each including

lectures...and at Trinity they do even less.... I have had 16 hours this term, and there seems no prospect of having less, but probably more. This does not sound much but it compares very unfavorably with...John's....[S]ince I have been in King's I have hardly done anything else, except write out things I thought of before.... It is not only that I don't get on with research, but I don't read enough useful literature. As I am mainly interested in philosophical questions nearly the whole of my teaching is quite discon-nected from my own work, and does not involve my reading or thinking of anything useful for it.... It is not that I dislike teaching, but that doing so much seems to interfere much too seriously with what I mainly want to do.

He asked if he might take a reduction in pay for a reduction in the number of hours. He didn't want to seem ungrateful, but he also didn't want to become 'dulled in brain and personality'. He ended the letter by saying: 'I haven't said anything about this to anyone, except I.A. Richards, because if nothing can be done it is obviously better for me not to appear discontented.'

Keynes had himself found teaching exhausting and by this time had farmed it all out to Gerald Shove. Nonetheless, he told Frank that he was asking for the impossible and advised him to simply knuckle down and get on with it. That's exactly what Frank did. And for the most part, he was very good at it.

Braithwaite remembered that one student, Jacob Bronowski (later of *Ascent of Man* fame), said Frank wasn't a good teacher, and Braithwaite himself said it was hard to imagine Frank identifying with the 'stupider' students and not breezing through explanations at incomprehensible speed. Tom Stonborough, Wittgenstein's nephew, had this experience. He had arrived from Vienna to study mathematics at Trinity in 1923, and in 1925 his supervisor sent him to Frank, as things were 'getting hot' for him—he was predicted to fail. By his own account, he was not up to the Mathematical Tripos and, anyway, was only interested in sport. Decades later, Tommy said it was like a beginner in tennis being sent to Björn Borg to learn how to play. Frank couldn't understand how Tommy couldn't understand the simplest things. Tommy said that mathematics, for Frank, was like a part of his body. He used it like his hands, without thinking. Despite the extra lessons, Tommy never got the hang of, or interest in, the subject, saying that he was unteachable and that he 'flunked Cambridge'. He later burned through his part of the Wittgenstein fortune, selling the Klimt portrait of his mother and the house that Wittgenstein designed. Frank agreed with Tom's self-assessment. He told Keynes that Tommy was 'nice but stupid'.

The more mathematically inclined students, on the other hand, thought Frank was a great teacher. Patrick Du Val, who went on to become a respected geometer, wrote of Frank's 'quiet voice, explaining, satisfying'. Richard Kahn, whom Frank supervised for the Mathematical Tripos Part I, said, well into his illustrious career as an economist, that it was an education from which he was still benefitting: 'Here was a great man who took me all alone one hour a week. . . . I regarded it as an enormous privilege.' Frank taught others who would also go on to success—Philip Hall in mathematics; Llewellyn Thomas in physics; Freddie Harmer in economics and the civil service; Henry Lintott in diplomacy. The brilliant geometer and inspirer of M.C. Escher's geometrical drawings, Donald Coxeter, who was in effect Senior Wrangler in 1928, learnt differential geometry from Frank.*

Ramsey had worried, before he started his teaching at King's, that Berry would be 'horrified' at how little applied mathematics he knew. But it turned out he could do it on his feet. Kahn said that all Frank knew of applied mathematics were Newton's three laws of motion, and that when he had to work out an applied problem, he did so by working it out from those first principles. Kahn's remarks were echoed by others:

> I remember his saying that he didn't know any applied maths, but he never failed to solve every applied question, & then laughed uproariously at what he said was a miracle. We got along famously, a very refreshing change from my previous five terms.

His students found him very easy to know. They liked his style—that of 'a large, untidy, shy & charming man with a wide and winning smile'. It was unusual and attractive to them. Some of them felt perfectly comfortable calling him by his first name. In an era in which the mathematics dons wore suits and formal manners 'rather like bankers', Frank was a standout.

He held his supervisions in his sparsely furnished and untidy study room, books and papers piled on the floor and on cupboard tops. The reports of his students gell into a coherent picture: 'One day an almighty crash behind me signalled that the law of gravity had cleared the top of the cupboard'; 'My visual memory of the supervisions is of his enormous frame sprawling in an armchair, laughing a great deal of the time'; he used a thick-nibbed fountain pen, 'making stabs at the ink bottle which

---

* Frank had one student who would become infamous—Alister Watson. He had encouraged the Apostles to elect Watson and he later employed him as an assistant to help him with marking and the like. Watson was an open Marxist, and from the early 1930s, he was a close friend of two Apostles in the Cambridge spy ring, Guy Burgess and Anthony Blunt, as well as of a third suspected spy (and another of Ramsey's friends), Dennis Proctor. Watson then left Cambridge for one of the most secret and important sections in NATO—the British Admiralty Signal and Radar Establishment. During Blunt's interrogation in 1965 by the British Security Services, he reluctantly fingered Watson, who was then interrogated at length and admitted to clandestine meetings with KGB agents, but not to passing on secrets. One of the senior British Security Services agents who tried to break Watson thought he was 'probably the most damaging of all the Cambridge spies'. Frank died just as the Cambridge spy ring was forming. It's safe to say that he wouldn't have been even tempted to join them, given his aversion to absolutist theories.

often had the cork in it'; his mathematical illustrations were accompanied by doodles and were a mess. His supervisions sometimes wandered off into talk of music and philosophy. That might have not been good preparation for the Tripos, but his supervisees felt it more profitable in other ways. And when he turned his attention to the maths and cleared up a student's confusion, he 'was awfully good at it', scribbling precisely understandable, analytic explanations.

His students were also consistent in reporting that, although they were awed by him, they were not frightened of him. One said this was because he had no interest whatsoever in dominating or embarrassing them. A South African under-graduate who had been made to feel like a 'low colonial fellow' by his previous supervisors, wished that he had been assigned earlier to the 'large, plump cheerful young man', who was so approachable and kind. Another said: 'He was always very friendly and human', 'not at all the "academic type"'. Another said that he might have been a paradigm of 'intellectual elitism', in the sense that he knew that he knew better than others about the right way to proceed mathematically, but he wasn't an elitist about people. He always 'took trouble' for his students, writing testimonials and letters of reference in a timely fashion, and taking pains to clear up their confusions. This was contrasted with Littlewood, who was singled out by some as not taking his supervisory duties 'at all seriously'. His friendliness was a contrast also with his severe and unemotional father's style of teaching.

In addition to his undergraduate supervisions, of which he had some experience at Girton, Frank was for the first time preparing and delivering lectures. He was unhappy with his initial assignments, as his favourite subjects had already been 'bagged'. So he taught some of the standard courses for the Mathematical Tripos: Theory of Equations, Solid Geometry, and Functions of a Complex Variable. Later he would teach other bread and butter courses, such as Differential Geometry, Functions of a Real Variable, Algebra, and Differential Calculus. Sometimes these were taught with others. Eventually those others included his old friend Max New-man, who in 1923 had been elected a Fellow of St. John's College, and in 1927 was made a lecturer in the Mathematics Faculty.

He was really happy when he bagged The Foundations of Mathematics, Russell's old course. The *Tractatus* scholar and eminent analytic philosopher Max Black was a student at Queens' College, Cambridge from 1927–30 and took it. His specialized subject in Schedule B of the Tripos was Mathematical Logic, which, as he put it, was 'then hardly pursued in England, although abroad actively researched in Europe'. Indeed, Black claimed 'There was no mathematical logic taught in England except in [my] third year when Ramsey began to be a strong influence.' Russell was not teaching. Whitehead had moved to Harvard in 1924, and had anyway left mathematical logic. Wittgenstein didn't count, as far as Black was concerned. He thought that although Wittgenstein was interested in the philosophy of mathematics, he didn't know much about the nuts and bolts of mathematics and logic.

Black found Frank 'a poor lecturer...but...a very, very intelligent, extraordinary man'. He took the Foundations of Mathematics course in the autumn of 1929, when Frank was ill—fatally ill, as it turned out. Perhaps that explains his verdict on his lecturing style. For others had a very different account. One student remembered:

> Chalk getting into his hair, all over his gown and suit, smudged over his glasses and face, and broken bits of chalk flying at all angles off the blackboard.... He generally had his hair in tufts all over the place. I remember him in a brown tweed suit, much more countrified than the conventional grey suits normally worn by other lecturers.... Shining through all this was a round cheerful face, and his style of lecturing was also cheerful; he imparted an enjoyment of his subject and spiced a clear exposition with little touches of humour.... Ramsey exuded some sort of personal charm into his lectures. It was like going into a friend's house, to go into his lecture room.

Others said that his lectures were aimed at the appropriate level of difficulty and that he was 'quiet, logical, and lucid'. He lectured by thinking on his feet, not by reading from notes, and had a habit of walking up and down in between the rows of students, smiling and talking. His audience was afraid to interrupt him, not because they thought he would react brusquely, but because he was 'superior' and they wanted to soak up his train of thought. Llewellyn Thomas took careful notes on the Foundations of Mathematics course in Lent term 1925. The notes still exist, and show that Frank's lectures were beautifully clear.

Thomas's notes also show that Frank's syllabus that year was ambitious beyond belief. On the reading list was the work of the French logician Jean Nicod; Frege's *Grundlagen der Arithmetik* (*The Foundations of Arithmetic*) and *Grundgesetze der Arithmetik* (*The Basic Laws of Arithmetic*); and *Introduction to Mathematical Philosophy* and *Principia Mathematica* by Russell. He must have chosen selections from these mammoth tomes, especially the Frege books, as they used an unfamiliar logical notation and weren't translated into English at the time. The lectures themselves featured a little Frege, and much Russell, Wittgenstein, Hilbert, Brouwer, and Weyl.

Sex from the Point of View of Society

Frank was still ruminating about where he stood with respect to women and the question of marriage, in practice and in principle. On 18 November 1924, shortly after his return from Vienna, he read a paper to the Apostles. It was a follow-up on a previous Apostles' discussion about sex and the individual. As with most of his Apostles papers, this one is untitled and unfinished. The topic was sex, not from the point of view of the individual, but from the point of view of society. It is a remarkable paper for a young man who wanted to follow his friends in sowing their wild oats, but wondered if such practices might have deleterious consequences for many women.

Frank made it clear that he wasn't going to consider sex in Freudian terms—in terms of 'what people desire or need'—but, rather, in terms of how society and its institutions should be arranged so that people might flourish. He noted that traditional religious morality was collapsing, although it still had sufficient strength to punish open violations of its code. Frank would soon have personal experience of breaking the rules and worrying about the consequences. But he had already had plenty of opportunity to see how his openly homosexual friends had to be wary in certain company. Personally, he was all for a relaxing of the old moral laws, and he certainly didn't believe in a church that felt authorized to lay them down. But he thought it important to examine whether the collapse of traditional morality was good from the point of society.

Frank first looked at the institution of marriage in economic terms. He supposed that it might be defended on the grounds that it serves as a kind of 'trade union', providing security for the majority of women and children. He suggested that there was something to the idea that marriage on the whole secures 'better terms' for women than they would have in free competition, since without the terms of marriage, the entire burden of providing and caring for children would fall on mothers. He was not so much talking about his own class here, where there was money to hire nannies and housekeepers. He was talking about whether traditional morality is better for the poorer parts of society, and hence better for society in general—whether an overturning of it, in the name of free sex, might have disastrous consequences.

He argued that in addressing this question, one had to consider what sort of system would have to be put in place to replace the old one. He noted that a shift was already afoot in which the burden of supporting children was falling more to the state and less on parents, with respect to 'schooling, doctoring and sometimes meals'. There was also 'considerable agitation for the adjustment of wages to family needs'. He went through the arguments for and against state support of children and, unsurprisingly, given his socialist inclinations, came out in support of it. Women should be directly paid by the state for having children, which would ensure that they ('the lower classes, anyhow') don't lose financial independence upon marriage. In what was an early, perhaps the earliest, analysis of the economics of marriage, child-bearing, and child-rearing, Frank argued that rates of pay should be varied and should be based on opportunity cost:

> the amount a woman is to be paid to bear and rear a child must, it would seem, depend on her social standing or perhaps on the amount she could have earned by adopting some profession other than that of motherhood.

This kind of system, he said, would only be workable once there was vastly diminished income inequality.

The question of whether society should get rid of moralistic feelings about monogamy was even more complex. Frank wondered whether negative outcomes might result if the institution of marriage were to 'disappear altogether', or if there were to be 'much more sexual intercourse outside of marriage' and easy divorce. His line of thought, accompanied with some hesitation, was: 'there may (I think) be reasonable apprehension about the position of women in such a state'. Perhaps many men 'would get tired of their wives and leave them lonely and poor in favour of someone younger and more attractive'. If marriage is viewed from the perspective of a market, then the traditional system includes a trade union. It imposes requirements on all its members, and even if some exceptions would in fact be harmless, the requirements have advantages. The marriage system 'secures better terms' for its female members.

Frank ended by asking a hard question. The Apostles had already made their decision about sex and the individual. They had already decided that the individual should have full freedom in pursuing his or her desires. But the Apostles must face up to a problem about sex from the point of view of society:

> In conclusion I want to raise rather a different question; if we decided that the traditional moral code is for the advantage of society, that a state in which it had disappeared would be worse than the present, should we then be justified or regard others as justified in refusing to sacrifice themselves for the general good and breaking the moral code?

He did not think the Apostles (himself included) could be at all certain that they were justified in flaunting traditional morality.[†]

[†] Margaret Paul misreads this essay, suggesting that her brother sided with traditional morality—that he disapproved of sex outside of marriage. She also misquotes it in a misleading way, replacing the 'others' in the above passage with 'women'.

As with many Apostles meetings, the question and vote were put in trashy and what we now take to be sexist language, in which the question was only sideways-on related to the content of the paper. We have to work quite hard to try to figure out the discussion. The question voted upon was: 'Be bad, sweet maid, and let the male be clever!' Someone called Thomson voted Yes. That is, let individual passion override the general good, but keep old gender roles in place. Lucas voted No, with the rider 'No better than she should be, but as clever as she can'. That seems like some kind of compromise: ditch conventional morality and gender roles to the extent that it is warranted. Braithwaite voted No, with a comment that seems to have been meant to be egalitarian: 'She should learn to grow a penis'. Sprott voted No, 'but if possible be not a maid'. Ramsey voted Yes, with an important exception: 'But not my wife'. That is, if traditional morality and gender roles are better for women, and hence for society, we must keep them. But he wasn't sure he was up to making the sacrifice.

Apostles papers and votes are not altogether reliable indicators of fixed positions. They were not intended for the light of day and there is a lot of showing off in the moment. But we can layer in Frank's Apostles papers, votes, and comments with what we know about his published work and behaviour, and get a clear enough view of his thoughts about sex, women, and society. He was all for overturning traditional morality in his private life, although till now he had only limited and miserable experience in this domain. He would write two Apostles papers on this topic—the one under discussion here and another, on culture and happiness, a year later. They were both about what we might call the paradoxes of progress, in which an advance is good for the individual but not good (or yet good) for society. He was especially concerned about the effect of progressive social practices on the poorer classes. These were hard questions, and he was determined to face them. It would have been around this time that, while staying with Roy Harrod in Oxford, Harrod took him to hear H.J. Paton talk on ethical obligation. Ramsey didn't take much part in the question-and-answer period, asking Harrod 'indignantly' afterwards why they discussed morality 'in terms of such a boring subject as keeping promises, instead of dealing with something interesting like fornication'.

Three days before presenting the paper on sex and society, Frank had met the woman who would be his wife. He was for the first time ever in a position in which he had some reason to speculate how he and a future wife might conduct themselves. Indeed, the paradox was one which would immediately be upon him. Frank's mother would be pressing the virtues of conventional morality on him, against all his instincts. He would act in just the way he voted. He and his wife would break with tradition. But as his analysis predicted, it would not be entirely easy.

10

PASSION FOUND

Lettice Cautley Baker

When he was a fresher in 1920, Frank had mentioned in his diary the 'very beautiful and rather nice' Miss Baker, treasurer of the Heretics Society. The following year, after his first Moral Sciences Club meeting, he spotted her again, and asked Braithwaite who she was. Braithwaite didn't know.

Lettice Cautley Baker was five years Frank's senior. Her mother, Frances Davies-Colley, was a Slade-trained amateur painter from a highly accomplished medical family. Lettice's father bought an oyster farm on Ross's Point, a beautiful bay five miles from Sligo on the west coast of Ireland. Lettice spent her childhood there, until her father threw himself under a train, upon which Frances took her small family to the next bay to set up a weaving shop. Lettice was in due course sent to the progressive English boarding school Bedales, where she was good at games and had a much better public school experience than did Frank. She would remain in England, but retain a strong connection to Ireland. Her mother and sister continued to live there, and the beauty and the political intensity appealed to her. In 1916, when she travelled home for the Easter school holiday, the train passed through a smoking Dublin, as Irish rebels attempted to overthrow British rule.

At Bedales, Lettice met Frances Marshall (later Frances Partridge), who would be at the centre of Bloomsbury's social and romantic intersections. They were not friends at school, Frances thinking Lettice a bit 'hearty' and bossy. But when they found themselves together in Cambridge at Newnham College, they reconnected to form an important relationship. Frances's undergraduate pocket diary has them meeting three or four times a week. The two of them made the most of the war's expansion of the freedoms and possibilities open to women. They spent a good deal of time flouting authority. Women students at the time weren't allowed to go to the theatre or visit a tea room without a chaperone. Lettice and Frances did much more, employing a hole in the fence of the dons' garden to return from late night sorties. Decades later, at the height of the 1960s sexual revolution, Lettice told the *Cambridge Times* that she and her friends had a 'good deal of giggles' over the new generation's attitude towards sex: 'They behave as if they discovered it.' There had been plenty of free love in the 1920s, albeit for a certain class, and kept secret from the college authorities.

Lettice was a highly intelligent woman, interested in psychology, philosophy, and the arts. Like Frank, her undergraduate academic record was achieved rather effortlessly. She did 'a certain minimum of work', and attained a first class mark in the Part I examinations in chemistry and biology for the Natural Sciences Tripos. Also like Frank, she felt the pull of the Moral Sciences, and unlike Frank, she made the switch to that Tripos. On 4 February 1921 she read a paper to the Moral Sciences Club, arguing that 'action is the be-all and end-all of all mental processes and that the ultimate purpose of all action is adaptation to environment'. The minutes of the meeting conclude with this passage: 'The one obstreperous mental element which refused to be fitted into the adaptive scheme was Aesthetics, and this served as the thin edge of a wedge, which, in the course of the discussion drove deep into the reader's defences.' A couple of weeks later, on March 12, Frank joined the Club, as a 'non-Moral-Science' student. That was an interesting near miss, as Frank would later mine similar ideas for intellectual gold.

Lettice worked in London for three years after graduation, where she gave vocational guidance tests in schools, and tried to help those leaving school at the age of fourteen to find a job that suited them. During this period, she lived in a cooperative house just off Gordon Square, the heart of Bloomsbury. Two of the house members were Janet Vaughan, a medical researcher who would go on to be Principal of Somerville College, Oxford, and her eventual husband David Gourlay. Lettice was leading a wild life—Gourlay said of her that she was the only person he knew who could sin with impunity. She remained an adventurer—funny, pleasure-loving, direct, and full of vitality. In 1969, at the age of seventy-one, she was stopped from getting into Cambodia in the last days of Prince Sihanouk's regime, because she carried a camera and was taken to be a journalist. She was indeed a professional photographer. She immediately arranged for another passport describing her occupation as 'housewife', and got into Cambodia, where she took hundreds of pictures. Also in her seventies, she surreptitiously climbed the scaffolding in King's Chapel to photograph the stained glass, and was locked in before she could get down.

Lettice was clearly a compelling person. She was involved with a string of younger men, before, during, and after her marriage to Frank. In the 1930s it would include Richard Braithwaite and, more seriously, Julian Bell, the adored son of Vanessa Bell and nephew of Virginia Woolf. But Frank would be the only man she ever married. Her extraordinary character is perhaps most succinctly indicated by the fact that Wittgenstein loved her, despite their alien personalities—her

Image 19 Lettice Cautley Baker.

free-wheeling ways with sex and his prudery, her messiness and his obsession with cleanliness. Wittgenstein remained close to Lettice after Frank's death, even though she became the lover of Julian shortly afterwards. Wittgenstein loathed him, expressing his scorn of the Apostles as 'all those Julian Bells'.

A Real Relationship

In 1924, Lettice had moved back to Cambridge to work in the University psychology labs. Frank returned from Vienna that autumn, declared cured of his crippling anxiety about sex. He proved his psychoanalyst right. Just over a month after his arrival home, on 14 November 1924, he saw Miss Baker at another Moral Sciences Club meeting. It was in McTaggart's rooms at Trinity, the meeting at which Moore read his famous 'A Defence of Commonsense'. Frank knew Moore's position well, and he could spend most of the evening stealing glances at Miss Baker. Lettice noticed the familiar man with the pale yellow tie staring in her direction, but she couldn't tell whether she was the object of his attentions, or her friend Beatrix Tudor-Hart. Frank disambiguated the situation by putting pen to paper late that night:

> Dear Miss Baker, I do not know if you remember me, but I did once meet you a long time ago in Ogden's rooms, & since then have always wished to pursue your acquaintance, but I have always been too timid to take any steps. I saw you this evening at the Moral Sciences Club & hoped that you were in Cambridge for some time & that we might perhaps meet.

He asked her to tea. Lettice replied the next day:

> Dear Mr. Ramsey,
>
> I recognized you last night at the meeting but could not fit your name to your face! Monday would be the best day for me about 4:30, as I have some work to do in the afternoon. My time is supposed to be occupied in research work at the psychological lab.
>
> Yours sincerely,
>
> Lettice C Baker

They had tea in his rooms at King's.

Lettice was in many ways perfectly suited to Frank. She was a 'confirmed' atheist, which she contrasted to Frank's 'militant' atheism. Her disregard of convention and her zest for life were attractive to Frank. Their social circles overlapped in a pleasing way, via the Bloomsbury group. Lettice hadn't yet met Virginia Woolf or Lytton Strachey, whereas Frank was already friendly with them through Keynes and the Apostles. But through Frances Marshall, Lettice was in with the younger Bloomsbury set. And Frances' sister Ray was married to David 'Bunny' Garnett, a central figure in that younger Bloomsbury generation. Bunny and Frank would become great friends, the two of them often playing croquet with the Penrose brothers.

The Bloomsburians were anything but conventional. Bunny Garnett was bisexual and having affairs across the playing field.* Keynes's diary catalogued his extraordinarily long list of male lovers, till he married Lydia Lopokova in 1925. Like many in this group, Lettice backed up her own free ways with a theory. She believed that

---

* In one of the most labyrinthine of Bloomsbury's relationships, Garnett, after Ray's death, would marry Angelica Bell, the child of his lover Duncan Grant and Vanessa Bell. Shortly after Angelica's birth he wrote to Lytton Strachey, with this prediction: 'Its beauty is the most remarkable thing about it. I think of marrying it: when she is twenty, I shall be 46 – will it be scandalous?' It was indeed scandalous.

wanting to possess or own someone was morally reprehensible, as was attendant jealousy about sexual matters. People should not be thought of as property.

Lettice and Frank did not stick to tea. Frank was in a rush, and in short order, they were lovers. Lettice happened to be writing an informal autobiography, something common at the time—Dick Pyke wrote one, as did Sebastian Sprott, who let his mother see part of it so she would know about his homosexuality. Frank was soon hoping Lettice would allow him to read hers. He wanted to learn about both her ex-lovers and her principles. After Frank's death (and Julian Bell's, in the Spanish Civil War), Lettice was still writing the autobiography, in Charleston, home of Vanessa and Clive Bell. She looked back on her first weeks with Frank, in her entirely forthright manner. She noted that a couple of weeks after they met, she dined, for the second time, with Frank in his rooms at King's:

> We decided to go to bed together that evening. I saw no particular reason to put it off longer & Frank was very impatient to do so. He was far too nervous to copulate in King's so we went round to my rooms in Trinity St. With little or no preliminaries we undressed, I shyly in the little bedroom & he in the sitting room. I slipped into bed but he came in quite naked & put on a French letter – completely unabashed. I was surprised at his absolute lack of physical shyness & ceased to be shy myself. After this I think we were never at all shy about anything to do with our bodies, though for some months I was occasionally shy or self conscious in conversation.

Lettice didn't think the first night was much of a success. But the next day, Frank wrote a long letter to Reik saying how happy he was and how grateful he felt to him. Lettice would say in her old age that 'the essential thing about Frank is that he was a very natural, uninhibited person'. But before his treatment with Reik, that naturalness did not extend to sex, as was illustrated when he visited the professional in Vienna. Reik certainly deserves some of the credit. But so does Lettice. As Frances Marshall put it in an interview in 2001, 'I think she broke him in as it were.'

There was, however, a terrible threat to their new happiness. A don could lose his job over such sins. In the summer of 1929, William Empson (later the great literary critic) would have his Bye Fellowship at Magdalene terminated and his name struck from all college records because his bedmaker found condoms—what the Magdalene Governing Body called 'engines of love'—in his rooms. Empson's mentor, I.A. Richards, was a Fellow of Magdalene, but he happened to be in China, too far away to try to intervene. Arthur, at the time, was President of the College. He was forever issuing dire warnings to Frank about the consequences of his immorality, and it is a reasonable surmise that he approved Empson's expulsion (the Governing Body minutes are silent on the details). Richards certainly worried about how Empson would fare under Arthur's 'pre-twentieth-century bachelor-schoolmaster's feeling and autocratic leanings'. The morals of Bloomsbury and the Apostles might have been free and easy, but the morals of the Cambridge colleges were anything but.

So Frank and Lettice tried to keep their relationship secret. They stayed away from King's. But even in Lettice's digs there were problems. She had a tiny flat in the attic of a house at 30 Trinity Street. The landlady was not pleased with Frank's visits. Not only did she personally disapprove, but to be aiding and abetting extra-marital sex could have landed her into trouble. She was the secretary for a Trinity don, and she worried that if word spread, her job could be imperilled.

Frank worried for his own job. Once, when he was leaving Lettice's flat just before midnight, he sent the empty milk bottles clattering down the street, causing heads to pop out of windows and him to fail to close the front door, as he bolted to King's. Lettice thought it funny at the time, lying in bed and laughing. But a policeman wandered by the open door and notified the landlady. Lettice nearly got evicted for that, and Frank was put in a panic.

The emotional seriousness of their relationship also moved at speed, despite the fact that Lettice was half-engaged to Dick Lithgow, a medical student. She had agreed to marry him while still at Newnham, but now, after three years in London and back in Cambridge, she was uneasy about his black periods and general moodiness. Decades later she recalled that when she met Frank, 'that settled it'. But in fact, it took some time to extract herself from the promise of matrimony and then from the relationship altogether. Apart from these complications, and apart from being distressed on the days in which Frank couldn't see her because he was too busy with work or too frightened about being caught out, the relationship went along, in Lettice's word, 'splendidly'. They talked about all manner of things so that 'time was always a continuous stream'. Lettice on occasion convinced Frank that his panic about losing his job was unreasonable. But he was never convinced for long. He knew that the college porters were not only charged with reporting the misbehaviour of undergraduates, but of Fellows as well.

In December, a month after meeting Frank, Lettice went to Ireland to see her mother. She and Frank were already addressing their letters to each other as 'My dearest' and 'Darling'. Lettice wrote from Ireland that 'Everything we have done together seems a kind of dream'; 'It has been heaven'. Frank was just as enthusiastic: 'Darling it is very wonderful. I think it is real too'. He was 'bored' without her, but nonetheless felt 'contented & that everything is really right, so long as you are still fond of me'. He signed off: 'Love (but there ought to be a stronger word) Frank'.

Frank had been completely open with Lettice about Margaret Pyke. While Lettice was away, Margaret and a friend came to have supper and play bridge, and Frank went round to see her on his own. He wrote to Lettice that it was curious to observe that the 'uncontrollable longing to kiss her' had disappeared and was replaced by 'a new element of vindictiveness in my feelings towards her'. But he assured Lettice that Margaret was 'very nice', and expressed the hope that Lettice would like her. Geoff, however, was another matter, dominating and without redemption:

> I can't forgive him for the loathsome way in which I discover[ed] he once talked to my mother about my passion for Margaret. He made jokes about it in the worst possible taste, to my mother too who took it so badly, and showed his great (unconscious?) enjoyment of the situation. He obviously likes contemplating the misery of his rivals.

He broke off this letter because he was writing from Howfield and the family had returned from church.

Their bond was already deep, yet companionable. Lettice sent Frank handmade squareword (a kind of crossword) puzzles to do, and instalments of her autobiography, which Frank found 'most interesting and vivid'. Lettice later said that 'he was shocked by parts of it, though at the same time interested and intrigued'.

Familial Storm

One might have thought that Frank would anticipate that his parents, especially Agnes, would be pleased. Their eldest son, now a don in Cambridge, was in a relationship with an educated, progressive, and unmarried woman. Agnes had thought his crush on Margaret Pyke highly inappropriate. Would not this new, healthier, relationship be welcome news to her? But Frank's instincts were to keep his parents in the dark. In one of his first letters to Lettice in Dublin over the Christmas separation, he wrote that he had 'invented things to tell my parents what I had been doing'. And now he lied that the letters with the Dublin postmarks were from Adrian Bishop, as Agnes was aware that Adrian was in Dublin. Frank knew that his parents strenuously disapproved of sex before marriage. He wrote Lettice from Howfield on Sunday, 28 December:

> I had a long argument with mother yesterday about free love and she maintained that it threatened the order of society and the security of women, and said she was sure my bark was worse than my bite or she would be in a perpetual state of agitation about me.

Agnes's argument that free love might endanger the security of society and women was precisely the one Frank had considered in his Apostles paper on sex from the point of view of society. No doubt he imbibed it from his mother. Agnes's disapproval of free love might have been partly political, but Arthur's was wholly religious and puritanical. He was still requiring his now fairly grown children, with the exception of Frank, go to church, and was not happy that at least one of them was radically non-conformist. Frank wrote to Lettice: 'Unlike yours, my sister (elder) has taken a turn for the bad; fallen under the influence of an evangelical parson and been confirmed; and now goes to church from choice instead of compulsion.'

Frank continued, even when Lettice was across the Irish Sea, to express his belief that they were taking too many risks in Cambridge. He was certain they would be eventually found out. He floated the idea that they should stop sleeping together, but neither of them was interested in that. He then suggested that perhaps they could arrange to meet for a long weekend in the countryside, while Lettice was en route from Dublin to Cambridge. Frank was setting off to visit Sebastian in Sussex and he would leave from there. Frank's 'authoritative and stupid' relations from the Wilson branch of the family were at Howfield for the holidays, and their presence only made him more lyrical about the prospect of getting away with Lettice. Frank planned the books he would bring for reading aloud—some Russian novels, his friend Morgan Forster's *Howards End*, and some books 'which David Garnett mentioned . . . when we had dinner with him'. Their Bloomsbury friends of course knew of their relationship. They could be trusted with such matters.

The holiday was not to go as planned. On 5 January, Frank wrote to Lettice to say that the previous day he had been caught in the rain, and on his return, put his coat in front of the fire without bothering to empty the pockets. One of them contained a letter from Lettice about their weekend away. It either fell out or Agnes extracted it. She defended her reading the letter by saying that she *always* read his letters. But Agnes knew that something was up with her eldest child, and the breach of privacy was not quite so innocent. On confirming her suspicions, she was beside herself, and had an awful row with Frank. She kept the matter from Arthur, which must have taken some effort, given her distress. Her reason was astounding. She thought he was the sort of man who might make a public fuss. It's hard to believe that Arthur would have been inclined to alert the authorities about his son's immoral relationship, putting his golden boy's job at King's in jeopardy. But Agnes knew him best, and she thought it within the realm of possibility.

Frank was thrown by his mother's reaction. He wrote to Lettice:

> She is so wretched and I am so sorry for her, that I promised to give up our holiday together. So that must be off. I'm so sorry; can you possibly forgive me?

He was also fretting that the location they had settled on wouldn't be safe from prying eyes:

> Also I rather have the wind up myself about being found out....I feel a little frightened because I remember one pious fellow of King's recommending to another The Dog and Duck as a place to stay at in the vac; and if we met either it would be all up with me.

The new Bloomsbury morality came up against the old Cambridge institutional morality, and the latter easily stared down the former.

Frank had a simple solution:

> What about marrying? It is risky, but what do you think? I don't feel sure of myself...It seems absurd not to go away as we planned, but I can't. I should be worrying so about mother, and possibly being caught. It's a shame for you. Darling, forgive me.

Lettice wrote the next day, saying that the news was 'miserably disappointing':

> Your letter feels like a lump of lead in my pocket and has put another lump of lead in my inside. But it's so much worse for you.

She agreed they should give up the weekend. But she was unhappy with Frank's mother. Being five years older than Frank, who was about to turn twenty-two, she was well past parental meddling, and she thought he should be too:

> But darling we shall have to think very much about the future. You won't find that I shall give you up so easily. We can't let parents spoil our lives—not that it's simple to go ones own way..... But I do feel that we must not give in easily or without sufficient thought.... I thought of writing to your mother, but I can't till I know what she knows and thinks.

She wondered whether Frank's mother knew that they had already spent a weekend together in London, as she couldn't really remember what she said in her 'unlucky letter'. But whatever was in that letter, she was not willing to let Agnes off the hook:

> She must have been already suspicious to read it—rather mean of her. Anyhow, dear, she should keep her own counsel!...Don't despair. It might be made worse. Think if we'd lived in Victorian times! Anyhow our friends won't despise us & we must find some way of making your mother reconciled. She is, after all, a reasonable person.

The anguished letters continued. Frank talked first to Peter Lucas and then to his mother about the marriage question. Agnes was 'not so averse' as Frank expected, but Peter counselled them to wait. Frank wrote Lettice with a 'definite proposal', which he immediately had second thoughts about.

Lettice was also of two minds. She had not been seeking a husband. Looking back on the events, she wrote:

> I was not in the least anxious to get married to anyone at that time. I was quite content to be on my own & I did not look on the men I met—even in phantasy—as possible husbands.

Moreover, if they were to marry, she felt there would have to be some agreements in place. One had to do with Frank's societies and dinners:

> Darling, we have a long way to go, you & I, before we are out of the wood. Don't imagine to yourself that marriage would settle all the difficulties. I should be even more of a strain as a wife. You would see much more of me, after all, I should want some attention. I shouldn't all at once be happy to let you go off to your old men every evening, or sleep in College most of the time!

But something 'much more fundamental' than dining with the old men at high table had to be 'tackled':

> Don't let yourself slide away... by thinking 'Oh it would be alright if we were married'. That's cowardly. And I recognize the same cowardice in myself. I feel that I want to solve all the problems too by getting married and at once. But try hard to dismiss the idea from my mind as it isn't a solution at any rate to my difficulties. You see, darling, I've just got out of 'Briary Bush'. I'm not going to walk straight into another. It's no use my giving up my freedom now that I've just won it, though I rather long to do so.... Nor could I cut myself off from Dick who has done a tremendous lot for us & really knows us inside out. I've hurt him a great deal already & he had retained his affection for me with absolutely no jealousy felt. He understands & knows about my love for you. Dick is my friend & I cannot go back on that. Anyhow at present you would be less prepared to let me spend time with him & possibly sleep with him occasionally, if we (you and I) were married, even though, as is the case, he makes absolutely no difference. All this I say prompted by reason & what I know of myself & you & because today you said again 'if we were married'— My emotions make me want to bind myself... to you at once with (ridiculous!) oaths and promises of everlasting fidelity & love. It suggests perfect bliss but my reason says this would be a cowardly & madly foolish course.

She was relieved to be extracting herself from the briary bush of a prospective marriage with her medical student, and she had other lovers, including their good friend Dick Pyke. Lettice was fully committed *by reason*, as well as desire, to the Bloomsbury idea that the bonds of love do not, and ought not, require sexual fidelity. If those bonds are strong enough, a relationship should have no problem accommodating others. She was not for settling into the monogamous marriage that Mrs. Ramsey wanted for her son.

They spent a day in London together, while Lettice was on her way back to Cambridge. It was a poor substitute for their holiday, and Frank was at first 'almost in a state of collapse with nervous worry and excitement'. They had to wait till the Easter vacation to finally get away. In the meantime, Frank remained concerned about his mother, and that someone at King's would discover his not-so-secret relationship with Lettice. This made the planning of the Easter vacation fraught. After failing to find friends who might go with them for cover, Frank wondered whether they should cancel. Lettice was steadier, and eventually, Frank simply lied to Agnes, saying that the party was larger than just the two of them. They travelled to Munich, where they purchased climbing boots (Frank having learned a lesson about proper mountain footwear), and made their way to the south of France. There they went off with rucksacks, finding inns as they walked. Frank's stressful term had resulted in bad skin and weight gain. There was a phrase in Cambridge: the new Fellow's stone—the 14 pounds a new don would pack on from dining in College. In Frank's case, it was the new Fellow's 3 stone. He now weighed 17 stone (240 lbs or 108 kilos), and each of his steps plunged him through the snow. Lettice was light enough to stay on top. The image is evocative of their emotional states at the time—Frank heavy with anxiety and the risks that came with their pre-marital liaison; Lettice skipping along the surface, resistant to the societal pressures and not terribly bothered by what people thought of her. Only after this trip did she tell her medical student definitively that she would not be marrying him.

Frank regained his health and vigour during this marvellous vacation. On their return, he was even more of the view that marriage was the only option for them, although the complexities of the situation made him toggle back and forth for a few weeks, changing his mind at lightning speed. There were anguished letters, written in the middle of sleepless nights, about what to do. Lettice began to worry that their relationship would be at a 'standstill' till they got married, and that became one of her 'chief reasons for wanting to marry now'. The stress of it all was affecting Frank's ability to work. That became another of his chief reasons for wanting to marry right away.

Finally, the question was settled. They would replace the gridlock with wedlock. But their marriage would not be a prison. It would be an open marriage. Frank told his parents of the first part of their decision. It was in the spring of 1924, after their Easter vacation:

> Dearest Mother,
> This is only to say that Lettice and I have decided to be engaged, but not necessarily to marry this summer.
> Love Frank
> I might come to lunch on Friday.

He went to Magdalene to tell Arthur, whose recollection of the discussion conveys a great deal about him:

> I remember how he came to my College room one morning early in the long vacation to tell me that he and Lettice wanted to be married in September and to discuss ways and means. He found me engaged in writing letters about rooms and lodgings to the parents of the freshmen coming up in October, a job that would not brook interruption. I told him that I must go on writing but, if he would sit down on the sofa and talk, I would undertake to listen to all he said and take my share in the conversation. So he did and I went on writing letters, addressing them, sealing them up and dropping them into a pile on the floor.

Michael thought the story was indeed 'rather like father'. Frank didn't expect any expression of emotion and, in Arthur's telling, Frank commented on how impressive it was that his father was able to divide his attention so well for the duration of the 90 minute conversation. He was probably relieved it went so peaceably.

Lettice was proved right about Agnes. She was a reasonable person. She immediately started to arrange a week in the Lake District. Agnes and Arthur drove Frank and Lettice up in their new (and first ever) car, joining Michael who was already there with a friend. Agnes did not, however, tell her husband that she suspected their son was sleeping with Lettice, as she still thought he 'would take a violent attitude'. Lettice later said that while Arthur and his side of the family were a 'rather inhibited, boring lot of people', and Arthur was particularly 'cramped', Agnes was the opposite. In Lettice's opinion, she was a splendid person—energetic, lively, and warm. She was 'worth twice' the value of Arthur. The two women became friends.

As A.C. Benson perceived, Arthur was a complex person. He cared intensely about his children, writing frequent letters to them when they were away. After Frank's death, he put together a loving scrapbook of his son's life. But he had a hard time expressing his emotions. His complexity can literally be seen on the pages in the scrapbook. He pasted in every letter he and Agnes had received from Frank, from the time he left for Sandroyd through to his many letters from Vienna. Then we find the above letter from Frank to Agnes announcing his intention to marry. What follows in the scrapbook are pictures of Frank as an infant and a boy, and then obituaries of him, with many blank pages left unpopulated. No pictures of Lettice, none of the two grandchildren who followed. It was as if Frank's life ended when he announced that he was to marry what Arthur suspected was an unsuitable woman.

The Stars Are as Small as Threepenny Bits

Despite their desire to marry quickly, the wedding took place not that summer, but a year later, in August 1925. In the months running up to the wedding, Ramsey was busy with work. In February, he presented to the brethren one of his most charming papers. He wrote it at speed, and left it untitled. The stated topic was what, if anything, can be the subject of meaningful debate. Its cheeky Apostolic style has led to misinterpretation. Braithwaite, as editor of the first volume of Ramsey's posthumously published essays, didn't help matters by slapping the title 'Epilogue' on it, and putting the paper at the end of the volume. That made it seem as if this paper was how Ramsey would have wanted to wrap up his whole body of work. But his most important ideas were still ahead of him in 1925, and this paper was an audacious talk to a group of insiders. Maria Carla Galavotti, when she published it in her collection of Ramsey's notes, gave it the title 'On There Being No Discussable Subject'. I will follow Galavotti, although it will be clear that the paper has a broader scope and that its meaning is not on its surface. It is in part a light-hearted jab at Wittgenstein, who had scorned the Apostles as having 'nothing to discuss'. More importantly, the paper is an attempt to address the question of happiness and the meaning of life, a topic at the front of Ramsey's mind as he started his new life with Lettice and settled in to his new job at King's.

Ramsey asks whether there is any subject the Apostles can discuss, and runs through various arguments for the conclusion that the group cannot discuss this, then that, then the next thing. He begins with the idea that 'we have really settled everything by realizing that there is nothing to know except science'. This is another implicit reference to Wittgenstein—in the *Tractatus*, he had delimited the scope of knowledge to the natural sciences. Ramsey says that since most of the Apostles are mere 'learners' when it comes to science, they can't even discuss that. All they can do is 'exchange information'. The same is true of history and politics, where the brethren are also not expert. He then turns to philosophy:

> this, too, has become too technical for the layman. Besides this disadvantage, the conclusion of the greatest modern philosopher is that there is no such subject as

philosophy; that it is an activity, not a doctrine; and that, instead of answering questions, it aims merely at curing headaches. It might be thought that, apart from this technical philosophy whose centre is logic, there was a sort of popular philosophy which dealt with such subjects as the relation of man to nature, and the meaning of morality. But any attempt to treat such topics seriously reduces them to questions either of science or of technical philosophy, or results more immediately in perceiving them to be nonsensical.

There go philosophy and ethics as subjects for discussion, courtesy of Wittgenstein. Either philosophy is meaningless, or it is reducible to science and logic, and thus too technical for the present company.

But is the situation really so dire for philosophy and ethics? Ramsey pauses on these topics, via a discussion of Russell, who had been presenting versions of a paper titled 'What I Believe' to various audiences, including the Apostles. The brethren also knew Russell's essay 'The Free Man's Worship', which presented a similarly depressing picture of the universe and the proper response to our place in it:

> [A]ll the labours of the ages, all the devotion, all the inspiration, all the noonday brightness of human genius, are destined to extinction in the vast death of the solar system, and...the whole temple of Man's achievement must inevitably be buried beneath the débris of a universe in ruins.... Only within the scaffolding of these truths, only on the firm foundation of unyielding despair, can the soul's habitation henceforth be safely built.

Ramsey notes that Russell is known for advancing an account of nature logically reducible to physics, physiology, and astronomy (as, roughly, did Wittgenstein and the Vienna Circle). He repeats that, on this picture, nature is discussable only by those with considerable technical expertise. All that might be left for discussion is 'the emphasis...laid on certain points, for instance, the disparity in physical size between stars and men'. Ramsey says he will return to this topic.

Russell was also presenting an account of value or ethics, which Ramsey tells us restricts questions of value to questions about human desires and how they might be satisfied. That makes ethics part of psychology. Ramsey then delivers a thought about Russell's position that has led commentators astray, making him seem on board with a position about ethics that is, in different ways, manifested by Russell, Ogden and Richards, Wittgenstein, and, later, the Vienna Circle. The famous passage is:

> Of course his main statement about value might be disputed, but most of us would agree that the objectivity of good was a thing we had settled and dismissed with the existence of God. Theology and Absolute Ethics are two famous subjects which we have realized to have no real objects.

It sounds like Ramsey is agreeing that since ethical statements can't be reduced to simple terms that correspond to objects in the world, they are either expressions of emotions (Ogden and Richards, and the Vienna Circle) or without sense (Wittgenstein). A.J. Ayer, R.M. Hare, and Alasdair MacIntyre thus take Ramsey to be one of the founders of emotivism in ethics. But Ramsey continues with his argument, and we must follow its winding course to see his real conclusion.

He turns to the subject matter of psychology. He says that most of the meetings of the Apostles deal with psychological questions. But the Apostles don't even try to discuss them in a scientific way. They merely compare their own experiences out of personal interest. Their arguments aren't real arguments—they are of the form where one person says 'I went to Grantchester this afternoon' and the other says 'No, I didn't', or someone says he would feel guilty if he were unfaithful and the other says *he* wouldn't feel guilty in the least. That's not really debating matters of psychology, it's just comparing notes about what one did this afternoon or how one feels about infidelity. Finally, Ramsey addresses the question of aesthetics and literature, which 'always excites us far more than anything else'. But here, too, there is a failure of real discussion: 'Our arguments are so feeble…what we really like doing is again to compare our experience', not getting into the psychological reasons why, for instance, 'certain combinations of colours give us such peculiar feelings'.

He sums up: 'there really is nothing to discuss'. The 'advance of science' and 'the decay of religion' 'have resulted in all the old general questions becoming either technical or ridiculous'. 'This process is the development of civilization which we have each of us to repeat in ourselves'. He says that while he had loved the Apostles' discussions when he started out at Cambridge, he now sees how they mostly just talk about themselves. And during his psychoanalysis, he learned that people don't know as much about themselves as they think.

This sounds rather like an indictment of the Apostles, along Wittgenstein's lines. But two months prior to reading 'On There Being No Discussable Subject', Ramsey had delivered his paper on sex from the point of view of society. It was a paper about the ethical consequences of the march of civilization, and its attendant repression of natural desires. Eight months after the paper on what can be discussed, he read 'Culture and Happiness' to the Apostles. It explored the same theme, trying to weigh the progress of society against the good of the individual who might not be able to keep up with it. In 'On There Being No Discussable Subject' he also talks about how the march of civilization is in tension with something—this time the discussion of science and other matters. Ramsey is far from making a straightforward claim that there is nothing to discuss. It seems that way only if we take the highest perspective—that of the collection of experts who know so much more than any individual. This is a variation of the tension that absorbed him in his two overt papers on civilization and the individual. In this third Apostles talk on the subject, he will resolve it in a new way.

The real point of the paper was still to come. Ramsey returned, as promised, to Russell's 'What I Believe'. He says that if he were to write such a *Weltanschauung* (a world-view) he would call it 'What I Feel', and if he were to quarrel with Russell's lecture, 'it would not be with what he believed but with…what he felt'. Now Ramsey gets down to his positive and interesting proposal. At first glance, it seems that one cannot quarrel with what another person feels. To do so either seems to begin another round of the 'I went to Grantchester'/'I didn't' routine, or, as Wittgenstein would have it, to try to talk about the ineffable. Wittgenstein's position in the *Tractatus* was that the world of the happy person is simply a different world to that of the sad person, with no discussion possible as to the merits of either world. It is to this debate that Ramsey makes an important contribution. His position is that one can in fact argue that one person's set of feelings or approach to life is better than another's.

Ramsey announces that he is going to conclude with some remarks about '*life* in general'. The conclusion is worth quoting at length. It tells us something important about Ramsey's approach to philosophy. Tilting at Kant, Russell, Wittgenstein and so many others who have come before him, he refuses to bend his philosophy to wonder. He prefers staying down to earth. It also tells us what Ramsey's state of mind was in February 1925, as he was coming to the decision to marry. It is also a poignant passage, since we know how Ramsey's world will end:

> Where I seem to differ from some of my friends is in attaching little importance to physical size. I don't feel the least humble before the vastness of the heavens. The stars may be large, but they cannot think or love; and these are qualities which impress me far more than size does. I take no credit for weighing nearly seventeen stone.
>
> My picture of the world is drawn in perspective, and not like a model to scale. The foreground is occupied by human beings and the stars are all as small as threepenny bits. I don't really believe in astronomy, except as a complicated description of part of the course of human and possibly animal sensation. I apply my perspective not merely to space but also to time. In time the world will cool and everything will die; but that is a long time off still, and its present value at compound discount is almost nothing. Nor is the present less valuable because the future will be blank. Humanity, which fills the foreground of my picture, I find interesting and on the whole admirable. I find, just now at least, the world a pleasant and exciting place. You may find it depressing; I am sorry for you, and you despise me. But I have reason and you have none; you would only have a reason for despising me if your feeling corresponded to the fact in a way mine didn't. But neither can correspond to the fact. The fact is not in itself good or bad;

it is just that it thrills me but depresses you. On the other hand, I pity you with reason, because it is pleasanter to be thrilled than to be depressed, and not merely pleasanter but better for all one's activities.

Of course, Ramsey really did believe in astronomy. His argument is something like the following. Those realist philosophers, such as Russell and Wittgenstein, who focus on whether a belief corresponds to objective facts in the world, are on the wrong track. Our feelings about the meaning of life can be evaluated, despite not corresponding to objective facts. They can be assessed in terms of whether they are more admirable or more conducive to a happy life. At the end of the last sentence in the passage quoted, he wrote and struck out 'which go more smoothly'. It is better to be optimistic than depressed, *as our activities will go more smoothly*. We can discuss or assess our feelings about the meaning of life, and ethics, in these terms—in terms of their impacts on human life and behaviour.

This view of the objectivity of questions about the meaning of life, and ethical questions more generally, is perfectly in line with Ramsey's view on beliefs arrived at by inductive inference. Recall that in his undergraduate papers, he treated induction as an indispensable form of reasoning for human beings, one that is justified because it leads us to successful action more than it leads us astray. Similarly, his point in 'On There Being No Discussable Subject' is that our fundamental attitudes toward life can be debated, justified, and criticized according to whether they promote or hinder human flourishing. This is how Ramsey can give reasons for his feelings about the meaning of life, and how he can give reasons for pitying Russell and Wittgenstein for their despair. We can deliberate about whether there is meaning in life, and, if so, what it consists in. We can ask, for instance: does the focus on the human angle rather than the astronomical angle result in a better life?

Ramsey's kind of objectivity for ethical matters is not the kind of objectivity that Moore was after—an objective good that we can somehow perceive.[†] Ramsey thought that Moore was after the kind of 'Absolute Ethics' which is like theology, a subject matter with no object. There is no God and there is no absolute good. Ramsey's reaction to the unavailability of that kind of objectivity is completely unlike Wittgenstein's position. To be sure, questions of ethics and the meaning of life cannot be answered with the kind of certainty that we might find in the primary language, which corresponds to objects in the world. But that does not mean there is nothing we can say. We can assess our ethical beliefs in terms of their

---

[†] Moore marked up pretty much everything in the Braithwaite volume of Ramsey's posthumously published papers, with two exceptions. One was a piece on pure mathematics. But the other, oddly, was this paper which addressed ethics and which was set against Moore's position.

effects. Ramsey's own assessment is that it is better to be an optimist, although, as with any matter, he might be wrong about that. It is an open question whether being 'thrilled' really is better for all of one's activities. All sorts of reasons will be in play, including ones that pull against him. Wittgenstein would argue that such optimism is a stupid optimism, not reverent enough about the weightiness of the problems we face.

There will also be debate about what counts as a good effect, and Ramsey was fully engaged in such discussions. His previous Apostles papers were serious examinations: of the duties of abstract thinkers to concretely improve the lot of others; of socialism and equality of income; and whether we should sacrifice our own progressive happiness for the greater good of a society that has not yet caught up to us. In 1928, his 'A Mathematical Theory of Saving' would launch a major discussion about intergenerational justice. And in his book, unfinished at his death, he was considering how to develop a theory of evaluation for ethics, and perhaps even aesthetics. He seems to have thought that there are principles about value that will lead to better outcomes—for instance, maximizing utility, social justice, and equality of income.

'A Mathematical Theory of Saving' would employ the term 'bliss' for the state in which savings would be unnecessary and all income would be devoted to consumption. In February 1925, Ramsey was in a different kind of state of bliss. Perhaps he was enjoying his new life a bit too much. The 17 stone he mentions in 'On There Being No Discussable Subject' is indicative of a kind of excess. But Ramsey was in full-life mode, getting as much from it as possible. Roy Harrod spoke of how his massive physique served to express his massive personality:

> He was of large build, his forehead was broad and his face intellectual, but simply drawn. His character too was simple: kind and good-hearted, natural and unaffected, he was not in the least degree spoilt by his precocity or the admiration of his seniors. He had a beautiful laugh, not loud or hearty, but sudden, genuine and convulsive; it sounded as if his huge frame was cracking under the strain of it.

That is as good a summary as any of Ramsey's character, which we find on full display in his paper on whether there is, after all, anything to discuss.

Freudian Theory

Also in February 1925, James Strachey wrote to his wife Alix about a new group in Cambridge, dedicated to the discussion of psychoanalysis. One requirement for membership was having been analysed:

They're starting a Ψα discussion society in Cambridge, consisting of Tansley, Lionel Penrose, Frank Ramsey, & a person at John's—some kind of science don who was analysed, I believe by Jones—called Harold Jeffreys. Rickman & I have been asked to join it also.

Ψα was a shorthand for psychoanalytic, and the group referred to it as the Psych An Society. Most of its members had significant experience and knowledge about Freudian practice and theory. Tansley, an old friend of Russell's, and one of the central figures in the new psychology, had been analysed by Freud himself. Freud also analysed James Strachey and John Rickman, both of whom were themselves practising psychoanalysts. Strachey and Rickman came down from London for the meetings, as did on occasion the two Glover psychoanalysts and Ernest Jones. Jones was at that point a close friend of Freud and the most internationally distinguished psychoanalyst in Britain. Jeffreys was a year into his analysis with Jones. Rickman made much of the group's being 'rigorous and rather select', rich not only with Freudian intelligentsia but also members of the Royal Society of London and those 'clearly headed in the same direction'.

Ramsey knew many of the members through his various Cambridge connections. He had been introduced to Rickman during his final Christmas holiday from Winchester, chatting to him not about Freud, but about his socialist and Quaker relief work in Russia. Tansley had been in Vienna during Ramsey's stay there. Ramsey had known Jeffreys, a mathematics fellow at St John's, since his undergraduate days, but mostly at a distance. Jeffreys had been working at the Meteorological Office and, until 1922, lived part time in London. He was a rugged northerner, a friend of Ogden's, and had been a fiancé of (and co-author with) Dorothy Wrinch, who had been responsible for getting the *Tractatus* published. But it was only now, through the Psych An Society, that they really got to know each other and discover a mutual interest in the philosophical foundations of induction and statistics.

The group met on Sunday nights. James Strachey would make a weekend of it, catching the Apostles' Saturday night meeting as well. Ramsey arranged for him (and Rickman) to stay at King's. On one typical occasion, Strachey arrived just in time to have dinner with Ramsey and Sprott on Saturday before the Apostles session. He breakfasted with Ramsey the next morning, met with the Psych An group all day till 11:00 that evening, and then breakfasted with Ramsey again the next morning, before catching his train back to London. Lettice was perhaps less than pleased, with all those old men at King's drawing away her husband's attention.

The first Psych An meeting was in Jeffreys's rooms on 2 March 1925, and at least once they met in Tansley's house in Grantchester. Coming back through the fields that evening, Ramsey helped Jeffreys by lifting his bicycle over all the gates in Grantchester Meadow. The conversation was serious, as Strachey recalled:

> A topic was taken at each meeting, announced beforehand, memoranda were some-times circulated; the theme was outlined before lunch, discussed casually in the after lunch walk, seriously tackled before, during and after tea and brought to a close usually before but sometimes after supper.

They didn't spend their time discussing their dreams or doing what Ramsey said the Apostles did—comparing their experiences. They were interested in psychoanalysis because their scientific curiosity extended to knowledge of the self. At the first meeting, Jeffreys spoke about how even socialists are resistant to the redistributive death duties, suggesting that the wish of the eldest son for his father's property was 'the modified expression of the childish wish for the mother'. Lionel Penrose gave talks about chess and the biological implications of the Pleasure–Pain principle. Susan Isaacs, the Freudian educational psychologist and head of the Malting House School, addressed them once. To add to the intellectual excitement, there was a scandal. Just as the group started to meet, Reik was sued by an American patient and barred from practising medicine. Freud publicly defended him. Ramsey read about the matter in the English papers and sought out back issues of the Austrian ones, to get additional information about the fate of his former analyst.

Ramsey was the least experienced in the group, having had just six months of analysis. He wasn't a regular attendee, perhaps because the meetings conflicted with those of the Heretics Society, perhaps because he simply wasn't as interested as the others. The group itself petered out after a year. For the handful of meetings he went to, however, Ramsey was an active participant. Strachey had a bright memory of a meeting in the middle of June:

> Yesterday there was a meeting of the Psych-An Society; and Rickman induced Frank to come to it. By a most curious chance it was by far the best meeting there's ever been: a paper was read by a curious friend of Rickman's—not a member—called Kapp ... He's ultimately some kind of foreigner (Jew) and by profession an optical engineer, I believe. But he evidently has immense knowledge of $\Psi\alpha$, of the most modern type, and produced a very clearly thought out & difficult paper on—heaven help me if I know what—something to do with Repression. My poor brain failed entirely. But Jones & the Glovers put up a very interesting discussion, which was just the right blend of the theoretical & clinical.—Frank was enthusiastic about it & said he thought it was the best discussion he'd ever heard at any such society & that not a single foolish remark had been made all the evening.

Kapp's paper, 'Sensation and Narcissism', was about how any check on the development of the ego is liable to result in the outbreak of morbid symptoms, as the ego seeks a new outlet.

Of all the members of the Psych An Society, it was Ramsey who most impressed Strachey:

> I was crushed by the unaccustomed intellectual level—especially of Ramsey. And it was rather like the third Act of Siegfried to hear the tone that he adopted about poor old Dr. Moore. He seemed on the whole to accept Ψα, but thought the theory very muddled. The theoretical work of the Prof's which he most admired was—Das Ich und das Es. He is thinking of devoting himself to laying down the foundations of Psychology. All I can say is that if he does *we* shan't understand 'em. He seems quite to contemplate, in his curious naif way, playing the Newton to Freud's Copernicus.

James wrote to Alix that Ramsey was also impressed with Freud's ('the Prof's') 'Instinct and its Vicissitudes', a paper on which Ramsey took careful notes. In it, Freud dealt with psychology 'in just the sort of "physics" way that Ramsey was recommending'. Ramsey thought psychology should be scientific—a theory that aims at 'laying down the foundations' and getting the facts about human motivation right.

A debate was raging at the time about whether Freud's theory was scientific enough, or even scientific at all. Tansley argued that it was, and that we should accept 'the essential body of Freud's doctrines as working hypotheses, without the help of which we cannot at present form a picture of many fundamental phenomena of the human mind'. Others argued that the evidence for Freud's theories was slim or even non-existent. Keynes put his oar in, pseudonymously, as 'Siela'. He wrote a letter to the *Nation and The Athenaeum*, describing Freud as 'one of the great disturbing, innovating geniuses of our age, that is to say as a sort of devil'. In Keynes's view, though Freud's theories would have to be drastically altered, they were nonetheless 'of great and permanent significance'.

Ramsey was of the same view. He saw Freud's theory of the mind, on which submerged desires find their outlet in dreams, neuroses, and unhappiness, as one that seemed to work in practice. It thus seemed to have some claim to truth as a scientific explanation of human behaviour. But he thought that the current stage of Freudianism was 'very muddled', and did not provide the best theory of the human mind. The competing theories seemed also to have some insight. The psychology that underpinned utilitarianism held that we desire to maximize our own pleasure or good, and it seems that sometimes we can figure out what is good, and try to maximize it. The new experimental psychology, which Lettice was engaged in, tried to find out what people actually desire. It was based on testing and measuring—as

Frances Marshall put it, galvanometers and 'sticking pins in yourself to see where you felt the heat'. It had some things in common with behaviourism, which requires an observable or operational definition of our mental states. In its extreme form, the theory says that mental states are identical to physical or behavioural states. Russell had been inclined towards a modest behaviourism in the 1920s and we shall see that Ramsey thought there was insight to be found here as well.

As was so typical of the way his mind worked, he didn't think that one theory had already nailed down the foundations of the human mind. He respected Freudian theory, without taking an obsequious attitude towards it. Just as he was a socialist who didn't believe in Marxist theory, he was interested in the study of human psychology without being an orthodox Freudian.

His friends knew that he wasn't fully signed up to Freud. A mere two months after psychoanalysis had cured him, James Strachey ran into Ramsey in a bookshop. Strachey reported his friend going on 'a long and violent tirade' about the 'active' technique, which had the analyst directly intervening in the patient's production of associations. He railed against English analysts, and said it was monstrous for an analysis to last more than six months. Strachey took him to have been 'simply hypnotized' by Reik. But this was an early sign that he was not buying Freudian theory wholesale. Kingsley Martin told this anecdote:

> I remember on one occasion Frank Ramsey rising in righteous wrath and roaring out: 'Don't worry whether what I have just said is due to my Oedipus complex or not. The question is whether it is *true*'.

Braithwaite said that Freud didn't influence Ramsey's philosophy at all. That's probably too strong a verdict. Ramsey thought that Freud made some real advances. One was the idea that the springs of human motivation often lie hidden in the subconscious and have to be brought into a light in which they can be seen and understood. Another was that fault lines run through a human psyche. Whether or not Freud described human motivation and these fault lines accurately, the mere highlighting of their existence provided a way of thinking and talking about the non-rational part of human desire and behaviour. That was a major step forward. But Ramsey's position was much like Keynes's. Psychoanalysis was a hypothesis to be tested and improved upon.

In the end, the psychological theory that Ramsey would take to be most promising was behaviourism. In 1928, his friend Roger Money-Kyrle published a paper titled 'The Psycho-Physical Apparatus: An Introduction to a Physical Interpretation of Psycho-analytic Theory' in the *British Journal of Medical Psychology*, in which he examined the idea that our subjective mental states have a corresponding brain state. Fifty years later, he republished it in his *Collected Papers*, and added a note: 'This paper is almost purely behaviouristic but I leave it in because Frank Ramsey liked it.' While the later Money-Kyrle might have found it too behaviouristic, it was far from 'purely' behaviourist. It argued that psychology and brain physiology are separate sciences, neither reducible to the other, and each throwing light on the other. That's why Frank Ramsey liked it. He would come to the view that the link between belief and behaviour was important, but complex.

Unlike many of the others in Psych An, Ramsey's interest in Freud was recent and not fully committed. There is nothing to suggest that he attended the Neurotics, a group which met in 1921 to discuss the new Freudianism. He remained sceptical of Lionel's propensity to talk about how the obsessional interest in tautology develops; or how the negation operator can be analysed in terms of repression; or how assertions, including those of the *Principia Mathematica*, are indicative of 'the aggressive, sadistic attitude towards external objects'. That was the stuff that had turned Lionel's brain to 'mush'.

But his own psychoanalysis had swiftly resolved his crippling anxiety about sex, and had enabled him to be in a happy relationship with a wonderful woman. During

Image 20 Harold Jeffreys and his bicycle.

the year that Psych An met, he was still anxious about things—his parents' acceptance of Lettice and whether the authorities at King's would find out that he was having premarital sex. However, these difficulties did not push him over any edge. They were within the realm of ordinary life. He would never again need medical help to solve his problems. Now his interest in psychoanalysis was scientific. Although Ramsey did not take on the rather ambitious project of laying down its foundations, he continued to think human psychology was an important domain of inquiry and that it was necessary (although probably not possible) for all of the rest of the sciences to come to a proper understanding of it.

Ψα, Utilitarianism, Feminism

Ramsey's approach to psychoanalytic theory is illuminated by the two papers he presented to the Apostles in which he utilized that theory. The first, read on 26 January 1924, imagined a conversation between himself and John Stuart Mill. They talked about the kind of 'mental crisis' both had had in their early twenties, crises to which young men, who had been hard-driven students in their early years, were prone. The paper was written before Ramsey was analysed and cured, but already he could see that his own crisis was only 'a mood', not 'a permanent depression'. This was obviously a highly personal essay.

In it, Ramsey criticized Mill's outdated associationist psychology in which continued exposure to an idea strengthens our belief and desires towards that idea. Psychology, he told Mill, had advanced since his day. He sympathized with the possibility that Mill would be put off by Freud's 'absurd metaphysics'. But he said that one mustn't forget that the Freudian is also a scientist, concerned with 'observing facts and inventing theories to fit them'. What the Freudians seem to observe is that our associations are formed early in life, and are not accessible to adult consciousness. We have to go deeper, with professional help, to the subconscious. Ramsey imagined that Mill would defend himself by saying that his psychology is like Newtonian mechanics, abandoned in favour of Einstein's, but so much easier to understand and still useful in ordinary life. Ramsey thought there might be something to that point.

He wholeheartedly agreed with Mill that happiness cannot be our direct aim in life. For only those who have their minds fixed on some object other than their own happiness can be happy: 'I do heartily agree that we must not too frequently ask ourselves or discuss with one another whether we are happy.' We must live 'spontaneously', only scrutinizing ourselves at infrequent intervals. Otherwise we run the danger of destroying our pleasure by immediately analysing it. Even after he had been cured by psychoanalysis, Ramsey would be wary of the constant self-scrutiny that Freudians seemed to require.

Ramsey's paper is not only of interest in understanding his approach to psychology, but also in understanding his relationship to utilitarianism. He took Mill to be advancing the theses that we are motivated to seek happiness and to avoid pain (that's utilitarian psychology), and the right thing to do in any circumstance is to maximize the greatest happiness for the greatest number (that's utilitarian ethics). He also took Mill to be adding the associationist idea that we must educate ourselves in a utilitarian direction, learning to associate pleasure with that which benefits the general whole, and pain with that which harms it. The associationist part of Mill's psychology might not have been in fashion, but the utilitarianism part certainly still had power. Utilitarianism dominated Cambridge, with Sidgwick as its recent local and prominent proponent. Even Moore advanced it, in chapter 5 of *Principia Ethica*. As Braithwaite put it, they were all disciples of Mill. Ramsey, especially, is thought by many to be as utilitarian as one can be.

Ramsey, however, took a step away from utilitarianism as a theory in this paper about Mill. He said to Mill, whether fairly or not: 'You put all your eggs in the same basket and to see a hole in it was a terrible shock.' He argued against 'single-minded devotion to the greatest happiness of the greatest number', on the grounds that single-minded devotion to any one value is wrong. The impulse, he said, explains why both Bolshevism and Christianity tend to produce 'fanatics' who are 'dangerous to their fellow-men'. Ramsey expressed a doubt that any great purpose—any one end—will withstand sustained questioning: 'I myself have been an enthusiast for the public welfare and for the discovery of mathematical truth, but neither of them lasted.' There is no ultimate, true end in life. To pursue such a thing is to be taken on a single track, certain to be a wrong track because of that very singularity.

On 24 November 1925, Ramsey read his second Freudian-tinged paper to the Apostles, 'Culture and Happiness'.[‡] In it, he revisited his argument in his sex from the point of view of society paper, delivered to the Apostles a year earlier. This time, the argument was put in 'Freudian language'—the language of instinct and its repression. Having finished his undergraduate degree, he 'took wings' at that meeting, after which he attended the Society less frequently and never again spoke from the hearthrug. In the sex and society paper, the question was whether the individual should suppress sexual desire for the sake of society. His mother's view, that free

[‡] As Forrester and Cameron note, Ramsey's paper is 'akin to Freud's *Civilization and its Discontents*, which had yet to be written'.

love was bad for women, loomed large in that paper. Ramsey's conclusion had been that he and his friends should sacrifice their desire for free sex for the good of society, although he was unsure about whether he could make the sacrifice himself. At that point, his life hadn't yet really started, as far as sex was concerned. Now he was in a passionate relationship, thanks to psychoanalysis.

'Culture and Happiness' explored Freud's idea that culture or civilization is an obstacle to happiness, which comes when we satisfy our instincts. Civilization results in cultivated desires and represses our infantile desires. This is why, as Ramsey put it, 'our pursuits so often seem not really worth while', as they seemed to him in 1924 and John Stuart Mill a century before. Reik had made a diagnosis of Ramsey in these terms. Ramsey's desire for philosophy was derived from a repressed infantile rivalry with his father and desire to kill him. He was therefore likely to identify 'someone like Wittgenstein' with his father and 'attach a most exaggerated importance to his every word'. In this paper, Ramsey accepted the Freudian framework and Reik's verdict.

Ramsey noted, as he had in the sex and society paper, that 'the kind of lives men lead changes much faster than do their instincts, which remain adapted to an earlier environment and become, so to say, out-of-date'. This raises the question of whether the burden of civilization—the guilt and repression that arises when we sublimate our instincts to education and culture—is bound to increase as society races ahead. Again in step with the earlier paper, he answered the question in the affirmative, with 'a general consideration of feminism'. For the burden of civilization, he asserted, 'has lately been and is still enormously increasing in the case of the female sex'. The position of women in England was especially bad, for the following reason:

> Englishmen are more homosexual, in a wide sense, than foreigners. I do not mean that they want to sleep with other men, but that their relations with men are more important to them than their relations with women.

Single-sex private education has led Englishmen, in Ramsey's account, to keep women away from their sporting fields, drawing rooms after dinner, and influential positions. He surmised that, because England was an outlier from Continental Europe in this respect, some of the most violent episodes in women's emancipation had occurred on home ground. This old system is slowly 'passing away', as civilization progresses. But he suggested that with emancipation and education, women's instincts for marriage and motherhood are sublimated, and they may become less happy. They will 'rival men in vocations for which they are, on the average, less fitted by nature'. They will decline to have sex with men, to marry, and to have children. Not only is this bad for women, but the English 'race' will be weakened.

These statements seem repugnant to us today. Margaret Paul, in her posthumously published account of her brother, takes this paper to be 'an attack on feminism'. But Ramsey's argument looks very different once we take seriously some important contextual matters, and carefully think through his argument. For one thing, in 'Culture and Happiness', Ramsey was explicitly employing a Freudian framework to make an argument he had made before. In 1925, Freud was arguing that women's nature was characterized by penis envy, rampant jealousy, self-loathing fueled by narcissism, and an emotion-driven lack of firm ethical principles. While Ramsey didn't adopt Freud's characterization of women, he did think women had a nature, and that it needed consideration. At the time, a debate was raging about the best kind of feminism to adopt. One camp advocated for equal wages and opportunities for women, the other argued that this was adopting male values and that women should 'stop looking at our problems through men's eyes'. The self-styled 'new feminists' argued that real equality meant preserving the natural differences between men and women and focusing on issues such as birth control and paying for the work of childcare, rather than on wage equality in the traditional job markets. Ramsey, far from attacking feminism, took a complex position between the two kinds of feminism then being debated.

Another piece of context that bears noting is that Ramsey's point that the emancipation of women will lead to fewer children being born into the English 'race' was a perfectly ordinary, and mild, one to make at the time. Social Darwinist explanations, now discredited, were then popular, as were those of its narrower cousin, eugenics. The former took the mechanisms of Darwin and applied them to social phenomena, while the latter focused on good stock for the progression of the race. When the Cambridge Eugenics Education Society was formed in 1911, Keynes was the treasurer, and the Cambridge welfare economist Pigou argued in the Report of the *Royal Commission on the Care and Control of the Feebleminded* that the costs of isolating the 'feebleminded' in institutions, where they could not reproduce, were well outweighed by the advantages to the quality of future society.

But the most important thing to consider in understanding Ramsey's position is that the *reason* he thought there was some merit to the conservative brand of feminism had entirely to do with the working class. In his paper on sex and society, he argued that, despite free love being good for his fellow Apostles and free-wheeling Bloomsbury friends, it was dangerous to women (and their children) in the 'lower classes'. For those women, monogamous and binding marriage served as a kind of trade union, offering protection from absconding husbands, and providing some economic security. His argument in 'Culture and Happiness' was also about feminism in 'general', not feminism for his friends. He had plenty of examples, close to hand, of women who were not 'average'—highly educated women perfectly suited to male-dominated professions and spheres of influence. There was his mother. There was Lettice. There were his Bloomsbury writer, artist, and psycho-analyst friends Vanessa Bell, Dora Carrington, Alix Strachey, and Virginia Woolf. There was Dorothea Morison, an economist of whom Frank thought highly and who would marry Richard Braithwaite. (Braithwaite himself was clear that he only heard thoroughly feminist talk from Ramsey.) There were the Girton College philosophers Dorothy Wrinch and Susan Stebbing. Like Keynes (and unlike Wittgenstein), Ramsey was enthusiastic about women's suffrage and the education of girls. He wrote to his mother in 1924 from Vienna after his sister Bridget had told him that their parents had sent the youngest, Margaret, to the Perse—a recently founded private school for girls. Even though it was quite a good school, Frank was apoplectic:

> for God's sake don't leave her long in that outrageous institution but send her somewhere where she'll learn something like the amount she's capable of. If she goes on like Gug [Bridget] it will be criminal of you.

He later taught Margaret geometry by offering her money to learn the equations. He wanted his sisters to be strong, smart, progressive women.

But this was not the lens he looked through in thinking about whether free love (the sex and society paper) or the sublimation of desire ('Culture and Happiness') was a good thing. The lens he chose was that of the impoverished working class. When he was a child, Ramsey had been taken by his mother to enough poorhouses and children's workhouses to know how precarious life could be for abandoned wives and children. When he was an undergraduate, he had been to enough trade union meetings to know that life was different on the other side of the economic and class divide. He married someone who helped poor children find a vocation. His second love would be a woman committed to eradicating slum housing and replacing it with something humane. Ramsey was not concerned, in these two papers, with his own elite group. He was concerned with women 'on the average', and right or wrong, he thought that they would suffer as civilization raced forward. In his paper on sex and society, he had argued that what is good for society might be in tension with sexual freedom and progress for some individuals. In this follow-up paper, he argued that what is good for some women (equal wages and opportunities) might be in tension with the happiness of most women.

In both papers, he expressed approval for progress. In the first, his approval took the form of saying that it was good that the moralizing force of religion was dying.

In 'Culture and Happiness', he asserted that the march of progress for women 'was bound to happen' and found that, despite its being bad for the race and for women, it 'to some extent, excites my imagination'. His conclusion is identical with that of the earlier paper:

> They [women] are taking upon themselves the burden of civilization and turning from sexual to intellectual activities which, though less satisfying, seem to me more excellent. We have here again, in opposition, culture and happiness, and what I really feel about that whole business is that I should like myself to be happy and other people to be ~~admirable~~ cultured.

He was arguing, in both talks, that feminism is progress, even if it makes most women unhappy until outdated social institutions and instincts catch up. The first presentation was planted in the soil of the economics of marriage, the other in Freudian concepts and terminology. Both argued that it's no good telling poor women who cannot free themselves of the bonds of their family, class, and nature that they should strike out on a radical path. Both probed the idea that perhaps people like him and his friends should wait until institutions and instincts caught up with progressive feminism. But he himself couldn't bear the sacrifice that seemed to be his duty.

The minutes of the second meeting record the impact of this year-long assault on his brethren. They read: 'Has Frank taughtoise?' Three (Thomson, Lucas, Ramsey) voted 'Yes', three (Keynes, Harmer, Watson) voted 'No'. Thomson's Yes was qualified by 'but to no porpoise'—that is, even those who accept Ramsey's argument (including Ramsey himself) won't change their behaviour.

He was a young man, trying to find his way in the sands of his psyche. He would not write such personal papers again. But concern for taking on topical and complex issues in ethics persisted. He would take them up in his 1927–28 papers on economics. And he would always show an impatience with philosophers who left the concrete world and thought about ethics only abstractly.

PART III

AN ASTONISHING HALF DECADE

11

SETTLING DOWN IN WORK
AND LIFE

Can Language and Logic Tell Us What There is in the World?

A t the same time as writing papers about happiness and the meaning of life, Ramsey was working on a technical paper in philosophy. It was an extension of some ideas of Wittgenstein's. He read it at the Moral Sciences Club's final meeting of the year, in May 1925. Unlike talks to the Apostles, which were often light of heart and weight, papers at the Moral Sciences Club were serious events. The Oxford philosopher H.H. Price wrote to Roy Harrod after a 1925 visit to Cambridge, giving a nice snapshot of the atmosphere:

> You'll be glad to hear that Dr. Moore got into one of his famous rages last Friday at the Moral Science Club. Your friend Miss Stebbing read a paper on Whitehead's theory of objects, which was really quite good. But in the discussion afterwards she was very stupid and pig-headed about objects and events....This drove Moore quite frantic. His cross-examination of her grew more & more ferocious, louder & louder, till at last he rose up, waved his arms about, and fairly roared out 'Oh Lord! If you can't see that!' He also climbed up on his chair and looked over the back of it, writhing about and contorting himself in the most extraordinary way, groaning and spluttering all the time....I must say, Miss Stebbing stood it very well....Her voice grew colder and colder and that was all.

Price didn't feel terribly sorry for Stebbing, since she 'herself tore Mr. Widgery to pieces in a heartless way the week before'.

When Ramsey's turn came, the meeting was held in his rooms at King's and the audience was large. Moore was in the chair. Ramsey's paper was about 'that great muddle the theory of universals', a topic Moore, Russell, and Johnson had wrestled with for decades. It was often put in terms of the question whether universal qualities, such as wisdom, are as real as particular individuals, such as Socrates. Russell, who provided the touchstone for Ramsey's paper, had argued that elementary facts include both particulars (objects that exist in space and time) and universals (properties that don't exist in space and time). We have seen that Ramsey rejected Russell's account of propositions as objectively existing entities. He now took on his theory of universals and particulars.

Because he was a new don, expectations were high, and Ramsey was concerned to meet them. At 2 am that night, after the event was over, he wrote an over-excited letter to Lettice. He was 'flattered' that so many people attended and thought the question and answer period afterwards a 'pleasant surprise'. The discussion

> was almost only with Moore who was very reasonable and intelligent, and seems to me to have improved a lot since I first knew him. I wasn't at all discomfited as I feared, and to one of my arguments against a theory of his he admitted he could see no answer. Whetnall asked a few questions, and Newman, Lionel and Wisdom made remarks, but they weren't tiresome. Towards 11 everyone departed except Moore, who stayed a little longer; I feel slightly in love with him. He is so frightfully nice. He asked for my paper for Mind to which I agreed. . . . I feel rather triumphant but also at a loose end; what shall I do without this paper to write? Answer: write a book. But I think it's so likely the whole thing's utter rot that it isn't a creditable thing to spend much time on. I do it very well according to the rules but it may be as futile as chess playing. (Though less bad for the temper as I do it better. I bite my nails when thinking about philosophy in just the same way as chess.) I am too excited to sleep. Discussing always has that effect.*

Moore might have had a reputation of having a go at others, but he was not inclined to attack Ramsey. As the editor of *Mind*, Moore exercised his executive authority on the spot and immediately bagged Ramsey's paper for the journal.

'Universals' is a gem in the history of analytic philosophy. Ramsey sets out and expands upon a position he discerned in Wittgenstein's work: that we cannot solve the question of universals and particulars by doing a priori metaphysics. I say 'discerned', because Wittgenstein was less than clear about the matter in the *Tractatus*. Indeed, a significant amount of text in Ramsey's 1923 Critical Notice is dedicated to showing that Wittgenstein was confused and conflicted on the issue of the structure of logical form. Was it subject–predicate in nature? Did it have to bottom out in particular, actually existing things?

Ramsey's argument in 'Universals' was that 'the whole theory of particulars and universals is due to mistaking for a fundamental characteristic of reality what is merely a characteristic of language'. Our language uses subject–predicate constructions, but we mustn't be misled by that accidental fact into thinking that the entities in the world must be of two distinct types: particulars and universals. We cannot read an ontology (the nature of the world) off of our language. For a proposition can be broken down in different ways, each depending on our 'interest' and each preserving meaning. Breaking down a proposition in three different ways would

---

* The 'Wisdom' is John Wisdom, a Moral Sciences student, contemporaneous with Ramsey. He would later become a Fellow at Trinity and a Wittgensteinian. Despite Wisdom being a regular at the Heretics Society, Ramsey seems to have been uninterested in him.

result, on the muddled theory of universals and particulars, in 'an incomprehensible trinity, as senseless as that of theology'.

If we cannot read the universal/particular distinction off ordinary language, Ramsey continued, then we are no more justified in reading it off our logic. On Russell's theory of the proposition (derived from Frege), what 'holds together' the various elements of the proposition, so to speak, is that predicates are incomplete symbols; similarly, the universals they denote are incomplete objects. But the symbolism of *Principia Mathematica*, Ramsey argued, doesn't tell us anything about the world. Russell grounds the distinction of universals and particulars not on an objective but on a subjective property—the mathematician's purposes. Ramsey argued that we needn't adopt the perspective of the mathematician. Philosophers might well have other purposes, and then they 'would invent a symbolism which was completely symmetrical as regards individuals and qualities'. Ramsey concluded that the distinction is grounded 'on human interests and needs'. Bringing human interests to metaphysics was a radical proposal in the Cambridge of Russell and Moore, as it had a trace of the kind of pragmatism of which they were so suspicious.

Ramsey anticipated a possible retort from Russell: we can ground the distinction between universals and particulars in a distinction between forms of atomic propositions. Ramsey registered his agreement with Wittgenstein that 'The truth is that we know and can know nothing whatever about the forms of atomic propositions'.

UNIVERSALS AND PROPOSITIONAL FUNCTIONS

Peter Sullivan, Professor of Philosophy, University of Stirling

In 'Universals' Ramsey challenges the presumption that 'there is a fundamental division of objects into two classes, particulars and universals'. By 'objects' he means the simple entities spoken of in basic statements. He straightaway puts aside as irrelevant to his concerns distinctions that might be proposed on 'physical' grounds (e.g. that a particular exists only at one place at a given time) or in relation to cognition (e.g. that a particular is an object of perception, a universal an object of thought). Ramsey's concern is whether there is a 'logical' basis for the distinction, one grounded in the different ways terms for particulars and universals function in basic statements.

One such ground that has been proposed is the contrast between two basic functions that must be performed in making any statement: one must *identify* what thing the statement concerns, and also *characterize* that thing as being one way rather than another; thus it is said, e.g., that in 'Socrates is wise' the name 'Socrates' identifies the person concerned, while the adjective 'wise' serves to characterize him. Against this proposal

Ramsey contends that identifying and characterizing are not *distinct* functions, to be parcelled out to different elements of a statement, but *connected* functions performed by every element of a statement: to characterize something *is* to identify a respect in which it is similar to others; to identify something as that which a statement concerns *is* to discern some common characteristic that statement shares with others. Ramsey's way of making this point is distinctive. He observes that the grammatical roles often associated with these supposedly distinct functions in statement-making can be trivially reversed: 'Socrates is wise' becomes 'Wisdom is a characteristic of Socrates' without altering what is said. But the point itself is not distinctively his. In different ways and in different terms Kant, his German and then British idealist successors, Frege (in his 'context principle'), and lately Evans (in his 'generality constraint') have all insisted that *any* element of discursive thought marks a point of identity amongst distinct thoughts; *every* concept is a 'one-over-many'. Accordingly Ramsey spends little time on this first point.

Ramsey's distinctive contribution is to separate the notion of generality involved in this first point from another, which is still too often confused with it. Frege, and in 1918 Russell, recognized that the kind of predicate to which a quantifier is attached in framing a generalization—as the quantifier '∀x' is attached to the predicate 'Philosopher (x) → Wise (x)' to form '∀x (Philosopher (x) → Wise (x))', or 'Every philosopher is wise' – has a special 'incompleteness': it cannot be recast as a self-standing term, nor can its meaning be counted an object. (Russell's paradox is enough to force this recognition, though as merely a symptom it is not itself enough to explain it.) Because an apparently simple predicate can also be used to frame a generalization, e.g. 'Everyone is wise', and because the role of 'wise' in that construction is not obviously different from its role in the singular 'Socrates is wise', the incompleteness of logically complex predicates—'propositional functions' in Ramsey's terminology—has been transferred to the simple adjectival or predicative terms occurring in such basic statements. The transference results in the notion of a kind of basic entity manifesting the special incompleteness of propositional functions, a *universal*. It is by being thus 'incomplete', it is then said, that the universal wisdom, or the simple adjective 'wise', serves as a 'one-over-many'.

Thus presented it is plain that this transference, and the notion of a universal it generates, is simply a 'muddle': it purports to explain as the special feature of just one kind of element in basic statements what is in fact a feature of every element. Ramsey's achievement in 'Universals' is to unpick this muddle, to explain the role of propositional functions in a way that distinguishes them clearly from any element in a basic statement, and thus to display the confusion in transferring the characteristic feature of the first to the second. Unfortunately—and no doubt partly because his essay was something of a rushed job, and not clearly structured so as to highlight its central arguments—his achievement is not widely recognized. Much contemporary work in philosophical logic and ontology perpetuates the muddle he exposed.

One might well ask why Ramsey didn't explicitly mention Frege as a target, alongside Russell. In the term he read 'Universals' to the Moral Sciences Club, he was teaching Frege in his Foundations of Mathematics course. But Frege hardly gets a mention in Ramsey's writings, and when he tells his diary that he is reading Frege, he is never specific about what he's reading or what he thinks about it. The answer may be as simple as this: Wittgenstein and Russell represented for Ramsey the modernization of Frege, and it was that newer position that he wanted to engage. Nonetheless, his silence about Frege remains a bit of a mystery.

A year after the Moral Sciences Club presentation, there was a symposium on 'Universals and the "Method of Analysis"' at the Joint Session of the Mind and Aristotelian societies—a major fixture on the philosophical calendar. Ramsey's 'Universals', which was published in *Mind* in 1925, was the basis of it. Ramsey was joined on the panel by Braithwaite and the Oxford philosopher and logician H.W.B. Joseph, and the contributions were published in the *Proceedings of the Aristotelian Society* in July 1926. Ramsey presented a position that was a little less strenuous than the one in 'Universals', stating that he was now doubtful about his assertion that we can't discover anything at all about atomic propositions. The discussion attracted considerable attention amongst the students in Cambridge. Joseph had initially demurred when Moore invited him to participate, saying that he was not competent in the language of Ramsey's paper, and began on the day by suggesting that he was unsure just what Ramsey's argument amounted to. In his reply, Ramsey agreed that Joseph had not understood him.

Ramsey would eventually distance himself from the logical atomist position which he built upon in 'Universals'. In 1925, when writing that paper, he was still trying to work his way through the implications of the *Tractatus* in a way that was amenable to Wittgenstein's project, not antithetical to it. But he never abandoned the rejection of a priori metaphysics that was so essential to 'Universals'. He always was more interested in finding out what is actually in the world than in surmising what must be in the world.

A Brief and Discordant Visit from Wittgenstein

Soon after Frank read 'Universals' to the Moral Sciences Club, he had to start thinking about his wedding, which was to take place on 21 August 1925 at Marylebone registry office in London. But Wittgenstein was coming to England for a long-negotiated stay, and Frank had to meet this commitment as well.

Frank had attempted, during his six months in Austria, to convince Wittgenstein to return to Cambridge and to his work in philosophy and logic. Wittgenstein contemplated at least a visit and had asked Frank to speak to Keynes about the conditions under which that could come about. He wanted assurances that Keynes would spend sustained time with him. Just as he had been in 1923, Keynes was wary of committing to too much, lest the burden become excessive. Frank had written Keynes from Vienna, relaying the message that Wittgenstein would like to stay with him at his country house:

> Russell he could no longer talk to, Moore he had some misunderstanding with, and there really only remain you and Hardy, and perhaps Johnson whom he would just like to see, but obviously they wouldn't get on.

A letter from Keynes to Wittgenstein at the end of December 1924 gives a good idea of the kind of mollifications that were required:

> I think that what you said is true. It is true that it would be no good on either side to meet in Cambridge casually. The only satisfactory way would be, if the conditions were such that conversation was unnecessary unless desired;—as for example, if you were to stay with me in the country when I was working (I generally take a house in August and September). Then perhaps you could work too,—and at any rate be just as morose as you might feel inclined, without upsetting anybody. Perhaps sometime under such conditions you will come?

The following July, Wittgenstein's mind was still not quite made up. His friend William Eccles was also pressing him to visit England. Wittgenstein wrote to Keynes, asking for further assurances about the invitation:

> Some weeks ago I got a letter from a friend of mine in Manchester inviting me to stay with him some time during my holidays. Now I'm not yet quite decided about whether I shall come or not but I should rather like to, if I could also see *you* during my stay (about the middle of August). Now please let me know FRANKLY if you have the slightest wish to see me. If you give me a negative answer I shan't mind in the least. Please write to me as soon as possible, as my holidays are rather short and I shall hardly have time enough to arrange for my journey.

Keynes replied positively and sent him some funds for his travel expenses.

Their efforts finally bore fruit—albeit bitter fruit—in August 1925. Wittgenstein happened to arrive two weeks after Keynes was married and three days before Frank's wedding. Lettice was returning from Ireland, and Frank had been organizing the ceremony, the honeymoon, and the renovations for their new flat. He was also dealing with how much to pay Lettice's landlady for the late notice of vacancy, and receiving and taking stock of a stream of gifts. He described himself to Lettice as insomniac and 'overdone' from the preparations and from missing her. Frank went to Sussex for the reunion with Wittgenstein while Lettice was en route back to Cambridge.

Keynes invited Braithwaite for the weekend, but he was unable to come. So Keynes asked his brother Geoffrey and his wife to join them to 'cushion' Wittgenstein's presence.

Virginia and Leonard Woolf stopped by. Bloomsbury—and Vanessa Bell especially—thought Lydia Lopokova, Keynes's new wife, was an uneducated chatterbox. The day before Wittgenstein arrived, Virginia had fainted at a party held at Charleston—a celebration of the Keynes's wedding and the birthday of Vanessa and Clive Bell's son Quentin. Things were already mighty tense without stirring Wittgenstein into the mix.

Frank could only join the gathering from Tuesday, the day of Wittgenstein's arrival, to Thursday. At first, everything was fine—in fact, better than fine. Frank wrote to Lettice:

> Here I am more taken out of myself by interesting conversation. I got here at tea time yesterday, and went for a long walk with Keynes and Wittgenstein and had a very good dinner.

But soon things deteriorated. The rain bucketed down, pinning them indoors. Wittgenstein resented the cushioning presence of Keynes's relations and neighbours and the fact that Keynes and Frank were distracted by other events in their lives. He made Lydia burst into tears by glaring at her and asking 'What do you mean?' when she remarked that a tree was beautiful. Frank wrote to Lettice that he got 'slightly heated because W said that Freud was morally deficient though very clever'.

Wittgenstein, however, was more than slightly heated. He would refuse to speak to Frank for four years. It wasn't the first time he gave the silent treatment to one of his friends, and it wouldn't be the last.[†] As Lettice put it later, he made 'a moral issue out of absolutely everything'. Frank was more weary than angry. Keynes had to go for a day's business in London, and Frank wondered to Lettice how he could possibly keep Wittgenstein entertained:

> How I shall amuse W I can't think because he is almost incapable of doesn't much like any but the most serious conversation, which tends to lead to such violent disagreement as to make it impossible. Also he doesn't like reading, being too lazy ever to try to understand a book but only occasionally using one as a text for his own reflections. He whistles marvellously.

Frank was right to be concerned. Wittgenstein's charming habit of whistling complex operas wasn't enough to keep the visit on the rails.

The moral issue Wittgenstein made on this occasion was certainly partly about Freud, as Frank reported. Wittgenstein was interested in the interpretation of dreams, and he thought that Freud was one of the few people who 'had something

---

[†] Once, on holiday with Wittgenstein, his dear friend David Pinsent attracted this punishment. His transgression was to take a touristy photo, putting Wittgenstein in a 'silent and sulky fit'.

to say'. But he was not so positive about other aspects of Freud. In a diary entry written three months after Ramsey's death, Wittgenstein revisited their quarrel and reiterated his view of Freud:

> Freud surely errs very frequently & as far as his character is concerned is probably a swine or something similar, but in what he says there is a great deal. And the same is true of me. There is a lot in what I say.

Frank, on the other hand, thought Freud a force for the good in finding the submerged levers with which to release a patient's problems. He had come through a long stretch in which he had terrible anxiety about sex, and been cured by one of Freud's students. Since he last saw Wittgenstein, his newfound freedom had resulted in a passionate relationship, and was about to culminate in an open marriage. He would have updated Wittgenstein at least on some of this. He may have said too much and incurred a second kind of moral censoriousness, not so much about Freud's character, but his own.

It is hard to tell much about Wittgenstein's sex life, except that he took the issue of sex so seriously that it disturbed him a great deal to talk about it. He might well have had some relationships with young men, and he was clearly smitten with at least one woman. One thing we know is that he thought marriage was sacred and not to be taken lightly. Part of this was religious—if you want to respect God, you need to respect his creatures. It would be to Lettice, in 1929, that he would confide his views on the sanctity of marriage. He would become very fond of her—one of the few close relationships he had with a woman. But at the time of this famous quarrel, Wittgenstein hadn't met her, and one suspects that the full force of his moralizing came crashing down on the head of Frank. If Frank told Wittgenstein that he was getting married partly out of fear of getting caught having pre-marital sex, that would have been more than enough to incur Wittgenstein's judgment that he was not respectful enough about marriage. But almost anything he said about that part of his life would have done the trick.

Another factor in the quarrel, unrelated to Freud, may have been that Frank was now less tolerant of being lectured at by Wittgenstein. Recall that while visiting Wittgenstein in Puchberg in 1924, Frank complained that if he suggested a question to Wittgenstein, he wouldn't listen to Frank's answer but started thinking of one himself. Frank had ceased to listen passively to Wittgenstein's answers, and the resulting 'violent disagreements' about serious matters were unsurprising.

Such a requirement for deference from younger scholars was not untypical of continental European academics, and Wittgenstein was part Continental in his temperament. Here is Ina Carnap, in 1960, writing to Peter Hempel, about a young colleague:

> I rather like him, an intelligent and modest man with a reverence and admiration for Carnap, which I find very agreeable. It has become somewhat rare, here quite young boys, Montague for instance, in the department, deem themselves a bit too equal for my taste. In general, this admiration one can still find in some of the foreigners: we had some Poles here who quite warmed my heart in that respect (with their respect).

Carnap and Hempel, two of the kindest, warmest members of the Vienna Circle movement, had been partially Americanized by this time, and may well not have shared Ina's ideas. But during Frank's time, they, along with Schlick, expected deference to Herr-Doktor-Professors. Perhaps this attitude was part of Wittgenstein's anger with Frank, although he at this time had no degree, never mind a professorship. For Frank, like the logician Richard Montague (who was thirty years old in 1960), had little by way of reverence, for heavenly or human gods. After the first flush of undergraduate awe for Wittgenstein, that emotion started to recede. He now considered himself pretty much equal to Wittgenstein (and more than equal to members of the Vienna Circle). He was always polite, but never deferential.

Frank left the gathering the day after the heated words with Wittgenstein, in order to make it to the registry office on Friday. There was little pomp and ceremony. Lettice said that Frank wouldn't have dreamt of being married in a church. She asked Frances Marshall to arrange the lunch party afterwards: 'Somewhere in Soho. Drink is essential.' Rather than a lunch party, Lettice's uncle, an eminent surgeon at Guy's Hospital, threw a reception for them at his house in Devonshire Place. Presumably there was drink. Lionel Penrose invented and made them a machine for solving quadratic equations as a wedding present. Frank's first teacher, Miss Sharpley, sent them an anthology of English verse that she'd compiled. They escaped on a walking holiday in the French and Italian Alps, after starting, as was the English post-wedding custom, with a night in a hotel in Dover. Frank brought his work along—no books, just 'various problems' he wanted to 'think out'.

He had not done as much work as he would have liked over the last year, what with the roil of emotion, and the toil of teaching and preparing their flat. He was keen to get on with it, and he was too busy to think much about the quarrel with his friend. But two years later, Wittgenstein was still refusing to engage in any direct communication. The story is interesting both as an illustration of how Frank was conciliatory in the non-intellectual parts of his life, and also as a window into the relations between Frank, Wittgenstein, and the Vienna Circle.

On 20 June 1927, Wittgenstein, Carnap, and Waismann met with Schlick at his house in Vienna. They discussed Ramsey's recently published 'The Foundations of Mathematics'. During the meeting, Wittgenstein registered an objection to the account of identity in Ramsey's paper. It was the first time Carnap met Wittgenstein, and he wrote in his diary afterwards that Wittgenstein was very interesting and original. But Carnap thought Wittgenstein's objections to Ramsey took the shape of Wittgenstein registering a rapid or impulsive position and then trying to find arguments for that assessment. One week later, on the 27th, they all met again, this time at Carnap's house. At this meeting, Wittgenstein dictated a letter to Schlick, for delivery to Ramsey. Carnap typed it up later that evening. Wittgenstein then wrote the opening and closing paragraphs by hand, and made revisions to the text he had dictated. He addressed it with a chilly 'Dear Mr. Ramsey' and asked Mr. Ramsey to send a response to the logical point not directly to him, but via Schlick.

Frank considered not following the instructions to write only to Schlick. It seemed ridiculous to him. He wrote two draft replies to Wittgenstein himself, apologizing for writing directly to him, and not to Schlick. He offered the rationale that Schlick 'won't know whether my answer is any good'. Schlick's 1918 *Allgemeine Erkenntnislehre (The General Theory of Knowledge)*, Ramsey said, contained some 'sad rubbish', although he was willing to consider the possibility that 'he may have got cleverer since then'. He also apologized for not having sent Wittgenstein a copy of 'The Foundations of Mathematics', citing this as the reason: 'because you were so annoyed with me when we were at Keynes's and I didn't think the paper would interest you much'.

In the end, he obeyed the instruction and sent his reply via Schlick. He tried to explain the awkward situation, but it's clear that he didn't know quite what to make of it himself:

> Dear Professor Schlick, . . .
>
> I had a letter the other day from Mr. Wittgenstein criticizing my paper 'The Foundations of Mathematics' and suggesting that I should answer not to him but to you. I should perhaps explain what you may have gathered from him, that last time we met we didn't part on very friendly terms, at least I thought he was very annoyed with me (for reasons not connected with logic), so that I did not even venture to send him a copy of my paper. I now hope very much that I have exaggerated this, and that he may perhaps be willing to discuss various questions about which I should like to consult him. But from the tone of his letter and the fact that he gave no address I am inclined to doubt it.

Wittgenstein's force of character enabled him to behave outrageously while often retaining the loyalty of the aggrieved. Frank was especially well-equipped to ride out his silence, having learnt how to keep his composure in the face of his father's sour periods. Wittgenstein's nephew Tommy, who knew the personalities of both his uncle and his former tutor, thought that while Frank had 'corners against which you could bump', no one could ever stay hurt or angry at him, as he was so likeable—'the most natural, good-natured, kind-hearted person you can imagine'. Frank remained polite, and in the end, Wittgenstein would relent.

Scholars have found the debate between Wittgenstein and Ramsey on identity difficult to reconstruct. In 'The Foundations of Mathematics', Ramsey had tried to improve upon Russell's *Principia Mathematica* by aligning it with the *Tractatus*. In that very specific context, he thought that Wittgenstein's account of identity ('a = b') was inadequate. Wittgenstein took an identity statement to be part of mathematics, and hence to consist of 'equations' and 'therefore pseudo-propositions', and he thought that the symbol '=' could be eliminated from logic without loss. Ramsey thought that identity statements were true, but trivially so—they were tautologies.

WITTGENSTEIN AND RAMSEY ON IDENTITY

Markus Säbel, Department of Philosophy, Humboldt University

Ramsey was one of few of Wittgenstein's contemporaries to seriously engage with one of the central logical doctrines in the *Tractatus*: the elimination of the identity sign. He saw that in the Tractarian framework the question of how to deal with identity boiled down to a dilemma between either accepting identity statements as atomic propositions or construing them as truth-functions of such. He argued that the first option was not available: when 'a' and 'b' are names of the same thing, the proposition a = b 'says nothing'; when they are names of different things, 'it is absurd'. The second option was taken in *Principia*, where identity was defined as indiscernibility with respect to predicative functions. But since any atomic predicate can be true or false of any object it can meaningfully be predicated of, there is nothing contradictory about two objects a and b sharing all their basic properties. Both Wittgenstein and Ramsey concluded that identity was not a propositional function at all but at best a metalinguistic device to express sameness of meaning.

One of the defects Ramsey saw in *Principia* was its failure to provide an extensional theory of classes. This problem was only exacerbated if one then tried to eliminate identity. Under the 'no-class theory', for any class to exist there needed to be a propositional function defining that class. But given two arbitrary objects a and b the only way to guarantee the existence of a defining function was to admit the function $\hat{x} = a \lor \hat{x} = b$. So unlike Wittgenstein, who had rejected logicism, Ramsey had to find some substitute for identity. His intriguing solution was the introduction of 'propositional functions in extension', which are arbitrary correlations between objects and

---

propositions. Using these functions (as indicated by a subscript 'e'), Ramsey proposed the formula $(\varphi_e).\varphi_e x \equiv \varphi_e y$ as a definition of x=y. (In the following I abbreviate this expression to Q(x,y).

Ramsey then argued that if 'x' and 'y' have the same meaning, Q(x,y) will be a product of expressions of the form $p \equiv p$, and so a tautology. If 'x' and 'y' have different meanings, there will be some function f_e in the range of φ_e such that $f_e x$ expresses some proposition p and $f_e y$ the negation of that proposition ¬p, so the product will be a contradiction. As Ramsey saw it, the behavior of Q therefore mirrored the behavior of identity in that Q(x,y) will be true (a tautology) if 'x' and 'y' refer to the same object, and false (a contradiction) if not. Ramsey concluded that Q could be used instead of identity to define classes, for example the class {a, b} by the function $Q(\hat{x}, a) \vee Q(\hat{x}, b)$. At the same time, the definition escapes Wittgenstein's objection against Russell's definition, because for two objects x and y, $(\varphi).\varphi x \equiv \varphi y$ (with ordinary functions) remains non-contradictory as required.

Some time in 1927, a copy of Ramsey's paper was transmitted to Wittgenstein by Schlick, prompting an incisive letter criticizing Ramsey's definition.[‡] In a nutshell, Wittgenstein's main contention in the letter is that Q(x,y) 'cannot be substituted for x = y'. Wittgenstein held that in order for any proposition to have sense, its negation couldn't be nonsensical. Consider now the case where 'a' and 'b' have different meanings. Wittgenstein grants that on this assumption there will be a 'critical function' such that $f_e a$ is p and $f_e b$ is ¬p. But is Q(a,b) really, as Ramsey has it, a contradiction? Q(a,b), with Q being offered as a definition of identity, should license the substitution of 'a' for 'b' in all contexts. Now if we substitute 'a' for 'b' in the critical function, we get not one but two senses for $f_e a$: p and ¬p. But by the lights of the *Tractatus*, a propositional sign that fails to have a definite sense is not a propositional sign at all, but simply nonsense. So Q(a,b) is not contradictory, but nonsensical.

Ramsey's initial response to this criticism was defiant, arguing that he didn't offer Q as a definition of identity but merely as 'an adequate substitute for x=y as an element in logical notation'. Ramsey was soon to grow doubtful about his logicist approach, although it's not clear that the exchange with Wittgenstein had much to do with it. Wittgenstein, for his part, kept returning to Ramsey's definition, trying out new arguments even after Ramsey's death.

Marriage, Their Way

Frank and Lettice settled into their version of married life. They rented one of Ogden's flats in the centre of town: Hoop Chambers on Bridge Street. On the ground floor was King and Harper's Garage, and every midnight, until they were

[‡] This letter seems to constitute Wittgenstein's first piece of philosophical writing after publication of the *Tractatus*, underscoring the role Ramsey played in bringing him back to philosophy.

used to it, they were woken by the great clutter of iron shutters being let down. Their new home was on two floors, with a nice sitting room. Lettice took care of the decoration and furnishing, given Frank's obliviousness to matters of style.

Lettice thought herself lucky that Hoop Chambers was hard to find, accessible only through a passageway in a side street. For the custom was that other don's wives stopped by unannounced. If they called and you were in, you had to invite them to tea. If you were out, they left a visiting card, and then you were required to go see them. Lettice hated these teas, not the least because they required that she 'actually put on a hat'. The whole business was terribly formal and conventional, as is illustrated by a story Dorothy Richards told of the college Fellows discussing in a committee meeting (!) what to do about Keynes's recent marriage to Lydia. One of them asserted that none of their wives would want to call on a woman 'of that kind', the problem having somehow to do with Keynes's well-known (and it seems, former) homosexuality. Another Fellow stood up and stormed out of the meeting saying 'And probably she wouldn't want to see them!'

Lettice and her new husband were perfectly suited to each other in being inclined to defy people's opinions of what their conduct and appearance should be. Lettice said Frank was 'very untidy', not caring 'a hoot about what he wore or what he looked like', and recalled someone saying 'why does Frank Ramsey always look so dirty and his wife looks like she has been pulled through a hedge backwards?' Philip Hall said that Frank sometimes looked as if he had crawled out of a dustbin. Lettice sewed her own clothes, some of them 'rather outlandish'.

They also, as agreed, defied convention in sexual matters. Here, unlike with their dress sense, they were in step with their friends. Affairs ran wild between the members of the extended Bloomsbury and Apostles circles. Some were heterosexual, some homosexual, and others not so easily classifiable. Alix Strachey was inclined to dress as a man. Frances Marshall was the lover of Ralph Partridge, who was married to Dora Carrington, who was in love with the resolutely homosexual Lytton Strachey, who had a passion for Ralph. Only after Strachey's death and Carrington's ensuing suicide were Frances and Ralph married (in 1933). Each had additional relationships outside their respective primary bonds. This privileged group was permitted to rebel as they pleased, as long as they didn't come too much to the notice of easily offended Cambridge colleges' sensibilities (or the law, in the case of homosexuals). They had to keep quiet in the college dining halls, or risk what Dora Russell called 'disastrous consequences'. But amongst themselves, they discussed their sexual adventures and were unabashed about taking pictures of naked outdoors frolicking.

Image 21 J.M. Keynes and Lydia Lopokova.

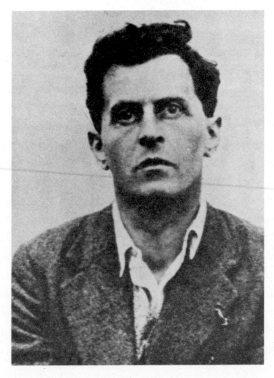

Image 22 Ludwig Wittgenstein, 1929.

Like Lettice, they often expressly articulated the moral principles that governed their behaviour. Bertrand Russell made his arguments for free love in print in his 1929 *Marriage and Morals*. Dora Russell put it this way: 'Bloomsbury people did get married, but it was part of the code to regard this as not very important in sexual ethics and certainly that was basic in my own code of conduct.' Here is Rupert Brooke to his then-lover, Phyllis Gardner, on his 'unconventional emotional life':

> There are two ways of loving: the normal and the wandering. Different kinds of character are drawn to each. The normal is to love and marry one person, and only him. The wandering is to take what one wants where one finds it, to be friends here, lovers there, married there, to spend one day with some, a week with others,—possibly a lifetime with others.

And here is George Mallory, the mountaineer, writing to Lytton Strachey in 1914, regarding Mallory's impending marriage:

> It can hardly be a shock to you that I desert the ranks of the fashionable homosexualists (and yet I am still in part of that persuasion) unless you think I have turned monogamist. But you may be assured that this last catastrophe has not happened.... This sentiment shocks me deeply—considering that I really am to be tied by the conjugal knot & actually to be blessed by the Church of England: but then the truth always is so shocking and probably nobody is monogamous.

Frank and Lettice also thought that probably nobody is monogamous, and lived accordingly. Lettice had a number of affairs, Frank perhaps only one.

Apart from its being open, their marriage was fairly ordinary. Frank had always enjoyed eating at King's high table, but he was happy to now do so less frequently. His attendance at the Apostles also became less regular. Part of the reason is that he wanted to be home with Lettice. But part was due to the fact that he started to think that many of the Apostles' discussions were boring. The worry he articulated in 'On There Being No Discussable Subject' was becoming more amplified. He felt the Apostles were just talking about themselves. Nonetheless, he went on those Saturday nights when a friend was giving a paper or when it was an undergraduate's first meeting.

The Ramseys' marriage was built upon many commonalities. One was the life of the mind. Frank had a vast quantity of books, and he and Lettice would read the novels to each other. They also shared a love of the outdoors. On holidays, they backpacked from village to village in various parts of the Alps, and when in Cambridge, they frequently took walks in the afternoons to Grantchester or along other parts of the river Cam. If there was a good frost, they skated the twenty miles from Cambridge to Ely, finishing with tea and crumpets toasted on the open fire, and cucumber sandwiches in houses cold as ice. They both loved music and the theatre, frequently attending concerts and shows in London. Frank could by himself make a comedy show successful—if he laughed, the whole audience would catch and join in. There was always a record playing in their home, and Frank was forever trying to find a better gramophone, spending hours getting the angle right on a new soundbox, or on some gadget to improve the bass. His musical tastes ran to Wagner, Beethoven, and Mozart. If he went to a Wagner opera, a sleepless night of racing brain followed.

They were also both dedicated to left-wing politics. In 1924, the first Labour Prime Minister, Ramsay MacDonald, had been elected, then defeated within the year. Unemployment and labour unrest were high, and a pay cut for miners tipped the country into the notorious General Strike and lockout of May 1926. Those on the right in Cambridge, the vast majority, followed Churchill's lead in viewing Bolsheviks or communists as the new enemy, and took the striking workers to be part of that enemy camp. A group of Cambridge dons formed a council, nicknamed the 'Soviet', and encouraged large numbers of undergraduates to help break the strike. Arthur, of all people, was the head of the Soviet, setting himself against his wife and both his sons.

Frank signed a letter in support of the strikers. His friend Dobb was at the centre of the Cambridge Bolshevik response and Frank did his bit on the margins. His view of strike-breakers had not changed from his Winchester days, when he had shouted 'Blacklegs!' at the school gate. He and Lettice made what was for them an agonizing decision to go see Wagner's Ring Cycle at Covent Garden in contravention of their principle not to use alternative transport. They had tickets for all five nights. Lettice recalled the conversations:

> Were we going to be blacklegs and be taken up in somebody's car? Or we were going to forgo our tickets? I'm afraid we were blacklegs.

But of course, this wasn't real blacklegging. They weren't driving trains, as were the Cambridge students under the direction of the Soviet. They must have detested Arthur's stance. Lettice said that Frank, although he wouldn't have hurt a fly, was violent in his opinions about politics, saying things like 'they ought to be shot' of those on the opposing side.

Frank and Lettice also shared a sensibility about people, reacting in similar ways to individuals and their circumstances. Lettice said that an essential thing about Frank was 'he was very good at using his great brain to pick out what was important in any human situation'. That mattered to her. The fact that he wasn't a sharp dresser or good at fixing things around the house mattered not a whit.

They were a modern couple in being committed to maintaining their independent lives and friendships. Frank saw a lot of Kingsley Martin, Philip Hall, and Ivor and Dorothy Richards. He was more and more impressed with Max Newman, and their intellectual relationship flourished. Lettice spent a lot of time with her old friends from Newnham. And they had a robust social life as a couple. With the Braithwaites, they punted and picnicked on the river. Sprott came to Cambridge often and joined bridge parties with Frank and Lettice. They threw and attended parties, which would often be a mix of their London and Cambridge friends. Sprott, Peter Lucas, Frances Marshall, the Penrose brothers, Pat Blackett, Dadie Rylands, and Desmond Bernal figured in their guest lists. Neither Frank nor Lettice cooked. A 'girl' came in and did that, which was standard practice for Cambridge academics. Their parties were renowned, not for the food, but for the intellectual conversation and the fact that they sometimes provided drink containing pure alcohol. When Lettice was in Ireland, Frank would have people to dine in College and he would go to parties on his own. One of many was in July 1926. He wrote to Lettice: 'Yesterday evening I went to a squash of physicists at Blackett's. He has a charming Gottingen professor staying there.'

Blackett and his wife, also named Pat, would come by to borrow gramophone records and Frank would distinguish them in his letters to Lettice as 'Pat Blackett (male)' or 'Pat Blackett (female)'.

Frances Marshall played a major role in their lives. By the time the Ramseys were in Hoop Chambers, Frances and Ralph were living in London, in a flat in the same house as James and Alix Strachey. There was much back-and-forth. When Frances and Ralph were having their flat renovated in 1926, they had an extended visit with Frank and Lettice in Cambridge, then, not yet having enough of each other, they all went to London to stay with Frances's mother. Ralph wrote to Lytton Strachey:

> I have had a fine dose of Ramsey this weekend—they followed us up to London and stayed at Brunswick Square. We went to Gerhardt's together and listened to Brahms, Schumann and Hugo Wolf.... On Wednesday we had a poker game with them and Bunny... where Frank, with the guffaws of a hippopotamus and terrible mathematical calculations, got all our money from us.

Frances provides one of the clearest pictures of Frank during his years of marriage. She described him as handsome, large, and full of life, with a tremendous sense of humour and a massive laugh that cracked his face. His voice was gentle and measured, quiet when it wasn't in gales of laughter, and his conversation was marked by a propensity to listen to people and consider what they had to say. He was not 'one of those volatile talkers' and did not 'show off' or try to convert people to his view, unlike some others. Frances had Russell and Wittgenstein in mind. Frances admired Frank's passion for abstract thought and his love of music.

It is interesting that Frances and others recollected that Frank was handsome. For he became less handsome as the years went on. He had a problem with his feet and needed orthotic shoes, which in those days were hideous. His face was at times ravaged by skin problems. And he was putting on the pounds. On one visit to London, Ralph, who was extremely fond of Frank, inadvertently wounded him by leaving a letter on the table that said: 'the Great Leviathan is here, eating us out of house and home'. On another occasion, Frances recorded in her diary:

> As with many great men (and I'm sure he is one) Frank is outwardly simple and unself-conscious. His tall ungainly frame becomes somewhat thicker at the hips; his broad Slavonic face always seems ready to break into a wide smile and his fine rapidly vanishing hair floats in wayward strands around his impressive cranium.

She also, in what sounds like a contradiction, called him 'touchingly ugly'. But the tension is a constant in how people, especially women, described him. Dorothy Richards said he was handsome and large. Lettice thought him good-looking, even though he had 'very poor' hair, soft and balding, and was 'not fat exactly', but there was 'plenty of him'. He gave the initial impression of clumsiness—he looked like 'he would knock over furniture in a room'. But in fact he was quite physically coordinated—he was quite a good lawn tennis player and had a delicate touch sharpening and changing a gramophone needle.

Frank and Lettice's married life was enmeshed not only with friends, but with family. Frank dropped in at Howfield frequently. Michael used to stop by Hoop Chambers and join whatever company was assembled in hanging about and chatting. Frank wrote to Lettice when she was away in 1925: 'Michael has got quite impossible, and when you out-argue him he says you haven't prayed enough.' But that seemed not to dim the warm feelings Frank and Lettice had for Michael.

There was more tension between the world-views of the senior and the junior Ramsey couples. When asked, decades later, how Lettice got on with her in-laws, Michael replied: a 'kindly tolerance'. Frank, he said, was very different from his parents and 'Lettice was still more sort of Frankish than Frank was.' Frank seems to have had a good relationship, mostly at a distance, with Lettice's mother in Dublin, although not with the physician she had married. Lettice disliked him intensely, and Frank referred to him as her 'brute step-father'.

Lettice continued to work and give talks, once to the Marshall Society, on the psychological aspects of helping young people choose a profession. Frank continued to berate himself for not doing enough work. In the summer of 1926, he wrote to Lettice while she was in Dublin:

> I am so idle about reading things which are boring....I decided to leave my L. Math. Soc. thing alone, but I've thought of ever so many ways in which, if I hadn't been damned slack, I'd have made it better. That always happens; at least, also with my universals paper. I never write anything except in a hurry because it is pressing, and am too slack & self-satisfied to improve it afterwards at my leisure...I am sometimes mentally blind about my work. It is awful...

This twenty-three year old had already published refutations of Douglas and Keynes; translated the *Tractatus* and written the most important commentary on it; published a long paper in the *Proceedings of the London Mathematical Society* that took on *Principia Mathematica* and had Russell's attention; and published a paper in *Mind* on universals that had warranted a session and a publication in the joint *Aristotelian* and *Mind* societies. No matter how productive he was, he would throughout his life think he was slack and idle.

Perhaps he felt that way because he didn't fill all the hours of the day with work. Frank wrote every morning, except when he had a 9 am lecture class. Holidays were no exception. When in Cambridge, he would go to his study at the top of the house straight after breakfast. He sat down and worked for three, never for more than four, hours. Then he went for walks or played tennis, after which he gave supervisions and lectures. When he was in a good groove with a piece of philosophy, he would sometimes start it up again after dinner, till the wee hours of the night. But most evenings, when they weren't at parties, he listened to music and read to Lettice. Those hours in the morning were the important ones, and were carefully set aside. Braithwaite was impressed at this regular and effective work regime, never having managed to organize himself in this efficient way.

As agreed, their marriage was an open one. We don't know how operatively open it was during the first two years of marriage, as the material evidence for various affairs only comes in 1927. But whatever the degree of extramarital activity, Frank and Lettice were devoted to each other and to their growing family. Jane was born a year into their marriage, on 12 October 1926. They didn't intend to have a child so soon, but, as Lettice put it, they were 'careless'.

One reason they had meant to wait was that money was tight. In the academic year 1926–27, Frank, with '0' years of seniority, had the second lowest pay (£260) of the twenty-two active lecturers in the Mathematics Faculty.[§] They economized on holidays by backpacking and staying wherever they could along the route. But at home, they weren't good budgeters. If Lettice spent over two pounds on a pair of shoes, Frank felt justified spending one pound for his boots and the remainder on a gramophone record. They kept separate bank accounts in an effort to keep these matters straight, but they had abandoned Frank's careful accounting of every shilling in favour of chaos in their household books. Frank sometimes checked his account, thinking that he would find a good amount of money there, only to find it empty.

They were nonetheless delighted about becoming parents. Jane arrived three weeks early. Lettice was at the theatre with a friend when she went into labour. She rushed to Howfield, where the birth was to take place. Their daughter came into the world weighing nine pounds, taking after the hearty Wilson side of the Ramsey family. (She, like her grandmother Agnes, would become a strong-minded woman, committed to justice).

Frank and Lettice named her Jane Elizabeth, the middle name after Frank's maternal grandmother. (It is possible that the middle name was also for Elizabeth Denby, of whom we will hear more.) Frances went to see Lettice soon afterwards and was taken by how Lettice 'seemed to make nothing of having babies'. Her employer, the Industrial Fatigue Board, gave her time off and allowed her to return, when she was ready, at whatever hours she liked. Frank and Lettice hired an eighteen-year-old girl to help out with the baby and managed just fine.

It turned out that parenthood was most definitely for them. Frances called Lettice an 'earth mother'. And Frank had always been good with children—his younger siblings, his godson David Pyke, and the neighbourhood youngsters. One of those neighbour children, Brian Reddaway, who grew up to be a well-known economist, recalled boarding at Howfield in the school holidays when he was nine, and Frank was nineteen. Brian was mathematically minded, and Frank was happy to patiently explain infinitely continuing fractions to him—how .99999...can be terminated in 1. Frances described Frank as a kind, if slightly abstracted father, not at all fierce. He was absolutely devoted to Jane. Lettice, Frances said, was much stricter, and they occasionally had rows about whether or not Frank was spoiling Jane.

[§] One woman, with nine years seniority, who also had been a Wrangler, was unjustly, but not unusually, paid less than Ramsey. One man was as well, but he was marked as ill.

Image 23 Frank and his two great loves: Lettice and Elizabeth.

Image 24 Lettice and Jane.

Frank was interested in the development of his new baby. He remarked to Sprott that Jane gave her life top marks: 'So far it is evident that her existence is to her a+. I wonder when it will cease to be so.' His existence too was an a+. Even his teaching was now easy. In August 1926, he wrote to Lettice: 'My pupils are very little trouble now I am in the swing of it.'

12

REVOLUTION IN PHILOSOPHY

'Facts and Propositions'

1926 was a turning point for Ramsey. He was unhappily occupied on a paper he was to present in Oxford at a meeting of the British Association for the Advancement of Science. It was titled 'Mathematical Logic' and was intended to be part of an accessible book on the foundations of mathematics, which he had promised to Ogden. An article in *The Times* advertised it as 'an attempt . . . to interest a wider circle in mathematical logic'. The paper and the proposed book tilled the same ground as his undergraduate thesis, 'The Foundations of Mathematics'. He dismissed the intuitionism of Brouwer and the formalism of Hilbert. He agreed with Wittgenstein about general propositions: 'the kind of fact asserted by a general proposition is not essentially different from that asserted by a conjunction of atomic propositions'. He peppered the paper with clever turns of phrase in an attempt to hold his broad audience.

But he didn't want to spend the next years on such efforts at popularization. He wrote to Lettice, asking her to stop him from taking on such assignments:

> Do encourage me not to accept engagements like this British Ass for a bit. It would be far better to do something no more tiresome which was paid, e.g. giving another course of lectures.

The days of Ogden setting him tasks, useful as they had been, were drawing to a close.

Ramsey delivered 'Mathematical Logic' in Oxford in August 1926 and was relieved to have it behind him. The event was not without its pleasures. He ran into his old friend from Trinity and Vienna, Roger Money-Kyrle, who was still deep into Freud, and reconnected with him. And the talk itself was a success. On his return, he wrote to Lettice, who was in Ireland:

> I have just got back from Oxford; I so wish I had you here to talk to about it. . . . I was really rather nervous about it. Anyway it was a success; Hardy and Neville both said

they enjoyed it, and I'm sure they meant it.... It is of course much longer than they expected, as it was ordinary prose without symbols... There were about 30-40 people there, mostly smiling at the right places! There wasn't any discussion except Hardy saying a few words of general agreement; Hardy proposed to call by name on any expert who was present but there wasn't one... Afterwards Hardy asked me to lunch, which was nice...

Eric Neville had been the colleague of Hardy's at Trinity who had persuaded the Indian prodigy Ramanujan to come to Cambridge. Neville and Hardy suggested that Ramsey's paper be published in the The Mathematical Gazette.

Ramsey was glad to place it there. But he remained unhappy with Ogden's idea of the larger book project. He extracted himself from it, explaining to Keynes in a letter written at the end of September 1926:

Thank you very much for your kind remarks about my Foundations of Mathematics. Some time ago I signed a contract with Ogden to publish a book about it but I have never got on with it and didn't promise it by any date. I am rather tired of it and can't get over some obstinate difficulties, so I have been doing more of other things, metaphysics and probability.

He would ultimately decide that the obstinate difficulties were well-founded and would abandon logicism in favour of intuitionism.

In the meantime, he got on with metaphysics and probability. Michael said that his brother wasn't ambitious; he was just fired up by his thoughts, which 'were authentic and imperative for him'. The profound questions of philosophy were what most fired him up, especially the nature of meaning and truth. In what would turn out to be the spectacularly productive year of 1926, Ramsey took on these questions in two papers—'Facts and Propositions' and 'Truth and Probability'. Both were heavily influenced by Wittgenstein and Russell. In 1926, Ramsey was estranged from Wittgenstein, but he was seeing Russell quite frequently. Not only was Russell occasionally at meetings of the Apostles, but Ramsey invited him to dinner at King's, and he visited him in London. After one meeting, Russell minuted 'Ramsey all morning talking mathematical logic'. But Ramsey was both building upon ideas in Russell and Wittgenstein and simultaneously breaking further away from these two major sources of inspiration. Together the two papers he wrote in 1926 form the beginning of his revolutionary attempt at linking truth with belief and action.

'Facts and Propositions' can be seen as Ramsey's official rejection of much of the logical analyst theory that so attracted Moore, Russell, Wittgenstein, and the Vienna Circle. Ramsey thought that his alternative would have significant payouts for seemingly intractable philosophical problems. By moving the discussion away from the truth of independently existing propositions and leaving the route clear for an analysis of true human belief, it would solve the problem of negation and make possible an understanding of partial belief.

One thing Ramsey wanted to preserve from Wittgenstein's system was its account of logical truths. In 'Facts and Propositions' he utilized it in a novel way. Wittgenstein had argued (in Ramsey's words) that 'a logical truth excludes no possibility and so expresses no attitude of belief at all'. Ramsey built on that idea to arrive at one of his most fruitful insights. Beliefs exclude possibilities. What it is to believe a proposition is, in large part, to take certain possibilities as alive or dead, and to behave accordingly. It is of the essence of a belief that it has a causal impact on our actions, and once we understand that, we have a way of identifying or individuating beliefs, as well as a way of measuring belief.

The paper begins with the statement: 'The problem with which I propose to deal is the logical analysis of what may be called by any of the terms judgment, belief, or assertion.' We have seen that, even as an undergraduate, Ramsey declined the standard Cambridge position that it is an objectively existing *proposition* that is true or false—he wanted no truck with such 'mysterious entities', 'so unlike anything else in the world'. In 'Facts and Propositions', Ramsey now adds that it is a mistake to try to analyse truth and falsity in terms of the correspondence of a proposition to a fact. For one thing, that would require us to posit mysterious negative facts in order to account for falsity. Even worse are the versions of the standard view that take truth and falsity to be primitive and unanalysable. They make the very difference between truth and falsity mysterious.

Ramsey took a different tack altogether, inspired by the founder of American pragmatism, C.S. Peirce and by Russell (who, in the 1921 *The Analysis of Mind*, had started to explore—but in the end rejected—the analysis of belief in terms of behaviour). Ramsey noted that belief seems to involve both subjective and objective factors, as well as some relationship between the two. When I believe that Caesar was murdered, it seems that this event involves, on the one hand, something subjective—'my mind, or my present mental state, or words and images in my mind'—and, on the other hand, something objective—'Caesar, or Caesar's murder, or Caesar and murder, or the proposition Caesar was murdered, or the fact that Caesar was murdered.' Ramsey then made a deflationary point that he is now well-known for:

there is really no separate problem of truth but merely a linguistic muddle... 'It is true that Caesar was murdered' means no more than that Caesar was murdered, and 'It is false that Caesar was murdered' means that Caesar was not murdered....

But Ramsey immediately followed this up with an argument that is not as well-remembered as his deflationary point. Once you have laid out the matter in this way, the problem of truth doesn't disappear. He prefaced his deflationary remark by saying that he should briefly discuss truth 'before we proceed further with the analysis of judgment', and he finished the whole discussion by concluding that 'if we have analysed judgment we have solved the problem of truth'. Yes, the assertion of the truth of *p* is equivalent to the assertion that *p*. But that leaves all the hard work still ahead of us. The deflationary move must be followed by an examination of belief, judgment, and assertion, which will provide us with a complete theory of truth.

Ramsey proceeded with that examination. Belief, he argued, involves a habit or disposition to behave. He gives the following example. If a chicken 'believes' that a certain caterpillar is poisonous, it abstains from eating that kind of caterpillar on account of the unpleasant experiences associated with that behaviour. But the chicken's behaviour has to be

> somehow related to the objective factors, viz. the kind of caterpillar and poisonousness. An exact analysis of this relation would be very difficult, but it might well be held that in regard to this kind of belief the pragmatist view was correct, i.e. that the relation between the chicken's behaviour and the objective factors was that the actions were such as to be useful if, and only if, the caterpillars were actually poisonous.

Chicken beliefs are not 'subject to logical criticism'. We are more interested in beliefs that 'are expressed in words, or possibly images or other symbols, consciously asserted or denied'. Such beliefs are not *reducible* to behaviour, for there is still a mental factor or an internal state involved. In later papers, Ramsey drops examples about chickens and turns to examples of human conscious belief. In 'Facts and Propositions', he gives a hint about how his example will evolve: 'the importance of beliefs and disbeliefs lies not in their intrinsic nature, but in their causal properties, i.e. their causes and more especially their effects'. The 'intrinsic nature' of human beliefs is the mental factor, but Ramsey will argue that it is too difficult to get a philosophical grip on that. We do better if we focus on the behavioural factor.

There are also objective factors to be taken into account. Ramsey may seem close to adopting a certain kind of pragmatist account of truth in 'Facts and Propositions': if a belief leads to successful action, it is true. But for his kind of pragmatism, the success of the action must be connected to the belief being related in the right way to the relevant objective factors. Whether or not Ramsey in fact went all the way to adopting such a pragmatist account of truth, he certainly adopted a pragmatist account of meaning or content, i.e. what it is that makes one belief equivalent to another:

> To be equivalent...is to have in common certain causal properties, which I wish I could define more precisely. Clearly, they are not at all simple; there is no uniform action which believing 'p' will always produce. It may lead to no action at all, except in particular circumstances, so that its causal properties will only express what effects result from it when certain other conditions are fulfilled. And, again, only certain sorts of causes and effects must be admitted; for instance, we are not concerned with the factors determining, and the results determined by, the rhythm of the words.

One can see why 'Facts and Propositions' sparked a research programme called 'success semantics', which argues that the contents or truth-conditions of our beliefs are those that explain the (typical) success of the actions they cause. Ramsey would not have signed up to the programme because one of its aims is to get rid of the mental factors in belief. But many have found it persuasive and found their inspiration in Ramsey.

SUCCESS SEMANTICS

Simon Blackburn, Bertrand Russell Professor Emeritus, University of Cambridge

In his famous example Ramsey imagines a chicken that may be said to believe that a foodstuff was poisonous if its action of avoiding it was useful if, but only if, the foodstuff was indeed poisonous. Generalizing he wrote that 'any set of actions for whose utility p is a necessary and sufficient condition might be called a belief that p, and so would be true if p, i.e. if they are useful'. His idea is congenial both to pragmatism, since it is what we do that determines what we believe, and to functionalism in the philosophy of mind, since it is the functions of states that identifies them as beliefs with particular contents.

A natural extension of Ramsey's insight looks to success in action as a key to interpreting the communications whereby such success is achieved. So, for example, we can interpret a particular kind of honey-bee dance as signalling the location and direction of a particular pollen source, if the bees witnessing the dance thereupon successfully fly off in the right direction for the right distance. Two people might succeed in meeting at Nelson's Column, and the explanation is that they communicated using a sentence containing the phrase 'Nelson's Column'. Success semantics is the enterprise of founding a theory of interpretation on this kind of explanation.

Ramsey's own phrasing suggested the idea that the content of a communication would be whatever was a guarantee of success in action based upon it. But that seems too strong, for a person can aim to do something in a way based on a true belief, and yet fail for other reasons. It is not an easy matter to repair this problem, partly because the world throws so many obstacles in our way, but partly because the 'holism of the mental' means that we may have other false beliefs in our mind that wreck our intentions even when these are triggered by a true belief. One suggested improvement is to avoid talk of guarantees, and content ourselves with explanation: the fact that their sentence contained 'Nelson's Column' explains two people's success in meeting, but it by no means guarantees it. Furthermore we can turn the holism of the mental into service, looking at a whole pattern of occurrences of a term, not only at individual pieces of communication one at a time, and then identifying the term's place in the whole pattern of communicative success.

William James preceded Ramsey in associating truth with success in action. But he unwisely made it seem that if enough satisfactions derived from a belief, that meant that it was true, and it is easy to counterexample that. Success semantics makes no such simple equation, but retains the essential insight that it is no coincidence that across the board we do better relying on true beliefs than false ones.

Ramsey ended 'Facts and Propositions' with two remarkable paragraphs. The first both paid homage to, and set him apart from, Wittgenstein:

> In conclusion, I must emphasize my indebtedness to Mr. Wittgenstein, from whom my view of logic is derived. Everything that I have said is due to him, except the parts which have a pragmatist tendency, which seem to me to be needed in order to fill up a gap in his system.

The gap that Ramsey saw in Wittgenstein's system is better described as a canyon, and Wittgenstein could not, in 1926, take the pragmatist suggestion to be a friendly amendment. (Only after a major shift in his thought, in the 1930s, could he do so.) We saw that in his 1923 Critical Notice of the *Tractatus*, Ramsey registered a worry that the picture theory was good only for elementary propositions, not for the whole range of meaningful and important beliefs. His proposal in 'Facts and Propositions' is that if we add pragmatism to the picture theory, we will have what we need. But adding pragmatism to the picture theory turns it into something altogether different.

The final paragraph announces the new direction Ramsey will be taking:

> My pragmatism is derived from Mr. Russell; and is, of course, very vague and undeveloped. The essence of pragmatism I take to be this, that the meaning of a sentence is to be defined by reference to the actions to which asserting it would lead, or, more

vaguely still, by its possible causes and effects. Of this I feel certain, but of nothing more definite.*

'Facts and Propositions' was presented at the July 1927 Joint Session of the Aristotelian and Mind Societies at Bedford College, London, with Moore responding. It was published in that year's *Proceedings of the Aristotelian Society*. Before the meeting, Ramsey wrote to Moore:

> Dear Moore,
>
> I wonder if we could discuss our symposium papers some time; I think conversation about it would be more useful than making speeches at a meeting.... Perhaps I might come and see you some evening?
>
> Yours Fraternally
>
> Frank Ramsey

It's not clear whether Ramsey and Moore discussed their ideas in advance, but the commentary was vintage Moore. He picked apart the many things Ramsey might have meant when he talked about 'facts' and he asserted that he could not believe that Ramsey could really want to analyse judgments, as opposed to propositions.

Another thing that Ramsey wanted to preserve from Wittgenstein's *Tractatus* was his account of universal generalizations as infinite conjunctions. He would later abandon this position. But in his discussion of generalizations in 'Facts and Propositions', Ramsey alighted on an important issue for quantified modal logic.

FRANK RAMSEY AND QUANTIFIED MODAL LOGIC

Timothy Williamson, Wykeham Professor of Logic, University of Oxford

In 'The Foundations of Mathematics' and 'Facts and Propositions' Ramsey followed Wittgenstein's *Tractatus* in analysing universal generalizations as conjunctions over all the things in the world. He discussed the objection that this would make it necessary what things there are, whereas really it is contingent. Rather than relying on Wittgenstein's dismissal of talk about what things there are as nonsense, Ramsey argued that, if such talk

---

* We have seen that Ramsey also got his pragmatism from C.S. Peirce. Russell, too, was influenced by Peirce. We know that in part from T.S. Eliot, who was a philosophy graduate student at Harvard when Russell gave the Lowell Lectures there in 1914 and then was on the scene in Cambridge and in Bloomsbury during Ramsey's time. It's not clear how much engagement there was between Ramsey and Eliot.

is allowed, then it *is* necessary what things there are. In doing so, he raised a central issue for what would now be called quantified modal logic, years before it was formalized by Barcan in 1946. In terms of Kripke's later possible worlds semantics for modal logic, the choice is between *constant domain semantics*, which requires all worlds in a model to have the same domain of individuals, and *variable domain semantics*, which does not. Ramsey's view corresponds to constant domain semantics. In responding to Ramsey at the Joint Session of the Aristotelian Society and Mind Association, G.E. Moore defended the view that it is contingent what things there are, which corresponds to variable domain semantics, though of course Ramsey and Moore were not thinking in such terms.

The difference between the two views has many repercussions for both quantified modal logic and modal metaphysics. In particular, Ruth Barcan (Marcus) postulated a principle now known as the *Barcan formula*, which says that if everything necessarily has a property F, then necessarily everything has F. Kripke showed that constant domain semantics validates the Barcan formula and its converse, while variable domain semantics invalidates both formulas (some compromises validate one but not the other). Their validity is an obvious consequence of Ramsey's view, for on his analysis the Barcan formula says that if every conjunct is necessary so is the conjunction, and its converse says that if the conjunction is necessary so is every conjunct.

Ramsey's argument for the necessity of what things there are anticipated another key issue in quantified modal logic and modal metaphysics: the treatment of identity. He used the premise that 'numerical identity and difference are necessary relations', in that facts of the form '$a = b$' and '$a \neq b$' are necessary facts. The necessity of identity was later proved by Barcan (Marcus), and the necessity of distinctness by Prior, on reasonable assumptions. Kripke (1980) strongly defended both principles against objections, although their exact form differs between constant domain and variable domain semantics. In effect, Moore noticed that point, agreeing with Ramsey that distinctness is a necessary *relation*, in the sense that if $a \neq b$ then necessarily if a and b both exist then $a \neq b$, but denying that distinctness is a necessary *fact*, for distinctness would fail if either a or b failed to exist.

At first sight, Moore's view—that it is contingent what things there are—looks much more consonant with common sense than Ramsey's, and most modal metaphysicians have gone Moore's way. Formally, however, Ramsey's approach to quantified modal logic is simpler and more elegant than Moore's. Ramsey's view can also be defended on metaphysical grounds. (See Williamson (2013) for further references.)

As with several other cases of Ramsey's farsightedness, his informal anticipation of quantified modal logic seems not to have had much influence. But his exchange with Moore brought a central issue into clearer focus than would be achieved again for another thirty years.

Measuring Belief in the Face of Uncertainty

In November 1926, Ramsey read 'The Idea of Probability' to the Moral Sciences Club. It was part of a long, rich paper titled 'Truth and Probability'. We can tell that it was completed after 'Facts and Propositions', for it solved the problem of partial belief and extended pragmatism, topics that were merely mentioned in 'Facts and Propositions'. The new paper made no gesture to Russell and only the weakest to Wittgenstein—a note in which Ramsey said that in one move in his argument, he was assuming Wittgenstein's theory of propositions, but the argument could be made to work with 'any other theory'. Those who built on 'Truth and Probability' set aside the Wittgensteinian framework as what Richard Jeffrey called 'a useless complication'. Nonetheless, in figuring out how to measure partial belief, Ramsey solved a major problem for Wittgenstein. Ramsey had seen in the Critical Notice of the *Tractatus* that the picture theory couldn't cope with beliefs such as '*p* or *q*', for if we believe '*p* or *q*', we don't fully believe *p* and we don't fully believe *q*. We require an account of partial belief.

Ramsey began the paper with his usual onslaught against Keynes's theory of probability. He then went on to do what Keynes had failed to do: measure partial belief and have it align with the world. There is no list of attendees at Moral Sciences Club meetings. All we know about this one is that Moore was in the chair, and that the meeting was in Braithwaite's rooms. We don't know for certain if Keynes was there to hear Ramsey treat induction not as 'lesser' or formal logic, but as the 'larger logic' of human reasoning. But the chances are that he was. For it seems that Keynes knew about Ramsey's theory before he presented it at the Moral Sciences Club. In May 1926, Keynes wrote to the German translator of the *Treatise*:

> Among those students in England for whose opinion I feel most respect I find a marked reluctance against abandoning some variant of the frequency theory. They admit that my criticisms hold good on the existing version, and they are not yet ready to prepare a version which can resist them.... I shall not be surprised if they prove right. I suspect, however, that the first step forward will have to come through progress being made with the partly psychological subject of vague knowledge.

A few months after Keynes wrote this letter, Ramsey read part of 'Truth and Probability' to the Moral Sciences Club, delivering that psychological account of vague or probabilistic knowledge, and linking partial belief to frequencies. Keynes, that is, had a heads-up that Ramsey was about to take the big step forward.

After Ramsey's death, Keynes gave a succinct and clear outline of the conflict between his logical theory of probability and Ramsey's subjective account:

> Ramsey argues, as against the view which I had put forward, that probability is concerned not with objective relations between propositions but (in some sense) with degrees of belief, and he succeeds in showing that the calculus of probabilities

simply amounts to a set of rules for ensuring that the system of degrees of belief which we hold shall be a *consistent* system. Thus the calculus of probabilities belongs to formal logic. But the basis of our degrees of belief—or the *a priori* probabilities, as they used to be called—is part of our human outfit, perhaps given us merely by natural selection, analogous to our perceptions or memories rather than to formal logic.... So far I yield to Ramsey—I think he is right.

The Moral Sciences Club minutes summarize Ramsey's path-breaking argument:

> He maintained that degrees of belief were to be measured by reference to willingness to bet, and that the laws of probability were laws of consistency in partial belief, and so a generalization of formal logic. Mr. Ramsey also asserted that induction, like memory, could not be justified by formal logic or formal probability. The discussion centred mainly on the possibility of numerical measurement of degrees of belief.

There is controversy about whether or not Keynes went over to Ramsey's view. Some of it rides on Keynes's worries about a strict utilitarian approach. But Ramsey, like Keynes, was a moderate utilitarian—remember that his imaginary conversation with John Stuart Mill and 'Truth and Probability' (and, we shall see, 'Mathematical Economics') raise problems for pure utilitarianism. Keynes would have known all of these papers—he would have known that Ramsey didn't think utilitarianism was the last word in ethics and that he didn't advocate a decision theoretic account of perfect rationality.

That said, Ramsey solved a major problem for utilitarianism. As he put it, the 'general psychological theory' that undergirds our actions is the utilitarian idea that

> We act in the way we think most likely to realize the objects of our desires, so that a person's actions are completely determined by his desires and opinions.... We seek things which we want, which may be our own or other people's pleasure, or anything else whatever, and our actions are such as we think most likely to realize these goods.

That last sentence makes it clear that Ramsey did not hold with the view of the 'Benthamists', as Keynes called them, who thought that people form beliefs or adopt plans for action on the basis of considerations about maximizing their own pleasure and minimizing their own pain. But on any version of utilitarianism, including Ramsey's, if we ought to regulate our conduct so that it maximizes our utility, then we need to be able to assess the varying degrees of probability of our beliefs' being true and the varying strength of our desires. It's completely unrealistic to go on full belief and full desire.

Psychological theories evolve, and Ramsey noted that even as he wrote, the Freudians were at the gates, arguing that our desires weren't so easily available to us. But he doubted that we could do without the notion of utility, in psychology or ethics, even if there is truth in other psychological theories and even if utility doesn't capture the whole of what we value. In 'Truth and Probability', and also in his later work in economics, he assumed the utilitarian psychological theory. Our beliefs and desires determine our actions, and those actions should be assessed in terms of whether they maximize what we want. In order to make such assessments, we have to be able to measure belief, isolate it from desire, and determine the impact of each on our choices.

Ramsey began with an examination of probability. Having re-demolished Keynes's theory, he moved on to the frequency theory, promoted by Cambridge's great logician, John Venn (of Venn Diagram fame), who had died only in 1923. The frequency theory uses the term 'probability' 'practically as a synonym for proportion'. It takes probability to be the observed frequency of occurrences of an event—say, a coin coming up heads. The frequentist, with Keynes, holds that probability is a matter of objective fact, but, unlike Keynes, thinks that probability relations are empirical. We can see that the coin lands heads half the time and then, as we continue to experiment, we eventually infer that the probability of its doing so is .5.

Keynes was right that Ramsey thought there was something worthwhile in the frequency theory. Ramsey said that the connection between frequencies and probabilities had an undeniable basis in ordinary language and was useful in all sorts of ways—in, for instance, physical science and everyday events, such as coin tosses. He also thought that our subjective degrees of belief should take account of the frequencies. But Ramsey didn't think that the frequency theory could stand on its own, for it can't provide an account of partial belief, nor an account of how an individual should make one-off decisions. He gave the following example:

> I am at a cross-roads and do not know the way; but I rather think one of the two ways is right. I propose therefore to go that way but keep my eyes open for someone to ask; if now I see someone half a mile away over the fields, whether I turn aside to ask him will depend on the relative inconvenience of going out of my way to cross the fields or of continuing on the wrong road if it is the wrong road. But it will also depend on how confident I am that I am right; and clearly the more confident I am of this the less distance I should be willing to go from the road to check my opinion.

The walker needs to make an assessment of the probabilities in a particular situation, and thinking about proportions in the long run is of no help at all. When the walker heads off to the right, he has some degree of belief or confidence (however he might have come to it), that this is the correct road, as well as some preferences about the relative inconveniences of getting lost and of going out of the way to ask directions. In order to make sense of probability in such contexts, we need to be able to measure degrees of belief.

The received view in Ramsey's day was that 'belief and other psychological variables are not measurable'—or if they are measurable, they must be measured introspectively, with each person looking inside his own mind and assessing the intensity of feeling that accompanies his belief in a given proposition. Ramsey thought the introspective method can't provide any enlightenment. Our perceptions of what goes on inside our minds are not only hard to access and study, but they are also unreliable. Even if we *could* ascribe numbers to intensity of feelings, we would be sure to get wildly inaccurate measurements. For instance, the beliefs we hold most strongly—the ones we take for granted—are often 'accompanied by practically no feeling at all'. Moore believed with complete certainty that he had two hands, but he usually didn't give it a thought, let alone have an intense feeling of confidence concerning it, unless he was giving a paper to the Moral Sciences Club on the topic of commonsense.

Thomas Bayes, in the 1700s, had set out a theorem for assigning the probability of a hypothesis on the basis of the available evidence—for updating an initial probability assignment in light of new evidence. The inputs of Bayesianism are subjective or human judgments of fact and value. Moving from one state of partial belief to another requires a way of comparing the relative strength of beliefs. In 'Truth and Probability', Ramsey took the mystery out of those subjective inputs. His solution employed the dispositional account of belief he announced in 'Facts and Propositions'. Degrees of belief can be measured and assessed by examining the disciplined connection between the inner states of beliefs and desires, on the one hand, and the outer states of behavior, action, and success, on the other.

Ramsey noted that there was 'an old established way of measuring a person's belief' by proposing a bet. The strict betting-with-money analogy, however, has defects. It can't cope with the diminishing marginal utility of money—how one feels about a bet of £1000 will vary depending on how poor or wealthy one is. It also can't cope with the fact that some people are more risk-averse than others, and with the fact that the very proposal of a bet might alter the person's beliefs. So, while 'fundamentally sound', the old established way is 'insufficiently general and ... necessarily inexact'.

Ramsey enlarged on the established view by invoking dispositions or habits, which go beyond betting:

> I use habit in the most general possible sense to mean simply rule or law of behaviour, including instinct: I do not wish to distinguish acquired rules or habits in the narrow sense from innate rules or instincts, but propose to call them all habits alike.

Beliefs are bets, but hardly ever are they literal gambles with money:

> Whenever we go to the station we are betting that a train will really run, and if we had not a sufficient degree of belief in this we should decline the bet and stay at home.

It was an idea whose time had come, although Ramsey happened to be first past the post. He was the first on record, in that Moral Sciences Club meeting, to propose a definition of probability as a numerical representation of an individual's subjective degree of belief. In Italy, the mathematician, statistician, philosopher, and economist, Bruno de Finetti, was on the same wavelength.

RAMSEY AND DE FINETTI

Colin Howson, Professor Emeritus, University of Toronto and London School of Economics

One of the most remarkable intellectual events of the twentieth century, that gala century for scientific advances, was the almost simultaneous development of a radically new theory of probability in the 1920s and '30s by Ramsey and de Finetti. The founding documents are Ramsey's 'Truth and Probability', written late in 1926 and published in 1931, and de Finetti's lectures at the Institut Henri Poincaré in Paris in 1935. Neither author was aware of the other's work, but so remarkable is the similarity between their accounts that both are credited with the authorship of this new theory, now widely known as *subjective Bayesianism* and numbering among its adherents a large and increasing galaxy of philosophers and scientists, among the latter probabilists, statisticians, biologists, physicists, economists, and AI workers.

The novelty of Ramsey's and de Finetti's approach lay in regarding probabilities simply as measures of agents' degrees of belief subject to what appears to be a rather weak consistency requirement. Both regarded an agent's degree of belief in a proposition A as measured by the odds on A which they would regard as fair (favouring neither side). Suppose however that it is possible to choose stakes which, in bets at an agent's supposedly fair odds, would guarantee a certain loss (say, giving odds of 2 to 1 on A and also on its negation): the agent would then be caught in a type of inconsistency, believing odds fair which can be shown for some combination of stakes to ensure a loss. Such a set of stakes is called a Dutch Book in betting parlance, and the constraint of consistency for supposedly fair odds (on finite sets of propositions) is simply that they should not be Dutch Bookable.

Now send odds Od, whose possible values vary from 0 to infinity, into the closed unit interval via the mapping Od/(1+Od); so zero odds go to 0, even money odds go to ½, and infinite odds go to 1. Such *normalized* odds are called *betting quotients*, and Ramsey and de Finetti proved, in somewhat different ways, the following fundamental result, often called the *Dutch Book theorem*, about an agent's consistent fair betting quotients/consistent degrees of belief: on any algebra of propositions these quotients obey the rules of finitely additive probability; and conversely, any finitely additive probability function on such an algebra delivers consistent evaluations on its members[†] (an algebra of propositions is a set of propositions, factored by logical equivalence, that includes the logically true proposition, and is closed under conjunction and negation). This theorem means that we can now simply talk about a consistent agent's *probabilities* P(A), P(B), P(C), etc. These are so-called *unconditional* probabilities, but there are also conditional probabilities of the form P(A|B), which Ramsey and de Finetti independently defined as an agent's fair betting quotient in a bet on A which wins if A and B are true, loses if A is false and B is true, and is cancelled if B is false. They each then proved that consistency requires the so-called *multiplication rule* P(A&B) = P(A|B)P(B) to hold.

Although Ramsey's and de Finetti's accounts endowed an agent's probabilities with a purely subjective status they knew that, far from rendering those quantities scientifically valueless, the condition of consistency combined with the rule of *conditionalization* supports a powerful new epistemology called *Bayesian epistemology*. Its scientific appeal lies principally in two features: (i) so-called *Bayesian networks* are not only extremely powerful diagnostic tools but also provide the formal basis of some of the most revolutionary developments in AI; (ii) in fairly general circumstances agents with different initial, or *prior*, probability functions will, with enough new information, find their updated probabilities converging; in this way, it is claimed, objectivity is realized as an emergent property of consistent subjective assignments.

The Polish probability theorist Janina Hosiasson was also on her way to the idea that probability is best thought of as subjective degree of belief. She went to Cambridge for the 1929–1930 academic year to work with Keynes on probability. Ramsey had yet to publish on the subject, whereas Keynes was well-known for his *Treatise*. It's likely that Hosiasson encountered Ramsey before he took ill and died. We know that she arrived in Cambridge at some point in the autumn term, for by 12 November she was attending philosophical lectures and events. A visiting graduate student from Oxford reported seeing two Polish philosophers, one of whom could only have been Hosiasson, on that date:

> There were two foreigners, a man and a woman, at Moore's lecture, whom I discovered afterwards to be Poles – the man a philosopher from the University of Cracow and the woman a mathematical logician from Warsaw.

Hosiasson went to Moore's discussion classes and 'raised a lot of points of detail', despite her shaky English. After Ramsey's death in January, Braithwaite showed her

[†] Ramsey's text only contains a proof of the first half of the theorem. The text is frustratingly full of proof-sketches and often simply statements of his results, but that is because he did not prepare it for publication. De Finetti proved a considerably more general version of this theorem (de Finetti (1972: 76–9).

the manuscript of 'Truth and Probability'. Four months later, she gave a talk to the Moral Sciences Club, and published it in the 1931 issue of *Mind*. In that paper, Hosiasson adopted something very much like Ramsey's idea of mathematical expectation. She expressed her debt to Ramsey's paper, and said that she had already been independently thinking along similar lines. She also noted that her position made sense only from a pragmatist perspective.

When she returned to Warsaw,[‡] Hosiasson gave a talk in which she reported on her time in Cambridge, and bemoaned the fact that little had remained of 'the logical school of Bertrand Russell'—only Ramsey's lectures in Foundations of Mathematics, and a few 'traces in different discussions and other lectures'. But Ramsey, she said, died a few days before his Lent Term lectures were to have begun and then there was nothing going on. Max Black said much the same thing:

> The sad thing for me was that he died in the course of that year.... He was to have been my examiner for Schedule B of the Tripos...Well, when Ramsey died...the official examiners for [the] mathematical Tripos couldn't think of anybody to substitute for him, setting the papers and grading them and so on. So Braithwaite approached me from the examiners and asked me to name somebody in mathematical logic who, in my judgment, would be competent to grade my answers. Isn't that extraordinary? The only person I could think of was Susan Stebbing, who had been the pupil...of Moore and had published a very good intermediate text, *Modern Introduction to Logic*.

As far as Hosiasson and Black were concerned, the logical school of Bertrand Russell had died with Ramsey.

The Birth of Expected Utility Theory

In Keynes's retrospective remarks on Ramsey in 1931, his willingness to yield to Ramsey's idea that probability is subjective was tempered by a scepticism about the

---

[‡] When she returned to Poland, Hosiasson married the mathematician Adolf Lindenbaum. Both were Jewish, and during the war they fled Warsaw only to be later captured and killed by the Gestapo—Janina was shot in 1942. She wrote a moving letter to Moore in 1940 asking for a reference for her appeal to the British Council for Assisting Refugee Philosophers. She also applied to the Rockefeller Foundation to be sponsored for the New School for Social Research's refugee scholar programme in New York. Carnap, Feigl, Hempel, Hook, Tarski, Nagel, Moore, Quine, and others wrote on her behalf. The New School accepted her, but didn't recommend that the Rockefeller Foundation provide any financial support. She continued to work while on the run, publishing a paper on confirmation in the 1940 *Journal of Symbolic Logic*, and giving her address as Vilna, Lithuania, where she had gone with the slim hope of surviving. Some of her work was published after her murder. See Galavotti (2014) for an account of her probability theory. Purdy and Zygmunt (2000) provide more on her life, as does Szubka (2018), who includes a transcription of the letter to Moore.

idea that we can determine whether it is rational to hold a particular degree of belief. Keynes concluded his remark as follows:

> But in attempting to distinguish 'rational' degrees of belief from belief in general he was not yet, I think, quite successful.

'Truth and Probability' proposed that we start with one's expectations, whatever they are, and move to the problem of explaining 'how exactly ... observation should modify my degrees of belief'. Thus was born modern subjective expected utility theory and rational choice theory, although we will see that Ramsey would not have been happy with what became of his ideas.

Ramsey took an expectation to be the combination of a habit (belief) with a feeling (preference or desire) and proceeded to disentangle the two. In effect, he pulled up by their bootstraps all the elements of a decision made under uncertainty by showing that we can measure an agent's values and beliefs by seeing how he acts. In betting terms, we can ask what the lowest odds are which he will accept: the 'probability of 1/3 is clearly related to the kind of belief which would lead to a bet of 2 to 1'. He then set out a framework that tells us what is rational, given an agent's beliefs and desires. Say you are at that crossroads, unsure of which path will get you to the parking lot most quickly. Say that, if you choose the shorter route, you will get 30 units of happiness or well-being, and if you choose the longer route, you will get 18 units. You have a degree of belief of 2/3 that the right-hand road is the shorter route, and 1/3 that the left-hand road is shorter. Ramsey's model lets you calculate your expected subjective utility for each option, and tells you that, given your beliefs and desires, it is rational for you to take the right-hand road.

Any axiomatization project rests on assumptions. Ramsey again questioned Keynes's assumption of the Principle of Indifference, which holds that when we have no relevant evidence of the probabilities of a particular ball in an urn being white or black, we are to assign equal probabilities to the two outcomes. Ramsey argued that it is not 'a matter of formal logic to say what should be a man's expectation of drawing a white or a black ball from an urn; his logical expectations may within the limits of consistency be any he likes'. Why assign equal probabilities to a white or black ball being drawn when we have no information about the proportion in the urn? Ramsey thought that Keynes's assignment of initial degrees of belief was 'meaningless'—we must start with our current state of knowledge and move forward from there.

Ramsey's own assumption was that we can make sense of what he called an ethically neutral proposition, whose truth or falsity is a matter of indifference to the agent. That gave him the anchor for the rest of the rankings. There has been hearty debate about which assumptions are more innocuous and elegant. Donald Davidson and Patrick Suppes argued for Ramsey's strategy and identified a chance event with an equally preferable possible world or a subjective probability of one-half. But they are by no means in the majority in thinking that this, amongst all the options, is the best assumption. The debate initiated by Ramsey lives on.

Ramsey's formal machinery was powerful, although, in the fashion so typical of him, he glossed over some important details, as if they were so easy that he needn't bother writing them out. Perhaps he would have taken the time to do so when he prepared the material for publication in the book he was writing when he died. In 'Truth and Probability', he sketched a representation theorem, on which if an individual's preferences satisfy some conditions, one can determine the individual's utilities. He was interested in making his model even more powerful. On a scrap of paper, he sketched a dynamic, rather than a static system. In another note, he came close to providing an account of exchangeability that allows us to connect subjective probabilities to statistical inferences and predictive success, showing how degrees of belief should be aligned to the available evidence. Another proved the value of collecting evidence, thus explaining, as Ramsey would put it, why we should continue to experiment. These notes were only published in the 1990s, completely lost to scholarship until then. W.E. Johnson had been on to the idea of exchangeability before Ramsey (and de Finetti) defined it. But the world of Bayesian decision theory had to wait till the 1950s for the point about evidence, when I.J. Good re-proved it.

RAMSEY'S PROBABILITY THEORY

Nils-Eric Sahlin, Professor and Chair of Medical Ethics Lund University

Ramsey showed that people's beliefs and desires can be measured with a betting method, and that given some principles of rational behaviour (e.g. that preferences are transitive) a measure of our 'degrees of belief' will satisfy the laws of probability. He gave us the theory of subjective probability; was the first to state the Dutch book theorem; laid the foundations of modern utility theory and decision theory; had a proof of the value of collecting evidence; took higher order probabilities seriously; and, in a derivation of 'the rule of succession', he introduced the notion of 'exchangeability'. Ramsey's theory is about as complete as any such theory could be.

Ramsey starts with the idea of a bet. Obviously, monetary outcomes will fail to give correct measures since money and utilities are not exchangeable. Ramsey ingeniously side-steps this issue by assuming there is an ethically neutral proposition believed to degree ½ (Axiom 1). This proposition is a clever and important device—a value-neutral, undisputed fair coin which enables value distances between all sorts of outcome to be measured, allowing us to scale the utilities of outcomes by comparing utility differences. The best-known theories of utility and decision-making (e.g. Savage's theory) have a problem with state-dependent utilities. Ramsey's use of preferences among bets to quantify value differences requires the states defining the bets to be value-neutral, thus avoiding this problem.

Degree of belief in a proposition is then given 'by the odds at which the subject would bet on p, the bet being conducted in terms of differences of value as defined'. Ramsey is using utilities to scale probabilities. He notes that the measure of degree of belief obtained is a probability measure obeying the axioms of probability theory.

Ramsey introduced the subjective expected utility model: $SEU(a_i) = P(s_1)u(o_{i1}) + P(s_2)u(o_{i2}) + \ldots + P(s_m)u(o_{im})$. Act a_i is preferred to a_j if and only if $SEU(a_i) > SEU(a_j)$. However, like all good mathematicians, he left some of the details of the proofs to the reader.

Later philosophers, statisticians, and economists rediscovered, reformulated, and generalized elements of Ramsey's theory. Some focused on utilities and personal probabilities, e.g. representation theorems (Fishburn). Others have tried to streamline the conceptual basis of the theory (Jeffrey), applying probabilities and utilities to the same type of entity, e.g. replacing concepts like *worlds* with *propositions*. Others still have attempted to generalize the theory by allowing the agent to express epistemic imprecision arising from the quality and quantity of information (Levi, Gärdenfors, and Sahlin).

Strait is the gate, and narrow is the way. All of these 'new' theories run into problems. They have had to assume that utilities and money are exchangeable, or that there are objective probabilities. Some are not fit for use (e.g. theories with too meagre ontologies). Others have run into counterexamples or given counterintuitive recommendations in consecutive choice situations, e.g. by violating one or other ordering or independence axiom (Seidenfeld).

Critics of John Stuart Mill objected to his preoccupation with Homo economicus. Ramsey, in a behaviouristic spirit, looked into the mind of this paragon of rationality. His theory is a descriptive theory, but it becomes normative when we put our trust in Homo economicus. Ramsey was a pragmatist. He believed in logic, science, and proven experience—a trinity without which pragmatism becomes wishy-washy and in whose absence the very idea of rational decision-making and inductive reasoning loses its meaning.

Part of the reason Ramsey's advances were only recognized decades after his death is that he declined to publish 'Truth and Probability'. He decided to expand and perfect it in a book by the same title. It was here, on the topics of truth and probability, that he intended to make his mark, and he intended to make it carefully. But he died in the middle of writing that book. The precursor to it, 'Truth and Probability', went into print in Braithwaite's 1931 collection of some of Ramsey's titled *The Foundations of Mathematics and Other Logical Essays*. But that was not the kind of volume that probability theorists would have read as a matter of course.

John von Neumann and Oskar Morgenstern went to press in 1944 with *Theory of Games and Economic Behaviour*, which had at its centre a near re-creation of Ramsey's formal results. Ramsey went unmentioned and they seemed determined to leave him out of the picture, even after it was pointed out that he had been the first to get the result. It was only in 1954, when the statistician Leonard Savage produced his own axiomatization of subjective probability, that Ramsey was cited. In 1959, Herbert Simon finally celebrated him.

It has seemed to some that von Neumann and Morgenstern must have known about Ramsey's paper. When asked, they said that they hadn't read Ramsey. But it is likely that Morgenstern, at least, knew of Ramsey in the 1920s and might have looked at Braithwaite's volume. Morgenstern was associated with the Vienna Circle, and was close to the mathematician Karl Menger, who was heavily involved in the debates about mathematics and probability in the Circle. The eminent British economist John Hicks wrote to Ramsey's friend Piero Sraffa in 1960, asking whether he might have been the conduit by which Ramsey's theoretical outlook was transmitted to von Neumann:

> You tell us that your work on the subject goes back a long way—you mention Frank Ramsey; is it possible that it was somehow through you and your mathematical friends that von Neumann got onto what is in so many ways a similar construction (It is understood that his paper was originally given at Princeton in 1932)? I have never been able to understand how he should have hit on it out of the blue.

We don't have an answer from Sraffa. But he knew Ramsey's theory well. In 1929, he met with Ramsey, Keynes, and Wittgenstein to discuss philosophy and probability. And he and Ramsey were planning further meetings with just the two of them.

It is also possible that Sraffa at some point himself, or via some mutual acquaintance, informed de Finetti of Ramsey's theory. It certainly looks like de Finetti followed Ramsey exactly in his operational definition of conditional probabilities as odds in called-off bets, as well as in placing at the centre of his position the idea that inconsistency was punishable by a Dutch Book. Of course, it's possible that conditions were ripe for the idea and that de Finetti and von Neuman reached their results independently.

Whatever the truth about who knew of Ramsey's results and when, Ramsey is now recognized as one of the architects of modern decision and rational choice theory. Variations and developments of his ideas still drive much of economics and social science.

'Too High a Standard to Expect of Mortal Men'

Though designing the house in which modern rational choice/utility/decision theory would inhabit, it is not clear that Ramsey would have chosen to reside there himself. For one thing, while he provided a logic of decision, he did not think that all human action and decision should be crammed into the strictures of rational choice theory, as many economists and social scientists today seem to assume. Utility, Ramsey saw, is not value neutral. In his 1928 work in economics, he would make it clear that choosing to maximize utility is a moral decision, one which puts utility before justice and equality.

For another, while Ramsey thought that we ought to focus on the aspect of belief that we can observe (behaviour), he was careful to stay away from *behaviourism*—the position that mental states, with all their richness, must, or can, be eliminated from our account of belief. Belief, on Ramsey's account, retains its subjective element—it is in part a 'feeling'. It's just that a theory of rational belief won't get far if it focuses on the 'feeling' aspect of belief. Ramsey also separated himself from cruder behaviourists by noting that 'in the course of trains of thought we believe many things which do not lead to action'. He did not assert that a belief *actually* has to lead to action. What he asserted is that a belief *would* lead to action in suitable circumstances—'we are concerned with dispositional rather than with actualized beliefs'.

Finally, Ramsey was clear that keeping one's degrees of belief consistent with the mathematics governing probability is highly idealized. We can't measure degrees of belief with precision, nor should we expect to. Such vagaries, he noted, are everywhere in scientific measurement. All we require is a 'sufficiently accurate' way of measuring belief that is easy to apply and is fit for our purposes. An ideal agent, having full or certain beliefs about every single thing, might always act in a way that he would expect to maximize utility. But people are far from ideal. They have imperfect evidence for their beliefs. That's one reason that most beliefs come in degrees:

> the ideally best thing is that we should have beliefs of degree 1 in all true propositions and beliefs of degree 0 in all false propositions. But this is too high a standard to expect of mortal men, and we must agree that some degree of doubt or even of error may be humanly speaking justified.

Human fallibility, in Ramsey's view, is not a friction that interferes with the smooth working of decision-making, but is the condition of humankind. Human psychology cannot be theorized away. Individuals will make different initial probability assignments, and strength of belief will vary from person to person, in ways partly driven by psychology.

Ramsey noted that our 'general psychological theory' will have to be updated as psychology advances—already 'many psychologists' would like to add 'unconscious desires' and 'unconscious opinions' to the utilitarian idea. In the meantime, and perhaps even in the long term, we have to use utilitarian psychology. He saw with clarity that his account of decision-making under uncertainty is true only 'in relation to this artificial system of psychology, which like Newtonian mechanics can...still be profitably used even though it is known to be false'. Similarly, while it is false to define rationality as the maximization of utility, it is a simplifying assumption that works well enough.

In 1957 Davidson and Suppes ran experiments at Stanford to see if they could verify Ramsey's formal theory, and established the discipline of experimental economics. That discipline has subsequently shown that human beings do not behave in anything like the way rational choice theory suggests. Even the simplest axioms are not followed. People often behave irrationally (for instance, when they fail to change their mind in light of evidence), even when they understand that they are being irrational. Ramsey would not be surprised at these results. We will see that he was brilliant at modelling economic interactions. But he recognized that these are ideal models and that failures of rationality are only to be expected. Beliefs are held by actual persons, not ideally rational automata. Ramsey didn't put forward his account of the rationality of partial belief as an empirical description of how people reason. Nor would he think that, for instance, nuclear powers should make their decisions based on what it would be rational for other nuclear powers to decide.

That does not mean we should not offer reasons to people based on what is rational to believe. When someone misestimates the probabilities of dying in an airplane crash as opposed to driving to the airport, we will want to put the actual probabilities to him in an effort to overcome his fears. We may not be successful, because all sorts of facts about his psychology, background, or ability to assess the evidence might get in the way. Ramsey would have been interested, and no doubt pleased, that much of contemporary cognitive behaviour therapy is based on the idea that a proper understanding of the facts can be crucial for altering crippling patterns of behaviour. For he argued that for a belief to be useful, it must be properly connected to the facts.

Keynes, in the 1930s, often said in his lectures that economists have to engage in scholastic, over-precise, exercises in order to clarify the 'fluffy grey lumps', the 'wooliness', or the unformed theories in their heads. They have to employ mathematics to get rid of those lumps. But the danger is that they get so mathematical that they 'precise everything away' and are left with a poverty of meaning. Keynes was paraphrasing directly from Ramsey here, who frequently warned against these polarities. Here is one passage from Ramsey in 1929:

> The chief danger to our philosophy, apart from laziness and wooliness, is *scholasticism*, the essence of which is treating what is vague as if it were precise and trying to fit it into an exact logical category.

Ramsey was well known for the idea that we need to avoid a false, mathematical sense of certainty about human matters. A decade after Ramsey's death, Wittgenstein was still talking of how Ramsey said that in philosophy one should be neither woolly nor scholastic.

So while Ramsey provided the formal machinery for the rational choice theorist, he would not have wanted to employ it to pretend that human reasoning does or should run in mechanical ways. Savage, von Neumann, and Morgenstern might have made claims about what rules people must follow if they are to be rational. But Ramsey was clear that no real person could have a set of beliefs that are perfectly coherent in terms of the probability calculus. His theory

> cannot be made adequate to all the facts, but it seems to me a useful approximation to the truth, particularly in the case of our self-conscious or professional life, and it is presupposed in a great deal of our thought.

To the extent we fall short of perfect coherence, we are less than fully rational. But not even in our self-conscious and professional lives as philosophers, economists, or mathematicans are we ever fully rational. In a 1928 elaboration on 'Truth and Probability', Ramsey said that he was talking about degrees of belief only in a simplified system 'to which those of actual people, especially the speaker, in part approximate'.

The point was agreeably illustrated by a paper Joan Robinson and Dorothea Morison (later Braithwaite) read to the Heretics Economics Section, just before Ramsey read 'Truth and Probability' to the Moral Sciences Club. They captivated the Heretics with an irreverent telling of 'Beauty and the Beast' in 'the jargon of orthodox economic theory' and on the 'assumption of perfectly rational man'. After making the bargain with the Beast and finding himself having to pay the price of his daughter in exchange for the rose, the protagonist quickly found the absurd balance of utility and disutility:

> The issue, therefore, seemed to depend on the degree of undesirability represented by the employment under consideration, and she ended her reflections with the following inquiry:

'Father, did you ascertain whether the beast was hairy?'

The merchant... was able to assure her that the degree of hairiness was not above the normal for that class of person.

Quickly balancing the factors relevant to the situation in light of this additional information, she finally replied: 'In these circumstances, I am just willing to accept the bargain'. At this moment they realized simultaneously that she was on the margin, for they did not omit to notice that an additional (small) increment of disutility would have outweighed the satisfaction to be obtained from obedience to filial duty.

Ramsey, too, was a Heretic. Human beings do not work the way ideal utilitarian theory has it, nor is there any value in trying to identify rationality with 'the opinion of an ideal person in similar circumstances'. To be sure, 'the highest ideal would be always to have a true opinion and be certain of it'; but 'this ideal is more suited to God than to man'. And Ramsey did not think that God existed.

Pragmatism: Logic and Truth for Humans

In 'Truth and Probability', Ramsey not only explicitly adopted a pragmatist account of how to identify the content of a belief (a belief is marked out by the actions that would manifest it), but he also started to articulate a pragmatist, demystified, account of what it is that makes a belief true.

After the point in the paper in which he delivered his account of how reasonable degrees of belief for an individual are those that conform to the logic of the probability calculus, Ramsey announced: 'What follows to the end of the section is almost entirely based on the writings of C. S. Peirce.' Here is Ramsey's rendering of Peirce's pragmatism:

We have... to consider the human mind and what is the most we can ask of it. The human mind works essentially according to general rules or habits.... We can therefore state the problem of the ideal as 'What habits... would it be best for the human mind to have?'

The problem of the ideal—the problem of truth—is linked to usefulness and to the most we can ask of the human mind. Some habits are a better basis for human action than others. Unlike Wittgenstein and the Vienna Circle circa 1926, Ramsey did not seek the holy grail of infallibility. Ramsey held that logic must reach for what is 'humanly speaking' right. Such a 'human logic or the logic of truth', which tells us how we should think, 'is not merely independent of but sometimes actually incompatible with formal logic'. Formal logic is the logic of consistency, but consistency is not enough for rationality. We also have to have habits of mind that reliably link our beliefs to the facts. It is these habits that are reasonable or unreasonable.

Ramsey's chicken example now becomes one about humans. He asks us to think of someone who, whenever he sees a yellow toadstool, infers that it is unwholesome. What would the optimal degree of belief be? Well, it will be best if his degree of belief is equal to the proportion of yellow toadstools that are in fact unwholesome. We need to align our subjective degree of belief with objective chances. We judge an inference

> accordingly as the degree of belief it produces is near or far from the actual proportion in which the habit leads to truth. We can then praise or blame opinions derivatively from our praise or blame of the habits that produce them.
>
> This is a kind of pragmatism: we judge mental habits by whether they work, i.e whether the opinions they lead to are for the most part true, or more often true than those which alternative habits would lead to.

His argument is similar to the justification of induction he gave when an undergraduate. Indeed, he reiterates that argument in 'Truth and Probability.' Induction can be justified as being a good habit:

> We are all convinced by inductive arguments, and our conviction is reasonable because the world is so constituted that inductive arguments lead on the whole to true opinions. We are not, therefore, able to help trusting induction, nor if we could help it do we see any reason why we should, because we believe it to be a reliable process.

We suppose that induction is reliable because the world is a certain way, and our past successes provide us with fallible evidence in support of that supposition. To ask that the conclusions of inductive arguments be proved independently 'is to cry for the moon'. Induction is, along with memory, among the 'ultimate sources of knowledge'. Induction and the beliefs it puts in place work well, and unless and until they fail to do so, we are justified in relying upon them:

> Induction is such a useful habit, and so to adopt it is reasonable. All that philosophy can do is analyse it, determine the degree of its utility, and find on what characteristics of nature it depends. An indispensable means for investigating these problems is induction itself, without which we should be helpless. In this circle lies nothing vicious.

He delivered a similar argument against skepticism. Russell had considered the following argument for scepticism in *The Analysis of Mind*. We have no way of knowing that the world did not begin five minutes ago, complete with history books, fossils, and all our memories. Ramsey agrees that there is no way of refuting such sceptical hypotheses, no way of showing that 'all our memories are not illusory'. But he asserts that 'no one regards it as a scandal to philosophy that there is no proof that the world did not begin two minutes ago'. Perhaps he should have said that no one *ought* to regard it as a scandal, for the sceptical impulse beats steadily in philosophy. But his point is one that every pragmatist makes: the mere possibility that all our memories might be illusory is not a good argument for actually doubting what we have ordinary reasons to believe.

Ramsey's position in 'Truth and Probability' is that beliefs are in part constituted by how they make people act, and truth is that property of beliefs that enables us to succeed in our actions. A belief combines with some set of desires, and the action following from it is successful only if the belief is true. Ramsey did not think that the truth of a belief *guarantees* successful action. For there may be all sorts of obstacles and mistakes that lead someone to act wrongly on a true belief, or accidents that make people act successfully on a false belief. The causal role of beliefs is a complex and holistic matter. What a given belief causes someone to do in a given situation will depend on all the other things the person believes and desires. And a belief can be true and still cause unsuccessful actions, because false beliefs may also play a role in causing those actions.[§]

In a 1982 interview, Braithwaite remarked on how surprised he was, when he went through Ramsey's papers after his death, at the extent of his pragmatism—'mathematical logicians are not usually pragmatists'. He had thought Ramsey was only a pragmatist about induction, an idea which appealed to Braithwaite, and which he would mine after Ramsey's death. Braithwaite was not himself inclined to take pragmatism farther than that. Hence the critical character of his remark in his obituary of Ramsey: 'Recently (in company with Bertrand Russell) he had been descending the slippery path to a sort of pragmatism.'

It may seem strange that Braithwaite didn't know the direction Ramsey's thought was taking. He was present when Ramsey read his paper on probability to the Moral Sciences Club. We don't know whether Ramsey read out the part that spoke to his debt to Peirce, but in 1929, the last year of his life, we know that he was making pragmatist arguments about a wide range of issues. The answer,

---

[§] Ramsey thus anticipated Donald Davidson's focus on the complex interchange between desire, belief, and action. Once Davidson had reinvented what he called 'the holism of the mental', he discovered that Ramsey had beaten him to it by seven decades. As Davidson (1999: 32) put it, he had joined the long list of thinkers who had fallen prey to the 'Ramsey Effect'.

I will suggest, is that a sensitive personal matter had intruded itself on the relationship between Ramsey and Braithwaite in 1929. They were not in the mood to talk to each other about philosophy. Braithwaite hadn't even been aware of the book project that was supposed to grow out of 'Truth and Probability', which was thoroughly pragmatist. He explained in a 1982 interview that he and Ramsey didn't talk very much about each other's positions. They were two young men who were trying to make names for themselves, in competition with each other. He also said that if Ramsey didn't talk to *him* about his book manuscript it was because he did not respect anyone's judgment on it.

But this is indeed strange. We will see that when Wittgenstein returned to Cambridge in 1929, Ramsey certainly talked to him about pragmatism. Why was Braithwaite in the dark? We shall also see that the sensitive personal matter caused Ramsey and Braithwaite to be estranged in 1929, making Braithwaite unaware of the philosophical direction in which Ramsey was travelling.

Braithwaite was right, though, that mathematical logicians were not usually pragmatists. Ramsey would spend much effort making his way down the path to what he intended to be a stable pragmatist patch of ground.

13

TWO CRISES

A Trifle, and Agnes is Dead

In August 1927, Agnes and Arthur Ramsey had a party for their silver wedding anniversary. The following day, they invited the pastor of their congregational church, his wife, and their Danish houseguest for a drive. Agnes and Arthur had purchased a motor car, a soft-roofed Morris Oxford, just before Frank and Lettice were married. Both of them drove the temperamental machine, which had a tendency to boil over and cut out on hills. Arthur had once broken his wrist on the crank shaft, which not infrequently would kick back. Agnes was the better driver of the two and was irritated by her husband's constant back-seat driving. She was even more annoyed when he took the wheel, for he was exceedingly cautious and nervous.

They picked up their guests on Lyndewode Road near the train station, and then drove out of Cambridge on the Huntington Road. The car was full. The road was straight and empty. Arthur was driving. He and the pastor were in the front seats. Agnes, the pastor's wife, and the Danish friend were in the back. They didn't get far before disaster struck. Arthur turned behind him to adjust his coat. The car, which was going at a good clip of 30 miles an hour, left the road and went up on the grass. To avoid hitting a telegraph pole, Arthur made a sudden attempt to straighten out. The car overturned, pinning four of the passengers underneath it, the reverend having been thrown clear. Arthur suffered broken ribs and the Danish woman incurred a serious head injury, from which she later died. Agnes was killed instantly. Her head and neck took the brunt of the impact. Arthur, in shock, said to the first man on the scene: 'It's such a little thing. I was trying to put my coat right.' Lettice later offered the comment that Agnes was killed 'very unnecessarily'.

The family was thrown into grief and crisis mode, with Frank in charge. He sent a telegram with the terrible news to Michael, who was just starting to train as a priest at Cuddesdon, near Oxford. Frank sat in the family home, Howfield, for two days, alternating between numb silence and howling like a dog. He said that his mother was the only person who really understood him. While he alone of the four siblings had an easy relationship with his difficult father, that relationship simply did not compare with the one he had with Agnes. She had been a major influence on his life.

Compounding his pain, Frank had to formally identify his mother's body, and was the first witness in the ensuing inquest. He responded to questions about Arthur's driving ability with a precisely measured volume of truth: he was 'an extremely careful driver'. The seven-member jury's verdict of accidental death was reported across the country. The *Aberdeen Post* ran the story under the headline 'Trifle Causes Smash'. Roy Harrod wrote to Keynes from Oxford, asking if the victim was Frank's mother, and Keynes replied that, alas, it was.

Agnes died in her prime, at the age of fifty-two. Her funeral was a large event, presided over by her brother Clifford, who had followed the family tradition into the Anglican priesthood. Attendance was high, as mourners from the University and the many public bodies in which Agnes was involved came out in strength. A memorial was set up in her name—a fund for working women to come to Cambridge for summer courses. Arthur contributed 100 pounds. Frank and Lettice pitched in as well.

Misery rolled through the family. Agnes's brother Kenny, who had introduced her to Arthur all those years ago at Fettes, was extremely upset. Bridget was just about to start her undergraduate studies at Newnham, and put it off for a year. She told Frank that she didn't want to go on living. Everything she did, she did because her mother wanted her to do it. Michael missed a term at Cuddesdon. His insomnia worsened and he started talking to himself. As the months went by his stammer got more pronounced and he became more skinny and nervous. The result was a mental collapse. One of Michael's biographers says of the car accident:

> The resulting turmoil, mental and emotional, ruined (the word is not too strong) his preparation to be a priest and blotted out his memory of Cuddesdon. He hardly ever spoke about his mother again. When his father died he burnt all the letters he could find.

Frank worried that his father would be overcome with guilt. But Arthur surprised everyone by thinking that it wasn't his fault, and not expressing any great remorse. The bereaved family would have to carry on in the face of Arthur's increasing remoteness. This was a difficult task. The youngest, Margie, was still a child, only nine at the time. She was now motherless and rattling around in the big house with her father, looked after by servants.

Frank and Lettice stepped up. They had been married two years. Jane was a year old. Although far from ideal, they decided they ought to move into Howfield. They gave up the Hoop Chambers flat and shifted to the family home, bringing with them, Margaret said, an immediate feeling of well-being, as well as Lettice's good artistic taste. They took over the drawing room, which had always been Agnes's preserve. Lettice turned it into an oasis. She changed the curtains, hung pictures, and furnished it nicely. No longer was it decorated on the principle that one ought to be able to throw a cup of coffee and have it unnoticed. They invited their friends for tea parties in the garden. There was life in the house.

Frank and Lettice did their best to be substitute parents to Margie. She recalled Frank's efforts when he discovered she knew no geography:

> To remedy matters he offered [me] half a crown—a big sum—for learning the counties of England and the countries of Europe.... He stood at one end of the drawing room laughing, making a great joke of it and holding up a large atlas.

Margie felt a bit stressed by him, as she wanted his good opinion and knew that the way to get it was to know things. Frank also took it upon himself to try to get Bridget back on the rails. They played tennis together, sometimes having a close match, despite Bridget's talent and Frank's increasing girth. Frank and Lettice took her on holidays, once walking in Cornwall, with Frank reading *War and Peace* to them in the evenings. Another time they went to Ireland, with a large party of friends. Bridget was quite religious at this time and not a great fit with those friends. But the kindness of this trip stayed with her all her life.

The attempt at making a happy home, however, did not work out. Margie felt neglected. There was simply no way for Frank and Lettice, two working people with a small child and active social lives of their own, to care for Margie the way her mother had cared for her. Arthur was awful to his son and daughter-in-law. He resented the re-decorating and wouldn't let it extend beyond the drawing room. He double-bolted every door to the outside, and there were constant complaints about Frank and Lettice not locking up properly. He didn't like the nursemaid who was taking care of Jane. Lettice, who was now in charge of household matters such as the catering, later said that Arthur was 'a very inhibited person' and 'not an easy man to get on with'. One of the things that irritated her was that there were 'a lot of things he thought he couldn't eat, but when he went abroad he ate them'. Thick soup was out of bounds because he couldn't tell whether anything in it had been ruined by contact with an onion. Mealtimes were rather sulky as a result. Michael returned to his old habit of getting up in the middle of an uncomfortable dinner to tear around the lawn, which was decidedly odder now that he was a young man. He was also getting into what Frank called 'comic arguments' with his father about ethics. He wrote to Lettice during one of her (now much-needed) times away:

> Michael got very excited and didactic and thought father a Pharisee and father thought Michael a dangerous Jesuit. Michael then kept father awake till 2 by jumping up and down overhead!

Presumably, Frank kept quiet about ethics. The difference between Michael and Arthur was internecine, between Anglican and Evangelical—not nearly the gulf between Arthur and his atheist son.

One of the difficult things about living in Howfield was Arthur's rudeness to Frank's and Lettice's visitors. He couldn't deal with the fact that there were people in his house who came and went as they pleased, and he let Frank and Lettice's friends feel his disapproval. He didn't even like his own children coming and going as they pleased. Frank and Lettice often returned late from parties, which enraged Arthur. Even Michael was a sinner in this respect. Frank wrote to Lettice that 'Mick isn't much use to Father; his movements are even less regular and explained beforehand than ours.'

Frank and Lettice bore the sacrifice as lightly as possible, it being less heavy for Frank, since he was fond of his childhood home. But their friends were concerned about how they were coping. When Lettice was in Dublin for the Christmas holidays, Frank wrote to her about a party he had been to at Dadie Ryland's, the King's literary and theatre scholar. Frank talked with Alister Watson about logic, and with other friends about their unhappy living situation. The opinion was voiced that

Image 25 Agnes Ramsey.

Image 26 Arthur Ramsey, 1927.

living at Howfield must be too much of a strain for Lettice. And it was. Lettice was returning from work, arranging meals for her picky father-in-law, and trying to raise a baby as well as a nine-year-old sister-in-law. She recalled with considerable restraint that it was 'a rather uneasy year', with two very different households living under the same roof, each with its own strong character. It simply didn't work. She was completely candid about how they weren't able to give Margie enough attention, and that Margie was not dealt a good hand. Frank's youngest sister was another casualty of Arthur's small adjustment of his coat.

'Thank Goodness We've Got into the Habit of Telling Each Other Everything'

Frances Marshall had a close-up view of the marriage of her old friend Lettice and her new friend Frank. She said that Lettice 'was not by nature a jealous person'. As they had agreed at the outset, neither partner was bound by the ties of sexual fidelity. Their way of being married was to give themselves licence to have extramarital relationships, while remaining committed and faithful to each other in a higher sense. While homosexuality was a part of their social world, so much that it hardly ever seemed relevant to either Frank or Lettice to mention which way or ways someone was inclined, it appears that they each conducted their affairs along only one gender dimension.

Those affairs inevitably made for some strains. But they worked them out. As far as Frances knew, there was never any serious question of their parting, not even in the major crisis of their marriage. That crisis was born of their different conceptions of what an ideal open relationship should be. Frank thought it meant they could each have more than one great love, and Lettice thought it meant they could each have a good number of less meaningful relationships.

Frank found another great love. Elizabeth Denby was a friend of Lettice's—they had lived together in a London cooperative house before Lettice returned to Cambridge. Elizabeth, like Lettice, was smart, educated, progressive in her politics, and older than Frank (in Elizabeth's case, by ten years). She moved in left-wing circles, only occasionally intersecting with Bloomsbury. One of her best friends was Marjory Allen, wife of the pacifist politician Clifford Allen, and a renowned architect of landscapes, children's playgrounds, and the 1948 Children Act. She described Elizabeth during the 1920s as 'a handsome, positive young woman from Yorkshire... manifestly a great original, with strong feelings, a ready gift of expression and an unerring eye for human needs'. Elizabeth had gone to the London School of Economics in 1916 to take a certificate in what is now called social work. She worked for the newly created Ministry of Labour until 1921. In 1923, she moved into the field in which she would make her mark: the replacement of slums with affordable city-centre terrace housing complete with vegetable patches, public open-air spaces, and inexpensive good furniture. After Frank's death, she was made a Fellow of the Royal Institute of British Architects and won one of the first Leverhulme Fellowships, to research and write *Europe Re-housed*. She went on to be important enough to have her own biography.

Elizabeth had been part of a large party that Frank and Lettice put together for a holiday in Ireland in the summer of 1926. Lettice was heavily pregnant with Jane—in her words, she was 'enormous', an 'absolute mountain'. Frank and Lettice borrowed Lettice's mother's little sports car and went off on their own to a remote island for a side-holiday. Neither had driven a car before, but Lettice took the wheel the fifty miles there and back on vague instructions from her mother: 'That thing's the brake' and 'If you want to change gears you've got to push your foot in.' Her driving was hair-raising, especially around the sharp corners on single-track roads. The car broke down, and they were stuck in an inn on the island for a week, living on bread, butter, lobster, and tea. Frank walked up a few mountains in the rain, alone, as Lettice was not in a fit state for such activities.

The rest of the holiday was uneventful. But Elizabeth, as Lettice put it, 'later became Frank's girlfriend'. He stayed at her London flat at 10 Red Lion Passage, near Bloomsbury, often enough to have some of his post sent there. Lettice had been trying to get Frank to agree to rent a small flat in London in order to facilitate their lifestyle. Frank was concerned about the cost. Of course, he was less in need of a flat, as Elizabeth had her own.

One imagines that this situation cannot have been entirely welcome for Lettice. No matter how easily she took childbirth and motherhood, it must have had some impact on the whirl of recreational sexual activity. Decades later, she would say that it was not jealousy she felt when Frank fell so hard for Elizabeth, but rather loneliness when he was with her. But the arrangement between Lettice and Frank was that they were not to look the other way—they were to have affairs and talk frankly to each other. And so they did. Some of those conversations were conducted via post, on those occasions when Lettice was visiting her mother in Ireland. Lettice kept those letters. We have, however, no access to Elizabeth's perspective. She instructed that her letters from Frank be destroyed upon her death, and Frank was not one for keeping correspondence.

The summer after the Ireland holiday, Lettice was again in Dublin. Frank was looking after Jane. But their nanny was on site and Frank could on occasion go to London, as well as entertain Sebastian when he came to visit. Frank wrote to Lettice about how it was going with Elizabeth—when the sex was good, when it was not; how much he missed Elizabeth when he returned to Cambridge, but at the same time was relieved to be back. They congratulated themselves on remaining devoted to each other while living in accord with their principles. At the beginning of August 1927, Frank wrote:

> I feel at the moment so glad not to be going to see her for a long time and to be going for a long holiday with you, darling. I wish you were here. I feel ours is fundamentally such a stable, calm, and happy relationship. I believe someday I shall be able to achieve calm happiness with E, too, but at the moment it is so exhausting. She is very tired and I get overexcited and then react like a small child, You know, she is very nice. You wrote her the most charming letter, darling.

The relationship with Elizabeth was not kept secret, but neither was it flaunted. Frank tried to keep his family in the dark. During Lettice's trip to Dublin, Elizabeth had to cancel a holiday, and Frank wondered whether she might come to Cambridge instead for the weekend. Elizabeth, however, thought Agnes might be 'disturbed'. Frank agreed. His mother wouldn't understand at all. Some of Frank's friends knew, others didn't. Braithwaite only heard about the affair well after it started and he said he knew Elizabeth really only by public reputation, for she was already a prominent civil servant. Frances Marshall did know her, and thought her capable, very pleasant, and not attractive or unattractive—a 'rather small, compact little person'. She was a career woman, she said. But the most important thing for Frances was that she was a threat to her dear friend Lettice: 'I wasn't frightfully keen, I suppose, on Elizabeth Denby.' Sebastian, who was also completely informed, and lunched whenever he could with Frank and Elizabeth, had a more charitable view.

The summer of 1927 was indeed happy and stable, but at the end of it, their lives were shaken up by Agnes's death. After the car accident and the move to Howfield, Frank and Lettice were under terrible strain. Perhaps it was that stress that resulted in the disturbance of their calm emotional waters. They both felt they had to escape Howfield over Christmas 1927. Lettice took Jane to Dublin and Frank went to the South of France with Elizabeth. Arthur, Michael, Bridget and Margaret spent the holidays with one of Arthur's sisters, where they had a thoroughly miserable time.

Frank and Elizabeth were agonizing about whether to end their relationship, but their holiday was very much that of a couple. They ran into Hugh Dalton, the Labour Member of Parliament and friend of Agnes's, along with his wife. Frank wrote to Lettice that the Daltons 'at first suspected nothing'. But after 'Poor E had a fearful string of embarrassing questions from Mrs. D', Frank had to ask Hugh to be discreet. His cooperation having been secured, they went to tea at the Daltons'. Frank, in his frequent letters to Lettice, recounted the incident, as well as intimate details of his sex life with Elizabeth, all the while making proclamations of his love for Lettice. In her own letters, Lettice hoped Frank was 'having a very nice time—not a rather nice one!' She was looking for her own romance, and informing Frank that thus far, she was having no luck. Whatever her precise feelings, Lettice sought to resolve them. And she did. In her next letter to Frank, she spoke of friends and relations, Jane, and trying to manage the Howfield household staff via the post. Then she added the following: 'During all this I'm running an affair of my own at hectic speed . . . with Liam O'Flaherty the writer'.

O'Flaherty, aged twenty-nine at the time, was already a major figure in Irish literature. His novel *The Informer*, about the moral dilemmas of a rebel during the Irish War of Independence, had won him the Tate Prize for fiction in 1925.* He was

* His cousin, the director John Ford, would make a classic and Academy Award winning film of the novel in 1935.

lithe and handsome with piercing eyes. A political firebrand, he had been active in the Irish struggle and in the founding of the Communist Party of Ireland. He was an exceptional and captivating person, and Lettice's affair with him was extraordinary. They had met at a dance, and within a week had been to bed together three times. Lettice wrote to Frank to tell him all about it. She didn't know what, if anything, would come of the affair, but she did know that she was attracted to Liam. In perfect symmetry with Frank's letters to her, she wrote that the affair did not affect their own relationship—'the serious part of my life'—and she was looking forward to seeing Frank soon. But she said she wanted to send her letter before Frank parted from Elizabeth, for it would make a difference to Frank's decision—she couldn't expect Frank to break off his relationship with Elizabeth while she was having her own with Liam. She hoped that Frank wouldn't be hurt, and ended with the postscript: 'Thank goodness we've got into the habit of telling each other everything.'

Lettice had had other affairs. But this one seemed different to Frank, for Lettice also told him that she had unprotected sex with Liam. Frank felt she was taking the possibility of a disease or a 'bastard child' rather lightly. He also felt she had betrayed their arrangement by moving out of their circle. He reacted, in the words of Frances Marshall, in a 'bull-like male way'. He lashed out with some nasty words about the Irish: 'their politics are mere assassination, their ethics superstition and their litera- ture fairytale'. The Catholic Church came in for special abuse. He complained that Lettice's mind was *not* on the serious part of her life:

> Frankly your letter gave me an awful shock, I can't see how you could imagine it wouldn't. I felt quite furious and still after a lot of reflection it seems to me very sickening, in fact, just bloody.

He had been on the verge of giving up Elizabeth and was looking forward to 'happy peace' again with Lettice. Their principles, he felt, were not working out so well in practice, and their open marriage was more precarious than they had cared to admit:

> Now you've completely messed it up again and I don't know where we stand at all. How can I go on with Elizabeth just until you get tired of Mr. O'Flaherty? It is too serious for her and for me to be played with in this way. It isn't a sort of little game, which is all a love affair seems to mean to you. ... I can't not feel concerned in what you do when I'm not there and I can't bear you to be (apparently) so cheap and nasty. I mean to go to bed with a man as soon as you meet him, like that, before you can possibly know whether he isn't an appalling cad....I can't help thinking of the possibility of your having a baby, which wasn't mine or even not certainly mine...I'm afraid you may think I'm the pot calling the kettle black, as far as the mere fact of

infidelity goes of course I am, but I don't really feel that is the point. The things that hurt me particularly are none of them applicable to my love for Elizabeth.

Although he apologized the next day for writing 'too crossly', and asked tenderly for news of Jane, Lettice was alarmed and did indeed think he was being rather hypocritical:

> My dear dear, what a dreadful letter you've written me.... I think you very hard on me and do think you rather a pot calling me a black kettle. I can't see that I've behaved badly in any way. I meet a perfectly delightful and interesting person and things go rather quickly. You know yourself that things can happen quickly. What about you and me? You had no guarantee that I was nice, nor did you want one at the time.... Perhaps I did not have enough resistance but then all the circumstances were against resistance on my part—you off with E, our conversations about wounded vanity, my loss of self confidence.... Darling, don't be so beastly to judge me. Don't talk so much about 'if our marriage was to go on'. If my letter shocked you, yours is a terrible shock to me. It seems so unlike you.

She told Frank that, in any event, she wouldn't be able to see Liam often, as he had been recently married. When she was in Ireland, they would be able to see each other only a few hours at a time, and he hardly ever came to London. They would probably 'end by being just very friendly'. In the meantime, Lettice said, it wouldn't be fair for her to ask Frank to give up Elizabeth. She did not want to give in to jealousy, and she did not want to replace their current arrangement with a monogamous one. She was hurt by the seriousness of the affair with Elizabeth, but made a fine distinction between envy and jealousy. If the hurt was due to envy, it could be remedied by her engaging in her own affair, but it was unacceptable for it to be caused by jealousy. She assured Frank that she was not pregnant. In an echo of Frank's Apostles' papers about the tension between traditional drives and modern ones, Lettice asserted: 'We're both more primitive than we thought.'

Emotions ran high on both sides. Letters flew back and forth, a dreadful row of recriminations, withdrawals of recriminations, and proclamations of love for each other. Frank reaffirmed that he and Elizabeth had decided to end their relationship: 'She had, to my surprise, absolutely forgotten that it was for your sake we were going to separate, and thought it was for hers and mine.' But that was an on-again, off-again decision, fluctuating mostly in light of whether Lettice was going to end things with Liam. They also debated the question of what kind of relationship was best for them as a couple. Lettice thought that a 'light affair which brings a lot of temporary happiness' was in order: it would not be 'permanently upsetting to us'. It was the seriousness of Frank's affair with Elizabeth that she found 'so hard to bear'.

Frank was of the view that 'lust and copulation without friendship are degrading and dangerous'. He was tired of the whole freedom business and thought it a threat to their marriage:

> I know I spoilt it originally, so I can't <u>blame</u> you, but it remains the fact that each blow weakens it; they don't cancel.
>
> Really, of course, I must blame myself for not knowing my own mind. I began it with E, but I find that in fact I can't stand the strain of this sort of polygamy and I want to go back to monogamy but it's now too late.... Are we going on having countless affairs? I pray not, for the sake of our children; parents must seem calm and reasonable not panicky.

Lettice caught whooping cough from Jane, and their return to Cambridge was delayed till the end of February. This was a long time to be separated, even at the best of times. It was especially difficult now that so much pressure was bearing down on their lives. They were living in an impossible situation at Howfield, trying to manage both a household and a distressed family. Their marriage was in trouble, and they couldn't sort it out long-distance. It was all too much for Frank. He stopped taking exercise. He became 'shy' of people, writing to Lettice: 'I mean to go into hall to-night if I have sufficient courage, but yesterday I funked it, and also ran away from Newman whom I saw coming down the road.'

He started lecturing again in the second week of January, after '10 weeks stagnation'. He was miserable, and bemoaned that there was no one in Cambridge he could talk to about what was going on. Lettice encouraged him to confide in any one of his large number of friends—she suggested Dadie Rylands, Ivor Richards, or Richard Braithwaite. Frank eventually talked to Peter Lucas, who lived in his own wide-open and often fraught marriage. Frank also discussed the relationship with Roger Money-Kyrle, who told him that if his own wife knew he had been unfaithful to her, as he had been occasionally 'in a light way', he thought 'she would leave him at once from hurt pride!' Frank's exclamation mark was an assertion that he and Lettice were much more sensible, much more decent than that. He decided that Money-Kyrle was 'astonishingly boring' and 'fearfully self-centred'.

Lettice stayed on a week after she was well enough to go home. A return to the restrictions of Howfield was not relished. She wanted to 'make hay', not so much with Liam, but at dances and a fancy-dress ball. Frank was not pleased, but, as requested, he packed up and sent her Hawaiian ensemble. Liam was absorbed with writing a novel and started to fail to keep assignations. Frank told Lettice that she should leave her lover, as there was no chance of a relationship of permanent value, which is what he thought ought to be the aim. Lettice told Frank that she felt like a 'small boat on a stormy sea' and badly wanted to return to her safe harbour. She hoped the gates would be open when she eventually made it home at the end of February.

They were indeed open, and the rupture was mended. Lettice was determined to make the situation with Elizabeth workable, and suggested to Frank that they become 'a happy trio'. She thought it would be 'rather difficult', more so for Elizabeth than for her, for Elizabeth 'would be the extra one, so to speak'. She floated a variation on the idea for a flat in London, in which Elizabeth would live permanently and Lettice would have a large semi-independent studio room for her own extra-marital life. It would make living in Howfield more bearable if she too had a regular escape route.

The flat was never acquired. They were saved by the death of Arthur's father. That freed up Arthur's sister Lucy to come and run the household. Having escaped her tyrannical father, Lucy now came to look after her tyrannical brother. In her view, it was better all round. Aunt Lucy was kind and everyone settled down well enough. But Margie had loved the year of Frank and Lettice living at Howfield, and was well aware that they had moved out because her father was impossible.

In June 1928, Frank, Lettice, and little Jane moved into a substantial three-storey house with a large garden, 4 Mortimer Road, near the green expanse of Parker's Piece. Frank had the window in the attic made bigger and now had a study in which he could work. He suggested some rules for future relationships, such as consulting with each other before getting involved with someone. Lettice agreed to them, although it's not clear they were strictly followed, and there would be bitter controversy over them in the last year of Frank's life. Frank stuck to his one, serious, relationship, and Lettice continued to have affairs, often borrowing Frances's London flat.[†]

One imagines the 'happy trio' was not so easy for Lettice. But she remained true to her principles. Frances Marshall recalled a weekend when she was visiting the Ramseys in Cambridge. She was told she had to share a bedroom with Elizabeth, which was irritating. But then 'there was a sort of swapping'. Lettice came into her bedroom and said that she would sleep there, as Elizabeth was going to sleep with Frank. They talked for hours about how Frank and Lettice had it all carefully worked out. When Frances woke up, Elizabeth's head was on the pillow next to her.

It also can't have been easy for Elizabeth. No matter the frequency of their times together, and the quality of her bond with Frank, she was still the other woman.

[†] Lettice's affair with Julian Bell did not start until after Frank's death. Bell was in Cambridge in 1929, but he was then otherwise engaged, including with his fellow Apostle Anthony Blunt. Lettice would be in effect widowed again, as Julian died fighting in the Spanish Civil War in 1937.

Frank's friends, and Lettice, referred to Elizabeth as 'Frank's girlfriend' or 'Frank's mistress'—or, if they were inclined to disapproval, as was the economist Joan Robinson, 'that girlfriend of his'. After he died, it seems that Elizabeth, who lived till the age of seventy-one, did not have another relationship.

Frank and Lettice did not think there was a whiff of indecency about their marriage, and apart from this, and one other, incident, it was strong, happy, and respectful. Lettice and Elizabeth continued to be friends. Frank and Lettice were back to thinking that they had matters very nicely, and ethically, settled. What they wanted, when they set out in their marriage, was a more expansive concept of love. It seemed to them that they achieved it. Frances Partridge and Richard Braithwaite both described a photo, from the now-missing album, of Frank walking between what Frances called his two great loves. They were walking on the river, Lettice and Elizabeth the same physical type and Frank towering over them.

Their worries seemed to be no longer about their sexual, but about their financial, affairs. When they moved to the Mortimer Road house, Frank couldn't see how they

Image 27 Elizabeth Denby.

could manage, since they had been spending nearly all their perfectly respectable income without having to pay rent. He wondered how they would do 'in a real house with several children'. But they weren't about to start economizing now. They continued with their parties and holidays. Frank joined some friends on a trip to the Tyrol in the summer of 1928, lugging his books up the mountain. He had a lot of work ahead of him and, although he didn't know it, precious little time to do it.

14

CAMBRIDGE ECONOMICS

Keynes and Pigou

1927–28 was a year of intense activity in economics for Ramsey. His work during this brief period has made him famous amongst contemporary economists. A striking number of innovations still in play are named after him and the two papers he wrote are still taught in economics graduate courses. One would think this would have him written into the intellectual history books, at the very least, histories of the Cambridge school of economics. But when he makes appearances in biographies and studies of Keynes, he is usually nowhere near centre stage, and two recent biographies of Pigou don't even have him in the index. That's something of a mystery. It can't be entirely explained by the fact that Ramsey was not a complete economist, with expertise and interests across its spectrum, like Keynes or Pigou. Nor can it be entirely explained by his early death. For even during his short lifetime his work in economics was taken to be important and he was a vital force in Cambridge economics. Moreover, in certain respects, he moved beyond his better-rounded and longer-lived mentors.

That school was perhaps even more self-contained than Cambridge philosophy. Its adherents were of the view that economics was not done very well anywhere else, although they did tolerate a few economists from Oxford. Alfred Marshall, the founder of the Cambridge school, had revolutionized the classical economics developed by Adam Smith, David Ricardo, and John Stuart Mill. His predecessors had analysed the production, distribution, and exchange of goods, arguing that the laws of supply and demand tell us that no more will be produced than can be sold, and that supply and demand determine market price. Marshall added to this analysis the role of money; extended the role of marginal analysis; showed how we can dispense with the idea that commodities and labour have real value; and tried to bring everything together into a unified theory.

That theory had a strong ethical character. Marshall had begun his education in philosophy and had been convinced by Sidgwick that the good was equivalent to the maximization of utility. Like Sidgwick and Mill, he argued that overall utility would be increased by improving the condition of the working classes. The new economics, in consort with progressive politics and education, was key to this mission. The Marxist economist Maurice Dobb surveyed the lay of the land in 1923: 'What the Cambridge school has done is to divest classical political economy of its more obvious crudities, to sever its connection with the philosophy of natural law, and restate it in terms of the differential calculus.' That calculus put marginal utility (the additional satisfaction gained from the consuming of one more unit of a good or service) equal to the marginal cost.

Ramsey's work in economics, even more than his work in philosophy, was influenced by those in his immediate circle. Marshall had retired in 1908. Keynes and Pigou were now the mainstays of the Cambridge School. Ramsey's work was also influenced by the times. The Cambridge economists were exploring solutions to the problems of Britain's post-war economy. The country had spent vast sums to fight the war and was now having to rebuild its industry. This period of reconstruction was at first marked by a spirit of optimistic hope of a return to pre-war economic conditions. By 1923–24, that optimism was beginning to waver. Keynes described his own generation as 'the last of the Utopians'. Ramsey's generation could not think of themselves as marching along the road of progress. The Great Slump, with its economic uncertainty; widespread unemployment; labour unrest; the first and short-lived Labour government of 1924; the 1926 General Strike; and runs on banks put an end to that. Indeed, Ramsey died just as the stock market crash of 1929 was starting to cause a global economic collapse. To many of his generation, the facts on the ground seemed to overturn received economic thinking. As Dobb put it in 1925, 'anti-laissez-faire' was becoming 'quite the fashion now in Camb'. 'Laissez-faire' was Keynes's preferred term for the economic orthodoxy that had dominated Britain. (Ramsey tended to use the term 'capitalism', and economists these days prefer 'market economy'.)

One particular piece of economic orthodoxy was the idea that market economies run in a circular way, like a finely built mechanical watch. Each element in a market, most notably supply and demand, is a part of the machinery, turning others, to make the whole economy function. For instance, when agents buy and sell with the aim of optimizing their own objectives, the prices that result are supposed to be set by supply and demand. The job of economists was to say how disturbances away from an equilibrium might be worked out, thus returning to a balance of forces in which supply and demand are balanced and there is more or less full employment.

The emerging position in the Cambridge School was that the economy did not run so flawlessly. The market economy simply was not producing a stable equilibrium, nor sufficient employment and income. As Keynes put it in 1923: 'Economists set themselves too easy, too useless a task if in tempestuous times they can only tell us that when the storm is long past the ocean is flat again.' In his 1926 pamphlet *The End of Laissez-Faire*, he argued that the decisions made by individuals, entrepreneurs, and businesses trying to optimize their own good were not guaranteed, or even likely, to produce the general good. Rather, government had to manage the economy. For instance, it had to step in to increase the level of employment, provide welfare benefits to the unemployed, and regulate interest rates and growth rates. Keynes wanted a managed economy, but still thought that financial markets were essential and, on the whole, benign.

When Ramsey was an undergraduate, Keynes had taken him under his wing. At that point, Ramsey already had strong opinions in favour of trade unions and progressive government intervention. He sporadically attended Keynes's Political Economy Club and the lectures that would become *A Treatise on Money*. By the time Ramsey was a young don at King's in 1927, Keynes was one of the country's foremost opinion-makers, not least because he was driving the economic policy of Lloyd George's Liberal Party. Ramsey and Keynes now interacted with each other whenever Keynes was in college, and also outside it, when Keynes mixed his Bloomsbury and economist friends at open house Sunday evenings, garden parties, and country weekends. The Ramseys were frequent guests, along with the economists Shove, Sraffa, Robertson, and Harrod.

Another major presence in Ramsey's economic thought was Arthur Pigou. Just a few years older than Keynes, he had become a Fellow of King's in 1902 and from 1908 was Marshall's successor as Professor of Political Economy. Like Keynes, Pigou sat on important public commissions, although he didn't enjoy them very much. He also had disagreements with Keynes—over, for instance, whether the pound sterling should return to being fixed to the price of gold, after its wartime depreciation. (Keynes lost the argument and accurately forecasted the ensuing disaster for workers.) But the two eminent King's economists were on the same page in advocating government intervention in the economy in order to make society better.

Pigou followed Marshall in taking 'better' as being the maximization of utility, and in aiming at the maximization of social, not individual, welfare. When social utility is the question, the answer seems to involve a redistribution of resources. For it is clear that the marginal utility of £100 for the rich person is less than it is for the poor person. Pigou's intellectual style was to ask whether a redistributive tax, a minimum income for the poor, or some other progressive measure would outweigh its social cost—would not take too big a piece out of the national dividend (the precursor of what is now called the gross national product). Pigou also thought, and here he was clearly following the intuitionist Moore, that we can perceive utility. He conceived of utility in a broad way as including pleasure, the quality of a person's ideals and character, love, and economic welfare. Only economic welfare seems to be measurable, as monetary values can be ascribed to goods. So Pigou, being an economist, focused on that particular slice of overall welfare, and assumed it was an adequate stand-in for utility.

One of Pigou's sustained projects during the 1920s was to develop Marshall's idea of 'externalities'—consequences (good or bad) for those who aren't party to a transaction. A factory owner might pollute the water, thereby imposing a cost on others. Pigou argued that the mitigation of such unintended costs often requires government intervention in the form of taxes or subsidies. Today the Pigou Club is a group of economists who support measures such as carbon tax policies and 'Pigovian taxes' are those designed to counter negative externalities. Another of Pigou's interests, articulated in the 1920 *The Economics of Welfare*, was that of fair distribution to future persons. He suggested that future persons should be treated equally with present persons and warned against the tendency of present generations to devote too few resources to investment, particularly in human capital. Dobb was right: thanks to Keynes and Pigou, anti-laissez-faire was quite the fashion in Cambridge.

Three Socialist Economists: Dobb, Sraffa, Ramsey

The Cambridge socialist economists were also important to Ramsey. They included his old friends from his days at the Heretics' Economic Section, Philip Sargant Florence and Maurice Dobb, and, more recently, the Italian economist Piero Sraffa. Ramsey also knew Joan Robinson, another well-known Cambridge socialist economist, from his undergraduate days. But she was in India during his burst of economic thought in 1927–28, and even when she was around, she seemed not to be on his radar. Perhaps that was because women weren't allowed to attend Keynes's Political Economy Club. Perhaps it was also because, unlike Dorothea Morison, who we know Ramsey thought an excellent economist, he took a dimmer view of Joan Robinson.

When they were undergraduates, Dobb had considerable influence on Ramsey, both by engaging with him about the kind of socialism that would be best, and by introducing him to workers' meetings. In the 1930s and 1940s, Dobb would be considered one of the most important Marxist economists of his century. In the mid-1920s, he was on his way to making that reputation. He published *Capitalist Enterprise and Social Progress* in 1925, *Russian Economic Development since the Revolution* in 1928, and popular books and pamphlets for workers' education on wages, money, prices, the development of capitalism, and much more.

Ramsey seems to have seen less of Dobb once he became a Fellow at King's. Sraffa, however, was very much in his orbit. He had been a friend of Antonio Gramsci, the founder and leader of the Italian Communist Party in fascist Italy, opening an account at a bookstore for Gramsci while he was in prison and supplying the pens and paper with which the famous *Prison Notebooks* were written. Sraffa had attacked Mussolini's policies and, to make matters worse in the eyes of the Fascists, he was a wealthy Jew. Mussolini was putting pressure on Sraffa about a piece he had written, on Keynes's invitation, for the *Manchester Guardian*. His position in Italy had become untenable and dangerous. In 1927, Keynes brought him to Cambridge, arranging a lectureship at the University and dining rights at King's.

Sraffa's 1926 article in Keynes's *Economic Journal*, 'The Laws of Return under Competitive Conditions', was well-known in Cambridge. He had noted a flaw in Marshall's (and Pigou's) theory that a firm will see diminishing returns as it grows in size. While Marshall had tried to explain the fact that firms were experiencing increasing revenue by reference to externalities or unintended causes, Sraffa had a more radical solution. Supply and demand, he argued, do not alone set the price of commodities. The exchange ratios of commodities must be explained on the basis of the physical characteristics of the production process. Because firms tend to grow and become monopolies, 'It is necessary to abandon the path of free competition and turn in the opposite direction, namely, towards monopoly'.

Sraffa, with the other Cambridge left-wing economists—including communists such as Dobb, Marxists such as Joan Robinson, and Guild Socialists such as Ramsey—thought their various proposals about state monopoly or income inequality could make the capitalist playing field fairer. They wanted to see a merging of a market economy and a socialist state. A capitalism that allows the unfettered play of private interests and private enterprise under competitive conditions was no good at all. But a regulated capitalism might well produce the greatest good for society. Even Dobb, who was keen on Soviet socialist planning and made extended trips in the late 1920s to see their results for himself, tried, in his 1925 doctoral dissertation, to marry Marx and Marshall. He had what Amartya Sen calls 'a complex attitude to the utility theory of value'.

Dobb thought that the utility theory of value rests on a psychology that narrows our desires and actions to what one bets on the market, or how one spends money, or the price one is willing to pay for some good. While this kind of 'empiricism traditional in Anglo-Saxon countries' has a basis in common sense, we mustn't turn that truism into a 'pretentious' final formula about a necessary equilibrium.

The tendency of the modern economist 'to make utility and disutility coincident with observed offers on the market' in effect makes him 'surrender, not...solve' 'the macroscopic problems of society'. But Dobb never became completely wedded to the opposing theory of value, the labour theory, which says that the value of a good or service is determined by the total amount of labour required to produce it.

Despite their heavy doses of moderation, Dobb and Sraffa were seen as fully signed up to Marxist ideology. After a college feast, a group including Sraffa, T.S. Eliot, and Newman went off to someone's rooms to talk. Eliot said afterwards that one of the things that made him different from the Marxists is that they were so certain of their beliefs. He was referring to Sraffa. Ramsey wasn't thought of in this way. He was considered (and considered himself) a socialist, but not a Marxist. After his schoolboy connection to the Glasgow Communist Party and his undergraduate association with Guild Socialism, he became rather allergic to ideology. He was not inclined to follow any party line. He certainly wasn't inclined to join the British Communist Party with Dobb.

The careers of these Marxists and communists tells us just how acceptable left-wing politics were in 1920s Cambridge. Sraffa got a University Lectureship in 1927, though he had to wait until 1934 before a college, Trinity, offered him a Fellowship. Similarly, Dobb's communism didn't scuttle his career but he, too, had to wait (till 1948) before a college offered him a Fellowship to complement his University Lectureship. When Trinity offered him the appointment, Dobb confessed to the conservative economist Dennis Robertson that he was a card-carrying member of the British Communist Party and would understand if the College were to withdraw their interest. Robertson is said to have replied: 'Dear Dobb, so long as you give us a fortnight's notice before blowing up the Chapel, it will be all right.'

Sraffa's nerves were a greater obstacle for him than his politics. Throughout 1927 and 1928 he regularly postponed his lectures and was granted leaves of absence from teaching. He was so notorious that his name became a noun—Braithwaite wrote to Keynes in 1928 that if he didn't soon figure out where to start in an upcoming talk, 'I may have to do a Sraffa.' In 1929, Keynes wrote to Lydia:

> Piero was...to have given his lecture to-morrow....He sat next to me in hall talking in high spirits and came to the combination room afterwards, then he rose from the table, delivered the whole of his dinner on the mat...and so won't lecture to-morrow after all! I am having (once more) to make the necessary announcement.

Perhaps Ramsey would have had better luck with his own appeal to Keynes for a teaching reduction had he deposited a few dinners on the mat.

But Sraffa did get to work, as Robinson put it, 'calmly committing the sacrilege of pointing out inconsistences in Marshall'. He argued that we should think of capital as inputs of labour and build our account of economic behaviour on that, rather than on the unrealistic assumptions about perfect competition that neo-classical economists held so dear. One pillar of the old economics had already been knocked down by the facts. Unemployment, on the orthodox view, should not really exist, yet it was galloping away. Sraffa attacked another—that profit is the reward for the productivity of capital—by arguing that profit comes from exploiting labour. His anxieties and his project of editing the works of Ricardo prevented these ideas being published in a timely fashion. They came out only in 1960 as *The Production of Commodities by Means of Commodities*.

Sraffa was one of Keynes's closest friends in Cambridge, and he would have an important, if fraught, intellectual relationship with Wittgenstein. He was also on excellent terms with Ramsey. The reader may recall from the Introduction that as Ramsey lay dying, he thought it 'mouldy' that he would have to cancel his planned meetings with Sraffa. And in that last year of Ramsey's life, the four—Keynes, Sraffa, Wittgenstein, and Ramsey—met, in what sometimes gets referred to as the 'Cafeteria Club', discussing Keynes's and Ramsey's theory of probability and Friedrich Hayek's theory of business cycles.

It's clear that Ramsey, like Dobb and Sraffa (and Moore) had a complex, pluralistic, view of value. In his 1924 Apostles paper, he castigated Mill for putting all his eggs in the utilitarian basket. During 1927–28, when his two important papers in economics were written, he was also working on a book in which he hoped to carve out a subtle, naturalist theory of value. He was going to start not with the transcendental, but with human psychology in all its complexity. He hardly mentioned utility in that book, keeping wide open the possibility that maximizing our desires might not be the whole, or even part, of the right story.

It may come as a surprise to economists that Ramsey shared with Dobb and Sraffa a scepticism about the utility theory of value. For he is considered a founding figure in two branches of utility theory economics, and his two famous papers were written in the neo-classical framework of individuals maximizing utility. But like Dobb and Sraffa, Ramsey employed utility analysis in the service of equality and socialism, and he did not think utility described the whole of what is good. We don't know where ultimately his views about the question would have landed, but we do know two things.

First, he was fully aware that the principle that agents act to maximize their utility is an ideal principle, not widely applicable in the real world. We cannot expect actual human beings to see all the implications of their body of belief and act accordingly.

(That is clear from 'Truth and Probability'.) Second, Ramsey was at home in the company that blended neo-classical economics and socialism. That is, he did not stop with the *efficient* outcome. He thought we have to adjust for inequalities of income, lack of imagination in considering future generations, etc. so as to bring about the *just* outcome. (That will become clear in his 'A Mathematical Theory of Saving'.)

Kingsley Martin said of Keynes that he wanted to 'save capitalism by altering its nature'. This holds also of Dobb, Sraffa, and Ramsey, who was more on the side of Dobb and Sraffa's socialism than Keynes's liberalism. He was more 'keen Labour', as Lettice put it, than Keynes, who was a keen Liberal. Keynes said that the '*class* war will find me on the side of the educated bourgeoisie'. Ramsey, who was so clearly a member of that educated middle class, tried to have some meaningful interaction with the working class. It began with his mother taking him to the workhouses, and continued with his undergraduate attendance at workers' meetings and his survey of unions. In his Apostles papers on the stresses that come with progress, he pressed the interests of the 'lower classes' on his well-heeled friends. In the class war, he was very much on the side of the underdog.

Image 28 Arthur Pigou.

The Thoroughbred

Schumpeter's description of Ramsey as a young racehorse, champing at the bit, is both evocative and apt. The Cambridge economists saw that he had speed, agility, and spirit, and they availed themselves of these talents. Keynes was especially alert to these qualities, and spotted them early. No review, no obituary, gets Ramsey as right as Keynes's.

It was an unusual friendship. Keynes was sophisticated, with a neat, languid, and loose-limbed manner, in contrast to Ramsey's unworldliness, untidiness, and ungainliness. There was a twenty-year age gap, as well as a wide experiential gap. Ramsey, as mere temporary resident and tourist, had observed the post-war inflation in Austria and Germany. Keynes had played a major role in advising the German government on how to stabilize the Deutschmark, and was famous for warning that in Austria, Russia, Turkey, and Hungary 'famine, cold, disease, war, murder, and anarchy are an actual present experience'.

But they also had a lot in common. Henry Lintott, a student of Frank's and later British High Commissioner to Canada, said that the only person he could compare Ramsey to, in temperament and ability, was Keynes. The comparison has a strong foundation in their histories. They both came from established Cambridge families with non-conformist roots. Their fathers were middling academics with considerable administrative abilities, and their mothers, political firebrands. They had been mathematically gifted scholarship boys at elite private schools (Eton for Keynes). Both had a vast breadth of interest in foundational theory—philosophy, mathematics, economics—which they combined with practical inventiveness and a commitment to putting their theories into practice.

They also both saw the economy as susceptible to the skilful pulling of policy levers, an approach which was the trademark of Keynesian economics. We must, however, keep in mind that Ramsey died before what we now think of as Keynesianism was fully developed. In the 1920s, Keynes was still claiming that the quantity theory of money could be employed to analyse business fluctuations. On that theory, a straightforward relationship exists between the amount of money in an economy and the price of goods and services. After a weekend at Keynes's country house in 1928, Ramsey wrote:

> I ought to have written before to say how very much I enjoyed the weekend.... And how exciting your quantity equation seemed; I wish I was sufficiently used to thinking about banking to appreciate it fully and make better criticisms. But I could see that it was a great advance.

Keynes was now very much in the habit of using Ramsey as a sounding board, asking him to work out a proof or take an idea in economics and test it mathematically. He would also frequently solicit Ramsey's opinion about papers submitted to the *Economic Journal*, of which he was editor.

A notable consultation occurred in the summer of 1928. Roy Harrod had given Keynes a draft paper, for consideration in the *Journal*. In it, Harrod put forward the concept of the marginal revenue curve and discussed it in different economic contexts. Keynes thought that part of the paper very good, but he had some concerns about Harrod's discussion of cartels. He invited the Ramseys to his country house for a weekend with the economist Hubert Henderson and his wife, telling Harrod that he would try out his argument on Ramsey and Henderson. Ramsey confirmed Keynes's worries about cartels, while agreeing with Keynes that the material on marginal revenue was 'very neat and nice'. He recommended that Keynes reject the paper as it then stood, and ask Harrod to resubmit after the cartel problems were ironed out. Harrod at the time happened to be having some personal difficulties and was close to a breakdown. He set aside the piece, replying to Ramsey's minor objections a year later, and the revised paper, 'Notes on Supply', was published in the June 1930 issue of the *Economic Journal*.* But Joan Robinson had got wind of Harrod's curve from Richard Kahn, and many credited her with it, much to Harrod's chagrin. Robinson said it was one of those instances 'when several explorers are surprised, and somewhat pained, on meeting each other at the Pole'.

Keynes wasn't the only Cambridge economist who enlisted Ramsey. In June 1928 Sraffa got Ramsey to help with the mathematics for his famous work on the determination of prices. In the Sraffa Papers there are a couple of notes in Ramsey's hand (one on the proverbial back of an envelope), with the equations which reduce the value of a commodity to the costs of producing it. Ramsey seems to have quickly corrected a mistake in Sraffa's initial attempt—a failure to distinguish between the quantity and price of a commodity. Then he showed Sraffa how to formulate the production of commodities in terms of simultaneous equations.

But while Keynes had a strong influence on Ramsey, Pigou had the strongest connection with Ramsey's work in economics. He was a tangled character, emotionally remote, shabbily dressed, and averse to talking shop when dining at King's. Indeed, he did all he could to avoid high table. Keynes once remarked to Lydia: 'Pigou was actually induced to come to lunch.' He was attracted to young men, and whether or not he acted on those attractions, he certainly didn't like women. Lettice

---

* Harrod himself told the story the following way. Discouraged by Ramsey's verdict and in poor health, he put the article in a drawer, and took the matter up with Ramsey eighteen months later. Ramsey 'recanted' and Harrod then re-submitted the article. The correspondence between them, however, shows that Ramsey saw from the beginning that the curve was important and that the required revisions could have been easily made.

was well aware of this, and Pigou seems never to have been a part of their socializing, nor weekends at Keynes's. But he and Ramsey had a serious intellectual relationship. Most of Pigou's correspondence and papers were destroyed, so we don't have much to go on. But there were at least two points of sustained personal contact. Pigou, a serious alpinist (he was a climbing partner of George Mallory), had Ramsey to stay at his cottage near Buttermere in the high hills of the Lake District, where they walked and talked economics. They also had rooms right next to each other in King's.

They worked together on what eventually became Pigou's 1928 *A Study in Public Finance*. Ramsey read parts of the book in draft and was thanked in the preface for his 'valuable suggestions'. Ramsey would pick up on that book's argument that saving should be exempt from income taxes. He also helped Pigou with modifications incorporated into the third edition of *The Economics of Welfare*, and supplied him with some mathematics for his work on credit and unemployment. When Pigou was writing 'The Statistical Derivation of Demand Curves', he wrote to Keynes that 'Ramsey, who I asked to vet my E.J. article, has now objected to parts 3 & 5, which I'm much too stupid to counter intelligibly in my present state'. He thought that he had just worded things badly, but 'the fact that it's not clear to Ramsey shows that it must be rewritten'. The paper appeared in the 1930 volume of the *Economic Journal*, presumably after it had passed Ramsey's vetting.

Ramsey thus was a collaborator in some of the most important economic developments in mid-1920s Cambridge. But, from a modern perspective (that is, from the point of view of what economists currently value), Ramsey soon surpassed his more senior colleagues. Not only was he more powerful at mathematical analysis, which was becoming increasingly necessary in order to model theories and discover their implications, but he also produced his own stunning results, going beyond what might be expected, beyond taking the next step in current thinking. He made leaps that still astonish. Once the world of economics caught up with him, Ramsey would be seen as a trailblazer in no less than three major problem areas in economics.

The first is the theory of choice under risk and uncertainty, worked out in the 1926 'Truth and Probability'. The second and third—optimal taxation theory and optimal savings theory—are the products of two papers he wrote for the *Economic Journal* in 1927. Ramsey was going to write just one paper, but Keynes told him that there was more than enough material for two. That was an understatement. Both papers were decades ahead of their time. They were tinged with philosophical analysis, and they were models, or simplifications of reality, while remaining very much tied to reality. Both had tremendous impact. Decades later in Cambridge, if economists employed an optimization model, they were said to be 'doing a Ramsey'. In France, the expression was 'à la Ramsey'. When the *Economic Journal* celebrated its

125th anniversary with a special edition in 2015, both of Ramsey's papers were included. That is, looking back over a century and a quarter, one of the world's best journals of economics decided that two of its thirteen most important papers were written by Frank Ramsey when he was twenty-five years old. The editors explained the unusual step of including two papers by one author: both initiated 'entirely new fields'. Austin Robinson said that Ramsey took economics to be 'a spare time, minor interest', secondary to his work in philosophy. He made quite good use of his spare time.

It wasn't until the 1950s, however, that Ramsey's work in economics was recognized outside of Cambridge. As in all his writing, Ramsey skipped lightly and quickly through highly technical matters. That footwork was too fast for most economists in the 1930s and '40s, but it impressed the technically inclined economists of the 1950s. It didn't help that the Great Depression followed shortly after Ramsey's death. It caused economists all over the world to be preoccupied with the immediate problem of unemployment, not the long-term rates of savings and taxation. It was only after the Second World War, when employment and prosperity were high, that economists could turn to consideration of Ramsey papers on optimal growth and distribution.

Image 29 Sraffa, Keynes and Dennis Robertson at Tilton, ca 1927.

15

RAMSEYAN ECONOMICS: THE FEASIBLE FIRST BEST

Optimal Taxation

Ramsey's first paper in the *Economic Journal* was titled 'A Contribution to the Theory of Taxation'. He had been heavily engaged with Pigou's public finance treatise, which tried to answer the question of how much and how best to tax. Ramsey's intellectual cylinders were firing on the question, and Pigou suggested that he write a paper. Pigou mentioned it to Keynes:

> Ramsey is writing out a paper on some results he got in the course of doing sums for me—with a marvellously simple generalized formula about taxes. Don't let him be too modest to produce it for the journal.

The idea that Ramsey thought his taxation paper not good enough to publish is almost comical. While *he* might have thought it a minor contribution to the theory of taxation, economists would later take him to have done something of major importance. He asked how we can minimize deadweight losses, or a fall in total surplus, when a given tax revenue needs to be raised. How can we raise that revenue in the most efficient way, the least costly in terms of individual utility? The solution he came to is now called Ramsey's Rule, and any research problem about optimal taxation policy is now called a Ramsey Problem.

In his 1923 Apostles paper 'Socialism and Equality of Income', Ramsey had argued for state ownership and control of industry. He had noted that the state would first have to buy out existing owners, and that the resulting inequality could be solved by taxation. He was also concerned in this early paper about the 'hereditary social classes', for it was inefficient to have 'fools'—the offspring of the rich—run our industries. The 'class system', he argued, is 'unjust', as it 'restricts equality of opportunity'. His argument was mostly a utilitarian one, but as was typical of him, it was joined by an argument about justice. Four years later, in 'A Contribution to the Theory of Taxation', he proposed to simplify the issue. He would 'neglect altogether' the question of whether income has been equitably distributed in the first place, as well as the differences in the marginal utility of money to different people. Here he was only doing the job of 'applying utilitarianism' to the problem of optimal taxation, making the assumption (which he knew to be false) that there was justice regarding income equality.

Ramsey argued that to optimize utility, we need an array of differentiated taxes. As Joseph Stiglitz, the American Nobel Laureate in Economics who built on Ramsey's paper, put it, Ramsey showed that

> A large number of small distortions, carefully constructed, is better than a single large distortion. And he showed precisely what these market interventions would look like.

We need a *system* of taxation, in which all goods are appropriately taxed, not a uniform tax. What is now known as Ramsey's Rule says that sales taxes 'should be such as to diminish in the same proportion the production of each commodity taxed'. When taxing commodities that are 'rivals for demand, like wine, beer and spirits, or complementary like tea and sugar, the rule to be observed is that the taxes should be such as to leave unaltered the proportions in which they are consumed'.

His position was that the consumption tax on each good should be inversely proportional to price elasticities. An elastic supply and demand curve occurs when the sale of a commodity is highly sensitive to small variations in price. The less elastic a commodity is, Ramsey argued, the more it should be taxed. The more elastic it is, the lower its tax rate should be. Inelastic goods can be taxed heavily without causing a deadweight loss. One consequence of his rule, he said, is that in some instances we might be justified in putting 'bounties' or subsidies on goods. It is 'perfectly possible' that a tax of 500 percent on whisky is right. What needs to be known is the elasticities of the supply and demand curves for whisky and its rivals.

Pigou was especially concerned about whether or not to tax savings—whether the redistributive fairness of taxing the savings of the rich outweighed the undesirable reduction of the national dividend. In 'A Contribution to the Theory of Taxation', Ramsey spoke briefly to whether his rule could be applied to savings and interest income. He treated savings as future consumption and suggested that, as with expenditure or current consumption, it should be taxed.

The paper was published in the *Economic Journal* in March 1927. When Pigou's book came out (the 1928 *Public Finance*), he summarized and defended Ramsey's approach. Ramsey's paper was hot off the press and had received its first citation. That would be one of a very few, for a very long time. In 1951, Paul Samuelson, in a widely circulated memorandum for the US Treasury, refined and re-energized

Ramsey's result (with a prompt from Harold Hotelling and John and Ursula Hicks). The entire field of optimal taxation now either follows the general outline of Ramsey's solution (in the case of public utilities, where it is called Ramsey Pricing) or uses it as backdrop to alternative solutions and new problems. Ramsey set the agenda that is still being pursued almost a century later, laying the foundation for the field of macro-public finance.

His approach would pave the way for progressive income taxes, indirect taxation, bequest taxes, and capital taxes. For once we articulate our concern with distributive justice and the need to fund public goods, we can figure out what can be achieved by the tax system while limiting the level of distortion. For instance, since the supply of land is inelastic, Ramsey's Rule would have it taxed more heavily than it is in most countries. This would be a progressive tax, for the inherited wealth that lies in land embeds inequality and restricts social mobility, just as he asserted in his 1923 paper to the Apostles.

THE LEGACY OF RAMSEY ON OPTIMAL TAXATION

Robin Boadway, David Chadwick Smith Professor Emeritus, Queen's University, Kingston

The terms 'Ramsey Tax Problem' and 'Ramsey Tax Rule' are part of the lexicon of the optimal tax literature. Consider a representative individual who obtains utility from the net consumption of n commodities, each of which is subject to a commodity tax. Lump-sum taxes and distributional considerations are ruled out, and the use of the revenues is neglected. The Ramsey tax problem asks how to extract a given amount of tax revenue with the least loss of utility to the representative individual. Utility functions are ordinal, so the loss of utility can be measured in monetary units.

The main results are as follows. For infinitesimal revenue requirements and taxes, optimal tax rates reduce the production of all commodities in the same proportion. Remarkably, if only a subset of commodities is taxed, this proportional reduction rule applies within the set of taxed commodities. Explicit solutions for tax rates are not presented, but in general one expects them to differ among commodities. In the case of discrete revenue requirements, these proportional reduction rules continue to apply if the utility function is quadratic. If commodities are independent and have their own demand and supply functions, optimal taxes satisfy an inverse elasticity rule: the optimal tax on each commodity is proportional to the sum of reciprocals of the sum of its demand and supply elasticities. Not surprisingly, the Ramsey Rule is alternatively described as the proportional reduction rule or the inverse elasticity rule. Its critical feature is the call for differentiated commodity tax rates.

Ramsey's results were largely neglected until the early post-war period, perhaps owing to the restrictive assumptions underlying them and the lack of familiarity among public finance economists of the mathematical techniques involved. (An exception is Hotelling (1932), who independently derived an optimal tax result similar to Ramsey's, and which too was neglected.) Four contributions refined and exploited Ramsey's insights.

Samuelson's 1951 memorandum to the US Treasury reformulated the Ramsey Rule using techniques of duality, a now-standard approach. (See also Boiteux (1951) who applied the Ramsey problem to public utility pricing.) Samuelson wrote the representative individual's utility in the indirect form as a function of consumer prices and maximized it with production possibilities as a constraint. This led to a set of equations that optimal taxes t_j should satisfy:

$$\sum_{j=1}^{n} s_{ij} t_j = -K$$

where s_{ij} is the compensated elasticity of demand for commodity i with respect to the price of commodity j. According to this condition, which is now thought of as the Ramsey Rule, optimal taxes should result in an equal proportionate reduction in the demand for all commodities if the individual is compensated to remain on the same indifference curve. Note that production elasticities do not appear in this expression. This proportionate reduction rule is not easy to interpret except in special cases: if preferences are additive in goods and quasilinear in leisure, the inverse demand elasticity rule applies; if goods are weakly separable from leisure and utility is homothetic in goods, commodity tax rates on goods should be uniform, or equivalently a proportional tax on income is optimal (Sandmo 1976).

A second contribution was Corlett and Hague (1953), who studied the effect on the representative individual's utility of incremental commodity tax reforms starting from uniform taxes. Using the simple case of two goods and leisure they showed using techniques similar to Ramsey's that utility would increase if the tax rate on the good most complementary with leisure were increased and the tax rate on the other good decreased so as to keep tax revenues constant. In effect, increasing the tax on the good most complementary with leisure indirectly taxes leisure, which is untaxed. The Corlett-Hague result has been used in many policy applications, including in an intertemporal setting similar to that originally considered by Ramsey.

The third extension of the Ramsey Rule was to a setting with heterogeneous individuals where the distribution of utility becomes relevant. While Ramsey's analysis required only the representative individual's utility function based on ordinal preferences, the objective function with heterogeneous individuals involves a social welfare function that requires measurability and interpersonal comparability of utilities. Diamond and Mirrlees (1971) derived a distribution-weighted analogue of the Ramsey Rule: the proportionate reduction in demand for a good is higher the more it is consumed by persons with lower social marginal utilities of income (i.e. the better-off). This overturned the prevailing wisdom popularized by Musgrave (1959) and Harberger (1971) that issues of equity and efficiency could be separated and dealt with in isolation by the tax system. Moreover, when government policies include not only commodity taxes but also an equal lump-sum transfer to all persons, the optimality of uniform commodity taxes becomes more likely. Deaton (1979) shows that in these circumstances, uniform taxes are optimal if household preferences are separable and quasi-homothetic in goods. Uniform commodity taxes combined with an equal lump-sum transfer is equivalent to a linear progressive (i.e., flat) income tax.

One final contribution cast further doubt on the Ramsey Rule's advocacy of differential commodity taxes. Atkinson and Stiglitz (1976) embedded commodity taxes into Mirrlees' model of optimal nonlinear income taxation. They showed that if goods are weakly separable from leisure in utility, commodity taxes used alongside an optimal income tax should be uniform. Weak separability is not very restrictive, and even if it does not literally apply, deviations from uniformity may not be worth the administrative effort.

The Ramsey Rule plays a limited role nowadays in tax policy debates. Tax reform proposals, such as the Mirrlees Review in the UK, typically argue for a uniform value-added sales tax system with minimal exceptions. Nonetheless, Ramsey's legacy remains intact. His contribution was instrumental in initiating the enormously influential and ongoing debate on optimal taxation.

Stiglitz called Ramsey's analysis of taxation 'the first successful exercise in second-best economics'. Economists employ the phrase 'second-best' to describe a state of affairs in which an ideal solution cannot be achieved. Ramsey had noted that lump sum taxes would be the best option, if all individuals were the same. It would not change any incentives. But individuals are not the same—in the real world, some are poor and unemployed, while others have vast sums of savings and ongoing earnings. So the first best solution is not workable. As James Meade argued, a policy that might optimize utility under a utopian model might make for less utility in the real world.

Ramsey's point was that we need a second best solution in which the distortion of variable taxation is introduced. Samuelson hit on a very nice way of characterizing his approach—so nice that it could well describe his attitude, not just in economics, but to all questions. He said that Ramsey provided

an analysis that still remains about the only substantive contribution to the theory of the second best (a subject better titled the 'theory of the *feasible* first best').

That phrase—the *feasible first best*—beautifully captures Ramsey's intellectual style. We are not after the ideal, the absolute, the certain rule or principle. We are after the feasible first best, which will be dependent on the circumstances that can actually hold. There is nothing more—nothing that goes beyond the feasible first best—at which we might aim. That is the optimal solution for the real world.

Ramsey saw that the feasible first best is a moving target, always evolving. We have to aim for what is *really* the best we can do, not merely what appears to be doable here and now. But we can't aim for what Ramsey called 'fairy tales'. As he remarked in another context, 'What we can't do, we can't do, and it's no good trying.' This is the great challenge for the pragmatist or naturalist—how to take seriously the facts of psychology, biology, the economy, and so on, without giving up on improvement or reaching higher. Indeed, it is the challenge of being human.

How Much Should We Save for Future Generations?

The second of Ramsey's two famous papers in the *Economic Journal*, 'A Mathematical Theory of Saving', addressed the question of how much should be saved for future generations. Individuals often save for their children. But Ramsey's question was: how much should *society* save? In putting the issue this way, he signalled the need for a political mechanism to ensure the welfare of future generations. The state must plan and intervene in individual choice via policy, rules, and incentives. For individuals, left to themselves, might not save the right amount.

One way of failing to save the right amount would be to save too much. Keynes had argued in *A Treatise on Money* that excess saving could cause a fall in output. But the error might come from the other direction—we might use up so much of our resources that we load excessive debt, environmental degradation, and other such burdens onto future generations. Ramsey had identified this problem in his 1923 'Socialism and Equality of Income', in which he argued that a socialist state would 'make a more farsighted use of our natural resources such as forests and minerals'. Decades later, Kenneth Arrow, Partha Dasgupta, and Geoffrey Heal would continue the discussion Ramsey started about how much natural capital we should save, including the topics of exhaustible resources, climate change, and nuclear waste disposal.

Five years after the 'Socialism and Equality of Income' paper, Ramsey set out to find a precise answer to the question of just how farsighted the state should be. As with his taxation paper, he put the question in terms of optimal or maximum utility over the long run. The very title of the savings paper asserts that he will be providing a mathematical analysis, which one cannot do without employing a utilitarian framework. His question was: How much of its income should a nation save in order to maximize utility over generations? Immediate consumption produces utility now and reduces it in the future (by reducing opportunities), and saving reduces utility now and increases it in the future. How much we should invest right now in goods such as the environment or scientific knowledge, which may have no immediate payoff but nevertheless may produce a big payoff for future generations? Should we discount the well-being of future generations? These are questions bred in the bone of utilitarianism and welfare economics.

In a characteristically charming way, Ramsey employed 'bliss' as the technical term for the situation in which saving would be unnecessary, and all income would be devoted to consumption. Bliss is beyond our reach, but we can measure, in a dynamic way, how close we are to it, and we can adopt policies to bring us as near as we can get. At each point in time, we can determine the trade-off between consumption and saving. His insight was that the difference between the upper-bound ideal and what we currently have is finite, and we can measure and improve upon it. In what we can now see as a signature move, Ramsey changed the question from one about an unreachable ideal to an answerable problem for finite human beings.

The optimal policy, Ramsey argued, is that we must not increase consumption in one generation to an extent that would decrease utility in the next generation to a greater extent. His conclusion was striking: to get the greatest amount of utility across generations, we ought to save over half our resources.

RAMSEY'S RULE

Partha Dasgupta, Frank Ramsey Professor Emeritus of Economics, University of Cambridge

How should we conceptualize human well-being over time and across generations? How ought the interests of people in the distant future to be taken into account when we make our own decisions? In which assets should that investment for the future be made? What should be the balance among private, public, and communitarian investments in the overall investment that a generation makes for the future?

In a remarkable paper, Frank Ramsey developed a framework in which each of these questions can be studied in a form that is precise and tractable enough to elicit answers. His approach was to apply Classical-Utilitarianism calculus to identify the best match from among attainable and desirable utility streams over time and across generations. The number of trails Ramsey laid was remarkable. In academic economics it is probably one of the dozen most influential papers of the twentieth century.

Ramsey responded to the question he posed—'How much of a nation's output should it save for the future?'—by constructing a model economy in which the planner maximizes the expected sum of the lifetime well-beings of all who are here today and all who will ever be born, subject to resource constraints. The future was assumed to be deterministic and indefinitely long; and population was assumed to be constant.

Let U be a numerical measure of utility. If C is consumption, utility is $U(C)$, which is assumed to be an increasing and strictly concave function. Ramsey assumed also that U is bounded above. Let B be the lowest upper bound of U and let $t \geq 0$ denote time. Ramsey's preferred position on national saving was that the future should not be discounted. Thus, the value of an infinitely long consumption stream, which we write as $\{C(t)\}$, is $V(0) = \int_0^\infty [U(C(t))]dt$. The economy is assumed to be endowed at $t = 0$ with the stock, K, of an all-purpose, non-depreciating commodity that produces output at each date. Output can be either invested so as to add to the commodity's stock or consumed immediately. The problem is to find the optimum allocation of output at each date between consumption and investment.

Ramsey noted that the infinite integral labelled $V(0)$ may not converge. When it doesn't, $V(0)$ is meaningless. To avoid the problem he reconstructed the utilitarian value of $\{C(t)\}$ to be $V(0) = \int_0^\infty [U(C(t)) - B]dt$. The thought behind the reconstruction is that in a productive economy there would be savings policies for which $C(t)$ rises to infinity at such a fast rate that the gap between B and U reduces to zero so fast that $V(0)$ is a finite quantity.

To illustrate Ramsey's analysis, we work with an example he studied. If Q is output, assume that

$$Q = \mu K, \quad \mu > 0 \tag{15.1}$$

In Equation (15.1) the productivity of capital (alternatively, the rate of return on investment) is μ and $dK(t)/dt$ is net investment at t. It follows that the economy's dynamics can be represented by the equation:

$$dK(t)/dt = \mu K(t) - C(t), \text{ and } K(0) \text{ is the initial stock of capital.} \tag{15.2}$$

We say $\{C(t)\}$ is a *feasible consumption stream* if it satisfies Equation (15.2). Ramsey's problem is to identify the feasible consumption stream $\{C(t)\}$ that maximizes $V(0)$.

A special form of U that Ramsey studied assumes $B = 0$ and

$$U(C) = -C^{-(\sigma-1)}, \quad \sigma > 1 \tag{15.3}$$

σ is the elasticity of marginal utility.

Let $\{C^*(t)\}$ denote the optimum consumption stream. Ramsey constructed a variational argument for identifying $\{C^*(t)\}$. He argued that the planner should require the marginal rate of ethically indifferent substitution between consumption at any two brief adjacent periods of time (which can be shown to be $\sigma[dC(t)/dt)/C(t)]$) to equal the marginal rate at which consumption can be transformed between those same pair of brief periods of time (i.e., μ). Thus $\{C^*(t)\}$ necessarily satisfies the condition that for all $t \geq 0$,

$$\sigma(dC(t)/dt)/C(t) = \mu \tag{15.4}$$

Equation (15.4) is the famous Ramsey Rule of optimum saving. The Rule equates the 'desirable' to the 'realizable' rate of exchange of consumption between every pair of brief adjacent periods of time. Integrating Equation (15.4) yields

$$C^*(t) = C^*(0)e^{[\mu/\sigma]t} \qquad (15.5)$$

Equation (15.5) says $C^*(t)$ grows exponentially at the rate μ/σ. Notice that although Equation (15.5) reveals the rate at which consumption ought to grow, it doesn't say what the initial level of consumption, $C^*(0)$, should be. That's an indeterminacy in the Ramsey Rule.

The simplest way to determine $C^*(0)$ is to deduce from Equations (15.2) and (15.5) that $K(t)$ ought to be made to grow at the same rate as $C^*(t)$. (The argument underlying this is complicated, and we suppress it for brevity.) Define the *saving rate*, s, as the proportion of output that is invested at each instant (i.e., $s = 1 - C(t)/Q(t)$). Then integrating Equation (15.1) yields

$$K(t) = K(0)e^{s\mu t} \qquad (15.6)$$

But because $C^*(t)$ and the optimum stock of capital $K^*(t)$ should grow at the same rate, Equations (15.5)–(15.6) say that the optimum saving rate, s^*, is

$$s^* = 1/\sigma < 1 \qquad (15.7)$$

Ramsey's model points to high saving rates. To illustrate, suppose $\sigma = 2$. Then Equation (15.7) says s^* is 50 per cent. Moreover, the closer σ is to 1, the nearer s^* is to 100 per cent. The subsequent literature on optimum saving has tried to find more realistic models, in which s^* is smaller.

Keynes was more involved in this second paper of Ramsey's than he had been with the first. On 28 June, the day Ramsey and Sraffa met about Sraffa's 'equations', Ramsey sent Keynes a draft of his savings paper:

Dear Maynard,

Here is an article which I hope you will think suitable for The Economic Journal. The mathematics is all very elementary, and the beginning part is fully explained for the sake of those who will read a little way.

Although the matter is terribly oversimplified, the equations must arise in any attempt to apply utilitarianism to saving and so far as I know they've never been treated before. The difficulty is to find simple results of sufficient generality to be interesting and yet not obvious. In this I think I've succeeded surprisingly well. To prove them is never hard, except when it comes to taxation which is very complicated and in which I've wasted a lot of time with only one achievement of any sort.

Of course, the whole thing is a waste of time, as I'm mainly occupied on a book about logic, from which this distracts me, so that I'm glad to have it done. But it's much easier to concentrate on than philosophy, and the difficulties that arise rather obsess me.

Yours ever,

Frank Ramsey

Keynes thought it was well worth Ramsey's time to temporarily put aside the more difficult matters of philosophy and get the savings paper into publishable shape. He had some comments with respect to the draft. One was that Ramsey's proof could be put in less technical, more intuitive, language. Keynes did just that, and it is Keynes's formulation that is now known as the Keynes–Ramsey Rule.

Keynes also suggested that Ramsey make explicit two assumptions in his paper: that 'the community will be always governed by the same motives in accumulation' and that 'no misfortunes occur to sweep away accumulations'. The first was uncontroversial as far as Ramsey was concerned. But the second was less so. Sidgwick was the first of the utilitarians to argue that we must be as concerned with 'the interests of posterity' as with current interests. But Sidgwick figured we must take account of uncertainty regarding the consequences of our actions for the future, and uncertainty even about the existence of people in the future. The utilitarian calculus, that is, seems to require that the well-being of future people should be given less weight than the well-being of people here and now. So Keynes thought that Ramsey should include a time-dependent discount factor, as 'the fear or the probability' that misfortunes will occur makes it 'rational to save at a slower rate than your formula would indicate'. Keynes had said in 1923 that 'the long run is a misleading guide to current affairs. In the long run we are all dead.' Ramsey might well have been registering a response to Keynes in his insistence on taking seriously those far down the road.

Pigou had argued in his 1920 *The Economics of Welfare* that discounting is a mistake in the calculation of utility, a mistake due to our inclination to employ a flawed 'telescopic' perspective:

> we see future pleasures…on a diminished scale…This reveals a far-reaching economic disharmony. For it implies that people distribute their resources between the present, the near future and the remote future on the basis of a wholly irrational preference.

We human beings often weigh even our own current pleasure as more significant than our own future pleasure, and we tend to see ourselves as more important than future people. That impulse, which Pigou took to be a weakness of will, usually turns out badly for individuals, as it will tend to suboptimal consumption patterns over time. The danger is amplified when we consider the utility of society as a whole, for we might be even more reluctant to save for faceless individuals in the distant future.

Ramsey agreed with Pigou that the optimal rate of savings is higher than people tend to think. He also agreed that we should not discount future generations. But he took a very different route to these conclusions. He thought it might make utilitarian sense for individuals to discount future people, as they care less about them than they care about themselves. That is, discounting needn't be a mistake in an individual's utility calculation. Towards the end of the paper, Ramsey included a rate of discount for individuals making intertemporal choices.

But *from the perspective of society*, it is indeed a mistake to discount future generations. The mistake isn't one of accounting nor of weakness of the will. Discounting future generations is 'a weakness of the imagination' and 'ethically indefensible' as a social policy. Yet again, we see Ramsey explore the tension between what is good for an individual and what is good for society. David Cass, who in 1965 built on Ramsey's account of savings, saw his strategy clearly:

> Ramsey had no discounting. He made a big point of talking about the correctness of the social welfare function from a moral viewpoint.

Tjalling Koopmans also noted that, with respect to discounting, 'on ethical grounds Ramsey would have none of this'.

Another way of seeing Ramsey's move is that he set out his problem in terms of the utilitarian calculus, but refused to confine himself to it. His question was not simply how to maximize utility over generations. He added a point about justice to the utilitarian calculus—an ethical point that stands above a calculation that would have us adding up the probabilities of disasters to determine whether to discount future generations' utilities. Ramsey was not a full-out utilitarian, to whom discounting is the obvious and correct thing to do. He did not think that the only value was utility, nor did he think that economics is all about efficiency and that somehow the quest for efficiency makes it a value-neutral science. His savings paper was concerned with intergenerational *justice*. This is perhaps why Richard Kahn, who had been Ramsey's student at King's, and whom Ramsey would support to become a Fellow in 1929, called it a 'very stratospheric' paper and 'a useful application of economics for a socialist state'.

Ramsey's eventual list of assumptions contained four: that our community goes on forever, seeking to maximize utility of its consumption and maintaining more or less the same size and the same capacity for enjoyment and aversion to labour; that no new technical innovations appear on the scene; that we can't go on forever being more and more in debt to foreign nations; and that utility is independent at various time points. He declined Keynes's advice to include a discount rate based on the probabilities of disasters. The final version of the paper spoke to the omission:

The most serious factor neglected is the possibility of future wars and earthquakes destroying our accumulations. These cannot be adequately accounted for by taking a very low rate of interest over long periods, since they may make the rate of interest actually negative, destroying as they do, not only interest, but principal as well.

Ramsey assumed that extinction is *not* on the horizon, although of course he knew that it was. This move was entirely consistent with one he made in his 1925 Apostles paper about the meaning of life. There he said: 'In time the world will cool and everything will die; but that is a long time off still, and its present value at compound discount is almost nothing.' His point in the Apostles paper was that we should not infer that 'the present is less valuable because the future is blank'. In the savings paper, his point is that the fact that the world will cool and die does not mean we should discount the well-being of future generations. Taken together, the two papers argue that the fact that the future is blank should not lead us to discount value now or later. All we can do is keep on with our practices and what is important to us. Ramsey thus anticipated the 'infinite life' assumption now adopted by many economic models, which hold that since we bequeath our resources to our descendants, it is as if we live an infinite life. Ramsey's friend Roy Harrod followed him on this matter. In a paper in 1938, and then in an important book in 1948, titled *Towards a Dynamic Economy*, he would argue against discounting, calling it a 'polite expression for rapacity and the conquest of reason by passion'.

DISCOUNTING OF FUTURE WELL-BEINGS

Partha Dasgupta, Frank Ramsey Professor Emeritus of Economics, University of Cambridge

Ramsey famously stated that discounting is 'ethically indefensible and arises merely from the weakness of the imagination'. This move has provoked more debate among economists and philosophers than any other feature of his theory of optimum saving. At the risk of generalizing wildly, economists have favoured the use of positive rates to discount future well-beings, whereas philosophers have insisted that the well-being of future people should be given the same weight as that of present people.

Ramsey considered a world with an indefinite future. This could appear to be an odd move, but it has a strong rationale. Suppose the decision maker, or planner, were to choose a horizon of T years. As she doesn't know when our world will end, she will want to specify the resources that should be left behind at T in case the world doesn't terminate then. But to find a justification for the amount to leave behind at T, the planner will need an assessment of the world beyond T. But that would amount to including the world beyond T. And so on.

Utility was taken by Ramsey to be an increasing numerical function of consumption (U(C)). It was assumed that the planner seeks to maximize the sum of utilities from the present to the indefinite future subject to resource constraints. The problem is, infinite sums don't necessarily converge to finite limits. So Ramsey supposed that utility is bounded above, say, by B. The planner's objective was then taken to be the sum of the shortfall of utility from B, the thought being that if, through the act of saving, consumption were allowed to increase at a sufficiently fast rate, the shortfall would tend to zero fast enough for the infinite sum to converge. Not only was the move on Ramsey's part ingenious, it also displayed his moral integrity. It would have been easy enough for him to ask the planner instead to discount future consumption and expand the range of circumstances in which utilitarianism provides an answer to her optimization problem. He chose not to do that.

Ramsey's intuition regarding the indefiniteness of the future was powerful, but in a paper that initiated the modern literature on the Ramsey Problem, Chakravarty (1962) observed that to rely exclusively on the condition Ramsey had identified as being *necessary* for a consumption stream to be the optimum for locating the optimum can lead to absurd results. In effect Chakravarty observed that infinite sums don't necessarily converge to finite values. What was needed was to de-link the question whether infinite well-being sums converge from the question whether optimum consumption streams exist. That insight was provided by Koopmans (1965) and von Weizsacker (1965).

What are we to make of the ethics of discounting the well-beings of future generations? Ramsey began by dismissing it but then studied it at the tail end of his paper. The matter cannot be settled without a study of production and consumption possibilities open to an economy. It has been shown by Dasgupta and Heal (1974) that, in the context of a simple model, if production requires produced capital and exhaustible resources, then optimum consumption declines to zero in the long run if future well-beings are discounted at a positive rate, but increases indefinitely if we follow Ramsey in not discounting future well-beings. The long-run features of optimum saving policies depend on the relative magnitudes of the rate at which future well-beings are discounted and the long-term productivity of capital assets.

Koopmans explored the general point in a remarkable set of publications on the idea of economic development, showing that it is foolish to regard any ethical principle (e.g., classical utilitarianism) as sacrosanct. One can never know in advance what it may run up against. We must play off one set of ethical assumptions against another in not-implausible worlds, see what their implications are for the distribution of well-being across generations, and then appeal to our intuitive senses before arguing over policy. Settling *ex ante* whether to use a positive rate to discount future well-beings could be a self-defeating move. Koopmans (1960, 1965) exposed internal contradictions in Ramsey's account and he (and subsequently Diamond (1965)) showed that if relatively weak normative requirements are imposed on the concept of intergenerational well-being in a deterministic world, equal treatment of the U-function across generations has to be abandoned. Koopmans's line of reasoning, concerning experimentation with alternative ethical principles would, of course, have been congenial to Ramsey.

In the end, Keynes applauded the paper, even if he never came round to Ramsey on the matter of discounting:

> [It is] one of the most remarkable contributions to mathematical economics ever made, both in respect of the intrinsic importance and difficulty of its subject, the power and elegance of the technical methods employed, and the clear purity of illumination with which the writer's mind is felt by the reader to play about its subject. The article is terribly difficult reading for an economist, but it is not difficult to appreciate how scientific and aesthetic qualities are combined in it together.

Pigou again cited Ramsey's paper. And in 1949, Ramsey's use of the catenary property (the U-shaped curve that a rope tethered at both ends makes when it sags in the middle) was a 'clue' that enabled Samuelson to arrive at his Turnpike Theorem:

> Just as a rope hangs toward the ground in a catenary, the optimal path arches toward the Bliss turnpike.

But only in the early 1960s did it become clear how extraordinarily fecund Ramsey's savings paper was. It was the natural starting point for studying the welfare economics of the long run, not only for pursuing optimum development in centrally planned economies, but also for use in social cost-benefit analysis of public investment in mixed economies and the choice of technology in labour-surplus economies. David Cass, in his 1960s Stanford PhD thesis, developed a well-received model of optimal growth. He found out about Ramsey's paper after he had written his first chapter. In an interview in 1998, he said that while his supervisor thought that his first chapter and the subsequent publication of it were 'absolutely seminal', when Cass found out about the Ramsey paper, his own view of his accomplishment dimmed:

> In fact I always have been kind of embarrassed because that paper is always cited although now I think of it as an exercise, almost re-creating and going a little beyond the Ramsey model.

Tjalling Koopmans reinterpreted and extended Ramsey's result, and showed that failure to apply a discount rate to future generations would require too much sacrifice from current ones. Kenneth Arrow argued that each generation should accord itself a slightly higher weight. Robert Solow showed that saving at Ramsey's rate, with no discounting of future generations, would be excessive for wealthy nations and would bankrupt poor nations, especially if the investments of each generation pay dividends in the future. Solow's solution is often called the Ramsey–

Solow optimizing model. Samuelson, Franco Modigliani, and others devised the overlapping generation model of the life-cycle theory of consumption, setting out how individuals and societies should plan their consumption and savings over time. Ramsey would have been pleased to see his principles being tested and refined in models and in practice.

His high rate of savings with no discounting was an effect of the fact that he was the first to set out a growth model. Others came along and made it better. As James Mirrlees put it, 'Ramsey's famous paper created the subject of optimum economic growth', but his assumptions were unrealistic. For Mirrlees, that was because they failed to account for how technological change has an impact on growth. He showed how to extend the model in order to do that. While it is true that Ramsey didn't take into account major technological advances and couldn't predict how the future would unfold, he did (in a letter to Harrod) joke that bliss might be achieved by 'enough appliances…e.g. the machine which puts your dinner on while you order it by telephone'.

Taxing Savings

At the end of his taxation paper, Ramsey had considered the question of whether savings should be taxed. His conclusion was that they should not be exempt from tax, but should be taxed at a lower rate than income from labour. The draft of the savings paper Ramsey sent to Keynes included two sections on the question. After some to-and-fro, Keynes asked that these sections be dropped. Ramsey was happy to comply, as he thought the mathematics complicated, and that he hadn't proved a sufficiently strong result. Had Ramsey continued to work on economics, perhaps he would have made a non-mathematical, political, argument for the taxation of savings. For despite being the most mathematically accomplished economist of his generation (and perhaps the next as well), we have seen that Ramsey did not think that all our conclusions had to come via mathematics.

The draft Ramsey sent to Keynes hasn't survived, but some extensive notes of Ramsey's on the taxation of savings have. Pedro Garcia Duarte has figured out which were the notes he made while helping Pigou with the topic and which informed the section of the savings paper cut by Keynes, and has published the missing sections. Once we take them into account, we can see that Ramsey had a research programme in economics, one heavily influenced by Pigou. It aligned well with his ideas about politics.

THE MISSING SECTION

Pedro Garcia Duarte, Department of Economics, University of São Paulo and INSPER

In his 1927 paper Ramsey derived mathematically a second-best taxation principle according to which goods should be taxed inversely to their demand (or supply) elasticities. He briefly considered an application of his result to the issue of taxing savings, but warned his readers that his paper had a static framework and, thus, 'we must suppose the taxes [are] imposed only for a very short time and that they raise no expectation of similar taxation in the future; since otherwise we require a mathematical theory considerably more difficult than anything in this paper'.

Pigou treated savings as a use of income and used Ramsey's result to conclude that because savings has a more elastic demand than consumption, it should be taxed at a lower rate than consumption. Ramsey did not dispute the soundness of this result, but disagreed that his mathematical treatment could support it. In producing his 1928 paper, with an intertemporal analysis of the allocation of consumption, Ramsey tried to extend his dynamic equations to consider the issue of taxing savings.

He considered the case of differentiated taxation by setting a positive constant tax rate on consumption which is partly remitted on savings. He then obtained the new equations describing the intratemporal allocation between consumption and labour and the intertemporal equation describing consumption allocation. He explained that the economy resource constraint here depended on the uses of the tax revenue raised by the government. He considered two cases. First, that 'the revenue is all *transferred* by the government back to the public in the form of pensions, dividends on war loan etc to be spent or saved by the public at its discretion'. This income is taxable and the resource constraint is the same as in the case of no taxation analysed in the 1928 paper. The second case considered the government expending the tax revenue 'on purposes separate from those on which the public spends its money, and that this government expenditure does not alter the utility of private incomes'. With a modified resource constraint Ramsey obtained a more complex mathematical system of equations and considered the simple case of a linear production function (as he did in the 1928 paper). In this case he added a further tax differentiation between earned and unearned incomes (i.e. labour and capital incomes).

Ramsey went on to analyse 'the problem of raising a given [tax] revenue with minimum sacrifice, distributional and administrative considerations being disregarded'. The first solution comes when all tax and remittance rates can be set independently. In this case, the best solution is not to tax earned income and make the tax on unearned income be offset by the remittance on savings. 'The revenue would in effect be raised entirely off capital existing at the time when tax is first imposed, and the taxation would have no "announcement effects," to use Prof. Pigou's phrase.'

323

The second solution refers to a case when earned and unearned incomes cannot be taxed at such different rates, and here is where Ramsey disagreed with Pigou's analysis. Supposing that both income types are taxed equally, Ramsey investigates whether 'a uniform income tax should be remitted on savings'. Pigou concluded that because the demand for savings is more elastic than that of consumption, 'that not merely should savings be altogether exempted from income tax but that they should actually be rewarded with a bonus; for on Prof. Pigou's view, unless exempted from income tax they are really taxed twice, once when originally made and again when they earn interest'. Ramsey argued that his 1927 analysis could not be applied to this case: 'The reason for this is that in a problem covering a considerable term of years saving cannot be considered simply as a use of income with its own utility. Its utility is indirect and arises from the consumption it makes possible later; it is therefore a part of the process of production rather than of that of consumption, and it is evident that the reasoning by which I proved the result to which Prof. Pigou refers cannot be applied at all', except in the case he considered in passing in the 1927 paper mentioned above. Ramsey argued that a new set of equations should be used to tackle this problem, which has an extremely complicated solution. As he wrote to Roy Harrod on 27 March 1929, 'I did a very elaborate treatment of taxation and savings which was cut out by Maynard; rightly as it was too involved in comparison with the conclusions which were feeble.'

This seems to be Ramsey's last communication about economics. In the year and a half that he had to live, he would do as he indicated to Keynes. He would focus on the foundational problems of philosophy. While Pigou, Shove, Dobb, Robertson, Sraffa, Austin Robinson, Kahn, and others continued to attend Keynes's Political Economy Club in 1928 and 1929, Ramsey's name appears and then is crossed out on the membership list, suggesting that they thought he would attend, but he didn't.

The volume of the *Economic Journal* of March 1927, in which Ramsey's taxation paper appeared, made mention of those who had taken out a subscription and joined the Royal Economic Society. One was his friend Dorothea Braithwaite. Another was Oskar Morgenstern, who intersected with the Vienna Circle and would go on with John von Neumann to reinvent (or perhaps resurrect) Ramsey's results in decision theory and to develop game theory. The December 1928 volume, in which Ramsey's savings paper appeared, noted his student Richard Kahn's membership in the Royal Economic Society and the death of Dorothea Braithwaite. Perhaps Ramsey would have eventually decided to join the Society and thus signal his intention to continue to work in economics. Perhaps the up-and-coming Kahn, or someone else, might have re-engaged his attention towards economics. Instead, the March 1930 volume would contain his obituary. It would be initialled by the editor of the *Journal*, Keynes, who wrote:

From a very early age, about sixteen I think, his precocious mind was intensely interested in economic problems. Economists living in Cambridge have been accustomed from his undergraduate days to try their theories on the keen edge of his critical and logical faculties. If he had followed the easier path of mere inclination, I am not sure that he would not have exchanged the tormenting exercises of the foundations of thought and of psychology, where the mind tries to catch its own tail, for the delightful paths of our own most agreeable branch of the moral sciences.... When he did descend from his accustomed stony heights, he still lived without effort in a rarer atmosphere than most economists care to breathe, and handled the technical apparatus of our science with the easy grace of one accustomed to something far more difficult.

The little that Ramsey wrote, when he was persuaded to turn his attention away from philosophy (and psychology, which he thought underpinned philosophy), was enough to establish a reputation in economics that shows no sign of diminishing. In 1966, Howard Raiffa, co-author of the classic 1957 *Games and Decisions*, which built on Ramsey's work, became the inaugural holder of the Frank Plumpton Ramsey Chair of Economics at Harvard University. In 1994, Partha Dasgupta became the inaugural Frank Ramsey Professor of Economics at the University of Cambridge. 'A Mathematical Theory of Saving' is often one of the first models taught in contemporary MA and PhD macroeconomics courses and is taught in almost all graduate public finance courses. Talk of optimal taxation continues to be peppered with 'Ramsey Problems' and 'Doing a Ramsey'. Even when we consider how little time Ramsey had left in which to work on the philosophy that really ignited him, it is impossible to agree with him that his excursion into economics was a waste of his time.

The Role of Mathematics in Economics

Keynes said that Ramsey occupied 'the border-country between Philosophy and Mathematics'. Wittgenstein would become contemptuous of Ramsey's residing in border-countries, thinking that he wasn't interested in the purity of philosophical problems. Ramsey begged to differ. He thought that disciplines flourished best when nourished by each other.

He also travelled the border-country between economics and mathematics. Various English paths had been cut through that territory by William Stanley Jevons in the 1870s and then by Edgeworth, Marshall, Keynes, and the logician W. E. Johnson (whose book Ramsey was reading, instead of going on that fatal mountain walk in Hintertux). But there was still some dispute in Ramsey's generation whether economics should be seen as a mathematical science rather than as a part of ethics and politics. Pigou wasn't trained in mathematics—he had read history at King's and had won prizes for literary compositions. Keynes thought that Pigou's mathematical analyses weren't up to much. Dennis Robertson, Gerald Shove, and Austin Robinson had all read classics. Some had a downright 'math phobia' and saw the lacunae as a virtue. Joan Robinson said 'As I never learnt mathematics, I have had to think.' In what sounds very much like a poke at Ramsey, she said in 1937: 'no amount of mathematical ingenuity can provide a criterion for deciding between the interests of one generation and the interests of its grandchildren'.

There was, however, a growing perception in Cambridge that economics needed more mathematical rigour. Dobb suggested that Mill's commonsense methods might 'be a cloak to a laziness of thought which harbours confusion as to what our propositions imply'. Economics would soon become highly mathematized, and Ramsey is often taken to have ushered in this new era. In 2006, the mathematician and game theorist Harold Kuhn could say:

> Although mathematics became the *lingua franca* of 20th century economics, only a handful of mathematicians have exerted a direct and lasting influence on the subject. They surely include Frank Plumpton Ramsey, John von Neumann, and John Forbes Nash Jr.

But while Ramsey certainly exerted a direct influence on mathematical economics, he would not have been on board with, for instance, Koopmans's 1957 endorsement of economic theory's transformation into a sequence of formalized, simplified models that seek to express a complicated reality.

Joan Robinson's scorning of mathematics was made less persuasive by her not knowing any. Ramsey possessed powerful mathematical abilities, as well as an exquisite sense of which technical results were important. His position regarding the place of mathematics in economics might be surprising to those who take him to be a founder of twentieth-century mathematical economics. Like Dobb, he thought that one ignores mathematics at one's peril, for the mathematics has to be right in order for progress in the real world to be made. And some real-world issues are going to be solvable by doing the maths—witness Ramsey's response to the Douglas Proposals. But he did not think that the mathematician could step in and solve all problems. He agreed with Keynes that we mustn't be so taken with the precision of mathematics that we erase the outlines of the very thing we are examining. As Ramsey so often put it, one mustn't be woolly, but one mustn't be scholastic either.

One of his reasons for warning against hyper-technicality was that the utilitarian tradition, the main employer of mathematics in economics, assumes some things about human psychology that might well be false: that we want to maximize pleasure; that we have an aversion to labour; and that the community will be always governed by the desire to maximize pleasure, which some economists interpret as the desire to accumulate money and the things it can buy. We have seen that Ramsey didn't think that utilitarianism was the final word on human motivation. But even were the utilitarian account of rationality more-or-less correct, people (including himself) do not always act rationally. He repeated that sentiment in his letter to Harrod about the taxation of savings: we don't know 'the effect it would have in practice, not supposing people to act so rationally'. He saw value in making a simplified utilitarian analysis that supposes that people act rationally. But he would have been unperturbed by later studies showing that people often behave in ways that go against the 'rational economic man'. Ramsey never thought that such a person could be anything but a highly idealized model of one kind of rationality—utilitarianism. In his entry to the 1929 edition of the *Encyclopedia Britannica* on 'The Foundations of Mathematics', he said, with respect to geometry: 'all that the mathematician can say is that if the axioms are true, then all the rest of geometry will be true also'. Whether the axioms are true 'lies with the physicist'. Similarly, he thought that all the mathematician can say in economics is that if the assumptions are true, then all the rest will be true. Whether the assumptions are true is a matter for psychology, philosophy, and ethics.

Ramsey explicitly addressed the topic of the role of mathematics in economics in a paper titled 'Mathematical Economics'. It was written over the same time he was working on his two mathematically accomplished articles for the *Economics Journal*. In November 1927, he read it to the Quintics Society, a Cambridge mathematical club. A year later, he presented it to at least two colleges—Sidney Sussex and the Trinity Mathematical Society, where his student, the brilliant geometer Donald Coxeter, was President and in the chair. The paper is nowhere to be found. But Ramsey's argument can be reconstructed from the minutes of the Quintics and Trinity meetings. In arguing that economics must always be tied to the world, not left to float mathematically above it, he made many of the points I have been extracting from his less explicit work.

The combined minutes report: 'After explaining the conception of the utility of a commodity, Mr. Ramsey dealt with the economic position of an isolated man, say Robinson Crusoe.' 'Crusoe could aim to maximize utility (for him, commodities) and minimize disutility (for him, work) fairly easily.' A man 'in society' aims to do the same in a more complex situation. He needs to factor in the prices of the commodities, his wages, and his unearned income in order to get to the marginal utility of money. 'Mr. Ramsey showed how the sale of any commodity was regulated by a supply curve and a demand curve, and how the producer's and consumer's surpluses can be read off from these'. He discussed 'Rent of Land, Taxation, Monopoly, Tariffs on foreign goods, and state ownership'. But 'in arguing about the welfare of the community as a whole', we have to assume that the utility is the same for everybody, and this assumption is 'quite unfair except when all the people were fairly well off'. Utility is different for a poor man and a rich man:

> For the rich man, it makes little difference how the last sixpence in his pocket is spent. The author held that direct taxation helps reduce these differences, but not much.

Ramsey 'showed to the satisfaction and gratification of the meeting how the running of the mines and the railways at a loss would benefit the community'. His conclusion was that while economics can be treated quantitatively, like hydrodynamics, the difficulty in doing so, just as in hydrodynamics, is that 'we do not get near actualities'. In hydrodynamics, we deal with perfect fluids, but water is not like that. In economics, we have to assume that everybody knows everything, and that there is equality of income, but people and societies are not like that.

The fact that the average of the very poor person's and the very rich person's utility is a malformed measure is a major problem for utilitarian economic analyses. Marshall had seen this clearly and thought that large enough numbers of people would enable us to get a meaningful average. Pigou had argued that if you reduce the differences in individual's utility through taxation and other measures, then your analysis will be more accurate. Ramsey thought such measures would not get us anywhere near an accurate calculation. Nonetheless, in his two papers for the *Economic Journal*, he produced utilitarian analyses in which he either neglected 'altogether questions of distribution and considerations arising from the differences in the marginal utility of money to different people' or introduced inequality among families in a brief extension of his intertemporal analysis, in order to show how his preceding analysis could be easily extended to different situations.

Each of these papers put forward what we today call social planner models, in which the planner's problem is to maximize utility across time, subject to the constraint of actual resources in the economy. One way of thinking about the solution to such a problem is to assume that a representative agent—an average person—can represent the utilities of all individuals. Although they differ, individuals act in a way that the resulting aggregate choices are mathematically equivalent to those of one fictional individual. Many economists take Ramsey to be a pioneer of this representative agent model, which is the central aspect of the economic model that bears his name—the Ramsey–Cass–Koopmans model.

The other way to solve the social planner's problem is to seek a utility function that's best in the eyes of the social planner. Other economists think this is what Ramsey was up to—that he focused on the social planner's perspective, again to the neglect of the differences in individuals. Kevin Hoover reads him this way, and disapproves:

> So why have intelligent economists come to believe so fervently both in the necessity of microfoundations and in the efficacy of the representative-agent model in providing them? Let me offer a speculation. One of the earliest examples of modern dynamic economics is found in Frank Ramsey's optimal savings problem.... Ramsey considered the problem of saving for an economy and imagined it to be a social planner's problem in which the utility function represented social preferences, without conjecturing how these might be related to the preferences of the members of society. Ramsey may well have thought (in the manner of Keynes) that the wise men of Cambridge could be trusted to know what was best for society independently of any direct knowledge of the lower classes. Push-pin may have been as good as poetry for Jeremy Bentham; but Bentham was an Oxford man. In Cambridge the poets ruled and aspired to rule the world. On Cambridge assumptions, there is no problem with what Ramsey did.

Hoover's speculation turns out to be unfair to Ramsey on a number of counts. In his Apostles papers, Ramsey argued passionately that one must take seriously the preferences of the lower classes, using that very phrase. He argued that sometimes their preferences will be in tension with progressive politics and that fact musn't simply be averaged away. In 'Mathematical Economics' he noted that the utility calculations of the poor will differ from those of the rich, limiting the use of mathematics in economics. However much some might despair over mainstream economics, and however much mathematically inclined economists might revere Ramsey, he can't be held responsible for how his work unfolded in the hands of others. Of course, he only hinted at these points in his two classic papers and the other papers are not easily accessible. And Ramsey's early death robbed him of the opportunity to stand back and make his background convictions clear in his handling of economic problems. So the misunderstandings are understandable.

So how should we think of Ramsey's approach? Perhaps it is best to say that he employed a mixed model, in which he was interested in social wellbeing (or social welfare), and in the relationship between a social utility function and individual utilities. As Duarte has argued, Ramsey, in his savings paper, took time discounting to be justifiable only at the individual level. From the perspective of society, he argued that generations ought to be treated equally and that time discounting is ethically indefensible. That is, there is some back-and-forth in this paper between social and individual utility. This is another manifestation of his ongoing concern about the tension between what is good in the long term for society and what is good for current individuals. While he wavered on this topic in his Apostles papers, in the savings paper he clearly comes down on the side of the long-term good of society.

Not only couldn't Ramsey predict how his work would be extended, he also couldn't anticipate how capitalism would evolve to put most of the riches in the pockets of the very few. But we know what he thought about unfettered capitalism in his time. With Marshall, Pigou, and Keynes, he thought that it needed heavy regulation. And, taking a step beyond them, he thought that justice required that we not look only to the calculation of efficient outcomes. We also have to look at things such as the challenges of income distribution in the name of public welfare and the morality of not caring about future generations. And we know what he thought about idealizations and other kinds of purely abstract problems. In some notes made when he was an undergraduate, he called them 'fairy tales':

> It is absolutely necessary in all political science to consider the relation of what you are saying to the two fundamental questions What is the world like? How can we make it better? People have so often set out to answer quite other and ridiculous questions; they have for example been puzzled by the so-called paradox of self-government; they have asked how can a man live in society and yet obey no one but himself...people who put questions like these do not want truth, they want fairy tales.

Ramsey insisted on being 'realistic'—he wanted his economic thinking to be about the *real* world. And he wanted to make the real world a better world. The economist must trade in idealizations, abstruse mathematics, and abstract ideas, and yet remain resolutely concerned with how to improve non-ideal situations. This was Sraffa's approach as well. In a 1931 unpublished manuscript, he argued that mathematics is a closed, self-contained structure. In economics, on the other hand, 'there must be a leak at one end or the other: the "closed system" is in communication with the world'. It is highly likely that such matters were the topics of conversation in 1929 when Ramsey, Sraffa, Keynes, and Wittgenstein talked about economics. For we will see that Ramsey and Sraffa both pressed Wittgenstein on the question on whether we could get anything realistic out of Wittgenstein's closed primary system in the *Tractatus*.

1928 RETURN TO MATHEMATICS

Not a Committee Man

When Ramsey's second economics paper was published at the end of 1928, he told Keynes he wanted to return to the foundational problems of philosophy. Ramsey's mind might now have been mostly in the land of philosophy, but his teaching and administrative duties were in mathematics. In 1928, he agreed to be Director of Studies at King's, the heavy job that Berry had been doing. And from the time he received his University Lecturership, he was part of the Mathematics Faculty's governing bodies, along with his father. If Arthur's presence was crimping for the younger Ramsey, there is no evidence of it. It appears that Arthur saved his rages for the family and Magdalene, sparing the Mathematics Faculty. But unlike Arthur, who is mentioned with great frequency in the Faculty's minute books, Frank's appearances are episodic. He attended the occasional meeting, starting in 1924, but wasn't interested in Faculty politics. He also found the standards for scholarship and integrity not up to his own, as is illustrated by an incident concerning the one and only PhD thesis he examined.

In June 1928, Frederick Maunsell submitted his PhD thesis. The title was 'An Extended Theory of Continued Fractions'. The eminent mathematician J.E. Littlewood was the supervisor. As required, Maunsell attested that the work was 'entirely original (except where reference in it is specifically made to other authorities)'. Ramsey and Littlewood were the examiners, the supervisor being on the examining committee in those early days of the Cambridge PhD. Ramsey knew the candidate fairly well, as they had been undergraduates together at Trinity. Maunsell was an older aristocratic ex-army officer and had been president of the Trinity Mathematical Society. As undergraduates, they had teamed up at that Society to argue against the rote and applied nature of the Mathematical Tripos, and they had both taken a run at a Trinity scholarship in 1921, with Ramsey coming first and Maunsell sixth.

One might surmise that it might have been awkward that one of these former classmates was now the examiner of the other. If so, it was nothing to match the awkwardness that arose between Ramsey and his former teacher Littlewood. Ramsey began his examiner's report by saying that Maunsell's main idea was 'an extraordinarily good one'. He went on:

> He would, in fact, have made a discovery of considerable importance, had he not been anticipated by Jacobi (Crelle's Journal vol LXIX). Mr. Maunsell's ignorance of this paper of Jacobi is the more remarkable, since he actually refers to it and also to Bachmann's Irrationale Zahlen in which it is fully described.

Ramsey had raised the issue in the viva. Maunsell defended himself by claiming that he only read the first few pages of Bachmann's paper and that, even though he asserted in the dissertation that his extension of continued fractions was more natural than Jacobi's, 'he never bothered to find out what Jacobi's was'. Ramsey held back from charging Maunsell with plagiarism, but the report suggested that the thesis should be failed:

> To sum up - his claim to a Ph.D rests on his independent discovery of an important idea, against which must be set his slackness in not reading Jacobi's paper, and his failure to display the ability required to deal with the problems raised.

Littlewood was disturbed by Ramsey's position. He said in his own examiner's report that he had only learned in the viva, from Ramsey, that Maunsell's result was already in the Jacobi paper, which Maunsell referred to at the beginning of his thesis. Littlewood conceded one thing: 'That M. should not have discovered this [that the result was in Jacobi] is highly reprehensible, and the examiners told him so.' But although 'the crime is bad', Littlewood argued that it was 'not quite as bad as it sounds', given some 'extenuating circumstances'. He set out those circumstances at length. They included Maunsell's proffered rationale; Littlewood's own culpability in suggesting the problem in the first place and in not being conscientious enough; and an account of how even eminent pure mathematicians don't see the connection between Jacobi and what Maunsell was trying to do. In his opinion, Maunsell had a 'happy-go-lucky temperament' with respect to research, but nonetheless, 'originality enough to rediscover a very important idea . . . although his slackness has put him in a position of some absurdity'. Littlewood ended his report with a defence of Maunsell's character and with the following extraordinary claim:

> In any case I should myself always vote for a man of his type, and I find his freshness and originality, even if it is combined with a touch of stupidity, more attractive and more hopeful than the rather depressing competence of the ordinary borderline candidate.

With that conclusion by the more senior Littlewood, Ramsey signed off on the thesis. Maunsell had already joined the mathematics department at University College, Southampton, and Ramsey may have thought it best, all round, to drop the matter. But he was unimpressed with Littlewood, with the Cambridge PhD, and with the Mathematics Faculty. Between the next meeting of the Faculty Board of Mathematics (in which the thesis was unanimously approved) and his death, Ramsey's name occurs not once in the Faculty's minute book—not as a supervisor, not as an examiner, not as an assessor of potential applicants, not even as being present at a Board meeting.

Littlewood was so bothered by the incident that he was still dissembling 25 years later in a lengthy section of his *A Mathematician's Miscellany*. What he says about Ramsey's 'highbrow' attitude is revealing of both his feelings about the young challenger and of the strength of that young challenger's feelings about the standards in the Faculty of Mathematics:

I suggested (*c.* 1923) a subject to X (one of about 10 research pupils), saying that as far as I know (I was frankly not an expert) the only relevant literature was a paper by Jacobi; I didn't think it *was* going to be relevant, but he was to read it. The thesis on its merits was more than adequate. My co-examiner F.P. Ramsey, who concealed behind his (then) contemptuous and 'King's' highbrow exterior a high standard of conscientiousness for himself and others, read Jacobi to the end, and found that all the important part of the thesis was there. Up to the point I had read, it looked very much as if there was nothing doing. X had read to this point, come to the same conclusion, *and read no further*. The paper does later take a quite unexpected turn. Ramsey, utterly shocked, obviously thought the case should be turned down. My view was that we should award the Ph.D for brains and promise (it was obvious that there was no deliberate fraud), and I was reporting 'yes' though with all the cards on the table. I told Ramsey I didn't expect others to necessarily agree with me, 'the Government Whips are off', and I said he should say 'no' if that was what he felt. He didn't. The next hurdle was the Degree Committee. I enlarged verbally on the case, and again said the Whips were off. Perhaps they had all had good lunches, but there was not only a majority vote 'for', but, what I would not have expected, unanimity...So X is a Ph.D (and on the whole has fully justified it).

Ramsey thought that reading to the end of the papers one cited was a basic requirement, not a display of over-conscientiousness.

As Ramsey became less involved with the Mathematics Faculty, he became more involved in the Moral Sciences Faculty. He would become the supervisor for just one PhD candidate, and it would be a philosophy thesis: Wittgenstein's.

The *Entscheidungsproblem*

It was in trying to solve a problem about the foundations of mathematics that Ramsey made his mark in pure mathematics. The *Entscheidungsproblem* (the decision problem) had been recently reinvigorated by David Hilbert at the 1928 International Conference of Mathematicians in Bologna. Hilbert had posed a question of any system of logic, such as that of *Principia*. Can we find a procedure or an algorithm to decide whether any well-formed statement in the system is a theorem or not? His very label for the problem pointed in the direction of his own answer. Hilbert thought that we *would* find a decision procedure—a method of giving an answer 'yes' or 'no' to whether a particular mathematical statement can be proven. In 1920, he had begun a program aimed at providing a set of consistent and complete axioms for all mathematics so that it could be mechanized and solved in a routine manner. In this way, he hoped to prove that there were no unsolvables in mathematics.

Max Newman attended the Bologna conference. Ramsey, who was well-connected with the Hilbert School, was no doubt excited to talk to Newman on his return from Bologna. Newman thought it was a 'madly exciting' time, and he took the philosophically-minded mathematicians, Ramsey (and later Alan Turing), to be 'tough guys'—sharp, confident, and dealing with the most difficult of issues. Newman was being modest in this interview in 1982. In 1928, he published an excellent paper on Russell which resulted in what we now call the Newman Problem. He would teach the Foundations of Mathematics course after Ramsey's death and inspire one of the attendees—Turing—to provide a proof that the *Entscheidungsproblem* couldn't be solved.

Wilhelm Ackermann, who had been a student of Hilbert's, had spent the first half of 1925 in Cambridge, the year he received his PhD from the University of Göttingen. Like Ramsey, he would do serious work on the *Entscheidungsproblem*. The two met during Ackermann's stay in Cambridge and one imagines they talked about the advances being made on the *Entscheidungsproblem* in Göttingen. Harold Langford, newly awarded Harvard PhD in hand, also came to Cambridge on a Sheldon Travelling Fellowship in 1924–25.* He was at the time heavily engaged in the *Entscheidungsproblem*, proving some early results. Langford attended Ramsey's lectures and had discussions with him. In 1928, Ramsey decided to make his own assault on the problem. He cited Langford's results, noted that Bernays and Schönfinkel, and Behmann, had solved various other parts of the problem. Ramsey solved another. He

---

* At that point, Langford could write to Sheffer that Ramsey was a 'disciple' of both Russell and Wittgenstein and that the tradition of mathematical logic in Cambridge was being maintained only by Ramsey. See Mancosu (2021).

RAMSEY'S PROOF

Steven Methven, Associate Researcher in Philosophy, Worcester College, University of Oxford

Construct some well-formed formula, S, of your favourite formal language, L. Now ask: is there a mechanical method—a decision procedure—whereby, in finite steps, I can unthinkingly determine whether or not S is a theorem? Put proof-theoretically, assuming the system sound and complete, can my method show whether or not S is provable from the axioms? That is a general statement of the decision problem.

It has two important features. First, one wants to know, of S, whether or *not* it is a theorem. Assuming completeness, one has a mechanical method for determining of S that it is a theorem *if* it is a theorem, namely the relevant proof system. If a proof of S exists, I will eventually find it by systematically applying the proof rules. But a proof procedure is only half a decision procedure (Quine 1950): if none exists, then, since there are infinitely many proofs, there is no point at which I will know to stop trying to find one. I'll keep searching forever.

Second, the procedure should be *mechanical*. Following Turing and Church, this notion has a formal definition. For any L there is a function f which, for any formula S of L, takes S as argument and yields '1' if its value of S is a theorem or '0' as its value otherwise. If f is effectively computable, then there is a procedure M consisting of a finite list of instructions—a program—which precisely articulates what is to be done at each step in computing f. Further, M must yield '1' or '0' as a value for *any* S in a finite number of steps, and it must not yield '1' or '0' for any input which is not a formula of L. So L is decidable if and only if f is effectively computable—computable by some M which satisfies all of these requirements. One example of a decision procedure for a formal language is the truth-table method for propositional logic.

The hunch in the early twentieth century was that formal languages *were* decidable, and logicians focused on finding decision procedures for specific families of sentences. Ramsey's L is first-order logic with identity, and his decision procedure concerns those sentences which, when in Prenex Normal Form, contain 0 or more existential quantifiers followed by 0 or more universal quantifiers. Earlier in 1928, Bernays and Schönfinkel constructed a decision procedure for the same class of sentences of first-order logic, but without identity. Ramsey's task was trickier: the addition of identity to the language increases the complexity of what it can express. Crucially, the satisfiability of sentences containing identity may vary with the cardinality of the domain.

Proposing a decision procedure is one thing, proving that it is such a procedure another. Ramsey's procedure involves, in several steps, a transformation of the candidate formula from which, ultimately, the cardinality of the domains on which it is satisfiable, if any, is determined by inspection. The real graft of the paper, however, involves proving that the procedure *is* a decision procedure for any sentence of the class mentioned above. To do this, Ramsey proved a novel combinatorial theorem, which later gave rise to a new branch of mathematics: *Ramsey Theory*.

pushed the *Entscheidungsproblem* to the wall and one gets the sense from the paper that he saw that the wall was unscalable via partial measures. That is, he may have intuited that the full *Entscheidungsproblem* was unsolvable.

Ramsey's 'On a Problem of Formal Logic' was read at the *London Mathematical Society* on 13 December, and was published posthumously in its *Proceedings*. Shortly after his death, it was shown that the general *Entscheidungsproblem* was unsolvable. Kurt Gödel made the first move just months after Ramsey died. Then it was Alan Turing's turn.

Turing came up to King's as a mathematics undergraduate in 1931. The fact that he was at King's would have pretty much guaranteed Ramsey as his supervisor. Turing attended Newman's Foundations of Mathematics lectures, the course that Ramsey had so happily 'bagged' and that likely would have remained his had he lived. Turing was appointed to a Fellowship at King's in 1935, at the age of 22, just a little older than Ramsey had been when he got his King's job. He went on to teach The Foundations of Mathematics course himself.

This was one of the most spectacular near-misses in the foundations of mathematics. For Turing was interested in precisely Ramsey's set of problems. Both were interested in solving the *Entscheidungsproblem*. Both were interested in the fundamental nature of mathematics. In 1933, Turing would read a paper to the Moral Sciences Club titled 'Mathematics and Logic', which took a stand against logicism. Ramsey, we shall see, would abandon logicism in 1929 and become interested in intuitionism. They would have had an awful lot to talk about and Ramsey of course would have joined Turing and Wittgenstein in their discussions about the foundations of mathematics and logic in the 1930s. As it turned out, it was left to Ramsey's student Alister Watson to introduce Turing and Wittgenstein and arrange a discussion group.

In 1936, Turing hammered the last nail into the coffin of Hilbert's project. He expressed the question in terms of whether there is a machine or mechanical process that could determine whether any computer program will finish running or not and definitively delivered the answer 'no' to this question. His paper was titled 'On Computable Numbers, with an Application to the *Entscheidungsproblem*'. The wall that Ramsey had seen was un-scalable. And seeds were planted for the birth of the computer.

There has been much speculation about what Ramsey would have thought about the Gödel and Turing results. Braithwaite characterized those results as more shocking than the Theory of Relativity. He thought they would have been a delight to Ramsey, so much so that he might have turned his energies back towards mathematics. One thing is not a matter of speculation. The Polish-born Cambridge philosopher Casimir Lewy, echoing his compatriot Janina Hosiasson, said that, had Ramsey lived, the breakdown in the study of mathematical logic in Cambridge wouldn't have occurred. Lewy tells the history as follows. Russell started the tradition. It was continued by Wittgenstein in the *Tractatus*. Ramsey was the heir.

When he died, Cambridge ceased to be one of the world centres for mathematical logic. (That was Hosiasson's very verdict when she was in Cambridge during Ramsey's illness and death.) Turing would have revived the tradition had he stayed, but he was soon off to Princeton, and then, famously, to Bletchley Park as a code-breaker.

That is another interesting site of surmise. Newman was Turing's mentor, and then one of the most important of the Bletchley Park code-breakers during the Second World War. His work led to the construction of Colossus, the first operational and programmable computer. Surely, had Ramsey lived, he would have joined his friends Newman and Peter Lucas, and his student Turing, at Bletchley Park. He had precisely that kind of quick and deep mathematical mind. In 1923 he noted, while visiting Wittgenstein, that the train from Vienna to Puchberg was slower than even the Cambridge to Bletchley train. One imagines he would have been on it frequently.

INCOMPLETENESS AND UNDECIDEABILITY: GÖDEL, NEWMAN, TURING

Juliet Floyd, Professor of Philosophy, Boston University

In 1931 Gödel proved the incompleteness of arithmetic for formal system P, obtained from *Principia Mathematica* by omitting ramification, taking natural numbers as the lowest type, and adding the Peano axioms of arithmetic. Pondering the model of sets definable in arithmetic he was led, *via* the Richard Paradox, to the undefinability of truth in P, and from there to P's *incompleteness*: if P is consistent, then there is a sentence R such that neither R nor $\neg R$ are formally derivable ('provable') in P. Key to the proof is Gödel's (effective) coding of the syntax of P with numbers. Metamathematical statements *about* P become interpretable as number-theoretic statements and can then be expressed *in* P.

Gödel constructs a sentence R that 'says', under coding, 'I am not provable', and then proves that if P is consistent, neither R nor its negation are provable in P. His Second Incompleteness theorem, that P cannot prove its own consistency, results from formalizing this proof. Since 'if P is consistent, then R is not provable' is formalizable and provable in P, if the consistency of P were provable in P, so would R be, a contradiction. Adding R to P yields a new and consistent system P_R, but it is incomplete by application of the same kind of argument. Adding $\neg R$ to P yields $P_{\neg R}$, also consistent yet incomplete. Adding P's consistency to P also yields a consistent but incomplete system Con_P. This process can be iterated indefinitely.

A question remains. Are these incompleteness phenomena about P and its extensions alone, or about *any* formalization of arithmetic? To settle this question, we must analyse the very idea of what a formal system (of the relevant type) *is*. To do that we cannot just write down another formal system. Philosophical work is needed.

Newman taught mathematical logic in 1934 and 1935 at Cambridge, adhering to the original Gödel paper, which he introduced by way of the *Entscheidungsproblem*. He pointed out that the case of one variable formula had been resolved. Ramsey's

'Foundations of Mathematics' is referred to, along with *Principia Mathematica*, Russell's *Introduction to Mathematical Philosophy*, the *Tractatus*, and Hilbert's, Bernays's and Church's work.

Gödel's 1930 completeness theorem (if the sentences of a formal theory are formally consistent, then they have a model) had made the *Entscheidungsproblem* tractable by reducing its original model-theoretic statement (to decide the validity of an arbitrary sentence of first order logic), to one of proof (to decide whether or not a particular sentence S in the language of the system is or is not derivable from the axioms). As had Hardy, Newman used the phrase 'mechanical' in presenting this formulation of the problem.

Turing attended Newman's course in the spring of 1935. Within a year he had resolved the pure *Entscheidungsproblem* (arbitrarily many variables) in the negative, narrowly anticipated by Church. Turing's mode of proof was so novel that at first Newman could not understand it. For Turing replaced 'is formally derivable in first order logic' by 'there is a machine that will determine...', modelling the idea of a formal system's *use* by analogizing it to a human 'computer' who calculates digits of a real number with pencil and paper, step-by-step, in a social world. (Wittgenstein later remarked: 'Turing's "Machines". These are *humans* who calculate'.)

A Turing 'machine' is a mathematized language-game: a finite table of commands expressed in quintuples of the form, e.g., $q_1 \, S_0 \, PS_1 \, Rq_2$, meaning 'when in configuration q_1 scanning an empty symbol print a "1", move right, and go into configuration q_2'. Gödelizing these formulations yields the idea of the stored-program computer: one that can operate on its own commands as well as its data inputs, and thus on its own hardware. Turing thereby characterized the 'Universal Machine' U: through coding, U can simulate any machine.

Turing then showed that if there were a decision method—a machine—that could generally determine whether or not an arbitrary machine ever prints a 0 (translatable into: whether or not a given sentence can be derived in a system formulated with first-order logic), one could then construct an ill-defined machine that eventually becomes stuck, ending in a circular loop. This shows that the basic notion is that of a partial, not a total function: some of the functions U 'computes' are not everywhere defined, so one cannot diagonalize out of the class of Turing-computable functions with another Turing 'machine'. Hilbert's *Entscheidungsproblem* is answered in the negative.

Turing had analysed the general notion of a formal system, thereby showing that Gödel's incompleteness theorem applies, not only to P, but to *any* such formulable system of arithmetic. The notion of 'Turing computable' is, as Gödel said, 'absolute': whether or not a function is Turing computable does not depend upon peculiar symbols of the language, the strength of the logic, or the laws of the formal system—in stark contrast to the notions of 'definability' and 'provability'. As Ramsey said in 'The Foundations of Mathematics', we need to dodge the paradoxical vaguenesses caused by our entanglements with language and meaning.

Turing also proved that the Turing-computable functions are exactly those calculable in Church's lambda-calculus, and exactly those calculable in the Herbrand-Gödel-Kleene equational systems. This extensional confluence lends weight to the idea that 'effectively computable' has been satisfactorily analysed (the so-called 'Church-Turing thesis').

Ramsey Theory

Ramsey came to two results in 'On a Problem of Formal Logic'. The first was to solve a part of the *Entscheidungsproblem*. While the world had to wait for Gödel, Church, and Turing to solve the whole of it (by proving that it couldn't be solved), matters were reversed for Ramsey's second result. A small handful of mathematicians had solved local problems as to how a particular combinatorial object must contain some smaller combinatorial object. In 1892, Hilbert got near to a general theorem, but apparently not even he appreciated the significance of his result. The topologist Issai Schur in 1916 and the Dutch mathematicians Pierre Baudet and B.L. Van der Waerden in the 1920s were making headway on individual problems. But the world of mathematics had to wait for Ramsey to provide a general proof.

Ramsey needed to prove a theorem (known as Ramsey's Theorem) as a step in his attempt to solve the *Entscheidungsproblem*. The proof was to be of great importance. In the early 1970s the American mathematicians Ronald Graham and Bruce Rothschild gave it momentum and a name: Ramsey Theory. It is a fruitful branch of mathematics which studies the conditions under which order, or patterns, must exist in a system.

It is often explained to undergraduates with this example. Take a party with at least 6 people. Consider any two of those people. They might be meeting for the first time (they are mutual strangers) or they might have met before (they are mutual acquaintances). Ramsey's Theorem tells us that in any such party, at least three are strangers or at least three are acquaintances. For if I go to such a party, I must know at least three others, or not know at least three others. If I know three of them, and two of the three know each other, then the theorem holds. If they don't know each other, the theorem also holds (for in that case we have three people who do not know each other). The situation is which I don't know three people mirrors the one in which I do.

We can run the example from the other direction. What is the smallest number of people at a party such that it is guaranteed that either three people all know each other, or three people do not know each other? It's a surprise that the answer is six—a very small number. One wouldn't guess that in a party of only six, either (at least) three people have never met or (at least) three people have all met each other.

Proofs within Ramsey Theory are sometimes expressed in graph theory, sometimes in number theory, sometimes in geometry. That is, the sets or structures in question can be points, numbers, or planes, and the puzzles can be represented by graphs or diagrams. All proofs start with a structure which is cut or partitioned into a number of pieces. Then it is determined how large the structure must be for at least one of the pieces to have an interesting property. For instance, consider a number of vertices in which each vertex is connected to every other vertex by an edge coloured either red or blue. How many vertices must there be order to ensure that there is always a monochromatic triangle with its edges either blue or red? The answer is six. That's a Ramsey number—the smallest number of vertices that all simple graphs of one order need so that they contain a particular sub-order.

Ramsey numbers are not easy to find. Even today we have only a handful, each discovery a small milestone in mathematics. That there are many open and stubborn problems in Ramsey Theory makes it a vital branch of mathematics. As Ronald Graham and Joel Spencer put it:

> Ramsey theorists struggle to figure out just how many stars, numbers or figures are required to guarantee a certain desired substructure. Such problems often take decades to solve and yield to only the most ingenious and delicate reasoning.

Like so much of Ramsey's formal work, there is an easily stated and important principle behind it. Complete disorder is impossible, for every large set contains a substructure with a regular pattern or cliques with a discernible pattern. That has led the mathematician Alexander Soifer to campaign that Ramsey's Theorem should really be named 'Ramsey's Principle'.

Again like so much of Ramsey's work, Ramsey's Theorem is a beautiful pure idea, but useful in the real world. Graham and Spenser say that it probes 'the ultimate structure of mathematics, a structure that transcends the universe'. This transcendent idea is heavily employed by engineers.

RAMSEY THEORY

Ronald Graham, Professor of Mathematics and Computer Science, University of California, San Diego

Ramsey's paper 'On a Problem in Formal Logic' was published in 1930 shortly after his death. Although it attracted relatively little attention at the time of its publication, the paper contained a profound generalization of what is often called the Box Principle (or Schubfach Prinzip). Since that time, it has inspired a dynamic branch of combinatorics known as Ramsey Theory. The underlying principle for Ramsey Theory can be succinctly summarized by the statement: 'Complete disorder is impossible'. While hints of this philosophy appeared earlier in the work of D. Hilbert, I. Schur and B. L. van Waerden, it wasn't until this thread was picked up by Paul Erdös and his colleagues that the field took off. In fact, Erdös introduced in 1947 his powerful technique now known as the Probabilistic Method in order to establish bounds for Ramsey numbers for graphs. Although Ramsey dealt with both finite and infinite sets in his paper, it is the finite versions that have especially challenged combinatorial mathematicians for the past 80 years. That is not to say that the many generalizations for Ramsey's theorem for infinite cardinals are not substantial. It is just that this branch belongs more to set theory than to combinatorics. As a simple example, it follows from Ramsey's theorem that for each integer n, there is a least number $R(n)$ so that if the edges of a complete graph on $R(n)$ vertices are arbitrarily coloured red or blue, then there must always be formed a smaller complete subgraph on n vertices such that all its edges have a single colour. It is easy to see that $R(3) = 6$ and it is not too hard to show that $R(4) = 18$. The best bounds known for $R(5)$ are $43 \leq R(5) \leq 48$ (it is conjectured that in fact $R(5) = 43$.) There seems to be no hope whatsoever that we will ever know the exact value of $R(6)$! A recurring theme in Ramsey Theory is the resilience of structure under partitions. This is seen to occur in many mathematical areas such as number theory, graph theory, geometry, analysis, etc. For example, it is known that if $2^{n+n^{0.8}}$ points are arbitrarily placed in the plane so that no three are collinear, then they must contain the vertices on a convex n-gon (however, 2^{n-2} points are not enough to force this to happen). Similarly, it is known that if the first $W(n)$ integers are coloured red or blue, then they must contain an arithmetic progression of length n with all elements having the same colour, where the best current upper bound on $W(n)$ is:

$$W(n) < 2^{2^{2^{2^{2^{2n+9}}}}}.$$

In the other direction, colouring the first 2^n integers is not enough to guarantee this conclusion. In fact, the author has made the (rash?) offer of $1000 to anyone who can prove (or disprove) that $W(n) \leq 2^{n^2}$ for all $n \geq 1$.

It has been noted that many results in Ramsey Theory require the use of a large number of alternating quantifiers in their statements, such as: 'For some m, there exists a $S(m)$ such that for any $n > m$, there is a $T(n)$ such that for some $k > T(n)$, there are integers $a_1 < a_2 < \ldots < a_k$ such that $\ldots$'. As a result, the proofs of such statements often require the use of highly recursive arguments which in turn can generate rather large bounds for when the desired conclusions hold. An extreme example of this occurs in a Ramsey Theory result concerning the necessary occurrence of a monochromatic planar 4-point configuration in any red-blue colouring of the diagonals of an N-dimensional cube. For this problem, it has been shown that this must always occur provided N is large enough. How large is 'large enough'? From the published proof it follows that this must happen when $N \geq$ **G** where **G** has become known as 'Graham's number' (see the Wikipedia entry for details). It was claimed that up to that time, this was the largest number that ever arose naturally in a mathematical proof! It is possible, however, that the conclusion for the theorem might actually hold for $N \geq 13$!

There is no doubt that Frank Ramsey's legacy in a myriad of disciplines will last for generations to come. It is equally certain that Ramsey's contributions to mathematics will be celebrated long after we are all gone.

The infinite version of Ramsey's theorem gave rise to the whole new subject of infinite combinatorics and 'Ramsey Cardinals'.

The time was right for progress in this direction, but as with the advances in the axiomatic treatment of subjective probability and the expected utility of preferences, Ramsey got there first. 'On a Problem of Formal Logic' was published, after his death, in the 1930 *Proceedings of the London Mathematical Society*. The eminent Norwegian logician Thoralf Skolem soon published his own version of Ramsey's Theorem, as did a brilliant group of Hungarian mathematicians, Paul Erdös, Esther Klein, George Szekeres, and Paul Turán. Who had been working on nearby topics, did the same. Turán's theorem, which he discovered in 1941, is an elegant example of a Ramsey theorem, showing the maximum number of edges that a graph on n vertices can have without having a clique of r vertices. It was the birth of extremal graph theory, with Erdös becoming one of its main proponents. Another Hungarian, Endre Szemeredi, would later prove a theorem on the existence of arbitrary long arithmetic progressions (settling a conjecture made by Erdös). By the end of the Second World War, Ramsey Theory was a thriving research programme, even if it would not be named for Ramsey for another two decades. For instance, Jeff Paris and Leo Harrington showed in 1977 that a variant of finite Ramsey's Theorem is a mathematically significant true sentence in the language of arithmetic whose truth cannot be proved in the most natural formal system for arithmetic.

There are parallels between Ramsey's stature in economics and in mathematics. His papers on optimal savings and taxation are Nobel prize worthy, in that offshoots won it for others. The same can be said for mathematics' high prize, the Fields Medal. Ramsey Theorists, such as Terrance Tao, have won it for recent developments. (Both prizes were established after Ramsey's death—1968 for the economics Nobel and 1936 for the Fields Medal.) And, just as Ramsey's work in economics was done on the side, distracting him from the foundations of thought, his work in pure mathematics was quite literally an aside. He had to prove a theorem on the way to solving a fragment of the *Entscheidungsproblem* in 'On a Problem in Formal Logic'. So he stepped away from the core of his argument and proved it, in eight pages. Those eight pages are Ramsey Theory, and they are the sum total of his publications in pure mathematics. What an astounding ratio of pages to importance.

The Bolshevik Menace

When Ramsey was writing 'Mathematical Logic' in 1926, he spoke of the 'obstinate difficulties' of the foundations of mathematics. One of the difficulties was Brouwer's denial of the law of excluded middle—the purported law of logic which states (in informal language) that every declarative proposition is either true or false. Since there is no proof that A or $\neg A$ holds for all of mathematics, intuitionists prefer not to assume the law. In his undergraduate thesis Ramsey had cheekily called intuitionism 'the Bolshevik menace of Brouwer and Weyl'. The idea that the ability of human beings to construct a proof has anything to do with mathematical truth or falsity was too revolutionary for him. But a year later, in 'Mathematical Logic', he expressed his disapproval of intuitionism more mildly: 'I cannot persuade myself that I do not know for certain that the "law of excluded middle" is true.' One can feel the slightest of wobbles in the double negative. Russell perceived it, noting after Ramsey's death that 'there is less certainty' in 'Mathematical Logic' regarding the rejection of intuitionism.

When Ramsey was writing his entry on the foundations of mathematics for the *Encyclopedia Britannica* in 1928, he was still exercised about Brouwer and Weyl. They propose

> to abandon many generally accepted parts of mathematics, and to retain only such propositions as they can prove without using the Law of Excluded Middle...They think that it is wrong to say that there is a number with a certain property...unless we have a definite construction for finding one.

And he was still dismissive about formalists like Hilbert. They

> hope to put an end to this disastrous scepticism by taking an altogether different view of what mathematics is. They regard it as merely the manipulation of meaningless symbols according to fixed rules.

Ramsey thought that a kind of scepticism loomed large for formalists. It seems that we could play any one of a number of meaningless games, and so, on their account, what passes as mathematics is no better than some other system. As Harold Jeffreys later put it, 'this seemed to me, and to him [Ramsey], that this is saying that it doesn't matter what you do with the bath water provided you make sure that the baby is thrown out'.

Hilbert tried to answer such charges in his meta-mathematics—his theory about the game of mathematics. He tried there to set out the general properties of axiomatic systems. That meta-mathematics, in Ramsey's words, consists of 'real assertions about mathematics' and tries to prove that 'this or that formula can or cannot be obtained from the axioms according to the rules of deduction'. Hilbert was confident that mathematics would be shown to be complete (every true statement in it can be proved), consistent (false statements cannot be arrived at by valid steps in the proof system), and decidable (that the *Entscheidungsproblem* would yield to a positive solution, showing that a decision procedure exists to prove, of any given statement, that it either is or is not derivable from the axioms).

In 'On a Problem of Formal Logic' Ramsey suggested that the answer to the *Entscheidungsproblem* was to be found in Wittgenstein. His encyclopedia article that year had ended abruptly with this very statement. In 1928, that is, he was still making the assertion, not shared by Wittgenstein, that we can extend the notion of a truth-functional tautology to all of mathematics.

But his position about the foundations of mathematics was in fact unsettled. Perhaps he was perturbed about the kind of problem Carnap identified. He said of Ramsey's attempt to save logicism in 'The Foundations of Mathematics': 'This happy result is certainly tempting', but 'we should not let ourselves be seduced by it'. It smacked too much of 'a platonic realm of ideas which exist in themselves independently of *if* and *how* finite human beings are able to think them'. Intuition-ism, Carnap said, has been called 'anthropological mathematics', but Ramsey's logicism might well be called 'theological mathematics'. Ramsey resolved the issues of *Principia*, but at a high cost.[†] We will see that Ramsey would also come to think that logicism was at a dead end. But unlike Carnap, who was moving away from logicism towards a kind of formalism, Ramsey was starting to think that intuition-ism wasn't such a menace after all.

Ramsey had finished his articles in economics, and was eager to return to these difficult and fundamental questions of mathematics and philosophy. In a great stroke of luck, his best interlocutor would soon be back in Cambridge. Together, he and Wittgenstein would make sparks fly and each, in their own distinctive ways, would move towards intuitionism and pragmatism.

[†] The context in which Carnap wrote was that Friedrich Waismann had employed one of Ramsey's moves, arguing the axiom of reducibility cannot be a logical principle because it is not a tautology. He thanked Carnap in that paper for helping him think through the problem. But in a 1930 symposium (published the following year in *Erkenntnis*), Carnap made it clear that he was sceptical about Ramsey's attempt to fix the theory of types. He said that Ramsey 'courageously' tried to solve Russell's problems by arguing that the circles of the set theoretic paradoxes are harmless, not vicious. On Ramsey's account, Carnap explained, when we say 'the tallest man in the room', the description is fine as it stands, for the person described already exists. The person is simply singled out, not created, by the description. Ramsey, he said, tried the same tactic for properties: the totality of properties already exists. That was the 'theological mathematics'. Carnap was relying both on Ramsey's 'The Foundations of Mathematics' and on Ramsey's 1928 letter to Fraenkel. See Waismann (1928); Carnap (1983 [1931]); Mancosu (2020).

WITTGENSTEIN COMES HOME

A Nervous Start

There had been little communication between Wittgenstein and his Cambridge friends after the disastrous 1925 visit at Keynes's country house. With respect to Frank, the silence was intentional—Wittgenstein was not speaking to him. Frank had thought he would go to Vienna after he received Wittgenstein's sniffy letter about the logic of identity, addressed to 'Dear Mr. Ramsey'. Surely, Frank thought, he could sort things out with his friend. His first plan, for the autumn of 1927, was cancelled due to the family crisis that followed his mother's death. He then considered going in the spring of 1928, but he doubted that Wittgenstein would 'consent to talk philosophy' with him, and Schlick, who *would* have talked philosophy with him, was away.

Wittgenstein was also thinking of coming to England, although not with a reconciliation with Frank in mind. He had had a rough time school teaching—an incident in which he hit a boy on the head resulted in a humiliating court case. He gave it up, and when he wrote to Keynes in the summer of 1927, he was in Vienna, designing and overseeing the building of a modernist house for his sister Gretl:

My dear Keynes,
It's ages since you have heard from me. . . . I won't try to explain my long silence. . . . [The house] will be finished about November and then I might take a trip to England if anybody there should care to see me. I should VERY much like to see you again and meanwhile to get a line from you.

Thus began a long correspondence about a return to Cambridge. In November 1928, Keynes expressed his feelings to Lydia:

A letter from Ludwig. . . . He . . . wants to come and stay with me here in about a fortnight. Am I strong enough? Perhaps if I do no work between now and then, I shall be.

Keynes summoned his strength, and a couple of months later, the arrival was imminent. On 17 January 1929, Keynes wrote to Lydia: 'Ludwig...arrives tomorrow ...Pray for me!' The next day, he wrote his famous line:

> Well, God has arrived. I met him on the 5:15 train. He has a plan to stay in Cambridge permanently.

As Robert Skidelsky, one of Keynes's biographers, put it:

> While God whistled Bach in the drawing room, Keynes crept to his study to write his letter to Lydia: 'I see that the fatigue is going to be crushing. But I must not let him talk to me for more than two or three hours a day'.

Wittgenstein needed a conversation partner, and Keynes was determined that it would not be him.

Frank, of course, was the obvious candidate. Just before Wittgenstein's arrival, Frank wrote a nervous letter to Keynes, uncertain of how he would be received by Wittgenstein, but keen to do whatever he could:

> Can I do anything to entertain Wittgenstein? I don't feel at all sure he wants to see me again, but I should love to do anything I can. There are lots of problems I should like his opinion on, though I fear he will find me so intolerably stupid that he won't want to talk about them.
>
> I'm not really extra busy at the beginning of term, and if he would like to stay here I should be only too delighted, though I should expect he would prefer to stay in college. But do let me know of anything I can do, and please give him in my name any invitation that would be tactful and convenient to him or you. And if you could let me know when he is coming to Cambridge as I shouldn't like too many avoidable engagements.

It would have been absurd for Wittgenstein to return to Cambridge and to philosophy, and yet not talk to the one person who understood him. Keynes made his move. He told Wittgenstein that he should try to forget about, or at least set aside, the Sussex visit and attempt to talk to Frank. He was pretty sure that they would be able to converse not just about logic, but other matters as well.

Keynes was proved right. He had a lunch party for Wittgenstein and perhaps it was on this occasion that Frank and Ludwig were reunited. What we know is that on 2 February, declaring himself to be 'not born to live permanently with a clergyman', Keynes shifted Ludwig to Mortimer Road. Although Frank and Lettice took to clergymen no more readily than Keynes, they became Wittgenstein's hosts until he found permanent lodging.

The move turned out beautifully. For not only could Wittgenstein talk with Frank, but he also liked Lettice very much. Keynes wrote to Lydia on 25 February:

> Last night Ludwig came to dinner. He was more 'normal' in every way than I have ever known him. One woman at last has succeeded in soothing the fierceness of the savage brute: Lettice Ramsey, under whose roof he stayed in the end for nearly a fortnight, before removing to Mrs. Dobb's.

It is remarkable that Wittgenstein was so fond of Lettice (and remained so long after Frank's death). Wittgenstein was not known for being well disposed towards women, and he tended to speak only of trifling matters in their presence. His physician, Edward Bevan, and his wife (with whom Wittgenstein lived at the end of his life) provide some insight into how Wittgenstein tended to behave towards some of the wives of his colleagues. When he went to Moore's house for philosophical discussions, he would open the front door without ringing the bell, walk straight past Mrs Moore, head in the air, leaving her exasperated in his wake. Frances Marshall, who was frequently at the Ramsey's in 1929 and so saw a lot of Wittgenstein, also reported his lack of genuine engagement with women. She recalled him as being 'tortured' and 'deeply twisted', in desperate need of psychoanalysis to sort out his sex life. She was always 'aware of suppressed irritability' in Wittgenstein, but 'In mixed company his conversation was often trivial in the extreme, and larded with feeble jokes accompanied by a wintery smile.'

Wittgenstein's relationship with Lettice was a different story. He confided in her about the most intimate matters. No doubt he would have been terribly upset to know that she immediately repeated their conversations to Frances Marshall. Frances reported in her diary that Wittgenstein 'confides in Lettice that he is in love with a Viennese lady, but he feels marriage to be sacred, and can't speak of it lightly'. This was Marguerite Respinger, a Swiss friend of Tommy's from Cambridge and the only woman in whom Wittgenstein seems ever to have had a romantic interest. His feelings towards her were indeed reverential. It is almost unbelievable, however, that it was Lettice to whom he confided, as she of all people did not take marriage to be sacred and was not the kind of person to disguise her views. Lettice even told Frances that she was tempted to have an affair with Wittgenstein.

Wittgenstein found his more permanent lodgings in a little cottage at the bottom of the garden of the Malting House School, where Maurice Dobb and his wife Phyllis lived. When asked what Wittgenstein was doing in Cambridge, Mrs. Dobb was known to reply: 'What he actually *does* is to bang the lavatory door at night.' But frustrated landladies aside, all was well with Wittgenstein. He even got over his allergy to the Apostles. They declared him 'absolved from his excommunication' (an excommunication that they had never officially recognized). Perhaps one should say, rather, that all was as well with Wittgenstein as it could be. A letter from Keynes to Wittgenstein in May illustrates the precariousness of his relationships, even at their best. Keynes had asked about Wittgenstein's finances with an eye to getting him a grant from Trinity, and a misunderstanding was the immediate result:

> Dear Ludwig,
>
> What a maniac you are! Of course there is not a particle of truth in anything you say about money.... No—it was not 'an undertone of grudge' that made me speak rather crossly when we last met; it was just fatigue or impatience with the difficulty, almost impossibility, when one has a conversation about something affecting you personally, of being successful in conveying true impressions into your mind and keeping false ones out. And then you go away and invent an explanation so remote from anything then in my consciousness it never occurred to me to guard against it!
>
> The truth is that I alternate between loving and enjoying you and your conversation and having my nerves worn to death by it. It's no new thing! I always have—any time these twenty years. But 'grudge' 'unkindness'—if only you could look into my heart, you'd see something quite different.

We will see that there were some tensions as well between Frank and Ludwig, some having to do with the kinds of matters Keynes referred to and some with matters of philosophy.

The PhD Saga

When Wittgenstein returned to Cambridge, he was forty years old, and didn't have any kind of degree. An academic job was impossible without one. So Keynes and Ramsey immediately set out to try to get him a degree on the basis of the *Tractatus*, as well as his pre-war time as an undergraduate in Trinity. At first, Moore stayed out of the whole business. In 1914 he had explored the possibility of getting Wittgenstein a Cambridge BA on the basis of his residency at Trinity and the notes on logic that Wittgenstein had dictated to him in Norway. But the rules had changed and that was no longer possible. When Moore gave this news to Wittgenstein in 1914, he received the following response:

> Dear Moore,
>
> Your letter annoyed me. *When I wrote Logik I didn't consult the regulations*, and therefore I think it would only be fair if you gave me my degree without consulting them so

much either! ... If I'm not worth your making an exception for me, *even in some STUPID details*, then I may go to Hell directly; and if I *am* worth it and you don't do it, then—by God—*you* might go there.

The whole business is too stupid and too beastly to go on writing about so—
LW

Moore did not take kindly to being told he could go to hell. He didn't reply to what he called Wittgenstein's 'violent letter of abuse', and the two had no contact until Wittgenstein returned in January 1929, when they happened to meet on a train.

By that time, Cambridge had introduced the PhD, and that was the route for Wittgenstein to take. He had been admitted in 1912 as an Advanced Student and did not need to be re-admitted. He was assigned a 'tutor' at Trinity—J.R.M. Butler, later Regius Professor of Modern History at Cambridge. This was standard procedure to help a student navigate administrative procedures. In Wittgenstein's case, the navigation involved filling out forms; showing that he met the residence requirements; and having it declared that the *Tractatus* could be his dissertation. It was decided that Ramsey would be his supervisor, in name only, as the thesis had already been completed and published. Wittgenstein was thirteen years older than his supervisor, but nonetheless, Ramsey was the obvious choice. He knew the *Tractatus* better than anyone else, and if it needed to be argued that it should suffice, he was the one to do it. He wrote to Sprott:

> I've been awfully busy this term and what spare time I've had has been rather occupied by Wittgenstein, who has arrived to finish the PhD he was at before the war. I am his supervisor! He is in much better spirits, and very nice, but rather dogmatic and inclined to repeat explanations of simple things. Because if you doubt the truth of what he says he always thinks you can't have understood it. This makes him rather tiring to talk to, but if I had more time I think I should learn a lot from discussing with him.

Wittgenstein was displeased about what he regarded as the trivial administrative requirements. Ramsey, as his supervisor, was working with Butler to ensure that the Board of Research Studies would take the residence requirement to have been satisfied and would take the *Tractatus* as a dissertation, all the while trying to assure Wittgenstein that any difficulties were surmountable. It took a few weeks before it was all settled. With respect to the residence requirements, Butler wrote to the Board of Research Studies precisely adding up the dates, with locations, of Wittgenstein's prior residence in Cambridge. He added: 'I look upon him rather as a distinguished "savant" than as an ordinary Research student, though of course the technicalities must be observed.'

An impressive battalion of philosophers—Moore, Ramsey, Braithwaite—was deployed to certify to the Board that the *Tractatus* was a suitable dissertation. Ramsey met with Raymond Priestley, the Antarctic explorer who was then head of the Board of Research Studies. Priestley told him that he agreed with his assessment of the *Tractatus*, and Ramsey took this to be conclusive. Priestley was a great admirer of Wittgenstein (he would offer his rooms for Wittgenstein's lectures and discussion classes in January) and Ramsey felt his conclusion on safe ground. The one remaining requirement was that every PhD had to come up with a summary of not more than 300 words for a University publication of abstracts. Wittgenstein didn't want to write one, so he suggested that the preface to the *Tractatus* serve as the summary. But it wasn't clear that the preface would be suitable, for while it contained a couple of short paragraphs that described the project, it also contained the acknowledgements and additional, rather idiosyncratic, prefatory remarks. It was also too long. The summary would have been thought the most minor of matters. So Ramsey and Butler started the formal process.

Braithwaite then told Ramsey that he had heard that C.D. Broad, who was on the Moral Sciences Faculty Board, was suddenly doubtful and needed to think the matter over. Broad's concern might have been that no new work was being produced for the PhD. Or he might merely have been out of sorts about Wittgenstein's return. In any event, it now seemed possible to Braithwaite that Broad might try to throw a spanner in the works before the matter even reached Priestley. That was not likely to be successful, even if he tried it, since the other philosophers, including Moore, would have been lined up against Broad. But Braithwaite alerted Wittgenstein to the possibility.

Wittgenstein's reaction was to pull out of an arranged dinner with Ramsey and write an angry letter to him. He accused him of not caring whether or not he got his PhD. (But in the next breath, he asked him to fix one more administrative matter with respect to his college fees.) The tone was fast and furious:

> I still can't understand the way you behaved in this matter, that's to say I can't understand how, being my supervisor & even—as I thought—to some extent my friend having been very good to me you couldn't care two pins whether I got my degree or not. So much so, that you didn't even think of telling Braithwaite that you had told me my book would count as a dissertation. (I afterwards remembered one day talking to you about it in hall & you saying 'it would be absurd to write another thesis now strai[gh]taway'.)—Now you'll want to know why I write to you all this. It is not to reproach you nor to make fuss about nothing but to explain why I was upset on saturday & couldn't have supper with you. It is allways very hard for a fellow in my situation to see that he can't rely on the people he would like to rely on. No doubt this is due to a great extent to the difference of nationalities: What a statement seems to

imply to me it doesn't to you. If you should ever live amongst foreign people for any length of time & be dependent on them you will understand my difficulty.

Yours

Ludwig

P.S. I find on looking at my College bills that I have informed you wrongly about the fees; they are altogether only 59£ not 70 or 80 as I thought.

Ramsey reacted with a long and careful letter. He began:

Dear Ludwig,

I really think it will be all right about your degree and that you need not worry. As for my own part in the matter I am extremely distressed to hear you find me unreliable, for I really don't think I have let you down by anything I have done or not done, and it seems to me there must be some misunderstanding between us.

He went on to explain how the only real question was 'the detail of whether the preface would do for a summary'. The matter with respect to Broad would be sorted out:

I did not take this very seriously, thinking that Broad was likely to change his mind being possibly actuated by a slight degree of malice which often prompts people to say something unpleasant which they never carry into act. Nor did I see anything I could usefully do; I do not know Broad well enough to be confident of improving matters by talking to him, supposing there to be any possibility of malice on his part; and when the matter came up at the Moral Sciences Board, I knew Moore, at any rate, would do everything possible in your interest.

He then gently corrected Wittgenstein's misunderstanding. He had indeed told Braithwaite that he had told Wittgenstein that the *Tractatus* would suffice for a dissertation. Then he genuinely apologized regarding the one charge of Wittgenstein's that might be justified, and finished with the most general of apologies:

Where I think you may be right to reproach me, is not for anything I have done or not done but for my attitude of mind, which was, I am very sorry to say, rather casual.... I thought the risk of anything going wrong was infinitesimal, and therefore tried to make as little of it as possible in what must have seemed the most unsympathetic way....

But, Ludwig, it really isn't true that I didn't care two pence whether you got your degree. I may not have realized *how* much it mattered, but I did mind about it, and I don't know how you can suppose I didn't. I must express myself very obscurely, and I get drawn into making excuses of a foolish kind. But it hurts me that you should suppose I do not feel the warmest friendship for you, or that you cannot rely on me.

If, after all, your book is not accepted as a dissertation, I shall have made the most serious mistake in thinking my conversation with Priestley proved that it would; but if, as I still think very unlikely, it should come to that I do hope you will believe that it was only a mistake and forgive me for it and for whatever else I have done or failed to do.

Yours ever,

Frank Ramsey

Frank was not fond of Broad, but he knew him well enough to accurately predict his behaviour. Broad kept quiet on the day, having earlier assured Butler, in writing, that Wittgenstein was 'of the highest distinction as a philosopher and...a thoroughly responsible person'. Broad himself ended up putting the case forward, and the Board of the Faculty of Moral Sciences unanimously approved Wittgenstein's admission as a research student with the exemptions that had been requested. All Wittgenstein had to do, in addition to passing the oral exam, was take care of that one small detail: submit a short summary.

Russell wrote to Moore on 29 May, four months after Wittgenstein's arrival in Cambridge, to say that he had just received a letter from Braithwaite asking him to join Moore in examining Wittgenstein's PhD. Russell worried that Wittgenstein's dislike of him, especially of the fact that he was not a Christian, would cause Wittgenstein to 'rush out of the room in the middle of the Viva, which I feel is the sort of thing he might do'. But on the day, there was no darting from the room. In telling the story to one of his biographers, Alan Wood, Russell said that Wittgenstein arrived 'in a funk.' After some pleasant chat as old friends, Russell said to Moore: 'Go on, *you've* got to ask him some questions—*you're* the Professor'. After a short discussion, the exam 'ended amicably with Wittgenstein putting an arm on each of his examiners' shoulders and saying 'Don't worry, I know you'll *never* understand it'. Moore concluded his examiner's report with: 'I am inclined to think that the dissertation as a whole is a work of genius, comparable with acknowledged philosophical masterpieces; but, even if that is not so, I feel quite sure that its quality is such that it would be a sheer absurdity not to grant the Ph.D degree to Mr. Wittgenstein.'*

The story ought to end there, but it doesn't. On 19 July, Priestley wrote to Wittgenstein, again requesting the required summary of his dissertation, not more than 300 words in length. It was already late, and Priestley asked for it to be

---

* This is usually misquoted as follows: 'It is my personal opinion that Mr Wittgenstein's thesis is a work of genius; but, be that as it may, it is certainly well up to the standard required for the Cambridge degree of Doctor of Philosophy.' Moore seems cheeky in this version, but in the accurate one, he seems a bit daunted.

produced as soon as possible, as he was 'anxious to proceed with the publication of the summary book'. Wittgenstein had brazenly suggested to him that he, Priestley, take the *Tractatus* out of the library, bowdlerize the preface, and write the summary himself. Priestley was contemplating doing that. When Wittgenstein received Priestley's letter, he, only slightly less brazenly, asked his supervisor to provide the summary.[†]

Ramsey decided to do the easiest, most effective thing. He wrote to Priestley on 7 August:

> Dear Mr. Priestley,
>
> Wittgenstein has asked me to send you a summary of his thesis, as he professes to be unable to give the time to it himself; so it seemed to me it would save trouble if I wrote one, of which I enclose two copies. I hope it will do, his book being really impossible to summarize intelligibly. The first paragraph must seem very odd, but is what I know he would have liked to have said.
>
> I'm sorry this is so very late, but I have only just got his letter asking me to do it.
>
> Yours sincerely,
> F.P. Ramsey

He enclosed a lovely summary of the *Tractatus*. The first paragraph, on the distinction between saying and showing, was as follows:

> This thesis deals with the problems of philosophy, and argues that their formulation depends on a misunderstanding of the logic of language. It proposes, therefore, to set a limit to what can be thought; or rather, not to what can be thought but to what can be expressed in language; for in order to set a limit to thinking we should have to be able to think both sides of this limit, to think, that is, what cannot be thought. The limit can therefore only be drawn in language and what lies beyond it is simply nonsense.

All requirements now met, Wittgenstein was granted the PhD. The philosopher Max Black, who was finishing his undergraduate degree in Cambridge at the time, said that from then on, 'he wanted to be called Doctor Wittgenstein. He was very sensitive about things like that.'

[†] Gabriel Citron has suggested to me that perhaps Wittgenstein's disinclination to write a summary stemmed from the fact that he considered the *Tractatus* to be in a certain sense unsummarizable and therefore took the attitude that if the University's bureaucracy demanded a summary, it was up to those who felt beholden to that bureaucracy to provide one. The problem with this reading is that Wittgenstein could have asserted that the *Tractatus* was impossible to summarize, but he didn't. He told Priestley that it was disagreeable and that he didn't have the time to do it.

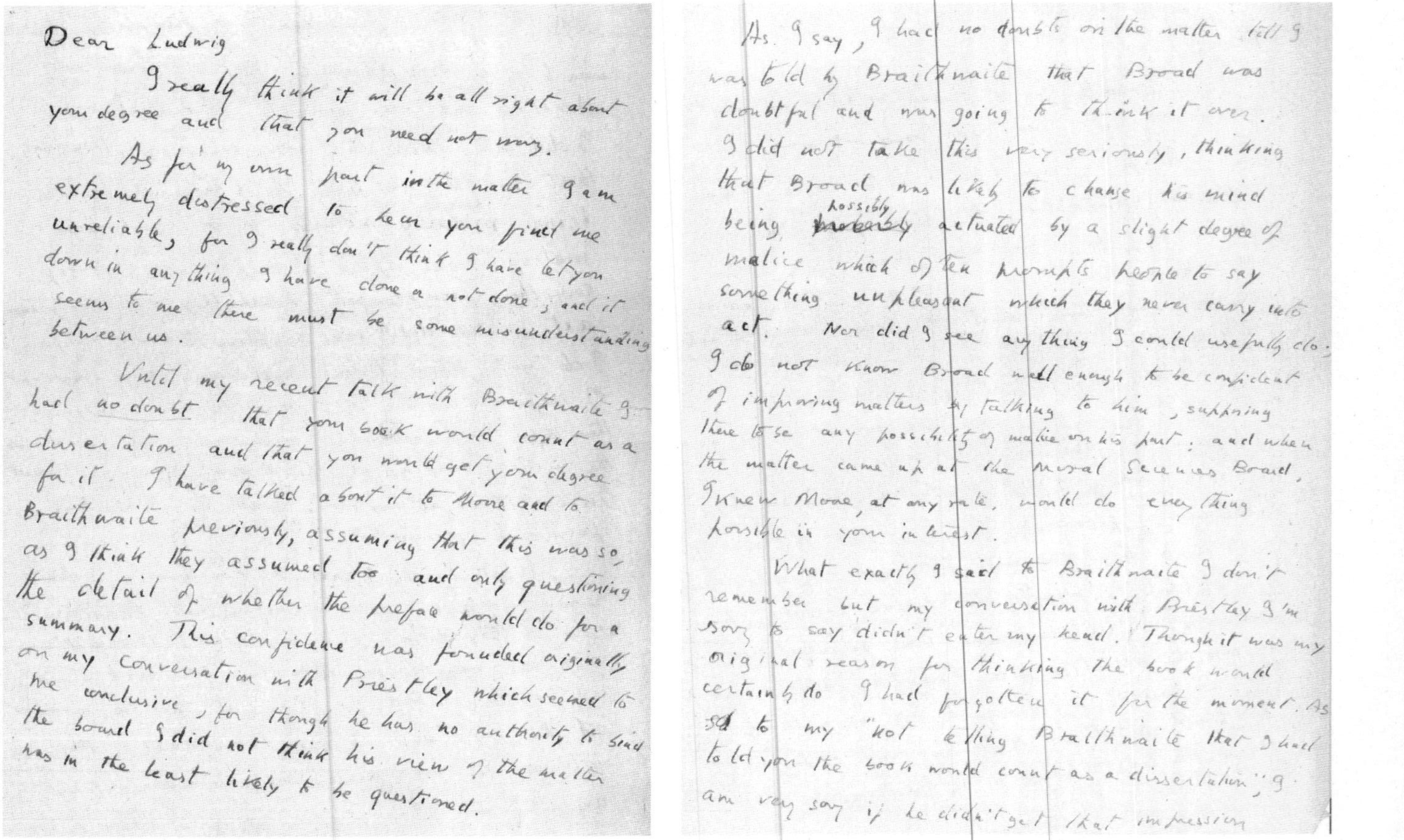

Dear Ludwig

I really think it will be all right about your degree and that you need not worry.

As for my own part in the matter I am extremely distressed to hear you feel me unreliable, for I really don't think I have let you down in anything. I have done a not done, and it seems to me there must be some misunderstanding between us.

Until my recent talk with Braithwaite I had no doubt that your book would count as a dissertation and that you would get your degree for it. I have talked about it to Moore and to Braithwaite previously, assuming that this was so, as I think they assumed too and only questioning the detail of whether the preface would do for a summary. This confidence was founded originally on my conversation with Braithwaite which seemed to me conclusive, for though he has no authority to said the board I did not think his view of the matter was in the least likely to be questioned.

As I say, I had no doubt on the matter till I was told by Braithwaite that Broad was doubtful and was going to think it over. I did not take this very seriously, thinking that Broad was likely to change his mind being possibly actuated by a slight degree of malice which often enough leads to say something unpleasant which they never carry into act. Nor did I see anything I could usefully etc. I do not know Broad well enough to be convinced of influencing matters by talking to him, supposing there were any possibility of making on his part: and when the matter came up at the Moral Science Board, I knew Moore at any rate, would do the right thing possible is your interest.

What exactly I said to Braithwaite I don't remember but my conversation with Priestley I'm sorry to say didn't enter my head. Though it was my original reason for thinking the book would certainly do I had forgotten it for the moment, as I say to my not telling Braithwaite that I had to let you the book would count as a dissertation, I am very sorry if it didn't get that impression.

Image 30 Letter from Frank to Ludwig. 'I really think it will be all right about your degree.'

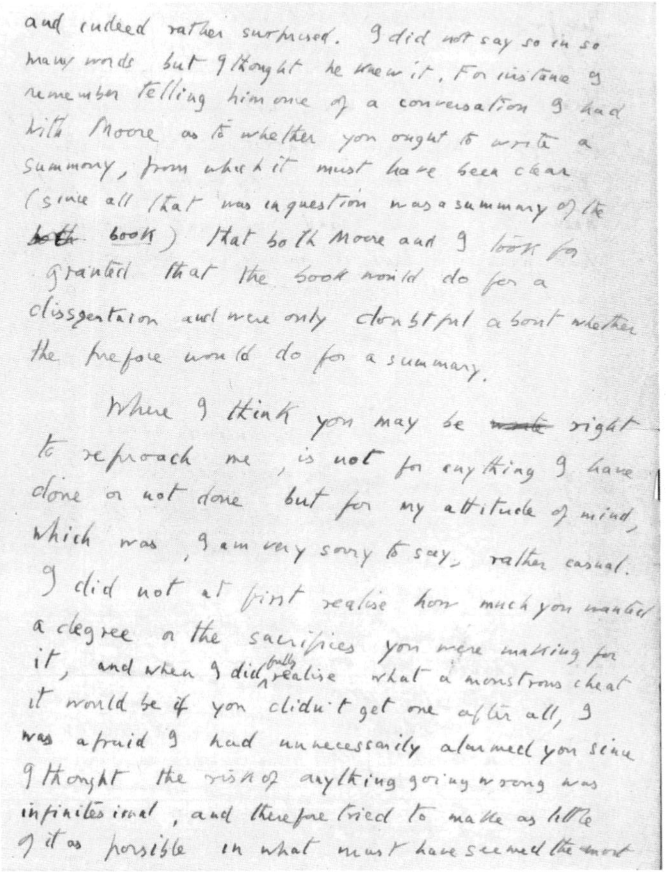

and ended rather surprised. I did not say so in so many words but I thought he knew it. For instance I don't remember telling him one of a conversation I had with Moore as to whether you ought to write a summary, from which it must have been clear (since all that I was suggestion was a summary of the both book) that both Moore and I took for granted that the book would do for a dissertation and were only doubtful about whether the preface would do for a summary.

Where I think you may be right to reproach me is not for anything I have done or not done, but for my attitude of mind, which was, I am very sorry to say, rather casual. I did not at first realise how much you minded a degree on the sacrifices you were making for it, and when I did fully realise what a monstrous thing it would be if you didn't get me after all, I was afraid I had unnecessarily alarmed you since I thought the risk of anything going wrong was infinitesimal, and therefore tried to make as little of it as possible in what must have seemed the most

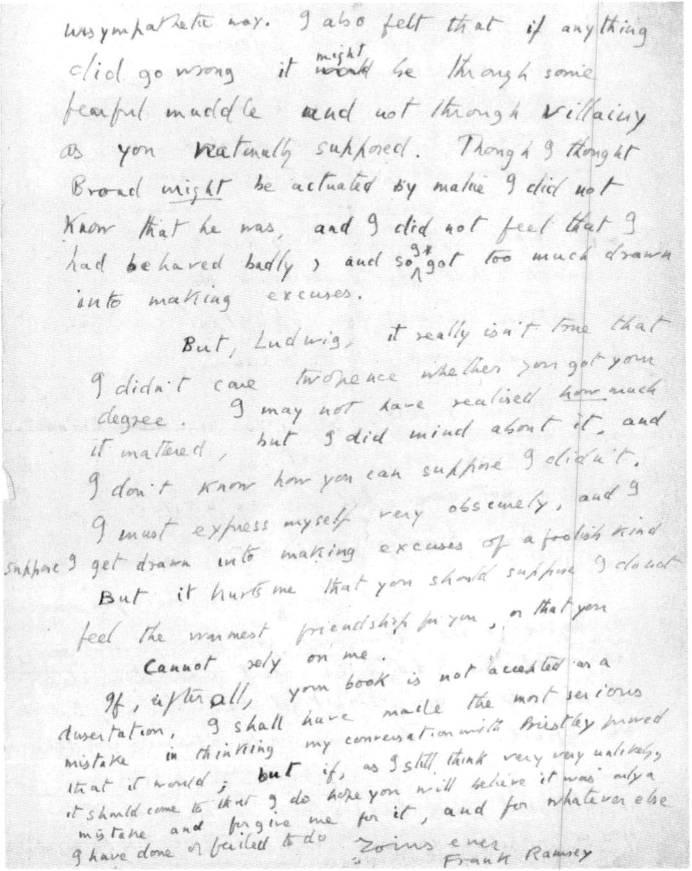

unsympathetic way. I also felt that if anything did go wrong it might not be though some fearful muddle as you ventually suspected. Though I thought Braine might be actuated by malice I did not know that he was, and I did not feel that I had behaved badly, and so got too much drawn into making excuses.

But, Ludwig, it really isn't true that I didn't care twopence whether you got your degree. I may not have realised how much it mattered, but I did mind about it, and I don't know how you can suppose I didn't. I don't express myself very obscurely, and I suppose I get drawn into making excuses I could not

But it hurts me that you should suppose I could feel the meanest friendliship for you, or that you cannot rely on me.

If, after all, your book is not accepted as a dissertation, I shall have made the most serious mistake in thinking my conversation with Priestley proved that it would; but if, as I still think very very unlikely, I do hope you will believe it was my mistake and forgive me for it, and for whatever else I have done or failed to do being

ever Frank Ramsey

Image 30 Continued

Philosopher Kings

The stimulating conversation that Ramsey had anticipated with Wittgenstein would be cut short. But they made the most of the time they had. They had a formal arrangement to meet once a week, to talk philosophy, in Ramsey's study at Mortimer Road. There were social occasions as well, with Wittgenstein coming to the Ramseys for casual dinners and more organized dinner parties, or just to listen to music on the gramophone. When you stir in meetings of the Moral Sciences Club, the meetings with Keynes and Sraffa, and so on, it's clear that Ramsey and Wittgenstein met almost daily. Some encounters were at odd hours. When Wittgenstein felt his philosophical writing was going well, he would make a good copy of his work and bring it over to Mortimer Road for safe-keeping, sometimes making his delivery after midnight.

There was a consensus amongst those who encountered the two of them together during that last year of Ramsey's life that Ramsey was one of the few philosophers Wittgenstein rated highly. Frances Marshall recalled Wittgenstein's visits to Mortimer Road: 'to see Frank and Wittgenstein together was nice because you felt they each admired the other enormously'. She said that Wittgenstein had a 'devotion to Frank'. Alister Watson recalled finding Ramsey and Wittgenstein in a railway carriage on the way to London—Ramsey was going through some material of Wittgenstein's, with Wittgenstein very attentive.

Some of Wittgenstein's own accounts of their relationship concur with these observations. He described his conversations with Ramsey:

> They're like some energetic sport and are conducted, I think, in a good spirit. There is something erotic and chivalrous about them. They educate me into a degree of courage of thinking.

Ramsey also had a devotion to Wittgenstein. He wrote in glowing support of Wittgenstein's application for a grant from Trinity, calling him a 'genius' and praising the intensity of his thought and commitment to pursuing a question to the very bottom. We will see that, outside of letters of recommendation, Ramsey found Wittgenstein's brooding over philosophical problems hard to take. But there is no doubting that Ramsey thought Wittgenstein the smartest person around.

Moreover, they seemed often to be on the same page. Wittgenstein said that it was as if Ramsey was taking his thoughts out of his own mouth and expressing them. As Russell put it, Wittgenstein always vehemently repudiated expositions of his doctrines by others, even when those others were ardent disciples. The only exception that I know of was F. P. Ramsey.

Max Black witnessed this harmony the very first time he saw Wittgenstein at the Moral Sciences Club. Wittgenstein was sitting on the floor, and when the paper was finished, he began

> to talk in a very strange and exciting sort of way. At one point, I remember [Wittgenstein] holding his neck with both hands and trying to stretch it to illustrate some point or other and it was very extraordinary, gripping. And then Ramsey... began to talk, and using the same notions, put them in respectable, dull, philosophical English. The two of them made an extraordinary team.

Ramsey, Black said, was more or less translating Wittgenstein. Arthur MacIver, an Oxford graduate student who visited Cambridge for the autumn and winter terms in 1929-30, also took Ramsey and Wittgenstein to be thinking in a similar way. He had known Ramsey at a distance at Winchester, and was very interested to observe him now. As far as he was concerned, both Ramsey and Wittgenstein were advancing a logically minded manner of doing philosophy. His first sighting of Ramsey was at the Moral Sciences Club:

> Afterwards I introduced myself to Ramsey and walked home with him as far as the R.C. church; he is now married, with two small children, and lives in Mortimer Road, overlooking Parker's Piece; he is still a very nice man and we discussed philosophical fundamentals, but we could never agree however long we argued; he belongs, with Wittgenstein, to the Cambridge 'Left Wing' and considers philosophy to be merely a matter of the right use of language, as also mathematics, all else being empirical science and such things as aesthetics merely complicated branches of psychology.

We'll see that MacIver didn't get either Ramsey or Wittgenstein quite right, but the impression that they were together on the radical wing of Cambridge philosophy is interesting. On a subsequent occasion, MacIver wrote in his diary that he perceived Ramsey and Wittgenstein to constitute the Cambridge way of doing philosophy:

> I greatly shocked Drury and Cornforth this morning by asserting that what Ramsey and Wittgenstein said last night was quite certainly false: I think they regarded such a saying as blasphemy. I find it very difficult to attack the presuppositions of Cambridge philosophy without offending Cambridge susceptibilities.

Both philosopher kings were well aware of their exalted reputations, and it seems that the only time Ramsey put on a swagger was, with Wittgenstein, at the Moral

Sciences Club. Wittgenstein was dismissive at what he took to be the stupidity of most of his colleagues, including Braithwaite, and let them know. Ramsey could also devastate a speaker. Harold Jeffreys recalled that after one paper, someone remarked that Ramsey had been contemptuous in the discussion, but that he had an awful lot to be contemptuous with. Sometimes Ramsey expressed his intellectual disapproval more quietly. When Braithwaite asked him why he didn't speak much at the Moral Sciences Club, he said it was because it often wasn't worth it. As Braithwaite put it, he was 'conscious of his abilities—it would have been foolish of him not to have been'.

Max Black recalled a paper C.D. Broad read at the Moral Sciences Club. It was a 'typical Broad-ish paper', 'carefully constructed' and 'rather dull':

> Ramsey and Wittgenstein, acting as a sort of team, attacked Broad and ended up by really devastating him. It was the first example I'd ever had of a complete blow-up of a respectable and in some ways very competent philosopher. And not only was Broad destroyed, but he and everybody else knew it. And he never came back to the Moral Sciences Club after that. He vented his spleen by making occasional very nasty remarks about the sycophantic episodes that were going in another part of the University.

Black didn't have much sympathy for Broad, as 'his so-called lecturing consisted of reading a text he would have already written out' and repeating 'every little bit of the text' three times, prefacing each bit with 'I believe...I believe...I believe...'. Black thought that Broad was 'very polite', but it was all on the surface—he was 'disgustingly uncivil, basically'. MacIver, too, was amazed at 'the meekness with which Broad lay down to Ramsey and Wittgenstein'. Henry Lintott reported: 'there's no doubt that the two of them thought themselves smarter, clever than the others'. That is in some tension with his saying of Ramsey, in the same breath:

> He was universally loved. I don't think that would be putting it too strongly . . . He was one of the nicest and most lovable people it's possible to know . . . the combination of charm and intelligence to that extent is very rare. . . . People weren't frightened of him . . . I can't remember him ever being sharp or bitchy or using his intelligence in a way to score off people. . . . almost too good to be true.

'What We Can't Say, We Can't Say, and We Can't Whistle It Either'

Ramsey and Wittgenstein didn't always operate in the unison described by Max Black, and when they didn't, the going could be rough. Lettice said that Wittgenstein would sometimes stride into Ramsey's study, not speak for half an hour except for muttering to himself 'I am such a heel', 'I am so horrible', all the while staring straight through Ramsey, and then eventually get into a huge philosophical wrangle with him. Ramsey found this trying. He wasn't alone. Braithwaite's view was that although Wittgenstein was the most original philosopher since Kant, he couldn't conceive of putting himself into another's position. Russell said that he knew of nothing more 'fatiguing' than disagreeing with Wittgenstein in an argument.

Ramsey was not willing to defer to Wittgenstein. Moore recalled that Wittgenstein once told him that in 1929 Ramsey said to him: 'I don't like your method of arguing.' Ramsey would puncture Wittgenstein's monologues—Lettice said that he would sometimes make Wittgenstein cry when they were arguing up in his study. One imagines these were tears of despair, when Wittgenstein could not get Ramsey to agree with him, or, as Wittgenstein would have it, understand him. Lettice also said that Wittgenstein could make Frank cry tears of frustration.

For, contrary to MacIver's impression, Ramsey and Wittgenstein were quite far apart in their views. While Ramsey thought Wittgenstein was an extraordinary philosopher, he had worries both about the style and content of his philosophy. In the end, well after Ramsey's death, Wittgenstein would finally hear and heed Ramsey's concerns about content, if not about style. The year 1929–30 was a crucial one in his philosophical development. It was then that he started to turn away from the logical, sparse landscape outlined in the *Tractatus* and gradually become more oriented towards ordinary human language, meaning as use, and the primacy of practice. This shift towards what we now think of as the later Wittgenstein was made under the influence of Ramsey. Wittgenstein acknowledged this in the preface of his most significant later work, posthumously published as *Philosophical Investigations*:

> since I began to occupy myself with philosophy again, sixteen years ago, I could not but recognize grave mistakes in what I set out in that first book. I was helped to realize these mistakes—to a degree which I myself am hardly able to estimate—by the criticism which my ideas encountered from Frank Ramsey, with whom I discussed them in innumerable conversations during the last two years of his life.

It may have felt like two years. But Wittgenstein returned to Cambridge on 17 January 1929, and Ramsey died on January 19, 1930. A year, almost to the day.

Piero Sraffa was the other person Wittgenstein thanked in his preface. Either through Keynes or Ramsey, or perhaps just by being at Trinity, Wittgenstein met Sraffa soon after he returned to Cambridge. They met regularly, sometimes alone, sometimes with Ramsey and Keynes. A famous story told by Norman Malcolm and G.H. von Wright gives us an idea of what Sraffa had to say about Wittgenstein's position. A central claim in the *Tractatus* was that the logical form of propositions must picture the structure of the world. One day, Sraffa made a contemptuous Italian gesture, brushing the underside of his chin with the outward sweep of the fingertips of his hand, and asked Wittgenstein 'What is the logical form of *that?*' His point was that we can express more than that which the *Tractatus* admits. Wittgenstein took this as almost a refutation. He said that talking with Sraffa made him feel like a tree whose branches had been cut off.

No date is given for this, but the slender evidence puts the conversation in the early 1930s. During the first year after his return to Cambridge, in 1929, Wittgenstein was not receptive to objections, and certainly not to refutations. He was still working within the parameters of the picture theory and trying to answer Ramsey's objections. The two papers he wrote in 1929 ('Lecture on Ethics' and 'Some Notes on Logical Form'), and the work he submitted to Trinity in 1930 for renewal of his funding, make that clear. Indeed, when he delivered 'Lecture on Ethics' to the Heretics Society in 1929, an undergraduate questioned something in the *Tractatus*, and, in Max Black's words: 'Wittgenstein was absolutely furious. He was striding off the stage, and he had to be forcibly held back and be persuaded that the man in question would apologize and that there was no malice behind it.' While he didn't storm out at Ramsey's objections, the fact that he was sometimes reduced to tears by them suggests a similar kind of anger at having his views questioned. It was only at the beginning of the 1930s, just after Ramsey died, that Wittgenstein began to understand that the *Tractatus* couldn't be fixed so as to be protected from objections, and began to accept criticism of it.

One might ask why Wittgenstein didn't simply take Sraffa's example to be another instance of something that can't be expressed in the primary language, like poetry or philosophy. The answer is that Ramsey had prepared the way for Wittgenstein to take Sraffa's gesture as a devastating criticism. Ramsey had been concerned, since his 1923 Critical Notice of the *Tractatus*, about those myriad propositions that cannot be expressed in the primary language. While Wittgenstein had been attentive to some of Ramsey's specific concerns about how the primary language is supposed to correspond to the world, only in 1929 would he properly take on board Ramsey's big objection to the distinction between saying and showing, and to his very conception of how to do philosophy. Once he truly took on board Ramsey's objections, Sraffa's gesture was the straw that broke the picture theory.

Those arguments that Ramsey made in 1929 against Wittgenstein were an onslaught. One venue for them was a piece titled 'Philosophy', perhaps intended to be included in the book he was writing. He opened a draft with a reprimand to Wittgenstein:

> Philosophy must be of some use and we must take it seriously; it must clear our thoughts and so our actions, ~~Otherwise it is mere chatter.~~ or else it is a disposition we have to check...i.e. the chief proposition of philosophy is that philosophy is nonsense. And again we must then take seriously that it is nonsense, and not pretend, as Wittgenstein does, that it is important nonsense!

We must avoid the 'absurd position' of the child in the following dialogue:

> 'Say breakfast.' 'Can't.' 'What can't you say?' 'Can't say breakfast.'

His most famous version of this objection to the saying/showing distinction is a quip made in another piece drafted in 1929. Wittgenstein was well-known for walking around Cambridge while whistling complex operas. Ramsey's zinger was:

> What we can't say, we can't say, and we can't whistle it either.

Ramsey was objecting to Wittgenstein's idea that philosophy is nonsense and should be abandoned. His objection was twofold. First, Wittgenstein could not *argue* for a particular view of the nature of meaning, if a consequence of that view is that the very argument for that account of meaning is meaningless. We do in fact understand Wittgenstein's philosophical argument. It is not a ladder that, once climbed, is kicked away. That was the force of those one-liners.

But the objection was not just that Wittgenstein was caught trying to do something he said couldn't be done. Ramsey also argued that Wittgenstein's whole approach was on the wrong track. One method of doing philosophy, 'Ludwig's', is to

> construct a logic, and do all our philosophical analysis entirely *unselfconsciously*, thinking all the time of the facts and not about our thinking about them, deciding what we mean without any reference to the nature of meanings.

The *Tractatus* tell us that a proposition is a picture of the world, and is disconnected to the self whose picture it is. As Wittgenstein accepted, this position leads to solipsism: 'The limits *of my language* mean the limits of my world.' But then how are we to bridge the chasm between ourselves and that world? How we can even make claims about that world? Wittgenstein's idea was that the subject isn't in the metaphysical world (as Ramsey put it, Ludwig's primary world 'contains no thought'). But Ramsey argued that this was a disastrous conclusion. We need to think about the human facts, not try to do the impossible—try to think about the facts somehow abstracted from all human understanding. In an undated note, Ramsey criticized the idea of having a 'first' or absolute philosophy and concluded:

> Our world is therefore a vague one and the precise is a fiction or construction. We cannot use Wittgenstein's notations like '.3 red /.7 blue'; what colour is that? I have no idea. I could only understand it by translating into intelligible terms.

Ramsey's verdict was that Wittgenstein's project of taking the propositions of science and ordinary life and exhibiting them 'in a logical system with primitive terms and definitions' results in a philosophy that is of not much use at all. In the same note, he said:

> The standardisation of the colours of beer is not philosophy, but in a sense it is an improvement in notation, and a clarification of thought.

Ramsey gave a number of examples where Wittgenstein's project fails—cases for which we need some sort of philosophical explication other than a strict definition. One invoked his daughter: when we try to explain what 'Jane's voice' is, we can't define it, since the constituents into which we would analyse it are highly specific sensations for which we have no name.

In addition to concepts too amorphous to analyse, Ramsey argued that sometimes 'nominal definition is inappropriate, and . . . what is wanted is an explanation of the use of the symbol'. We shouldn't seek definitions of Moore's kind, which purport to tell us what we have always meant by a proposition. And we shouldn't seek, as Wittgenstein does, a strict logic of our language. Rather, Ramsey argued, we should seek explications that 'show how we intend to use them in future'. So often, 'we are forced to look not only at the objects we are talking about, but at our own mental states'. Yet another note provides a beautiful summary of his argument:

> We cannot really picture the world as disconnected selves; the selves we know are in the world. What we can't do we can't do and it's no good trying. Philosophy comes from not understanding the logic of our language; but the logic of our language is not what Wittgenstein thought. The pictures we make to ourselves are not pictures of facts.

Philosophy must not neglect the 'subjective side'. If it is construed solely as the search for precise definitions or analyses of concepts, too often it will not be true to the complexity of those concepts. It is clear that in 1929, Ramsey was making the point that Sraffa would later press on Wittgenstein—that he should move away from a closed logical-physical system to an open organic system. While the primary language might be fit for some propositions, the secondary system, full of generality, vagueness, and human inference, is more important.

Ramsey admitted to having once been under the sway of Wittgenstein's conception of philosophy:

> I used to worry myself about the nature of philosophy through excessive scholasticism. I could not see how we could understand a word and not be able to recognize whether a proposed definition of it was or was not correct. I did not realize the vagueness of the whole idea of understanding, the reference it involves to a multitude of performances any of which may fail and require to be restored.

But now Ramsey has moved far away from this conception of philosophy. He sees that trying to construct an ideal definition in a perfect language is 'treating what is vague as if it were precise and trying to fit it into an exact logical category'. And he sees that Wittgenstein's dumping of all propositions that go beyond the primary language into the bin of various kinds of nonsense is far too crude. We need to think about the propositions that are not strictly true: the 'multitude of performances' of philosophy, ethics, generalizations, counterfactual conditionals, scientific theories, and so on.

Some of Ramsey's Cambridge friends quite clearly understood that Ramsey was taking on Wittgenstein. In November, when Wittgenstein gave his talk on ethics to the Heretics, the room was packed. Julian Bell wrote a long and clever poem about the event, titled 'An Epistle', in the style of Alexander Pope's satirical addresses to particular friends. When it was published in 1930 in *The Venture*, a Cambridge magazine, its subtitle was 'On the Subject of the Ethical and Aesthetic Beliefs of Herr Ludwig Wittgenstein (Doctor of Philosophy) to Richard Braithwaite ESQ, MA (Fellow of King's College)'. Bell had intended to address the poem to Ramsey. (He knew him well through the Apostles and because Ramsey had helped him with his PhD dissertation, 'Some Applications of Ethics to Politics'.) Ramsey died as the poem was going to press, and Bell thought it best to make the change. But it clearly was Ramsey, and his antipathy to Wittgenstein's idea that the important truths of ethics and philosophy could only be shown, not said, that was the impetus for 'An Epistle'. The following passage from the Epistle is about Herr Wittgenstein, and makes Ramsey's point that Wittgenstein was in fact saying things that he declared unsayable:

For he talks nonsense, and he statements makes
Forever his own vow of silence breaks:
Ethics, aesthetics, talks of day and night,
And calls things good or bad, and wrong or right.
The universe sails down its charted course,
He smuggles knowledge from a secret source:
A mystic in the end, confessed and plain,
He's the old enemy returned again;
Knowing by his direct experience
What is beyond all knowledge and all sense.

So, how, we might ask, could MacIver, and so many after him, think that Ramsey was on board with Wittgenstein's project in the *Tractatus*? For example, Wittgenstein's biographer, Ray Monk, says that Ramsey was 'unable to follow [Wittgenstein] in his radical departures from the theory of the *Tractatus*' and suggests that Ramsey may be the stupid man in a dream, reported by Wittgenstein to his diary in 1929:[‡]

This morning I dreamt: I had a long time ago commissioned someone to make me a water-wheel and now I no longer wanted it but he was still working on it. The wheel lay there and it was bad; it was notched all around, perhaps in order to put the blades in (as in the motor of a steam turbine). He explained to me what a tiresome task it was, and I thought: I had ordered a straightforward paddle-wheel, which would have been simple to make. The thought tormented me that the man was too stupid to explain to him or to make a better wheel, and that I could do nothing but leave him to it. I thought: I have to live with people to whom I cannot make myself understood. That is a thought that I actually do have often. At the same time with the feeling that it is my own fault.

But it is clear that in 1929 Ramsey was not making notches in the *Tractatus*, trying to fit new blades, unable to see that Wittgenstein was abandoning his position. Ramsey was the one who tried to convince Wittgenstein that the *Tractatus* was broken, and it was he who was leading Wittgenstein to a position that took seriously the 'vagueness' and 'the multitude of performances' involved in our understanding. Braithwaite published 'Philosophy' in his 1931 volume of Ramsey's papers, so Ramsey's approach to philosophy, so radically opposed to that of the *Tractatus*, wasn't hiding anywhere.

The explanation of how Ramsey is so often taken to be in agreement with the *Tractatus* is hinted at by Wittgenstein's other biographer, Brian McGuinness. During their year of intense philosophical conversation, Ramsey 'was (almost) the enemy,

---

[‡] Monk also thinks it possible that Wittgenstein thought that *he* was the one who kept tinkering with the broken machine.

though no doubt the enemy within'. Ramsey was used to thinking in terms of Wittgenstein's framework. It was part of his philosophical upbringing and it had become part of his language and thought. It is unsurprising that he used Wittgenstein's concepts. But what he was doing in 1929 was employing Wittgenstein's own categories of primary and secondary language in order to convince him that he had to focus on the latter, not the former. In Ramsey's terminology, he convinced Wittgenstein to be more of a pragmatist. Wittgenstein admitted as much in the *Philosophical Investigations*:

> F.P. Ramsey once emphasized in conversation with me that logic was a 'normative science'. I do not know exactly what he had in mind, but it was doubtless closely related to what only dawned on me later: namely, that in philosophy we often *compare* the use of words with games and calculi which have fixed rules, but cannot say that someone who is using language *must* be playing such a game.—But if you say that our languages only *approximate* to such calculi you are standing on the very brink of a misunderstanding. For then it may look as if what we were talking about were an *ideal* language. As if our logic were, so to speak, a logic for a vacuum.

The day after Ramsey's death, Wittgenstein came close to admitting that Ramsey had had this effect on him. The first positive mention of pragmatism in Wittgenstein's oeuvre comes on that day. Wittgenstein had just given his first lecture since his return to Cambridge. Moore was in the audience, and his notes indicate that the lecture (which may have been prepared in advance) was in step with the *Tractatus*. But that evening, Wittgenstein made a long and substantial entry in his notebook, and what he wrote sheds light on how Ramsey had influenced him:

> Sentences—that is, what we ordinarily call so: the sentences of our everyday use—seem to me to work differently from what in logic is meant by propositions. And this is due to their hypothetical character. Events do not seem to verify or falsify them in the sense I originally intended—rather there is, as it were, still a door left open. Verification and its opposite are not the last word. . . . When I say 'There is a chair over there', this sentence refers to a series of expectations. I believe I could go there, perceive the chair and sit on it, I believe it is made of wood and I expect it to have a certain hardness, inflammability etc. If some of these expectations are disappointed, I will see it as proof for retaining that there was no chair there.
>
> Here one sees how one may arrive at the pragmatist conception of true and false: A sentence is true as long as it proves to be useful.
>
> Every sentence we utter in everyday life appears to have the character of a hypothesis . . .
>
> The point of talking of sense-data and immediate experience is that we are looking for a non-hypothetical representation.
>
> But now it seems that the *representation* loses all its value if the hypothetical element is dropped, because then the proposition does not point to the future any more, but it is,

as it were, self-satisfied and hence without any value. . . . And it is through the telescope of expectation that we look into the future. It makes no sense to speak of sentences, if they have no instrumental value. The sense of a sentence is its purpose.

This notebook entry is riveting for anyone interested in the relationship between Ramsey and Wittgenstein. For in it, Wittgenstein adopts Ramsey's account of a belief as an expectation with which we meet the future. He also clearly signals his move, which would be made over the next decade, to the idea that the meaning of an expression is its use or its purpose. In this notebook entry, he calls the position pragmatism—the position Ramsey had been pressing on him all year.

Over the next decade, Wittgenstein would gradually move away from the *Tractatus* and to what we think of as the later Wittgenstein. Perhaps once the person who kept urging the move was dead, Wittgenstein could drop his defences and take on the suggestion. Indeed, he took it on so wholeheartedly that by the end of 1932, it seems that he was re-writing history and saying that Ramsey stole these ideas from him. Neurath wrote to Carnap: 'Wittgenstein is again worried about plagiarism. He claims, so I was told that the papers [Nachlass] of Ramsey contain Wittgenstein's ideas, noted carefully by Ramsey'. But if Wittgenstein was talking about the ideas outlined in his notebook entry, the charge of plagiarism is completely out of line. Those ideas were clearly articulated in Ramsey's writing (for instance, in 'Truth and Probability') during the years Wittgenstein had exiled him—years in which Wittgenstein himself was not doing any philosophy.

A Clash of Intellectual Temperaments

The fact that Wittgenstein was influenced by Ramsey does not mean that he immediately or entirely went over to Ramsey's way of thinking. For a few years following Ramsey's death, Wittgenstein mostly expressed repulsion about it. These two great philosophers understood each other well and had much in common both early on (when Ramsey was attracted to Wittgenstein's ideas in the *Tractatus*) and in 1929 (when Wittgenstein was attracted to Ramsey's pragmatism). But they had very different temperaments. Frances Marshall describes the differences in personal temperaments:

[Wittgenstein] almost had a sort of persecution mania. . . . He looked so deeply unhappy a lot of the time. I think he must have felt, in some way, the world was not his friend. Whereas in Frank's great moon face there was a sort of serenity and this wonderful great smile and this great laugh.

The differences in philosophical temperament were just as striking. In exploring them, we not only see why Wittgenstein felt reluctant to side with Ramsey, but we get insight into each of these important philosophers and into the profound questions with which they were engaged. Ramsey might have encouraged Wittgenstein's shift away from the primary language and towards the multiplicity of our practices, but when the shift was finally and decisively made in the mid-1930s, there was still considerable distance between their approaches to philosophy.

Once their conversation had been put to an abrupt end by Ramsey's death, and once Wittgenstein had started along his new trajectory, he had critical things to say about Ramsey. On 27 April 1930, three months after Ramsey died, Wittgenstein looked back on their relationship in a long diary entry:

> Ramsey's mind repulsed me. When I came to Cambridge 15 months ago I thought that I would not be able to have dealings with him, for I had such unpleasant memories of him from our meeting 4 years ago with Keynes in Sussex. But Keynes, whom I told this, said to me he thought that I should well be able to talk with him & not just about logic. And I found Keynes's opinion confirmed. For I could communicate quite well with R. about some things. But in the course of time it did not really go well, after all. R's incapacity for genuine enthusiasm or genuine reverence, which is the same, finally repulsed me more & more. On the other hand I had a certain awe of R. He was a very swift & deft critic when one presented him with ideas. But his criticism didn't help along but held back and sobered. That short period of time, as Schopenhauer calls it, between the two long ones when some truth appears first paradoxical & then trivial to people, had shrunk to a point for R. And so at first one labored arduously for a long time in vain to explain something to him until he suddenly shrugged his shoulders about it & said this was self-evident, after all. But he wasn't insincere about this. He had an ugly <u>mind</u>. But not an ugly soul. He truly relished music & with understanding. And one could see by looking at him what effect it had on him. Of the last movement of one of Beethoven's last quartets, a movement he loved perhaps more than anything else, he told me that it made him feel as if the heavens were open. And that meant something when he said it.

There is much to explore in this passage. One thing we get from it is that Wittgenstein didn't think Ramsey helped him *advance* his project—he only threw sobering obstacles in its way. He repeated the charge:

> A good objection helps one forward, a shallow objection, even if it is valid, is wearisome. Ramsey's objections are of this kind. The objection does not seize the matter by its root, where the life is, but so far outside that nothing can be rectified, even if it is wrong. A good objection helps directly towards a solution, a shallow one must first be overcome and can, from then on, be left to one side. Just as a tree bends at a knot in the trunk in order to grow on.

Wittgenstein never said what, exactly, those objections were. But we know how they went, from Ramsey's papers and notes. Some were the local objections contained in Ramsey's 1923 Critical Notice. There was also the more general objection that Wittgenstein's attempt to secure foundations for knowledge in the *Tractatus* was a failure. For if there are foundations, they underpin only a small subset of our beliefs—tautologies and perhaps some very simple observation statements. Our actual language is too rich to be expressed in an infallible elementary language. These are the objections that eventually made Wittgenstein see that ordinary human language and practices had to be front and centre in his philosophy. Ramsey, that is, thought that Wittgenstein's philosophy *needed* sobering up. It needed to become more realistic. In 1929, he was no longer trying to advance Wittgenstein's project, but upend it.

The long passage also alludes to a difference in intellectual temperaments. While Wittgenstein might have been starting to see the point of Ramsey's objections, he felt that Ramsey didn't have the appropriate reverential attitude to the seriousness of the philosophical problems. He felt that Ramsey didn't understand the profound implications of there being no absolute standard for assessing beliefs. Wittgenstein would proceed to try to get to the bottom of these problems in, for instance, his famous rule-following argument in the *Philosophical Investigations*. If there is nothing that grounds a rule, then a chasm opens up about how we can know the meaning of any of our concepts. He didn't think that a Ramseyan appeal to usefulness got anywhere near the true depths of the problem. In 1931, Wittgenstein remarked:

> Ramsey was a bourgeois thinker. i.e. he thought with the aim of clearing up the affairs of some particular community. He did not reflect on the essence of the state—or at least he did not like doing so—but on how *this* state might reasonably be organized. The idea that this state might not be the only possible one partly disquieted him and partly bored him. He wanted to get down as quickly as possible to reflecting on the foundations—of *this* state. This is what he was good at & what really interested him; whereas real philosophical reflection disquieted him until he put its result (if it had one) on one side as trivial.

Wittgenstein contrasted a bourgeois criticism with a 'radical' one. Wittgenstein's complaint seems to be that Ramsey was too interested in the scientific inclination to better understand the nature of the way things actually are, not the philosophical inclination to question whether that's possible. Wittgenstein thought: 'The philosopher is not a citizen of any community of ideas. That is what makes him into a philosopher.' Ramsey would have responded by saying that if philosophy must be severed from our world, and from trying to making things better in that world, then it's not worth doing. In an interesting twist, Wittgenstein, of course, argued in the

Tractatus that philosophy is not worth doing—it's nonsense. He held on to this idea in his later work, even when he rejected his argument for it (the picture theory and its distinction between saying and showing). Philosophy, for the later Wittgenstein, is a kind of therapy aimed at curing one from asking philosophical questions. He counselled students not to do philosophy, but to do something worthwhile.

There is no definitive answer as to which philosophical world-view is right—Ramsey's 'realistic' attempt to provide a philosophy for the real world or Wittgenstein's quest to get to the bottom or the 'essence' of all states. No doubt one's own intellectual temperament will direct one's assessment of these two approaches. But one thing we can say is that Ramsey very clearly saw the profound problems. He saw them and thought they had to be answered on a human scale.[§]

Wittgenstein's commitment to reverence and Ramsey's commitment to being realistic manifested itself not only in different philosophical approaches but also in different styles of thinking. Ramsey was impatient with Wittgenstein's method of asking about alternative possibilities and approaching a matter again and again from multiple angles. The silences and heavy thinking in the Mortimer Road study seemed to him an exaggeration. Wittgenstein's student and friend Rush Rhees reported the following conversation with Wittgenstein:

> He told me that Frank Ramsey, when they discussed in 1929, could never understand why Wittgenstein kept coming back again to the same point, although from a different angle. Ramsey called this 'messing about'.

What Ramsey called 'messing about', Wittgenstein called 'gnawing' at a problem. Moore, in Wittgenstein's opinion, was inclined to gnaw at a problem, but didn't have enough talent to achieve clarity by this approach. Wittgenstein thought that he himself could at times do it. But at least Moore saw 'how difficult it is to see the truth'. Wittgenstein held that 'you can't think decently if you don't want to hurt yourself'—if you don't want to suffer. He included Ramsey in the camp that took philosophy to be too easy and not to have the required angst about philosophical problems. Ramsey thought that Wittgenstein's suffering over a philosophical problem was excessive. They would both come to the same general conclusions about there being no foundations for knowledge, except for human ones. But Ramsey would be cheerful about that, and Wittgenstein anguished.

[§] One might argue that the later Wittgenstein came to similar, indeed, more radical, conclusions. He suggests (for instance, in section 241 of *Philosophical Investigations*) that the only thing that underpins our practices is a 'form of life'.

This difference bears out Wittgenstein's feeling that philosophy is a deeply personal matter, expressive of one's most inner being. His own personality was, as Max Newman, said, 'pure' (and 'strange'). He was reverent about religion, music, and much else. It is unsurprising that he took philosophy to be a pure endeavour which respected the profound nature of the problems and the difficulty of getting to the bottom of things. Ramsey's way of doing philosophy expressed his personality as well. He did indeed have a streak of irreverence in him. With respect to religious morality, a number of his friends recalled that he used to find it highly comic that his little brother was a cleric. With respect to philosophy, Ramsey thought that it was hard, but on the whole enjoyable, and he found the painful and obscure way in which Wittgenstein came to his ideas exasperating. While Wittgenstein was irritated by Ramsey's optimistic attitude towards the problems of philosophy, Ramsey was irritated by Wittgenstein's idea that we must honour the insolubility of the problems of philosophy. He saw Wittgenstein as wallowing in those problems and thought that Wittgenstein's quest for pure originality was the wrong—indeed, impossible—way to do philosophy.

Another way Wittgenstein sometimes put his objection was that Ramsey was in tune with the general approach of contemporary civilization, namely, he had signed up to the aim of progress. Wittgenstein, on the other hand, took himself to be at odds with the spirit of the times: 'For me on the contrary clarity, transparency, is an end in itself.' Ramsey 'wants to move forward', 'while I remain steadfast at a few signs and two steps in the calculus'. Wittgenstein was right here too. Ramsey did insist that philosophy must be of some use, and that the philosopher is 'in the ordinary position of scientists of having to be content with piecemeal improvements'. In contrast to Wittgenstein's ideas that there might be important ethical or spiritual nonsense before which we should simply stand in inarticulate awe, or that we should cease to do philosophy now that Wittgenstein has shown it to be nonsense, Ramsey thought that we can and must make an effort to spell out the norms that govern thought and action. This attitude—that one can make progress in the problems of philosophy, even the profound ones—was an anathema to the later Wittgenstein, who would argue that philosophers should be like therapists, convincing those who were in the grip of a philosophical problem to stop banging their heads against it.

A further point of friction concerned the role of others in philosophy. Wittgenstein thought that philosophy must flow directly, and from scratch, from the mind of an individual philosopher. As Gilbert Ryle put it, Wittgenstein thought that people who 'studied other philosophers' were, by virtue of doing so, themselves 'unauthentic philosophers'. Historical precedents were worse than irrelevant. To place oneself in a tradition was almost a betrayal of the enterprise of pure thought.

Ramsey didn't think this way. He was happy to acknowledge that he had predecessors, most significantly Russell, Peirce, and Wittgenstein himself. He did not take himself to be the sole origin of and solution to philosophical problems. He saw that there were no blank slates on which to inscribe one's theory, and took himself as part of an ongoing enterprise of philosophical inquiry. As a result, Wittgenstein thought that Ramsey wasn't original enough:

> Ramsey lacks originality; he is unable to see something as new as if he were the first to take it and would not have settled yet how to deal with it.

In one sense of the word 'original' (not Wittgenstein's), Ramsey was strikingly original across a number of disciplines. But some people are attracted to Wittgenstein's sense of originality because it fits their conception of a genius—an oracular presence without precedents. It is clear, however, that Wittgenstein initially got his problems from Russell and Frege, and that he shared some things with the Vienna Circle. He too was part of an ongoing tradition of philosophical thought, even if he made striking proposals within it.

This brings us to another way Wittgenstein considered Ramsey not really to be a philosopher. He was too interested in what Keynes called the borderlands between philosophy, mathematics, and economics. Wittgenstein thought the philosopher should steer clear of them. In 1944, he told Rush Rhees that Georg Kreisel was the most able philosopher he had met who was also a mathematician. Rhees replied: 'More able than Ramsey?' Wittgenstein said: 'Ramsey?! Ramsey was a mathematician!' He was levelling this charge in 1933 as well:

> One of the temptations that we must resist while philosophizing is to think that we must make our concepts more exact than they are, according to the current state of our insight. This deviation leads to a kind of mathematical philosophy, which believes that it must solve mathematical problems to achieve philosophical clarity. (Ramsey). We need only a correct description of the status quo.

This seems rather rich, as it was Ramsey who accused Wittgenstein of scholasticism or over-precision and encouraged him to focus on the status quo, or our actual practices. When Rhees recalled that Wittgenstein himself came to see that the *Tractatus* 'had too much the look and character of a scientific treatise, trying to establish results', that clarity had come courtesy of Ramsey.

In the same vein, Wittgenstein charged Ramsey with being too interested in science, and in utilizing one's scientific understanding of the world for benefit. In Wittgenstein's opinion, that simply was not philosophy. He told Rhees:

Philosophy is contemplative; and so not scientific. It is concerned with pointing out other possibilities; other ways in which it might be done.

In 1930, he said:

It is all one to me whether the typical western scientist understands or appreciates my work since in any case he does not understand the spirit in which I write.

Science, Wittgenstein thought, threatens our capacity for wonder: 'In order to marvel human beings...have to wake up. Science is a way of sending them off to sleep again.'

An exchange of letters between Moore and Sydney Waterlow sheds further light on how Ramsey and Wittgenstein had clashing intellectual temperaments. Waterlow had been an undergraduate in classics at Trinity and an editor at the *International Journal of Ethics*, but had left the academic world to work in the diplomatic service. He was a presence in Ramsey's circles, although uneasily so. He was still mortified that he had not been made an Apostle and Virginia Woolf described him as 'a kind of spaniel who follows anybody who will beat him'. Waterlow was a disciple of Wittgenstein's. He wrote to Moore of how he had become overwrought when hearing Wittgenstein being discussed:

I have a vivid memory of a wet afternoon—it seems to me a long time ago—when I listened to you and Norton discussing Wittgenstein. I may say now that my excitement on that occasion was so great that I lost control; it was all I could do not to be sick and to faint in your house.

That was Waterlow's idea of genius—someone who might make others faint with their wisdom. Wittgenstein inspired (perhaps even required) that kind of personality cult. Ramsey, despite worrying about what he felt was an ugly 'ambition' when he was an undergraduate, was not in the business of attracting acolytes.

On 31 March 1931, Waterlow, having just read Ramsey's papers collected in *The Foundations of Mathematics and other Logical Essays*, started a correspondence with Moore about the debate between Wittgenstein and Ramsey. Waterlow was on Wittgenstein's side: Wittgenstein was 'right in substance', 'however flawed his expression may be'. A couple of months later, after discussing the matter with Moore in person, he wrote:

My dear Moore,

I would have written before this to try to arrange another meeting, but I wanted to tell you what I thought about Ramsey, and so I put it off from day to day, finding it ever more difficult to say. I see I must take more time to get my ideas about R—which means my ideas about everything—clearer, and meanwhile is there any possibility of your being persuaded to come here soon, if only to help me?...If you come, please bring Wittgenstein's book with you.... If I say that my outstanding impression on a first reading of Ramsey is the contrast between his quite extraordinary powers & his immense vitality on the one hand, and on the other the poverty of his Weltanschauung, I don't much advance matters. For what is it to have a Weltanschauung? Yet I feel sure it is wrong that there should be such a contrast; something has gone terribly wrong. His drift towards stating everything in 'pragmatic' terms could not, however arguable, put the wrong right; of that I feel equally sure, for I still obstinately cling, like you...to the conviction that there is objective truth, goodness, etc. But what I mean by clinging to such conceptions as 'absolute' & 'objective', I haven't the faintest idea.

Moore was not able to visit to have the discussion 'about first and last things' with Waterlow. But he replied as follows:

I quite agree with what you say about Ramsey. I think his Weltanschauung, without objective values, is very depressing. Wittgenstein finds this too: he calls Ramsey a 'materialist'; and what he means by this is something very antipathetic to him. Yet he himself doesn't believe in objective values either! He thinks they're nonsense, but important nonsense. For my part, I still believe what I believed when I wrote Principia Ethica. I gather this doesn't at all satisfy you; but I can't believe any more.

Waterlow ignored Moore's swipe at Wittgenstein's idea that there were important kinds of nonsense. Moore at least was on Wittgenstein's side against Ramsey, with whom Waterlow was getting more exercised: 'there is a cocksureness in his attitude, which I feel to be cosmically inappropriate'. Nonetheless, Waterlow felt that Ramsey had been destined for great things before fate intervened: 'A Russell or a Keynes can never grow out of that pertness—there is no principle of growth in them—but R. seems to have been so good that he might have, had he lived.'

What an illuminating snapshot of how Ramsey was viewed by those who were searching for the Absolute. The shared worry of Waterlow and Moore (and attributed also to Wittgenstein) is that Ramsey's world-view, in trying to account for value in terms of what is best for human beings, is left devoid of 'objective' or 'absolute' or *real* value. This is the criticism Wittgenstein articulated by calling Ramsey a 'materialist', and Waterlow articulated by saying that he was drifting towards stating everything in pragmatic terms. Ramsey would have replied that he was not a materialist—he did not *reduce* value to behaviour or action. He was trying to show how the idea of what works best for humans is baked into objectivity and normativity. He was trying to set out the profound truth that the search for knowledge can only be conducted and analysed in human terms.

Ramsey would also have vigorously defended the relative sparseness of his world-view as compared to Wittgenstein's. Wittgenstein's world view in 1929 was somehow populated (on the other side of the thinkable) by the mystical, religious, and unknowable. It was marked by the quality Keats called *negative capability*—being 'capable of being in uncertainties, mysteries, doubts, without any irritable reaching after fact and reason'. Wittgenstein thought it only right to reside in this place of wonder, whereas Ramsey sought to resolve mysteries. He thought it almost a cheat to rest content with something like Wittgenstein's important nonsense or Moore's unanalysables. His worry about Moore was the worry gestured at in the above correspondence: what kind of property could Moore's unanalysable goodness be?

All this evidence from the 1930s—what Wittgenstein said and what those on his side of the debate said on his behalf—indicates an intensity of feeling about the philosophical disagreements between Wittgenstein and Ramsey. But if Wittgenstein's attitude towards Ramsey shortly after his death reflected the sting of the battle of his enemy from within, it eventually softened. As the years went by, he focused less on the enemy aspect and more on the fact that Ramsey and his ideas had been important to him. The logician Georg Kreisel said that in the 1940s, Wittgenstein talked 'quite a lot about Ramsey to me, with absolutely unbounded admiration'. By the 1940s, in Kreisel's telling, Wittgenstein was impressed by Ramsey's ability to solve problems and express his opinions with great certainty, never having to stop in the middle of a sentence to correct his thoughts. Kreisel remembered Wittgenstein bemoaning his own 'clumsy' and 'roundabout' way of communicating. By the 1950s, Wittgenstein could preface the *Philosophical Investigations* with his acknowledgement of Ramsey's influence to a degree that he was 'hardly able to estimate'.

We don't know how their different approaches would have affected their conversations, careers, and indeed, the history of philosophy, had Ramsey lived. In 1939, Carew Meredith, the Irish logician who had been a near contemporary of Ramsey's at Winchester and Trinity, echoed something that Braithwaite frequently said. Meredith wrote a letter to James Smith, a Shakespeare scholar who had been an undergraduate with them at Trinity. Moore had just resigned his chair of philosophy and Wittgenstein had been named as his successor. Meredith wrote: 'No. I did not know that Wittgenstein had succeeded Moore. One feels that, but for Ramsey's death, W. would have been confined to his proper sphere.' Meredith may not have appreciated the size of Wittgenstein's proper sphere. He is one of the most important figures in the history of philosophy. We needn't take the side of Meredith and Braithwaite and think that Ramsey was better than Wittgenstein. We can, though, reasonably say that, had he lived, Ramsey's sphere would have been as large as Wittgenstein's.

We can also say that, had Ramsey not died so young, the new generation of Cambridge philosophers would have had an alternative model for how to do philosophy. Casimir Lewy, a student of Wittgenstein's, recalled an incident when Wittgenstein was told of Susan Stebbing saying something 'almost hagiographic' about Ramsey. Wittgenstein made disparaging movements with his hands, meant to show that *he* didn't think Ramsey 'a great philosophical genius'. It seems that Wittgenstein thought that hagiography was to be reserved for thinkers such as himself—those who gnawed away at a problem in order to get to its very root. That became a model of how philosophy was to be conducted. Perhaps Ramsey's more cheerful and straightforward style would have provided an alternative and welcome exemplar.

The Infinite

At the beginning of the intellectual relationship between Ramsey and Wittgenstein, the direction of influence was very much Wittgenstein imparting his vision of the logical structure of the world to Ramsey. At the end, it was the other way around, with Ramsey imparting his pragmatism to Wittgenstein. But there was one further point of influence between these two, with the lines less clearly drawn.

In July of 1929, Wittgenstein gave a talk at the preeminent annual philosophy conference in Britain—the Joint Session of the Aristotelian Society and Mind Association, which was being held in Nottingham. He had told the organizers he would read a paper on logical form, a piece he had written soon after his return to Cambridge. It tried to make more concrete some ideas in the *Tractatus*, as well as solve the colour exclusion problem that Ramsey had raised in his Critical Notice.

Ramsey wasn't certain he'd be able to attend the conference. Wittgenstein wrote to Russell, asking him to come to Nottingham, as he was sure no one would understand him. He also said that he wasn't going to talk about logical form after all. Since the Joint Session had advertised 'Some Remarks on Logical Form', and since Wittgenstein had sent them the paper in advance as required, that's what they published in the *Proceedings*. Wittgenstein couldn't have been pleased, for by that point he thought the paper problematic. (In 1933 he would call it 'weak'.) We have seen that Ramsey had been chipping away at Wittgenstein's confidence in the *Tractatus* over the previous six months. But Ramsey had also been engaging with Wittgenstein in a more positive way about a different topic. It was a discussion that provoked both of them to explore intuitionism in the foundations of mathematics. What Wittgenstein talked about when he arrived in Nottingham was infinity.

In the spring of 1928, he had gone to a lecture by Brouwer in Vienna titled 'Mathematik, Wissenschaft und Sprache' ('Mathematics, Science, and Language'), and then met with Brouwer. In the lecture, Brouwer gave a philosophical overview of his intuitionism, stressing the role of the ideal mathematician's mind in creating mathematical truth.** The lecture seems to have re-ignited Wittgenstein's passion for philosophy and spurred his return to Cambridge. Herbert Feigl, who was a member of the Vienna Circle, had attended the lecture as well, and described Wittgenstein's excitement at the café afterwards:

> Suddenly and very volubly Wittgenstein began talking philosophy—and at great length. Perhaps this was the turning point, for ever since that time, 1929, when he moved to Cambridge University Wittgenstein was a philosopher again, and began to exert a tremendous influence.

One of Wittgenstein's biographers, Ray Monk, says that the paper Wittgenstein delivered in Nottingham has been lost. Another, Brian McGuinness, suggests that a draft of the talk was likely dictated to Ramsey and can be found in some notes in Ramsey's hand. The notes do seem to be a copy of something Wittgenstein said or wrote. They are very much in Wittgenstein's voice, in German, with Ramsey's interventions in English, and chunks of the text appear elsewhere in Wittgenstein's writing. Wittgenstein told F.R. Leavis at midnight on the eve of his departure for Nottingham that he was setting off to lodge a fair copy of his work with Ramsey for safe-keeping. Perhaps these notes are the result of an all-night session.

One thing is certain. In 1929, Ramsey and Wittgenstein talked a lot about infinity and intuitionism. There are those notes in Ramsey's hand. There is also testimonial evidence. In 1972, Rush Rhees reported on his conversations with Wittgenstein:

> Wittgenstein said often that Ramsey used to say, in discussion, 'I seem to mean something by it' (perhaps some proposition having to do with infinity in mathematics); or perhaps: 'it does mean something to me'. This was almost like speaking of how it looked to him. At any rate, it is not a way of deciding whether the expression you contemplate does mean anything or not. And Wittgenstein's move was always to ask, 'Well, what do you do with it?' To find what it means, consider its application.

This report is four decades after the fact, and it is muddled in an interesting way. Wittgenstein decisively made the move to link meaning and use only after Ramsey's death. It was Ramsey who, in 1929, was saying that if you want to know what something means, consider its application in action. Perhaps Rhees was reading

---

** As Mancuso (2020) shows, Ramsey thought that Wittgenstein had been leaning towards intuitionism before then. In a 1928 letter to Fraenkel, he wrote: '[Wittgenstein's] conclusions were more nearly those of the moderate intuitionists; what he thinks now I do not know. In any case I haven't seen him since 1925'.

Wittgenstein's later work into his 1929 conversation or perhaps Wittgenstein himself pre-dated his conversion to Ramsey's view. Alternatively, perhaps Wittgenstein was in fact already into Ramsey's mindset in 1929, throwing Ramsey's own principles back at him when it came to the nature of infinity.

We have seen that in 'The Foundations of Mathematics' and subsequent papers on the subject, Ramsey argued for logicism, scorning intuitionism as the 'Bolshevik menace'. In August 1929, he wrote two long notes which mark a change of mind. He titled them 'Principles of Finitist Mathematics' and 'The Formal Structure of Intuitionist Mathematics'. In them, he actively explored intuitionist mathematics, opting mostly for Weyl's introduction rules and arriving at his own substitution rules. Philip Hall would say that during Ramsey's day intuitionism was not taken seriously in England. But Ramsey and Wittgenstein were together changing that.

Their conversations about the infinite were not, it seems, arguments of the sort they had over the *Tractatus* and over pragmatism. They seem to have been more a cooperative working through of the issues, trying to come to a conclusion. Wittgenstein recalled one:

> I said on one occasion that no extensional infinite existed. Ramsey replied, Can't one imagine a man living for ever, i.e. simply never dying, and isn't that extensional infinity? And, to be sure, I can imagine a wheel turning and never stopping. There is a strange difficulty here: it seems to me nonsense to say that there are in a room an infinite number of bodies, as it were by accident. On the other hand I can think in an intentional manner of an infinite law (or an infinite rule) that always produces something new—ad infinitum—but naturally only what a rule can produce, i.e. constructions.

In both Wittgenstein's and Rhees's recollections, Ramsey seems to be pushing against Brouwer's intuitionism, arguing that we do mean something by the infinite, even if some claims about the infinite are not decidable.

One might wonder if Ramsey really did become an intuitionist as opposed to merely exploring how such a mathematics would go. One might also wonder whether he intended to marry logicism with a finitist logic. The answers to both queries seem to be negative. With respect to the second, Ramsey seems to have taken logicism, intuitionism, and formalism to be in strict opposition to each other. With respect to the first, we will see when we turn to 'General Propositions and Causality', written some time in 1929, that Ramsey argued that an infinite statement goes beyond what we can express and hence is not a proposition that can be strictly true or false. He made the point in those August 1929 notes as well. A universal generalization cannot be the sum of an infinitely large number of singular judgments, as 'the mind cannot attain to any such infinite conception'. All this left Ramsey feeling 'without a clear conception of the nature and purpose of mathematics'. He came to the conclusion that

> We cannot…assume that mathematical propositions in general can be made arguments to truth-functions and treated by the propositional calculus, but must examine the question afresh.
>
> Our old conception that the 'propositions' of mathematics expressed each a true judgment has been destroyed and we have as yet nothing to put in its place.

That is a radical change. Mathematics might not, after all, be expressible in the primary language.

In his book manuscript, which he was writing at the same time, he made the further intuitionist move of considering whether the law of excluded middle failed to hold of some propositions. Ramsey, that is, was now tempted to go over to the Bolshevik finitism—the position that in mathematics we can only go as far as our human intelligence will take us.††

This may seem like a sudden move. Russell certainly thought so. In 1931, he reviewed Braithwaite's edition of Ramsey's posthumously published papers. His opening line marked the great personal loss: 'In reading this book, it is impossible not to be perpetually haunted by the tragedy of Ramsey's death.' He then expressed bewilderment at Braithwaite's announcement in the introduction that Ramsey had been 'converted to a finitist view'. The reader, Russell said, 'is placed in something of a difficulty'. Ramsey must have 'found flaws' in the argument he made in 'The Foundations of Mathematics', 'but we are not told what these flaws were'.

The explanation for Russell's bewilderment is, I think, as follows. In the last years of Ramsey's life, Russell was busy with his family and running his experimental school, not closely attached to Cambridge and the work going on there. He simply would not have heard or read much, if anything, of Ramsey's commitment to pragmatism. Intuitionism can be seen as an expression in the philosophy of mathematics of the general pragmatist position that truth does not go beyond potential human experience. In 1929, Ramsey started to see that perhaps he needed to be as radical in mathematics as he was in philosophy.

Wittgenstein would never become a card-carrying intuitionist (he once said that intuitionism is 'all bosh'). But he would remain intensely engaged with what

---

†† The relationship between intuitionism and finitism is not straightforward, partly because the extension of the term 'finitism' is open to debate. In Cambridge of the 1920s, the terms were employed as Ramsey does: loosely and often equivalently.

RAMSEY AND INTUITIONISM

Mathieu Marion, Professor of Philosophy of Logic and
Mathematics, Université du Québec à Montréal

In his early papers on 'The Foundations of Mathematics' (1925) and 'Mathematical Logic' (1926), Ramsey wished to improve *Principia Mathematica*, and defend its logicism against competing foundational programmes, such as Hilbert's formalism and Brouwer's intuitionism. Initially, Ramsey adopted Wittgenstein's view of the quantifiers in the *Tractatus* as 'logical products' and 'sums', with universality being expressed, for predicate F, as an infinite conjunction:

$$F(a) \wedge F(b) \wedge F(c) \wedge \dots$$

And existence as an infinite disjunction:

$$F(a) \vee F(b) \vee F(c) \vee \dots$$

Wittgenstein appears not to have noticed that Frege had already provided in the *Begriffschrift* (§ 11) a rule of generalization: that one can derive $A \to \forall x\, F(x)$ from $A \to F(a)$, if a does not occur in A and stands only in argument places in $F(a)$. In absence of this rule, however, one has at most that a universality implies any of his instances:

$$\forall x\, F(x) \to F(a), \tag{1}$$

and the product becomes infinite. Likewise, without a rule of existential elimination, all one has is that an instance implies existence:

$$F(a) \to \exists x\, F(x), \tag{2}$$

and, the disjunction being infinite, it cannot sum up all the disjuncts.

Ramsey knew two alternatives to Wittgenstein. The first was Skolem, who proposed in a paper where he introduced primitive recursive arithmetic (1923) to simply do away with the quantifiers. Wittgenstein already hinted in the *Tractatus* at a logic-free equation calculus for arithmetic. Ramsey thought this to be 'ridiculously narrow', and wanted the convenience afforded by quantifiers.

In two of his last papers, 'Principles of Finitist Mathematics' and 'The Formal Structure of Intuitionist Mathematics', he showed signs of agreement with the other alternative. Hermann Weyl, in 'On the New Foundational Crisis in Mathematics' (1921), had suggested that universality should be understood in analogy with bank drafts, as 'instructions for judgments', while existence would be a 'judgment abstract', classical existence being compared to a treasure map that does not tell us where the treasure is. These explanations happen to justify (1) and (2) above. Weyl claimed further that (1) and (2) cannot be negated since one could not, say, survey infinitely many disjuncts, so the Law of Excluded Middle would not hold.

It is in this paper that Weyl declared that he was now siding with Brouwer. Intuitionistic logic is characterized by the rejection of the universal applicability of the Law of Excluded Middle, $A \lor \neg A$. With the classical form of *reductio ad absurdum* one can prove A assuming $\neg$ A, and then derive an absurdity, which means one cannot assert $\neg$ A, i.e., $\neg\neg$ A, which would imply that one can assert A in virtue of a principle equivalent to the Law of Excluded Middle:

$$\neg\neg A \rightarrow A$$

But Brouwer could not accept that one could assert some 'positive' A, without any construction, simply because the assumption of its contradictory leads to absurdity. Later work by Kolmogorov and others led to Heyting presenting the standard axiomatic formulation for intuitionistic logic in 1930, just after Ramsey's death. Quantifiers were not well understood in the 1920s. It is only in the mid-1930s that Gentzen supplied introduction and elimination rules for the quantifiers in accordance with Heyting's axioms—by adding to (1) and (2) the missing rules of generalization and existential elimination.

It seems that Ramsey wanted to obtain an intuitionistic arithmetic starting from Skolem's primitive recursive arithmetic, adding to it Weyl's rules for quantifiers. In intuitionism, however, the Law of the Excluded Middle applies to atomic formulas, and if quantifiers are in 'prenex normal form', then no indirect inferences as above are possible and the theory remains constructive. This is what Ramsey captured. But he did not provide a rule of existential elimination and restricted himself to quantifiers in 'prenex' form, so that the result is not the full intuitionistic arithmetic. In 'Principles of Finitist Mathematics', he stated that his rules give 'all the logical modes allowed by the finitists', but if he meant 'intuitionism', the claim was inaccurate.

Ramsey knew about Weyl's views in 1925–26, so what made him change his mind in 1928–29? It seems to have been the result of changes in his underlying conception of theories visible in a note in his manuscript *On Truth* and 'Theories'. According to a view originating in Hertz and Campbell, a 'primary system' of true or false observational statements is entailed, via a 'dictionary', by a 'secondary system' of hypotheses, and Ramsey described the latter not as statements or propositions, but, adapting Weyl's expression, as 'rules for judging' or 'formulas from which we derive propositions'. In 'General Propositions and Causality', he also took them to be 'maps by which we steer', and developed allied qualms of a pragmatic nature about the infinity of the above products and sums: if these 'hypotheticals' were to be infinite, one would not be able to steer by them, and this is why he denied them the status of propositions and, as with Weyl above, the possibility of applying the Law of Excluded Middle to them.

In 1929, Ramsey had many discussions with Wittgenstein, whose manuscripts show that he was coming to similar views on 'hypotheses' as 'laws for the construction of expectations', but it appears that Ramsey had reached some of these ideas prior to their discussions.

he took to be Brouwer's argument that it is a mistake to think of the infinite as a very large finite. And he would say, at some point between 1937 and 1944, that 'mathematics is after all an anthropological phenomenon', which the reader will recall was Carnap's characterization of intuitionism.

There is dispute about the direction of influence between Ramsey and Wittgenstein on the matter of intuitionism. The question of who more heavily influenced the other on this topic, however, is best answered by saying that their views evolved together.

18

'THE PROBLEM OF PHILOSOPHY MUST BE DIVIDED IF I AM TO SOLVE IT'

On Truth

In 1928, Keynes had encouraged Ramsey to come down from the unforgiving heights of philosophy and move towards economics, where he so agreeably blended theory and practice. But Ramsey declined. He stayed in the rarefied air, even if he didn't think it as devoid of oxygen as Wittgenstein might have thought. In the last year of his life, he made remarkable progress in solving some of the most fundamental problems of philosophy. This work, while unfinished and frustratingly incomplete, buzzes with the energy of someone who is on to something important.

Ramsey intended his book to be the main vehicle of his ideas. He started to write it in 1927, soon after he finished 'Truth and Probability'. In January 1928, as the tide of emotion over their respective affairs was receding, he wrote to Lettice in Dublin:

> I am thinking this weekend of taking up my book again. I've got most of the next 3 days (counting Sunday) free for it.

A weekend here and there is better than nothing, but it's not much time in which to write your magnum opus. And he was starting to think it would indeed be something of lasting value:

> I feel rather excited about my book, and clearer about the difficulties in planning it, i.e I see new difficulties, I haven't solved them. Everything turns so on everything else that it is hard to see how you can arrange it satisfactorily.

So Ramsey started to clear the decks. In May 1928, he cancelled his book contract with Ogden on the foundations of mathematics. Then he applied to King's for some leave, and got it. He told Sprott in March 1929: 'Next term I...have been let off supervision on the pretext of writing my book'. His students were shifted to Philip Hall, a newly elected and reclusive mathematics Fellow, who had been one of Ramsey's first students. Although King's continued to pay into his pension during his leave, they held back his stipend. It was precious and hard-won time. Ramsey made the most of it. He was charged with energy and he felt that he was finally tying things together.

Ramsey intended his book to be a substantial expansion and improvement of 'Truth and Probability', and he planned to give it the very same title. When Nicholas Rescher and Ulrich Majer edited the book for publication in 1991, they asserted that Ramsey realized that the problem of truth was difficult enough to merit a stand-alone treatment, so he split the project in two—first he would write a book on truth and then one on logic and probability. The editors published what they took to be the intended book—drafts of five short chapters mostly on the nature of truth. They gave it the title *On Truth*.

But there is reason to believe Ramsey meant to write the more expansive *Truth and Probability*. First, there is no title other than *Truth and Probability* in Ramsey's manuscripts—indeed, there is a draft table of contents which includes chapters on probability, partial belief, generality, causality, the nature of knowledge, induction, and more. Second, during 1928–29, he wrote a vast amount of philosophy and there is no evidence that he had any intention of submitting these pieces, say, to *Mind*. Indeed, he published no philosophy at all from 1927 to his death, suggesting that all his philosophical writing during this period was intended for the book. (The 1928 'On a Problem in Formal Logic' was a paper in the foundations of mathematics and wouldn't have been suitable for the book.)

Third, it is not clear from the organization of Ramsey's papers that only the five chapters on truth were meant to form the book. We know from a microfilm copy which resides in the Cambridge University Library that the Ramsey Papers at the University of Pittsburgh aren't in the order they were when Lettice put them up for sale. Braithwaite looked after Ramsey's papers until he died, then they went to Lettice, perhaps getting re-ordered even during those transitions. And the Pittsburgh collection is not complete—a few papers remain in the Cambridge University Library and some were sold or given away before the Pittsburgh acquisition.

Finally, it's hard to believe that Ramsey intended to sit on his novel approach to probability and partial belief, which was receiving so much attention from Keynes and others. He would have wanted to improve and publish that. He was writing notes in September 1929 suggesting that he thought parts of his paper on probability needed revision. He was worried about the idea that psychologists might measure degrees of belief by looking at external behaviour, as the science wasn't up to it. All this suggests that Ramsey did intend to write the whole *Truth and Probability*, and that papers such as 'Theories', 'Philosophy', and 'General Propositions and Causality' were designed to be part of it.

When the five draft chapters were published as *On Truth*, philosophers paid it surprisingly little attention. That may have been because it came out with a press that assigned it a hefty price tag. But more likely it was because most philosophers who looked at it didn't know what to make of it, just as Russell didn't know what to make of Ramsey's turn to finitism in mathematics. They already had a settled view of Ramsey, from Braithwaite's hand-picked selection of papers in *The Foundations of Mathematics and other Logical Essays*. They took Ramsey's axiomatization of choice, naturalized account of meaning as success, and account of scientific theories as isolated pieces of work, and as being in the spirit of the early Wittgenstein and the Vienna Circle. The position presented in the five chapters (which I will call *On Truth*, since they now get referred to as that) jarred with this received view of Ramsey.

In the book, Ramsey promises to solve the problem of truth, which he takes to be the hardest problem of philosophy—'How difficult the problem is may be judged from the fact that in the years 1904–25, Mr Bertrand Russell has adopted in succession five different solutions of it.' One of Russell's attempts, Ramsey thought, was on the right track. Russell had suggested in *The Analysis of Mind* (1921) that two things about truth can hold simultaneously: (1) *human judgments* are the things that are true or false; and (2) true judgments are nonetheless connected to the way things are. In *On Truth*, Ramsey tried to show how truth is a property of our fallible human judgments, yet is objective. Because he died before the book was finished, we have to make educated guesses as to how he would have shown that this 'naturalist' or 'pragmatist' account of truth is coherent and preferable to its competitors.*

Part of *On Truth* was a restatement of some of Ramsey's earlier ideas. Propositions do not exist as independent entities: 'it is only the hardiest verbalists who can persuade themselves "that the earth is flat" is the name of something real'. Truth is not a relation between a proposition and a fact, but is primarily an attribute of 'thoughts and opinions and only derivatively of sentences'. The very '*meaning*' of

---

* He thought that Russell's position was 'in general' naturalist, but it was 'peculiar' in that some things he accepted, such as Keynes's objective probability relations, were in tension with that naturalism. Russell, for his part, seems to have been unfazed about being associated with Ramsey's pragmatism.

'belief' is tied up with dispositions to act. But the meaning of belief is not reduced to action, for belief is also a feeling or a mental state.

Much of the book, however, was strikingly novel, especially at two points. First, Ramsey was now explicitly concerned with the normative domain, including ethics and aesthetics. He was extending his reach to include moral philosophy, so much so that Henry Lintott surmised that had Ramsey lived, he, rather than Braithwaite, would have ended up the Knightbridge Professor of Philosophy, which was then a chair in moral philosophy.

Second, he now positioned the discussion of truth in the context of the three main candidate theories of truth: coherence (idealism), correspondence (realism), and pragmatism (naturalism). He staked out the territory:

> With regard to the meaning of any concept of value such as goodness, beauty, truth or validity there are three main schools of opinion which may, perhaps, be called idealist, realist and naturalist. With the idealists such as Green, Bradley, and Bosanquet I shall not deal; their writings seem to me to be almost entirely nonsense; the living issue is between the realists and the naturalists.

Some Realists, he said, take truth and validity to 'involve in their ultimate analysis one or more distinctively logical predicates or relations, such as a unique kind of correspondence or indefinable probability relations'. This kind of realist holds that 'truth or validity are unanalysable' (such as Moore on the good and Keynes on probability). Other realists take truth to be a matter of propositions hooking on to the independently existing world (such as the early Russell and the Wittgenstein of the *Tractatus*). Ramsey did not adopt either kind of realism in this book. He chose amongst his old arguments, and put the chosen ones in new, confident ways. For instance, with respect to Wittgenstein's picture theory, consider the belief that Jones is a liar or a fool. It seems that Wittgenstein must explain the truth of this belief by appeal to its corresponding to the 'disjunctive fact' that Jones is either a liar or a fool. But there are no such strange things in the world as facts like these. Anyway, what could this relation between a belief and the world be? Does a belief resemble the world? Ontological accounts of truth, such as the correspondence theory, which single out a particular kind of entity as the one required to ground the truth of any proposition, do not make good on their promise to set out in a clear way how a proposition might get the world right. The appeal to some kind of relation between a belief and reality amounts to 'shirking our duty' because that relation itself is so problematic. Ramsey's own position is 'superior' to the correspondence view because it is 'able to avoid mentioning either correspondence or facts', two philosophically problematic notions.

He also employed a version of his old objection to Keynes's objective probability relations against the correspondence theory. Just as we do not actually appeal to objectively existing probability relations between statements when we assess likelihoods, an appeal to correspondence to facts simply does not figure in what we do when we use the word 'true':

> If I make a judgment, and claim that it is true, this cannot be because I see that it corresponds to a fact other than itself; I do not look at the judgment and the fact and compare them.

But Ramsey was equally loath to have truth rest in an all-encompassing and inescapable subjective sphere, whose relation to the concrete world is in principle incapable of discovery. The coherence theory, which holds that truth must 'lie within the circle of our beliefs and not pass outside them to an unknowable reality' is no good. 'The beliefs of a man suffering from persecution mania may rival in coherence those of many sane men but that does not make them true.'

The solution to the problem of truth, Ramsey argued, lies in a naturalism or pragmatism. He was not interested in the kind of pragmatism that Russell, Moore, and others were bashing—the kind that holds truth to be whatever happens to work. MacIver reported going to a lecture of Broad's in 1929, where that kind of pragmatism was being dismissed:

> Broad was criticising Pragmatism, and that so unfairly that even I, who do not love the Pragmatists, was offended, and Cornforth, who does not ordinarily take notes of lectures, filled his note-book with swear-words.

What is 'ludicrous', Ramsey said, is not 'the general idea' of pragmatism, but 'the way in which William James confused it especially in its application to religious beliefs'. What Ramsey (and Russell, Moore, and Broad) didn't like was James's suggestion that if a belief in God is useful for me, I ought to believe that it is true.

Ramsey began his own version of pragmatism with an affirmation of the core insight of the tradition—the dispositional account of belief that he himself had been championing over the past two years:

> To say a man believes in hell means, according to the pragmatists that he avoids doing those things which would result in his being thrown into hell.

He then stated that the pragmatist must acknowledge that truth and usefulness are tied to the way things are, a point he made in 'Facts and Propositions' with the chicken whose avoidance of certain caterpillars will be useful only if those caterpillars are in fact poisonous. In *On Truth*, his example is the hellish one:

> Such conduct will be useful to the man if it really saves him from hell, but if there is no such place it will be a mere waste of opportunities for enjoyment.
>
> But besides this primary utility there are other ways in which such conduct may or may not be useful to the man or others; the actions from which a belief in hell would cause him to abstain might bring disasters in their train either for him or for others even in this present life. But these other consequences of the belief, whether useful or not, are clearly not relevant to its...truth....William James...included explicitly these further kinds of utility and disutility, which must obviously be excluded if pragmatism is to have any plausibility, and thought that the truth of the belief in hell depended not on whether hell in fact existed but on whether it was on the whole useful for men to think it existed.
>
> Such absurdities...form no part to the essential pragmatist idea, even if they constitute its chief attraction to some minds;...we shall see that pragmatism has a considerable contribution to make.

The good kind of pragmatism, according to Ramsey, holds that when we talk about the usefulness of a belief that *p*, we must consider whether or not *p*—in this case whether there really is a hell. He did not want to turn his back on our connection to objective reality. For that would be turning against the 'realistic spirit'—it would fail to capture the way we really use the concept of truth. The correspondence theory must be brought on board 'in a vague sense'. Like pragmatism, it 'is not simply to be mocked at'. He put the point differently in different drafts, but the sentiment was always the same: 'this talk of correspondence, though legitimate and convenient for some purposes, gives...not an analysis of truth but a cumbrous periphrasis, which it is misleading to take for an analysis'. Sure, a true belief is one that 'corresponds to the facts'. But we cannot specify that any further than to say that correspondence is the type—'or types, since [it] may be different with different forms of belief'—of relation between thinking that such-and-such is the case and such-and-such's actually being the case.

On Ramsey's theory of truth, truth is a property of 'mental states', but it is not a property of just *any* kind of mental state. For one thing, the mental state must have propositional reference: it must be 'necessarily a belief that something or other is so-and-so': for instance, beliefs 'that the earth is round' or 'that free trade is superior to protection'. He was interested in the range of so-and-sos to which the truth predicate can be applied—in exploring propositional reference without any preconceived notion of what its objects must be. That's why he included beliefs about goodness and perhaps even beauty in his provisional list.

Ramsey thought that propositional reference was not the only important thing regarding belief and truth: 'So important is this character of propositional reference, that we are apt to forget that belief has any other aspects or characters.' Another vital aspect of true belief is that only those mental states with 'affirmative or assertive character' can be true—not my *hope* that I will win the lottery or my *wondering* whether I will do so. A true belief also has 'the felt quality…characteristic of assertion as opposed to doubt or inquiry', as well as 'effects on subsequent thought and conduct'.

As always, Ramsey made his deflationist point: 'A belief is true if it is a belief that p, and p.' This 'is merely a truism, but there is no platitude so obvious that eminent philosophers have not denied it'. It is 'so obvious that one is ashamed to insist on it, but our insistence is rendered necessary by the extraordinary way in which philosophers produce definitions of truth in no way compatible with our platitudes'. These barbs were meant for the idealist, who takes truth and reality to be entirely mental, and also for James, who seemed to suggest that whatever works for you or me is true. Then, again as usual, Ramsey noted that setting out the truism 'is a very small part and much the easiest part' of the analysis of truth. We now need to ask what is it for a belief to be a belief *that p*.

It is here that pragmatism moves into the foreground for Ramsey. It is not possible to understand the 'truth or falsity of thoughts without considering the effects they have on our acting either directly or indirectly through dispositional beliefs'. The pragmatists, he says, 'had a laudable desire for an account of truth which went deeper than the mere formal reduction of truth to reference'. The non-ludicrous pragmatist acknowledges the truism and goes beyond it by telling us what it is for a particular belief to be the belief that it is. That explanation will appeal to the belief's causes and effects.

Ramsey reiterated what he said in 'Truth and Probability' about how complex it will be to unpack the content of any particular belief. Someone's belief cannot be understood as a simple disposition to act, since in any given case the particular act it issues in will depend on what other mental states accompany it:

[No] particular action can be supposed to be determined by this belief alone; his actions result from his desires and the whole system of his beliefs, roughly according to the rule that he performs those actions which, if his beliefs were true, would have the most satisfactory consequences.

As he put it in 'Philosophy', also written in 1929, 'meaning is mainly potential'.

TRUTH AND CONTENT

Ian Rumfitt, Senior Research Fellow, All Souls College, Oxford

At the time of his death, Ramsey had in hand a book with the working title *Truth and Probability*. The extant drafts of the first five chapters have been published as *On Truth* and comprise one of the most tantalizing fragments in the history of philosophy. In it we see Ramsey advancing a brilliant answer to one of the subject's central questions, recognizing clearly the further problem that his answer poses, but fatally postponing the full development of a solution.

The question that gets answered is 'What is truth?' Ramsey takes truth, and falsity, to apply primarily to what he calls 'beliefs and judgments', mental states and events which possess both 'propositional reference'—i.e. are beliefs or judgments *that* such-and-such is the case—and 'some degree of the affirmative character' 'that is present in thinking that, but absent in wondering whether'. As Ramsey observes, if a man 'believes that A is B, his belief will be true if A *is* B and false otherwise. It is clear', he continues, that we have here 'the meaning of truth explained, and that the only difficulty is to formulate this explanation strictly as a definition'. His solution is to invoke the higher-order quantification used in Russell's logic: 'In Mr Russell's symbolism:

B is true:=: $(\exists p)$. B is a belief that p & p. Df'.

We may similarly define falsity by:

B is false:=: $(\exists p)$. B is a belief that p & $\neg p$.

Brilliant as it is, this solution is incomplete. As A.N. Prior showed in his *Objects of Thought*, Ramsey's definitions lead to paradoxes if the sentences that may be substituted for the variable 'p' are themselves permitted to contain such notions as 'is a belief that p'. The problem of restricting the range of 'p' without unnecessarily comprising the application of truth and falsity remains open.

Even if a satisfactory restriction is found, however, Ramsey's definitions raise a new question: what is it for a belief to be a belief that p? Ramsey was well aware that his account would be unsatisfactory without an answer: 'Truth, it will be said, consists in a relation between ideas and reality, and the use without analysis of the term "propositional reference" simply conceals and shirks all the real problems that this relation involves.'

Ramsey begins to address the new question in Chapter III of *On Truth*, 'Judgment'. A belief, he notes, is a disposition to think and act in certain ways, and its propositional reference, i.e. its content, 'is evidently derived from that of the resultant thoughts or assertions'. Furthermore, the content of a man's beliefs 'is to be defined in terms of the reference of his thinking or the meaning of his words'. In fact, none of what Ramsey proposes here is at all evident. Many philosophers hold that an assertion's content derives from that of the belief it would express if sincere, not vice versa. Again, many hold that content attaches more securely to a persisting disposition than to a fleeting thought. In any event, Ramsey offers no account of the putative determinants of a belief's content. We are not told what it is for words to mean what they mean, or for a thought to refer to something. Ramsey is aware of the lacuna and promises further details later, but in the material we have the promise is not kept. Chapter IV rebuts the objection that there must be radical differences between accounts of content for factive mental states, such as knowledge, and for non-factive states, such as mere opinion. Chapter V addresses questions about the metaphysics of events, including mental events. The discussion is always interesting but it keeps Ramsey from returning to the central unresolved issues about the determination of content.

Many of his followers, indeed, think he took a wrong turn in switching his focus from the contents of beliefs to those of related thoughts and assertions. For them, a belief is a disposition to act, and its content is to be explicated in terms of the panoply of actions that it may cause, when combined with various desires. In my view, this focuses too narrowly on what lies downstream from a belief, which is not *simply* a disposition to act—like a mere penchant—but also a rational response to perception and other evidence. It is in the nexus of what rationally prompts beliefs, and what actions they cause, that we may hope to discern the determinants of their contents.

In *On Truth*, Ramsey was reaching for a unified account of inquiry. His idea was brash, although he suggested it was common knowledge. He asserted that logic is on a par with aesthetics and ethics:

> It is a commonplace that Logic, Aesthetics, and Ethics have a peculiar position among the sciences: whereas all other sciences are concerned with the description and explanation of what happens, these three normative studies aim not at description but at criticism. To account for our actual conduct is the duty of the psychologist; the logician, the critic, and the moralist tell us not how we do but how we ought to think, feel, and act.

The logic he is talking about is his 'human logic', which he had noted (in 'Truth and Probability') might be in tension with formal logic. He was now moving at speed in the opposite direction from Wittgenstein and the Vienna Circle, who took logic to provide a value-neutral descriptive language for science. Ramsey agreed with Wittgenstein that there is a distinction to be made between what is *strictly* true/false and what is not. The tautologies of deductive logic and mathematics, and perhaps some direct observational beliefs are strictly true/false. Outside of that domain lies what we know probabilistically. That's the vast bulk of our belief.

Ramsey could have confined the word *truth* to the strict domain, and called beliefs in the secondary domain warranted, correct, right, or assertible. But instead, he usually used the word truth to mark the aim of all propositions, and argued that each science must answer for its own 'domain' the question 'what is true?' His project was to offer a unified account of how various kinds of statements might aim at truth, for 'the whole purpose of argument is to arrive at truth'. 'Science' is to be taken 'in its widest sense'. It includes logic, ethics, and perhaps even aesthetics. All of these are both 'normative' and 'definable in (ordinary factual) natural terms'.

Ramsey thought that we must begin with natural terms, such as facts about human psychology, but we will not end with them:

> The three normative sciences: Ethics, Aesthetics and Logic begin ... with psychological investigations which lead up, in each case, to a valuation, an attribution of one of the three values: good, beautiful, or rational, predicates which appear not to be definable in terms of any of the concepts used in psychology or positive science. I say 'appear' because it is one of the principal problems of philosophy to discover whether this is really the case.[†]

He remained staunchly non-reductionist: value can't be reduced or boiled down to human psychology, but neither can it be pulled apart from human psychology. He again expressed doubt that we had in hand the best psychological theory: since 'psychologists grossly neglect the aspects of their subject which are most important to the logician', philosophers have to take on some of the psychological work themselves.

In taking on the question of value in this manner, Ramsey was engaging with the most difficult problem in the British empiricist tradition. Hume had asked in 1739 whether we can get an 'ought' from an 'is'. Can facts about how people act give us any clue as to how they ought to act? Moore put the challenge to the empiricist in an 'open question argument'. When faced with an attempt to identify the good with any natural property such as utility or what human beings desire, we can always ask whether such natural properties really are good. Moore thought that empiricists fail to see that this is always an open question, and thus make the 'naturalistic fallacy'. Moore's own answer was to posit a non-natural, indefinable, property of goodness.

In Ramsey's day, empiricists were answering 'no'—we can't get an ought from an is. Ethics consists of either: (i) statements about what people actually approve of, not what they ought to approve of—that is, ethics is an empirical science; or (ii) expressions of emotions or feelings—to say that an act is odious is to say 'Boo-hiss!' to it, and to say that an act is good is to say 'Hurrah!'; or (iii) nonsense. Each of these options was embraced by one or another member of the Vienna

---

[†] The statement that logic is a normative science comes directly from Peirce.

Circle. The second was initially put forward by Ogden and Richards and christened 'emotivism' in ethics. The third was Wittgenstein's position.

Ramsey was inclined to answer 'yes'. Beliefs about values 'are definable in natural terms', but they nonetheless are oriented towards the way things are. He was concerned with 'the relations between man and his environment', and this environment includes both the physical and the social world. But he certainly did not think he was committing any kind of naturalistic fallacy. He read Moore as saying that the naturalistic fallacy is 'believing that the very meaning of good is desired or pleasure or satisfying'. Ramsey thought that such an extreme naturalist would have to say that the good life is the life of a pig whose impulses are satisfied. As Mill, saw, the naturalist can be more sophisticated than that. Ramsey's account of the good would be more subtle. It would unpack the complex relationship between behaviour, psychology, value, and facts. It would rest on a general account of truth on which 'copying and pragmatism are both elements in the true analysis which is exceedingly complicated, too complicated for us to hope to give it accurately'.

We can see from the fact that he crossed out 'beauty' in the passage quoted above that he wavered about whether judgments about aesthetics are part of our natural, yet epistemically evaluable body of knowledge. Aesthetics at the time was a fast-moving subject, with fresh ways of verse and painting upending the old. Blooms-bury was at the centre of the new wave. Keynes had a magnificent collection on his walls—Cézanne, Matisse, Braque, and Picasso. Roger Fry painted in what he called a post-impressionist style; the painting of Dora Carrington and Roland Penrose was surrealist; and Vanessa Bell's abstractionist. Clive Bell and Roger Fry wrote books and gave lectures on the new art. These shifting tastes might have led Ramsey to think that questions about whether something was genuinely beautiful or not had no true or false answer. But some judgments seemed to be objective—those about the beautiful movement of one of Beethoven's last quartets, and the hideous pictures in the church in Austria where Ramsey's friend Fryer was buried. Ramsey was unable to finish his complicated analysis of truth, but one suspects that the matter of aesthetics would have been the most complex.

Ramsey's naturalist theory of truth remained hidden for decades. After his death, Braithwaite sorted through the great number of notes and half-written papers in his chaotic rooms at King's and in his home study, and pulled out for posthumous publication the manuscripts he thought were interesting and could stand on their own. He said that when he read what he took to be the draft chapters of the book manuscript, he didn't trust his own judgment about their value. So he asked Moore. They decided that they weren't publishable, because Ramsey kept saying that this or that problem would be discussed in the next chapter, and those next chapters were never written. But it's also the case that Braithwaite didn't know what to make of the pragmatist position articulated in the manuscript. In 1929, when Ramsey's position was really coming together, all the hours he had for philosophizing were absorbed by Wittgenstein, with little room left for Braithwaite. And as Braithwaite himself put it, he didn't really discuss philosophy with Ramsey because they were both trying to establish their independent reputations.

The handful of Ramsey's papers and notes Braithwaite did publish made a tremendous impact on analytic philosophy. But once they are read in light of the book project, it seems that many analytic philosophers have misunderstood their hero. For they have taken Ramsey to be trying to reduce various kinds of propositions to the primary language, or failing that, to be giving them a pragmatist construal on which they are mere second-rate or quasi-propositions. But in the book, he was presenting a general theory of truth, on which a true belief is one which fits with the facts and with successful human action.

Some major questions loom over this unfinished theory. Ramsey didn't work out his dispositional account of belief in any detail, and it is no trivial task to do so. Neither did he work through what it is for a belief to really work, or to really be connected to the facts. Hence, it is not clear whether he would have been able to resist the slide into Jamesian pragmatism, or the idealism he thought such nonsense. Both Ramsey and Peirce were making the attempt to hold on to a thin concept of fact and yet have the truth of beliefs be connected to what works. The debate over whether that's possible continues to this day, and no doubt into the future, as the deepest philosophical questions always do.

Scientific Theories and Entities

The most influential of the pieces selected by Braithwaite was the paper we know by the title 'Theories'. The manuscript itself has gone missing, so we don't know whether the title was Ramsey's or whether it was supplied by Braithwaite. Ramsey wrote a number of notes on scientific theories, laws, and entities in the last two years of his life. The problem he was grappling with was how we should think of science, since much of it goes beyond the pristine primary language of observation and logic.

The first piece, dated March 1928, is 'Universals of Law and Fact'. Ramsey suggested here that a law of nature is a consequence of a set of axioms in a simple deductive system in which we know everything. Our ideal or complete theory of the world would give us the laws of science. But he then wrote a spate of pieces that moved away from that idea: 'Theories', 'Causal Qualities', 'General Propositions and

Causality', and material on scientific laws in the book manuscript. That is, he moved away from the idea, present in the early Wittgenstein and amplified by the Vienna Circle, that science is built up deductively from a foundation of logic and experience. At the time of his death, he hadn't fully nailed down what he thought about the matter. He left it hanging in the book manuscript, starting the discussion, but wondering whether it might be 'better postponed for another occasion'. We don't know whether 'Theories' was part of that further discussion. Figuring out where Ramsey stood with respect to one of his most famous contributions is a challenge.

In the book manuscript, he identified an 'objection from the philosophy of science'. Ramsey had read Norman Campbell's book on physics, and might have discussed the matter with Campbell, who had been at Trinity. He had seen first-hand, in the Cavendish Laboratory with J.J. Thomson, the rise of atomic theory and quantum mechanics. What could be the meaning of their elusive terms and hypotheses, so untethered to the observable facts? The problem was older than the new physics: Mach had asked the question about atoms, and concluded there were none. Campbell's solution was to say that when we introduce or postulate a new unobservable or theoretical entity, such as an electron, the entity is hypothetical or fictional, and a kind of dictionary can translate the fictional theoretical terms into observable terms. He also argued that it is the whole theory that is true or false, not the theoretical statements by themselves.

In 'Causal Qualities', Ramsey seemed to agree with Campbell:

The truth is that we deal with our primary system as part of a fictitious secondary system. Here we have a fictitious quality [mass], and we can have fictitious individuals. This is all made clear in my account of theories.

Then he made his own contribution: it is the consequences of the theory that matter, and those consequences may end up meeting the future so well that the theoretical terms can be thought of as referring to something real. In the book manuscript, he reiterated this idea, but distanced himself from the 'fictionalist' label. He now objected to the idea that this 'large body of sentences' only 'appear to express judgments', but really 'may not express judgments at all'. Fictionalism reminded him of Wittgenstein's claim that some pseudo-propositions are unsayable, yet important. Ramsey didn't want to write off theoretical language as a special kind of nonsense.

With this context in place, let us turn to the famous paper. Ramsey started 'Theories' as follows:

Let us try to describe a theory simply as a language for discussing the facts the theory is said to explain.

This is the assumption of the early Wittgenstein and the Vienna Circle. Let's assume that facts are expressible in the 'universe of discourse which we will call the *primary system*'—they are expressible in simple observational propositions that are strictly true or false. The problem from the philosophy of science is that scientific laws and theories go beyond what can be built up from the primary language. Ramsey expressed this concern in his 1923 Critical Notice of the *Tractatus*, and in 1929, it had not yet been laid to rest.

He then argued that when we try, we can indeed construct a theory out of simple observational facts, using a set of axioms and a dictionary that translates the primary language into the secondary language. But he asserted that these definitions are not necessary for the 'legitimate use of the theory'. It is merely 'instructive' to show how such definitions could be set out. Part of the instruction was to show how it might be done, for Russell, Carnap, and others 'seem to suppose that we can and must do this'. It's interesting that he included Russell here. Looking back, we might think that Russell had already left that position behind him, but Ramsey knew him well and thought otherwise. Ramsey was certainly right about Carnap—only in the mid-1930s did he start to abandon the view that every term must be definable by the observational language.

Another part of the instruction was negative. Ramsey thought that the project wouldn't work. One obstacle, perhaps surmountable, is that it would be impossibly complicated. For instance, if the primary language is concerned with a series of experiences, it needs 'time order' and a structure for things like colour and smells. But the really insurmountable obstacle is that 'if we proceed by explicit definition we cannot add to our theory without changing the definitions, and so the meaning of the whole'. That would be a disaster, for we need to be able to explain how a concept such as mass both evolves and retains its meaning. The theory of mass and the observations it is based on have changed and will continue to change. On the explicit definition account of scientific theories, it seems that every time the theory changes, the new theory ceases to refer to the entities referred to by the older version and hence, we can't explain how the theory of mass gets improved upon.

These worries led Ramsey to the view that all 'useful theories' must have 'more degrees of freedom' than the primary system—the 'dictionary alone does not suffice'. Neither does the dictionary plus the axioms, unless we are happy confining ourselves to a finite, primary system much less rich than the theory itself. That kind of impoverished system would be of 'no use at all'. There would be no point in having a secondary system—no point in having a scientific theory—unless it went beyond a catalogue of the facts.

Having dismissed the explicit definition account of scientific theories, Ramsey, in a new and exciting move, instructed the empiricist on how to think of theories and

unobservable entities. A theory is a system of judgments or beliefs, whose consequences will meet the future successfully or not. We employ the theory as a
shorthand expression of all those judgments. An unobservable theoretical term
such as *electron* plays a role in a long and complex formal sentence which contains
both theoretical and observational terms. Such a sentence is now called a Ramsey
Sentence. It will start with: 'There are things which we call electrons, which . . .', and
will go on to tell a story about those electrons.[‡] We assume there are electrons for
the sake of the story, just as we assume there is a girl when we listen to a story that
starts 'Once upon a time there was a girl, who . . .'. Additions to the theory are not
'strictly propositions by themselves just as the different sentences in a story beginning
"Once upon a time" do not have complete meanings and so are not propositions
by themselves.' Nonetheless, we commit ourselves to the existence of the entities in
our theory, knowing that if the theory gets overthrown, so will our commitment to
its entities. In the meantime, we use the theory. We don't, however, treat it as a fiction,
for unlike the bedtime story, we believe in the entities in our scientific story.

Any additions to the theory are to be made within the scope of the quantifier that
says that there exists at least one electron. That is, we can revise the theory. It can evolve
while still being about the original entities. Definitions, Ramsey said in 'Philosophy',
'are to give at least our future meaning, and not merely to give any pretty way of
obtaining a certain structure'. Ramsey's kind of definition tells us how to go on using
a term by making more precise the vague and complex concept or entity it stands for.
We are to treat our theory of the world as an evolving existential statement.

RAMSEY SENTENCES

Stathis Psillos, Professor of Philosophy of Science and Metaphysics, University of Athens

'The best way', Ramsey suggested in *Theories*, 'to write our theory seems to be this ($\exists$ α,
β, γ): dictionary · axioms'. His main point is this: the excess content of the theory over
whatever is captured in the 'primary system' (empirical laws and singular observational
consequences) is seen when the theory is formulated as expressing an existential
judgment. This is the origin of Ramsey Sentences. The theoretical terms and predicates

[‡] The process of converting such a narrative form of a theory into a second order logic of
properties is called Ramsification. And Ramsey Sentences are also used in the philosophy of mind
to define mental states by their causal role.

(featuring in the 'secondary system' of the theory) can be dispensed with and be replaced by existentially bound variables. Seen as a judgment, then, the theory asserts that there are entities that satisfy it and refers to them without naming them but via variables.

In order to get the Ramsey Sentence ^RT of a (finitely axiomatizable) theory T we conjoin the axioms of T in a single sentence, replace all theoretical predicates with distinct (second-order) variables u_i, and then bind these variables by placing an equal number of existential quantifiers $\exists u_i$ in front of the resulting formula. Suppose that the theory T is represented as $T(u_1,\ldots,u_n; o_1,\ldots,o_m)$, where T is a purely logical m+n-predicate. The Ramsey-sentence ^RT of T is: $\exists u_1 \exists u_2 \ldots \exists u_n T(u_1,\ldots,u_n; o_1,\ldots,o_m)$.

The Ramsey Sentence ^RT of theory T has the same deductive structure as T and is a logical consequence of T. It also has exactly the same first-order observational consequences as T. So ^RT is empirically adequate iff T is empirically adequate. Besides, if $^RT_1$ and $^RT_2$ are compatible with the same observational truths, then they are compatible with each other. Hence, ^RT can replace T in formal reasoning as well as for the purposes of prediction and control. However, the Ramsey Sentence of T has excess content over the 'primary system' of T by referring to whatever entities satisfy the theory. A theory, then, need *not* be a definite description to be (a) truth-valuable, (b) ontically committing, and (c) practically useful. Besides, if we take a theory as a *dynamic* entity (something that can be improved upon, refined, modified, changed, enlarged), we are better off if we see it as a *growing existential sentence*. Ramsey can be seen as a realistic pragmatist: what matters, in the end, is getting the phenomena right but in order to get them right we have to get the world (in some sense) right.

Rudolf Carnap used Ramsey Sentences in his attempt to draw the analytic-synthetic distinction within a theory. A theory T is logically equivalent with the conjunction ^RT & $(^RT{\rightarrow}T)$, where $^RT{\rightarrow}T$ says that *if* there is some class of entities that satisfy the Ramsey Sentence, *then* the theoretical terms of the theory denote the members of this class. For Carnap, the Ramsey-sentence of the theory captured its factual content, and the Carnap-sentence $^RT{\rightarrow}T$ captured its analytic content. According to structural realists, the Ramsey Sentence captures the proper content of the theory: scientific theories issue in existential commitments to unobservable entities but all non-observational knowledge of unobservables is *structural knowledge*, i.e., knowledge of their higher-order (or structural) properties and not of their first-order (or intrinsic) properties.

In 'Theories' we again see that, for Ramsey, questions of usage—in this case, how we use a scientific theory—are more important than questions of metaphysics. The metaphysics of Russell and the Vienna Circle, interesting as it was to him, cannot provide enough to go on in real life and real science. We must see theories as being true or false, not in the strict, atomist sense, but in a pragmatist sense.

Ramsey's solution to the objection from the philosophy of science rests on the idea of holism. Like Campbell, Duhem, Poincaré, and later Quine, he saw that we need to consider the whole theory in order to make sense of the meanings of its parts: 'no proposition of the secondary system can be understood apart from the whole to which it belongs'. Propositions about Zeus do not appear in any of our theories about how the world is, so the proposition 'sacrifices will bring the thunderbolts to an end' makes little sense. He employed holism to explain how there is meaning to our belief that the back of the moon is not made of green cheese, despite the fact that, in his time, it couldn't be observed:

> If our theory allows as a possibility that we might go there or find out in any other way, then it has meaning. If not, not; i.e. our theory of the *moon* is very relevant, not merely our theory of things in general.

Our theory of the moon, and of solid bodies more generally, will tell us something about the likely constitution of the moon's far side—the whole theory gives meaning to beliefs about the unobservable part of the moon and speaks to whether they are true or false. Our best theory says that the far side of the moon is not made of green cheese. Its surface may be unobservable, but we have beliefs about it as part of what Arthur Fine has called our natural ontological attitude. Returning to the example of electrons, the entities that we should believe in are the ones our best system would admit. That does not mean that we *know* that electrons exist. David Lewis coined the term 'Ramseyan humility' to mark Ramsey's idea that we must not foreclose on the possibility that our theory will not be uniquely determined, or that it might be determined in a way we do not anticipate. But, as Stathis Psillos put it, Ramsey thought that we must nonetheless be 'bold' in affirming in our theories that entities (including unobservable ones), relations, causes, properties, and so on, exist.

One consequence of Ramsey's view is that rival scientific theories might give quite different meanings to theoretical terms. But it would be a mistake to think that the theories aren't really in conflict because they are incommensurable. For Ramsey was also arguing in 1929 that, in putting forward different theories, we *disagree*. That disagreement is made manifest by the fact that the adherents of the rival theories will face the future differently, expecting different experiences and results. Some of them will be right and some wrong, and the future will let us know which.

The Afterlife of Ramsey Sentences: The Vienna Circle and Beyond

Carnap's 1928 *Der Logische Aufbau Der Welt* (*The Logical Construction of the World*) is one of the classics of the Vienna Circle and of analytic philosophy. It argued that classes of experience are constructed out of individual time slices of sensory experiences; then concepts such as blue are built up; then objects; then higher concepts. Ramsey said in 'Theories' that Carnap supposed that we can and must be able to define scientific theories in terms of a primary system of experiences.

As Keynes saw so clearly, Ramsey had been moving in the opposite direction, 'departing...from the formal and objective treatment of his immediate predecessors'. Ramsey and Wittgenstein had started off by helping Russell perfect the system of *Principia Mathematica*. The effect, said Keynes, was

> gradually to empty it of content and to reduce it more and more to mere dry bones, until finally it seemed to exclude not only all experience, but most of the principles...of reasonable thought. Wittgenstein's solution was to regard everything else as a sort of inspired nonsense, having great value indeed for the individual, but incapable of being exactly discussed. Ramsey's reaction was towards what he himself described as a sort of pragmatism, not unsympathetic to Russell, but repugnant to Wittgenstein....Thus he was led to consider 'human logic' as distinguished from 'formal logic'.

By 1929, Ramsey had indeed found the reductionist approach of Russell, which had been amplified by Wittgenstein in the *Tractatus* and Carnap in the *Aufbau*, to be a sack of dry bones. In 'Philosophy', written in this last year of his life, he argued that any attempt to analyse 'This patch is red' into 'a theoretical construction' of an infinite class of points on a visual field would be 'giving up philosophy for theoretical psychology'. A theory of how a perception is logically constructed will always fall short.[§] Carnap and Wittgenstein make a 'mistake' because the subject or the perceiver is not in their picture, but is somehow meant to be standing outside it. On such a view, we have no real explanation of perceptual experience or, for that matter, of how we come to know anything about the world. In one of the few of his notes mentioning Carnap, Ramsey said:

> Solipsism in the ordinary sense in which as e.g. in Carnap the primary world consists of my experiences past present and future will not do. For this primary world is the world about which I am now thinking.

Such realist (as opposed to *realistic*) philosophies were not to Ramsey's liking.

That's not to say that Ramsey denied there was any value to be found in these realist philosophers. He was still mining Russell for ideas—indeed, he found a strain of pragmatism in Russell's work. Wittgenstein was still his most important philosophical interlocutor. He also shared quite a bit with the Vienna Circle, including a facility with logical methods. Many of the problems that exercised the Vienna Circle

---

[§] Ramsey's friend Max Newman delivered a paper to the Moral Sciences Club in December 1927, published in *Mind* in April 1928. It argued that the structuralism of Russell, Carnap, and Eddington fails. We cannot define objects by locating them in the structure of a theory because structure alone does not uniquely pick out a set of objects. Ramsey didn't think much of structuralism either, but he was silent on Newman's paper. See Blackburn (forthcoming) and Misak (forthcoming).

were Ramsey's problems too. Some of their answers were the same. For instance, both Ramsey and the Circle were incredulous about Wittgenstein's idea that there is something inexpressible yet important—that we can peer through the boundary fence of thought, glimpse the unsayable, and stand in awe of it.

Ramsey liked the members of the Circle he had come in contact with, and desired more frequent exchanges. In July 1927, he had invited Schlick to present a paper at the Moral Sciences Club. Schlick's wife accompanied him to Cambridge, and the two couples got along very well. Ramsey wrote to Schlick in the spring of 1928:

> Dear Professor Schlick,
>
> I must first thank you for the card you sent us at Christmas; it was very kind of you to remember us.
>
> I am thinking of coming to Vienna almost immediately, and wonder whether, if I did, you or any of your circle would be able to spare a little time to talk philosophy with me. If you could, I should be extremely grateful as I get very little stimulus here and make no progress.

Schlick was away during Ramsey's proposed dates, and invited him to come and stay some other time.

But all these commonalities notwithstanding, Ramsey's philosophical instincts were not those of the 1920s Vienna Circle.** Ramsey never said much about their work, a silence which in itself is an indication of intellectual distance. And what little he did say was not positive. We have already seen that upon his first meeting Schlick in 1924, Ramsey said that he was not a very good philosopher, and later repeated that judgment to Wittgenstein. With respect to Carnap, Ramsey wrote to Schlick towards the very end of his life about the *Aufbau*:

> I feel very guilty that I've not yet written a review of Carnap's book, which is really inexcusable. I found it very interesting, though some things I thought certainly wrong and others I felt very doubtful about.

He told Schlick that he wanted to get 'clear about the truth of these things' himself before writing about the merits and the doubtful points in Carnap's book. Ramsey took notes on the *Aufbau*, and we can see from them that some of his worries were about the specifics of Carnap's attempts to construct the world from an observation language—for instance, Carnap's analysis of a note as a class of sounds with certain well-defined properties. As Ramsey put it in 'Theories', such constructions are bound to be almost impossibly complex and yet still leave out far too much.

** The Vienna Circle gradually liberalized their position in light of criticism after Ramsey's death, and some members moved towards positions that would have been more congenial to Ramsey.

Carnap had a long life and hence ample time to assess Ramsey. He acquired a copy of Braithwaite's 1931 volume of Ramsey's papers, and he read it carefully. His marginalia indicate how far apart he and Ramsey were in the early 1930s. He annotated pretty much the whole of the book, except for Ramsey's undergraduate paper on the foundations of mathematics, which he already knew inside and out. The more recent, previously unpublished, material was new to him. Where Braithwaite noted in his introduction that Ramsey had been moving towards pragmatism, Carnap registered his surprise with an exclamation mark in the margin. 'General Propositions and Causality' also attracted a number of '!'s. That paper, we will see, is one of Ramsey's most pragmatist pieces, in which he argued that many sentences express cognitive attitudes without being strict propositions, and that scientific and causal statements are not strict propositions, but rules for judging.

Carnap paid close attention to 'Theories' as well. He wasn't at the time receptive to Ramsey's idea that we could boldly refer to unobservable entities by thinking about a theory as a long sentence which supposes the existence of such entities. But Carnap would soon start to relax his reductionism and advocate a principle of tolerance with respect to theory choice. Ramsey's paper would become more interesting to him. But on his first reading, he didn't know what to make of it.

Fifteen years later, his friend and fellow logical empiricist Carl Hempel heard of Ramsey's 'Theories' from Braithwaite's 1946 Tarner Lectures. In the 1950s Carnap and Hempel each started to employ Ramsey's idea. In 1956 Hempel sent Carnap a draft of his 'The Theoretician's Dilemma: A study in the logic of theory construction', where Hempel coined the term 'Ramsey Sentence'. Carnap wrote to Hempel, saying that his paper had prompted him to go back to the Braithwaite volume and see that he had 'neatly underlined' the important passages in 'Theories'. He expressed his gratitude for being prevented from presenting Ramsey's idea as his own. In 1966, Carnap sent Braithwaite his *Philosophical Foundations of Physics*, which had a chapter titled 'The Ramsey Sentence'. Ramsey's idea, two decades after he had floated it, had finally been widely taken up.

Indeed, it became famous amongst philosophers. In 1970, the American metaphysician David Lewis wrote 'How to Define Theoretical Terms'. Lewis, unlike the 1928 Carnap, didn't want to eliminate theoretical terms by translating them into an observational language, but rather, wanted to define newly introduced theoretical terms via the original terms of the theory. The meaning of the term 'electron', he argued, is generated by the theory or Ramsey Sentence that describes it. Lewis took his own project to be a 'vindication' of theoretical entities. Ramsey might well have been happy with that. Just as he cleared induction of suspicion and showed that it was a reasonable habit, he wanted to show how scientific theories should be thought of as reasonable habits with which we meet the future. This approach doesn't aim at reducing theories, laws, general propositions, or induction to observation and logic, thereby showing how they are part of the furniture of the world. Rather, this approach says that if they are essential to our reasoning, inductive conclusions, causal laws, and scientific theories are vindicated, and if our best theory tells us that theoretical entities are real, they are as real as it gets. That was an aspect of what Lewis called 'Ramseyan Humility'. We don't know the intrinsic properties of things, but only their causal impacts on each other and on us. Ramsey had floated this idea (about induction) when an undergraduate. Four decades later, it was taken up in the way he had intended.

Lewis enhanced the reputation of yet another idea in Ramsey's papers on scientific laws and causation. Braithwaite had decided not to publish 'Universals of Law and Fact' in *The Foundations of Mathematics and Other Logical Essays*, perhaps because Ramsey's 1929 work had rejected the deductivism in it. But Braithwaite alluded to the note in his introduction, and in the early 1970s, Lewis was 'intrigued' and asked if he might see it. Braithwaite agreed, telling him that he mustn't publish any of it, for copyright reasons. In the 1973 *Counterfactuals*, Lewis recounted how Braithwaite had 'permitted me to read a short unpublished note, written by Ramsey', and he went on in that book to expand upon Ramsey's idea and make the view his own. The laws of nature are those that belong to the deductive system with the best combination of simplicity and strength. Hugh Mellor included 'Universals of Law and Fact' in his 1978 and 1990 volumes of Ramsey's papers, its fame having preceded its publication.

The System with which We Meet the Future

Ramsey dropped the deductivism in 'Universals of Law and Fact', but he retained an important place for the idea of our best system or theory. 'General Propositions and Causality' is dated September 1929, during his sabbatical leave, the last term he was able to do any work. It is one of his richest papers, and speaks to a variety of propositions that do not fit into the primary system. He spends the most time on universal generalizations and scientific laws, which range over infinite domains. One approach to such propositions is to adopt an instrumentalism on which they aren't genuine propositions, but rather, mere tools to be judged in terms of whether they work. That was a view attractive to Wittgenstein at times in 1929–32, and perhaps even in the *Tractatus*. It was also attractive to some members of the Vienna Circle.

Ramsey had raised the problem of scientific laws in his Critical Notice of the *Tractatus*. Over the next years, he put in place the makings of his own solution to the problem—our beliefs (save logical, mathematical, and perhaps some straightforward observational beliefs) are habits upon which we act. The vast bulk of our beliefs are instruments that are evaluated in terms of how well they work. Now he was ready to unpack this idea explicitly in a piece he might well have intended to be part of his book. Ramsey didn't give the manuscript a title. Braithwaite gave it one—'General Propositions and Causality'—when he prepared it for publication. But Ramsey's manuscript is about much more than that.

Ramsey opened with this rather audacious sentence:

> The problem of philosophy must be divided if I am to solve it: as a whole it is too big for me. Let us take first the meaning of general propositions.

Ramsey, or perhaps even Braithwaite, lightly crossed out the first sentence. It was Braithwaite who certainly revised the second one: he replaced the 'let us take first', with 'let us consider'. So the published paper, after Braithwaite's heavy editorial hand, starts with 'Let us consider the meaning of general propositions.'

Braithwaite's intervention clouds the fact that Ramsey was giving in this paper a general account of belief as habit or disposition. He took the 'problem of philosophy' to be the problem of truth and of the kinds of propositions that can aspire to it. That's clear from his book project. In 'General Propositions and Causality', he started on the problem of philosophy by looking at law-like general propositions, such as 'All men are mortal' or 'Arsenic is poisonous'. Can such a statement, which ranges over an infinite number of individuals, be seen as true or false, given that there is no way to conclusively check whether all human beings (past, present, and future) die or whether all samples of arsenic are in fact poisonous?

Open generalizations seem simply to be predicating the same property of one thing after another, and Wittgenstein's view in the *Tractatus* was that they were infinite conjunctions. In the 1927 'Facts and Propositions', Ramsey too had tried to cram general propositions into the primary language in this way. Now his view had changed. He noted that there was no problem in taking generalizations to be conjunctions if they range over a finite domain, such as 'Everyone in Cambridge voted'. We can understand that as: Russell voted, and Moore voted, and Hardy voted, and so on. But an open generalization 'always goes beyond what we know or want'. It cannot be thought of as a conjunction, for we lack the symbolic power or the capacity to express an infinite statement. Other attempts to make sense of them, such as grounding a law by appeal to a connection between universals or appealing to the idea of an infinite collection, are 'nonsense':

> The analogies are misleading, difficult though they are to escape, and emotionally satisfactory as they prove to different types of mind. Both these forms of 'realism' must be rejected by the realistic spirit.

It is here, on the topic of talking about an infinite collection, that Ramsey made his famous quip against Wittgenstein: 'But what we can't say we can't say, and we can't whistle it either.'

In urging us to adopt a 'realistic spirit', Ramsey meant to remind us that philosophy must be tied to our practices. A philosophical theory must not neglect the facts of our experience in favour of a theoretical construction, such as the metaphysics of a purportedly existing universal (such as 'humanness' and 'mortalness') or the metaphysics of an exact isomorphism between propositions and reality. Both those kinds of realism (as opposed to *realistic* theories) require us to divorce ourselves from the very features of our experience we wished to examine in the first place. Ramsey thought that Russell, Moore, and Wittgenstein, in adopting versions of realism, turned their backs on actual human practices and inquiry. His alternative account of law-like generalizations would not make this mistake.

In delivering that alternative account, Ramsey first argued that law-like generalizations can't be 'eliminated and replaced by the primary propositions which serve as evidence for them'. We cannot analyse generalizations away as 'superfluous':

> [A]part from their value in simplifying our thought, they form an essential part of our mind. That we think explicitly in general terms is at the root of all praise and blame and much discussion.

They are indispensable, just like inductive conclusions. Without laws, or rules, or general truths, we cannot assess any singular statement. So how are these essential propositions to be understood? Here Ramsey made one of his most interesting pragmatist moves. An open generalization, in his view, 'expresses an inference we are at any time prepared to make, not a belief of the primary sort'. The same holds for causal statements and the laws of nature. They, too, are 'rules for judging', or rules with which we meet the future, or rules that we 'trust'. This is an epistemic, as opposed to metaphysical, conception of law or necessity, inspired by both Peirce and Weyl. We must examine causality and necessity from the agent's perspective.

The question arises as to whether such rules can be true or false. They certainly can't be seen as such if truth is restricted to propositions in the primary language. In another novel move, Ramsey asserted that 'Many sentences express cognitive attitudes without being propositions'. Such beliefs can be evaluated. An onlooker can approve or criticize them 'and he may be in the right without having *proof* on his side'. Think about the countless and diverse ways my belief that all humans are mortal will play out. We can tell whether I have the belief by observing my actions—I will be disposed to assert that all humans are mortal in appropriate circumstances; I will be prepared to offer reasons for my belief; I will disagree with those who assert the contrary; I will drive my car carefully around those pedestrians I wish to remain alive; I will not treat myself as an immortal exception; I may despair about the meaning of life. That is the dispositional or pragmatist analysis of belief. And my belief can be *evaluated* in terms of whether it fits with experience—whether it is reliable or not. That last idea is the pragmatist account of truth, at least as it appears in the best reading of Peirce.

Part of the way that beliefs can express cognitive attitudes without being part of the primary language is that they

> form the system with which the speaker meets the future; they are not, therefore, subjective in the sense that if you and I enunciate different ones we are each saying something about ourselves which pass by one another like 'I went to Grantchester', 'I didn't'.

If you and I meet the future with different systems, then we *disagree*—we assume that the future will be compatible with one of our systems but not the other. Our beliefs are not subjective, as they are in the non-dispute about who went to Grantchester, which turns on different people uttering 'I went to Grantchester'.

Ramsey gave another example of how non-primary beliefs can be cognitive, which again puts into sharp relief the fact that it was Braithwaite who made the paper's conclusions seem to apply only to one kind of belief—general propositions and the causal laws based on them. Ramsey's second example is about conditionals or statements of the form: if *p* then *q*. These statements, he argued, also require a pragmatic (sometimes now called an epistemic or commitment-based) account. Formal logic's truth table for the material conditional has 'if *p* then *q*' being false only when *p* is true and *q* is false. So formal logic has the following sentence coming out true: If the moon is made of green cheese, then $2+2=4$. The antecedent ('the moon is made of green cheese') is false, so the whole conditional comes out true, despite the fact that there is no connection between the composition of the moon and the truth of $2+2=4$. This particular example is due to the pragmatist Clarence Irving Lewis, who argued against the material conception of the conditional. Ramsey knew his work—recall I.A. Richards's story about how as a schoolboy Ramsey delighted in solving the logic problems in A *Survey of Symbolic Logic*. In that book Lewis called the results that follow from the truth table definition of the conditional 'peculiar' and 'useless'. Ramsey agreed. On his 'human logic', a conditional is a rule for judging. When I accept the conditional 'if p then q', I commit myself to acquiring the disposition to judge q whenever I judge p. That disposes of the peculiar instance above, for I won't judge the moon to be made of green cheese. Ramsey's position is concerned with what I'm rationally committed to. I might not in fact acquire the disposition to judge q whenever I judge p, because I might be irrational or inattentive. But that doesn't affect my rational commitment.

Ramsey's next example is an especially tricky kind of conditional. He argued that even a counterfactual conditional, where the antecedent is false, can be a cognitive, evaluable, attitude. Like making inductive conclusions and universal generalizations, counterfactual reasoning is indispensable, for 'We cannot blame a man except by considering what would have happened if he had acted otherwise.' He considered a man who doesn't eat a certain cake, and thinks that were he to eat it, he would be made ill. Ramsey argued that we have different 'degrees of expectation' as to the outcome, and in disputing about the proper degree of expectation we can 'introduce any fact we know, whether he did or could know it'. If the man knew that I carefully baked the cake with the finest ingredients, that I'm an excellent baker, that I know he has no food allergies or aversions, and that I bear no ill will toward him, we might judge that he is irrational in maintaining his worry about the cake. If all these things hold, but he doesn't know them, then we might merely judge him mistaken. The fact that we can 'dispute with him or condemn him' requires explanation, which is unavailable to those who think of conditionals in terms of strict logic, as opposed to human logic.

In a now-famous footnote, Ramsey suggested that when someone evaluates a conditional 'if p, then q', they are hypothetically adding the antecedent p to their stock of knowledge and then seeing if q would also be in their stock of knowledge. Robert Stalnaker in 1968 proposed a theory of truth conditions for indicative conditionals on the basis of that footnote. What is now known as the Ramsey Test for Conditionals is a method for determining whether we should believe a conditional. We add p, hypothetically, to our given body of belief. If the acceptance of p leads to a contradiction within that body of belief, we make adjustments, as minor as possible, within the existing body of belief in order to restore consistency. Then we ask whether q is acceptable in the revised body of belief.

Ramsey also made suggestive remarks about the distinctions between cause and effect, and between a 'fixed' past and 'open' future. For Ramsey, these distinctions rest on the viewpoint of human beings, not on the metaphysics of causation and time. Moore, in a 1933 discussion at the Moral Sciences Club, 'defended a view of causality of the type of Ramsey's'. It would have been fascinating to hear that conversation and discover what philosophers in the 1930s, including Wittgenstein, thought of Ramsey's position. For it then dropped out of view, only to be resurrected decades later.

RAMSEY'S PRAGMATISM ABOUT CAUSATION AND TIME

Huw Price, Bertrand Russell Professor of Philosophy, University of Cambridge

Ramsey is famous as a pioneer of 'subjectivism' about probability—the view that the philosophy of probability begins with the psychology of decision. Far less well known is his analogous view about causation.

In 1913 Russell dismissed causation altogether. Physics, he argued, shows us a time-symmetric world of bare associations: 'The law of causality...surviv[es], like the monarchy, only because it is erroneously believed to do no harm'. Why then do we think that we can affect the future but not the past? Russell attributes it to 'the accident that memory works backward and not forward'.

Ramsey doesn't mention Russell, but his investigation of lawlike generalizations leads him into similar territory. He agrees that we shouldn't count causes among the furniture of the world. As with probability, the interesting questions are matters of psychology. But Ramsey turns to agency, not memory: 'from the situation when we are deliberating seems to me to arise the general difference of cause and effect'.

Ramsey notes that some probabilities look different from the agent's perspective than from a third-person perspective. He takes this distinction to explain why we take the past to be fixed: '[A]ny possible present volition of ours is (for us) irrelevant to any past event. To another...it can serve as a sign of the past, but to us now what we do affects only the probability of the future.' The distinction turns on the fact that for the agent herself, whether she acts a certain way is not an epistemic matter—'not...an intellectual problem'. 'In a sense', as Ramsey puts it, 'my present action is an ultimate and the only ultimate contingency.'

Decades later, other philosophers stumbled towards the link between causation and agency. For Nancy Cartwright it grounds an argument for causal realism. Cartwright agrees with Russell that physics describes a world of bare correlations, and that '[c]ausal principles cannot be reduced to laws of association'. But she maintains that causation is 'needed to ground the distinction between effective strategies and ineffective ones'. Moving barometer needles is an ineffective strategy for controlling the weather, despite the correlation between the two. We need real causal laws to explain such facts, Cartwright maintains.

How then, as Hartry Field puts it, to reconcile 'Cartwright's points about the need of causation in a theory of effective strategy with Russell's points about the limited role of causation in physics'? Field calls this 'the central problem in the metaphysics of causation'.

For Ramsey it isn't a matter of metaphysics at all. We won't find causal asymmetry or the distinction between past and future by doing metaphysics. We should look instead to the psychology of agency. The distinction between correlations that support effective strategies and those that don't is explained by the difference between probability from the agent's perspective and probability from the third-person perspective. An agent sees her own actions as 'interventions', in the terminology of recent agentive theories of causation such as those of Pearl and Woodward. Again, Ramsey's pragmatism avoids the need to treat intervention as a metaphysical primitive, with no foundation in physics.

In 'Philosophy', Ramsey argued that the philosopher must 'take our problems as a whole and jump to a simultaneous solution'. In the manuscript Braithwaite titled 'General Propositions and Causality', he was doing just that. His aim was to eventually solve 'the problem of philosophy' by taking all manner of propositions, and showing how their meaning is grounded not in their reducibility to the primary language, but in their being habits of action. He asserts this overarching claim in two places in 'General Propositions and Causality':

> since all belief involves habit, so does the criticism of any judgment whatever, and I do not see anything objectionable in this.
>
> it belongs to the essence of any belief that we deduce from it, and act on it in a certain way.

Ramsey's pragmatist position was coming into clear shape. He ended the manuscript with another example of how counterfactual propositions can be evaluated. This time, he answered that tenacious problem from the philosophy of science. He answered it with Peirce's pragmatist idea that we hope that inquiry would eventually settle our questions:

> Suppose the human race for no reason always supposed strawberries would give them stomach-ache and so never ate them; then all their beliefs, strictly so-called, e.g. that if I eat strawberries I shall have a pain, would be true; but would there not really be something wrong? Is it not a fact that if they had eaten them they wouldn't have had a pain? No, it is not a fact; it is a consequence of my rule.... If we regarded the unfulfilled conditional as a fact we should have to suppose that any such statement as 'If he had shuffled the cards, he would have dealt himself the ace' has a clear sense true or false,

which is absurd. We only regard it as sense if it, or its contradictory, can be deduced from our system.... But their system, you say, fitted all the facts known to them; if two systems both fit the facts, is not the choice capricious? We do, however, believe that the system is uniquely determined and that long enough investigation will lead us all to it. This is Peirce's notion of truth as what everyone will believe in the end; it does not apply to the truthful statement of matters of fact, but the 'true scientific system'. What was wrong with our friends the strawberry abstainers was that they did not experiment. Why should one experiment? To increase the weight of one's probabilities...

'Strictly' speaking, speaking from the perspective of the *Tractatus* and the material definition of the conditional, the strawberry abstainers' belief that if they eat strawberries, they will be sick, is true, since the antecedent is false (they never eat strawberries). That is a major problem with the material conditional. Moreover, there is also something wrong with a realism that says there are facts about what would have happened had someone eaten a strawberry. On Ramsey's alternative, we don't appeal to such bizarre counterfactual facts. We appeal to how we actually make inferences about counterfactuals. We look to what can be deduced from our best system of belief or our best theory. The strawberry-abstaining community can be criticized for their belief that eating strawberries causes stomach-ache, for if they had experimented they might have come to a better theory.

All sorts of statements not reducible to the primary language—open generalizations, inductive conclusions, conditionals, and statements about causes and theoretical entities—will be part of our best system. We expect, moreover, that our natural ontological attitude will prevail—that, in the end, our beliefs about causes, for instance, will be left in place. This position stands in sharp contrast to Wittgenstein's. Wittgenstein asserted in the *Tractatus* that 'Superstition is the belief in the causal nexus.' The untenable position one lands in, if restricted to the primary language, is that our beliefs about most things will be superstitions.

Ramsey capped off his run of brilliant papers in September 1929 with a note on knowledge. The standard definition of knowledge is that it is true justified belief. This definition has proven to be susceptible to a modern industry of counterexamples—situations in which we have true justified belief, but we wouldn't say that we know what we believe. Russell had been advancing such counterexamples since his 1912 *The Problems of Philosophy*. Later, he came up with this one. Alice sees a clock that reads two o'clock, and believes that the time is two o'clock, and it is in fact two o'clock. But unknown to Alice, the clock she's looking at stopped twelve hours ago. Alice thus has an accidentally true, justified belief, but not knowledge.

Ramsey's note on the topic was a mere page and a half long, but there was a lot in it and it has stood the test of time. It is the founding document of reliabilist theories of knowledge. Knowledge, he suggested, is what enables us to reliably act in the future, consolidating all our various kinds of belief. It is to be thought of in terms of good habits with which to meet the future. Ramsey replaced 'justified' in the standard definition of knowledge with 'obtained by a reliable process', and made the counterexamples disappear. His new account of knowledge is obviously in step with his pragmatism. Perhaps less obviously, it is also connected to his work on probability. We get reliability, or we increase the weight of our probabilities, by experimenting and measuring success. Probability and experimentation are at the very heart of knowledge.

Braithwaite rued not developing Ramsey's ideas in greater detail and depth, saying that he had instead spent too much time trying to figure out Wittgenstein. At Braithwaite's eightieth birthday party, A.J. Ayer said a similar thing: it was a great pity that Cambridge philosophers had spent the 1930s 'chewing over Wittgenstein when they ought to have been chewing over Ramsey'. But a generation later, Braithwaite's teaching of Ramsey's ideas would have a significant effect, and there would be plenty of chewing-over Ramsey in Cambridge by eminent philosophers such as Jonathan Bennett, Simon Blackburn, Edward Craig, Ian Hacking, Hugh Mellor, Huw Price, and Bernard Williams. Another generation follows, and, in any event, Ramsey's influence has spread well beyond the Cambridge fens.

THE END AND MEANING
OF A LIFE

A Summer of Family and Friends

The extraordinary last year of Frank's life was busy with important non-philosophical matters as well. In March 1929, Sarah was born in the Mortimer Road house. Frank and Lettice took the birth of their second child in the same easy manner as the first. Frank was going to squeeze in a weekend's visit to Sebastian Sprott just before the due date, but had to write to him: 'I'm most awfully sorry but the situation is quite changed as the doctor has now decided to produce Lettice's baby artificially on the Thursday before Easter or as soon after as the stuff works.' He said they would love to have Sebastian to stay the weekend after Easter, but couldn't be certain it would be manageable. Sarah was born without additional incident, and became a delightful baby with a head of curls.* Frank's friends and family refer to a photograph of him romping in their garden with his two little daughters, Jane on his back and Sarah in his arms, perfectly capturing his joy at being a father. The picture has unfortunately gone missing, along with the entire photo album of Frank and Lettice's married life.

Frank and Lettice resumed their social lives. The children could be left with the nanny, and they could go out for the evening or even the weekend. They also had people to stay at Mortimer Road. Frances Marshall was often there. Lionel Penrose's wife Margaret remembered visiting for a weekend and having Frank burst in on her while she was in the bath.

Bloomsbury figured large. In 1928, Dora Carrington had been in and out of King's College, painting a work of art over most of Dadie Rylands' rooms—the door frames and panels, the fireplace mantel, and the tiny alcove that Dadie used as a bar. Frank was in and out of Dadie's rooms as well, which were not far from his own. The Ramseys added Carrington and Rylands to their pack of close Bloomsbury friends, and by the summer of 1929, Frank and Lettice were frequent guests at the

---

* Sarah would contract polio while cycling in France and die within a week, at the age of twenty.

country homes of the Bloomsbury set—most often Bunny Garnett's Hilton Hall, a beautiful seventeenth-century house just outside of Cambridge.

Beakus Penrose, brother of Lionel and central Bloomsbury figure, bought a 16mm film camera in the summer of 1929. A number of short silent films, featuring murder and mayhem, were scripted and directed by Bunny Garnett. The first films were produced at Hilton Hall, with later ones at Ham Spray, the country house of Lytton Stratchey, Dora Carrington, and Ralph Partridge. Four survive at the National Film & Television Archive. They appeared in a 1995 exhibition titled 'Carrington' at the Barbican Art Gallery and are easily found on the Internet under the title 'When Beakus Came to Stay'. At least one of the films, 'Dr. Turner's Mental Home', was screened at the London residence of Virginia and Leonard Woolf. They offer us moving pictures of Frank's friends and settings.

The very first of the productions took place at the beginning of July, at a weekend gathering at Hilton Hall. Frank and Lettice were there, and the party saw 'quite a lot' of Wittgenstein, although he wasn't present for the filming. The script was based on a Penrose family story in which two teetotal aunts poured the wicked contents of the family's fine wine cellar down the drains. Both Beakus and Alec Penrose were there to provide factual details. Lettice played the role of one of the aunts, and Frank was the cellarman with a long apron and rolled-up sleeves. Frances Marshall reported in her diary:

> I simply had to spend my time merrily running through hayfields and scampering over fences, or bounding into Alec's arms—and very silly I looked too.

Frances annoyed the others by refusing to continue when darkness fell. But she took and preserved some photos, one of the few glimpses we get of Frank and Lettice after 1928.

It wasn't acting ability that endeared Frank to the Bloomsbury crowd. Bunny Garnett summed up their attraction:

> Of all our visitors from Cambridge I have no doubt that Frank Ramsey had the most remarkable brain. . . . There was something a bit abnormal about Frank. He was so huge in body and in mind, so much bigger and better than the rest of us, that I suspected that like the Bramley Seedling apple he might be a diploid, that is to say his cells might have double the number of chromosomes as those of ordinary men. If it were true it would have accounted for his immense tree-trunk arms and legs, carthorse's bottom, and great genial face surmounted by a big broad forehead. . . . But this precocious intelligence was combined with a childlike innocence. . . . When I brought to his notice some ordinary tale of petty self-seeking, self-deception, egoism or malice, Frank was at

first astounded. Such things did not seem possible to him up there, in the heights. Then he would realise the full implications and humour of folly and silliness, and the self-defeating nature of selfishness and spitefulness, and God-like, his great innocent face would become wreathed in smiles ... his chuckle was the chuckling of a god.

The summer of 1929 was not all Bloomsbury high-jinks. Some of their friends were in turbulent phases of their lives, and the Ramseys were there to support them. Most awful was the death of Dorothea Braithwaite of a brain tumour. They had the distraught Richard over for dinners and walks. They also were involved with the extended Ramsey family, who were still in rocky emotional states. Frank and Lettice frequently went to Howfield for Sunday lunch, and took Margie to her sporting events and to the cinema. Michael was not in great shape. In January 1928, he had given a speech at the Union. Frank attended it, and wrote to Lettice about the debacle:

> Poor Mick is very sorry for himself; he spoke last night in the Union on disestablish-ment and broke down after about ten minutes; his mind stopped working altogether and he found himself saying 'in 1919 the Enabling Act was passed' and quite unable to remember what the Enabling Act was (of course it's a thing he's as familiar with as his a,b,c, it is the foundation of the present constitution of the church). So he stopped and walked out. Father (who was there) attributed it to his drinking too much at dinner. Michael thinks he ought to go to a mental specialist; he has been getting more and more excitable lately and ineffective running up and down more and more. I agree with him but there will be some dispute as to whom he ought to go to.

Lettice agreed that Michael 'ought to go see a psychoanalyst', as 'he must be very repressed—no outlet at all'. No sexual outlet, she meant. She worried about his 'odd mannerisms' and that he wasn't at all 'normal'—'worse than you even were I should have thought'. Lettice thought that perhaps psychoanalysis could cure Michael as it had Frank, but it had to be the right kind:

> Don't let him go to see one of those religious people if possible—though I suppose they might understand his type and make suggestions which would be acceptable or in accordance with Mick's Conscious Self.

Frank made the suggestion to Michael, although he did think that his brother's tactic of repressing his emotions was to some extent effective. He wrote to Lettice that Michael 'may have found a satisfactory remote solution for himself which isn't worth disturbing'. Michael eventually went to a religious analyst who told him that he was sexually underdeveloped and ought to find some female company. The analyst thought Michael so interesting that he asked if he might use his case anonymously in a lecture. Michael pulled himself together, and eventually married and became the Archbishop of Canterbury. He was one of the most effective and progressive heads of the Church of England, set against apartheid in South Africa, the war in Vietnam, the death penalty, religious fundamentalism, laws criminalizing homosexuality, and the Pope's encyclical banning birth control.

Frank and Lettice rented a cottage south of Dublin, at Cahor Point, in the summer of 1929. They had made trips to the Irish countryside in 1925 and 1926, and were keen to return. They included people in need of a holiday. Richard Braithwaite was one, and remembered feeling a 'miserable widower', glad of the opportunity to temper his crushing grief. He and Lettice would start an affair shortly after this trip.

They brought Frank's sister Bridget along as well, and she too remembered the generosity well into her old age. Dick Pyke joined the party. So did the free-thinking Beatrix Tudor-Hart and her child. Beatrix was part of a famous left-wing London family and had been the inaugural principal teacher at the Russells' experimental Beacon Hill School. She helped out with the Ramsey children, who must have had a grand time, as Beatrix would later make her name with a theory about how children learn through play.

Image 31 Frank reading while on a walking holiday in the Alps.

Image 32 Hilton Hall Filming, 1929, from left to right: Bunny Garnett, Angus Wilson (?), Frances Marshall, Beakus Penrose, Ray Marshall, Frank, Lettice.

The adults also had a grand time, despite the heat and the fact that the cottage was full of fleas. They got used to both. Some Irish friends of Lettice's were in a nearby cottage, and together the big group irritated and scandalized the neighbours with their loud partying and nude bathing. Bridget remembered the holiday as full of jolly meals and naked people lying about on the beach. She slept in the room next to Lettice and Frank, and she thought them lucky to have so much to say to each other so early in the morning.

There were quieter activities as well. They played bridge while flicking the fleas off. Frank kept up his morning work regime. Braithwaite said that he wrote 'vigorously' during the holiday. He had a lot of philosophy on the boil.

Fatal Illness

The warm weather over the holiday in Ireland seemed to follow Frank and Lettice to Cambridge. September and the first weeks of October were unusually warm and sunny. Frank was working at pace, writing a vast number of notes and drafts for his book project.

The pace of their social lives remained strong as well. Frank invited Moore to dine with him at the King's Audit Feast on November 14, a seven-course dinner accompanied by seven fine wines. He caught a chill after this feast. Even though Frank was feeling poorly, Wittgenstein continued to come by Mortimer Road—his pocket diary records visits on 20, 23, and 28 November. Perhaps they talked about the quarrel Wittgenstein was having with the Moral Sciences Club. On 19 November, MacIver had told his diary:

> The secretary of the Moral Science Club has complained to Broad about Wittgenstein's presence at the 'supplementary meeting' a fort-night ago and Broad has passed this on to Moore and Moore to Wittgenstein, with the result that Wittgenstein is now holding little meetings of protest with everyone he meets. We are to gather for further discussion in Drury's rooms on Thursday evening.

Perhaps they talked some philosophy on the first two occasions. But by 25 November, Frank was not in any state to have serious conversation. He declined an invitation from Moore:

> Thank you very much for asking me, but I can't come this week either as I'm still in bed having now got jaundice, which has prevented my getting fit at all after my previous fever, so I'm not really up to any sort of discussion and I'm sorry to say don't know when I shall be.

Frank had for years signed off his letters to Moore with endearments, but this one ends with the formal 'Yours sincerely', suggesting a low state of mind indeed.

Nothing much was made of his illness at this point. It was simply said, as Michael recalled, 'Frank's got jaundice.' Lettice came down with the flu herself, and to give her a rest, Frank was moved to Howfield. He got yellower and yellower. Frances Marshall remembers him and his eyeballs being 'bright yellow', and his skin being an orange copper colour.

On 4 December, Michael wrote to his father to say that he was sorry to hear that Frank was still ill. Wittgenstein visited on 5 December. On the 10th, Frank wrote to Schlick to say that his pupil, Alister Watson ('quite good', but not 'really brilliant'), wanted to go to Vienna after Christmas to study mathematics. He then issued his apology for being late with the review of Carnap's *Aufbau*:

> I am very sorry and will do it when I next have leisure. At the moment I am in bed with a very severe attack of jaundice...

There is nothing in the letter that suggests pessimism about his prognosis, only a weariness with the illness dragging on. It was interfering with a great deal of work. His book might have been at the very front, but the queue was long. He was on the docket to read a paper at the Aristotelian Society in the new year and he and Sraffa had arranged to meet regularly. He was planning similar meetings with Moore, who said after Frank died:

> In the course of the twenties I had a good deal of discussion with him, and, just before his final illness, he proposed that we should meet regularly once a week to discuss philosophical questions together. How I wish those discussions had taken place! I think that I might really have learnt a great deal from them.

And of course, he intended to keep talking to Wittgenstein.

Come Christmas, he was still in bed, but still very much himself. On New Year's Day, he was up to ribbing his brother about whether he had managed to replace his unsatisfied lust by employing the trick of contemplating the oneness of God. But a week later, he wrote to Lettice from Howfield, mentioning that his doctor had come:

> My love,
> ... So glad to hear you're better; do be careful.... I've had a bad night and a goodish one. Have you anything to read? I will try to get the library books changed but I don't know what for. Cooper came yesterday and was rather dismal, knocked me off meat. I think Sraffa's getting out of question, also beginning work at beginning of term. It is mouldy. Could you write to your stepfather and find out anything more definite about his notions on jaundice.
> I've had a nice book from Mick—Oxford Book of German Verse. Wish I'd got one for him in time. I do like a sunny day like this even when in bed, don't you.
> Want my shaving things soon.
> Much love from
> Frank

It was the last letter he would write to her, or to anyone.

Lettice contacted her uncle, Robert Davies-Colley, a senior surgeon at Guy's Hospital in London. He had hosted her and Frank's wedding reception. Davies-Colley knew a thing or two about disorders of the liver—his own father, also a surgeon, had died of liver cancer at the age of fifty-eight. Davies-Colley came up on 10 January to examine Frank and immediately arranged for him to be taken by ambulance to Guy's Hospital in London. Harold Jeffreys visited him there and found him looking very yellow, but 'all there mentally'. Davies-Colley suspected that a stone might be blocking Frank's bile ducts and operated on him. Wittgenstein must have asked Lettice for a full account, as she apologized for the delay when she wrote to him on Wednesday, 15 January:

> Frank was operated on Saturday afternoon, because, after 8 weeks in bed he showed no improvement. My uncle, who's a surgeon, came from London to see him and thought that he should be brought to London to Guy's hospital. So we took an ambulance & came. Then there was a consultation with a physician (as opposed to a surgeon) & firstly they agreed that an op would be best. They found his gall bladder very inflamed & are draining it. There was no stone. I have seen Frank twice today, for a few moments. He is still too much under the effect of drugs to like any company...The dose of morphia that is always given after an op had a bad effect on him & he had to have something to counteract it.
>
> I write again, darling, & tell you how things go. I feel it is a comfort to have something definite done anyhow & I think Frank feels the same.

Frank seemed to his family to be in reasonable shape after the operation. A telegram was sent to Howfield to say that it was definitely not a stone. Michael had over the prior week received a dizzying series of letters and telegrams from his father. After the operation, he was reassured: 'Heard from father that Frank's operation had gone successfully.'

But the operation had not been successful. Lettice asked Frances to be with her. Frances arrived at the hospital to find her friend in a hot little room

> compulsively writing postcards and crying a little now and again. Very sensibly she at once asked me not to be sorry for her—in words at least—as it only made her lose control. She found it easier to talk about the medical aspect; so she told me of the history of the illness in detail and even talked a little about what she would do if he died.

Frank was lying nearby in a screened-off room, his breathing distressed. Frances cancelled her plans to go to the Ham Spray country house with Ralph. She spent the night at her mother's, the house where Lettice had lodged for a year before returning to Cambridge and meeting Frank. The next morning, Frances returned to find 'the cold and somewhat menacing eyes of a doctor in a white overall' looking over Frank's screen as he was given a blood transfusion and then had 'another slight operation'.

During the Christmas break, Wittgenstein had been in Vienna visiting his family, and having conversations with Schlick and Waismann. Upon his return, he joined

Frances and Lettice in their vigil. On Friday, 17 January, Wittgenstein seemed to miss a pre-planned meeting in Cambridge which was to decide on the timing of his first lectures. MacIver wrote in his diary, with no inkling that anything was wrong with his old schoolmate Frank Ramsey:

> 17th. Back to Bateman Street for tea, which I had to have early, because all who were to attend Wittgenstein's lectures were told to meet in Braithwaite's rooms to arrange the time at five o'clock to-day. I was a little late and found a crowd there, who had already almost decided on the times from five to six o'clock on Mondays and from five to seven o'clock on Thursdays.

Braithwaite must have known why Wittgenstein was not in town, and how dire things were.

Frances said that it was clear that Wittgenstein shared with her both an immense personal sadness, as well as sympathy for Lettice. But he made poor and flippant jokes, perhaps to disguise emotions he couldn't cope with, or perhaps to help Lettice keep her composure. Frances found them disconcerting and in bad taste. Wittgenstein departed for Cambridge on Saturday the 18th, as Braithwaite's crowd had decided that his first lecture would be on Monday. Frances and Lettice saw him off at the rail station, where they had sausage rolls and sherry in the buffet. The two women went back to the hospital.

Wittgenstein arrived in Cambridge in time to attend Moore's discussion class on Saturday. MacIver recorded in his diary that, after Janina Hosiasson started things off, 'Wittgenstein began to talk and talked for the rest of the hour, bringing the discussion back to the old question of tooth-ache which ate up so much time last term.' Moore had been talking about the difference between the verb 'to know' in its various tenses and Wittgenstein was wrestling with whether 'I know I right now have a toothache' can mean anything, since it seems an utterly private thought. He seems to have kept his thoughts about Frank's condition to himself as well.

When Lettice and Frances returned from dropping Wittgenstein at the station, Frank was in the grip of delirium, although he sounded, from a distance, perfectly reasonable. Frances was 'moved by the extremely gentle, cultivated sound of his voice, coming from behind the screen':

> I was painfully conscious of the struggle for life going on, and could not help unreasonably feeling that Frank was too civilized and intelligent to have a fair chance in that savage battle. The sounds of his laboured breathing and hiccups were worse than before.

The next day Arthur wrote to Michael that Frank's condition had become critical and there was only a slight chance of recovery. A few hours later, a telegram arrived:

> Frank slightly better, though condition very critical. Important not alarm him, so Bridget not allowed to see him; better not come unless prefer.
>
> Father.

Michael preferred to disregard his father's suggestion. He caught the overnight train to London, but was too late.

Frank's sheer excess of powers came to a stop in the early hours of Sunday, 19 January. Frances was having a restless night at home when her mother came in to deliver the news and to say that Lettice needed her. Frances was devastated, as she realized that she loved Frank even more than her dear friend Lettice.

Lettice wrote to Wittgenstein on Monday, her handwriting distressed and difficult to decipher:

> Dearest Ludwig,
>
> After you left I went to bed & slept a bit & was woken up to say that Frank was conscious. He was hardly conscious & gradually fell into a daze & then faded away quietly & died at 4:10 am.
>
> I _did_ appreciate you coming & you gave me great courage, dear Ludwig. I hope I shall see you again soon.
>
> I have no plans at present—I cannot imagine life without Frank. And I don't know when I shall dare to come back to Cambridge. It's all too impossible & unreal.
>
> I hope your lecture went well. Write to me here. They will know where I am.
> With love, Lettice

She added a postscript after returning from the funeral, saying 'I hold my head high as you said . . . . so far'. Wittgenstein gave his lecture that day. It was standard Tractarian fare, but by 25 January, he was telling his class that he had given up on many points he had expressed in the _Tractatus_. Indeed, in his notebook after the 20 January lecture, he wrote positively about pragmatism for the first time. Perhaps his friend's death released Wittgenstein so that he could, at least temporarily, shake his aversion to seeing his position as part of an ongoing tradition—one that included Frank Ramsey.

The news hit Cambridge like a sledgehammer. On Friday, 17 January, Keynes had written to Lydia in London, saying that 'Everybody is in an excellent temper with no rows or controversies ahead, so I just sit hour after hour in the combination room'. The peace in the King's Fellows' room was soon shattered. Keynes's next letter to Lydia began:

> My dearest darling,
> Frank Ramsey died last night. We are all very much overwhelmed by feelings about it. All yesterday the news seemed desperate. He was in his way the greatest genius in the college and such a dear creature besides. Poor Lettice and her two babies.

Keynes broke the news to his colleagues, telephoning those who had a special connection to Frank. When he rang Richard Kahn, Keynes was terribly upset. Kahn said that not only did Keynes have high expectations of Frank doing important work in economics, but he lost one of his great friends at King's, someone with whom he often enjoyed a laugh.

Braithwaite broke the news to others. The curtness of his postcard to Sprott reflects his mood, which was complicated by the fact that he was then estranged from Frank because of his affair with Lettice:

> Sunday
> Frank Ramsey has died. When they operated for his jaundice (on Tuesday) they found some horrible condition of the liver. He died early this morning in London at Guys.
> Richard Braithwaite

Lytton Strachey wrote to Dadie Rylands:

> The loss to your generation is agonizing to think of—and the world will never know what has happened—what a light has gone out. I always thought there was something of Newton about him—the ease and majesty of the thought—the gentleness of the temperament...

And he wrote to his lover Roger Senhouse to say that he and Dadie were 'wretched about it':

> It really was a dreadful tragedy, he was a real genius, and a most charming person—infinitely simple and modest, and at the same time obviously a great intellect.... The loss to Cambridge is incalculable.

MacIver read the obituary over breakfast in *The Times* on 20 January, and was very surprised, as he had only heard from Cornforth the day before that Frank was ill. He then went to Wittgenstein's lecture:

> Wittgenstein had already begun to lecture when I got to the room in the Arts School, but I took no notes to-day and found it rather distressing to listen, for the poor man was terribly nervous and I thought at first that he would not spin out the hour.

The next day Drury expressed scepticism when MacIver remarked that Wittgenstein had seemed nervous. Perhaps what MacIver saw as nervousness was grief.

Michael led the early morning requiem mass at King's College on 21 January, as he did the funeral later that day at Golders Green in London. He didn't give himself the luxury of thinking that his brother was up in heaven and reunited with his mother—on the contrary. These two deaths were the only occasions on which Michael felt doubt about the existence of God, so unjust did they seem. By the time he became the head of the Church of England, Michael's doubts were resolved. But he would forever upset his conventional critics by saying that he hoped and expected to meet atheists in heaven—for if anyone would be in heaven, it would be Frank.

The next day, Wednesday, 22 January, there was a memorial service at King's. Frank's ashes were buried with his mother's in the St. Giles' and St. Peter's Burial Ground (now the Ascension Parish Burial Ground) in Cambridge, just off the road Frank would have walked to get to Girton when, as a schoolboy, he was tending the garden and as a recent graduate, he was teaching the students. At the cremation, Lettice was utterly crumpled up with grief, and Michael was so upset that he ran out of the church. Elizabeth Denby was there, 'entirely in the correct manner in all the novels—the mistress sitting in the back', said Braithwaite. Frances understood that Elizabeth 'was very much in love with Frank', but she was feeling upset for Lettice, and thought, rather unkindly, that Elizabeth seemed to be trying to draw attention to herself. Elizabeth's best friend's daughter asserted that Elizabeth, who never married, loved Frank till the day she died, in 1965.

Michael said that all of Cambridge attended the memorial service. But it is not clear that Wittgenstein was there, or at the funeral. He doesn't get a mention in any of the accounts of these events, and he was someone whose presence was usually mentioned. His emotions were perhaps too extreme. He told Frank's family, as well as his own sister Gretl and his friend Desmond Lee, that Frank ought not to have died—that the medical situation was mishandled. Frank's sisters remembered that he wrote a terrible letter to their father, saying that Arthur had failed to get Frank proper medical treatment and so was responsible for his death. The gratuitous cruelty leaves one aghast. Wittgenstein was notoriously and severely self-critical. But he seems not to have understood that extending his brand of moral self-criticism to others was itself not very moral.

Fine obituaries of Frank were written by Keynes and Braithwaite. Life in Cambridge lumbered on. Frank's undergraduate students were transferred to Philip Hall. On Friday, 31 January 1930, Wittgenstein gave a talk to the Moral Sciences Club at the first meeting of the term, titled 'Evidence for the Existence of Other Minds'. Frances tried to help Lettice pick up the pieces of her life. Richard Braithwaite took her abroad to cheer her up and during the holiday proposed marriage. Lettice considered it—and may have even agreed—but in the end unhitched herself from an arrangement made in grief.[†]

When the Oxford philosopher J.N. Findlay visited Wittgenstein in February, he reported that 'The grievousness of the recent death of Ramsey hung like a cloud over Cambridge, and had demoralized everyone.'

Cause of Death

Theories abound as to the precise cause of death. Frank's parents were always concerned about his health. He was born with jaundice and had digestive troubles when young, and some have suggested there was a chronic liver disease. Sraffa had a more picturesque way of putting the hypothesis: Ramsey, he said, was far too big, physically and mentally, to survive long in this world. But jaundice in newborns was common in the early 1900s, and Frank's state of health as an adult was robust. Francis Marshall didn't remember him ever being ill and Desmond Lee remembered him in 1929 as having 'tremendous vitality'. He was vigorously swimming and walking in Ireland during his last summer. His final illness was not likely the endgame of something chronic.

Another possibility is gallstones. As an adult, Frank retained the big appetite he had developed at Winchester. While in Vienna in 1924, he wrote in reply to a query from his parents:

> I don't know if I'm fat or thin! I only take about 1 hr walk daily for exercise but don't eat much except eggs mayonnaise and whipped cream. This place just flows with whipped cream.

[†] Lettice would go on to live a prominent life as a renowned portrait photographer. Wittgenstein for a long time remained attached to her, even residing with her the following autumn. A diary entry at the beginning of October 1930 registered his fondness: 'Then to Cambridge where I am staying with Lettice who is very friendly & good to me. I told her about Marguerite & our difficulties.' Lettice was one of the few people who could deliver reprimands to Wittgenstein. She once wrote to him about his taking offence at her expressing happiness that he had received more funding from Trinity than he had expected: 'Dear Ludwig, I was glad to get your letter. Yes, you did hurt me very much indeed. I don't know how you can have thought even for a moment that my motives were anything other than friendly towards you. Why should I want to know your affairs for any other reason than interest in you? When I talked of your money matters I was only feeling pleased that you would get more than you expected. . . . I'm very sorry you were offended, Ludwig. But I do think it was very touchy of you. Why you should be so suspicious of my motives I can't think.' Eventually Wittgenstein cut her out of his life. He had left some furniture with her while he was between addresses, including a foul bathmat, which Lettice threw out. When Wittgenstein got his new rooms in Trinity, he wanted it back, and took Lettice's crime to be unforgivable.

James Strachey noticed during Frank's time in Vienna that his young friend seemed unhealthily 'swollen & stiff'. And once he got to King's, the fare was rich and plentiful—Keynes was always complaining that the college food and drink were bad for one. That only accelerated Frank's becoming overweight. MacIver described him just weeks before his illness:

> Broad was reading a paper to the Moral Science Club in his own room and there was an enormous crowd collected there. An enormous man like a cross between a light-house and a balloon—like a Zeppelin set up on end—who came in with Wittgenstein, I did not at first recognize, but it was Ramsey. Braithwaite was in the chair and is also a large man, but not as large as Ramsey.

While the probability is low that gallstones could have plagued a twenty-six-year-old man, Frank's oft-changing girth increased that risk. But no stone was found.

Wittgenstein wasn't the only one to cite some kind of medical malpractice as the cause of death. Lionel Penrose, who as his brother Beakus put it, always talked about Frank with 'such reverence and interest', thought he was operated on when he shouldn't have been. At the time of Frank's death, Lionel had a medical degree and he might have known that surgery for advanced liver disease is dangerous. There is some suggestion that Lionel might have been wracked with guilt about not having been there to step in and save his friend.

Lettice said that Frank 'died of an infected liver'. There was a post-mortem examination, and the death certificate cited the first cause of death as cholangitis, an ascending bacterial infection within the system of ducts linking the gallbladder, liver, and pancreas. The infection, however, was likely not bacterial cholangitis, which advances rapidly. Frank's illness stretched over many weeks—too long for cholangitis.

While one can't be certain, the infection might well have been Leptospirosis, or Weil's Disease, caused by bacteria carried by the urine of animals.[‡] While quite rare, and still hard to diagnose, it is sometimes found in the River Cam, in which Frank loved to swim. His course of illness seems to follow Weil's Disease near perfectly. There are three phases, particularly in younger persons, if left untreated. First there is an acute fever phase. That would be the 'chill' Frank caught after the King's feast. Then there is a brief recovery, followed by a prolonged and worsening jaundice. Then there

---

[‡] If this is right, Margaret Paul was not far off. After Hepatitis A and B had been distinguished and it had been shown that the latter deadly form was carried by water rats in the Cam, she surmised that viral hepatitis was the cause of death. But death from acute viral hepatitis is extremely rare and accompanied by encephalopathy, manifested by mental slowing and confusion. That did not characterize Frank's final days.

is liver failure, kidney failure, and often meningitis. The autopsy showed both Frank's liver and kidneys to be affected, as Braithwaite relayed to Kingsley Martin:

> Frank Ramsey became ill with what appeared to be simply jaundice in the middle of Nov. It went on and did not get better, and in January it was decided to operate to remove a small stone or something which was suspected to be stopping up the bile duct. But nothing was found, and instead the whole liver and kidneys were found in a frightful condition, and he died a few days later (without much pain and without believing he was seriously ill). No one thought that he was dangerously ill till three days before his death.

One thing that might speak against the hypothesis is that these bacteria don't survive long in cold water and the onset of illness is quite soon after exposure, from two days to four weeks. Could the Cam have been warm enough for Frank to have been swimming in October and for the bacteria to survive? The answer is yes: it happens that from 9 to 18 October of that year, unseasonably mild weather hung over the whole of the UK.

The decision to operate might have seemed reasonable given the course of his condition, but performing surgery in the setting of such a damaged liver undoubtedly hastened his death. It may have been that no treatment available at the time could have saved him at that point. The first antibiotic had been discovered by Fleming in 1928, but wasn't purified for use until 1940. Life support machines had yet to be invented. But it is not clear that Frank was indeed suffering from what Davies-Colley told Arthur was 'a degenerative disease of the liver which was bound to end fatally'. The one thing that is clear is that the decision to operate was an error of judgment, possibly fatal.[§]

The Meaning of Life: Russell, Wittgenstein, Ramsey

Braithwaite ended his obituary of Ramsey thus:

> Unlike many intellects, his had not been garnered into print; and the best of his mind is utterly destroyed. Such an event would lead us to question the 'purpose' or the 'meaning' of life, had not Frank Ramsey taught us that these are nonsense questions.

While this is a clever way to end an obituary, it is not quite right. Ramsey did not think it was nonsense to ask about the meaning of life.

[§] After this book was published, Trisha Greenhalgh was able to unearth Ramsey's case notes from Guy's Hospital archives. See Misak, Naylor, Tonelli, Greenhalgh, and Foster (forthcoming) for an analysis of the case history and the conclusion about the decision to operate. The Case Notes tell us that Lettice got the date of the surgery muddled, understandably, given the dire circumstances. The surgery was on Tuesday the 14th.

Braithwaite was referring to Ramsey's 1925 Apostles talk in which he argued, cheekily, that ethics, along with much else, was not a subject discussable by the Apostles. But it is worth revisiting the very end of that paper, where Ramsey took a serious turn and made an argument about the very meaning of life. He put his point in the context of where he seemed 'to differ from some of my friends'. One of those friends was Russell, who in 'What I Believe' and 'The Free Man's Worship', tried to carve out a place for human value in a godless universe. The result was what Braithwaite called a 'temperamental pessimism' about man's place in the vast emptiness. The other friend was Wittgenstein, who hated the fact that Russell wrote of such 'intimate' matters, and made that distaste clear to him. One thing Wittgenstein objected to was Russell's assumption that the universe was godless. But Wittgenstein managed to re-enchant the world, yet remain in despair. He agreed with Russell that gloom or (as William James put it) a 'sick soul' was a natural response to the human condition. By confronting despair, Wittgenstein came to religiosity. Ramsey was attracted neither to Wittgenstein's mysticism, nor to his distressed outlook. And, while just as much an atheist as Russell, he didn't think one had to quail in front of the fact that the world will cool and die (or now, more likely, heat and die).

His own approach was in line with the rest of his philosophy. We can evaluate the various outlooks on life and see which have the best consequences. In his assessment, the key to meaning in life is to be optimistic, thrilled, and actively trying to improve conditions for people now and in the future. Live as fully and as ethically as you can, was his conclusion. Ramsey understood that inequalities get in the way of being thrilled by life. He put much effort into trying to make the world a fairer place. He also understood that individuals' psychological makeups have an impact on whether one is depressed or not. His own tendency was to be cheerful—he was remembered as always smiling and looking rather pleased, not so much with himself but with things in general. He knew that Wittgenstein was not so disposed. But Ramsey too had periods of crippling anguish, and he thought that one should try to improve one's life by engaging with what clinical psychology has to offer and by trying to be happy. If psychology can help change our outlook for the better, we should avail ourselves of it, as he had.

Such assessments are of course open to challenge. Wittgenstein judged Ramsey's idea of the meaning of life to be impoverished—recall that he said that Ramsey failed see the value of reverence, except with respect to music. Russell too addressed Ramsey head on. In 1959, looking back on his own philosophical development, he said he simply did not feel what Ramsey felt: 'I find little satisfaction in contemplating the human race and its follies.' Both he and Wittgenstein wanted more than that. But Ramsey's point is a deep one. We cannot have more than what is best for human beings. No God, no 'oneness' of Michael's, no yearning for perfection in logic and philosophy will inject a transcendent meaning into our lives. The search for the transcendent, Ramsey thought, is misguided. We have what we have, and we must find meaning within it.

Keynes, perceptive as always, compared Ramsey to David Hume: 'Ramsey reminds one of Hume more than of anyone else, particularly in his common sense and sort of hard-headed practicality.' The similarities are indeed striking, despite the two centuries between these two great naturalist philosophers. Hume and Ramsey both resisted scepticism by turning their backs on the quest for certainty.§ They both made their major contributions to philosophy before the age of twenty-seven and extended their intellectual reach into economics. Both were clever wits, with large girths. They were also atheists, able to turn their humour on religion, and unafraid of a godless death. They both enjoyed life, while also being susceptible to the low spirits that come from trying to think hard about fundamental questions.

Frank Ramsey had many good reasons to be thrilled and optimistic about his life. His marriage was excellent, as was the relationship with his second great love. He had two daughters on whom he doted. In his view, philosophers, mathematicians, and economists could and should solve problems, and he solved plenty of them, in ways that would write his name in permanent marker on the history of those disciplines. In one of his first letters to Lettice, he wrote that he was putting the finishing touches on his essay, 'The Foundations of Mathematics'. He told her that the paper was important to him, not for the prospect of getting the Smith's Prize, but 'as a sort of self-expression'. When he thought about suicide, not as a serious possibility, but more abstractly, he would think

> that I must at least wait till I had written down my ideas, because they mustn't be wasted! Then I always went on to say that anyhow apart from these ideas I've had a very good education which mustn't be wasted by my dying before I turn it to advantage.

Ramsey's ideas weren't wasted. We have seen in this biography that an astounding number of them lived on, and have aged well. He might have had a short life, but his thoughts have had a long one.

He also would have appreciated more light-hearted and sentimental things about the afterlife of his work. It would have pleased him that the first volume of his papers was edited by his friend Braithwaite and published by his mentor Ogden in the series in which Wittgenstein's *Tractatus* had appeared. His former

§ Ramsey took careful notes on Hume's *Treatise of Human Nature*, singling out the idea that some principles are such that we cannot do without them.

student Alister Watson corrected the proofs. Lettice gave Wittgenstein a copy of that volume, inscribing it simply: 'Ludwig from Lettice. May 1931'.** Ramsey might even have let roar one of his great laughs about the fact that, although sales were slow in the first decades, by the 1980s, original copies had been stolen from all the Cambridge libraries, including those of King's College and the Moral Sciences Library. Even Braithwaite's own copy had been stolen by a pupil.

The question 'What might have been?' looms large, and many have offered answers. Braithwaite asserted that Ramsey might have discovered the Gödel result first and, with Newman and Turing, developed the idea of computability. He also thought Ramsey would have been delighted with the decision and game theory that arose from von Neumann, especially John Nash's solution to the puzzle of how a group of rational bargainers, acting with their individual interests in mind, would interact. But all this is speculative. Indeed, we have seen that Ramsey did not think that payoff maximizing strategies were what we should (or could) be aiming at. For that reason, he would not have thought that human decision-making could be explained by an equilibrium point in which each player pursues his or her best strategy, on the assumption that every other player is pursuing his or her best strategy.†† He may well have defined formal rationality with payoff maximizing, but he thought that fallible humans would be mistaken to think they should or could aspire to such ideal rationality. That doesn't mean he wouldn't have been thrilled at the cleverness of game theory.

There are, however, a few things we can say with some confidence about what might have been. One is that Ramsey and Wittgenstein would have continued to influence each other. Another is that Ramsey would have written that review of Carnap's *Aufbau* and would have had an impact on how the Vienna Circle's pro-gramme evolved. For the Circle was always interested in what Ramsey had to say. We have seen that they pored over 'The Foundations of Mathematics' shortly after Ramsey published it in 1926 and that they remained engaged with his work. In 1932, A.J. Ayer, the English upholder of the Circle's position, read a paper to the Moral Sciences Club 'in which he defended Ramsey's view of general propositions against the Oxford view that they assert a necessary connection between universals'. (This was just before Ayer's first meeting with the Vienna Circle.) Carnap and Hempel, of course, made use of Ramsey sentences in the 1950s. No doubt their exchanges would have borne more fruit, had Ramsey lived.

** Wittgenstein's copy of *The Foundations of Mathematics* was once on the market at Christie's, listed for £2500. Its present whereabouts are unknown to me.

†† There is no evidence that Ramsey read von Neumann's paper in which he presented the min-max theorem (von Neumann 1928). It was an attempt to solve a simpler but similar problem—two-person, zero-sum games, where if one person wins, the other must lose.

Another thing we can say is that, given Ramsey's love of travel and interest in American philosophers and logicians, he might well have made his way across the Atlantic, as did Russell, Moore, Schlick, Wittgenstein, and Carnap. This would have spread his influence, widened his interests, and loosened his ties to Cambridge analysis even further. Those ties bound him to one of the richest traditions in the history of thought, and also provided the resistance against which he could carve out his own positions. But progress is often made with exposure to outside influences, and one imagines that both he and the Americans would have benefitted from sustained contact.

The last words should be Ramsey's. An excerpt from the passage quoted in Chapter 10 provides the best, and most poignant, expression of his view of the meaning of life, in perfect alignment with his realistic, feasible first-best approach to philosophy:

> In time the world will cool and everything will die; but that is a long time off still, and its present value at compound discount is almost nothing. Nor is the present less valuable because the future will be blank. Humanity, which fills the foreground of my picture, I find interesting and on the whole admirable. I find, just now at least, the world a pleasant and exciting place. You may find it depressing; I am sorry for you, and you despise me....On the other hand, I pity you with reason, because it is pleasanter to be thrilled than to be depressed, and not merely pleasanter but better for all one's activities.

AFTERWORD TO THE PAPERBACK EDITION

One of the pleasures of writing a biography is sleuthing for buried secrets and one of the frustrations is knowing that some will remain resolutely inaccessible. Hence I was intrigued and pleased to receive an email after the hardback publication of this book, which uncovered a significant piece of new information, filling in some gaps in my story of Ramsey's life and providing further insight into how and why Ramsey's place in the history of analytic philosophy unfolded as it did.

In the 1980s, two people were working on biographies of Ramsey. One was the DPhil student Laurie Kahn, who abandoned the project mid-decade and returned to the United States, after interviewing Ramsey's siblings, friends, and colleagues and compiling a great deal of other important material about Ramsey's life. The other was Margaret Paul, Ramsey's youngest sister, who was in the happy position of having access to sources such as family documents and recollections. In the late 1980s, she received an advance from Duckworth, her publishers, in order to employ a research assistant. Her book, perhaps not quite in a finished state, was posthumously published as *Frank Ramsey: A Sister's Memoir* in 2012 by Smith Gordon.

Margaret Paul's research assistant was Christopher Collins—at the time a Nuffield College graduate student, later an Oxford lecturer in Politics, later recruited to help Margaret Thatcher write her memoirs, now head of the Margaret Thatcher Foundation. It was he who sent me the email about something interesting that didn't make it into Margaret Paul's book. Lettice and Richard Braithwaite, he said, had engaged in an affair in 1929. Frank was so upset by it that it caused the friendship to rupture. Braithwaite felt terrible about the whole mess in the decades following Frank's death and didn't want to talk, hear, or even think about it. He had kept the letters Frank and Lettice had written to him in 1929, but denied Margaret Paul access to them. Then he destroyed them, Chris says, having held onto them for 50 years, to Margaret Paul's distress. When I received Chris's email, I asked Laurie Kahn about whether she knew of the liaison. She remembered Lettice "dancing around" this particular issue. As far as I know, no written documentation of the affair remains.

The relationship must have started right after the Ramseys' rather raucous summer holiday in Ireland, to which the recently bereaved Braithwaite was invited.

When interviewed by Laurie Kahn 50 years later, he recalled that invitation as being exceedingly generous, as he was a 'miserable widower' and not good company. Frank's sister Bridget, who was very religious at the time, was also invited, and she recalled thinking on that holiday that Frank and Lettice had a wonderful relationship, despite what she must have thought was the general immorality of their lifestyle—there was a fair bit of Bloomsburyish naked dancing and lounging about on that holiday. Bridget had the room next to Frank and Lettice and in her interview with Laurie Kahn the memory was still strong of how much they had to say to each other so early in the mornings.

In Chris's telling, which he got from Margaret Paul, Frank felt betrayed about the affair with Braithwaite because it broke what few rules or taboos there were in their open marriage—that one party wasn't to have a relationship with the close friend of the other. If that's right, then Frank's understanding of the rules had changed since 1926. At that point, during the first, well-documented, crisis in their marriage, he thought they had agreed on the opposite principle: that their affairs must stay within their circle, and not move out of it. (Other principles, articulated by Lettice, were: neither party owns the other; they tell each other everything about their affairs; and jealousy is an unwarranted and unethical response to extramarital activities.) Frank's relationship with Elizabeth Denby was thus fine, as Elizabeth had been a London flatmate of Lettice's and remained a friend, however strained that friendship might have become once Lettice proposed they become a 'happy trio'. But Lettice's wild affair with a famous Irish novelist she met while visiting her mother on her own in Ireland, was not fine. Braithwaite was very much in their circle, so Frank's sense of betrayal would be unwarranted on the principles he articulated in 1926.

There is a second, slightly different, candidate for the cause of Frank's hurt. Chris also remembered Margaret saying that 'Braithwaite was no catch' and that Lettice had her choice of men. But she chose *him* because he was Frank's friend, in order to get under his skin. If intending to hurt Frank was indeed part of her motivation for the affair, the explanation is likely that Lettice herself was hurt by Frank's deep relationship with Elizabeth Denby.

It would appear that the principled open marriage envisioned by Lettice and Frank remained imperfectly realized. Since Frank was generally against idealised 'fairytales' and in favour of realistic theories, it should have come as no surprise to him that such a triangle might prove unstable. In Chapter 9, I discuss how he worried about whether it was ethical for progressives such as the Apostles to abandon established but non-ideal values about 'fornication' outside of marriage in favour of radical utopian ones. He argued that the imperfect values protect working class women and children and that their own elite subclass of privileged Bohemians needed to take that fact seriously. He concluded, cheekily and in advance of finding a relationship of his own, that it was wrong to try to upend traditional morality, but that he and his future wife might not be able to resist the ideal open lifestyle. He should have been unsurprised that such an ethically and emotionally fraught issue could not be straightforwardly resolved by adopting some absolute principles.

But while the affair appears to have indeed got under Frank's skin, his wrath seems to have been directed not towards Lettice, but at Braithwaite. During the run-up to Frank's death in January 1930, there is only evidence of tenderness and care between Frank and Lettice, whereas Chris recalls Margaret Paul believing that savage things were said and written between Frank and Braithwaite. (Perhaps Braithwaite had told her that or shown her some of the correspondence.) Then Frank died, with the rift still very much unresolved.

Chris reports that Margaret Paul had difficulty writing about Frank and Lettice's marriage, the openness of which she disapproved. She thought the marriage disastrous for her brother and blamed Lettice—she was 'very anti-Lettice'. In Margaret's view, Frank had not wanted an open marriage, but it had been forced on him by Lettice in an aggressive manner that was impossible to refuse. This coheres with other things that were said to me while I was writing the biography—that Margaret Paul felt sorry for her brother, as he was forced by Bloomsbury's morality to live in a terrible and unworkable open marriage. He was taken in by the times.

The contemporaneous evidence, however, goes against the grain of Margaret Paul's judgment. The letters, diaries, and recollections of friends make it clear that, while the idea of an open marriage was due in the first instance to Lettice's strongly held principles, Frank was very happy to go along with it. As we know, a year after the wedding, he began that relationship with Elizabeth Denby, which ended only with Frank's death in 1930 and remained the only serious relationship in Elizabeth's much longer life. Indeed, Margaret Paul herself seemed at the time to have a positive view of their relationship. She was only 12 when her brother died and she may well have been innocent of the inner workings of his and Lettice's marriage until much later. After their mother's death in an automobile accident in 1926, Frank and Lettice moved into the family home largely to look after the 10 year old Margaret. She remembered 'a general feeling of well-being' during that year and when a spinster aunt relieved Frank and Lettice by moving in to look after the household, she told Laurie Kahn that it was to her 'great sorrow—I loved having them there.'

So Margaret's idea that the marriage was a disaster for her brother developed later in life, perhaps once she knew of its non-conformism. One contributing factor seems to have been, as Chris put it, that as an adult, she could not herself conceive of an open marriage as meaningful or real. But another set of reasons for Margaret's 'anti-Lettice'

Image 33 Richard Braithwaite, photographed by Lettice Ramsey

position may have come into play in the weeks immediately after Frank's death. She may have been scandalized, along with the rest of their family, about the behaviour of Lettice and Braithwaite. They went abroad on holiday and during the trip Braithwaite proposed marriage. Lettice considered it, but in the end declined. Of course, if Chris Collins' story is right, it makes that behaviour understandable. Absent knowledge of their affair, these two recent widowers seem either callous or desperate.

Is the story of the affair not merely someone's best recollection, a quarter century on, of things that were thought a half century after the events? And why bring up something that Braithwaite and Lettice preferred to keep quiet? The answer to these legitimate questions is that the affair is important not only because of what it tells us about a vital part of Frank's life and not only that it explains some events, such as the holiday and consideration of marriage that occupied Braithwaite and Lettice in early 1930. It also explains something significant about the way Ramsey's work was received by subsequent generations of philosophers.

I had been bewildered by the fact that Braithwaite knew so little about Ramsey's pragmatism during 1929. When asked about this gap in his knowledge by Laurie

Kahn in 1982, he replied gruffly that he and Frank had been two young men in a hurry, competing for the same things, and they didn't talk to each other about their work. I expressed some mild scepticism about this in Chapter 18, saying that Ramsey's philosophical views were no secret and surmising that perhaps Braithwaite was sidelined by Wittgenstein in 1929. But if Ramsey was angry with Braithwaite during that year, they would not have been talking about philosophy and the mystery of Braithwaite's ignorance is solved.

Even more importantly, Braithwaite became Ramsey's editor and interpreter after his death. (He also based some of his own work on the ideas of his old friend, continuing what he took to be Ramsey's legacy.) Because they were not talking in 1929, when Ramsey was hammering Wittgenstein with pragmatist arguments and formulating his own pragmatist account of belief and truth, that aspect of his position never got articulated by Braithwaite and went under-recognised for decades. As I argue in Chapter 18, Braithwaite's heavy editorial hand on some of the unfinished manuscripts and his decision to not publish anything from the book Ramsey was working on when he died sent the world of philosophy up blind alleys when it came to understanding Ramsey. Had Lettice not been involved with Braithwaite, she might have left Ramsey's papers with Keynes, who was the one person who really understood his work. Such are the contingencies that determine the course of reputations and how the history of thought is understood.

ENDNOTES

These endnotes are meant for the scholar who wants to track down direct quotes or be satisfied that my assertions are grounded. A list of abbreviations and details are to be found at the front of the book and in the Bibliography.

Preface

'Have you had any more success at this trick?' he asked!: Paul (2012: 262–3).
'my little brother the curate': TFL MS/COLL/735: 9/12.
from sheer excess of powers: Schumpeter (1933: 656).
his wide temples and broad, smiling face: Keynes (1972 [1930]: 336).
presented more elegantly, by Frank Ramsey: Davidson (1999: 32).
at the heart of his theories: Methven (2015: 51); GC: 160.
'Frank Ramsey was a genius by all tests for genius': Samuelson (1986 [1982]: 97).
'very accessible to his fellow human beings': TFL MS/COLL/735: 13/21B.
the new Cambridge school of literary criticism: BTTS.
she didn't think it would be possible: TFL MS/COLL/735: 13/10A.
'never solemn about anything either': TFL MS/COLL/735 13/4A.
'a total lack of uppishness': BTTS.
to have as big a heart as possible: Redpath (1990: 33).
'devastating laugh': Braithwaite (1930); (1931: 78).
'He shook with laughter': TFL MS/COLL/735: 13/32A.
it sounded just like Frank Ramsey: TFL MS/COLL/735: 13/44A.
paragraph ending: to rectify misleading impressions: Paul (2012); Hemming (2015); Cameron and Forrester (1999; 2008); Forrester and Cameron 2017).
soul of the person who holds it: Fichte (1982 [1797]: 16).
does not see that any explanation is needed: Moore (1931: vii–viii).
making desultory observations: Harrod (1951: 653).
'Would Ramsey think that?': TFL MS/COLL/735: 13/15B.
various matters as late as 1953: Lewy (1962).
were at least in their late seventies. : TFL MS/COLL/735: 13/33A.
the other great love of his life: TFL MS/COLL/735/8/9.
burned, on her instructions, after her death: Paul (2012: 241).

Chapter 1

the English intellectual aristocracy: Annan (1955: 244).
Frances Darwin, granddaughter of Charles Darwin: TFL MS/COLL/735: 13/23A.
when they were all youngsters: TFL MS/COLL/735: 9/9.

'may have been saying or writing in Trinity': Keynes (1972 [1931]: 336).
'caring for the underdog': BTTS.
a great joy to us both: KCA FPR/2/1/2/58.
as a step to a headmastership: TFL MS/COLL/735: 12.
principles of Marx is education: ASP/FPR.1983.01: 07-02-78.
never an issue that threatened their relationship: BTTS.
'B. could never have done that if Frank had been alive': Garnett (1962: 50).
who held considerable land after the 1066 Conquest: Paul (2012: 1).
an 'exceedingly rigorous' way: TFL MS/COLL/735: 9/20.
'ebullient members of the upper middle class': Paul (2012: 3).
'over-confident in their opinions': TFL MS/COLL/735: 13/5A; Paul (2012: 1).
the Daily Mail called him 'England's darling': MCA F/oMP/IV/6/11: 138.
'occasionally wrathful but an extraordinary teacher': TFL MS/COLL/735: 13/31A.
and say 'We'll have that boy': TFL MS/COLL/735: 13/31A.
hell-fire and eternal punishment: TFL MS/COLL/735: 9/20.
engages with Charlie and the boys 'in quest of sport': TFL MS/COLL/735: 9/20.
'socialists and liberals' were 'miserable worms': TFL MS/COLL/735: 9/20.
I had my triumph and made the most of it: TFL MS/COLL/735: 9/20.
'got me rooms at Oriel College': TFL MS/COLL/735: 9/20.
looking back through rose-tinted glasses: TFL MS/COLL/735: 9/21.
regarded all the women in the family as his slaves: Paul (2012: 1, 4); TFL MS/COLL/735: 13/5A.
a different girl coming every half hour: TFL MS/COLL/735: 13/5A.
used to go boating with Dodgson: TFL MS/COLL/735: 13/12B.
'continue to shake hands only': Paul (2012: 16).
Alice's Adventures in Wonderland, fondly inscribed: TFL MS/COLL/735: 13/9A.
the move is something of a mystery: TFL MS/COLL/735: 13/9A; Paul (2012: 16).
the Cambridge Association for Women's Suffrage: CA/455/Q1/Q2/Q3/Q12/Q13.
who made the Labour Party in Cambridge great: Manning (1970: 41).
Christmas day to serve plum pudding: TFL MS/COLL/735: 13/5A, 13/9A.
'good old Ginger' and 'good old Bertie': Manning (1970: 59–60).
Kim Philby and Guy Burgess: Boyle (1979).
the Tories were 'the stupid party': TFL MS/COLL/735: 13/22A.
with a powerful sense of humour: Chadwick (1998: 5).
such intimate matters with her children: TFL MS/COLL/735: 13/9A.
a kiss could cause a pregnancy: TFL MS/COLL/735: 9/9; Paul (2012: 18).
others saw her as formidable and over-bearing: TFL MS/COLL/735: 13/15B; 13/23A.
'the time and ability to show me how to do them': MCA F/oMP/IV/6/11: 32.
hire private tutors out of their own pocket: MCA F/oMP/IV/6/11: 52
coming fifth in the final examinations: TFL MS/COLL/735: 11.
Arthur Ramsey 'was all eye and moustache': Chadwick (1998: 4).
A.S.R. (Arthur Stanley Ramsey) to them: Simpson (1962: 63).
'"addressed anyone other than a relation by his Christian name"': Morshead (1995: 42).
after the first world war: MCA F/oMP/IV/6/11: 100.
Margaret asserted that he voted against the women: Paul (2012: 6).
play on the common, Jesus Green: TFL MS/COLL/735: 13/21A.
always in the same pew: TFL MS/COLL/735: 13/15B.
read the Bible as a family every morning: Simpson (1962: 37).
but never prohibited them: TFL MS/COLL/735: 13/9A.

sitting on the stage with Agnes: CA: 455/Q2.

Agnes was the dominating party: TFL MS/COLL/735: 13/26A.

'read at a fast dictation speed': TFL MS/COLL/735: 13/44A; 11.

the College prospered under his rod: TFL MS/COLL/735: 11.

'Resurgence of Magdalene College Cambridge': *The Times*, 3 Jan. 1955.

set against new notions and notations: TFL MS/COLL/735: 13/39B.

'by virtue of those very qualities': MCA Benson Diaries/143/51, Mar. 1914, also 156/24, Dec. 1915.

'a look of hatred' all too frequently from Arthur: MCA Benson Diaries/149/39, Dec. 1914.

indulgence in tobacco: MCA Benson Diaries/164/12–13, Feb. 1917.

'But of course he was Ramsey's pupil!': MCA Benson Diaries/143/53, Mar. 1914.

'contemptuous virtue and complacent commonsense': MCA Benson Diaries/121/18, Apr. 1911.

'the lower regions of the heart': MCA Benson Diaries/132/7, Aug. 1914.

he informally offered Arthur the Presidency: MCA Benson Diaries/156/32, Dec. 1915.

he sent for Arthur as he lay dying: Newsome (1980: 377).

real affection and tenderness: MCA Benson Diaries/174/45–46, May 1924.

walk out in a leonine sort of way and give one his paw: MCA Benson Diaries/164/Feb. 1917/21.

a belief in culture by his clever family: MCA Benson Diaries/174, Mar. 1924/13.

'despise the things which others understand': MCA Benson Diaries/156/27, Dec. 1915.

other people are comfortable: MCA Benson Diaries/145/10, May 1914; Dec. 1915; 20 Feb. 1917/1; 141/42, Nov. 1913.

Agnes sometimes left the table in tears: Paul (2012: 10).

run around the garden in an agitated state: TFL MS/COLL/735: 13/7B; Paul (2012: 13).

'if the conversation bored or displeased him': Paul (2012: 14).

dined in College two or three nights a week: TFL MS/COLL/735: 13/9B.

'piggyback trots' round the gardens: Simpson (1962: 35).

a bowl of light bulbs: Chadwick (1998: 6).

paragraph ending: the wall above the veranda: TFL MS/COLL/735: 13/5A; 13/5A; 9/9; 13/22A; 13/22B; 13/5A; 13/7B; 13/13B; 13/2B; 13/20A.

'old Professor Ramsey's home': TFL MS/COLL/735: 1/2.

a quiet and contained exterior: TFL MS/COLL/735: 13/36B.

other forms of high culture: TFL MS/COLL/735: 13/36A, 36B.

they welcomed me warmly and I'm glad I went: MCA Benson Diaries/172/10, Oct. 1924.

was unkind, but not unfair: TFL MS/COLL/735: 13/22A.

'you can't marry your mother till she's a widow?': Paul (2012: 23).

So he must be a conservative: MCA F/oMP/IV/6/11: 171.

'and made them harangue one another': MCA F/oMP/IV/6/11: 171.

and soft voices and accents: TFL MS/COLL/735: 9/9.

the terminology of disability used to describe it: Chadwick (1998: 7).

as a Winchester school friend put it: TFL MS/COLL/735: 13/27B.

it was time to go to Chapel: TFL MS/COLL/735: 13/9A; Simpson (1962: 35).

Agnes was understandably offended: TFL MS/COLL/735: 13/9A; Paul (2012: 104).

chortling when one came up which he had had before: MCA F/oMP/IV/6/11: 114.

billboards from his pram: KCA FPR 2/1/1.

teaching them French verbs: TFL MS/COLL/735: 13/23A.

rid the school of all frivolity and joy: TFL MS/COLL/735: 13/21A; 1/18; 1/19.

mostly delivered by Cambridge undergraduates: TFL MS/COLL/735: 9/11.

The boys were suitably impressed: TFL MS/COLL/735: 13/21A; 1/18.

'attention to sartorial matters had no place in his life': TFL MS/COLL/735: 1/18.

'intellectually he outshone us all': TFL MS/COLL/735: 1/19.

I am utterly miserable: Chadwick (1998: 9).

'whips lots of people': KCA FPR/2/1/1.

the boy had two strokes with a hard cricket stump: TFL MS/COLL/735: 13/31A.

'my tail-end was lamentably short of skin': TFL MS/COLL/735: 9/10.

'kind of friends with lots of boys': KCA FPR 2/1/1/.

eyes blinking whenever he had to take off his glasses: TFL MS/COLL/735: 1/18.

more about the result of the match than the examination: KCA FPR 2/1/1.

He ate and drank little. Then fled: MCA Benson Diaries/154/41, Aug. 1915]

the milk of human kindness in one human unit: KCA FPR/2/1/1.

'strenuous in all games': The Sandroyd, Summer Term, 1915.

eyes blinking through his specs: TFL MS/COLL/735: 1/25.

older boys, especially if they were pretty: TFL MS/COLL/735: 13/31B.

Frank discovered he was hopeless at it: TFL MS/COLL/735: 13/9A.

Chapter 2

those terrifying lists of names: Manning (1970: 52).

men in khaki and military carriages of all sorts: WCA. Report of Head Master, 1915.

where it grew to 1600 beds: MCA F/oMP/IV/6/11: 200, 205.

'I walked about with Brown a lot': KCA FPR/2/1/2.

great interest for boys of scholarly mind: Stevens (1998: xvi).

'punished in the traditional manner': TFL MS/COLL/735: 1/25.

'argument of the friendliest kind': TFL MS/COLL/735: 1/24.

father radical etc: WCA: Housemaster's Election Book, G5/1/118/134.

'Ramsey was an adult at the age of twelve': TFL MS/COLL/735: 1/25.

a bit remote and self-contained: TFL MS/COLL/735: 13/26A.

concerned about being part of a conversation or not: TFL MS/COLL/735: 13/18B.

an especially 'mucky meal': KCA FPR/2/1/2.

'it was always full of bristles': WCA Rex Herdman: Winchester: During and After the First World War, 1916–1921: 23–4.

from the school shop were always hungry: TFL MS/COLL/735: 1/23; 13/26A.

he remained hungry all his life: TFL MS/COLL/735: 1/23.

'I am having a ripping time', he reported: KCA FPR/2/1/2.

'for the sake of example': KCA FPR/2/1/2.

treated so badly in their chambers: TFL MS/COLL/735: 1/23.

'I thought he was fifteen.': MCA F/oMP/IV/6/11/208.

'O, Ramsey, Ramsey'!: KCA FPR/2/1/2.

'the masters simply taught': TFL MS/COLL/735: 13/28B.

better at washing up in hot water: TFL MS/COLL/735: 1/23; 13/23A; 13/28A.

beatings and spankings to their 'inferiors': TFL MS/COLL/735: 1/23.

serious offences such as stealing: TFL MS/COLL/735: 1/24.

'the nastiest man in College': KCA KCA FPR/2/1/2.

'a picturesque villain': TFL MS/COLL/735: 9/12.

easier for them to go to sleep: KCA FPR/2/1/2.

'did not agree with the new bedtime regime: TFL MS/COLL/735: 1/23.

and was not looked upon kindly: TFL MS/COLL/735: 1/24.

I yawned up to books which made him think I was tired !!!!!!??!?!?: KCA FPR/2/1/2.

'we had pupils resident here almost continuously': KCA FPR/2/1/2.

a 'butt', an object of teasing: TFL MS/COLL/735: 13/23A.

unusual boys tend to get picked on: TFL MS/COLL/735: 13/30A.

'even a year or two mattered very seriously': TFL MS/COLL/735: 1/22.

that we had never seen on any other boy: TFL MS/COLL/735: 13/31B.

'although I do not think that Frank did': TFL MS/COLL/735: 1/23.

Some of his classmates called him 'Frink': TFL MS/COLL/735: 13/28B; 1/22; 1/25.

'good natured chaffing': TFL MS/COLL/735: 13/28B, 13/23B, 13/26A; 13/30A; 1/22.

did not like being made fun of: TFL MS/COLL/735: 9/13.

whether the other boys were 'ragging' or teasing him: KCA FPR/2/1/2.

a 'real egghead'—a 'phenomenon': TFL MS/COLL/735: 13/31B.

I doubt if he had many close friends: TFL MS/COLL/735: 1/23.

a lifelong dislike of bullies: TFL MS/COLL/735: 13/9A, 9B.

hope he will have a good rest: KCA FPR/2/1/2.

'fairly when he gets the chance': WCA Canvas Book, 1919, F4/1/71.

ran the College sick-house: TFL MS/COLL/735: 1/23.

a loner, also became a friend: TFL MS/COLL/735: 13/30A.

the unpleasant gaze of suspicion: Siepmann (1955: 27).

Wanted to see her 'so badly': KCA/FPR/2/1/2.

would always feel paternal towards her: TFL MS/COLL/735: 9/9.

£100 to Arthur to tide him over: Newsome (1980: 324).

He is doing excellent work: KCA FPR/2/1/2.

the foundations of mathematics in the original: TFL MS/COLL/735: 9/14.

'his answers are sometimes too condensed': KCA FPR/2/1/2.

in the garden in his spare time—approved: GCA GCGB 5/2/2/1/1.

a new periodical, The Cambridge Magazine: Florence (1977: 16).

his magazine could go to press: Forrester and Cameron (2017: 116).

not to be 'egged' into war: Newsome (1980: 309).

'a king ping pong player': Black (2014: 49).

smuggled heroin in the heels of those shoes: TFL MS/COLL/735: 13/2A.

a reward for philosophical instruction: Warburg (1959: 93).

'His activity was immense': Warburg (1959: 92).

when annoyed, which was not unusual: Warburg (1959: 92).

preferable, as he would tell us, to the real article: Dora Russell (1975: 43).

Left about 11:30: TFL MS/COLL/735: 12.

his Magdalene undergraduate days: TFL MS/COLL/735: 13/4A.

a pillar in Trinity's Nevile's Court: Gardiner (1988: 71).

bursts of laughter at our astonishment: Richards (1977: 103).

substituted Kant's Critique of Pure Reason: Richards (1977: 103), Samuelson (1986 [1982]: 97).

It seems most disgraceful bullying but he is very brave: KCA FPR/2/1/2.

this went too far: Franke (2008: 78), Martin (1966: 106).

'raised considerable hump, especially off Vino': TFL MS/COLL/735: 12.

'Major Robertson can't prevent me by force': KCA FPR/2/1/2.

'Feel rather flattered': TFL MS/COLL/735: 12.

and remembered as highly unusual: TFL MS/COLL/735: 13/29A; 13/30A.

he was an exception to it: TFL MS/COLL/735: 13/36A.

'they all got to Frank without difficulty': TFL MS/COLL/735: 1/22.

stood at the gate shouting 'blacklegs!': TFL MS/COLL/735: 1/23.
would subscribe to socialism: TFL MS/COLL/735: 1/25.
'as I have often done in conversation': KCA FPR/2/1/2.
'a most formidable indictment of Bolshevism': WCA *The Wykehamist*, no. 580, 19 Feb. 1919:
    308–09; Winchester College Debating Society minute book.
defeated in the voting 34 to 18: TFL MS/COLL/735: 13/26A.
'accusations of Bolshevism': WCA*The Wykehamist*, no. 580, 19 Feb. 1919: 318.
further strikes were imminent: WCA *The Wykehamist*, no. 588 2 Dec. 1919: 415.
'a frontal attack on Trade Unions': WCA *The Wykehamist*, no. 589 16 Dec. 1919: 421.
not inclined to aggressive war: Paul (2012: 64).
'really cares about social questions': KCA FPR/2/1/2.
'always on the side of liberty': KCA FPR/2/1/2.
his own public school debates, at Repton: Chadwick (1990:12).
'teach Frank and Michael to dance on my grave!': TFL MS/COLL/735: 13/9A.
after Uncle Charlie disowning me as a nephew it seems unnecessary: KCA FPR/2/1/2.
and cricket ('made 19, took 5 wkts'): TFL MS/COLL/735: 12.
Lost a bet about Monty's letter: TFL MS/COLL/735: 13/21A.
tried to teach her maths: TFL MS/COLL/735: 13/9B.
'I should clamber to get to Germany': KCA FPR/2/1/2.
('slack bowels McDowell'): TFL MS/COLL/735: 13/23A.
Die Philosophischen Prinzipien der Mathematik: KCA FPR/2/1/2.
'we ought to help them do it better, not fight them': KCA FPR/2/1/2.
he would become an economist: TFL MS/COLL/735: 9/11.
Weyl's *Raum, Zeit, Materie*, and much else: TFL MS/COLL/735: 12.
'a good deal for 5 weeks': KCA FPR/2/1/2.
the abstract and concrete questions: KCA FPR/2/1/2.
He then crossed them out: TFL MS/COLL/735: 12.
Peterhouse, Queens', and Magdalene: KCA FPR/2/1/2.
making the examiners 'feel small': KCA FPR/2/1/3.
as he did Asquith for being 'solitary': KCA FPR/2/1/3.
'There seems little to say except what I read': KCA FPR/2/1/3.
he admitted he could be proved wrong: TFL MS/COLL/735: 12.
when all life lies before him: KCA FPR/2/1/3.

Chapter 3

'We really live in a great time for thinking': KCA FPR/5/2/.
argue with *him* than at crushing *you*: Keynes (1972 [1938]: 438).
'now an academic figure at Cambridge': Bell, A. (1977: 280).
'a disregard for other people's opinions': Bell, C. (1956: 48).
'abler than he was': Blanshard (1980: 80–82).
a 'puritan and a precisian': Keynes (1972 [1938]): 435.
wrote invisibly on the blackboard with his finger: Gardiner (1988: 69).
three contradictory senses in a single page: Martin (1966: 101–2).
'even how contemptible': Moore (1899: 181).
'but must be immediately recognised': Moore (1899: 180).
never, by any definition, make their nature known: Moore (2004 [1903]: 7).

what Moore called the 'Naturalistic Fallacy': Moore (2004 [1903]: 9–10).

shines like a sword between the lines: Holroyd (2011: 90).

'the opening of a new heaven on a new earth': Keynes (1972 [1938]): 435.

the way they conducted their lives: Woolf (1960: 148). See also Bell, C.(1956).

useless and impossible to argue: Keynes (1972 [1938]: 436–37).

various topics of philosophy were...the orthodoxy: Braithwaite (1933: 1).

'a kind of reality not belonging to anything else': Russell (1986 [1918]: 234).

Paragraph ending: 'that truth might be analysed as one of those incomplete symbols or expressions': Russell (1906: 46); EBR; TS.

'pathological state of agitation': Rhees (1981: 2).

abandon engineering to study with Russell: Monk (1990: 30–35).

his lectures were bad: McGuinness (1988: 141).

I understood his state of mind: Hermine Wittgenstein (1981: 5).

'he has accomplished nothing and never will': Monk (1990: 65).

don't let yourself be put off by that: MCI: 86.

supplied many of the theories contained in them: Russell (1986 [1918]: 160).

God bless you: WCL: 88.

I *could* come to you I would do it: WCL: 89.

and so was not much use: WCL: 101.

'to Russell through me': WCL: 90.

'a very thorough explanation': WCL: 91.

even if it does get printed!: WCL: 93.

'thinking the book of first-class importance': WCL: 96.

more severe and intense: TFL MS/COLL/735: 13/37A.

'It is VERY hard not to be understood by a single soul!': WCL: 98.

he has become a complete mystic: WCL: 112.

Weyl's *Raum, Zeit, Materie*: KCA FPR/1/1/1; TFL MS/COLL/735: 12.

does the barber shave himself?: Russell (1986 [1918]: 228).

this volume was nearing completion: Frege (2013 [1893, 1903]: 253).

'may yet be literally nonsense': EBFM: 83.

To the laws of logic: Frege (2013[1893, 1903]).

Frege's definition of numbers: Whitehead and Russell (1910–13); see Russell (1919) for an accessible introduction.

Chapter 4

marked in some way: TCL Rec 22.5, 6–8.

It was too much: Macmillan (1973).

'he was much younger than anybody else there': TFL MS/COLL/735: 13/39B.

lasting depression and breakdown: Wright (2010: 42); TFL MS/COLL/735: 9/17.

shaking a misbehaving student: TFL MS/COLL/735: 13/6A.

shirked their duty during the war: TFL MS/COLL/735: 13/40A.

huddled together for self-protection: TFL MS/COLL/735: 13/41A.

'We had had the war to end all wars': TFL MS/COLL/735: 13/35B.

My time at Newnham was spent dancing: 'Cambridge's Own First Lady,' *The Times*, c. 1969; reprinted online at <http://www.stephenburch.com/lettice/lettice.htm>

'all we cared about in our partners was their technical ability': Chisholm (2009: 32).

their agonized love affairs: TFL MS/COLL/735: 13/4B.

conduct, politics, and literature: Woolf (1966 [1924]: 320–21).

would have made their parents faint: Nicholson (2003).

felt 'free and authentic': Gardiner (1988: 62–3).

kept Magdalene's outdated requirement in place: Lambeth Palace Archives, Ramsey 1: 7.

'a remarkable young man has just come up': TFL MS/COLL/735: 9/19.

'total disregard of the conventions': Gardiner (1988: 61); Wright (2010: 49–50).

'he was profoundly influenced by him': Cameron and Forrester (2008: 199).

an intellectual, but a friendly one: TFL MS/COLL/735: 13/35B.

lording it over anyone: TFL MS/COLL/735: 9/11.

the Russian dancer Lydia Lopokova: Skidelsky (1992: 35); Chisholm (2009: 35, 104).

cant and flapdoodle: KCA FCP 8/4/1.

he was still in his teens: Martin (1966: 108–9).

one set of shabby clothing: Martin (1966: 90); Rolph (1973: 68).

his Marxist convictions: Boyle (1979: 47); see also Brown (2005: 26).

inherited his wei-chi board: TFL MS/COLL/735: 9/8.

recollected no personal contact: TFL MS/COLL/735: 2/1–4.

integrated with the rest of the family: TFL MS/COLL/735: 13/21B.

'hold himself in readiness to play at short notice anytime': KCA FPR/5/2.

moved quite fast for a large man: TFL MS/COLL/735: 13/2B.

Russell, who was living in London, but coming to Cambridge on occasion: KCA FPR/4/1.

'always provide him with something to work at': MCA F/oMP/IV/6/11: 226.

'is merely a collection of standardized puzzles': TCL Rec.11.1

a 'sideshow', as his brother put it: TFL MS/COLL/735: 13/21B.

through his Cambridge connections: TFL MS/COLL/735.

An occasional guest at Howfield: TFL MS/COLL/735: 8/8) 13/22A.

'the course was not a success and he gave it up': KCA FPR/5/2/259.

he could avoid his father's lectures: TFL MS/COLL/735:/9/8.

Frank's supervisor for analysis: KCA FPR/5/2/263.

the edge of a sheer cliff: Dora Russell (1975: 74).

make up for idleness last term: KCA FPR/1/1/1.

'an Intuitionist proper': KCA FPR/1/1/1.

Guild Socialism gets an excited paragraph: KCA FPR/1/1/1.

and not the form of Government: Martin (1966: 111).

the government moved to 'smash the unions': Martin (1966: 114, 161).

'Am sceptical about class war theory': KCA FPR/1/1/1.

spend time with the speaker afterwards: KCA FPR/1/1/1.

proportions in which the various parties are represented: ASP/FPR.1983.01: 006-07-09.

the quarterly meeting to-morrow evening: KCA FPR/1/1/1.

the assistants 'fear the sack': ASP/FPR.1983.01: 006-07-05.

'Douglas Credit Power and Democracy. Seems confused rubbish': KCA FPR/1/1/1.

'almost word perfect' on Russell: TFL MS/COLL/735: 13/42A, 43A.

'that ghastly shit McTaggart': Delany (1986: 44).

'as Richards and Ogden will be there arguing': TS: 380; KCA FPR/1/1/1.

indicates my insertion: ASP/FPR.1983.01:7 007-01-01.

the best claim to correctness: Braithwaite (1970 [1961]: 25).

a concept that applies to nothing: ASP/FPR.1983.01: 7 007-01-19.

a new sort of logical construction. [l.c.]: ASP/FPR.1983.01: 7 007-01-84.

'[...infinitely divisible as they are spatially]': ASP/FPR.1983.01: 7 007-01-103, 106.

of which I was quite unconscious: Moore (1968 [1942]: 35).

will I suppose stir me up: KCA FPR/1/1/1.

'finding anyone who could say whether it was correct or not': KCA FPR/2/1/3.

an additional 'mark of distinction': Ordinances of the University of Cambridge, 1920: 78–83.

joining the elite London clubs: TFL MS/COLL/735: 13/32B.

'run to the lavatory instead of speaking': Martin (1966: 96).

the Union was largely a waste of time: KCA FPR/1/1/1.

But that too didn't last long: TCL Rec.13.5.

'That Democracy is the Rule of Force and Fraud': TCL Rec 8.10, 122, 160.

merely for the 'recognition': KCA FPR/1/1/1.

'to argue with Dobb': KCA FPR/1/1/1.

their meetings were on Sunday nights: Russell (1977: 83).

200 undergraduates were members: Franke (2008: 56).

was a frequent attendee: TFL MS/COLL/735: 9/11.

chain-smoking, direct-speaking path: Niehans (1990: 304), Scitovsky (2002 [1989]: 63).

it will never be found again: Dora Russell (1975: 43).

'match her attitude to her audience': Gardiner (1988: 75).

I think he's great: KCA FPR/1/1/1.

but simply an 'emotional aura': Ogden and Richards (1923: 125n).

his own criticisms of Moore from Ramsey: TFL MS/COLL/735: 13/41B, 42B.

'the assumption of a rational economic man': Sargant Florence (1968: 237).

he would have to ask her as well: TFL MS/COLL/735: 13/13A.

'stuck in my gizzard as a student': Joan Robinson (1978: x).

finding the pages completely blank: Martin (1966: 108).

Miss Baker and Sprott are Moral Scientists: KCA FPR/1/1/1.

the effort of answering a question: TFL MS/COLL/735: 13/11A.

interacting mostly with his colleagues at Trinity: TFL MS/COLL/735: 13/42B.

waiting list constructed for those deemed also worthy: KCA RFK/3/15/3; TFL MS/COLL/735: 13/42A; KCA RFK/3/15/8.

where they were right and wrong: TFL MS/COLL/735: 13/42A.

'could be rather devastating if people advanced silly views': Blaug (1990: 42).

Keynes would sum up in friendly but utterly devastating fashion: Robinson (1947: 27).

the final word in conversations: TFL MS/COLL/735: 13/40A.

domestic mystification or even discord: TFL MS/COLL/735: 1/13.

'the society of equals enjoying each other's foibles': Woolf (1940: 51).

corporate bond which I have known in my life: Sidgwick and Sidgwick (1906: 34–35).

detachment and interest scarcely possible in later life: Russell (2000 [1967]: 58).

very nice and liking the society: BL Add MS 60712: 78.

which was politely declined: See Paskauskas (1993: 498, 500).

you ought to be able to get rid of guilt: Martin (1966: 110).

Russia had an oral fixation, and so on: BK Martin Papers, 9.

'perhaps we were not really "directing ourselves" at all': Martin (1966: 112).

'As philosophy, no: as a penny dreadful, yes': KCA KCAS/39/1/16.

the 'task of alleviating the suffering of humanity': ASP/FPR.1983.01: 007-06-01.

'Deteriora sequor': KCA KCAS/39/1/16.

'Socialism and Equality of Income': ASP/FPR.1983.01: 007-06-04.

declared the Society a complete waste of time: KCA JMK/PP/45/349/12.

'had not yet made their toilets': Monk (1990: 67).

'sheer love of argument seemed to him intolerable': McGuinness (2006: 19).
What will happen I don't know: BL/Add/MS/60732, 32–3.
had been in 1855: Levy (2005: 50).
the idea of telling the unpopular truth: Martin (1966: 109).
'up and down a Lake District peak each day, just for the fun of the thing': Martin (1966: 69).
various states of emotional disturbance: BK Martin Collection, Sussex University. 7/10.
the rest of us into Germany: KCA FPR/2/1/3.
the sharp sword of Cambridge intellectualism: Martin (1966: 110).
'always very pessimistic on the subject of holidays': Paul (2012: 105).
pink Frank were always showing through: Martin (1966: 109).
his Italian was quite good: TFL MS/COLL/735: 13/2B.
Peano in the original: TFL MS/COLL/735: 13/2B.
'without drying and stayed in them all evening!': Paul (2012: 136).
guided them over the frontier the next day: BTTS; TFL MS/COLL/735: 9/8.
he had a very simple character: TFL MS/COLL/735: 13/21B.
without being accompanied by a desire of getting ahead: TFL MS/COLL/735: 13/22A.
'recognized as able than to be able': KCA FPR/1/1/1.
guts to talk to a doctor: KCA FPR/2/1/1.
relieves the sexual impulse: Courtesy of Stephen Burch.
much older in many ways: Rolph (1973: 92).
kinds of judgments were entirely subjective: TFL MS/COLL/735: 13/41B.

Chapter 5

a peculiar and decisive authority: *The Cambridge Review*, 31 Jan. 1930, p. 216.
he would just point it out: TFL MS/COLL/735: 13/40A.
advanced some way into mathematics: Harrod (1951: 321).
his manuscript back when you have finished with it: KCA JMK/TP/1/1/19.
'cannot remember before the war': KCA JMK/TP/1/1/19.
made the same mistake each time: KCA JMK TP/1/1/19.
invited them to lunches in his rooms: TFL MS/COLL/735: 13/33A.
Cambridge should be renamed 'Keynesbridge': Martin (1966: 103).
'it is impossible to praise too highly': Russell (1922b: 119, 125).
'the very continuous chain...of Cambridge thought': Moggridge (1992: 364).
'probability-relation in terms of simpler ideas': Keynes (1973 [1921]: 8).
each of these alternatives have an *equal* probability: Keynes (1973 [1921]: 44–45).
'shook my beliefs about it': TFL MS/COLL/735: 13/41A.
'Napoleon was a great general': KP: 220.
strange correspondence with degrees of belief: NPPM: 274.
was his first target: CN 473.
'relates any two given propositions': TP: 57.
'hypothetical degree of belief': TP: 59.
logical relation between them that constitutes such support: Bateman (1996: 62ff.).
evidently may not be true: ASP/FPR.1983.01: 007-06-02.
the failure of attempts of formulate it, is hardly good enough: ASP/FPR.1983.01: 007-06-02.
'nothing to distinguish the wise man from the fool': ASP/FPR.1983.01: 007-06-02.
Rylands voted No: KCA KCAS/39/1/16.
the theory becomes vague and muddled: ASP/FPR.1983.01: 007-06-02.

'more plausible psychologically': KCA JMK/TP/1/1/19.
induction being reasonable this is a reasonable argument: ASP/FPR.1983.01: 007-06-02.
I feel great confidence that they are wrong: Moggridge (1992: 364–65).
'which caused the stitches to run': Bell, C. (1956: 59).
Keynes felt that he had a satisfactory answer to it: Harrod (1951: 141).
'not too technical for a valuable discussion': CUL/Min.IX.42.
'so unlike anything else in the world': NP: 112.
(... forward to the future) to be related: NP: 109.
'no proposition entertainable by us can be infinitely complex': NP: 109.
each of which is 'of great importance': NP: 110.
'referential characters or references': NP: 110.
point to an objective proposition: NP: 113.
'only pretends to have analysed' them: NP: 113.
hoped the paper would be published: KCA/FPR/1/1.
'p coheres' are not equivalent to 'p': NP: 118.
the prosentential theory: Hacker (1996: 71); Baldwin (2013: 444); Frápolli (2005).
belief in this way is awfully difficult: KCA FPR 4/1; TS.
a mysterious entity not easy to identify: ASP/FPR.1983.01: 007-06-02.
Zion in defense of his economic theories: Soifer (2009: 293).
were suspicious: See, for instance, *Guildsman*, Feb. 1921.
'he thought that Bertrand Russell should be told of it': Cole (1920).
£100, a huge amount at the time: TFL MS/COLL/735: 13/2A.
agreed with Douglas that 'capitalism is obnoxious': ASP/FPR.1983.01: 004-10-02.
'the capitalistic system and of Labour itself': ASP/FPR.1983.01: 004-10-02.
If he convinces the Almighty he may get his way: ASP/FPR.1983.01: 004-10-02.
'diminishes A by precisely the amount it increases it': ASP/FPR.1983.01: 004-10-02.
'is always obscure and often absurd': DP: 335.
'flaw in the Douglas argument': DP: 336; DP 335.
and the ratio is unity: DP: 336–7.
being paid at time T: DP 338.
a quarter of cost price: DP 339–40.
Ramsey wrote to the editor (Ogden): OF Ramsey letter dated 30/1/22.
trouncing of Douglas in the *New Statesman*: Dobb (1922).
notice that he was exceptional: TFL MS/COLL/735: 13/41B.
'Ramsey's complicated mathematical analysis': Hiskett and Franklin (1939: vii).
not to waste his pounds: KCA FPR/5/2/295; 310.
I'm thinking of giving a week to those problems: TFL MS/COLL/735: 4/15.

Chapter 6

but I can't help believing it: WCL:89).
'a Spinozistic ring': MBP/14/21/2466/5.
'your conscience will allow you to': WCL: 100.
that will be a judgment too: WCL: 118.
with Russell on his *Principia* in 1916: Lenzen (1971).
I mean the sort of thing in the enclosed...: von Wright (1973: 3).
to write a thick book: WCL: 137.

'Ramsey will say "all wrong" now leaving us all alone in our opinions': OF: Box 59.

'difficulties which their victims are trying to solve': RMM:109.

studying [in *The Meaning of Meaning*]: Richards (1977: 102).

clear that there was a possibility: BTTS.

'the Trinity mathematical prodigy': LWG: From Charles K. Ogden 3.5, 1922.

'he meant by it, but he'd forgotten': MBP/14/21/2466/19/129–30.

'as regards translation of terms': WCL: 130.

in the dark about the translation: TFL MS/COLL/735: 13: 42A.

a shorthand writer who then typed it up: KCA FPR/5/2/316.

Ogden was at his side: McGuinness (1988: 298).

despite having 'an awful job': von Wright (1973: 21).

'equal authority with the original': McGuinness (1988: 298).

he had not been at all involved in the process: TFL MS/COLL/735: 13: 41A.

'Wittgenstein in Red': letters 19 Jan., 9 Feb., 23 Feb., 16 Mar., 18 Mar., 13 Apr., 27 Apr., 18 May, and 8 June 1962; 18 Feb., 7 Mar., 11 Mar., 18 Mar., and 15 Apr., 1965; 31 Oct. 1968; and 9 Oct. 1970.

'a more exact translation': von Wright (1973: 10); letter quoted in the TLS correspondence, 18 May 1962 and 18 Mar. 1965.

philosophy was just as he wanted: BL RP 6160 (iii)/47; T: 2.15.

Published the correspondence: von Wright (1973).

preparation of the book for the press: T, prefatory note.

They didn't answer: von Wright 1973: 73, Brian McGuinness conversation.

since Kant's *Critique of Pure Reason*: See the letter published in Besomi (2003: 35).

discussions at Cambridge since it was written: KCA JMK/PP/45/349/25.

paragraph ending: 'it cannot be *said*, but shows itself': T 1.2; 2–2.13; 2.221; 2.222; 2.1511–1515, 2.21; 2.061; 5.632–633, 5.2; 5.6; 5.64; 5.62.

it is raining or not raining: T 4.461.

complex propositions from simple ones: T 4.461.

paragraph ending: would remain a sticking point: T 6.375; 6.2; 6. 13; 6.2341; 6.24; von Wright (1973: 44).

paragraph ending: it is the mystical: T 6.41; 6.42; 6.421, 6.432; 6.521–22.

'*palpably* on that of the elementary propositions': T 4.411.

paragraph ending: 'networks' to describe the world: T 5.1361; 6.341; 6.35.

the only strictly correct method: T 6.53.

thereof one must be silent: T 6.53–7.

paragraph ending: that might clarify thoughts: T 4.113–14; 4.112.

'evident that there is no such problem': CN: 469.

'and false if ¬p': CN: 469.

'logically completely in order': T: 5.5563.

and the structure of the fact: CN: 465.

if you break them you are not playing bridge': P: 7.

'common between the picture and the world': CN: 468.

'intrinsically impossible to discuss': CN: 468.

the only impossibility that of contradiction': CN: 473.

opaque and blurred: T: 4.112.

'without some further explanation of "clarity"'. CN: 4.76.

completely analysed elementary proposition: CN: 469.

'these constitute the Mystical': CN: 472.

and Ramsey's Critical Notice: TFL MS/COLL/735: 13/43A.
on Wittgenstein, at least up until 1929: MCI: 223.
'easily the best candidate': MCA F/oMP/IV/6/11: 228.
a first in either or both: MCA F/oMP/IV/6/11: 228.
the rest of this one in German: WCL: 139.
his general appearance is athletic: KCA FPR/2/1/3.
Ludwig introduced him to his friend the pianist Rudolf Koder: LWG: To Rudolf Koder 24.2.1929.
'they are part of the symbolism': TFL MS/COLL/735: 5.
fifty-five pages of notes and reflections: Josef Rothhaupt (1996: 46) argues that items 002-29-01,
    002-28-01, 002-27-01, and 002-26-01 in the Ramsey Papers constitute these notes.
a great man but beside W!: KCA FPR/2/1/3.
stand up to his uncle: TFL MS/COLL/735: 13/37A, 36A.
more difficult meaning which he also believes: KCA FPR/2/1/3.
he had done with Russell before the war: Monk (1990: 217).
the Tractatus, which then you can have: LWG: To Hermine Wittgenstein, Sep. or Oct. 1923.
    Michael Nedo translation.
decide certainly to send it to him: KCA FPR/2/1/3.
very much wants to see you again: WCL: 145.
'Keynes has never written to W': KCA FPR/2/1/3.
you could come into society gradually: WCL: 145.
'to get into any trouble': LWG: From Frank Plumpton Ramsey: 27.12.1923.
'Peirce, who is surprising good in parts': KCA FPR 1/1/1.
the whole volume, taking extensive notes: ASP/FPR.1983.01: 005-30-01.
'doubt in our hearts': ASP/FPR.1983.01: 005-30-01.
'because his personality is different': Schiller (1939: 178).
truth and reality are 'wholly plastic': Schiller (1902: 61).
'genuinely new' point to be its theory of truth: James (1975–88, vol. 1: 260–1; 1907).
Good bye, Russell! : James (1975–88, vol. 12: 379; 1909).
a whole at all. Bah! : James (1975–88, vol. 11: 538–9; 1908).
one that would be 'indefeasible': Peirce (1931–58, vol. 6: §485; 1908).
not 'extraneous to the facts': Peirce (1982–, vol. 3: 253; 1877).

Chapter 7

'nice, but religious': KCA FPR/2/1/1/.
Maynard Keynes's rooms in King's: Martin (1966: 102).
the clever talk about art: TFL MS/COLL/735: 14A.
Newman said that he was far too serious for that: TFL MS/COLL/735: 13/6A.
mine her Cambridge acquaintances for this use: Nicolson (1977: 386, 374, 379, 383, 572–73).
modelled after Frank and his wife Lettice: Meisel and Kendrick (1985: 19); Rosenbaum (2015
    [1995]: 179).
'egregiously academic types' in To the Lighthouse: Meisel and Kendrick (1985: 19).
Honest I should say, a true Apostle: Bell, A. (1978: 231).
other 'young and brilliant people': Bell, Q. (1972: 90).
thought Strachey's book 'very amusing indeed': TFL MS/COLL/735: 13/2A.
'common bond of Cambridge intellectuals': Martin (1966: 102).
Bernal put it, was the new religion: Brown (2005: 41).

write probably less to you: Paul (2012: 140).

the side of the great ox Ramsey: Paul (2012: 140).

Yours fraternally, Frank Ramsey: BL/Add/MS/60692 8. f. 54.

'Wish she were more sensible': KCA FPR/1/1/1.

'the sharpness of his intellect': TFL MS/COLL/735: 13/40A.

and done a fair amount of work: WCL: 143.

a good civil service job during the war: Hemming (2015: 112).

They were well-known in Cambridge: Brown (2005: 59).

knew and admired her: TFL MS/COLL/735: 8/9; TFL MS/COLL/735: 13/9A.

his obedience to strict laws: Hemming (2015: 118).

'Jew Hunt!' or 'Pyke hunt!': Hemming (2015:119).

'SUFFERING IN A PRISON CELL': The Daily Chronicle, Monday, 26 July 1915.

more convinced that he was a German spy: Hemming (2015: 6).

no censure, no punishment: Hemming (2015: 133ff.).

make her name in educational theory: Hemming (2015: 151).

fit into any other establishment: TFL MS/COLL/735: 9/26.

'Timmy, please do not insert that stick in Stanley's eye': Meisel and Kendrick (1985: 205).

whopping bill delivered to his parents: TFL MS/COLL/735: 9/26.

'How can we make you make us do what we don't want to do?': Gardiner (1988: 73).

a wonderful time at her tennis parties: TFL MS/COLL/735: 13/2B, 43A.

with 'a perfect classical profile': TFL MS/COLL/735: 13/2A.

with David in the garden at Howfield: TFL MS/COLL/735: 13/5A.

'Do you think once would make any difference?': KCA FPR/1/1/1.

with some frequency been portrayed as such: Hemming (2015) and Forrester (2004).

and David made his inspection: Gardiner (1988: 72).

'He felt he had no property rights in her': KCA FPR/1/1/1.

Glover prescribed a 'sleeping draught': KCA FPR/1/1/1.

'I decided to stop it and go back to sea': KCA FPR/1/1/1.

'the meaning of life and his relation to other people': KCA FPR/2/1/3.

nice to me during my trip[os]: KCA FPR/1/1/1.

coming first in Schedule B: Paul (2012: 140); KCA 5/2/43.

try to accumulate it: KCA FPR/2/1/3.

came to giving him some teaching: KCA FPR/1/1/1.

Frank's fondness for his wife: TFL MS/COLL/735: 9/11.

'the only unoriginal thing he had ever done': Hemming (2015: 3).

'seemed to think it might be a good idea': KCA FPR/1/1/1.

'things of which I should be ashamed': KCA FPR/1/1/1.

and last, not to do them: KCA FPR/1/1/1.

his son 'was not very happy himself': KCA FPR/S/2/336.

'some other more unsatisfactory attachment': KCA WJHS/85.

But I'm afraid you won't agree with this: WCL: 147.

'he came in sight and recognized me': KCA FPR/2/1/3.

seven years writing his book: KCA FPR/2/1/3.

an appointment was far from certain: KCA FPR/1/1/1.

'merely doing it to avoid starvation': KCA FPR/1/1/1.

after a Commemoration Dinner: CUL/Ms Add. 8330 8R/3/1.

'more responsive than ever before': KCA WJHS/85.

but only a little 'unbalanced': TFL MS/COLL/735: 13/4B.

forty per cent of his patient load: Forrester (2004: 3).
nice, as I like them: KCA FPR/5/2/393.
'the great psychoanalyst Dr. Wilhelm Stekel': TFL/Coxeter Fonds/B 2006-0023/003.
elected to a King's Fellowship in mathematics: KCA FPR/5/2/347.
poured them wine till 3 am: KCA FPR/5/2/347-51.
after a little I lost my fear: KCA WJHS/85.
he would contract gonorrhoea: LRA.
going to the opera almost every night: TFL MS/COLL/735: 13/10A.
chess in their heads, no board needed: Gardiner (1988: 62).
a mathematics undergraduate at Trinity: WCL: 145.
as exhausting and intense as her brother: KCA FPR/5/2/361.
fallen in love with Wittgenstein's powerful sister': McGuinness (2006:19).
they had anything like an affair: Brian McGuinness conversation.
his boyishness and mothered him a bit: TFL MS/COLL/735: 13/36B, 37B.
'the feeling of superiority towards foreigners': TFL MS/COLL/735: 13/36B.
'his colleagues have so often been demonstrated': Paskauskas (1993: 732, 272).
analytically, that all was for the best: Meisel and Kendrick (1985: 86).
prejudice against foreigners I think: KCA FPR/5/2/347-8.
Das Trauma der Geburt. It is superb: KCA WJHS/85.
'a Jew (but all the good ones are)': KCA FPR/5/2/349.
a disagreeable joke about his nose: Paul (2012: 167).
'was then substantial if superficial': Warburg (1959: 30).
'something to be said for Flora Woolf': Bell, A. (1977: 6).
the Irish different, and not in a good way: KCA FPR/2/2/1/4.
saying violently anti-Semitic things: See Skidelsky (1992: 238f.).
on the basis of political and religious affiliation: KCA FPR/5/2/418.
out of Vienna and support them upon arrival: See Edmonds (2020).
'serious conversation is almost impossible': KCA WHJS/85.
no critical capacity or commonsense!: KCA FPR/2/350.
a dream of family conflict: Cameron and Forrester (2008: 200).
inductive reasoning was where the erotic resided: Penrose (1927).
and oh! I like him awfully: Paul (2012: 172).
juggling with words, and his quick, satirical wit: Bowra (1966: 272).
encounter them only once, for a few minutes: KCA FPR/5/2/407.
took this to be a flaw in his character: Paul (2012: 174).
one of Tehran's most expensive hotels: Mitchell (2009: 130).
imitate a sergeant major superbly: Paul (2012: 172).
Theory of Functions of a Complex Variable: KCA FPR/5/2/364.
'he didn't seem to me much of a philosopher, but a very nice man': KCA FPR 5/5/434.
as exhausting now as it was at first: KCA FPR/5/2/362.
argue much but go on to something else: KCA FPR/5/2/359-372.
'I'm quite happy you needn't worry': KCA FPR/5/2/416.
don't want to go on but can't stop...: KCA WJHS/85.
you get bored with the subject: TFL MS/COLL/735: 13/18A.
'disgust and repugnance at them': Tansley (1925: 567).
by choice on the wild side: Sargant Florence (1968: 228).
The verdict as to its death: under-nourishment: Wright (2010: 47).
he was weaned, and so on: KCA FPR/5/2/395.

'I mean, any longer than a day or two': KCA FPR/5/2/397.
'but that isn't psychoanalysis': KCA FPR/5/2/347.
exaggerated importance to his every word: NPPM: 320.
'I am slightly attracted to him physically': KCA/WJHS/85.
ill written and unintelligible and unconvincing: KCA FPR/5/2/467.
the least idea how he did it: KCA FPR/5/2/372.
be careful and take stock of yourself: KCA FPR/5/2/415-16.
people were as complicated as that: TFL MS/COLL/735: 13/43B.
to be so wise and to be unphilosophical: KCA JMK/PP/45/190/1/123.
the most selfish man he had ever met: TFL MS/COLL/735: 13/2A.
As Tommy put it, 'He was not tolerant': TFL MS/COLL/735: 13/37A.
dominate and who would imitate him: TFL MS/COLL/735: 13/37A.
wangled for him: Ground and Flowers (2016: 163).
the mainstay of our conversation: WCL: 150.
pushing something too heavy uphill: KCA FPR/2/360.
But he is no good for my work: KCA FPR/5/2/398.
he talked on his old lines: WCL: 147.
(and to the kindred Berlin Circle): Christoph Limbeck-Lilienau uncovered the story and
    translated the relevant letters.
very intelligent and sophisticated mind: ASP/HR-016-42-16.
'during his last stay in Vienna': EC: 21–599.
'would certainly be kind enough to arrange for some copies': VCA: 123/Wittg-1.
'as Mr. Ramsey tells me': BRA: M31.
'deepest' work of 'the new philosophy': EC: 21–599.
'The totality of true propositions is the total natural science': T 2.223, 4.11.
pseudo-propositions, devoid of content: Carnap (1963: 25).
'new theories of propositions and their relations to facts': CUL/BOGS 2 1920-37/1925.
same idiocies at one indefinitely: KCA WHJS/85.
'He is a very clever Jew, amusing and interesting': KCA FPR/5/2/454.
There was no ground at all in front!: KCA FPR/5/2/455.
a frightening ledge, again, with any misstep a fatal one: TFL MS/COLL/735: 13/22B.
All of which seems fairly reasonable: Meisel and Kendrick (1985: 112).
'we couldn't have gone deeper': Meisel and Kendrick (1985: 108).
which she declined: Meisel and Kendrick (1985: 107); Hemming 2015: 138).
stopped some from repeating it: Forrester and Cameron (2017: 401).
forbidden Frank from writing to her during his time in Vienna: KCA FPR/5/2/375.
Perhaps we'd better all go on to Reik: Meisel and Kendrick (1985: 157).
'something definite within two or three weeks': KCA FPR/5/2/400.
£300 coming when he received the Fellowship: KCA FPR/5/2/402.
and don't seem likely to just yet: KCA FPR/5/2/403.
the ability to snap someone up like that: TFL MS/COLL/735: 13/41B.
he upset the natural order of things: TFL MS/COLL/735: 9/16.
Carried Ayes 12. No 1: KCA KCGB/6/14/1/3.
advertised the first external Fellowship: Wilkinson (1980: 82).
and out of sorts, in second place: Rolph (1973: 107); TFL MS/COLL/735/13/2A.
'fearing pedantic interpretation of our statutes': Wilkinson (1980: 100).
'there had been some terribly anxious moments': KCA FPR/5/2/404.
'Frank Ramsey to a fellowship, which satisfies me': KCA JMK/PP/45/190/1/134.

filling a Fellowship when one became vacant: KCA KCGB/5/1/4/9.
'at King's starting with this coming term': von Wright (1973: 86).
'there is no vacant fellowship yet but will be in a few months': KCA FPR/5/2/404.
Carried. Ayes 11, Noes 1: KCA KCGB/6/14/1/3.
the youngest University Lecturer in the Faculty of Mathematics: CUL/Comm B.7.3.
what its like lecturing, how fast I go etc: KCA FPR/5/2/469.

Chapter 8

so far I've only had one year: KCA FPR/5/2/446.
'(and all in Germany or Austria, those foes of civilization!)': KCA FPR/5/2/446.
as the generation he criticized dies: WCL: 145.
without breakfast; a very hard day's work: KCA FPR/1/1/1.
the American logician Henry Sheffer: KCA FPR/1/1/1.
'Why not put Wittgenstein into the bibliography?': BR 9/22/24, BR 8 12/3/24, BR 9 12/23/24.
'contributed valuable criticisms and suggestions': Whitehead and Russell (1925: xiii).
'put in the Axiom of Reducibility': von Wright (1973: 84).
'deserted altogether its line of approach': FM: 164.
take no account of Wittgenstein's work at all: CUL/Ms Add. 8330 8R/3/1.
'such parts of Wittgenstein that I want to use for my own stuff': KCA FPR/5/2/464.
difficulties generated by the paradoxes: FM: 184, 187.
the 'doubtful' axiom of reducibility: CUL/Ms Add. 8330/8R/3.
as much 'ordinary meaning' as any other concept: FM: 165.
'the methods fail to conform to their private prejudices': FM: 166.
'there is no reason whatever to suppose it true': FM: 174–75; ML: 228.
all were examples of a vicious-circle principle: FM: 187.
'faulty ideas concerning thought and language': FM: 184.
though Wittgenstein himself didn't accept it: PPO: 336.
(we don't know which) 'may be wrong': KCA FPR/2/2/1.
'I corrected the proofs 2 days ago': KCA FPR/2/1/3.
'some obstinate difficulties': KCA JMK/L/26/56.
'won't perhaps do for the Smith's prize': KCA JMK/L/26/23/73-74.
to look at the matter in a new way: KCA JMK/L/26/56.
'who the hell was the expert that they had consulted!': TFL MS/COLL/735: 13/16A.
he didn't care much about the Smith's Prize: KCA 2/2/1.
knows enough about it to give me useful advice: TFL MS/COLL/735: 4/15.
'he might help to get it published': KCA 2/2/1.
'to send him it with Russell's letter': KCA 2/2/1.
fourteen pages of close notes on the paper: TCL Broad C1/64.
definition of logic as tautology to mathematics: Russell (1931: 477).
'highly interesting article in the London Math Soc': KCA FPR/2/2/2.
is Abraham (at the time, Adolf) Fraenkel: Mancosu (2020).
'We talked about Wittgenstein and Ramsey. Very interesting': ASP/RC-025-72-06: 42-01-1927
    bis 061927/769.
confined to simple arithmetic: FM: 180.
'consists entirely of tautologies in Wittgenstein's sense': EBFM: 831.

a fundamental turning point in philosophy: See Hahn, Carnap, and Neurath (2012 [1929]).

'also compatible with the empiricist position': Hahn (1980 [1931]: 34).

frequently expressed opinion: Hahn, Carnap, and Neurath (1929: 318); Glock (2008: 80–1).

primacy of the primary language: 'The primacy of the primary' is due to David Stern, in conversation.

same thing of *a* as φ*b* does of *b*': FM: 213.

'expressed by using names alone': FM: 201.

'extension between propositions and individuals': FM: 215.

to individuals *x*: FM: 215.

paragraph ending: 'which *expresses* that proposition': FM: 201; FM: 198; FM: 199.

'an intelligible notation': FM: 204.

years after Ramsey's death: CUL/Ms Add. 8875 13/39, CUL/Ms Add. 8830/17/1/100.

Behmann's alternative proposal for solving the problem. See Mancosu (2020).

Chapter 9

about the financial situation of the world: TFL MS/COLL/735: 13/32A.

added to the pleasure of the company: TFL MS/COLL/735: 13/44A.

he might have been malicious about: TFL MS/COLL/735: 13/2B; 13/32A.

next morning with the thought still percolating: TFL MS/COLL/735: 13/2B.

Keynes, Sheppard, Lowes Dickinson: TFL MS/COLL/735: 13/21B.

'not so interesting as Frank': Hill and Keynes (1989: 261).

rather than take the one he did: Chadwick (1998: 20), 13/9B.

even though his friend was a formidable player: King's FCP 6/1/143/1/4: letter from Ralph Partridge to Frances Marshall, 8 July 1925.

'Ramsey passed it as substantially sensible': TFL MS/COLL/735: 4/1.

Oxford and Cambridge for intellectually rich weekends: KH 205; TFL MS/COLL/735: 3/26.

an imitator of Marie Laurencin: MCI: 226.

with what I mainly want to do: KCA JMK/PP/45/262/1.

explanations at incomprehensible speed: TFL MS/COLL/735: 13/41B.

unteachable and that he 'flunked Cambridge': TFL MS/COLL/735: 13/36A; 1/2.

Tommy was 'nice but stupid': Ground and Flowers (2015: 163).

'quiet voice, explaining, satisfying': 'On a Philosopher Dying': *The Cambridge Review*, KCA FPR/2/486.

'regarded it as an enormous privilege': TFL MS/COLL/735: 9/16.

learnt differential geometry from Frank: TF/UTA 1183–3: B 2006–0023/003.

from those first principles: TFL MS/COLL/735: 9/16.

change from my previous five terms: TFL MS/COLL/735: 1/27.

Frank was a standout: TFL MS/COLL/735: 1/28.

'most damaging of all the Cambridge spies': Wright 1987: 256.

'cleared the top of the cupboard': TFL MS/COLL/735: 1/28.

more profitable in other ways: TFL MS/COLL/735: 1/27; 13/24A.

precisely understandable, analytic explanations: TFL MS/COLL/735: 13/14A.

dominating or embarrassing them: TFL MS/COLL/735: 1/27.

so approachable and kind: TFL MS/COLL/735: 1/27.

'not at all the "academic type"': TFL MS/COLL/735: 1/28.

an elitist about people: TFL MS/COLL/735: 13/18A.

not taking his supervisory duties 'at all seriously': TFL MS/COLL/735: 1/29.
had already been 'bagged': KCA FPR/5/2/414.
'Ramsey began to be a strong influence': MBP/14/21/2466/19/22 and 76.
the nuts and bolts of mathematics and logic: MBP/14/21/2466/19/125.
'very, very intelligent, extraordinary man': Black [1973] (2014): 65.
to go into his lecture room: Paul (2012: 187).
was 'quiet, logical, and lucid': TFL MS/COLL/735: 1/27.
rows of students, smiling and talking: TFL MS/COLL/735: 13/12A.
soak up his train of thought: TFL MS/COLL/735: 13/12B.
Introduction to Mathematical Philosophy and *Principia Mathematica*: TFL MS/COLL/735: 3/1.
Russell, Wittgenstein, Hilbert, Brouwer, and Weyl: TFL MS/COLL/735: 8/5–6.
arranged so that people might flourish: NPPM: 325.
financial independence upon marriage: NPPM: 328.
other than that of motherhood: NPPM: 327–28.
breaking the moral code?: NPPM: 328.
in the above passage with 'women': Paul (2012: 201).
with an important exception: 'But not my wife': KCA KCAS/39/1/16.
'with something interesting like fornication': Harrod (1971:49).

Chapter 10

who she was. Braithwaite didn't know: KCA FPR/1/1/1; TFL MS/COLL/735: 13/43B.
Irish rebels attempted to overthrow British rule: TFL MS/COLL/735: 13/7A.
a bit 'hearty' and bossy: Chisholm (2009: 35); TFL MS/COLL/735: 13/10A.
three or four times a week: KCA FCP 7/2/1; FCP 3/2/1.
'They behave as if they discovered it': TFL MS/COLL/735: 1/11.
knew who could sin with impunity: Paul (2012: 239).
she made the switch to that Tripos: LRA.
'all action is adaptation to environment': CUL/Min.IX.42.
as a 'non-Moral-Science' student: CUL/Min.IX.42.
nephew of Virginia Woolf: Stansky and Abrahams (2012: 141ff.).
his obsession with cleanliness: TFL MS/COLL/735: 9/9.
'all those Julian Bells': McGuinness (2006: 26); TFL MS/COLL/735: 13/10B.
that we might perhaps meet: KCA FPR 2/2/1/1/1.
Yours sincerely, Lettice C Baker: KCA FPR/2/3/1.
contrasted to Frank's 'militant' atheism: TFL MS/COLL/735: 13/7A.
croquet with the Penrose brothers: TFL MS/COLL/735: 13/7B.
attendant jealousy about sexual matters: LRA.
she would know about his homosexuality: KCA FPR/1/1/1.
Lettice would allow him to read hers: KCA FPR/2/2/1/3.
'will it be scandalous?': Spalding (1997: 215).
shy or self conscious in conversation: LRA; TFL MS/COLL/735: 13/32B; Forrester (2004:15).
'a very natural, uninhibited person': BTTS; TFL MS/COLL/735: 13/3A, 32B.
'she broke him in as it were': Forrester and Cameron (2017: 403). Interview by John Forrester.
the Governing Body minutes are silent on the details: MCA B/605 fol. 86r.
too far away to try to intervene: Stansky and Abrahams (2012: 62).
bachelor-schoolmaster's feeling and autocratic leanings': Paul (2012: 13).

lying in bed and laughing: Paul (2012: 198).
when she met Frank, 'that settled it': TFL MS/COLL/735: 13/7A.
then from the relationship altogether: TFL MS/COLL/735: 13/7A, LRA.
he was never convinced for long: LRA.
'Love (but there ought to be a stronger word) Frank': KCA FPR/2/2/1/3.
contemplating the misery of his rivals: KCA FPR/2/2/1/3.
found 'most interesting and vivid': KCA FPR/2/2/1/4.
'at the same time interested and intrigued': LRA.
'invented things to tell my parents what I had been doing': KCA FPR/2/2/1/2.
Adrian was in Dublin: KCA FPR/2/2/1/3.
a perpetual state of agitation about me: KCA FPR/2/2/1/3.
'goes to church from choice instead of compulsion': KCA FPR/2/2/1/4.
'we had dinner with him': KCA FPR/2/2/1/4.
might make a public fuss: TFL MS/COLL/735: 13/3A.
can you possibly forgive me?: KCA FPR/2/2/1/6.
a shame for you. Darling, forgive me: KCA FPR/2/2/1/6.
it's so much worse for you: KCA FPR/2/3/2.
till I know what she knows and thinks: KCA FPR/2/3/4.
after all, a reasonable person: KCA FPR/2/3/4.
immediately had second thoughts about: KCA FPR/2/2/1/10; TFL MS/COLL/735: 13/32A.
even in phantasy—as possible husbands: LRA.
a cowardly & madly foolish course: KCA FPR/2/3/7.
'collapse with nervous worry and excitement': LRA.
that she would not be marrying him: TFL MS/COLL/735: 13/3A.
I might come to lunch on Friday: KCA 5/2/470.
dropping them into a pile on the floor: MCA F/oMP/IV/6/11: 231.
indeed 'rather like father': TFL MS/COLL/735: 9/11.
he 'would take a violent attitude': LRA.
'worth twice' of Arthur: TFL MS/COLL/735: 13/3A, 32B.
'nothing to discuss': BL/Add/MS/60732, 32–3.
All they can do is 'exchange information': DS: 245.
more immediately in perceiving them to be nonsensical: DS: 246.
the soul's habitation henceforth be safely built: Russell (1985 [1903]: 66–67).
we have realized to have no real objects: DS: 246–7.
founders of emotivism in ethics: Ayer (1949: 171); Hare (1959: 570); MacIntyre (1981: 20).
he wouldn't feel guilty in the least: DS: 247.
'each of us to repeat in ourselves': DS: 248.
no discussion possible as to the merits of either world: T: 6.43.
better for all one's activities: DS: 249–50.
cracking under the strain of it: Harrod (1951: 320–21).
I have been asked to join it also: Meisel and Kendrick (1985: 219).
those 'clearly headed in the same direction': Rickman (1950: 281).
his socialist and Quaker relief work in Russia: TFL MS/COLL/735: 12.
before catching his train back to London: Meisel and Kendrick (1985: 222–23).
all the gates in Grantchester Meadow: TFL MS/COLL/735: 13/16A.
usually before but sometimes after supper: Rickman (1950: 281).
'the childish wish for the mother': Forrester and Cameron (2017: 419).
the Malting House School, addressed them once: TFL MS/COLL/735: 13/16A.

Freud publicly defended him: KCA 2/2/1/20.

the Austrian ones, to get additional information: KCA 2/2/1/20.

remark had been made all the evening: Meisel and Kendrick (1985: 288–89); Kapp (1925).

the Newton to Freud's Copernicus: Meisel and Kendrick (1985: 223).

'way that Ramsey was recommending': Meisel and Kendrick (1985: 232).

'many fundamental phenomena of the human mind': Tansley (1925: 567).

nonetheless 'of great and permanent significance': Keynes (1925).

'see where you felt the heat': TFL MS/COLL/735: 13/11A.

an analysis to last more than six months: Meisel and Kendrick (1985: 153).

'The question is whether it is *true*': Martin (1966: 110–11).

didn't influence Ramsey's philosophy at all: TFL MS/COLL/735: 13/42A.

'leave it in because Frank Ramsey liked it': Money-Kyrle (1978 [1928]: 16n1).

'the aggressive, sadistic attitude towards external objects': Penrose (1927: 47ff.).

in their early years, were prone: ASP/FPR.1983.01: 007-06-03.

they were all disciples of Mill: TFL MS/COLL/735: 13/41B.

'the greatest happiness of the greatest number': ASP/FPR.1983.01: 007-06-03.

'dangerous to their fellow-men': ASP/FPR.1983.01: 007-06-03.

put in 'Freudian language': ASP/FPR.1983.01: 007-06-03.

'our pursuits so often seem not really worth while': ASP/FPR.1983.01: 007-06-05.

'which had yet to be written': Forrester and Cameron (2017: 404).

'become, so to say, out-of-date': ASP/FPR.1983.01: 007-06-05.

'a general consideration of feminism': ASP/FPR.1983.01: 007-06-05.

than their relations with women: ASP/FPR.1983.01: 007-06-05.

to be 'an attack on feminism': Paul (2012: 219).

lack of firm ethical principles: Freud (1961 [1925]: 251, 257); Rathbone (1925: 52); Marouzi
(forthcoming).

the quality of future society: Pigou (1909: 14–15).

(and who would marry Richard Braithwaite): TFL MS/COLL/735: 13/43B.

heard thoroughly feminist talk from Ramsey: TFL MS/COLL/735: 13/41B.

it will be criminal of you: KCA FPR/5/2/406.

money to learn the equations: Paul (2012: 245).

and other people to be ~~admirable~~ cultured: ASP/FPR.1983.01: 007-06-05.

Chapter 11

colder and colder and that was all: KH 201; TFL MS/COLL/735: 13/8A.

the audience was large: CUL/Min.IX.42.

'that great muddle the theory of universals': U: 30.

Discussing always has that effect: KCA FPR/2/2/1/11.

'merely a characteristic of language': U: 13.

'senseless as that of theology': U: 14.

grounded 'on human interests and needs': U: 25.

'nothing whatever about the forms of atomic propositions': U: 29.

two classes, particulars and universals': U: 8.

without altering what is said: U: 12.

amongst the students in Cambridge: TFL MS/COLL/735: 13/42A.

competent in the language of Ramsey's paper: TFL MS/COLL/735: 3/26.

surmising what must be in the world: See MacBride (2018: 182) for this way of putting the point.

but obviously they wouldn't get on: WCL: 150.

under such conditions you will come?: WCL: 155.

enough to arrange for my journey: WCL: 155.

the preparations and from missing her: KCA FPR/2/2/1/16–17.

but he was unable to come: KCA JMK/PP/45/349.

Virginia and Leonard Woolf stopped by: McGuinness (2012b: 5–6).

an uneducated chatterbox: TFL MS/COLL/735: 13/27A.

Vanessa and Clive Bell's son Quentin: Skidelsky (1992: 208).

a tree was beautiful: Skidelsky (1992: 208).

'morally deficient though very clever': KCA/FPR/2/2/1.

'a moral issue out of absolutely everything': TFL MS/COLL/735: 13/7B.

He whistles marvellously: KCA/FPR/2/2/1.

'silent and sulky fit': Monk (1990: 86).

few people who 'had something to say': LAPR: 41.

There is a lot in what I say: PPO: 17.

sanctity of marriage: Partridge (1981: 159).

in that respect (with their respect): ASP/RC.1974.01: 102-13-30.

expected deference to Herr-Doktor-Professors: See Edmonds (forthcoming).

dreamt of being married in a church: BTTS.

'Somewhere in Soho. Drink is essential': KCA FPR/2/3.

English verse that she'd compiled: KCA 2/2/1/15.

'various problems' he wanted to 'think out': KCA 2/2/1.

directly to him, but via Schlick: WCL: 158–61.

'he may have got cleverer since then': WCL: 160–61.

I am inclined to doubt it: VCA/114-Ram-1.

'kind-hearted person you can imagine': TFL MS/COLL/735: 13/36B.

'it is absurd': FM: 179.

in bringing him back to philosophy: For Wittgenstein's letter, see NPPM: 339–41. For Ramsey's response, see Iven (2015: 98–100).

new arguments even after Ramsey's death: See PR: 141–43 and PG: 315–18.

she 'actually put on a hat': TFL MS/COLL/735: 13/7B.

'And probably she wouldn't want to see them!': TFL MS/COLL/735: 13/4B.

crawled out of a dustbin: TFL MS/COLL/735: 13/3A; 13/7A; 13/12A.

some of them 'rather outlandish': TFL MS/COLL/735: 13/7B.

what Dora Russell called 'disastrous consequences': Russell (1977: 88).

'basic in my own code of conduct': Dora Russell (1975: 69).

possibly a lifetime with others: Beckett (2015: 121–23).

'finally solve all philosophical problems': CN: 465.

probably nobody is monogamous: The Guardian, 27 May 2015: 'Mallory's camp correspondence for auction'.

Apostles were just talking about themselves: TFL MS/COLL/735: 9/10.

or when it was an undergraduate's first meeting: TFL MS/COLL/735: 13/7A.

would read the novels to each other: TFL MS/COLL/735: 9/16.

the whole audience would catch and join in: TFL MS/COLL/735: 13/2A.

some gadget to improve the bass: KCA 2/2/1/20: 13/3A, 32B.

the right in Cambridge, the vast majority: TFL MS/COLL/735: 13/12A.

against his wife and both his sons: Paul (2012: 224), Simpson (1962: 57).
a letter in support of the strikers: Paul (2012: 224).
we were blacklegs: TFL MS/COLL/735: 13/3A.
those on the opposing side: TFL MS/COLL/735: 13/3A.
'important in any human situation': TFL MS/COLL/735: 13/3A.
Pat Blackett, Dadie Rylands, and Desmond Bernal: TFL MS/COLL/735: 13/18A.
standard practice for Cambridge academics: TFL MS/COLL/735: 13/3A.
provided drink containing pure alcohol: TFL MS/COLL/735: 13/35B.
charming Gottingen professor staying there: KCA FPR/2/2/1/21.
'Pat Blackett (male)' or 'Pat Blackett (female)': KCA 2/2/2.
all our money from us: Paul (2012: 221–22).
laugh that cracked his face: TFL MS/COLL/735: 13/10A.
Frances had Russell and Wittgenstein in mind: TFL MS/COLL/735: 13/10A.
needed orthotic shoes: TFL MS/COLL/735: 13/2B, 44A.
'eating us out of house and home': TFL MS/COLL/735: 13/10A.
strands around his impressive cranium: McGuinness (2006: 20).
Handsome and large: TFL MS/COLL/735: 13/4A.
there was 'plenty of him': BTTS; TFL MS/COLL/735: 13/7A; TFL MS/COLL/735: 13/7A.
gramophone needle: BTTS, TFL MS/COLL/735: 13/2B; 13/28B.TFL MS/COLL/735: 13/41A.
in hanging about and chatting: TFL MS/COLL/735: 13/22A.
'he says you haven't prayed enough': KCA FPR/2/2/1/20.
'Lettice was still more sort of Frankish than Frank was': TFL MS/COLL/735: 13/22B.
her 'brute step-father': KCA FPR/2/2/1.
helping young people choose a profession: TFL MS/COLL/735/8/14.
my work. It is awful: KCA/FPR/2/2/1/20.
he gave supervisions and lectures: TFL MS/COLL/735: 13/2B.
listened to music and read to Lettice: BTTS; TFL MS/COLL/735: 13/2B.
the remainder on a gramophone record: KCA FPR/2/2/1/13.
but he was marked as ill: CUL/Comm/B.7.3.
only to find it empty: KCA FPR/2/2/1/25.
delighted about becoming parents: TFL MS/COLL/735: 13/7B.
'committed to justice': http://www.leeds.ac.uk/secretariat/obituaries/2010/obituary7153.html
'seemed to make nothing of having babies': TFL MS/COLL/735: 13/10A.
at whatever hours she liked: TFL MS/COLL/735: 13/3A.
Frances called Lettice an 'earth mother': TFL MS/COLL/735: 13/10A.
how. 99999...can be terminated in 1: TFL MS/COLL/735: 13/13B.
whether or not Frank was spoiling Jane: TFL MS/COLL/735: 13/3A; TFL MS/COLL/735: 13/10B.
'when it will cease to be so': KCA WHJS/85.
'now I am in the swing of it': KCA FPR/2/2/1.

Chapter 12

'interest a wider circle in mathematical logic': KCA FPR/2/2/1.
'asserted by a conjunction of atomic propositions': ML: 240.
e.g. giving another course of lectures: KCA FPR/2/2/1.
Hardy asked me to lunch, which was nice: KCA FPR/2/2/1.
other things, metaphysics and probability: KCA JMK/L/26/56.
'were authentic and imperative for him': TFL MS/COLL/735: 13/22A.

'Ramsey all morning talking mathematical logic': BRA: RA3/1027/250357, Mar. 1926 letter.

'expresses no attitude of belief at all': FP: 47.

'any of the terms judgment, belief, or assertion': FP: 34.

'so unlike anything else in the world': NP: 112.

'the fact that Caesar was murdered': FP: 34.

'means that Caesar was not murdered': FP: 38.

'we have solved the problem of truth': FP: 39.

the caterpillars were actually poisonous: FP: 40.

the rhythm of the words: FP: 44.

success of the actions they cause: Blackburn (2005), Dokic and Engel (2001), Mellor (2005), and Whyte (1990).

'if they are useful': FP: 40.

fill up a gap in his system: FP: 51.

Yours Fraternally Frank Ramsey: CUL/Ms Add. 8330 8R/3/.

engagement there was between Ramsey and Eliot: Linsky and Levine (forthcoming).

by Barcan in 1946: Barcan (1946).

some compromises validate one but not the other: Barcan (1946); Kripke (1963).

paragraph ending: either *a* or *b* failed to exist: Barcan (1947); Prior (1956); Kripke (1980).

work with 'any other theory': TP: 73.

called 'a useless complication': Jeffrey (1983: 57); also Davidson and Suppes (1956).

the 'larger logic' of human reasoning: TP: 82.

psychological subject of vague knowledge: KCA JMK/TP 1/2.

numerical measurement of degrees of belief: CUL/Min.IX.43.

think most likely to realize these goods: TP: 69.

'practically as a synonym for proportion': TP: 54.

the road to check my opinion: TP: 70–1.

'belief and other psychological variables are not measurable': TP: 62.

'accompanied by practically no feeling at all': TP: 65.

propose to call them all habits alike: TP: 90–91.

decline the bet and stay at home: TP: 79.

Institut Henri Poincaré in Paris in 1935: It appeared first in French as de Finetti (1937) and in English as de Finetti (1964).

despite her shaky English: MCI: 217; 219.

only from a pragmatist perspective: Hosiasson (1931: 36).

Lent Term lectures were to have begun: Hosiassonówna (1930–31). Translation courtesy of Tadeusz Szubka.

'*Modern Introduction to Logic*': Black [1987]2014: 65.

not yet, I think, quite successful: Keynes (1972 [1931]: 338–39).

'observation should modify my degrees of belief': TP: 88.

'lead to a bet of 2 to 1': TP: 67.

initial degrees of belief was 'meaningless': TP: 88.

a subjective probability of one-half: Davidson and Suppes (1956: 264).

he needn't bother writing them out: TP: 76.

we should continue to experiment: NPPM: 279–84.

lost to scholarship until then: See Sahlin (1990b); NPPM: 279–87; Good (1967).

before Ramsey (and De Finetti) defined it: De Finetti (1928).

paragraph ending: ordering or independence axiom, (Seidenfeld): Fishburn (1981); Levi (1974); Gärdenfors and Sahlin (1982); Seidenfeld (1988).

with homo economicus: for the use of this term, see Persky (1995).
paragraph ending: Herbert Simon finally celebrated him: von Neumann and Morgenstern (1944); Kuhn (2009: 296); Simon (1959).
hit on it out of the blue: Kurz and Salvadori (2003: 234).
it is in part a 'feeling': TP: 66.
paragraph ending: most beliefs come in degrees: TP: 65–68; FP: 34; TP: 65; TP: 68; TP: 63.
error may be humanly speaking justified: TP: 80.
'unconscious opinions' to the utilitarian idea: TP: 69.
'even though it is known to be false': TP: 69.
could verify Ramsey's formal theory: Davidson and Suppes (1957).
with a poverty of meaning: Rymes (1989: 102).
fit it into an exact logical category: P: 7.
neither woolly nor scholastic: LWG: MS 163: 57v. 1941.
a great deal of our thought: TP: 69.
'especially the speaker, in part approximate': C: 104.
obtained from obedience to filial duty: Robinson (1978: 273).
'an ideal person in similar circumstances': TP: 89.
'this ideal is more suited to God than to man': TP: 89–90.
be best for the human mind to have?: TP: 90.
habits that are reasonable or unreasonable: TP: 87.
blame of the habits that produce them: TP: 92.
those which alternative habits would lead to: TP: 93–94.
we believe it to be a reliable process: TP: 93.
among the 'ultimate sources of knowledge': TP: 93.
In this circle lies nothing vicious: TP: 93–94.
the world did not begin two minutes ago': TP: 93.
'mathematical logicians are not usually pragmatists': TFL MS/COLL/735: 13/42A.
'the slippery path to a sort of pragmatism': Braithwaite (1930: 216).
did not respect anyone's judgment on it: TFL MS/COLL/735: 13/42B.

Chapter 13

her husband's constant back-seat driving: TFL MS/COLL/735: 13/3A; Paul (2012: 242).
Cambridge on the Huntington Road: TFL MS/COLL/735: 13/15A.
'I was trying to put my coat right': Simpson (1962: 64).
Agnes was killed 'very unnecessarily': TFL MS/COLL/735: 13/3A.
numb silence and howling like a dog: TFL MS/COLL/735: 9/9.
the only person who really understood him: TFL MS/COLL/735: 8/9; 13/22A.
he was 'an extremely careful driver': Paul (2012: 243).
the headline 'Trifle Causes Smash': *Aberdeen Journal*, Wednesday 17 Aug. 1927.
Keynes replied that, alas, it was: KH 10. 19/8/27.
he burnt all the letters he could find: Chadwick (1998: 32).
not expressing any great remorse: TFL MS/COLL/735: 13/10A; TFL MS/COLL/735: 13/3A; TFL MS/COLL/735: 13/ 32B.
her mother wanted her to do it: TFL MS/COLL/735: 13/9A.
as well as Lettice's good artistic taste: TFL MS/COLL/735: 13/5A.
holding up a large atlas ...: Paul (2012: 245).

way to get it was to know things: TFL MS/COLL/735: 13/5A.

stayed with her all her life: TFL MS/COLL/735: 13/9A.

Margie felt neglected: Paul (2012: 244–45).

ruined by contact with an onion: TFL MS/COLL/735: 13/3A; TFL MS/COLL/735: 13/32B.

odder now that he was a young man: TFL MS/COLL/735: 13/3A.

jumping up and down overhead!: KCA FPR/2/2/2.

children coming and going as they pleased: TFL MS/COLL/735: 13/3A.

'explained beforehand than ours': KCA FPR/2/2/2.

Margie was not dealt a good hand: TFL MS/COLL/735: 13/3A.

'unerring eye for human needs': Allen and Nicholson (1975: 84).

important enough to have her own brief biography: Darling (2005).

Ireland in the summer of 1926: TFL MS/COLL/735: 13/7B.

'enormous', an 'absolute mountain': TFL MS/COLL/735: 13/7B.

'you've got to push your foot in': TFL MS/COLL/735: 13/7B.

'later became Frank's girlfriend': TFL MS/COLL/735: 13/7B.

loneliness when he was with her: Paul (2012: 198).

You wrote her the most charming letter, darling: KCA FPR/2/2/2.

Agnes might be 'disturbed': KCA FPR/2/2/2.

already a prominent civil servant: TFL MS/COLL/735: 13/44A.

a 'rather small, compact little person': TFL MS/COLL/735: 13/10A.

'I suppose, on Elizabeth Denby': TFL MS/COLL/735: 13/10A.

they had a thoroughly miserable time: Paul (2012: 244).

Frank had to ask Hugh to be discreet: KCA FPR/2/2/2.

'not a rather nice one!': KCA FPR/2/3.

'Liam O'Flaherty the writer': KCA FPR/2/3.

'the habit of telling each other everything': KCA FPR/2/3.

in a 'bull-like male way': TFL MS/COLL/735: 13/10A.

very sickening, in fact, just bloody: KCA FPR/2/2/2.

It seems so unlike you: KCA FPR/2/3.

unacceptable for it to be caused by jealousy: KCA FPR/2/3.

'permanently upsetting to us': KCA FPR/2/3.

she found 'so hard to bear': KCA FPR/2/3.

seem calm and reasonable not panicky: KCA FPR/2/2/2.

'I saw coming down the road': KCA FPR/2/2/2.

'fearfully self-centred': KCA FPR/2/2/2.

Elizabeth 'would be the extra one, so to speak': KCA FPR/2/2/2.

In her view, it was better all round: TFL MS/COLL/735: 13/9B.

then 'there was a sort of swapping': TFL MS/COLL/735: 13/10B.

Joan Robinson, 'that girlfriend of his': TFL MS/COLL/735: 13/13A.

Frank towering over them: TFL MS/COLL/735/13/0A; TFL MS/COLL/735: 13/44A.

Chapter 14

Pigou don't even have him in the index: Aslanbeigui and Oakes (2015), Kumekawa (2017).

'restate it in terms of the differential calculus': Shenk (2013: 28).

'the last of the Utopians': Keynes (1972 [1938]: 447).

becoming 'quite the fashion now in Camb': Shenk (2013: 30).

'the storm is long past the ocean is flat again': Keynes (1971[1923]:65).
'opposite direction, namely, towards monopoly': Sraffa (1926: 542).
'a complex attitude to the utility theory of value': Sen (1990: 144).
'the macroscopic problems of society': Dobb (1929: 506, 519).
He was referring to Sraffa: TFL MS/COLL/735: 13/20A.
'blowing up the Chapel, it will be all right': Sen (1998).
'I may have to do a Sraffa': KCA PP/45/42.
to make the necessary announcement: Skidelsky (1992: 290).
'the sacrilege of pointing out inconsistences in Marshall': Robinson (1978: ix).
Friedrich Hayek's theory of business cycles: Canterbery (2018: 74); Skidelsky (1992: 292);
    Newman (1982: 42).
'save capitalism by altering its nature': Martin (1946).
Keynes, who was a keen Liberal: TFL MS/COLL/735: 13/3A.
'the side of the educated bourgeoisie': Davenport-Hines (2015:128).
'anarchy are an actual present experience': Keynes (1971[1919]: 162).
temperament and ability, was Keynes: TFL MS/COLL/735: 13/24A.
that it was a great advance: KCA JMK/L/28/56. (Dated 3 Aug. 1928.)
'very neat and nice': See KCA JMK/EJ/1/3/85–92; Besomi (2003): letter 154.
much to Harrod's chagrin: Aslanbeigui and Oakes (2009: 37–39).
'meeting each other at the pole': Robinson (1993)[1969]: xiv.
a commodity to the costs of producing it: TCL Sraffa D1/54.
in terms of simultaneous equations: Kurz and Salvadori (2001: 262–4); TCL Sraffa/D3/12/2/28.
when dining at King's: Skidelsky (1992: 287); TFL MS/COLL/735: 13/32B; TFL MS/COLL/735:
    13/41B.
'Pigou was actually induced to come to lunch': KCA JMK/PP/45/190/4/15.
Harrod then re-submitted the article: Harrod (1951: 159–60).
could have been easily made: Besomi 2003: lxviii, 95–102, 109–12, 222–4; Moggridge 1992: 210.
Lettice was well aware of this: Kumekawa (2017: 14); TFL MS/COLL/735: 13/32B.
they walked and talked economics: TFL MS/COLL/735: 13/40A.
preface for his 'valuable suggestions': Pigou (1928: v).
'Ramsey shows that it must be rewritten': KCA JMK/EJ/1/3/12–15.
the expression was 'à la Ramsey': Dasgupta (1993: 5), Gaspard (2003: 433).
initiated 'entirely new fields': Royal Economic Society: Introduction. https://www.youtube.
    com/watch?v=ko1ITPG6F58.
secondary to his work in philosophy: TFL MS/COLL/735: 13/40A.

Chapter 15

modest to produce it for the journal: Bridel and Ingrao (2005: 156).
'restricts equality of opportunity': ASP/FPR.1983.01: 007-06-04.
market interventions would look like: Stiglitz (2015: 236).
'the production of each commodity taxed': TT: 47.
'the proportions in which they are consumed': TT: 59.
Harold Hotelling and John and Ursula Hicks: Duarte (2010).
duality, a now-standard approach: Republished verbatim in Samuelson (1986).
'the first successful exercise in second-best economics': Stiglitz (2015: 237).
less utility in the real world: Meade (1955: 102).

(the 'theory of the *feasible* first best'): Samuelson (1986 [1982]: 76).

what Ramsey called 'fairy tales': ASP/FPR.1983.01: 006-07-10.

'and it's no good trying': NPPM: 51.

'such as forests and minerals': ASP/FPR.1983.01: 007-06-04.

nuclear waste disposal: Arrow (1966), (1999a), Dasgupta and Heal (1974), Dasgupta (1993), (2005).

save over half our resources: Braithwaite (1930: 216).

Yours ever, Frank Ramsey: Keynes (1983: 784).

existence of people in the future: Sidgwick (1907: 414).

'a slower rate than your formula would indicate': Keynes (1983: 785).

'in the long run we are all dead': Keynes (1971 [1923: 65).

the basis of a wholly irrational preference: Pigou (1920: 25).

'ethically indefensible' as a social policy: MTS: 543.

function from a moral viewpoint: Cass (1998: 538).

'Ramsey would have none of this': Cass (1998: 538), Koopmans (1976: 219).

'a useful application of economics for a socialist state': TFL MS/COLL/735: 9/16.

interest, but principal as well: MTS: 549.

conquest of reason by passion: Harrod (1938: 404; 1948: 39).

not discounting future well-beings: Solow (1974).

combined in it together: Keynes (1972 [1930]: 335–36).

arches toward the Bliss turnpike: Samuelson (1972 [1965]): 93).

in centrally planned economies: Chakravarty (1962).

public investment in mixed economies: Arrow and Kurz (1970).

technology in labour-surplus economies: Little and Mirrlees (1974).

going a little beyond the Ramsey model: Cass (1998: 538).

sacrifice from current ones: Koopmans (1960); Koopmans (1965).

accord itself a slightly higher weight: Arrow (1999b).

pay dividends in the future: Solow (1986).

consumption and savings over time: Attanasio (2015).

extend the model in order to do that: Mirrlees (1967: 95).

'while you order it by telephone': Besomi (2003: 104).

has published the missing section: NST.

one heavily influenced by Pigou: Collard (1996), Gaspard (2003), Duarte (2009a).

'more difficult than anything in this paper': TT: 59.

paragraph ending: consider the issue of taxing savings: Pigou (1928); NST.

'utility of private incomes': NST: 474.

'to use Prof. Pigou's phrase': NST: 476.

paragraph ending: conclusions which were feeble: NST: 476, 477, 477; Besomi (2003: 104).

crossed out on the membership list: KCA RFK/3/15/1; KCA RFK/3/15/6.

accustomed to something far more difficult: Keynes (1972 [1930]: 335).

'the border-country between Philosophy and Mathematics': KCA TP/1/1/19.

downright 'math phobia': Weintraub (1993: 167).

'As I never learnt mathematics, I have had to think': Skidelsky (1992: 703).

'one generation and the interests of its grandchildren': Robinson (1970 [1937]: 52).

'confusion as to what our propositions imply': Dobb (1929: 506).

von Neumann, and John Forbes Nash Jr: Soifer (2009: 292).

seek to express a complicated reality: Koopmans (1957: 142).

'not supposing people to act so rationally': Besomi (2003: 105–6).

'the rest of geometry will be true also': EBFM: 82.

The combined minutes: TCL Rec.11.2/104–6; TFL MS/COLL/735: 2/9.
enable us to get a meaningful average: Marshall (1920).
then your analysis will be more accurate: Pigou (1920).
differences in the marginal utility of money to different people: TT: 47.
the Ramsey-Cass-Koopmans model: Samuelson (1943); (1986 [1982]), Solow (1994).
neglect of the differences in individuals: Hoover (2001: 83).
no problem with what Ramsey did: Hoover (2001: 83).
time discounting is ethically indefensible: Duarte (2016).
they want fairy tales: ASP/FPR.1983.01: 006-07-10.
'in communication with the world': Davis 2017.

Chapter 16

sparing the Mathematics Faculty: Paul (2012: 11).
interested in Faculty politics: TFL MS/COLL/735: 13/43A.
'(... specifically made to other authorities)': CUL/BOGS 2 1920–38/1105.
Ramsey coming first and Maunsell sixth: TCL REC 47.1.
'he never bothered to find out what Jacobi's was': CUL/BOGS 2 1920–38/1105.
deal with the problems raised: CUL/BOGS 2 1920–38/1105.
competence of the ordinary borderline candidate: CUL/BOGS 2 1920–38/1105.
(and on the whole has fully justified it): Littlewood (1986: 142–43).
Max Newman was in attendance: Hodges (1983: 91); KCA FPR/1/1/1.
dealing with the most difficult of issues: TFL MS/COLL/735: 13/39B.
lectures and had discussions with him: Mancosu (2020).
took a stand against logicism: Hodges (1983: 86).
his energies back towards mathematics: TFL MS/COLL/735: 13/42B.
logic in Cambridge wouldn't have occurred: TFL MS/COLL/735: 9/16.
even the Cambridge to Bletchley train: KCA FPR/2/1/3.
'These are *humans* who calculate': RPP: section 1096.
1920s were making local headway: Soifer (2011: 3).
the most ingenious and delicate reasoning: Graham and Spencer (1990: 80).
Ramsey's Theorem should really be named 'Ramsey's Principle': Soifer (2009: 264).
'structure that transcends the universe': Graham and Spencer (1990: 80).
'the Bolshevik menace of Brouwer and Weyl': FM: 219.
'the "law of excluded middle" is true': ML: 229.
regarding the rejection of intuitionism: Russell (1931: 478).
definite construction for finding one: EBFM: 84.
meaningless symbols according to fixed rules: EBFM: 84.
'provided you make sure that the baby is thrown out': TFL MS/COLL/735: 1/1.
'axioms according to the rules of deduction': EBFM: 84.
'theological mathematics': Waismann 1928; Carnap (1983 [1931]: 50).

Chapter 17

talked philosophy with him, was away: VCA: 114-Ram-2.
meanwhile to get a line from you: MCI: 162.
no work between now and then, I shall be: JMK/PP/45/190/4/89.

'Ludwig...arrives tomorrow...Pray for me!': JMK/PP/45/190/4/106.
a plan to stay in Cambridge permanently: JMK/PP/45/190/4/107.
'more than two or three hours a day': Skidelsky (1992: 291).
shouldn't like too many avoidable engagements: JMK/PP/45/349/59.
about logic, but other matters as well: PPO: 15.
that Frank and Ludwig were reunited: TFL MS/COLL/735: 13/18B.
'not born to live permanently with a clergyman': Skidelsky (1992: 292).
nearly a fortnight, before removing to Mrs. Dobb's: KCA JMK/PP/45/190/4/124.
leaving her exasperated in his wake: TFL MS/COLL/735: 13/15B.
'aware of suppressed irritability' in Wittgenstein: TFL MS/COLL/735: 13/10A.
'marriage to be sacred, and can't speak of it lightly': Partridge (1981: 159).
his feelings towards here were indeed reverential: See Wittgenstein's photo album, Michael
    Nedo collection.
she was tempted to have an affair with Wittgenstein: Chisholm (2009: 129).
'What he actually *does* is to bang the lavatory door at night': Kaap (2003:144).
(an excommunication that they had never officially recognized): KCA KCAS/39/1/17.
my heart, you'd see something quite different: WCL: 170.
go on writing about so—LW: WCL: 73.
Wittgenstein's 'violent letter of abuse': WCL: 75.
I should learn a lot from discussing with him: KCA WHJS: 85.
'of course the technicalities must be observed': TCL Wittgenstein 401.
lectures and discussion classes in January: Moore (1954: 3–4).
not 70 or 80 as I thought: WCL: 164.
Frank was not fond of Broad: KCA/FPR 1/1/1.
'thoroughly responsible person': TCL Wittgenstein 401. J.R.M. Butler letter of 23 Feb. 1929.
with all the exemptions he had requested: CUL/BOGS 2 1920–37/1925.
'I feel is the sort of thing he might do': CUL/Ms Add. 8330 8R/33/34.
'Don't worry, I know you'll *never* understand it': Wood (1957: 156).
'the Ph.D degree to Mr. Wittgenstein': CUL/BOGS 2 1920–37/1925.
'the publication of the summary book': CUL/BOGS 2 1920–37/1925.
Priestley was contemplating doing that: LWG: From Raymond Edward Priestly 3.8.29.
Yours sincerely, F.P. Ramsey: CUL/BOGS 2 1920–37/1925.
beyond it is simply nonsense: CUL/BOGS 2 1920–37/1925. For the entire summary, see Misak
    (2016a: 123).
'very sensitive about things like that': Black [1987] 2014: 53.
Ramsey's study at Mortimer Road: TFL MS/COLL/735: 11; 8/15; TFL MS/COLL/735: 13/7B.
listen to music on the gramophone: TFL MS/COLL/735: 13/24A.
Ramsey and Wittgenstein met almost daily: TFL MS/COLL/735: 9/11; TFL MS/COLL/735: 8/9.
making his delivery after midnight: Leavis (1981: 74).
Wittgenstein had a 'devotion to Frank': TFL MS/COLL/735: 13/10A; Partridge (1981: 159),
    Chisholm: (2009: 129).
with Wittgenstein very attentive: TFL MS/COLL/735: 13/18A. See also Leavis (1981: 63–64), TFL
    MS/COLL/735: 9/8.
a degree of courage of thinking: MS 105, p. 4 (7/2/1929).
pursuing a question to the very bottom: Moore (1954: 3).
out of his own mouth and expressing them: MS 105, p. 4 (7/2/1929).
exception that I know of was F. P. Ramsey: Russell (1959: 84).
made an extraordinary team: Black [1987] (2014: 50–1).

merely complicated branches of psychology: MCI: 213.

without offending Cambridge susceptibilities: MCI: 213.

most of his colleagues, including Braithwaite: TFL MS/COLL/735: 13/42B; TFL MS/COLL: 9/10.

awful lot to be contemptuous with: TFL MS/COLL/735: 13/16A.

'foolish of him not to have been': TFL MS/COLL/735: 13/2B.

going in another part of the University: Black (1987) (2014: 51).

'the meekness with which Broad lay down to Ramsey and Wittgenstein': MCI: 214.

almost too good to be true: TFL MS/COLL/735: 13/24A.

paragraph ending: disagreeing with Wittgenstein in an argument: TFL MS/COLL/735: 13/2B; 3/26.

'I don't like your method of arguing': Moore (1954: 3).

paragraph ending: cry tears of frustration.: TFL MS/COLL/735: 13/7B; TFL MS/COLL/735: 13/2B.

innumerable conversations during the last two years of his life: PI: §4.

Wittgenstein 'What is the logical form of *that*?': Malcolm (1958: 69).

a tree whose branches had been cut off: von Wright (2001 [1955]: 14f.).

puts the conversation in the early 1930s: CV: 16, 1931; BRA: MS:157b, 5v, 1937.

'there was no malice behind it': Black [1987] 2014:57.

Sraffa's gesture as a devastating criticism: Jacquette (1997: 186f.), one of the very few Wittgenstein scholars to see the profound influence of Ramsey on Wittgenstein, makes a similar point.

that it is important nonsense!: ASP/FPR.1983.01: 006-02-03.

'What can't you say?' 'Can't say breakfast.': P: 6.

and we can't whistle it either: GC: 146.

without any reference to the nature of meanings: P: 5.

The limits of my language mean the limits of my world': T: 5.6; T 5.62.

this was a disastrous conclusion: ASP/FPR: 003-30-05.

translating into intelligible terms: NPPM: 55.

a philosophy that is of not much use at all: P: 1.

and a clarification of thought: NPPM: 55.

'an explanation of the use of the symbol': P: 3.

'show how we intend to use them in future': P: 1.

'but at our own mental states': P: 5.

ourselves are not pictures of facts: NPPM: 51.

neglect the 'subjective side': P: 6.

fail and require to be restored: P: 1–2.

'into an exact logical category': P: 7.

What is beyond all knowledge and all sense: WCL: 176.

the feeling that it is my own fault: Monk (1990: 276).

'though no doubt the enemy within': McGuinness (2006: 25).

a logic for a vacuum: PI: § 81.

sense of a sentence is its purpose: Nedo (1996, vol. 2: 174–75); LW: MS 107.

'noted carefully by Ramsey': VCA: Neurath to Carnap from 22 Oct. 1932, trans. Christoph Limbeck-Lilienau.

this wonderful great smile and this great laugh: TFL MS/COLL/735: 13/10A.

meant something when he said it: PPO: 15.

knot in the trunk in order to grow on: Monk (1990: 259).

(if it had one) on one side as trivial: CV: 24.

a bourgeois criticism with a 'radical' one: DA: Rush Rhees to C. Drury 21 Feb. 1970.

'what makes him into a philosopher': Z: §455.

Ramsey called this 'messing about': WPCR: 62.

'how difficult it is to see the truth': PPO: 301.

if you don't want to suffer: Malcolm (1958: 40); Citron (2019).

'pure' (and 'strange'): TFL MS/COLL/735: 13/39B.

his little brother was a cleric: TFL MS/COLL/735: 13/24A.

'For me on the contrary clarity, transparency, is an end in itself': CV: 9.

'a few signs and two steps in the calculus': LW: MS 111: 66.

'content with piecemeal improvements': P: 6.

doing so, themselves 'unauthentic philosophers': Ryle (1970: 11).

settled yet how to deal with it: LWG: MS 111.

Wittgenstein said: 'Ramsey?! Ramsey was a mathematician!': Monk: (1990: 498).

a correct description of the status quo: LW: MS 115: 71.

'look and character of a scientific treatise': DA: Rush Rhees to C. Drury 12 Aug. 1968.

other ways in which it might be done: WPCR: 36.

understand the spirit in which I write: CV: 9.

'a way of sending them off to sleep again': CV: 7.

'a kind of spaniel who follows anybody who will beat him': Nicolson (1977: 80).

be sick and to faint in your house: CUL/Ms Add. 8330 8W/8/25.

'however flawed his expression may be': CUL/Ms Add. 8330 8W/8/25.

I haven't the faintest idea: CUL/Ms Add. 8W/8/28.

'about first and last things' with Waterlow: CUL/Ms Add. 8W/8/28.

but I can't believe any more: Paul (2012: 117).

'I feel to be cosmically inappropriate': CUL/Ms Add. 8330 8W/8/29.

'so good that he might have, had he lived': CUL/Ms Add. 8330 8W/8/29.

'irritable reaching after fact and reason': Keats (1899: 277).

'with absolutely unbounded admiration': TFL MS/COLL/735: 19A.

echoed something that Braithwaite frequently said: BTTS.

'W. would have been confined to his proper sphere': TCL SMIJ 1/61.

think Ramsey 'a great philosophical genius': TFL MS/COLL/735: 9/16.

certain he'd be able to attend the conference: KCA WJHS/85.

he would call it 'weak': M: 415.

and then met with Brouwer: Marion (2008: 102).

philosopher again, and began to exert a tremendous influence: Feigl (1981: 64).

Wittgenstein delivered in Nottingham has been lost: Monk (1990: 273).

some notes in Ramsey's hand: ASP/FPR: 004-23-01; McGuinness (2006: 24); and Methven
(forthcoming) for a translation of and commentary on the notes.

a fair copy of his work with Ramsey for safe-keeping: Leavis (1981: 74).

consider its application: WPCR: 54.

The Formal Structure of Intuitionist Mathematics': ASP/FPR.1983.01: 006-06-1; ASP/
FPR.1983.01: 006-06-07.

intuitionism was not taken seriously in England: TFL MS/COLL/735: 9/9.

naturally only what a rule can produce, i.e. constructions: MCI: 23.

the mind cannot attain to any such infinite conception': NPPM: 203.

we have as yet nothing to put in its place: NPPM: 204.

paragraph ending: 'we are not told what these flaws were': Russell (1931: 478); Braithwaite (1931b:
xii); Russell (1931: 477).

intuitionism is 'all bosh': LFM: 237.

on the matter of intuitionism: See Majer (1991); Marion (1995); Sahlin (1997); McGuinness (2006).

Carnap's characterisation of intuitionism: RFM: VII–33.

Chapter 18

3 days (counting Sunday) free for it: KCA FPR/2/212.
how you can arrange it satisfactorily: KCA FPR/2/2/2.
'the pretext of writing my book': KCA WHJS: 85.
one of Ramsey's first students: TFL MS/COLL/735: 13/24A; KCA KCAR 4/1/1/139.
they held back his stipend: KCA KCGB/5/2/1/7.
'in succession five different solutions of it': OT: 15.
paragraph ending: belief is also a feeling or a mental state: OT: 85; 84; 44–5.
which was then a chair in moral philosophy: TFL MS/COLL/735: 13/24A.
associated with Ramsey's pragmatism: OT: 83; Russell (1931).
between the realists and the naturalists: OT: 82.
(e.g., the early Russell and the Wittgenstein of the *Tractatus*): OT: 83.
two philosophically problematic notions: OT: 90.
the judgment and the fact and compare them: OT: 39.
paragraph ending: 'but that does not make them true': OT: 25; 94.
filled his note-book with swear-words: WCL: 212.
'especially in its application to religious beliefs': OT: 91.
pragmatism has a considerable contribution to make: OT: 91–92.
paragraph ending: such-and-such's actually being the case: OT: 11; OT: 91; OT: 19; OT: 90.
'belief has any other aspects or characters': OT: 85.
paragraph ending: a belief to be a belief *that p*: OT: 12–14.
paragraph ending: the belief's causes and effects: OT: 101; 91–2.
would have the most satisfactory consequences: OT: 45.
'meaning is mainly potential': P: 1.
'but absent in wondering whether': OT: 8.
'explanation strictly as a definition': OT: 9.
'B is a belief that *p* & *p*. Df': OT: 15.
such notions as 'is a belief that *p*': Prior (1971).
'problems that this relation involves': OT:14.
or the meaning of his words: OT: 45.
how we ought to think, feel, and act: OT: 3.
paragraph ending: 'definable in (ordinary factual) natural terms': OT: 3; OT: 4; OT: 4; bracketed
  portion original.
to discover whether this is really the case: OT: 4.
any clue as to how they ought to act?: Hume (1739: Book III, Part I, Section I).
includes both the physical and the social world: OT: 4.
'desired or pleasure or satisfying': ASP/FPR.1983.01: 006-07-08.
'too complicated for us to hope to give it accurately': OT: 42.
and those next chapters were never written: TFL MS/COLL/735: 13/42B.
TFL MS/COLL/735: 13/43A.
'objection from the philosophy of science': OT: 35.
who had been at Trinity: Campbell (1920).
all made clear in my account of theories: CQ: 137.
really 'may not express judgments at all': OT: 34.
discussing the facts the theory is said to explain: TH: 112.
paragraph ending: others 'seem to suppose that we can and must do this': TH: 129; 120.
paragraph ending: beyond a catalogue of the facts: TH: 122ff; 130.

'complete meanings and so are not propositions by themselves': TH: 131.

'any pretty way of obtaining a certain structure': P: 1.

not merely our theory of things in general: TH: 134.

the ones our best system would admit: Fine (1984).

David Lewis coined the term 'Ramseyan humility': Lewis (2009). The paper was presented as his Gareth Evans Memorial Lecture in 2002 and published posthumously.

things, relations, causes, properties, and so on, exist: Psillos (2006: 85–6).

'human logic' as distinguished from 'formal logic': Keynes (1972 [1931]: 338).

'giving up philosophy for theoretical psychology': P: 4.

the world about which I am now thinking: NPPM: 66.

present a paper at the Moral Sciences Club: VCA: 114-Ram-1.

very little stimulus here and make no progress: VCA: 114-Ram-2.

and others I felt very doubtful about: VCA: 114-Ram-4.

sounds with certain well-defined properties: ASP/FPR: 003-28-01.

also attracted a number of '!'s: ASP/RC.1974.01:111-F-110.

Braithwaite's 1946 Tarner Lectures: Psillos (1999: 46).

started to employ Ramsey's idea: Carnap (1958); Hempel (1958).

prevented from presenting Ramsey's idea as his own: ASP/RC.1974.01: 102-13-53.

a 'vindication' of theoretical entities: Lewis (1970): 427.

mustn't publish any of it, for copyright reasons: TFL MS/COLL/735: 13/43A.

expand upon Ramsey's idea and make the view his own: Lewis (1973: 73ff.).

its fame having preceded its publication: Ramsey (1978), (1990).

paragraph ending: 'and we can't whistle it either': GC: 146; 160.

paragraph ending: 'from the agent's perspective.': GC: 153; 154; 146; 149; 151.

'Many sentences express cognitive attitudes without being propositions': GC: 147.

'without having *proof* on his side': GC: 147.

appears in the best reading of Peirce: See Misak (2016).

'I went to Grantchester', 'I didn't': GC: 149.

the conditional 'peculiar' and 'useless': Lewis (1918: 326).

strict logic, as opposed to human logic: GC: 154–55.

counterfactuals on the basis of that footnote: Stalnaker (1968).

whether *q* is acceptable in the revised body of belief: Stalnaker (1968), Harper (1976).

'defended a view of causality of the type of Ramsey's': CUL/Min.IX.42.

paragraph ending: 'works backward and not forward': Russell (1913: 1); Russell (1913: 20).

'difference of cause and effect': GC: 158.

'the only ultimate contingency': GC: 158.

paragraph ending: Cartwright maintains: Cartwright (1979: 419-420).

'metaphysics of causation': Field (2003: 443).

paragraph ending: no foundation in physics: Pearl (2000); Woodward (2003).

deduce from it, and act on it in a certain way: GC: 150, 159.

increase the weight of one's probabilities: GC: 161.

'Superstition is the belief in the causal nexus.': T 5.1361.

true, justified belief, but not knowledge: Russell (1948: 113).

made the counterexamples disappear: K: 110.

'ought to have been chewing over Ramsey': TFL MS/COLL/735: 13/42B; 43B.

Chapter 19

'or as soon after as the stuff works': KCA KCRC/WHJS/85.
burst in on her while she was in the bath: TFL MS/COLL/735: 13/6A.
'When Beakus Came to Stay': https://www.youtube.com/watch?v=FFOOG9PjlJc.
he wasn't present for the filming: Partridge (1981: 159). TFL MS/COLL/735: 13/10A.
and very silly I looked too: KCA/FCP/6/1/142/1.
refusing to continue when darkness fell: Chisholm (2009: 125).
his chuckle was the chuckling of a god: Garnett (1962: 49–50).
dispute as to whom he ought to go to: KCA FPR/2/2/2.
accordance with Mick's Conscious Self: KCA FPR/2/3.
'which isn't worth disturbing': KCA FPR/2/2/2.
ought to find some female company: KCA FPR/2/2/2.
use his case anonymously in a lecture: Lambeth Palace Archives, Ramsey 1: 24.
opportunity to temper his crushing grief: TFL MS/COLL/735: 13/44A.
say to each other so early in the morning: TFL MS/COLL/735: 13/9A.
'vigorously' during the holiday: TFL MS/COLL/735: 9/8.
accompanied by seven fine wines: CUL/Ms Add./8330/8R/3; KCA KCAR/5/4/1/2.
caught a chill after this feast: TFL MS/COLL/735: 13/8A.
Drury's rooms on Thursday evening: WCL: 219.
I'm sorry to say don't know when I shall be: CUL/Ms Add. 8330/8R/3.
Michael recalled, 'Frank's got jaundice': TFL MS/COLL/735: 13/22A.
his skin being an orange copper colour: TFL MS/COLL/735: 13/10A.
he was sorry to hear that Frank was still ill: Lambeth Palace Archives, Ramsey 1: 28.
in bed with a very severe attack of jaundice: VCA: 114-Ram-4.
really have learnt a great deal from them: Moore (1968 [1942]: 35).
Much love from Frank: KCA FPR/2/2/2.
yellow, but 'all there mentally': TFL MS/COLL/735: 13/16A.
anyhow & I think Frank feels the same: TFL MS/COLL/735: 4/7.
say that it was definitely not a stone: TFL MS/COLL/735: 13/13A.
'Heard from father that Frank's operation had gone successfully': Paul (2012: 266).
little about what she would do if he died: Chisholm (2009: 129–30).
before returning to Cambridge and meeting Frank: TFL MS/COLL/735: 13/7A.
'another slight operation': Partridge (1981: 166).
from five to seven o'clock on Thursdays: WCL: 229.
disconcerting and in bad taste: TFL MS/COLL/735: 13/10B.
'tooth-ache which ate up so much time last term': WCL: 229.
hiccups were worse than before: Partridge (1981: 166).
better not come unless prefer. Father: Paul (2012: 267).
Frank even more than her dear friend Lettice: Chisholm (2009: 129).
With love, Lettice: TFL MS/COLL/735: 4/7.
many points he had expressed in the Tractatus: WCL: 231–32.
about pragmatism for the first time: LW: MS 107; Misak (2016).
'hour in the combination room': KCA JMK/PP/45/190/4/188.
Poor Lettice and her two babies: KCA JMK/PP/45/190/4/190.
With whom he often enjoyed a laugh: TFL MS/COLL/735: 9/16.

this morning in London at Guys. Richard Braithwaite: KCA WJHS/85.
the gentleness of the temperament: Holroyd (2011: 655).
The loss to Cambridge is incalculable: Levy (2005: 614–15).
he would not spin out the hour: WCL: 229.
it would be Frank: Chadwick (1998: 44).
'mistress sitting in the back', said Braithwaite: TFL MS/COLL/735: 13/44A.
to be trying to draw attention to herself: TFL MS/COLL/735: 13/10A.
loved Frank till the day she died, in 1965: Paul (2012: 241).
Cambridge attended the memorial service: Paul (2012: 267).
the medical situation was mishandled: TFL MS/COLL/735: 13/19A; 13/37B; 9/8; 9/10.
and so was responsible for his death: TFL MS/COLL/735: 9/9; 13/37B.
students were transferred to Philip Hall: TFL MS/COLL/735: 1/27.
'Evidence for the Existence of Other Minds': CUL/Min.XI.43.
from an arrangement made in grief: TFL MS/COLL/735: 13/10A.
'Marguerite & our difficulties': PPO: 47, Monk (1990: 258).
'and had demoralized everyone': Ground and Flowers (2016: 677).
suggested there was a chronic liver disease: Sahlin (1990a: 221).
'suspicious of my motives I can't think': TFL MS/COLL/735: 4/8.
Lettice's crime to be unforgivable: (TFL MS/COLL/735, 13/7B, Michael Nedo conversation).
to survive long in this world: Michael Nedo conversation.
remember him ever being ill: TFL MS/COLL/735: 13/10B.
in 1929 as having 'tremendous vitality': TFL MS/COLL/735: 9/10.
This place just flows with whipped cream: KCA FPR/5/2/406.
unhealthily 'swollen & stiff': Meisel and Kendrick (1985: 153); TFL MS/COLL/735: 13/14A.
also a large man, but not as large as Ramsey: WCL: 212.
step in and save his friend: TFL MS/COLL/735: 9/17; Roger Penrose conversation.
viral hepatitis was the cause of death: Paul (2012: 264).
dangerously ill till three days before his death: Paul (2012: 264).
mild weather hung over the whole of the UK: https://www.metoffice.gov.uk/binaries/content/
   assets/mohippo/pdf/c/2/oct1929.pdf
'a degenerative disease of the liver which was bound to end fatally': MCA F/0MP/IV/6/11: 286.
Ramsey taught us that these are nonsense questions: Braithwaite (1930: 216).
Braithwaite called a 'temperamental pessimism': KCA RBB/2/1.
made that distaste clear to him: McGuinness (1988: 108ff.).
a natural response to the human condition: McGuinness (1988: 156).
with himself but with things in general: TFL MS/COLL/735: 9/9.
'contemplating the human race and its follies': Russell (1959: 97).
'sort of hard-headed practicality': Keynes (1970 [1931]: 339).
some principles are such that we cannot do without them: ASP/FPR.1983.01: 003-10-01.
dying before I turn it to advantage: KCA FPR/2/2/1/3.
Alister Watson corrected the proofs: TFL MS/COLL/735: 9/10.
had been stolen by a pupil: TFL MS/COLL/735: 13/42B.
individual interests in mind, would interact: TFL MS/COLL/735: 13/43B; 13/42B.
'assert a necessary connection between universals': CUL/Min.IX.42.

ILLUSTRATION SOURCES

Note: The publisher and author have made every effort to trace and contact all copyright holders before publication. If notified, the publisher and author will be pleased to rectify any errors or omissions at the earliest opportunity.

Image 1   Frank, crop from Winchester College photo, 1916. Courtesy of Winchester College.

Image 2   Frank, happy at home, with his parents and sisters, c. 1919. Courtesy of Anne Paul Jones.

Image 3   Winchester College House, Frank in glasses, with chin up, near top row, 1919. Courtesy of Winchester College.

Image 4   Frank half-heartedly in fancy dress, 1919. Courtesy of Winchester College.

Image 5   College prefects, 1920. Frank top row, third from left. Igor Vinogradoff next to him on the left; Richard Pares on the ground, right; Sylvester Gates, 'the nastiest man in College' seated third from left; Foot, seated, second from right. Courtesy of Winchester College.

Image 6   Richard Braithwaite. Reproduced by permission of the Master and Fellows of Kings College, Cambridge.

Image 7   Lionel Penrose. Courtesy of the Penrose family.

Image 8   Tsemou Hsu/Xu Zhimo. Courtesy of Historic Collection / Alamy Stock Photo.

Image 9   G.E. Moore. Copyright © National Portrait Gallery, London. Reproduced by permission.

Image 10   I.A. (Ivor) Richards. Courtesy of Mark Kauffman / The LIFE Images Collection via Getty Images.

Image 11   Bertrand Russell and Dora Black. Courtesy of Hulton Archive / Stringer via Getty Images.

Image 12   Frank with Irene Martin and Kingsley Martin on holiday in Bavaria, 1921. Courtesy of Dorothy Woodman papers (SxMs95) University of Sussex Special Collections at The Keep.

Image 13   Dorothy Wrinch. Reproduced by permission of the Master and Fellows of St John's College, Cambridge.

Image 14   Dora Carrington, Steven Tomlin, Sebastian Sprott, and Lytton Strachey. Courtesy The Picture Art Collection / Alamy Stock Photo.

Image 15   Margaret and Geoffrey Pyke. Courtesy of the Pyke family.

Image 16   Frank, c. 1924. Courtesy of Stephen Burch.

Image 17   Moritz Schlick. Vienna University Archives.

Image 18   Hans Hahn. Vienna University Archives

Image 19   Lettice Cautley Baker. Courtesy of Stephen Burch.

Image 20   Harold Jeffreys and his bicycle. Reproduced by permission of the Master and Fellows of St John's College, Cambridge.

Image 21   J.M. Keynes and Lydia Lopokova. Reproduced by permission of the Master and Fellows of King's College, Cambridge.

Image 22   Ludwig Wittgenstein, 1929. Courtesy of Pictorial Press Ltd / Alamy Stock Photo.

Image 23   Frank and his two great loves: Lettice and Elizabeth. Archive Centre, King's College, Cambridge, FCP/7/2/3 p 34. Permission of estate of Francis Partridge

Image 24   Lettice and Jane. Archive Centre, King's College, Cambridge, FCP/7/2/3 p 34. it s source will have to be described: Permission of estate of Francis Partridge

Image 25   Agnes Ramsey, undated. Courtesy of Stephen Burch.

Image 26   Arthur Ramsey, 1927. Reproduced by permission of the Master and Fellows of Magdalene College, Cambridge.

Image 27   Elizabeth Denby. Reproduced by permission, The Architects' Journal, 11 June 1942.

Image 28   Arthur Pigou. Courtesy of Chronicle / Alamy Stock Photo.

Image 29   Sraffa, Keynes and Dennis Robertson at Tilton, ca 1927. Archive Centre, King's College, Cambridge, JMK/PP/94/443

Image 30   Letter from Frank to Ludwig. 'I really think it will be all right about your degree.' Archives of Scientific Philosophy, University of Pittsburgh Library System. Reproduced by permission of the University of Pittsburgh.

Image 31   Frank reading while on a walking holiday in the Alps. Courtesy of Stephen Burch.

Image 32   Hilton Hall filming, 1929, from left to right: Bunny Garnett, Angus Wilson (?), Frances Marshall, Beakus Penrose, Ray Marshall, Frank, Lettice. From Frances Partridge Photo Albums by Frances Partridge. Published by Frances Partridge, 1929. Copyright © Frances Partridge. Reproduced by permission of The Estate of Frances Partridge, c/o Rogers, Coleridge & White Ltd, 20 Powis Mews, London W11 1JN.

Image 33   Richard Braithwaite. NPG x31078 Richard Bevan Braithwaite by Ramsey & Muspratt bromide print on tissue mount, 1930s © Peter Lofts Photography / National Portrait Gallery, London

BIBLIOGRAPHY

1. Cited Works of Ramsey and Wittgenstein

1.1 Frank Ramsey

1921 (cited as NP). 'The Nature of Propositions'. Read to the Moral Sciences Club in 1921. (Published posthumously in 1991 in NPPM, 86–103, as well as in OT, 107–19.)

1922 (cited as DP). 'The Douglas Proposals'. *The Cambridge Magazine* 11/1: 74–6. (Reprinted in *Precursors in Mathematical Economics: An Anthology*. Ed. William J. Baumol and Stephen M. Goldfeld. London: The London School of Economics and Political Science, 1968, 335–40.)

1922 (cited as RT). 'Mr. Keynes on Probability'. *The Cambridge Magazine* 1/1: 3–5. (Reprinted in *British Journal for the Philosophy of Science* 40 (1989): 219–22.)

1922 (cited as TS). 'Truth and Simplicity'. *British Journal for the Philosophy of Science*, with a preamble by Arnold Koslow 58 (2007): 379–386.

1923 (cited as CN). Critical Notice: *Tractatus Logico-Philosophicus*, by Ludwig Wittgenstein'. *Mind* 32/128: 465–78.

1924 (cited as RMM). 'Review of C. K. Ogden and I. A. Richards, *The Meaning of Meaning*'. *Mind* 33/129: 108–9.

1925 (cited as DS). 'On There Being No Discussable Subject'. Read to the Apostles in 1925. Published posthumously under the title 'Epilogue' in Ramsey (1931). (Reprinted as 'Epilogue', in Ramsey 1990, 245–50.)

1925 (cited as FM). 'The Foundations of Mathematics'. *Proceedings of the London Mathematical Society* s2-25/1: 338–84. (Reprinted in Ramsey 1990, 164–224.)

1925 (cited as U). 'Universals'. *Mind* 34/136: 401–17. (Reprinted in Ramsey 1990, 8–30.)

1926 (cited as ML). 'Mathematical Logic'. *The Mathematical Gazette* 13: 185–94. (Reprinted in Ramsey 1990, 225–44.)

1926 (cited as UMA). 'Universals and the "Method of Analysis"'. *Aristotelian Society Supplementary Volume* 6: 17–26. (Reprinted in Ramsey 1990, 31–3.)

1927 (cited as FP). 'Facts and Propositions'. *Aristotelian Society Supplementary Volume* 7: 153–70. (Reprinted in Ramsey 1990, 34–51.)

1926 (cited as TP). 'Truth and Probability'. Selections read to the Moral Sciences Club in 1926. Published posthumously in Ramsey (1931). (Reprinted in Ramsey 1990, 52–95.)

1927 (cited as TT). 'A Contribution to the Theory of Taxation'. *The Economic Journal* 37/145: 47–61.

1928 (cited as C). 'Chance'. Published posthumously in Ramsey (1931). (Reprinted in Ramsey 1990, 104–9.)

1928. (cited as MTS). 'A Mathematical Theory of Saving'. *The Economic Journal* 38/152: 543–59.

1928. (cited as NST). 'Notes on Saving and Taxation' in 'Frank Ramsey's Notes on Saving and Taxation' Pedro Garcia Duarte (ed.) *History of Political Economy* 41/3: 471–89, 2009.

1929 (cited as EBFM). 'Mathematics, Foundations of'. *Encyclopedia Britannica*, 14th ed. Vol. 15, 82–4.

1929 (Cited as EBR): 'Russell, Bertrand Arthur William', *Encyclopedia Britannica*, 14th ed. Vol. 19, 678.

1929 (cited as GC). 'General Propositions and Causality'. Published posthumously in Ramsey (1931). (Reprinted in Ramsey 1990, 145–64.)

1929 (cited as K). Published posthumously in Ramsey (1931). (Reprinted in Ramsey 1990, 110–11.)

1929 (cited as OT). *On Truth*. Published posthumously. Ed. N. Rescher and U. Majer. Dordrecht: Kluwer, 1991.

1929 (cited as P). 'Philosophy'. Published posthumously in Ramsey (1931). (Reprinted in Ramsey 1990, 1–8.)

1929 (cited as TH). 'Theories'. Published posthumously in Ramsey (1931). (Reprinted in Ramsey 1990, 112–37.)

1930. 'On a Problem of Formal Logic'. *Proceedings of the London Mathematical Society* s2–30/1. 264–86.

1931. *The Foundations of Mathematics and Other Logical Essays*. Ed. R. B. Braithwaite. London: Routledge and Kegan Paul.

1978. *Foundations: Essays in Philosophy, Logic, Mathematics and Economics*. Ed. D. H. Mellor. Cambridge: Cambridge University Press.

1990. *Philosophical Papers*. Ed. D. H. Mellor. Cambridge: Cambridge University Press.

1991 (cited as NPPM). *Notes on Philosophy, Probability and Mathematics*. Ed. M.-C. Galavotti. Naples: Bibliopolis. (This is a collection of various, mostly unpublished notes by Ramsey.)

1.2 Ludwig Wittgenstein

1921. 'Logisch-Philosophische Abhandlung'. In *Annalen der Naturphilosophie*. Leipzig: Reinhold Berger for Verlag Unesma G.m.b.H. XIV, 3/4: 185–262. (Subsequently translated as Wittgenstein 1922 and 1961 [1922].)

1922 (cited as T). *Tractatus Logico-Philosophicus*. Trans. C. K. Ogden. London: Routledge and Kegan Paul.

1933 (cited as M). Letter to the Editor. *Mind*, 42/167: 415–16.

1961 [1922]. *Tractatus Logico-Philosophicus*. Trans. D. F. Pears and B. F. McGuinness. London: Routledge and Kegan Paul, 1961.

1967. *Lectures & Conversations on Aesthetics, Psychology, & Religious Belief*. Ed. C. Barrett. Oxford: Basil Blackwell.

1970 [1967] (cited as Z). *Zettel*. Paperback reprint. Ed. G. E. M. Anscombe and G. H. von Wright. Trans. G. E. M. Anscombe. Berkeley & Los Angeles: University of California Press, 1970.

1974 (cited as PG). *Philosophical Grammar*. Ed. R. Rhees. Trans. A. Kenny. Oxford: Basil Blackwell.

1975 (cited as PR). *Philosophical Remarks*. Ed. R. Rhees. Trans. R. Hargreaves and R. White. Oxford: Basil Blackwell.

1976 [1939] (cited as LFM). *Lectures on the Foundations of Mathematics, 1939*. Ed. Cora Diamond. Chicago: University of Chicago Press, 1976.

1980 (cited as RPP). *Remarks on the Philosophy of Psychology, Volume I*, eds G.E.M. Anscombe and G. H. von Wright, trans., G. E. M. Anscombe, Basil Blackwell, Oxford.

1983 (cited as RFM) *Remarks on the Foundations of Mathematics*. 2nd ed. Ed. G.H. von Wright, Rush Rhees; G.E.M. Anscombe. Cambridge, Mass.: MIT Press.

1998 [1980] (cited as CV). *Culture and Value*. Ed. G. H. von Wright in collaboration with H. Nyman. Trans. P. Winch. Rev. 2nd ed. Oxford: Basil Blackwell, 1998.

LWG: Wittgenstein (1993) Gesamtbriefwechsel (Complete Correspondence). Innsbrucker Electronic Edition. (2nd Release). Brian McGuinnes, Monika Seekircher, Anton Unterkircher (Eds). Charlottesville, Va: InteLex.

2009 [1953] (cited as PI). *Philosophical Investigations*. Rev. 4th ed. Trans. G. E. M. Anscombe, P. M. S. Hacker, and Joachim Schulte. Chichester, West Sussex: Wiley-Blackwell, 2009.

2. Other Works Cited

Allen, Marjorie and Mary Nicolson (1975). *Memoirs of an Uneducated Lady*. London: Thames and Hudson.

Annan, Noel (1955). 'The Intellectual Aristocracy'. In *Studies in Social History: A Tribute to G. M. Trevelyan*. Ed. J.H. Plumb. London: Longmans.

Arrow, Kenneth J. (1966). 'Discounting and Public Investment Criteria'. In *Water Research*. Ed. Allen V. Kneese and Stephen C. Smith. Baltimore, MD: Johns Hopkins University Press, 13–32.

Arrow, Kenneth J. (1999a). 'Discounting, Morality and Gaming'. In *Discounting and Intergenerational Equity*. Ed. Paul Portney and John Weyant. Washington D.C.: Resources for the Future, 13–21.

Arrow, Kenneth J. (1999b). 'Inter-generational Equity and the Rate of Discount in Long-term Social Investment. In *Contemporary Economic Issues* (pp. 89–102). Palgrave Macmillan, London.

Arrow, Kenneth J. and Mordecai Kurz (1970). *Public Investment, the Rate of Return and Optimal Fiscal Policy*. Baltimore: Johns Hopkins University Press.

Aslanbeigui, Nahid and Guy Oakes (2009). *The Provocative Joan Robinson: The Making of a Cambridge Economist*. Durham: Duke University Press.

Aslanbeigui, Nahid and Guy Oakes (2015). *Arthur Cecil Pigou*. London: Palgrave Macmillan.

Atkinson, Anthony B. and Joseph E. Stiglitz (1976). 'The Design of Tax Structure: Direct vs. Indirect Taxation'. *Journal of Public Economics* 6: 55–75.

Attanasio, Orazio (2015). 'Frank Ramsey's A Mathematical Theory of Saving'. *The Economic Journal*, 125: 269–94.

Ayer, A. J. (1949). 'On the Analysis of Moral Judgements'. *Horizon* 117: 171–84.

Baldwin, Thomas (2013). 'G.E. Moore and the Cambridge School of Analysis'. In *The Oxford Handbook of the History of Analytic Philosophy*. Ed. Michael Beaney. Oxford: Oxford University Press, 430–50.

Barcan, R. C. (1946). 'A Functional Calculus of First Order Based on Strict Implication'. *Journal of Symbolic Logic* 11/1: 1–16.

Barcan, R. C. (1947). 'The Identity of Individuals in a Strict Functional Calculus of Second Order'. *Journal of Symbolic Logic* 12/1: 12–15.

Bateman, B. W. (1996). *Keynes's Uncertain Revolution*. Ann Arbor: University of Michigan Press.

Beckett, Lorna (2015). *The Second I Saw You: The True Love Story of Rupert Brooke and Phyllis Gardner*. London: British Library.

Bell, Anne Olivier (ed.) (1977). *The Diary of Virginia Woolf, vol. 1: 1915–1919*. London: The Hogarth Press.

Bell, Anne Olivier (ed.) (1978). *The Diary of Virginia Woolf, vol. 2: 1920–1924*. London: The Hogarth Press.

Bell, Anne Olivier (ed.) (1980). *The Diary of Virginia Woolf, vol. 3: 1925–1930*. London: The Hogarth Press.

Bell, Clive (1956). *Old Friends: Personal Recollections*. London: Chatto and Windus.

Bell, Quentin (1972). *Virginia Woolf: A Biography, vol. 2 1912–1941*. London: The Hogarth Press.

Besomi, D. (ed.) (2003). *The Collected Interwar Papers and Correspondence of Roy Harrod, vol. 1: Correspondence, 1919–35*. Cheltenham: Edward Elgar.

Black, Max ([1987] (2014). *A Memoir*. Ed. Susanna Eve. King of Prussa, Penn: Modino.

Blackburn, Simon (2005). 'Success Semantics'. In *Ramsey's Legacy*. Ed. Hallvard Lillehammer and D. H. Mellor. Oxford: Oxford University Press, 22–36.

Blackburn, Simon (2021) 'Review of Misak *Frank Ramsey: A Sheer Excess of Powers*'. *Mind*, https://doi.org/10.1093/mind/fzaa093

Blanshard, Brand (1980). 'Autobiography'. In *The Philosophy of Brand Blanshard*. The Library of Living Philosophers. Ed. Paul Arthur Schlipp. LaSalle: Open Court, 1–186.

Blaug, Mark (1990). *John Maynard Keynes: Life, Ideas, Legacy*. London: St Martin's Press.

Boiteux, Marcel (1951). 'Le "Revenue Distribuable" et les Pertes Economiques'. *Econometrica* 19 (April): 112–33.

Bowra, Maurice (1966). *Memories: 1898–1939*. London: Weidenfeld and Nicolson.

Boyle, Andrew (1979). *The Climate of Treason*. London: Hutchinson.

Braithwaite, Richard (1930). 'Frank Plumpton Ramsey'. *The Cambridge Review*, 31 January: 216.

Braithwaite, Richard (1931a). 'Frank Plumpton Ramsey'. *Journal of the London Mathematical Society*, series 1, 6/1: 75–8.

Braithwaite, Richard (1931b). 'Editor's Introduction'. In F. P. Ramsey, *The Foundations of Mathematics and other Logical Essays*. London: Routledge and Kegan Paul, ix–xiv.

Braithwaite, Richard (1933). 'Philosophy'. In *University Studies: Cambridge 1933*. Ed. H. Wright. Cambridge: Nicholson and Watson, 1–32.

Braithwaite, Richard (1970 [1961]). 'George Edward Moore, 1873–1958'. Originally published in *The Proceedings of the British Academy*, 47. Reprinted in *G. E. Moore: Essays in Retrospect* (Muirhead Library of Philosophy). Ed. A. Ambrose and M. Lazerowitz. London: George Allen and Unwin, 1970, 17–33.

Bridel, P. and B. Ingrao (2005). 'Managing Cambridge Economics: The Correspondence between Keynes and Pigou'. In *Economists in Cambridge: A Study through Their Correspondence, 1907–1946*. Ed. M. C. Marcuzzo and A. Rosselli. London: Routledge, 149–73.

Brown, Andrew (2005). *J. D. Bernal: The Sage of Science*. Oxford: Oxford University Press.

Cameron, L. and J. Forrester (2008) 'Tansley's Psychoanalytic Network: An Episode out of the Early History of Psychoanalysis in England'. *Psychoanalysis and History* 2/2: 189–256.

Cameron, L. and J. Forrester (1999). '"A Nice Type of the English Scientist": Tansley and Freud'. *History Workshop Journal* 48: 65–100.

Campbell, Norman (1920). *Physics: The Elements*. Cambridge: Cambridge University Press.

Canterbery, E. Ray (2018). *Inequality and Global Supra-surplus Capitalism*. Singapore: World Scientific Press.

Carnap, Rudolf (1928). *Der Logische Aufbau der Welt*. Leipzig: Felix Meiner Verlag.

Carnap, Rudolf (1958). 'Beobachtungssprache und Theoretische Sprache'. *Dialectica* 12/3–4: 236–348.

Carnap, Rudolf (1963). 'Intellectual Autobiography'. In *The Philosophy of Rudolf Carnap*. The Library of Living Philosophers. Ed. Paul Arthur Schilpp. La Salle, IL: Open Court, 859–1013.

Carnap, Rudolf (1983 [1931]). 'The Logicist Foundations of Mathematics'. Originally published in *Erkenntnis*. Reprinted in *Philosophy of Mathematics: Selected Readings*, 2nd ed. Ed. Paul Benacerraf and Hilary Putnam. Cambridge: Cambridge University Press, 41–52.

Cartwright, N. (1979). 'Causal Laws and Effective Strategies'. *Noûs* 13: 419–37.

Cass, David (1998). 'Interview with David Cass, conducted by S. Spear and R. Wright'. *Macroeconomic Dynamics* 2/4: 533–58.

Chadwick, Owen (1998). *Michael Ramsey: A Life*. London: SCM Press.

Chakravarty, S. (1962). 'The Existence of an Optimum Savings Programs'. *Econometrica* 30/1: 178–87.

Chisholm, Anne (2009). *Francis Partridge: The Biography*. London: Weidenfield and Nicolson.

Citron, Gabriel (2015). 'Wittgenstein's Philosophical Conversations with Rush Rhees (1939–50): From the Notes of Rush Rhees', ed. Gabriel Citron, *Mind* 124: 493, January 36–7.

Citron, Gabriel (2019). 'Honesty, Humility, Courage, and Strength: Later Wittgenstein on the Difficulties of Philosophy and the Philosophical Virtues'. *Philosopher's Imprint* 19/25: 1–24.

Cole, G. D. H. (1920). Review of Douglas, *Credit-Power and Democracy*. *The Guildsman*: July 1920.

Collard, David (1996). 'Pigou and Future Generations: A Cambridge Tradition'. *Cambridge Journal of Economics* 20: 585–97.

Corlett, W. J and D. C. Hague (1953). 'Complementarity and the Excess Burden of Taxation'. *Review of Economic Studies* 21: 21–30.

Darling, Elizabeth (2005). '"The Star in the Profession She Invented for Herself": A Brief Biography of Elizabeth Denby, Housing Consultant'. *Planning Perspectives* 20/3: 271–300.

Dasgupta, P. (1993). 'Population, Resources, Knowledge and Destitution: The Making of an Economist'. In *The Makers of Modern Economics*. Ed. Arnold Heertje. Hempel Hempsted: Harvester.

Dasgupta, P. (2005). 'Three Conceptions of Intergenerational Justice'. In *Ramsey's Legacy*. Ed. Hallvard Lillehammer and D. H. Mellor. Oxford: Oxford University Press, 149–69.

Dasgupta, P. and G. Heal (1974). 'The Optimal Depletion of Exhaustible Resources'. *The Review of Economic Studies* 41: 3–28.

Davenport-Hines, Richard (2015). *Universal Man: The Seven Lives of John Maynard Keynes*. London: William Collins.

Davidson, Donald (1999). 'Intellectual Autobiography of Donald Davidson'. In *The Philosophy of Donald Davidson*. Library of Living Philosophers. Ed. Lewis Edwin Hahn. Chicago and LaSalle, IL: Open Court, 3–70.

Davidson, Donald and Patrick Suppes (1956). 'A Finitistic Axiomatisation of Subjective Probability and Utility'. *Econometrica* 24: 264–75.

Davidson, Donald and Patrick Suppes (1957). *Decision Making: An Experimental Approach*. Stanford: Stanford University Press.

Davis, J. B. (2019). 'Sraffa on the Open vs. Closed Systems Distinction and Causality'. *Research in the History of Economic Thought and Methodology* 35: 153–170.

Deaton, Angus (1979). 'Optimally Uniform Commodity Taxes'. *Economics Letters* 2: 357–61.

de Finetti, Bruno (1928). 'Funzione Caratteristica di un fenomeno aleatorio'. In *Atti del Congresso Internazionale dei Matematici*. Bolongo: Zanichelli, 179–90.

de Finetti, Bruno (1937). 'La prévision: ses lois logiques, ses sources subjectives'. *Annales de l'Institut Henri Poincaré* 17: 1–68.

de Finetti, Bruno (1964). 'Foresight: Its Logical Laws, Its Subjective Sources'. In *Studies in Subjective Probability*. Ed. H. E. Kyburg and H. Smokler. New York: Wiley, 93–158. (English translation of de Finetti 1937.)

de Finetti, Bruno (1972). *Probability, Induction, and Statistics*. New York: John Wiley.

Delany, Paul (1986). 'Russell's Dismissal from Trinity: A Study in High Table Politics'. *Russell* 6/1: 39–61.

Diamond, Cora (1995). 'Throwing Away the Ladder: How to Read the *Tractatus*'. In *The Realistic Spirit: Wittgenstein, Philosophy, and the Mind*. Cambridge, MA: MIT Press, 179–204.

Diamond, Cora (2011). '"We Can't Whistle it Either": Legend and Reality'. *European Journal of Philosophy*, 19/3: 335–56.

Diamond, Peter (1965). 'The Evaluation of Infinite Utility Streams'. *Econometrica* 33/1: 170–7.

Diamond, Peter A. and James A. Mirrlees (1971). 'Optimal Taxation and Public Production II: Tax Rules'. *American Economic Review* 61: 261–78.

Dobb, Maurice (1922). 'The "Douglas Credit Scheme"'. *New Statesman*, 18 February.

Dobb, Maurice (1929). 'A Sceptical View of the Theory of Wages'. *Economic Journal* 39: 506–19.

Dokic, J. and P. Engel (2001). *Frank Ramsey: Truth and Success*. London: Routledge.

Duarte, Pedro Garcia (2009a). 'Frank P. Ramsey: A Cambridge Economist'. *History of Political Economy* 41/3: 445–70.

Duarte, Pedro Garcia (ed.) (2009b). 'Frank Ramsey's Notes on Saving and Taxation'. *History of Political Economy* 41/3: 471–89.

Duarte, Pedro Garcia (2010). 'Beyond Samuelson's Chapter on Ramsey'. *History of Economic Ideas* 18/3: 121–59.

Duarte, Pedro Garcia (2016). 'A Path Through the Wilderness: Time Discounting in Growth Models', *History of Political Economy* 48/2: 265–306.

Edmonds, David (forthcoming). *The Murder of Professor Schlick (and the rise and fall of the Vienna Circle)*. Princeton: Princeton University Press.

Feigl, Herbert (1981). *Inquiries and Provocations: Selected Writings 1929–1974*. Ed. Robert S. Cohen. Dordrecht, the Netherlands: D. Reidel Publishing Company.

Fichte, J. G. (1982 [1797]). 'First Introduction to the Science of Knowledge'. In *The Science of Knowledge*. Trans. P. Heath and J. Lachs. Cambridge: Cambridge University Press, 1982, 3–28. (Originally published in German in 1797.)

Field, H. (2003). 'Causation in a Physical World'. In *The Oxford Handbook of Metaphysics*. Ed. M. Loux and D. Zimmerman. Oxford: Oxford University Press, 435–60.

Fine, Arthur I. (1984). 'The Natural Ontological Attitude'. In J. Leplin (ed.), *Scientific Realism*. Berkeley, CA: University of California Press, 261–77.

Fishburn, P.C. (1981). 'Subjective Expected Utility: A Review of Normative Theories'. *Theory and Decision* 13: 139–99.

Florence, P. Sargant (1968). 'The Cambridge Heretics: 1909–1932'. In *The Humanist Outlook*. Ed. A. J. Ayer. London: Pemberton, 225–39.

Florence, P. Sargant (1977). 'Cambridge 1909–1919 and Its Aftermath'. In *C. K. Ogden: A Collective Memoir*. Ed. P. S. Florence and J. R. L. Anderson. London: Elek Pemberton, 13–55.

Forrester, John (2004). 'Freud in Cambridge'. *Critical Quarterly* 46/2: 1–26.

Forrester, John and Laura Cameron (2017). *Freud in Cambridge*. Cambridge: Cambridge University Press.

Franke, Damon (2008). *Modern Heresies: British Literary History 1883–1924*. Columbus: Ohio State University Press.

Frápolli, M. J. (ed.) (2005). 'Ramsey's Theory of Truth and the Origins of the Prosentential Account'. In M. J. Frápolli (ed.), *F. P. Ramsey: Critical Reassessments*. London: Continuum, pp. 133–8.

Frege, Gottlob (2013 [1893, 1903]). *Basic Laws of Arithmetic*. Ed. and trans. Philip A. Ebert and Marcus Rossberg. Oxford: Oxford University Press.

Freud, Sigmund (1961 [1925]). 'Some Psychical Consequences of the Anatomical Distinction between the Sexes'. Reprinted in *The Standard Edition of the Complete Psychological Works of Sigmund Freud*, vol. XIX. Ed. and trans. James Strachey in collaboration with Anna Freud. London: The Hogarth Press, 1961, 248–58.

Galavotti, Maria Carla (ed.) (2006). *Cambridge and Vienna: Frank P. Ramsey and the Vienna Circle*. Dordrecht: Springer.

Galavotti, Maria Carla (2014). 'Probabilistic Epistemology: A European Tradition'. European Philosophy of Science: Philosophy of Science in Europe and the Viennese Heritage. Ed. M. C. Galavotti, E. Nemeth, F. Stadler. Springer. 78–81.

Galavotti, Maria Carla (2017a). 'On Some French Probabilists of the 20th Century: Fréchet, Borel, Lévy'. *Proceedings of the 15th International Congress in Logic, Methodology and Philosophy of Science*. Ed. H. Leitgeb, I. Niiniluoto, P. Seppälä, and E. Sober. London: College Publications, 155–73.

Gärdenfors, Peter and Nils-Eric Sahlin (eds) (1982). 'Unreliable Probabilities, Risk Taking, and Decision Making' *Synthese* 53/3, 361–86.

Gardiner, Margaret (1988). *A Scatter of Memories*. London: Free Association Books.

Garnett, David (1962). *Familiar Faces*. London: Chatto and Windus.

Gaspard, Marion (2003). 'Ramsey's Theory of National Saving: A Mathematician in Cambridge'. *Journal of the History of Economic Thought* 25/4: 413–35.

Glock, Hans-Johann (2008). 'The Development of Analytic Philosophy: Wittgenstein and After'. In Dermot Moran (ed.), *The Routledge Companion to Twentieth Century Philosophy*. London, 76–117.

Good, I. J. (1967). 'On the Principle of Total Evidence'. *British Journal for the Philosophy of Science* 17: 319–21.

Graham, Ronald and Joel Spencer (1990). 'Ramsey Theory'. *Scientific American* 263/1: 80–5.

Ground, I. and F. A. Flowers (2016). *Portraits of Wittgenstein*. 2 vols. London: Bloomsbury.

Hacker, P. M. S. (1996). *Wittgenstein's Place in Twentieth-Century Analytic Philosophy*. Oxford: Blackwell.

Hahn, Hans (1980 [1931]). 'Discussion about the Foundations of Mathematics'. In Brian McGuinness (ed.), *Empiricism, Logic and Mathematics*. Vienna Circle Collection, vol. 13. Dordrecht: Springer.

Hahn, Hans, Rudolf Carnap, and Otto Neurath (1929). *Wissenschaftliche Weltauffassung. Der Wiener Kreis*. Vienna: Wolf. (Partially translated as Hahn, Carnap, and Neurath 1973 [1929]; fully translated, with revisions, as Hahn, Carnap, and Neurath 2012 [1929].)

Hahn, Hans, Rudolf Carnap, and Otto Neurath (1973 [1929]). 'The Scientific Conception of the World: The Vienna Circle'. In O. Neurath, *Empiricism and Sociology*. Ed. M. Neurath and R. S. Cohen. Dordrecht: D. Reidel, 1973, 299–318.

Hahn, Hans, Rudolf Carnap, and Otto Neurath (2012 [1929]). 'The Scientific World-Conception: The Vienna Circle'. In F. Stadler and T. Uebel (eds), *Wissenschaftliche Weltauffassung. Der Wiener Kreis*. Vienna and New York: Springer, 75–116.

Harberger, Arnold C. (1971). 'Three Basic Postulates for Applied Welfare Economics'. *Journal of Economic Literature* 9: 785–97.

Hare, R. M. (1959). 'Broad's Approach to Moral Philosophy'. In Paul Arthur Schilpp (ed.), *The Philosophy of C. D. Broad*. Library of Living Philosophers. New York: Tudor, 563–77.

Harrod, R. F. (1938). 'Scope and Method of Economics'. *The Economic Journal* 48/191: 383–412.

Harrod, R. F. (1948). *Towards a Dynamic Economy*. London: Macmillan.

Harrod, R. F. (1951). *The Life of John Maynard Keynes*. London: Macmillan.

Harrod, R. F. (1971). *Sociology, Morals and Mystery*. London: Macmillan.

Hemming, Henry (2015). *The Ingenious Mr. Pyke*. New York: Public Affairs.

Hempel, Carl G. (1958). 'The Theoretician's Dilemma: A Study in the Logic of Theory Construction'. *Minnesota Studies in the Philosophy of Science* 2: 173–226.

Hill, Polly and Richard Keynes (eds) (1989). *Lydia and Maynard: The Letters of Lydia Lopkova and John Maynard Keynes*. London: Andre Deutsch.

Hiskett, W. R. and J. A. Franklin (1939). *Searchlight on Social Credit*. London: P. S. King and Sons, Ltd.

Hodges, Andrew (1983). *Alan Turing: The Enigma of Intelligence*. London: Unwin.

Holroyd, Michael (2011). *Lytton Strachey: The New Biography*. London: Chatto & Windus.

Hoover, Kevin (2001). *The Methodology of Empirical Macroeconomics*. Cambridge: Cambridge University Press.

Hosiasson, Janina (1931). 'Why Do We Prefer Probabilities Relative to Many Data?' *Mind* 40(157): 23–36.

Hosiasson-Lindenbaum, Janina (1940). 'On Confirmation'. *The Journal of Symbolic Logic* 5(4): 133–48.

Hosiassonówna, Janina (1930–1931). 'Studya filozoficzne w Cambridge'. *Ruch Filozoficzny* 12: 218–20.

Hotelling, Harold (1932). 'Edgeworth's Taxation Paradox and the Nature of Demand and Supply Functions', *Journal of Political Economy* 40: 577–616.

Hume, David (1739). *The Treatise of Human Nature.* London.

Iven, M. (2015). 'Er "ist eine Künstlernatur von hinreissender Genialität"'. *Wittgenstein-Studien* 6/1: 83–174.

Jacquette, Dale (1997). *Wittgenstein's Thought in Transition.* West Lafayette, IN: Purdue University Press.

James, William (1975–88). *The Works of William James.* 18 vols. Ed. F. H. Burkhard et al. Cambridge, MA: Harvard University Press.

Jeffrey, Richard (1983). *The Logic of Decision.* 2nd ed. Chicago: University of Chicago Press.

Kapp, Reginald O. (1925). 'Sensation and Narcissism'. *The International Journal of Psycho-Analysis* 6: 292–9.

Kaap, Yvonne (2003). *Time Will Tell: Memoirs.* London: Verso.

Keynes, J. M. (1920). *The Economic Consequences of the Peace.* New York: Harcourt, Brace and Howe.

Keynes, J. M. (1923). *A Tract on Monetary Reform.* London: Macmillan.

Keynes, J. M. (1925). 'Freudian Psycho-analysis'. *The Nation & The Athenaeum,* 29 August, 37/22: 643–4. (Keynes published this using the nom de plume 'Siela'.)

Keynes, J. M. (1972 [1930]). 'F.P. Ramsey'. *Economic Journal,* 157–40 (1930): 154. Reprinted in *Essays in Biography. The Collected Writings of John Maynard Keynes,* vol. 10. Ed. Elizabeth Johnson and D. E. Moggridge. London: Macmillan, 335–6.

Keynes, J. M. (1972 [1931]). 'Review of the Foundations of Mathematics'. *The New Statesman,* 3 October, 1931. Reprinted in *Essays in Biography. The Collected Writings of John Maynard Keynes,* vol. 10. Ed. Elizabeth Johnson and D. E. Moggridge. London: Macmillan, 336–9.

Keynes, J. M. (1972 [1938]). 'My Early Beliefs'. Reprinted in *Essays in Biography. The Collected Writings of John Maynard Keynes,* vol. 10. Ed. Elizabeth Johnson and D. E. Moggridge. London: Macmillan, 433–50.

Keynes, J. M. (1973 [1921]). *A Treatise on Probability.* Reprinted in *The Collected Writings of John Maynard Keynes,* vol. 8. London: Macmillan.

Keynes, J. M. (1983). *Economic Articles and Correspondence: Investment and Editorial. The Collected Writings of John Maynard Keynes,* vol. 12. Ed. D. E. Moggridge. London: Macmillan.

Klagge, James and Nordmann, Alfred (eds) (2003). *Ludwig Wittgenstein: Public and Private Occasions.* Lanham, MD: Rowman & Littlefield.

Koopmans, Tjalling (1957). *Three Essays on the State of Economic Science.* McGraw-Hill.

Koopmans, Tjalling (1960). 'Stationary Ordinal Utility and Impatience'. *Econometrica* 28/2: 287–309.

Koopmans, Tjalling (1965). 'On the Concept of Optimal Economic Growth'. *Pontificiae Academiae Scientiarum Scripta Varia* 28/1: 225–300. (Reprinted in Tjalling Koopmans, *The Econometric Approach to Development Planning.* Amsterdam: North Holland, 1966.)

Kripke, Saul A. (1963). 'Semantical Considerations on Modal Logic'. *Acta Philosophica Fennica* 16: 83–94.

Kripke, Saul A. (1980). *Naming and Necessity.* Oxford: Blackwell.

Kumekawa, Ian (2017). *The First Serious Optimist: A. C. Pigou and the Birth of Welfare Economics.* Princeton: Princeton University Press.

Kuhn, Harold W. (2009). 'Reflections on Ramsey and Economics'. In Soifer (2009), 291–6.

Kurz, Heinz D. and Neri Salvadori (2001). 'Sraffa and the Mathematicians: Frank Ramsey and Alister Watson'. In T. Cozzi and R. Marchionatti (eds), *Piero Sraffa's Political Economy: A Centenary Estimate*. London: Routledge, 254–84.

Kurz, Heinz D. and Neri Salvadori (2003). 'Sraffa and von Neumann'. In Heinz D. Kurz and Neri Salvadori (eds), *Classical Economics and Modern Theory: Studies in Long-Period Analysis*. London: Routledge, 217–37.

Leavis, F. R. (1981). 'Memories of Wittgenstein'. In Rush Rhees (ed.), *Ludwig Wittgenstein: Personal Recollections*. Oxford: Basil Blackwell, 63–82.

Lenzen, Victor. (1971). 'Bertrand Russell at Harvard'. *Russell: The Journal of Bertrand Russell Studies*, o.s. 3: 4–6.

Levi, Isaac (1974). 'On Indeterminate Probabilities'. *Journal of Philosophy* 71: 391–418.

Levy, Paul (ed.) (2005). *The Letters of Lytton Strachey*. London: Penguin.

Lewis, C. I. (1918). *A Survey of Symbolic Logic*. Berkeley: University of California Press.

Lewis, David (1970). 'How to Define Theoretical Terms'. *The Journal of Philosophy* 67/13: 427–46.

Lewis, David (1973). *Counterfactuals*. Oxford: Blackwell.

Lewis, David (2009). 'Ramseyan Humility'. In D. Braddon-Mitchell and R. Nola (eds), *Conceptual Analysis and Philosophical Naturalism*. Cambridge, MA: The MIT Press, 203–22.

Lewy, Casimir (ed.) (1962). *The Commonplace Book of George Edward Moore: 1919–1953*. London: Allen & Unwin.

Little, I. M. D. and J. A. Mirrlees (1974). *Project Appraisal and Planning for Developing Countries*. London: Heinemann.

Littlewood, J. E. (1986). *Littlewood's Miscellany*. Ed. Béla Bollobás. Cambridge: Cambridge University Press. (A revised and expanded version of Littlewood's 1953 *A Mathematician's Miscellany*.)

MacBride, Fraser (2018). *On the Genealogy of Universals: The Metaphysical Origins of Analytic Philosophy*. New York: Oxford University Press.

MacIntyre, Alasdair (1981). *After Virtue*. London: Bloomsbury.

Macmillan, Harold (1973). 'Oxford Before the Deluge'. *History of the University* Seminar, 14 March, 1973. HUA Recording.

Majer, Ulrich (1991). 'Ramsey's Theory of Truth and the Truth of Theories: A Synthesis of Pragmatism and Intuitionism in Ramsey's Last Philosophy'. *Theoria* 57/3: 162–95.

Malcolm, Norman (1958). *Ludwig Wittgenstein: A Memoir*. Oxford: Oxford University Press.

Mancosu, Paolo (2020) 'Three Letters on the Foundations of Mathematics by Frank Plumpton Ramsey'. *Philosophia Mathematica*, 28, 1–27.

Mancosu, Paolo (2021) 'An essay review of three books on Frank Ramsey', *Philosophia Mathematica*, 29/1 110–150.

Manning, Leah (1970). *A Life for Education: An Autobiography*. London: Victor Gollancz.

Marouzi, Soroush (forthcoming). 'Frank Plumpton Ramsey and the Politics of Motherhood', *Journal of the History of Economic Thought*.

Marion, Mathieu (1995). 'Wittgenstein and Finitism'. *Synthese* 105/2: 141–76.

Marion, Mathieu (2008). 'Brouwer on "Hypotheses" and the Middle Wittgenstein'. In M. van Atten, P. Boldini, M. Bourdeau, and G. Heinzmann (eds), *One Hundred Years of Intuitionism (1907–2007)*. Publications des Archives Henri Poincaré/Publications of the Henri Poincaré Archives. Birkhäuser Basel.

Marshall, Alfred (1920). *Principles of Economics*. 8th ed. London: Macmillan.

Martin, Kingsley (1946). 'John Maynard Keynes'. *The New Statesman and Nation* 31/792 (Apr. 27): 295.

Martin, Kingsley (1966). *Father Figures: A First Volume of Autobiography, 1897–1931*. London: Hutchinson.

McGuinness, Brian (1988). *Wittgenstein: A Life*. London: Duckworth.

McGuinness, Brian (2006). 'Wittgenstein and Ramsey'. In *Cambridge and Vienna: Frank P. Ramsey and the Vienna Circle*. Ed. M. C. Galavotti. Dordrecht: Springer, 19–28.

McGuinness, Brian (ed.) (2012a). *Wittgenstein in Cambridge: Letters and Documents 1911–1951*. Oxford: Blackwell.

McGuinness, Brian (2012b). 'Introduction'. In McGuinness (2012a), 1–7.

McGuinness, Brian (ed.) (2016). 'Arthur MacIver's Diary: Cambridge (October 1929–March 1930', *Wittgenstein Studien*, 201–55.

Meade, James E. (1955). *Trade and Welfare. The Theory of International Economic Policy*, vol. 2. Oxford: Oxford University Press.

Meisel, Perry and Walter Kendrick (1985) (eds). *Bloomsbury/Freud: The Letters of James and Alix Strachey, 1924–1925*. New York: Basic Books.

Mellor, D. H. (1978). 'Better Than the Stars'. Broadcast on BBC Radio 3: 27 February, 1978. (Available online: http://www.dspace.cam.ac.uk/handle/1810/3484.)

Mellor, D.H. (1995). 'Cambridge Philosophers I: F.P. Ramsey'. *Philosophy* 70: 243–62.

Mellor, D. H. (2005). 'What Does Subjective Decision Theory Tell Us?' In H. Lillehammer and D. H. Mellor (eds). *Ramsey's Legacy*. Mind Association Occasional Series. Oxford: Clarendon Press, 137–48.

Methven, S. J. (forthcoming) 'Ramsey's Record? Wittgenstein on Infinity and Generalisation'.

Methven, S. J. (2015). *Frank Ramsey and the Realistic Spirit*. London: Palgrave Macmillan.

Mirrlees, James (1967). 'Optimum Growth when Technology is Changing'. *Review of Economic Studies* 34/1: 95–124.

Misak, Cheryl (2016). *Cambridge Pragmatism: From Peirce and James to Ramsey and Wittgenstein*. Oxford: Oxford University Press.

Misak, Cheryl (forthcoming) 'Ramsey and the Newman Problem'.

Mitchell, Leslie (2009). *Maurice Bowra: A Life*. Oxford: Oxford University Press.

Misak, C. Naylor, C.D. Tonelli, M.R, Greenhalgh, T. and Foster G. (forthcoming) 'What—or who—killed Frank Ramsey? Some reflections on cause of death and the nature of medical reasoning'.

Moggridge, D. E. (1992). *Maynard Keynes: An Economist's Biography*. London: Routledge.

Money-Kyrle, Roger ([1928]1978) 'The Psycho-Physical Apparatus: An Introduction to a Physical Interpretation of Psycho-analytic Theory'. In *The Collected Papers of Roger Money-Kyrle*. Ed. Donald Meltzer. Clunie Press, 16–28.

Monk, Ray (1990). *Ludwig Wittgenstein: The Duty of Genius*. New York: The Free Press.

Moore, G. E. (1899). 'The Nature of Judgment'. *Mind* 8/30: 176–93.

Moore, G. E. (1927). 'Facts and Propositions – II'. *Proceedings of the Aristotelian Society, Supplementary Volume* 7: 171–206.

Moore, G. E. (1931). 'Preface'. In F. P. Ramsey, *The Foundations of Mathematics and other Logical Essays*. London: Routledge and Kegan Paul, vii–viii.

Moore, G. E. (1968 [1942]). 'An Autobiography'. In *The Philosophy of G. E. Moore*. The Library of Living Philosophers. Ed. P. A. Schilpp. La Salle, IL: Open Court, 1–39.

Moore, G. E. (1954). 'Wittgenstein's Lectures in 1930–33. *Mind* n.s. lxiii/249, 1–15.

Moore, G. E. (2004 [1903]). *Principia Ethica*. Reprint. Mineola, NY: Dover Publications.

Morshead, O. (1995). Arthur Stanley Ramsey, 1867–1954. *Magdalene College Magazine and Record*. 86, 41–4.

Musgrave, Richard A. (1959). *Theory of Public Finance*. New York: McGraw-Hill.

Nedo, Michael (1996—). Ed. L. Wittgenstein, *Wiener Ausgabe*, Vienna: Springer-Verlag.

Newman, Peter (1982). 'Ramsey, Frank Plumpton'. In J. Eatwell, M. Milgate, and P. Newman (eds), *The New Palgrave: A Dictionary of Economics*, vol. 4. London: Macmillan, 41–6.

Newsome, David (1980). *On the Edge of Paradise: A.C. Benson: The Diarist*. London: John Murray.

Nicolson, Nigel (1977). *A Change of Perspective: The Letters of Virginia Woolf, Vol. III: 1923–1928*. London: The Hogarth Press.

Niehans, J. (1990). *A History of Economic Theory: Classic Contributions, 1720–1980*. Baltimore: Johns Hopkins University Press.

Ogden, C. K. and I. A. Richards (1923). *The Meaning of Meaning: A Study of the Influence of Language upon Thought and of the Science of Symbolism*. New York: Harcourt Brace.

Partridge, Francis (1981). *Love in Bloomsbury: Memories*. London: Gollancz.

Pascal, Fania (1981). 'Wittgenstein: A Personal Memoir'. In Rush Rhees (ed.), *Ludwig Wittgenstein: Personal Recollections*. Oxford: Basil Blackwell, 26–62.

Paskauskas, Andrew (1993). *The Complete Correspondence of Sigmund Freud and Ernest Jones, 1908–1939*. Cambridge, MA: Harvard University Press.

Paul, Margaret (2012). *Frank Ramsey (1903–1930): A Sister's Memoir*. Cambridge: Smith-Gordon.

Pearl, J. (2000). *Causality*. New York: Cambridge University Press.

Peirce, Charles Sanders (1931–58). *Collected Papers of Charles Sanders Peirce*. 8 vols. Ed. C. Hartshorne and P. Weiss (vols. I–VI), A. Burks (vols. VII–VIII). Cambridge, MA: Belknap Press. (References to this work include the original year of composition of the referenced passage.)

Peirce, Charles Sanders (1982–). *The Writings of Charles S. Peirce: A Chronological Edition*. Gen. ed. E. Moore. Bloomington: Indiana University Press. (References to this work include the original year of composition of the referenced passage.)

Penrose, L. (1927). 'Some Psycho-analytical Notes on Negation'. *International Journal of Psycho-Analysis* 8: 47–52.

Persky, Joseph. 'Retrospectives: The Ethology of Homo Economicus'. *The Journal of Economic Perspectives* 9/2: 221–31.

Pigou, Arthur C. (1909). 'The Economic Aspect of the Problem'. In *The Problem of the Feeble-minded: An Abstract of the Report of the Royal Commission on the Care and Control of the Feeble-minded*. Ed. Mrs. Walter Slater. London: P. S. King, 97–101.

Pigou, Arthur C. (1920). *The Economics of Welfare*. London: Macmillan.

Pigou, Arthur C. (1928). *A Study in Public Finance*. London: Macmillan.

Price, H. (1993). 'The Direction of Causation: Ramsey's Ultimate Contingency'. In D. Hull, M. Forbes, and K. Okruhlik (eds), *PSA 1992, vol. 2*. East Lansing, Michigan: Philosophy of Science Association, 253–67.

Price, H. (2014). 'Where Would We Be without Counterfactuals?' In M. C. Galavotti, D. Dieks, W. Gonzalez, S. Hartmann, T. Uebel, and W. Weber. (eds), *New Directions in the Philosophy of Science*. Cham, Switzerland: Springer, 589–607.

Price, H. and B. Weslake (2009). 'The Time-Asymmetry of Causation'. In H. Beebee, C. Hitchcock, and P. Menzies (eds), *The Oxford Handbook of Causation*. Oxford: Oxford University Press, 414–43.

Prior, A. N. (1956). 'Modality and Quantification in S5'. *Journal of Symbolic Logic* 21: 60–2.

Prior, A. N. (1971). *Objects of Thought*. Ed. P.T. Geach and A.J.P. Kenny. Oxford: Oxford University Press.

Psillos, Stathis (1999). *Scientific Realism: How Science Tracks Truth*: London: Routledge.

Psillos, Stathis (2006). 'Ramsey's *Ramsey Sentences*'. In M. C. Galavotti (ed.), *Cambridge and Vienna: Frank P. Ramsey and the Vienna Circle*. Dordrecht: Springer, 67–90.

Purdy, Robert and Zygmunt, Jan (2000). Adolf Lindenbaum, 'Metric Spaces and Decompositions'. In Urszula Wybraniec-Skardowska (ed.), *The Lvov-Warsaw School. Past and Present*. New York: Springer.

Quine, W. V. O (1950). *Methods of Logic*. Cambridge Mass.: Harvard University Press.

Redpath, Theodore (1990). *Ludwig Wittgenstein: A Student's Memoir*. London: Duckworth.

Rhees, Rush (ed.) (1981). *Ludwig Wittgenstein: Personal Recollections*. Oxford: Basil Blackwell.

Richards, I. A. (1977). 'Co-Author of The Meaning of Meaning'. In P. S. Florence and J. R. L. Anderson (eds), *C. K. Ogden: A Collective Memoir*. London: Elek Pemberton, 96–109.

Rickman, John (1950). 'Susan Sutherland Isaacs, *C.B.E., M.A., D.Sc. (Vict.), Hon. D.Sc. (Adelaide)*'. *The International Journal of Psycho-Analysis* 31: 279–85.

Robinson, E. A. G. (1947). 'John Maynard Keynes, 1883–1946'. *The Economic Journal* 57/225: 1–68.

Robinson, Joan (1970 [1937]). 'The Economic System in a Socialist State'. In E. Homburger, W. Janeway, and S. Schama (eds), *The Cambridge Mind: 90 Years of the Cambridge Review: 1879–1969*. London: Jonathan Cape.

Robinson, Joan (1978). *Contributions to Modern Economics*. Oxford: Basil Blackwell.

Robinson, Joan (1993)[1969]. *The Economics of Imperfect Competition*, London: St. Martin's Press.

Rolph, C. H. (1973). *Kingsley: The Life, Letters and Diaries of Kingsley Martin*. London: Penguin.

Rosenbaum, Stanford P. (2015 [1995]). 'Wittgenstein in Bloomsbury: 1911–1931'. Reprinted in I. Ground and F. A. Fellows III (eds), *Portraits of Wittgenstein*, vol. 1. Rev. ed. London: Bloomsbury.

Rothhaupt, Josef (1996). *Farbthemen in Wittgenstein's Gesamtnachlass*. Weinheim: Beltz Athenaum.

Russell, Bertrand (1906). 'On the Nature of Truth'. *Proceedings of the Aristotelian Society* 7: 28–49.

Russell, Bertrand (1913). 'On the Notion of Cause'. *Proceedings of the Aristotelian Society, New Series* 13: 1–26.

Russell, Bertrand (1919). *Introduction to Mathematical Philosophy*. London: Allen and Unwin.

Russell, Bertrand (1922a). 'Introduction'. In Ludwig Wittgenstein, *Tractatus Logico-Philosophicus*. London: Routledge & Kegan Paul, 7–23.

Russell, Bertrand (1922b). Review of John Maynard Keynes, *A Treatise on Probability*. *The Mathematical Gazette* 11/159: 119–25.

Russell, Bertrand (1931). *The Foundations of Mathematics and Other Logical Essays*, Frank Plumpton Ramsey'. *Mind* 40/160: 476–82.

Russell, Bertrand (1948). *Human Knowledge: It's Scope and Limits*. London: Allen and Unwin.

Russell, Bertrand (1959). *My Philosophical Development*. London: Routledge.

Russell, Bertrand (1985 [1903]). 'The Free Man's Worship'. Reprinted in *The Collected Papers of Bertrand Russell*, vol. XII. London: Routledge, 62–72.

Russell, Bertrand (1986 [1918]). 'The Philosophy of Logical Atomism'. Reprinted in *The Collected Papers of Bertrand Russell*, vol. VIII. London: Routledge, 157–244.

Russell, Dora (1975). *The Tamarisk Tree*. London: Elek/Pemberton.

Russell, Dora (1977). 'My Friend Ogden'. In P. S. Florence and J. R. L. Anderson (eds), *C. K. Ogden: A Collective Memoir*. London: Elek Pemberton, 82–96.

Ryle, Gilbert (1970). 'Autobiographical'. In O. P. Wood and G. Pitcher (eds), *Ryle*. London and Basingstoke, Macmillan, 1–15.

Rymes, Thomas (1989). *Keynes: Lectures 1932–35*. London: Macmillan.

Sabbagh, Karl (2013). *Shooting Star: The Brief and Brilliant Life of Frank Ramsey*. Amazon Digital Services LLC.

Sahlin, Nils-Eric (1990a). *The Philosophy of F. P. Ramsey*. Cambridge: Cambridge University Press.

Sahlin, Nils-Eric (1990b). 'Weight or the Value of Knowledge'. *British Journal for the Philosophy of Science* 41: 1–4.

Sahlin, Nils-Eric (1997). '"He Is No Good for My Work". On the Philosophical Relations between Ramsey and Wittgenstein'. *Poznan Studies in the Philosophy of the Sciences and the Humanities* 51: 61–84.

Samuelson, Paul A. (1943). 'Dynamics, Statics, and the Stationary State'. *Review of Economics and Statistics* 25/1: 58–68.

Samuelson, Paul A. (1951). 'Theory of Optimal Taxation'. Unpublished memorandum for the U.S. Treasury, published as Samuelson, Paul A. (1986), 'Theory of Optimal Taxation'. *Journal of Public Economics* 30: 137–43.

Samuelson, Paul (1972 [1965]). 'A Catenary Turnpike Theorem Involving Consumption and the Golden Rule'. In *The Collected Scientific Papers of Paul A. Samuelson*, vol. 3. Ed. Robert Merton. Cambridge, MA: MIT Press, 93–103.

Samuelson, Paul (1986 [1982]). 'A Chapter in the History of Ramsey's Optimal Feasible Taxation and Optimal Public Utility Prices'. In *The Collected Scientific Papers of Paul A. Samuelson*, vol. 5. Ed. Kate Crowley. Cambridge, MA: MIT Press, 76–100.

Sandmo, Agnar (1796). 'Optimal Taxation: An Introduction to the Literature'. *Journal of Public Economics* 6: 37–54.

Savage, L. J. (1954). *The Foundations of Statistics*. New York: Dover.

Schiller, F. C. S. (1902). 'Axioms and Postulates'. In *Personal Idealism: Philosophical Essays*. Ed. H. Sturt. London: Macmillan, 47–133.

Schiller, F. C. S. (1939). *Our Human Truths*. New York: Columbia University Press.

Schumpeter, J. A. (1933). 'Review of Keynes' *Essays in Biography*'. *The Economic Journal* 43/172: 652–7.

Scitovsky, Tibor (2002 [1989]). 'My First Encounter with Joan Robinson'. In *Joan Robinson: Critical Assessments of Leading Economists*. Ed. Prue Kerr. London: Routledge, 63–4.

Seidenfeld, T. (1988). 'Decision Theory without "Independence" or Without "Ordering": What Is the Difference?' *Economics and Philosophy* 4: 267–90.

Sen, Amartya (1990). 'Dobb, Maurice Herbert'. In J. Eatwell, M. Milgate, and P. Newman (eds), *The New Palgrave: Marxian Economics*. London: Macmillan, 141–7.

Sen, Amartya (1998). 'Biographical'. Published online: <http://www.nobelprize.org/nobel_prizes/economic-sciences/laureates/1998/sen-bio.html>

Shenk, Timothy (2013). *Maurice Dobb: Political Economist*. London: Palgrave.

Sidgwick, A. S. and Sidgwick, E. M. (1906). *Henry Sidgwick: A Memoir*. London: Macmillan.

Sidgwick, H. (1907). *The Methods of Ethics*, 7th Edition. London: Macmillan.

Siepmann, Eric (1955). *Confessions of a Nihilist*. London: Victor Gollancz.

Simon, Herbert A. (1959). 'Theories of Decision-Making in Economics and Behavioural Science'. *The American Economic Review* 49/3: 253–83.

Simpson, James (1962). *The Hundredth Archbishop of Canterbury*. London: Harper and Row.

Skidelsky, R. (1992). *John Maynard Keynes: The Economist as Saviour, 1920–1937*. London: Macmillan.

Skolem T. (1967) [1923]. 'The Foundations of Elementary Arithmetic Established by Means of the Recursive Mode of Thought, without Use of Apparent Variables Ranging over Infinite Domains'. In J. van Heijenoort (ed.), *From Frege to Gödel. A Sourcebook in Mathematical Logic, 1879–1931*, Cambridge MA, Harvard University Press, 303–33.

Soifer, A. (2009). *The Mathematical Coloring Book—Mathematics of Coloring and the Colorful Life of its Creators*. New York: Springer.

Soifer, A. (ed.) (2011). 'Ramsey Theory Before Ramsey, Prehistory and Early History'. In A. Soifer (ed.), *Ramsey Theory—Yesterday, Today, and Tomorrow*. New York: Springer, 1–25.

Solow, Robert M. (1974). 'Intergenerational Equity and Exhaustible Resources'. *The Review of Economic Studies* 41: 29–45.

Solow, Robert M. (1986). 'On the Intergenerational Allocation of Natural Resources'. *The Scandinavian Journal of Economics* 141–9.

Solow, Robert M. (1994). 'Perspectives on Growth Theory'. *Journal of Economic Perspectives* 8/1: 45–54.

Spalding, Frances (1997). *Duncan Grant: A Biography*. London: Chatto.

Sraffa, Piero. (1926). 'The Laws of Returns under Competitive Conditions'. *The Economic Journal* 36/144: 535–50.

Sraffa, Piero. (1960). *The Production of Commodities by Means of Commodities: Prelude to a Critique of Economic Theory*. Cambridge: Cambridge University Press.

Stalnaker, Robert (1968). 'A Theory of Conditionals'. In N. Rescher (ed.), *Studies in Logical Theory* (*American Philosophical Quarterly*, monograph series, 2. Oxford: Basil Blackwell, 98–112.

Stansky, Peter and William Abrahams (2012). *Julian Bell: From Bloomsbury to the Spanish Civil War*. Stanford: Stanford University Press.

Stevens, Charles (1998). *Winchester Notions: The English Dialect of Winchester College*. London: The Athlone Press.

Stiglitz, Joseph E. (2015). *In Praise of Frank Ramsey's Contribution to the Theory of Taxation*. The Economic Journal 125: 235–68.

Szubka, Tadeusz (2018). 'List Janiny Hosiasson-Lindenbaum Do George Edward Moore'. *Filozofia Nauki* 26/1 [101]: 129–41.

Tansley, A. G. (1925). 'Psycho-analysis'. *The Nation & the Athenaeum*, 8 August: 656–7.

Taylor, Gabriele (2006). 'Frank Ramsey: A Biographical Sketch' in Galavotti, (2006), 1–18.

von Neumann, John (1928). *Zur Theorie der Gesellschaftsspiele*, Math. Ann. 100: 295–320.

von Neumann, John and Oskar Morgenstern (1944). *Theory of Games and Economic Behavior*. Princeton: Princeton University Press.

von Weizsacker, C.C. (1965). 'Existence of Optimal Programs of Accumulation for an Infinite Time Horizon'. *Review of Economic Studies*, 32/2: 85–104.

Von Wright, G. H. (1973). *Letters to C. K. Ogden with Comments on the English Translation of the 'Tractatus Logico-Philosophicus'*. Ed. G. H. von Wright, with an appendix of letters by Frank Plumpton Ramsey. Oxford: Basil Blackwell.

Waismann, Friedrich (1928). 'Die Natur des Reduzibilitätsaxioms'. In *Monatshefte für Mathematik und Physik*, 35: 143–5.

Warburg, Fredric (1959). *An Occupation for Gentlemen*. London: Hutchinson.

Weintraub, E. R. (1993). *General Equilibrium Analysis: Studies in Appraisal*. Ann Arbor: University of Michigan Press.

Weyl, H. (1921) [1998]. 'On the New Foundational Crisis in Mathematics'. In P. Mancosu (ed.), *From Brouwer to Hilbert. The Debate on the Foundations of Mathematics in the 1920s*, Oxford, Oxford University Press, 86–118.

Whitehead, Alfred North and Bertrand Russell. 1910–13. *Principia Mathematica*. Vols 1, 2, and 3. Cambridge: Cambridge University Press.

Whyte, J. T. (1990). 'Success Semantics'. *Analysis* 50/3: 149–57.

Wilkinson, L. Patrick (1980). 'A Century of King's 1873–1972'. Cambridge: University Press for King's College, Cambridge.

Williamson, Timothy (2013). *Modal Logic as Metaphysics*. Oxford: Oxford University Press.

Wittgenstein, Hermine (1981). 'My Brother Ludwig'. In Rush Rhees (ed.), *Ludwig Wittgenstein: Personal Recollections*. Oxford: Basil Blackwell, 1–13.

Woodward, J. (2003). *Making Things Happen: A Theory of Causal Explanation*. Oxford: Oxford University Press.

Woolf, Leonard (1960). *Sowing: An Autobiography of the Years 1880 to 1904*. London: The Hogarth Press.

Woolf, Virginia (1927). *To The Lighthouse*. London: Hogarth Press.

Woolf, Virginia (1940). *Roger Fry: A Biography*. London: Hogarth Press.

Woolf, Virginia (1966 [1924]). 'Mr. Bennett and Mrs. Brown'. Reprinted in *Collected Essays*, vol. 1. London: Hogarth Press, 319–37.

Wright, Bertha (2010). *Bad Aunt Bertha: The Memoirs of Bertha Wright*. Cambridge: Biograph.

Wright, G. H. von (2001 [1955]). 'A Biographical Sketch. Revised ed. In Norman Malcolm, *Ludwig Wittgenstein: A Memoir*, 2nd ed. Oxford: Clarendon Press, 2001, 1–20.

Wright, Peter (1987). *Spycatcher*. Australia: Heinemann.

Young, W. Allen (1921). *Dividends for All: Being an Explanation of the Douglas Scheme*. London: Cecil Palmer.

NAME INDEX

Note: Tables, figures, and boxes are indicated by an italic 't', 'f', and 'b' respectively, following the page number. Bolded page numbers indicate that the person/group is properly introduced on that page.

For the benefit of digital users, indexed terms that span two pages (e.g., 52–53) may, on occasion, appear on only one of those pages.

O'Flaherty, Liam 289–93
Officers' Training Corps, the 26–7, 30, 35, 43–4
Ogden, C.K. 3, 5, **38**, 42–3, 47–8, 59, 89, 93–6, 114, 123, 126–7, 129–34, 140, 143–4, 151, 183, 186–7, 194, 206, 216–17, 221, 246–7, 256–7, 382–3, 391–2, 428
Oppenheimer, J. Robert 96–7
Ostwald, Wilhelm 129

Pares, Richard 45, 51f
Paris, Jeff 342
Partridge, Frances *see* Marshall (Partridge), Frances
Partridge, Ralph 148–9, 247, 412
Pate, Miss 131
Paton, H.J. 202
Paul, Margaret (Ramsey) 3, 6–10, 13, 17–18, 35, 163, 166, 229–30, 283–6, 289, 293, 413, 422
Peano, Giuseppe 106, 337b
Pearl, Judea 407b
Pears, David 132
Peirce, C.S. 117, 130, 143, 258, 261–2, 278, 280–1, 370–1, 393, 404–5, 408–9
Penrose, Alec 74, 99, 412
Penrose, Bernard ('Beakus') **78**, 206, 251, 412, 415f, 424
Penrose, Elisabeth 166–8
Penrose, James 166–8
Penrose, Lionel 55–6, 73–4, **78**–80, 82f, 94, 99–101, 106, 109, 159–61, 164–5, 206, 221–2, 243, 251, 411, 424
Penrose, Roland 75, **78**, 206, 251, 392
Perry, Ralph Barton 61
Peterhouse, Cambridge 50
Philby, Kim 11
Piaget, Jean 39, 152
Pigou, Arthur 122, 180–1, 193, 229, **296**, 300, 303f, 305–6, 308–10, 317–18, 321–2, 323b, 324–6, 328, 330
Pigou Club, the 299
Piketty, Thomas 88n.‡
Pinsent, David 241n.†
Plompton, Sir Edward 6
Poincaré, Henri 65, 397–8
Political Economy Club 95, 97, 113, 298–9, 324
Pollard, Samuel 50, 83, 85
Portman Clinic, the 154
Pound, Ezra 122
Potter, Michael 185–6b
Price, H.H. 134, 235
Price, Huw 407b, 410
Priestley, Raymond 350, 352–3
Prior, A.N. 262b, 389b
Proctor, Dennis 197n.*
Prokofiev, Sergei 162
Psillos, Stathis 396b, 398
Psych An Society, the 221–3
Pyke, David 151–4, 254

Pyke, Dick 141, 153–6, 159, 163–4, 207, 212–13, 414
Pyke, Geoffrey **150**, 159, 159f
Pyke, Margaret 80–1, **150**, 159, 159f, 177, 183, 208–9

Queens' College, Cambridge 50, 198–9
Quine, W.V. 270n.‡, 335b, 397–8
Quintics Society, the 327

Rackham, Clara 10
Raiffa, Howard 325
Ramanujan, Srinivasa 84, 257
Ramsey, Adam Averall 4, 8–9
Ramsey, Agnes (Wilson) 3–9, 12–14, 17–23, 26, 31–2, 35–6, 38, 46–50, 74–5, 77, 104–7, 141, 147, 149–51, 156–8, 163, 166–9, 182, 187, 202, 209, 227–30, 254, 282–4, 285f, 288–9, 303–4, 345, 422
Ramsey, Arthur 3–4, 6–**11**, 17–24, 28–32, 35–6, 39, 41–4, 46, 50, 52, 74–5, 77, 80–1, 83–4, 91, 106–7, 110, 140, 154–5, 157–8, 163, 167–9, 176, 178, 180, 195, 198, 207–10, 214–15, 228, 244–5, 250, 282, 286f, 289, 293, 331, 413, 416, 418, 420, 422, 425
Ramsey, Bridget 3, 5, 11, 17–19, 23, 47–8, 156–8, 229–30, 283–4, 289, 414–15, 420, 422
Ramsey, Frank (brother to Arthur Stanley Ramsey) 9
Ramsey, Jane 253–5, 283–4, 287–9, 291–3, 362, 411
Ramsey, Lettice (Baker) 96, 106–7, 177, **203**–9, 205f, 209, 215, 221, 223–6, 229–30, 236, 240–3, 246, 256, 282–6, 303, 305–6, 346–7, 358–9, 382–4, 411, 415–24, 415f, 427–8
Ramsey, Lucy 8–9, 293
Ramsey, Margaret ('Margie') *see* Paul, Margaret (Ramsey)
Ramsey, Michael ('Mick') 3–6, 11, 17–20, 22, 46, 78, 80, 106–7, 176, 194, 214, 252, 257, 282–5, 289, 413–14, 416–18, 420, 422, 426–7
Ramsey, Phebe 8–9
Ramsey, Sarah 411
Rank, Otto 162–3
Ravel, Maurice 162
Reddaway, Brian 97, 254
Redmayne, Paul 103–5
Reichenbach, Hans 173
Reidemeister, Kurt 174
Reik, Theodor **162**–164, 167–9, 175–7, 207, 222, 224, 228
Rendall, Monty 26
Rescher, Nicholas 383
Respinger, Marguerite 347
Rhees, Rush 132, 369, 371–2, 376–7
Rhodes, Cecil 8
Ricardo, David 296, 302
Richards, Dorothy Pilley 75–6, 159, 247, 251–2
Richards, I.A. **41**–2, 75–6, 89, 92f, 94–5, 106–7, 126, 130–1, 159, 196, 207–8, 216–17, 251, 292, 391–2, 405–6
Rickman, John 100, 221–2

SUBJECT INDEX

Note: Tables, figures, and boxes are indicated by an italic "*t*", "*f*", and "*b*", respectively, following the page number.

For the benefit of digital users, indexed terms that span two pages (e.g., 52–53) may, on occasion, appear on only one of those pages.